T0359327

AUSTRALIAN
MINI
THE FUTURE OF AUSTRALIAN ENGLISH
OXFORD
THESAURUS

AUSTRALIAN
MINI
THE FUTURE OF AUSTRALIAN ENGLISH
OXFORD
THESAURUS

Compiled by Anne Knight

OXFORD
UNIVERSITY PRESS
AUSTRALIA & NEW ZEALAND

OXFORD
UNIVERSITY PRESS

Oxford University Press is a department of the University of Oxford.
It furthers the University's objective of excellence in research,
scholarship, and education by publishing worldwide. Oxford is a registered
trademark of Oxford University Press in the UK and in certain other
countries.

Published in Australia by
Oxford University Press
Level 8, 737 Bourke Street, Docklands, Victoria 3008, Australia

© Oxford University Press 2004

The moral rights of the author have been asserted.

First published 2004
Reprinted 2004 (twice), 2005 (twice), 2006, 2007, 2008, 2009, 2010, 2011, 2012, 2013,
2014, 2015, 2016, 2017, 2018, 2019 (twice), 2020, 2022, 2024

This thesaurus is based on the *Australian School Dictionary and Thesaurus*
compiled by Anne Knight.

National Library of Australia Cataloguing-in-Publication data

    Australian mini Oxford thesaurus.

    ISBN 978 0 19 555025 2.

    1. English language – Synonyms and antonyms. 2. English
    language – Australia – Synonyms and antonyms. I. Knight, Anne.

423.1

Reproduction and communication for educational purposes

The Australian *Copyright Act 1968* (the Act) allows a maximum of one chapter
or 10% of the pages of this work, whichever is the greater, to be reproduced
and/or communicated by any educational institution for its educational purposes
provided that the educational institution (or the body that administers it) has
given a remuneration notice to Copyright Agency Limited (CAL) under the Act.

For details of the CAL licence for educational institutions contact:

Copyright Agency Limited
Level 15, 233 Castlereagh Street
Sydney NSW 2000
Telephone: (02) 9394 7600
Facsimile: (02) 9394 7601
Email: info@copyright.com.au

Typeset by Promptset Pty Ltd
Printed in China by Golden Cup Printing Co Ltd

Oxford University Press Australia & New Zealand is committed to
sourcing paper responsibly.

MIX
Paper
FSC   FSC® C110497

Preface

The *Australian Mini Oxford Thesaurus* is an alphabetical collection of words with their synomyns (words of the same or nearly the same meaning). Each entry provides a set of words of similar or related meaning to the word you look up, so that you can choose the word which best expresses what you want to say. You may want to find an alternative word for an overused one, a more formal word for an everyday word, a slang alternative to a standard word, or a more specific word for a general one.

In using the thesaurus it is important to recognise that perfect synonyms—words that have exactly the same meaning and are substitutable in any context—are in fact rare. Care must be taken in order to select the most appropriate word for the particular context, and it is wise to check the meaning and usage of any unfamiliar word in a dictionary.

Guide to the thesaurus

formal adjective (*a formal occasion*) ceremonial, official, solemn, stately; (*a formal manner*) ceremonious, conventional, dignified, pompous, prim, proper, punctilious, reserved, starchy, stiff, stilted, strait-laced.

kind noun brand, breed, category, class, classification, form, genre, genus, ilk (*informal*), make, nature, order, set, sort, species, strain, style, type, variety.

kind adjective affectionate, altruistic, amiable, attentive, avuncular, benevolent, benign, big-hearted, caring, charitable, compassionate, considerate, fatherly, friendly, generous, genial, gentle, good, good-natured, gracious, helpful, hospitable, humane, kind-hearted, kindly, lenient, loving, merciful, motherly, neighbourly, nice, obliging, philanthropic, soft-hearted, sympathetic, tender-hearted, thoughtful, understanding, unselfish, warm-hearted, well-meaning.

Guide to the thesaurus

Cross-reference: printed in small capitals and introduced by 'see' or 'see also'. Provided at some entries instead of, or to supplement, a list of synonyms.

king noun monarch, ruler, sovereign, see also *RULER*.
□ **kingly** adjective regal, royal.

opt verb (*opt for*) choose, decide on, go for, pick, select, settle on, vote for.

weapon noun (*weapons*) armaments, arms, munitions, weaponry.

Sense number: where a word has more than one meaning, the different senses of the word are numbered.

wear verb **1** be attired in, clothe yourself in, don, dress in, have on, put on, sport. **2** abrade, corrode, eat away, erode, grind down, rub away, scuff, wear away, wear down. **3** endure, last, stand up, survive. □ **wear off** decrease, diminish, dwindle, fade, lessen, subside. □ **wear out 1** become shabby, become threadbare, fray, wear thin. **2** drain, exhaust, fatigue, tire out, weary.

Phrase: where a word is used as part of a phrase, the phrase is printed in bold and found at the entry for the main word in the phrase. Synonyms are given for the phrase.

wear noun **1** apparel (*formal*), attire (*formal*), clobber (*slang*), clothes, clothing, dress, garb, garments, gear (*informal*), raiment (*old use*). **2** damage, deterioration, disrepair, wear and tear.

Guide to the thesaurus

Part of speech: the headword is followed by a label indicating its part of speech, for example *noun*, *verb*, *adverb*, *adjective*, *preposition*, *pronoun*, *interjection*, or *conjunction*.

weary *adjective* all in (*informal*), beat (*slang*), dog-tired, done in (*informal*), drained, drowsy, exhausted, fagged out (*informal*), fatigued, jaded, knackered (*slang*), pooped (*informal*), sleepy, spent, tired, whacked (*informal*), worn out, zonked (*slang*). □ **weariness** *noun* exhaustion, fatigue, languor, lassitude, lethargy, listlessness, tiredness.

weary *verb* drain, exhaust, fatigue, sap, tire, wear out.

Derivatives: derivatives of the headword are included in some entries and are printed in bold, followed by their synonyms.

Usage label: if a synonym is restricted in use, it is followed by a label printed in italics in brackets. Words may be restricted to a particular region or subject area, or may be classed as formal, informal, slang, old use, or derogatory. *Informal* indicates that the word is normally used in informal or spoken English rather than formal writing, while *slang* warns that it is used very informally, or restricted to a particular group. A *derogatory* use is one that is intentionally insulting.

Proprietary terms

This book includes some words which are, or are asserted to be, proprietary names or trade marks. Their inclusion does not imply that they have acquired for legal purposes a non-proprietary or general significance, nor is any other judgement implied concerning their legal status. In cases where the editor has some evidence that a word is used as a proprietary name or trade mark this is indicated by the label *trade mark*, but no judgement concerning the legal status of such words is made or implied thereby.

Aa

abandon verb **1** abdicate, cancel, chuck in (*informal*), discontinue, drop, forgo, give up, quit, resign, scrap, surrender, throw in (*informal*), waive, yield. **2** (*abandon a person*) desert, ditch (*informal*), forsake, jilt, leave, leave in the lurch, run out on (*informal*), walk out on (*informal*); (*abandon a place*) evacuate, leave, quit, vacate.

abate verb decrease, die down, ease, moderate, subside, weaken.

abbey noun convent, friary, monastery, nunnery, priory, religious house.

abbreviate verb abridge, contract, cut, reduce, shorten, truncate.

abbreviation noun acronym, contraction, shortening.

abdicate verb quit, resign, stand down, step down; see also RENOUNCE.

abdomen noun belly, gut (*informal*), insides (*informal*), intestines, paunch, stomach, tummy (*informal*).

abduct verb carry off, kidnap, seize, snatch (*informal*).

abet verb aid, assist, encourage, help, incite, support.

abhor verb abominate, detest, hate, loathe, recoil from, shrink from. ◻ **abhorrent** adjective abominable, detestable, disgusting, hateful, horrid, loathsome, odious, repugnant, repulsive, revolting.

abide verb **1** dwell, live, remain, reside, stay. **2** bear, endure, put up with, stand, stomach, suffer, take, tolerate. ◻ **abide by** accept, adhere to, agree to, comply with, conform to, follow, keep to, obey, observe, stick to.

abiding adjective endless, enduring, eternal, everlasting, lasting, permanent, steadfast, unending.

ability noun **1** capability, capacity, potential, power, strength. **2** aptitude, capacity, cleverness, competence, expertise, facility, flair, genius, gift, knack, know-how, potential, proficiency, prowess, skill, talent.

able adjective **1** allowed, authorised, available, eligible, fit, free, permitted. **2** accomplished, adept, adroit, capable, clever, competent, gifted, intelligent, proficient, qualified, skilful, talented.

abnormal *adjective* anomalous, atypical, bizarre, curious, deviant, eccentric, exceptional, extraordinary, freakish, irregular, odd, peculiar, queer, rare, singular, strange, uncommon, unconventional, unnatural, unusual, weird. □ **abnormality** *noun* anomaly, deformity, irregularity, malformation, peculiarity.

abolish *verb* cancel, do away with, eliminate, end, eradicate, extinguish, get rid of, put an end to, remove, stamp out, wipe out. □ **abolition** *noun* cancellation, elimination, ending, eradication, removal.

abominable *adjective* abhorrent, appalling, atrocious, base, contemptible, despicable, detestable, disgusting, execrable, foul, hateful, heinous, horrible, loathsome, obnoxious, odious, repugnant, repulsive, terrible, vile.

abominate *verb* abhor, detest, hate, loathe.

aboriginal *adjective* earliest, first, indigenous, native, original.

abortion *noun* (*when spontaneous*) miscarriage, (*when induced*) termination.

abortive *adjective* failed, fruitless, futile, ineffective, unsuccessful, vain.

abound *verb* **1** be abundant, be plentiful, flourish, proliferate, thrive. **2** be full, overflow, swarm, teem.

about *preposition* **1** around, close to, near. **2** concerning, connected with, dealing with, involving, on, regarding, relating to.

about *adverb* **1** almost, approximately, around, more or less, nearly, roughly. **2** around, hereabouts, near, nearby. □ **be about to** be going to, be on the brink of, be on the point of, be on the verge of, be ready to.

above *preposition* **1** higher than, on top of, over, superior to. **2** beyond, exceeding, greater than, higher than, more than, over.

above *adverb* **1** on high, overhead, upstairs. **2** before, earlier, previously.

above board *adjective* clean, fair, honest, honourable, legal, legitimate, open, straight.

abrasion *noun* graze, lesion, scrape, scratch.

abridge *verb* abbreviate, condense, cut, edit, reduce, shorten, trim.

abroad *adverb* overseas.

abrupt *adjective* **1** hasty, precipitate, quick, rapid, sharp, sudden, swift, unexpected. **2** blunt, brisk, brusque, curt, gruff, impolite, rude, short.

abscond *verb* bolt, disappear, do a bunk (*slang*), escape, flee, make off, nick off (*Australian slang*), run off, shoot through (*Australian informal*).

absence *noun* **1** absenteeism, non-attendance, truancy. **2** dearth, deficiency, lack, want.

absent *adjective* away, elsewhere, missing, off.

absent *verb* □ **absent yourself** play hookey (*informal*), play truant, skive off (*informal*), stay away, wag (*informal*).

absent-minded *adjective* abstracted, daydreaming, distracted, dreamy, far-away, forgetful, inattentive, oblivious, preoccupied, scatterbrained, scatty (*informal*).

absolute *adjective* **1** complete, downright, out-and-out, outright, perfect, positive, pure, sheer, thorough, total, unmitigated, unqualified, utter. **2** autocratic, complete, omnipotent, sovereign, supreme, total, unconditional, unlimited, unqualified, unrestricted.

absolution *noun* forgiveness, pardon, remission.

absolve *verb* **1** acquit, clear, exonerate, forgive, pardon, vindicate. **2** discharge, excuse, exempt, free, release, set free.

absorb *verb* **1** (*absorb liquid*) draw up, mop up, soak up, suck up, take up; (*absorb information*) assimilate, digest, take in. **2** captivate, capture, engage, engross, interest, monopolise, occupy, preoccupy. □ **absorbing** *adjective* captivating, engrossing, fascinating, gripping, interesting, riveting.

abstain *verb* (*abstain from*) avoid, decline, desist from, do without, forgo, go without, refrain from.

abstinence *noun* non-indulgence, self-denial, sobriety, teetotalism, temperance.

abstract *adjective* academic, conceptual, intangible, intellectual, theoretical.

abstract *noun* outline, précis, résumé, summary, synopsis.

absurd *adjective* comic, crazy, farcical, foolish, funny, illogical, inane, laughable, ludicrous, mad, nonsensical, outrageous, preposterous, ridiculous, senseless, silly, strange, stupid, unreasonable, zany.

abundance noun heaps (*informal*), lashings (*informal*), loads (*informal*), lots (*informal*), oodles (*informal*), plenty, stacks (*informal*), tons (*informal*), wealth.

abundant adjective ample, bountiful, copious, generous, lavish, liberal, overflowing, plentiful, profuse, teeming.

abuse verb **1** exploit, misuse. **2** assault, damage, harm, hurt, ill-treat, maltreat, mistreat, molest. **3** attack, be rude to, curse, denigrate, disparage, insult, revile, slander, swear at.

abuse noun **1** assault, exploitation, ill-treatment, maltreatment, mistreatment. **2** calumny, curses, denigration, insults, invective, obscenities, revilement, slander, swearing, vilification, vituperation. □ **abusive** adjective derogatory, disparaging, foulmouthed, impolite, insulting, obscene, offensive, pejorative, rude, scornful, scurrilous, slanderous.

abyss noun bottomless pit, chasm, hole.

academic adjective **1** educational, pedagogic, scholastic. **2** bookish, erudite, highbrow, intellectual, learned, scholarly, studious. **3** abstract, hypothetical, speculative, theoretical.

accelerate verb **1** go faster, quicken, speed up, step on it (*informal*). **2** expedite, hasten, speed up, step up.

accent noun **1** brogue, dialect, intonation, pronunciation. **2** emphasis, prominence, stress.

accent verb accentuate, emphasise, stress.

accentuate verb accent, draw attention to, emphasise, highlight, stress, underline.

accept verb **1** get, receive, take. **2** agree to, consent to, go along with, put up with, reconcile yourself to, resign yourself to, take, tolerate, welcome.

acceptable adjective adequate, admissible, appropriate, passable, pleasing, proper, satisfactory, seemly, suitable, tolerable.

access noun admission, admittance, approach, entrance, entry, way in.

access verb retrieve.

accessible adjective attainable, available, handy, obtainable, retrievable.

accessory noun **1** attachment, extension, extra, fitting. **2** abetter, accomplice, assistant, associate, confederate, partner.

accident *noun* calamity, catastrophe, disaster, misadventure, misfortune, mishap; (*a car accident*) collision, crash, pile-up (*informal*), prang (*slang*), smash.

accidental *adjective* chance, coincidental, fluky, fortuitous, inadvertent, serendipitous, unexpected, unforeseen, unintentional, unplanned.

acclaim *verb* applaud, cheer, clap, hail, praise, salute, welcome. □ **acclaim** *noun* acclamation, applause, approval, commendation, ovation, praise, welcome.

acclimatise *verb* adapt, adjust, become accustomed, become inured, get used.

accolade *noun* acclaim, compliment, honour, praise, tribute.

accommodate *verb* **1** billet, board, house, put up, take in. **2** furnish, grant, provide, supply.

accommodation *noun* billet, digs (*informal*), home, house, housing, lodgings, premises, quarters, residence.

accompany *verb* **1** attend, be with, chaperone, escort, go with, partner, tag along with, travel with. **2** back up, play with, support. □ **accompaniment** *noun* background, backing, support.

accomplice *noun* abetter, accessory, assistant, collaborator, helper, partner, sidekick (*informal*).

accomplish *verb* achieve, attain, bring off, carry out, complete, do, effect, execute, finish, fulfil, perform, succeed in. □ **accomplishment** *noun* ability, achievement, attainment, deed, exploit, feat, gift, skill, talent.

accomplished *adjective* able, adept, brilliant, consummate, experienced, expert, gifted, proficient, skilful, skilled, talented.

accord *noun* agreement, compact, pact, treaty. □ **of your own accord** off your own bat, of your own free will, of your own volition, spontaneously, unasked, voluntarily, willingly.

accord *verb* agree, be consistent, coincide, concur, correspond, harmonise, tally.

accordingly *adverb* consequently, hence, so, therefore, thus.

accost *verb* bail up (*Australian*), buttonhole, confront, hail, stop, waylay.

account *noun* **1** bill, invoice, receipt, statement. **2** chronicle, description, explanation, history, log, narrative, record, report, story, tale. □ **take into account** allow for, consider, take into consideration.

account verb □ **account for** excuse, explain, give grounds for, justify.

accountable adjective answerable, liable, responsible.

accumulate verb **1** acquire, amass, collect, gather, hoard, pile up, stockpile, store up. **2** accrue, build up, grow, increase, multiply, pile up. □ **accumulation** noun buildup, collection, heap, hoard, mass, pile, stack, stockpile, store.

accurate adjective careful, correct, exact, factual, faithful, meticulous, perfect, precise, right, spot on (informal), true. □ **accuracy** noun correctness, exactitude, exactness, faithfulness, fidelity, meticulousness, precision, truth.

accusation noun allegation, charge, imputation, indictment.

accuse verb blame, charge, denounce, impeach, incriminate, indict, point the finger at (informal).

accustom verb (accustom to) acclimatise to, adjust to, familiarise with, habituate to, inure to, make used to.

accustomed adjective customary, established, expected, familiar, fixed, habitual, normal, regular, set, usual.

ace noun champion, expert, master, star, winner.

ache noun **1** discomfort, hurt, pain, pang, soreness. **2** agony, anguish, distress, grief, misery, pain, sorrow, suffering.

ache verb be painful, be sore, hurt, pound, throb.

achieve verb accomplish, attain, carry out, fulfil, reach, realise, succeed in. □ **achievement** noun accomplishment, attainment, deed, feat; see also SUCCESS.

acid adjective **1** acidic, sharp, sour, tangy, tart, vinegary. **2** acerbic, bitter, caustic, cutting, sarcastic, sharp, stinging.

acknowledge verb **1** accept, admit, agree, allow, concede, confess, grant, recognise. **2** answer, reply to, respond to. □ **acknowledgement** noun **1** acceptance, admission, confession. **2** answer, reply, response. **3** appreciation, credit, notice, recognition, reward, thanks.

acme noun apex, climax, culmination, height, peak, pinnacle, summit, top, zenith.

acquaint verb (acquaint with) advise of, enlighten about, familiarise with, fill in on (*informal*), inform of, make aware of, tell. □ **be acquainted with** be aware of, be familiar with, be versed in, know.

acquaintance noun associate, colleague, contact.

acquire verb buy, collect, come by, gain, get, obtain, pick up, procure, purchase, secure. □ **acquisition** noun accession, possession, purchase.

acquit verb absolve, clear, exonerate, let off, release, vindicate.

acrimonious adjective bitter, cutting, embittered, hostile, nasty, spiteful, tart, virulent.

acrobat noun gymnast, tightrope walker, trapeze artist.

across preposition over, through, throughout.

act noun **1** accomplishment, achievement, action, deed, exploit, feat, undertaking. **2** decree, edict, law, statute. **3** performance, routine, show, sketch, skit. **4** deception, front, hoax, pretence, sham, show.

act verb **1** behave, conduct yourself. **2** appear, impersonate, perform, play, portray. **3** function, have an effect, operate, work. **4** fake, feign, make believe, pretend, sham.

acting adjective deputy, interim, provisional, substitute, temporary.

action noun **1** activity, motion, operation, performance, practice, work. **2** act, deed, effort, endeavour, exploit, feat, move, step, undertaking. **3** battle, combat, conflict, fighting, warfare. **4** lawsuit, litigation, proceedings, prosecution. **5** activity, adventure, drama, events, excitement, happenings, incidents.

activate verb actuate, set off, start, switch on, trigger, turn on.

active adjective **1** busy, diligent, dynamic, energetic, full of beans (*informal*), hard-working, hyperactive, industrious, involved, lively, occupied, participating, sprightly, spry, strenuous, vigorous, vivacious. **2** functioning, operative, working.

activist noun agitator, campaigner, crusader, firebrand, lobbyist, militant, protester, stirrer.

activity noun **1** enterprise, hobby, occupation, pastime, project, pursuit, undertaking, venture. **2** action, bustle, exercise, exertion, hurly-burly, hustle, industry, liveliness, movement.

actor *noun* actress, performer, player, star, trouper; (*group of actors*) cast, company, troupe.

actual *adjective* authentic, confirmed, factual, genuine, real, true, verified. □ **actually** *adverb* genuinely, indeed, in fact, really, truly.

acute *adjective* **1** excruciating, extreme, intense, keen, piercing, severe, sharp, shooting, stabbing. **2** astute, canny, clever, discerning, discriminating, incisive, keen, penetrating, perceptive, sharp, shrewd, subtle.

adamant *adjective* determined, firm, immovable, inflexible, intransigent, resolute, resolved, stubborn, unyielding.

adapt *verb* adjust, alter, change, convert, edit, modify, remake, rewrite, transform; (*adapt to*) acclimatise to, accustom to, adjust to, become accustomed to, get used to. □ **adaptable** *adjective* accommodating, amenable, easygoing, flexible, malleable, versatile.

add *verb* affix, append, attach, combine, join, tack on. □ **add to** augment, enlarge, increase, swell. □ **add up** calculate, compute, count, reckon, sum, total, tot up (*informal*), work out. □ **add up to** amount to, come to, make, total.

addendum *noun* appendix, postscript, supplement.

addict *noun* (*a TV addict*) devotee, enthusiast, fan, fanatic, freak (*informal*), lover, nut (*informal*), (*a drug addict*) druggie (*informal*), junkie (*slang*), user (*informal*). □ **addicted** *adjective* dependent on, hooked on (*slang*). □ **addiction** *noun* dependence, habit, obsession.

addition *noun* **1** calculation, computation, totalling, totting up (*informal*). **2** (*an addition to a document*) appendix, attachment, codicil, postscript, rider, supplement; (*an addition to a building*) annexe, extension, wing. □ **additional** *adjective* added, backup, extra, further, more, new, other, supplementary.

address *noun* **1** abode (*old use*), domicile, location, residence. **2** discourse, lecture, oration, sermon, speech, talk.

address *verb* **1** lecture, speak to, talk to. **2** apply yourself to, attend to, devote yourself to, focus on, tackle, turn to.

adept *adjective* accomplished, capable, competent, expert, masterful, masterly, proficient, skilful, skilled, talented.

adequate *adjective* acceptable, all right, enough, fair, OK (*informal*), passable, satisfactory, sufficient, tolerable.

adhere *verb* **1** attach, cling, hold fast, stick. **2** (*adhere to*) abide by, comply with, follow, keep to, stick to.

adhesive *adjective* gummed, sticky.

adhesive *noun* cement, fixative, glue, gum, paste.

adjacent *adjective* adjoining, bordering, contiguous, neighbouring, next-door.

adjoin *verb* abut on, be adjacent to, be next to, border on.

adjourn *verb* break off, defer, discontinue, interrupt, postpone, put off, suspend.

adjudicate *verb* arbitrate, judge, referee, umpire. □ **adjudicator** *noun* arbitrator, judge, referee, umpire.

adjust *verb* **1** arrange, regulate, set, tune. **2** adapt, alter, change, fit, modify, reshape, tailor. **3** acclimatise, adapt, become accustomed, get used, reconcile yourself.

ad lib *adverb* extempore, impromptu, off the cuff, off the top of your head (*informal*).

ad lib *verb* extemporise, improvise, play it by ear (*informal*).

administer *verb* **1** carry out, deal out, dispense, give, hand out, mete out, provide. **2** conduct, control, direct, govern, look after, manage, operate, oversee, run, supervise.

administration *noun* **1** control, direction, management, running, supervision. **2** government, ministry, regime. □ **administrator** *noun* chief, controller, director, executive, governor, head, manager, superintendent.

admirable *adjective* commendable, excellent, exemplary, honourable, laudable, praiseworthy, worthy.

admire *verb* appreciate, approve of, esteem, idolise, look up to, praise, regard highly, respect, revere, think highly of, venerate. □ **admiration** *noun* approval, commendation, praise, respect, veneration. □ **admirer** *noun* (*a woman's admirer*) beau, boyfriend, lover, suitor, sweetheart; (*an actor's admirer*) devotee, fan, follower, supporter.

admission *noun* **1** access, admittance, entrance, entry. **2** acceptance, acknowledgement, confession, declaration, disclosure, statement.

admit *verb* **1** allow in, let in, permit entry, take in. **2** accept, acknowledge, concede, confess, grant, own up.

admittance noun access, admission, entrance, entry.

admonish verb chide (old use), rebuke, reprimand, reproach, reprove, scold, tell off (informal), tick off (informal).

ado noun bother, commotion, fuss, kerfuffle (informal), to-do, trouble.

adolescence noun puberty, teens, youth. □ **adolescent** adjective teenage, youthful. □ **adolescent** noun minor, teenager, youngster, youth.

adopt verb accept, approve, assume, choose, embrace, endorse, espouse, ratify, take up, use.

adore verb 1 cherish, dote on, idolise, love. 2 exalt, extol, glorify, hallow, honour, laud (formal), magnify (old use), praise, revere, venerate, worship. □ **adorable** adjective appealing, cute (informal), darling, dear, delightful, irresistible, likeable, lovable, lovely, sweet (informal).

adorn verb array, deck out, decorate, festoon, ornament.

adult noun grown-up. □ **adult** adjective developed, full-sized, fully grown, grown-up, mature.

adulterate verb contaminate, dilute, pollute, water down, weaken.

adultery noun infidelity, unfaithfulness.

advance noun 1 breakthrough, development, headway, improvement, progress. 2 addition, gain, increase, rise. 3 loan, prepayment. □ **in advance** ahead, beforehand, up front.

advance verb 1 approach, go ahead, go forward, go on, make headway, move forward, proceed, progress. 2 lend, prepay.

advanced adjective 1 complicated, difficult, hard, higher. 2 avant-garde, innovative, modern, new, progressive, revolutionary, sophisticated, up to date.

advantage noun asset, benefit, blessing, bonus, boon, gain, help, plus. □ **take advantage of** capitalise on, cash in on, exploit, make the most of, make use of, use.

advantageous adjective beneficial, favourable, good, helpful, profitable, useful, valuable.

advent noun appearance, arrival, coming, dawn.

adventure noun 1 escapade, experience, exploit, incident. 2

danger, excitement, risk, uncertainty. □ **adventurous** *adjective* bold, brave, daring, enterprising, intrepid, venturesome.

adversary *noun* enemy, foe, opponent, rival.

adverse *adjective* bad, detrimental, harmful, ill, injurious, unfavourable, untoward. □ **adversity** *noun* affliction, calamity, catastrophe, disaster, distress, hardship, misfortune, trouble.

advertise *verb* **1** announce, make known, proclaim, publicise. **2** market, plug (*informal*), promote, push (*informal*), tout. □ **advertisement** *noun* ad (*informal*), advert (*informal*), announcement, blurb, commercial, notice, plug (*informal*), promotion, publicity, trailer.

advice *noun* **1** counsel, guidance, opinion, recommendation, suggestion, tip. **2** information, news, notification, word.

advisable *adjective* expedient, judicious, politic, prudent, recommended, sensible, wise.

advise *verb* **1** counsel, recommend, suggest, urge, warn. **2** acquaint (with), inform, notify, tell. □ **adviser** *noun* consultant, counsellor, guide, mentor.

advocate *verb* be in favour of, champion, endorse, favour, recommend, support.

advocate *noun* **1** backer, champion, promoter, proponent, supporter. **2** attorney (*American*), barrister, counsel, lawyer.

aegis *noun* auspices, patronage, protection, sponsorship.

aerial *adjective* bird's-eye, overhead.

aerial *noun* antenna.

aeroplane *noun* see AIRCRAFT.

afar *adverb* far away, far off.

affable *adjective* amiable, amicable, congenial, cordial, courteous, easygoing, friendly, genial, good-tempered, kindly, pleasant.

affair *noun* **1** activity, business, case, concern, episode, event, happening, incident, interest, matter, occurrence, operation, thing, undertaking. **2** fling, liaison, love affair, relationship, romance.

affect *verb* **1** concern, have an effect on, have an impact on, impinge on, touch. **2** attack, damage, infect, strike. **3** disturb, move, stir, touch, upset.

affected *adjective* artificial, fake, feigned, insincere, phoney (*informal*), pretended, sham, studied, unnatural.

affection noun caring, fondness, liking, love, tenderness, warmth.

affectionate adjective caring, devoted, doting, fond, kind, loving, tender-hearted, warm-hearted.

affiliated adjective allied, associated, connected.

affinity noun **1** attraction, fondness, liking, rapport, sympathy. **2** closeness, connection, correspondence, likeness, relationship, resemblance, similarity.

affirm verb assert, confirm, declare, state, swear.

affirmative adjective agreeing, assenting, favourable, positive.

affix verb add, append, attach, fasten, join, stick, tack.

afflict verb affect, distress, oppress, plague, strike, torment, trouble. □ **affliction** noun adversity, distress, hardship, illness, misery, misfortune, pain, sickness, suffering, trouble.

affluent adjective moneyed, opulent, prosperous, rich, wealthy, well-heeled (informal), well off, well-to-do.

afford verb bear the expense of, manage, pay for, spare.

affront verb insult, offend, outrage, scandalise.

affront noun insult, offence, slap in the face (informal), slight, snub.

afraid adjective alarmed, anxious, apprehensive, fearful, frightened, nervous, panic-stricken, scared, terrified, timid, worried. □ **be afraid** be apologetic, be regretful, be sorry, regret.

aftermath noun after-effects, consequences, follow-up, outcome, sequel, upshot, wake.

afterwards adverb after, later, next, subsequently.

again adverb **1** afresh, anew, another time, once more. **2** also, besides, furthermore, in addition, moreover.

against preposition anti, averse to, in opposition to, opposed to, opposing, versus.

age noun days, epoch, era, period, time. □ **ages** plural noun an eternity (informal), donkey's years (informal), yonks (slang).

age verb develop, grow older, mature, mellow, ripen.

aged adjective elderly, old, retired.

agency noun bureau, business, company, firm, office, organisation.

agenda noun list, plan, programme, schedule.

agent *noun* **1** broker, delegate, envoy, go-between, intermediary, middleman, negotiator, proxy, representative, spokesperson. **2** intelligence officer, mole (*informal*), spy.

aggravate *verb* **1** compound, exacerbate, inflame, intensify, worsen. **2** annoy, bother, exasperate, get on someone's nerves, irritate, provoke, rile (*informal*), vex.

aggregate *adjective* combined, cumulative, total, whole.

aggressive *adjective* **1** attacking, bellicose, belligerent, combative, hostile, militant, pugnacious, warlike. **2** assertive, forceful, insistent, persistent, pushy, self-assertive, zealous.

aghast *adjective* appalled, dismayed, horrified, shocked, stunned.

agile *adjective* flexible, limber, lissom, lithe, nimble, quick-moving, sprightly, spry, supple.

agitate *verb* **1** disturb, excite, fluster, perturb, ruffle, stir up, trouble, unsettle, upset, work up, worry. **2** campaign, lobby, protest, stir. **3** beat, churn, shake, stir, toss, whisk. □ **agitator** *noun* activist, campaigner, demagogue, firebrand, lobbyist, protester, rabble-rouser, stirrer.

agony *noun* anguish, distress, pain, suffering, torment, torture. □ **agonising** *adjective* acute, excruciating, harrowing, intolerable, painful, severe, unbearable.

agree *verb* **1** be of the same mind, be unanimous, concur, see eye to eye. **2** (*agree to come*) consent, promise, undertake; (*agree to a plan*) accede to, accept, acquiesce in, allow, approve, assent to, back, consent to, endorse, grant, OK (*informal*), support. **3** accord, be consistent, be in harmony, coincide, conform, correspond, fit, harmonise, match, suit, tally.

agreeable *adjective* **1** amenable, in accord, in agreement, in favour, willing. **2** amiable, congenial, friendly, likeable, nice, pleasant.

agreement *noun* **1** accord, concord, consensus, harmony, unanimity. **2** accord, arrangement, bargain, compact, contract, covenant, deal, pact, settlement, treaty.

agriculture *noun* agribusiness, farming.

aground *adverb & adjective* beached, grounded, marooned, shipwrecked, stranded.

ahead *adverb* **1** in advance, in front, in the lead. **2** forwards, on, onwards.

aid noun **1** assistance, backing, collaboration, cooperation, encouragement, help, succour, support. **2** charity, contribution, donation, funding, grant, relief, sponsorship, subsidy, support.

aid verb abet, assist, back, collaborate with, contribute to, cooperate with, encourage, facilitate, give to, help, lend a hand to, promote, relieve, subsidise, succour, support.

aide noun assistant, helper.

ailing adjective crook (Australian informal), ill, indisposed, infirm, poorly, sick, unwell.

ailment noun affliction, complaint, condition, disease, disorder, illness, indisposition, infection, infirmity, malady, sickness, trouble.

aim verb **1** direct, focus, level, point, train. **2** aspire, endeavour, intend, plan, purpose, seek, strive, try.

aim noun ambition, design, end, goal, intention, object, objective, plan, point, purpose, target.

aimless adjective drifting, goalless, pointless, purposeless.

air noun **1** aerospace, atmosphere, sky. **2** breeze, draught, wind. **3** melody, strain, tune. **4** ambience, appearance, atmosphere, aura, feeling, impression, look, mood.

air verb **1** freshen, open up, ventilate. **2** express, get off your chest, make known, reveal, say, tell, vent, voice.

aircraft noun (kinds of aircraft) aeroplane, airliner, airship, biplane, bomber, fighter, glider, helicopter, jet, jumbo jet, jump jet, microlight, monoplane, plane, seaplane, turbojet.

airport noun aerodrome, airfield, airstrip, landing strip.

airtight adjective hermetically sealed, impermeable.

airy adjective breezy, draughty, fresh, ventilated, well-ventilated.

aisle noun corridor, gangway, gap, passage, passageway, path.

alarm noun **1** alert, bell, signal, siren, tocsin, warning. **2** anxiety, apprehension, consternation, dismay, dread, fear, fright, panic, terror, trepidation, worry.

alarm verb agitate, dismay, disturb, frighten, panic, perturb, petrify, put the wind up (informal), scare, startle, terrify, unnerve.

album noun **1** book, display book. **2** collection, compilation, disc, record, recording.

alcohol noun booze (*informal*), drink, grog (*Australian informal*), liquor, spirits, wine.

alcoholic adjective intoxicating, spirituous.

alcoholic noun boozer (*informal*), dipsomaniac, drunk, drunkard, soak (*informal*), sot, wino (*informal*).

alcove noun bay, niche, nook, recess.

alert adjective attentive, awake, aware, careful, observant, on the ball (*informal*), on the lookout, on your guard, on your toes, ready, vigilant, wary, watchful.

alert noun alarm, signal, siren, warning.

alert verb caution, forewarn, prepare, warn.

alias noun assumed name, false name, nickname, nom de plume, pen-name, pseudonym, stage name.

alien noun **1** foreigner, outsider, stranger. **2** extraterrestrial.

alien adjective **1** exotic, foreign, outlandish, strange, unfamiliar. **2** contrary, foreign, inconsistent, uncharacteristic.

alienate verb antagonise, estrange, turn away, turn off.

alight adjective ablaze, blazing, burning, on fire.

alight verb **1** descend, disembark, get down, get off. **2** land, perch, settle.

align verb **1** line up, straighten up. **2** affiliate, ally, associate, join, side.

alike adjective akin, comparable, equivalent, identical, indistinguishable, similar, synonymous.

alive adjective **1** animate, breathing, existing, live, living, quick (*old use*), surviving. **2** (*alive to*) alert to, aware of, conscious of, mindful of, sensitive to. **3** (*alive with*) crawling with (*informal*), full of, packed with, swarming with, teeming with.

all adverb □ **all right 1** acceptable, fine, OK (*informal*), passable, satisfactory. **2** fine, OK (*informal*), safe, safe and sound, unharmed, uninjured, unscathed.

allay verb alleviate, calm, diminish, ease, lessen, quell, reduce, subdue.

allegation noun accusation, assertion, charge, claim, statement.

allege verb affirm, assert, avow, claim, declare, profess, state.

allegiance noun devotion, duty, faithfulness, fidelity, loyalty.

allegory noun fable, parable.

allergy *noun* reaction, sensitivity.

alleviate *verb* assuage, diminish, ease, lessen, mitigate, moderate, reduce, relieve, soften.

alley *noun* back street, lane, passage, passageway, path.

alliance *noun* affiliation, association, coalition, confederation, league, partnership, union.

allocation *noun* allotment, allowance, cut (*informal*), lot, portion, quota, ration, share, slice (*informal*).

allot *verb* allocate, apportion, assign, dispense, distribute, dole out, give out, mete out, ration, share out.

allotment *noun* **1** block, lot, plot, section (*Australian historical*). **2** allocation, allowance, quota, ration, share.

allow *verb* **1** approve, authorise, enable, let, permit. **2** allocate, allot, assign, give, grant, permit, provide.

allowance *noun* allocation, allotment, annuity, benefit, dole, endowment, grant, payment, pension, pocket money, portion, quota, ration, stipend, subsidy. ◻ **make allowances for** allow for, bear in mind, make concessions for, take into account, take into consideration; see also EXCUSE.

allude *verb* (*allude to*) hint at, mention, refer to, touch on. ◻ **allusion** *noun* hint, intimation, mention, reference.

alluring *adjective* attractive, beguiling, captivating, charming, enchanting, fascinating.

ally *noun* associate, colleague, confederate, friend, partner.

ally *verb* affiliate, band together, combine, join forces, side, team up, unite.

almighty *adjective* all-powerful, omnipotent, sovereign, supreme.

almost *adverb* all but, approximately, close to, nearly, not quite, practically, virtually, wellnigh.

alone *adjective* apart, by yourself, isolated, on your own, separate, single, solitary, solo, unaccompanied, unaided, unassisted; see also LONELY.

alongside *preposition* adjacent to, beside, close to, next to.

aloof *adjective* cool, distant, remote, stand-offish, unapproachable, unfriendly, unsociable, unsympathetic.

aloud *adverb* audibly, out loud.

also *adverb* additionally, as well, besides, furthermore, in addition, moreover, too.

alter *verb* adapt, adjust, amend, change, convert, modify, remodel, reshape, revise, transform, vary.

altercation *noun* argument, barney (*informal*), clash, disagreement, dispute, fight, quarrel, row, scrap (*informal*), set-to, squabble.

alternate *adjective* every other, every second.

alternate *verb* change, interchange, oscillate, rotate, swing, switch, take turns, vary.

alternative *adjective* **1** different, other, second. **2** non-conventional, unconventional.

alternative *noun* choice, option, possibility.

altitude *noun* elevation, height.

altogether *adverb* **1** all told, in all, in total, in toto. **2** absolutely, completely, entirely, perfectly, quite, thoroughly, totally, utterly, wholly.

always *adverb* **1** consistently, every time, invariably, regularly. **2** constantly, continually, continuously, eternally, forever, perpetually, repeatedly. **3** in any case, in any event, whatever happens.

amalgamate *verb* blend, combine, incorporate, integrate, join, merge, mix, unite.

amass *verb* accumulate, collect, gather, heap up, hoard, pile up, stock up, store up.

amateur *noun* dabbler, dilettante, layman, layperson, nonprofessional. □ **amateurish** *adjective* clumsy, incompetent, inexpert, unprofessional, unskilful.

amaze *verb* astonish, astound, bewilder, confound, dumbfound, flabbergast, nonplus, overwhelm, shock, stagger, startle, stun, stupefy, surprise, take aback. □ **amazement** *noun* astonishment, bewilderment, shock, stupefaction, surprise, wonder.

ambassador *noun* attaché, consul, diplomat, envoy, legate, plenipotentiary, representative.

ambiguous *adjective* equivocal, imprecise, indefinite, uncertain, unclear, vague.

ambition *noun* **1** drive, enterprise, enthusiasm, get-up-and-go (*informal*), motivation, push, zeal. **2** aim, aspiration, desire, dream, goal, intention, object, objective, purpose.

ambitious *adjective* **1** aspiring, eager, enterprising, go-ahead, high-flying, keen, pushy, zealous. **2** bold, challenging, daring, difficult, formidable, grandiose.

amble *verb* & *noun* dawdle, ramble, saunter, stroll, walk, wander.

ambush *noun* snare, trap.

ambush *verb* attack, ensnare, lie in wait for, pounce on, swoop on, trap, waylay.

ameliorate *verb* enhance, improve, make better, upgrade.

amend *verb* adapt, adjust, alter, change, correct, edit, improve, modify, rectify, revise. □ **make amends for** atone for, compensate for, expiate, make reparation for, make restitution for.

amenity *noun* convenience, facility, feature.

amiable *adjective* affable, agreeable, amicable, friendly, genial, good-natured, kind, kindly, pleasant.

amicable *adjective* cordial, friendly, harmonious, peaceful.

amiss *adjective* awry, defective, faulty, incorrect, out of order, wrong.

ammunition *noun* bullets, cartridges, grenades, missiles, projectiles, rounds, shells, shot, shrapnel.

amnesty *noun* pardon, reprieve.

among *preposition* amid, amidst, amongst, in the middle of, in the midst of, surrounded by.

amorous *adjective* affectionate, loving, passionate, tender.

amount *noun* extent, lot (*informal*), mass, measure, quantity, sum, total, volume.

amount *verb* □ **amount to** add up to, come to, equal, make, total.

ample *adjective* **1** abundant, bountiful, copious, enough, generous, lavish, liberal, plentiful, profuse, sufficient. **2** big, large, stout.

amplify *verb* **1** boost, enhance, increase, intensify, magnify, strengthen. **2** add to, develop, elaborate on, enlarge upon, expand, fill out, supplement.

amputate *verb* chop off, cut off, remove.

amuse *verb* cheer up, delight, divert, entertain. □ **amusing** *adjective* comical, diverting, droll, entertaining, farcical, funny, hilarious, humorous, laughable, ludicrous, priceless (*informal*), ridiculous, witty, zany.

amusement *noun* **1** delight, enjoyment, entertainment, fun, hilarity, merriment, mirth, pleasure, recreation. **2** distraction, diversion, entertainment, game, hobby, interest, pastime, sport.

anaemic adjective colourless, pale, pallid, pasty, sickly, wan, white.

analogy noun comparison, likeness, metaphor, parallel, resemblance, similarity. □ **analogous** adjective akin, comparable, corresponding, like, parallel, similar.

analyse verb **1** break down, dissect, divide, separate, take apart. **2** examine, interpret, investigate, study. □ **analysis** noun breakdown, examination, interpretation, investigation, study.

anarchy noun chaos, confusion, disorder, lawlessness.

ancestor noun forebear, forefather, predecessor, progenitor. □ **ancestry** noun ancestors, blood, descent, extraction, forebears, genealogy, lineage, origin, pedigree, roots, stock.

anchor verb fasten, moor, secure, tie up.

ancient adjective **1** antiquated, antique, archaic, obsolete, old, old-fashioned, out-of-date. **2** bygone, early, former, old, olden, prehistoric, primeval, primitive, primordial.

ancillary adjective auxiliary, subordinate, subsidiary, support, supporting.

anecdote noun narrative, story, tale, yarn (informal).

angel noun archangel, cherub, messenger of God, seraph. □ **angelic** adjective **1** celestial, cherubic, heavenly, seraphic. **2** good, innocent, kind, pure.

anger noun annoyance, displeasure, exasperation, fury, indignation, ire, irritation, outrage, pique, rage, temper, vexation, wrath.

anger verb annoy, bug (informal), displease, enrage, exasperate, gall, incense, infuriate, irritate, madden, outrage, pique, provoke, rile (informal), vex.

angle noun **1** bend, corner. **2** approach, outlook, perspective, point of view, position, slant, standpoint, viewpoint.

angle verb slant, slope, tilt, turn, twist.

angry adjective annoyed, bad-tempered, cross, displeased, enraged, exasperated, furious, hot under the collar (informal), incensed, indignant, infuriated, irascible, irate, irritated, livid (informal), mad (informal), outraged, resentful, riled (informal), ropeable (Australian informal), shirty (informal), snaky (Australian informal), up in arms, wild, wrathful. □ **be angry**, **become angry** blow your stack (informal), blow your top (informal), do your block (Australian *informal*), do your lolly (*informal*), explode, flare up, flip your lid (*informal*), fly off the handle (*informal*), freak (out) (*informal*), fume, get steamed up (*informal*), go crook (*Australian informal*), go off the deep end (*informal*), hit the roof (*informal*), lose your temper, rage, rave, seethe.

anguish *noun* agony, distress, grief, misery, pain, sorrow, suffering, torment, torture, woe.

animal *noun* beast, brute, creature; (*animals*) fauna, livestock, wildlife.

animate *adjective* alive, breathing, live, living, sentient.

animate *verb* buck up (*informal*), energise, enliven, excite, fire up, galvanise, inspire, liven up, motivate, perk up (*informal*), rouse, stimulate. □ **animated** *adjective* active, bright, energetic, enthusiastic, excited, exuberant, lively, passionate, spirited, vigorous, vivacious. □ **animation** *noun* dynamism, energy, enthusiasm, excitement, liveliness, spirit, verve, vigour, vitality, vivacity, zest.

animosity *noun* acrimony, antagonism, antipathy, bitterness, enmity, hatred, hostility,

ill will, malevolence, malice, rancour, resentment.

annex *verb* conquer, occupy, seize, take over, take possession of.

annexe *noun* addition, extension, wing.

annihilate *verb* destroy, eliminate, eradicate, exterminate, extinguish, get rid of, kill, liquidate, murder, obliterate, slaughter, wipe out.

anniversary *noun* birthday, jubilee.

annotation *noun* comment, explanation, footnote, note.

announce *verb* advertise, broadcast, declare, disclose, divulge, make known, proclaim, promulgate, publicise, publish, report, reveal, tell. □ **announcement** *noun* advertisement, bulletin, communiqué, declaration, disclosure, notice, notification, proclamation, pronouncement, publication, report, statement.

announcer *noun* broadcaster, compère, disc jockey, DJ, herald, master of ceremonies, MC, newsreader, presenter.

annoy *verb* aggravate (*informal*), anger, badger, bother, bug (*informal*), distress, drive someone mad (*informal*), drive someone up the wall (*informal*), exasperate, gall, get on someone's nerves, get under someone's skin (*informal*), get up someone's nose (*informal*), harass, hassle, infuriate, irk, irritate, madden, nark (*informal*), needle (*informal*), pester, pique, plague, provoke, rankle, rile (*informal*), rub someone up the wrong way (*informal*), trouble, try, upset, vex, worry. □ **annoyed** *adjective* angry, cheesed off (*slang*), cranky, crook (*Australian informal*), cross, displeased, exasperated, fed up (*informal*), irritated, mad, miffed (*informal*), narked (*informal*), needled (*informal*), peeved (*informal*), put out, riled (*informal*), shirty (*informal*), upset, vexed.

annual *adjective* yearly.

annul *verb* abolish, cancel, invalidate, nullify, rescind, revoke, void.

anoint *verb* grease, oil, rub, smear.

anomaly *noun* abnormality, deviation, inconsistency, irregularity, oddity, peculiarity.

anonymous *adjective* incognito, nameless, unidentified, unknown, unnamed.

another *adjective* **1** additional, extra, further, second. **2** alternative, different.

answer *noun* **1** acknowledgement, rejoinder, reply, response, retort, riposte. **2** explanation, solution.

answer *verb* acknowledge, rejoin, reply, respond, retort. □ **answer back** argue, be cheeky, contradict, disagree, talk back. □ **answer to** conform to, correspond to, fit, match.

answerable *adjective* accountable, liable, responsible.

antagonism *noun* animosity, antipathy, conflict, discord, friction, hatred, hostility, opposition, rivalry.

anthem *noun* canticle, chorale, hymn, psalm.

anthology *noun* collection, compendium, compilation, miscellany, selection, treasury.

anticipate *verb* **1** forestall, preempt. **2** expect, forecast, foresee, predict.

anticlimax *noun* comedown, disappointment, flop (*informal*), let-down.

antics *plural noun* capers, fooling around, mischief, pranks, shenanigans (*informal*), tomfoolery, tricks.

antidote *noun* antitoxin, antivenene, corrective, countermeasure, cure, remedy.

antipathy *noun* abhorrence, aversion, detestation, dislike, hatred, hostility, loathing, revulsion.

antiquated adjective ancient, antediluvian (*informal*), antique, archaic, behind the times, obsolete, old, old-fashioned, outdated, outmoded, out of date, prehistoric, primitive, quaint, unfashionable.

antique adjective ancient, antiquated, archaic, old, old-fashioned, veteran, vintage.

antique noun collectable, collector's item, heirloom, relic.

antiseptic noun bactericide, disinfectant, germicide.

antisocial adjective inconsiderate, offensive, unfriendly.

antonym noun opposite.

anxious adjective **1** afraid, apprehensive, concerned, fearful, nervous, tense, troubled, uneasy, uptight (*informal*), worried. **2** desirous, desperate, eager, keen, longing, wanting. □ **anxiety** noun apprehension, concern, dismay, disquiet, dread, foreboding, fear, misgiving, nervousness, stress, tension, trepidation, uneasiness, worry.

apart adverb **1** independently, separately. **2** asunder, into pieces. □ **apart from** aside from, except, excluding, not counting, not including, other than, save.

apartment noun bedsit (*British*), condominium (*American*), flat, home unit (*Australian*), penthouse, unit (*Australian*).

apathy noun coolness, impassivity, indifference, listlessness, passivity, unconcern. □ **apathetic** adjective impassive, indifferent, listless, passive, unconcerned, unemotional, uninterested, unmoved, unresponsive.

ape verb copy, imitate, mimic.

aperture noun crack, gap, hole, opening, slit.

apex noun acme, crest, height, peak, pinnacle, summit, tip, top, vertex, zenith.

apologetic adjective contrite, penitent, regretful, remorseful, repentant, sorry.

apologise verb beg pardon, express regret, repent, say sorry.

apostle noun evangelist, messenger, missionary.

appal verb disgust, dismay, horrify, outrage, shock, sicken, terrify. □ **appalling** adjective abominable, atrocious, awful, dire, dreadful, frightful, ghastly, hideous, horrendous, horrible, outrageous, repulsive, shocking, sickening, terrible.

apparatus noun appliance, contraption, device, equipment, gear, instrument, machine, machinery, tool.

apparent adjective **1** clear, conspicuous, discernible, evident, manifest, obvious, patent, plain, unmistakable, visible. **2** ostensible, outward, seeming, superficial.

apparition noun ghost, hallucination, phantom, spectre, spirit, spook (informal), vision.

appeal verb **1** apply, ask, beg, entreat, implore, petition, plead, request, solicit. **2** attract, entice, fascinate, interest, lure, tempt.

appeal noun **1** call, entreaty, petition, plea, request. **2** attraction, charm, fascination, interest, temptation.

appear verb **1** arrive, attend, be present, come, emerge, front up (informal), materialise, show up, surface, turn up. **2** give an impression of being, look, seem. **3** act, perform, play, star, take the part of.

appearance noun **1** advent, arrival, coming. **2** air, aspect, demeanour, expression, look, manner, mien. **3** front, guise, illusion, impression, pretence, semblance, show.

appease verb calm, mollify, pacify, placate, quiet, quieten, soothe, tranquillise.

appendix noun addendum, addition, attachment, supplement.

appetising adjective appealing, delicious, mouth-watering, palatable, tasty, tempting. ▢ **appetiser** noun aperitif, hors d'oeuvre, starter.

appetite noun craving, desire, fondness, hunger, inclination, keenness, liking, longing, passion, relish, stomach, taste, thirst.

applaud verb acclaim, approve, clap, commend, compliment, congratulate, give someone a big hand (informal), give someone an ovation, praise. ▢ **applause** noun clapping, hand (informal), ovation, plaudits; see also APPROVAL.

appliance noun apparatus, contraption, device, equipment, gadget, implement, instrument, machine, utensil.

applicable adjective apposite, appropriate, fitting, germane, pertinent, relevant, suitable.

applicant noun candidate, competitor, entrant, interviewee, job-seeker.

application noun **1** appeal, claim, petition, request, submission. **2** assiduity, commitment, dedication, diligence, effort, industry, perseverance, persistence.

apply verb **1** put on, smear, spread. **2** administer, employ, enforce, exercise, put into effect, use, utilise. **3** be relevant, concern, pertain, refer, relate. **4** (apply for) ask for, audition for, put in for, register for, request, seek, solicit.

appoint verb **1** choose, designate, elect, name, nominate, select. **2** arrange, assign, decide on, determine, establish, fix, organise, settle on.

appointment noun **1** arrangement, assignation, date, engagement, interview, meeting, rendezvous. **2** choice, election, selection. **3** job, office, position, post, situation.

appreciable adjective considerable, noticeable, perceptible, significant, substantial.

appreciate verb **1** be grateful for, be thankful for, cherish, prize, think highly of, treasure, value. **2** acknowledge, comprehend, realise, recognise, understand. **3** escalate, gain, go up, improve, increase, inflate, mount, rise. □ **appreciative** adjective grateful, obliged, thankful.

apprehend verb **1** arrest, capture, catch, detain, nab (informal), nail, nick (slang), seize, take into custody. **2** comprehend, grasp, perceive, realise, understand.

apprehension noun **1** anxiety, concern, dread, fear, foreboding, nervousness, trepidation, uneasiness, worry. **2** appreciation, comprehension, realisation, recognition, understanding. **3** arrest, capture, seizure. □ **apprehensive** adjective afraid, anxious, edgy (informal), fearful, frightened, nervous, troubled, uneasy, worried.

apprentice noun beginner, cadet, learner, novice, probationer, pupil, tiro, trainee.

approach verb **1** advance, come near, draw near, loom, near. **2** appeal to, apply to, ask. **3** go about, handle, set about, tackle. □ **approachable** adjective accessible, affable, easygoing, friendly.

approach noun **1** advance, advent, arrival, coming, nearing. **2** access, entry, way, way in. **3** attitude, manner, method, procedure, style, technique, way.

appropriate adjective applicable, apposite, apropos, apt, befitting, fitting, pertinent, proper, relevant, right, seemly, suitable, timely.

appropriate *verb* commandeer, confiscate, requisition, seize, take; see also STEAL.

approval *noun* **1** acclaim, acclamation, admiration, applause, appreciation, approbation, commendation, favour, praise. **2** acceptance, agreement, assent, authorisation, blessing, consent, endorsement, go-ahead, OK (*informal*), permission, ratification, sanction, support, validation.

approve *verb* **1** (*approve of*) acclaim, admire, applaud, be pleased with, commend, favour, like, praise. **2** agree to, allow, assent to, authorise, back, consent to, endorse, pass, permit, ratify, sanction, support, validate.

approximate *adjective* ballpark (*informal*), close, estimated, inexact, rough. □ **approximately** *adverb* about, almost, approaching, around, circa, close to, nearly, roughly.

apron *noun* pinafore.

apt *adjective* **1** inclined, liable, likely, tending. **2** applicable, apposite, appropriate, apropos, felicitous, fitting, relevant, suitable. **3** bright, clever, intelligent, quick, sharp, smart.

aptitude *noun* ability, capability, capacity, facility, flair, gift, knack, skill, talent.

arbitrary *adjective* capricious, chance, indiscriminate, random, subjective, unreasoned, whimsical. □ **arbitrator** *noun* adjudicator, arbiter, judge, referee, umpire.

arc *noun* arch, bend, bow, crescent, curve.

arcade *noun* cloister, colonnade, gallery, mall, passage, portico, walk.

arcane *adjective* abstruse, esoteric, inscrutable, mysterious, obscure, secret.

arch *noun* **1** archway, span, vault. **2** arc, bow, curve, semicircle.

arch *verb* bend, bow, curve, hump.

arch *adjective* mischievous, playful, roguish, saucy, teasing.

archaic *adjective* ancient, antiquated, antique, obsolete, old, olden, old-fashioned, outmoded, out of date.

archetype *noun* model, original, pattern, prototype, standard.

archives *plural noun* annals, chronicles, documents, papers, records, registers.

ardent *adjective* avid, eager, earnest, enthusiastic, fervent, impassioned, keen, passionate, vehement, zealous.

ardour *noun* eagerness, earnestness, enthusiasm, fervour, keenness, passion, warmth, zeal.

arduous *adjective* difficult, exacting, exhausting, formidable, gruelling, hard, herculean, laborious, onerous, strenuous, taxing, tough.

area *noun* **1** extent, measurement, size. **2** district, locality, neighbourhood, precinct, quarter, region, territory, vicinity, zone. **3** place, space, spot.

arena *noun* amphitheatre, field, ground, pitch, ring, stadium.

arguable *adjective* contentious, controversial, debatable, disputable, doubtful, moot, uncertain.

argue *verb* **1** barney (*informal*), bicker, debate, differ, disagree, dispute, feud, fight, haggle, have words, quarrel, quibble, row (*informal*), spar, squabble, wrangle. **2** assert, claim, contend, declare, maintain, reason, show.

argument *noun* **1** altercation, barney (*informal*), blue (*Australian informal*), clash, controversy, debate, disagree-ment, dispute, feud, fight, quarrel, row (*informal*), spat (*informal*), squabble, tiff, wrangle. **2** case, defence, grounds, justification, reason, reasoning.

argumentative *adjective* belligerent, contentious, contrary, disputatious, pugnacious, quarrelsome.

arid *adjective* barren, desert, dry, infertile, lifeless, parched, unproductive, waste, waterless.

arise *verb* **1** appear, come up, crop up, emerge, occur, originate, present itself. **2** get up, rise, stand up.

aristocracy *noun* elite, gentry, nobility, peerage, upper class.

aristocrat *noun* grandee, lady, lord, noble, nobleman, noblewoman, peer, peeress. □ **aristocratic** *adjective* blue-blooded, courtly, high-born, noble, titled, upper-class.

arm *noun* **1** appendage, forelimb, limb, tentacle (*of an octopus*). **2** (*arm of a tree*) bough, branch, limb.

arm *verb* equip, furnish, provide, supply. □ **armed forces** air force, armed services, army, defence forces, forces, marines, military, navy, services, troops.

armada *noun* convoy, fleet, flotilla, navy, squadron.

armistice *noun* ceasefire, peace, peace treaty, truce.

armour *noun* chain mail, mail, protective covering.

arms *plural noun* **1** armaments, firearms, weapons. **2** coat of arms, crest, emblem, insignia, shield.

army *noun* **1** armed forces, armed services, military, soldiers, troops. **2** crowd, horde, host, mob, multitude, throng.

aroma *noun* bouquet, fragrance, odour, perfume, savour, scent, smell. □ **aromatic** *adjective* fragrant, pungent, spicy, strong-smelling.

around *adverb & preposition* **1** (*travel around*) about, all round, here and there, hither and thither. **2** (*stay around*) about, at hand, close by, in the vicinity, near, nearby. **3** (*around 500*) about, approximately, circa, close to, nearly, roughly. **4** (*a screen around the bed*) encircling, on all sides of, round, surrounding.

arouse *verb* awake, awaken, excite, inspire, provoke, rouse, stimulate, stir up, waken, wake up.

arrange *verb* **1** array, categorise, classify, display, dispose, group, lay out, line up, order, organise, position, put in order, rank, set out, sort. **2** contrive, fix, organise, plan, prepare, schedule, settle, set up, wangle (*slang*). **3** adapt, orchestrate, score, set. □ **arrangement** *noun* **1** array, categorisation, classification, display, grouping, layout, line-up, order, organisation, set-up, system. **2** agreement, bargain, contract, deal, plan, provision, settlement, understanding. **3** adaptation, orchestration, setting, version.

array *noun* arrangement, collection, display, exhibit, line-up, series, show.

array *verb* adorn, attire, clothe, deck, dress, garb, robe.

arrears *plural noun* **1** back pay, debt, outstanding amount. **2** accumulation, backlog, build-up, pile-up. □ **in arrears** behind, behindhand, late, overdue.

arrest *verb* **1** apprehend, capture, catch, collar (*informal*), detain, nab (*informal*), nail, nick (*slang*), seize, take into custody. **2** block, check, curb, halt, inhibit, prevent, retard, stem, stop.

arrive *verb* appear, come, disembark, enter, get in, land, roll up (*informal*), show up, touch down, turn up; (*arrive at*) come to, get to, hit, make, reach. □ **arrival** noun advent, appearance, approach, coming, entrance, entry.

arrogant adjective cocky, conceited, condescending, contemptuous, disdainful, egotistic, haughty, high and mighty, lofty, overbearing, presumptuous, proud, scornful, self-important, snobbish, snooty (*informal*), stuck-up (*informal*), supercilious, vain.

arsenal noun ammunition dump, armoury, arms depot, magazine, ordnance depot, store.

arsonist noun firebug (*informal*), pyromaniac.

art noun craft, flair, gift, knack, skill, talent, technique, trick.

artful adjective astute, clever, crafty, cunning, deceitful, ingenious, scheming, shifty, shrewd, sly, tricky, wily.

article noun **1** essay, feature, item, piece, report, story, write-up. **2** item, object, piece, thing.

articulate adjective clear, coherent, comprehensible, eloquent, fluent, intelligible, lucid, understandable.

articulate verb enunciate, pronounce, say, speak, utter.

artifice noun dodge (*informal*), ruse, stratagem, subterfuge, trick, wile.

artificial adjective **1** bogus, counterfeit, fake, false, imitation, man-made, manufactured, mock, phoney (*informal*), pseudo, sham, synthetic. **2** affected, false, feigned, forced, hollow, insincere, phoney (*informal*), pretended, simulated, skin-deep, superficial.

artisan noun craftsman, craftswoman, technician, tradesman, tradeswoman.

artist noun **1** (*kinds of artist*) cartoonist, engraver, graphic designer, illustrator, painter, photographer, sculptor. **2** artiste, entertainer, musician, performer.

artistic adjective aesthetic, attractive, beautiful, creative, decorative, imaginative, tasteful.

artless adjective genuine, guileless, honest, ingenuous, innocent, natural, open, simple, sincere, straightforward, unaffected, unsophisticated.

ascend verb climb, go up, mount, rise, scale, soar.

ascent noun climb, gradient, hill, incline, rise, slope.

ascertain verb confirm, determine, discover, establish, find out, identify, learn, uncover, verify, work out.

ascetic adjective abstemious, austere, frugal, harsh, puritanical, self-disciplined, spartan, strict, temperate.

ascribe verb attribute, impute, put down.

ash noun (ashes) cinders, embers, remains.

ashamed adjective abashed, embarrassed, humiliated, mortified, red-faced, shame-faced, sheepish.

aside adverb away, out of the way, to one side, to the side. □ **aside from** apart from, besides, in addition to, other than.

ask verb 1 enquire of, inquire of, interrogate, query, question, quiz. 2 appeal, apply, beg, beseech, demand, entreat, implore, petition, plead, pray, request, seek, solicit, supplicate. 3 invite, summon.

askew adjective awry, cock-eyed (informal), crooked, lopsided, on an angle, out of line, slanting.

asleep adverb & adjective dormant, dozing, hibernating, napping, resting, sleeping, slumbering, snoozing. □ **fall asleep** doze off, drop off, flake out (informal), go to sleep, nod off.

aspect noun 1 angle, detail, facet, feature, side. 2 orientation, outlook, prospect, view.

aspiration noun aim, ambition, desire, dream, goal, hope, longing, objective, wish, yearning.

aspire verb (aspire to) aim for, desire, hanker after, hope for, long for, set your sights on, wish for, yearn for.

ass noun 1 donkey, jackass (male), jenny (female). 2 see FOOL.

assail verb assault, attack, bombard, lay into, set upon. □ **assailant** noun assaulter, attacker, mugger.

assassin noun executioner, hit man (slang), killer, murderer.

assassinate verb execute, kill, murder, slay.

assault noun attack, blitz, charge, incursion, offensive, onslaught, raid, strike.

assault verb assail, attack, beat up, hit, molest, mug, rape, set upon, strike.

assemble verb 1 accumulate, bring together, collect, come together, congregate, flock, gather, group, marshal, meet, mobilise, muster, rally, round up, swarm, throng. 2 build, construct, erect, fabricate, fit together, make up, manufacture, put together.

assembly noun conference, congregation, congress, convention, council, crowd, gathering, group, meeting, mob, multitude, rally, synod, throng.

assent verb accede, accept, acquiesce, agree, approve, consent, permit, sanction.

assent noun acceptance, accord, acquiescence, agreement, approval, consent, permission, sanction.

assert verb allege, argue, attest, claim, contend, declare, insist, maintain, proclaim, state, swear.

assertive adjective aggressive, authoritative, bold, dogmatic, forceful, insistent, pushy, self-assertive, strong-willed.

assess verb appraise, calculate, compute, estimate, evaluate, gauge, grade, judge, mark, rate, reckon, value, work out.

asset noun advantage, benefit, blessing, boon, help, strength. □ **assets** plural noun capital, holdings, means, possessions, property, resources, securities, wealth.

assiduous adjective diligent, hard-working, indefatigable, industrious, persevering.

assign verb 1 allocate, allot, deal out, dispense, distribute, give out. 2 appoint, delegate, designate, nominate, select.

assignment noun homework, job, project, task, work.

assimilate verb absorb, digest, take in; see also LEARN.

assist verb abet, advance, aid, back, collaborate with, cooperate with, help, lend a hand, relieve, serve, succour, support. □ **assistance** noun aid, backing, backup, collaboration, cooperation, help, reinforcement, relief, service, succour, support.

assistant noun abetter, accessory, accomplice, aide, auxiliary, deputy, helper, offsider (Australian), sidekick (informal), subordinate, underling.

associate verb 1 connect, identify, link, relate. 2 consort, fraternise, hang around (informal), hang out (informal), hobnob, keep company, mix, socialise.

associate noun colleague, co-worker, fellow-worker, partner, workmate; see also COMPANION.

association noun 1 alliance, body, club, federation, group, league, organisation, society, union. 2 connection, link, relation, relationship, tie-up.

assorted *adjective* different, diverse, miscellaneous, mixed, sundry, varied. □ **assortment** *noun* array, collection, hotch-potch, medley, miscellany, mixture, potpourri, range, selection, variety.

assuage *verb* alleviate, appease, ease, quench, relieve, slake, soothe.

assume *verb* **1** believe, expect, guess, imagine, presume, presuppose, suppose, surmise, think. **2** accept, adopt, take on, undertake. **3** acquire, adopt, affect, put on. □ **assumption** *noun* guess, hypothesis, presumption, presupposition, supposition, surmise, theory.

assurance *noun* **1** commitment, guarantee, oath, pledge, promise, undertaking. **2** aplomb, confidence, poise, self-assurance, self-confidence.

assure *verb* **1** declare, give your word, guarantee, pledge, promise, swear, vow. **2** ensure, guarantee, make sure of, secure. □ **assured** *adjective* bold, cocksure, confident, cool, self-assured, self-confident, unafraid.

astonish *verb* amaze, astound, confound, dumbfound, flabbergast, nonplus, shock, stagger, startle, stun, stupefy, surprise, take aback.

□ **astonishment** *noun* amazement, surprise, wonder.

astray *adverb* □ **go astray** be lost, be mislaid, be misplaced, go missing, go walkabout (*informal*).

astronaut *noun* cosmonaut, spaceman, spacewoman.

astronomical *adjective* colossal, enormous, exorbitant, huge, incredible (*informal*), massive, unbelievable, vast.

astute *adjective* canny, clever, discerning, intelligent, knowing, observant, perceptive, quick, sharp, shrewd, sly.

asylum *noun* **1** protection, refuge, safety, sanctuary, shelter. **2** lunatic asylum (*old use*), mental home, mental hospital, mental institution, psychiatric hospital.

asymmetrical *adjective* irregular, lopsided, unbalanced, uneven.

atheist *noun* see NON-BELIEVER.

athletic *adjective* active, brawny, husky, muscular, robust, sporty (*informal*), strapping, strong.

athletics *plural noun* games, races, sport, sports, track and field events.

atmosphere *noun* **1** aerospace, air, heavens, sky. **2** air, ambience, aura, climate, environment, feeling, mood, tone, vibes (*informal*).

atone verb (*atone for*) compensate for, expiate, make amends for, make up for, pay for, pay the penalty for.

atrocious adjective (*an atrocious crime*) abominable, appalling, barbaric, brutal, cruel, despicable, evil, heinous, horrific, monstrous, savage, vicious, wicked; (*atrocious weather*) bad, dreadful (*informal*), foul, shocking (*informal*), terrible (*informal*), unpleasant.

atrocity noun crime, cruelty, evil, horror, offence, outrage.

attach verb affix, append, bind, connect, couple, fasten, fix, glue, join, link, pin, secure, staple, stick, tack, tie. □ **attachment** noun accessory, appendage, extra, fitting. □ **attached to** close to, devoted to, fond of.

attack noun 1 ambush, assault, blitz, bombardment, charge, foray, incursion, invasion, offensive, onslaught, raid, rush, sortie, strike. 2 bout, fit, outbreak, seizure, spell.

attack verb 1 ambush, assail, assault, beat up, besiege, bombard, fall upon, invade, molest, mug, pounce on, raid,

set about (*informal*), set upon, storm, strike. 2 condemn, criticise, denounce, knock (*informal*), malign, pan (*informal*), revile, slam (*informal*), slate (*informal*), vilify. □ **attacker** noun aggressor, assailant, assaulter, mugger.

attain verb accomplish, achieve, arrive at, gain, obtain, reach.

attempt verb endeavour, strive, try, venture.

attempt noun bid, effort, endeavour, go, try.

attend verb 1 (*attend to a problem*) deal with, handle, see to, take care of; (*attend to the teacher*) heed, listen to, pay attention to, take notice of. 2 appear at, be present at, go to, show up at (*informal*), turn up at, visit. 3 care for, look after, take care of, tend, wait on. 4 accompany, chaperone, escort, guard.

attendant noun aide, assistant, chaperone, companion, escort, helper, servant, steward, usher.

attention noun care, concentration, concern, heed, notice, regard, thought. □ **pay attention** attend, concentrate, listen, pay heed, watch.

attentive adjective alert, awake, aware, careful, diligent, mindful, observant, vigilant, watchful; see also CONSIDERATE.

attest verb affirm, assert, certify, confirm, swear to, testify to, verify, vouch for.

attic noun garret, loft.

attire noun apparel (formal), clothes, clothing, costume, dress, garb, garments, gear (informal), outfit, raiment (old use), wear.

attitude noun demeanour, disposition, feeling, frame of mind, manner, mien, mood, opinion, outlook, position, stance, stand, standpoint, thoughts, view, viewpoint.

attract verb allure, appeal to, draw, entice, fascinate, interest, lure, pull. □ **attractive** adjective alluring, appealing, beautiful, bonny (Scottish), captivating, charming, comely, enchanting, enticing, fascinating, fetching, good-looking, handsome, interesting, inviting, irresistible, lovely, nice, pleasant, pleasing, pretty, striking, stunning, sweet (informal), tempting, winsome.

attraction noun **1** allure, appeal, attractiveness, charm, enticement, fascination, lure, pull. **2** crowd-pleaser, draw-card, feature, interest.

attribute verb ascribe, credit, impute, put down to.

attribute noun characteristic, feature, property, quality, trait, virtue.

audacious adjective adventurous, bold, brave, confident, courageous, daredevil, daring, fearless, game, heroic, intrepid, plucky, reckless, venturesome. □ **audacity** noun boldness, cheek, effrontery, gall (slang), hide (informal), impertinence, impudence, insolence, nerve, temerity.

audible adjective clear, discernible, distinct, perceptible.

audience noun congregation, crowd, listeners, spectators, viewers.

audit noun check, examination, inspection, review, scrutiny.

audit verb check, examine, go over, inspect, review, scrutinise.

audition noun screen test, test, trial, try-out.

auditorium noun hall, theatre.

augment verb add to, boost, eke out, increase, supplement, swell.

augur verb be a sign of, bode, foreshadow, portend, presage, promise.

august adjective dignified, grand, imposing, impressive, majestic, noble, venerable.

aura noun air, ambience, atmosphere, feeling, mood, spirit, vibes (*informal*).

auspices plural noun aegis, authority, control, patronage, protection, sponsorship.

auspicious adjective favourable, promising, propitious.

austere adjective abstemious, ascetic, frugal, hard, harsh, plain, puritanical, restrained, rigorous, self-denying, self-disciplined, severe, simple, spartan, strict.

authentic adjective actual, dinkum (*Australian informal*), genuine, real, true, trustworthy.

authenticate verb certify, confirm, endorse, prove, substantiate, validate, verify, vouch for.

author noun biographer, composer, creator, dramatist, essayist, novelist, playwright, poet, writer.

authorise verb allow, approve, commission, empower, entitle, give permission for, OK (*informal*), license, permit, sanction.

authoritarian adjective autocratic, bossy, dictatorial, dogmatic, domineering, severe, strict.

authority noun **1** command, control, dominion, influence, jurisdiction, power, right, sovereignty, supremacy. **2** arbiter, connoisseur, expert, judge, pundit, scholar, specialist.

autocratic adjective absolute, despotic, dictatorial, domineering, high-handed, imperious, tyrannical.

automatic adjective **1** automated, computerised, electronic, mechanised, programmed, pushbutton, self-operating, self-regulating. **2** instinctive, involuntary, mechanical, reflex, spontaneous, unconscious, unthinking.

autonomous adjective free, independent, self-governing.

autopsy noun necropsy, postmortem.

autumn noun fall (*American*).

auxiliary adjective ancillary, assisting, backup, helping, reserve, supplementary, support, supporting.

auxiliary noun aide, assistant, helper.

available adjective accessible, at hand, at your disposal, free, handy, obtainable, ready, usable.

avalanche noun deluge, flood, inundation, torrent.

avenge verb get even for, get your own back for (*informal*), repay, take revenge for; see also RETALIATE.

average *adjective* **1** mean. **2** intermediate, mediocre, medium, middling, normal, ordinary, regular, standard, usual.

averse *adjective* disinclined, loath, opposed, reluctant, unwilling.

aversion *noun* antipathy, dislike, hatred, hostility, loathing, revulsion.

avert *verb* **1** turn away. **2** fend off, prevent, stave off, ward off.

aviator *noun* airman, air-woman, aviatrix (*female, old use*), flyer, pilot.

avid *adjective* eager, enthusiastic, fervent, keen, passionate, zealous.

avoid *verb* **1** cold-shoulder, elude, give a wide berth to, ignore, keep away from, leave alone, shun, steer clear of. **2** bypass, circumvent, dodge, escape, evade, get out of, shirk, sidestep, skirt. **3** abstain from, eschew, keep off, refrain from.

awake *verb* arouse, awaken, rouse, stir, wake, wake up.

awake *adjective* conscious, open-eyed, sleepless, wakeful, wide awake.

award *verb* accord, allot, assign, bestow, confer, give, grant, present.

award *noun* badge, colours, cup, decoration, honour, medal, prize, scholarship, trophy.

aware *adjective* (*aware of*) acquainted with, alert to, alive to, conscious of, familiar with, informed about, mindful of, sensible of.

awe *noun* admiration, amazement, fear, respect, reverence, veneration, wonder.

awe-inspiring *adjective* amazing, astonishing, awesome, breathtaking, impressive, magnificent, marvellous, stupendous, wonderful, wondrous (*poetical*).

awesome *adjective* daunting, fearsome, formidable, intimidating, overwhelming, terrible.

awful *adjective* **1** abominable, appalling, atrocious, bad, deplorable, disgusting, dreadful, foul, frightful, ghastly, horrible, lousy (*informal*), nasty, rotten (*informal*), shocking, terrible, unpleasant. **2** big, excessive, huge, impressive, inordinate, large, tremendous. □ **awfully** *adverb* **1** abominably, appallingly, atrociously, badly, deplorably, dreadfully, frightfully, horribly, lousily (*informal*), nastily, poorly, reprehensibly, shockingly, terribly, unpleasantly. **2** exceedingly, extremely, really, terribly (*informal*), very.

awkward *adjective* **1** cumbersome, difficult, hard, inconvenient, ticklish, tricky, troublesome, unmanageable, unwieldy. **2** bumbling, bungling, clumsy, gauche, gawky, ham-fisted (*informal*), maladroit, uncoordinated, ungainly. **3** embarrassed, ill at ease, self-conscious, uncomfortable, uneasy.

awry *adverb* **1** askew, crookedly, on an angle, out of line, unevenly. **2** amiss, wrong.

axe *noun* adze, battleaxe, chopper, cleaver, hatchet, mogo, tomahawk.

axe *verb* abolish, cancel, discontinue, do away with, eliminate, get rid of, give the chop (*informal*), remove, scrap, terminate, wind up.

axiom *noun* fundamental, principle, truth; see also PROVERB.

axle *noun* arbor, rod, shaft, spindle.

Bb

babble *verb* **1** chatter, gabble, gibber, jabber, mumble, yabber (*Australian informal*). **2** burble, gurgle, murmur.

baby *noun* babe, bairn (*Scottish*), child, infant, toddler, tot. □ **babyish** *adjective* childish, immature, infantile, juvenile, sooky (*Australian informal*).

babysitter *noun* carer, childminder, minder, nanny, sitter.

back *noun* **1** end, rear, tail; (*of a ship*) poop, stern. **2** backbone, spinal column, spine, vertebral column.

back *adjective* dorsal, hind, rear. □ **backblocks** back of beyond, backwoods, bush (*Australian*), interior, never-never (*Australian*), outback (*Australian*), the sticks (*Australian informal*), up country, Woop Woop (*Australian informal*).

back *verb* **1** move backwards, reverse. **2** aid, assist, encourage, endorse, help, promote, sponsor, subsidise, support, underwrite. **3** bet on, gamble on. □ **backer** *noun* benefactor, patron, promoter, sponsor, supporter, underwriter. □ **back away** move backwards, pull back, recoil, retire, retreat, withdraw. □ **back down** back-pedal, backtrack, concede, give in, submit, surrender, yield. □ **back out of** escape from, get out of, go back on, renege on, withdraw from, wriggle out of.

□ **back up** affirm, confirm, corroborate, document, reinforce, second, substantiate, support, verify.

backbone noun **1** spinal column, spine, vertebral column. **2** courage, determination, fortitude, grit, guts (*informal*), pluck, resolve.

backfire verb boomerang, fail, rebound, recoil.

background noun **1** backcloth, backdrop, setting. **2** circumstances, context, environment, setting. **3** education, experience, history, training, upbringing.

backing noun aid, approval, assistance, endorsement, funding, help, patronage, sponsorship, subsidy, support.

backlash noun counteraction, reaction.

backlog noun accumulation, arrears, build-up, stockpile.

backpack noun haversack, knapsack, pack, rucksack.

backward adjective **1** rearward, regressive, retrograde, retrogressive, reverse. **2** handicapped, retarded, slow, underdeveloped, undeveloped.

backwards adverb in reverse, rearwards. □ **backwards and forwards** back and forth, hither and thither, to and fro.

bacterium noun bug (*informal*), germ, microbe, microorganism.

bad adjective **1** defective, deficient, faulty, inadequate, incompetent, inferior, poor, shoddy, substandard, unacceptable, unsatisfactory, unsound. **2** abhorrent, abominable, atrocious, awful, base, beastly, corrupt, criminal, cruel, deplorable, depraved, despicable, detestable, disgraceful, dishonest, dishonourable, evil, hateful, immoral, infamous, loathsome, malevolent, malicious, mean, nasty, naughty, notorious, reprehensible, sinful, ungodly, unrighteous, unworthy, vile, villainous, wicked. **3** appalling, awful, dire, disastrous, dreadful, frightful, ghastly, grave, hideous, horrendous, horrible, horrific, nasty, serious, severe, shocking, terrible. **4** ailing, crook (*Australian informal*), diseased, ill, indisposed, off colour, poorly, sick, unhealthy, unwell. **5** damaging, dangerous, deleterious, destructive, detrimental, harmful, hurtful, injurious, ruinous, unhealthy. **6** decayed, foul, mildewed, mouldy, nauseating, noxious, obnoxious, off, offensive, on the nose (*Australian informal*), putrid, rancid, repulsive, revolting, rotten, spoiled, stinking, tainted, vile. □ **bad-tempered** adjective angry, cantankerous, crabby, cranky, cross, crotchety, grouchy, gruff, grumpy, hot-tempered, ill-tempered, irascible, irritable, moody, peevish, petulant, quarrelsome, shirty (informal), short-tempered, snaky (Australian informal), snappy (informal), stroppy (informal), sullen, surly, testy.

badge noun crest, emblem, insignia, logo, medal, shield, sign, symbol.

badger verb bully, harass, hassle (informal), hound, nag, pester.

baffle verb bamboozle (informal), bewilder, confound, confuse, flummox (informal), mystify, perplex, puzzle, stump.

bag noun receptacle; (kinds of bag) attaché case, backpack, briefcase, carpet bag, carry bag, case, dilly bag (Australian), duffel bag, grip, handbag, haversack, holdall, kitbag, knapsack, pack, port (Australian), pouch, purse (American), rucksack, sack, satchel, schoolbag, shopping bag, shoulder bag, suitcase, swag (Australian), travelling bag, tucker bag (Australian informal).

baggage noun bags, cases, luggage, suitcases, trunks.

baggy adjective floppy, loose, roomy, shapeless.

bail noun bond, guarantee, security, surety.

bail verb □ **bail out** assist, help, relieve, rescue.

bail verb □ **bail up 1** hold up, rob, stick up (informal). **2** buttonhole, corner, detain, waylay.

bait noun attraction, decoy, enticement, lure, temptation.

bait verb badger, goad, provoke, tantalise, tease, torment.

bake verb **1** cook, roast. **2** fire, harden.

balance noun **1** equilibrium, poise, stability, steadiness. **2** scales, weighing machine. **3** difference, excess, leftovers, remainder, residue, rest, surplus.

balance verb cancel out, counteract, counterbalance, equalise, even out, level, neutralise, offset. □ **balanced** adjective even-handed, fair, impartial, unbiased.

balcony noun **1** deck, terrace, veranda. **2** gallery, the gods (informal), upper dress circle.

bald adjective hairless, shaved.

bale *noun* bundle, pack, package, parcel, truss.

bale *verb* □ **bale out** eject, jump out, parachute.

ball *noun* bead, drop, globe, orb, pellet, sphere.

ball *noun* dance, formal, social.

ballerina *noun* ballet-dancer, dancer.

balloon *verb* billow, bulge, puff out, swell.

ballot *noun* election, plebiscite, poll, referendum, vote.

balm *noun* balsam, embrocation, liniment, ointment, salve.

balmy *adjective* gentle, mild, pleasant, warm.

bamboozle *verb* baffle, bewilder, cheat, con (*informal*), confound, deceive, dupe, fool, hoax, hoodwink, mislead, mystify, perplex, puzzle, take in, trick.

ban *verb* forbid, outlaw, prohibit, proscribe.

ban *noun* boycott, embargo, moratorium, prohibition, proscription, veto.

banal *adjective* clichéd, commonplace, hackneyed, humdrum, trite, unimaginative, uninteresting, unoriginal.

band *noun* belt, circle, cord, elastic, hoop, ligature, line, loop, ribbon, ring, strap, string, strip, stripe, tie.

band *noun* **1** body, bunch, clique, company, gang, group, mob, pack, party, push (*Australian old use*). **2** ensemble, group, orchestra.

band *verb* affiliate, ally, associate, gather, group, join, team up, unite.

bandage *noun* dressing, gauze, plaster, tourniquet.

bandit *noun* brigand, buccaneer, bushranger, criminal, crook (*informal*), desperado, gangster, highwayman, outlaw, pirate, robber, thief.

bandstand *noun* platform, rotunda, stage.

bandy *adjective* bandy-legged, bow-legged.

bandy *verb* circulate, pass, spread.

bane *noun* curse, plague, scourge, trial, woe.

bang *noun* **1** blast, boom, clap, clatter, crash, detonation, explosion, pop, report, shot, thud. **2** blow, bump, hit, knock, punch, whack.

bang *verb* **1** bash, hammer, hit, knock, pound, punch, slam, strike, thump. **2** blast, boom, crash, detonate, explode, pop.

bangle noun anklet, armlet, bracelet.

banish verb cast out, deport, dismiss, drive out, excommunicate (*from a church*), exile, expatriate, expel, oust, remove, send away, transport.

banisters plural noun handrail, railing, stair-rail.

bank noun 1 brink, edge, embankment, shore, side, slope, verge. 2 mass, mound, pile. 3 group, row, series, set.

bank verb 1 accumulate, amass, collect, heap, pile, stack. 2 incline, lean, list, pitch, tilt.

bank noun kitty, pool, reserve, store.

bank verb deposit, invest, put aside, save. □ **bank on** bargain on, count on, depend on, pin your hopes on, rely on.

bankrupt adjective broke (*informal*), bust (*informal*), failed, in liquidation, insolvent, ruined.

banner noun 1 flag, pennant, standard. 2 placard, sign.

banquet noun dinner, feast, meal, repast (*formal*).

banter noun badinage, chiacking (*Australian informal*), jesting, joking, kidding (*informal*), raillery, repartee, ribbing (*informal*), teasing.

baptise verb christen; see also NAME.

bar noun 1 (*a wooden or metal bar*) bail, batten, beam, block, girder, pole, rail, rod, stake, stick; (*a bar of soap*) block, cake, hunk, lump, piece, slab. 2 counter, saloon. 3 barrier, block, hindrance, impediment, obstacle, obstruction, restriction.

bar verb 1 block, impede, obstruct. 2 ban, exclude, forbid, keep out, outlaw, prevent, prohibit.

barbaric adjective 1 barbarian, barbarous, primitive, savage, uncivilised, uncultivated, uncultured, wild. 2 barbarous, brutal, cruel, inhuman, rough, savage, vicious.

barber noun haircutter, hairdresser.

bard noun minstrel, musician, poet, troubadour.

bare adjective 1 denuded, exposed, naked, nude, stripped, unclothed, uncovered, undressed. 2 empty, unfurnished, uninhabited, unoccupied, vacant. 3 bald, plain, unadorned, unembellished, unvarnished. 4 basic, meagre, mere, scant. □ **barely** adverb hardly, only just, scarcely.

bare verb expose, reveal, show.

barefaced *adjective* blatant, brazen, downright, flagrant, shameless, unconcealed, undisguised.

bargain *noun* **1** accord, agreement, compact, contract, covenant, deal, pact. **2** giveaway (*informal*), good buy, snip (*informal*), special, steal (*informal*).

bargain *verb* barter, discuss terms, haggle, negotiate. □ **bargain for** anticipate, be prepared for, envisage, expect, foresee.

barge *verb* bump, collide, crash, knock, lurch, slam. □ **barge in** burst in, butt in, interrupt, intrude.

bark *noun* bay, bow-wow, growl, woof, yap, yelp. □ **bark** *verb* bay, growl, woof, yap, yelp.

barn *noun* outbuilding, outhouse, shed.

barney *noun* altercation, argument, fight, quarrel, row, squabble.

barrack *verb* (*barrack for*) cheer on, egg on, encourage, support.

barracks *noun* billet, camp, garrison, quarters.

barrage *noun* **1** barrier, dam, wall. **2** battery, bombardment, fusillade, gunfire, hail, onslaught, salvo, volley.

barrel *noun* **1** butt, cask, drum, hogshead, keg, tun.

barren *adjective* **1** arid, bare, desert, infertile, lifeless, unproductive, waste. **2** childless, infertile, sterile.

barricade *noun* barrier, blockade, fence.

barricade *verb* block off, fence off, obstruct, shut off.

barrier *noun* **1** bar, barricade, boom, fence, gate, obstruction, partition, rail, screen, wall. **2** bar, block, hindrance, impediment, obstacle, restriction, stumbling block.

barrister *noun* advocate, attorney (*American*), counsel; see also LAWYER.

barrow *noun* **1** wheelbarrow. **2** cart, handcart.

barter *verb* exchange, swap, trade.

base *noun* **1** bottom, foot, foundation, pedestal, plinth, stand, support. **2** camp, depot, headquarters, installation, post, station.

base *verb* build, establish, found, ground, root.

base *adjective* bad, contemptible, cowardly, despicable, dishonourable, evil, ignoble, immoral, low, mean, selfish, shabby, sordid, underhand, wicked.

basement noun cellar, crypt, vault.

bash verb assault, attack, batter, beat, clout, hit, mug, punch, strike, thump.

bash noun blow, hit, knock, punch, thump.

bashful adjective coy, demure, diffident, reserved, reticent, self-conscious, sheepish, shy.

basic adjective central, elementary, essential, fundamental, key, necessary, primary, radical, root, rudimentary, underlying. □ **basically** adverb at bottom, at heart, essentially, for the most part, fundamentally.

basin noun **1** bowl, container, dish, font. **2** sink, washbasin, washbowl.

basis noun base, beginning, footing, foundation, grounds, premise, principle, starting point, support.

bask verb sunbake, sunbathe, sun yourself, warm yourself.

basket noun carrier, hamper, pannier, punnet.

bass adjective deep, low, sonorous.

bat noun club, racquet, stick.

batch noun bunch, collection, group, lot, number, set.

bathe verb **1** bogey (Australian), paddle, swim, take a dip. **2** clean, cleanse, rinse, wash.

bathers plural noun bathing costume, bathing suit, bikini, cossie (Australian informal), one-piece, swimmers (Australian informal), swimming costume, swimsuit, togs (Australian informal), trunks, two-piece.

baton noun cane, rod, staff, stick, truncheon, wand.

batter verb abuse, assault, bash, beat, belt (slang), clobber (slang), hit, pound, pummel, strike, thump, wallop (slang), whack.

battery noun group, sequence, series, set.

battle noun action, affray, campaign, clash, combat, conflict, confrontation, crusade, encounter, engagement, fight, fighting, fray, hostilities, offensive, skirmish, strife, war, warfare.

battle verb see FIGHT.

battler noun fighter, struggler, toiler, worker.

battleship noun see WARSHIP.

bauble noun decoration, ornament, trinket.

baulk verb hesitate, jib, prop, pull up, shy, stop.

bawl verb **1** bellow, cry out, roar, shout, yell. **2** cry, howl, sob, wail, weep.

bay noun **1** bight, cove, estuary, gulf, inlet. **2** alcove, compartment, niche, nook, recess.

bay *noun* bark, cry, howl, yelp. □ **keep at bay** see WARD OFF (at WARD).

bazaar *noun* charity sale, fair, fête, flea market (*informal*), garage sale, jumble sale, trash and treasure market.

be *verb* **1** be alive, dwell, exist, live, remain, reside. **2** be found, be located, be situated, sit. **3** fall, happen, occur, take place.

beach *noun* coast, sands, seashore, seaside, shore, strand.

beacon *noun* flare, lighthouse, signal fire, signal light, signal station.

bead *noun* **1** (*beads*) necklace, necklet, rosary. **2** bubble, drop, droplet.

beaker *noun* cup, glass, tumbler.

beam *noun* **1** board, girder, joist, plank, rafter, support, timber. **2** gleam, ray, shaft, streak, stream.

beam *verb* **1** grin, smile. **2** broadcast, emit, radiate, send out, transmit.

bear *verb* **1** bring, carry, convey, deliver, take, transport. **2** carry, hold up, support, sustain, take. **3** have, possess,

show, wear. **4** abide, cope with, endure, put up with, stand, stomach, suffer, take, tolerate. **5** bring forth, give birth to, have, produce.

bearable *adjective* acceptable, endurable, sustainable, tolerable.

beard *noun* facial hair, goatee, whiskers, ziff (*Australian slang*).

bearing *noun* **1** air, behaviour, carriage, demeanour, deportment, manner, mien, posture, stance. **2** connection, relation, relationship, relevance. **3** (*bearings*) location, orientation, position, whereabouts.

beast *noun* **1** animal, brute, creature, quadruped. **2** brute, fiend, monster, savage. □ **beastly** *adjective* **1** animal, bestial. **2** (*informal*) abominable, awful, disgusting, hateful, horrible, mean, nasty, rotten, unpleasant.

beat *verb* **1** bash, baste, batter, belt (*slang*), cane, clobber (*slang*), clout (*informal*), club, cudgel, drub, flog, hit, knock, lash, lay into (*informal*), pound, quilt (*Australian slang*), slap, smack, smite, spank, stoush (*Australian slang*), strike, thrash, thump, thwack, trounce, wallop (*slang*), whack, whip. **2** agitate, mix, stir, whip, whisk. **3** flutter, palpitate, pound, pulsate, throb, thump. **4** clobber (*slang*), conquer, crush, defeat, euchre, get the better of, lick (*informal*), outdo, outstrip, outwit, overcome, overwhelm, prevail over, pulverise, rout, slaughter, stonker (*Australian slang*), surpass, thrash, triumph over, trounce, vanquish, win against. □ **beat up** assault, attack, bash up, batter, mug, thrash.

beat noun **1** accent, pulse, rhythm, stress. **2** circuit, course, path, round, route.

beautiful adjective appealing, attractive, bonny (*Scottish*), captivating, charming, comely, delightful, exquisite, fair (*old use*), fetching, fine, glorious, good-looking, gorgeous, handsome, irresistible, lovely, pleasing, pretty, radiant, stunning.

beautify verb adorn, decorate, embellish, enhance, improve, prettify, smarten up, titivate (*informal*), tizzy up (*Australian*).

beauty noun attractiveness, elegance, glamour, glory, good looks, handsomeness, loveliness, magnificence, prettiness, radiance, splendour.

because conjunction as, for, since. □ **because of** as a result of, by reason of, on account of, owing to, thanks to.

beckon verb gesture, motion, signal.

become verb **1** change into, develop into, grow into, turn into. **2** befit, be right for, flatter, look good on, suit. □ **becoming** see ATTRACTIVE (at ATTRACT), SUITABLE. □ **become of** befall (*formal*), happen to.

bed noun **1** (*kinds of bed*) berth, bunk, camp bed, cot, cradle, crib, divan, folding bed, four-poster, futon, hammock, sofa bed, stretcher, trundle bed, waterbed. **2** border, patch, plot, strip. **3** bottom, channel, course. **4** base, bottom, foundation.

bedclothes plural noun bedding, bed linen, bedspread, blankets, covers, linen, pillows, quilt, sheets.

bedlam noun chaos, confusion, madhouse (*informal*), mayhem, pandemonium, rumpus, uproar.

bedraggled adjective dishevelled, messy, ruffled, scruffy, unkempt, untidy, wet.

bedroom noun chamber (*old use*), dormitory.

bee noun bumble-bee, drone, honey bee, queen, worker. □ **bee-keeper** noun apiarist.

beefy adjective brawny, burly, hefty, muscular, nuggety (Australian), solid, stocky, strapping, strong, sturdy, thickset.

beer noun ale, bitter, lager, stout.

befall verb come about, come to pass, crop up, eventuate, happen, occur, take place.

befitting adjective appropriate, becoming, fitting, proper, right, seemly, suitable.

before adverb beforehand, earlier, formerly, hitherto, in the past, previously.

before preposition **1** earlier than, prior to. **2** ahead of, in front of.

beforehand adverb ahead, earlier, in advance, in anticipation, in readiness.

befriend verb look after, make a friend of, take care of, welcome.

beg verb **1** cadge, scrounge, sponge. **2** ask, beseech, entreat, implore, plead, pray, request.

beget verb **1** father, procreate, sire. **2** breed, bring about, cause, create, engender, generate, give rise to, produce, result in.

beggar noun **1** cadger, down-and-out, mendicant, scrounger, sponger, tramp.

2 fellow, person, rascal, wretch (informal).

begin verb **1** commence, create, embark on, establish, found, get going, get under way, inaugurate, initiate, introduce, kick off (informal), launch, open, originate, set up, start. **2** appear, arise, commence, crop up, emerge, originate, spring up, start.

beginner noun apprentice, learner, new chum (Australian informal), novice, recruit, starter, tiro, trainee.

beginning noun **1** birth, commencement, creation, dawn, founding, genesis, inception, introduction, onset, opening, origin, outset, rise, root, source, start, starting point. **2** introduction, opening, preamble, preface, prelude, prologue.

begrudge verb envy, grudge, mind, object to, resent.

behalf noun □ **on behalf of** as a representative of, for, representing.

behave verb **1** (of a person) act, conduct yourself, react; (of a machine) function, operate, perform, run, work. **2** be polite, be well-mannered, mind your manners. □ **behaviour** noun actions, conduct, demeanour, deportment, manners.

behead verb decapitate, guillotine.

behind adverb **1** at the back, at the rear, in the back, in the rear. **2** in arrears, behindhand, late, overdue.

behind preposition **1** after, at the back of, at the rear of, beyond, following, on the far side of, on the other side of. **2** less advanced than, trailing. **3** at the bottom of, underlying. □ **behind a person's back** covertly, deceitfully, in secret, secretly, slyly, sneakily, surreptitiously. □ **behind the times** antediluvian, antiquated, obsolete, old-fashioned, outdated, outmoded, out of date.

behold verb observe, see, survey, view, witness.

beige adjective biscuit, buff, coffee, fawn, neutral.

being noun **1** existence, life. **2** animal, creature, entity, individual, living thing, mortal, person.

belch verb **1** bring up wind, burp (*informal*). **2** discharge, emit, give off, send out, spew.

belief noun **1** confidence, credence, faith, reliance, trust. **2** conviction, credo, creed, doctrine, dogma, faith, ideology, opinion, persuasion, philosophy, religion, view.

believe verb accept, be certain of, be convinced of, be sure of, credit, have faith in, rely on, trust. □ **believable** adjective acceptable, convincing, credible, plausible. □ **believer** noun adherent, convert, disciple, follower, supporter, zealot.

belittle verb denigrate, depreciate, disparage, knock (*informal*), put down, run down, sling off at (*Australian informal*).

bell noun alarm, carillon, chime, knell, peal, ring, signal, tocsin.

belligerent adjective **1** aggressive, argumentative, bellicose, hostile, provocative, pugnacious, quarrelsome, truculent. **2** fighting, militant, warmongering, warring.

bellow verb bawl, roar, scream, shout, yell.

belly noun abdomen, guts (*informal*), paunch, stomach, tummy (*informal*).

belong verb go, have a place. □ **belong to 1** be owned by, be the property of. **2** be a member of, be a part of, be associated with.

belongings plural noun chattels, effects, gear (*informal*), goods, possessions, property, stuff (*informal*), things (*informal*).

beloved *adjective* adored, cherished, darling, dear, loved, precious, treasured.

below *adverb* beneath, downstairs, downstream, underneath.

below *preposition* beneath, less than, lower than, under, underneath.

belt *noun* **1** band, cummerbund, girdle, sash, strap. **2** area, district, region, strip, zone.

belt *verb* beat, flog, hit, lash, strap, thrash, whip.

bemused *adjective* bewildered, confused, perplexed, puzzled.

bench *noun* **1** form, pew, seat, settle. **2** counter, table, work surface, worktop. **3** judges, magistrates.

bend *verb* **1** angle, arch, bow, buckle, contort, curl, curve, distort, flex, kink, loop, turn, twist, veer, warp, wind. **2** bow, crouch, duck, hunch, incline, kneel, lean, stoop.

bend *noun* angle, arc, corner, crook, curve, kink, loop, turn, twist.

beneath *preposition* **1** below, under, underneath. **2** unbefitting, unfit for, unworthy of.

benefactor *noun* backer, donor, patron, philanthropist, sponsor, supporter.

beneficial *adjective* advantageous, constructive, favourable, good, helpful, positive, profitable, rewarding, useful, valuable.

beneficiary *noun* heir, heiress, inheritor, legatee, recipient.

benefit *noun* **1** advantage, asset, blessing, boon, help, profit, use. **2** allowance, assistance, dole (*informal*), handout (*informal*), income support, payment.

benefit *verb* **1** advance, aid, assist, further, help, serve. **2** gain, profit.

benevolent *adjective* benign, caring, charitable, compassionate, friendly, generous, good, gracious, helpful, humane, humanitarian, kind, kindly, liberal, magnanimous, merciful, philanthropic, warm-hearted.

benign *adjective* **1** benevolent, caring, compassionate, genial, gentle, good, gracious, humane, kind, kind-hearted, kindly, lenient, merciful, softhearted, sympathetic, tenderhearted, warm-hearted. **2** harmless, non-malignant.

bent *adjective* arched, bowed, contorted, crooked, curved, distorted, hunched, twisted, warped. □ **bent on** determined on, intent on, set on.

bent *noun* ability, aptitude, flair, gift, inclination, leaning, liking, skill, talent.

bequeath *verb* hand down, leave, make over, pass on, will.

bequest *noun* endowment, gift, inheritance, legacy, settlement.

bereaved *adjective* orphaned, widowed.

bereft *adjective* (*bereft of*) deprived of, devoid of, lacking, robbed of, without.

berserk *adjective* beside yourself, crazy, demented, deranged, frantic, frenzied, insane, mad, maniacal, manic, wild.

berth *noun* **1** bed, bunk. **2** anchorage, dock, landing stage, moorings, pier, quay, wharf.

berth *verb* anchor, dock, land, moor, tie up.

beseech *verb* appeal to, ask, beg, entreat, implore, plead with, pray, supplicate.

beside *preposition* alongside, close to, near to, next to. □ **beside the point** immaterial, irrelevant, unconnected.

besides *preposition* apart from, aside from, as well as, excluding, in addition to, not counting. □ **besides** *adverb* also, anyway, furthermore, in addition, in any case, moreover, too.

besiege *verb* **1** blockade, encircle, encompass, lay siege to, surround. **2** assail, badger, beleaguer, beset, harass, hound, pester.

besotted *adjective* enamoured, infatuated, smitten (*informal*).

best *adjective* finest, first-rate, foremost, greatest, leading, optimal, optimum, pre-eminent, superlative, supreme, top, top-notch (*informal*), unequalled, unrivalled, unsurpassed.

bestial *adjective* animal, beastly, brutish, depraved, inhuman, savage, wild.

bestow *verb* award, confer, give, grant, present.

bet *noun* **1** flutter (*informal*), gamble, punt, risk, wager. **2** stake, wager.

bet *verb* **1** gamble, punt, risk, stake, venture, wager. **2** be certain, be convinced, be sure, predict.

betray *verb* **1** be disloyal to, denounce, dob in (*Australian informal*), double-cross, grass (on) (*slang*), inform on, rat on (*informal*), shop (*informal*), tell on (*informal*). **2** blab, disclose, divulge, expose, give away, let slip, reveal, tell. □ **betrayal** *noun* denunciation, disloyalty, perfidy, treachery, treason, unfaithfulness.

better *adjective* **1** finer, greater, superior. **2** cured, fitter, healed, healthier, improved, on the mend (*informal*), recovered, stronger, well. □ **get better** convalesce, improve, rally, recover, recuperate. □ **get the better of** beat, conquer, defeat, outdo, outwit, overcome.

better *verb* beat, do better than, exceed, improve on, surpass, top.

beverage *noun* drink, liquid, refreshment.

bevy *noun* collection, company, gathering, group, mob (*Australian*).

beware *verb* be careful, be cautious, be on your guard, be wary, look out, mind, take heed, watch out.

bewilder *verb* baffle, bamboozle (*informal*), confound, confuse, nonplus, perplex, puzzle, stump.

bewitch *verb* **1** cast a spell on, jinx (*informal*), point the bone at (*Australian*). **2** beguile, captivate, charm, delight, enchant, enthral, entrance, fascinate, spellbind.

beyond *preposition* farther than, further than, over, past.

bias *noun* **1** favouritism, inclination, leaning, partiality, prejudice, slant. **2** angle, cross, diagonal, slant. □ **biased** *adjective* distorted, one-sided, partial, prejudiced, slanted, unbalanced, unfair.

Bible *noun* Holy Writ, Scripture, the Scriptures, the Word of God.

bicycle *noun* bike (*informal*), cycle, push-bike (*informal*), two-wheeler (*informal*); (*kinds of bicycle*) BMX, moped, mountain bike, penny farthing, racing bike, tandem.

bid *noun* **1** offer, proposal, submission, tender. **2** attempt, effort, try.

bid *verb* offer, proffer, propose, tender.

bid *verb* **1** ask, command, instruct, invite, order, tell. **2** say, tell, wish.

big *adjective* **1** ample, astronomical, broad, bulky, colossal, considerable, enormous, fat, gargantuan, giant, gigantic, ginormous (*slang*), great, hefty, huge, hulking, humungous (*slang*), immeasurable, immense, incalculable, jumbo (*informal*), king-sized, large, lofty, mammoth, massive, mighty, monstrous, monumental, outsize, prodigious, sizeable, spacious, staggering, stupendous, substantial, tall, tidy (*sum*), tremendous, vast. **2** critical, grand, great, important, major, momentous, significant, vital. **3** elder, grown-up, older.

bigoted *adjective* biased, dogmatic, intolerant, narrow-minded, opinionated, prejudiced.

bilious *adjective* ill, nauseous, queasy, sick.

bill *noun* **1** account, invoice, statement, tab (*informal*). **2** advertisement, flyer, notice, placard, poster. **3** draft legislation, proposed legislation. **4** banknote, note.

billet *verb* accommodate, house, lodge, put up.

billow *verb* balloon, puff out, rise, roll, surge, swell.

billycart *noun* go-cart, hill trolley.

bin *noun* can, container, crate, receptacle, skip, tin.

bind *verb* **1** bandage, cover, dress, swathe, wrap. **2** attach, connect, fasten, hold together, join, link, secure, strap, tie, truss. **3** compel, constrain, force, oblige, require. □ **binder** *noun* cover, file, folder.

bind *noun* difficulty, dilemma, fix, jam (*informal*), predicament, quandary, spot (*informal*).

binge *noun* bender (*slang*), fling, orgy, spree.

binoculars *plural noun* field glasses, opera glasses.

biography *noun* life story, memoirs, profile, reminiscences.

bird *noun* birdie (*informal*), chick, cock, fledgling, fowl, hen, nestling. □ **bird's-eye view** aerial view, overhead view.

birth *noun* **1** childbirth, confinement, delivery, labour, nativity. **2** beginning, creation, founding, genesis, origin, start. **3** ancestry, blood, descent, extraction, lineage, origin, parentage, pedigree, stock. □ **give birth to** bear, bring forth, deliver, produce, reproduce.

biscuit *noun* bickie (*informal*), cookie, cracker, wafer.

bisect *verb* cut in half, halve.

bistro *noun* bar, brasserie, café, restaurant.

bit *noun* **1** chip, crumb, fragment, iota, jot, morsel, particle, piece, portion, scrap, segment, skerrick (*Australian informal*), slice, speck. **2** jiffy (*informal*), minute, moment, second, tick (*informal*). □ **bit by bit** by degrees, gradually, little by little, progressively.

bitchy *adjective* catty (*informal*), malicious, mean, nasty, spiteful, vindictive.

bite *verb* **1** champ, crunch, gnaw, munch, nibble. **2** nip, sting, wound.

bite *noun* **1** nip, sting, wound. **2** morsel, mouthful, piece.

bitter *adjective* **1** acrid, harsh, sharp. **2** (*bitter memories*) distressing, galling, heartbreaking, painful, poignant, sad, sorrowful, unpleasant; (*bitter comments*) acrimonious, embittered, hostile, rancorous, resentful, spiteful, vicious, virulent. **3** biting, cold, freezing, harsh, piercing, sharp.

bizarre *adjective* curious, eccentric, fantastic, grotesque, odd, outlandish, peculiar, strange, unusual, weird.

blab *verb* **1** disclose, divulge, let out, reveal. **2** blow the gaff (*slang*), let the cat out of the bag (*informal*), spill the beans (*slang*), squeal (*slang*), tattle, tell, tell tales, tittle-tattle.

black *adjective* **1** dark, dusky, ebony, inky, jet-black, moonless, pitch-black, raven, sable, sooty, starless, swarthy. **2** blackened, dirty, filthy, grimy, grubby, sooty. **3** depressed, dismal, gloomy, glum, lugubrious, melancholy, sad, sombre. **4** angry, furious, glowering, hostile, menacing, sullen, threatening.

black *verb* **black out** collapse, faint, flake out (*informal*), lose consciousness, pass out (*informal*), swoon.

blacken *verb* **1** darken, dirty, soil, stain. **2** defame, denigrate, discredit, libel, malign, slander, smear, speak ill of, sully, tarnish.

blackguard *noun* knave (*old use*), miscreant, rascal, rogue, scoundrel, villain.

blacklist *verb* ban, bar, blackball, boycott, debar, exclude, ostracise, veto.

blackmail *verb* hold to ransom, threaten. ☐ **blackmail** *noun* extortion.

blade *noun* **1** cutting edge, edge. **2** frond, leaf, shoot.

blame *verb* accuse, charge, condemn, criticise, find guilty, hold responsible, make accountable, reproach, reprove.

blame *noun* censure, criticism, culpability, fault, guilt, liability, rap (*informal*), reprimand, reproach, reproof, responsibility.

blameless *adjective* guiltless, innocent, irreproachable, unimpeachable.

bland *adjective* flavourless, insipid, mild, plain, tasteless, uninteresting, wishy-washy.

blank *adjective* **1** clean, empty, plain, unfilled, unmarked, unused. **2** deadpan, emotionless, expressionless, impassive, poker-faced, vacant, vacuous.

blank *noun* gap, space, void.

blanket *noun* **1** cover, covering, rug. **2** cloak, covering, layer, mantle, sheet.

blanket *adjective* comprehensive, general, inclusive, overall.

blare *verb* blast, boom, resound, roar, sound, trumpet.

blasé *adjective* bored, indifferent, nonchalant, unexcited, unimpressed, uninterested.

blasphemy *noun* disrespect, impiety, irreverence, profanity, sacrilege. □ **blasphemous** *adjective* disrespectful, impious, irreligious, irreverent, profane, sacrilegious, ungodly.

blast *noun* **1** draught, gust, rush. **2** detonation, discharge, explosion. **3** blare, boom, honk, toot.

blast *verb* blow up, destroy, detonate, explode. □ **blast-off** *noun* launch, lift-off, take-off.

blatant *adjective* barefaced, flagrant, obvious, open, overt, unashamed, unconcealed.

blaze *noun* conflagration, fire, flames, inferno.

blaze *verb* burn, flame, flare, glow, shine.

blazer *noun* coat, jacket.

bleach *verb* blanch, fade, lighten, peroxide, whiten.

bleak *adjective* **1** bare, barren, chilly, cold, desolate, windswept, wintry. **2** black, depressing, dismal, dreary, gloomy, grim, hopeless, unpromising.

bleary *adjective* blurred, cloudy, filmy, fuzzy, misty, watery.

bleed *verb* haemorrhage, lose blood.

bleep *noun & verb* beep, signal.

blemish *noun* blotch, defect, discoloration, disfigurement, fault, flaw, imperfection, mark, scar, spot, stain.

blend *verb* combine, fuse, incorporate, integrate, mingle, mix, synthesise.

blend *noun* amalgam, combination, composite, compound, fusion, mix, mixture, synthesis.

bless *verb* consecrate, dedicate, hallow, sanctify. □ **blessed** *adjective* **1** beatified, consecrated, hallowed, holy, revered, sacred, sanctified. **2** fortunate, happy.

blessing *noun* **1** benediction, grace, prayer, thanksgiving. **2** asset, boon, gift, godsend, help. **3** approval, consent, favour,

OK (*informal*), sanction, support.

blight noun **1** disease, fungus, mildew, pestilence, rust. **2** affliction, bane, curse, plague, scourge.

blight verb damage, dash, frustrate, mar, ruin, spoil, wreck.

blind adjective **1** sightless, unsighted, visually impaired. **2** mindless, uncritical, unreasoning, unthinking. □ **blind alley** cul-de-sac, dead end, no through road.

blind verb see DAZZLE.

blind noun holland blind, screen, shade, shutter, venetian blind, vertical blind.

blink verb flash, flicker, glimmer, shimmer, sparkle, twinkle, wink.

bliss noun delight, ecstasy, euphoria, happiness, heaven, joy, paradise, pleasure, rapture. □ **blissful** adjective delightful, happy, heavenly, joyous, rapturous, wonderful.

blister noun bubble, swelling.

blithe adjective carefree, careless, casual, cheerful, gay, happy, heedless, indifferent, joyous, light-hearted, merry, nonchalant.

blitz noun attack, campaign, crackdown (*informal*), offensive, onslaught.

bloated adjective distended, enlarged, inflated, puffed up, swollen.

blob noun bead, dollop, drop, globule, splash, splotch, spot.

block noun **1** bar, brick, cake, chock, chunk, cube, hunk, ingot, slab, wedge. **2** barrier, blockade, obstacle, obstruction. **3** acreage, allotment, plot, section (*Australian historical*).

block verb bar, blockade, bung up, choke, clog, fill up, halt, hamper, hinder, hold back, impede, jam, obstruct, stop, stop up. □ **blockage** noun barrier, block, blockade, bottleneck, impediment, jam, obstacle, obstruction, stoppage.

blockade noun barricade, barrier, block, siege.

bloke noun boy, chap (*informal*), character, fellow (*informal*), guy (*informal*), man.

blond, blonde adjective fair, flaxen, golden, light, tow-coloured.

blood noun **1** gore. **2** ancestry, birth, descent, family, kindred, kith and kin, line, lineage, parentage, race, relations, relatives, stock.

blood-curdling adjective chilling, frightening, hair-raising, horrific, horrifying, spine-chilling, terrifying.

bloodshed *noun* carnage, killing, massacre, murder, slaughter, slaying, wounding.

bloodthirsty *adjective* brutal, ferocious, fierce, homicidal, murderous, sanguinary, savage, vicious.

bloody *adjective* **1** bleeding, bloodstained. **2** cruel, gory, sanguinary, violent.

bloom *noun* blossom, bud, flower.

bloom *verb* blossom, burgeon, flower.

blossom *noun* bloom, flower.

blossom *verb* **1** bloom, burgeon, flower. **2** bloom, develop, flourish, grow, thrive.

blot *noun* **1** blotch, mark, smudge, splotch, spot, stain. **2** blemish, defect, eyesore, fault, stain.

blot *verb* **1** smudge, spot, stain. **2** absorb, dry, soak up. □ **blot out** cover, efface, mask, obliterate, obscure, wipe out.

blotch *noun* blemish, blot, mark, patch, spot.

blouse *noun* shirt.

blow *verb* **1** breathe out, exhale, puff. **2** blast, bluster, gust, roar, whistle. **3** carry, convey, drive, move, send, sweep, waft. **4** blare, blast, play, sound, toot. □ **blow out** extinguish, put out, snuff. □ **blow up 1** enlarge, expand, fill, inflate, pump up, swell. **2** exaggerate, magnify, overstate. **3** detonate, explode, go off. **4** blast, bomb, burst apart, destroy, shatter.

blow *noun* **1** bang, bash, belt (*slang*), box, buffet, clout (*informal*), hit, king-hit (*Australian informal*), knock, punch, rap, slap, smack, stroke, thump, thwack, wallop (*slang*), whack. **2** body blow, bombshell, calamity, disappointment, disaster, misfortune, setback, shock, upset.

blubber *noun* fat, flab

bludge *verb* **1** idle, loaf, skive (*informal*), slack, take it easy. **2** borrow, cadge, scab (*Australian slang*), scrounge, sponge. □ **bludger** *noun* freeloader (*informal*), hanger-on, idler, layabout, loafer, parasite, shirker, slacker, sponger.

bludgeon *noun* see CLUB.

blue *adjective* **1** aqua, aquamarine, azure, cobalt, indigo, navy (blue), powder blue, Prussian blue, royal blue, sapphire, sky blue, turquoise, ultramarine. **2** depressed, despondent, downcast, down in the dumps (*informal*), gloomy, low, melancholy, sad, unhappy. **3** bawdy, coarse, dirty, indecent, lewd, obscene, risqué, rude.

blueprint *noun* design, outline, pattern, plan, scheme.

bluey *noun* drum (*Australian*), matilda (*Australian*), shiralee (*Australian*), swag (*Australian*).

bluff *verb* deceive, dupe, fake, feign, fool, hoodwink, mislead, pretend, sham, take in, trick.

bluff *noun* deception, pretence, sham, trick.

bluff *noun* cliff, escarpment, headland, precipice, scarp.

blunder *noun* blue (*Australian informal*), booboo (*slang*), bungle, clanger (*informal*), gaffe, howler (*informal*), mistake, slip-up (*informal*).

blunder *verb* lumber, lurch, stagger, stumble.

blunt *adjective* **1** dull, unsharpened. **2** abrupt, candid, curt, direct, frank, open, outspoken, upfront (*informal*).

blunt *verb* dull.

blurred *adjective* blurry, confused, dim, distorted, foggy, fuzzy, hazy, indistinct, misty, out of focus, unclear.

blurt *verb* (*blurt out*) blab, burst out with, call out, utter.

blush *verb* colour, flush, glow, go red, redden.

blustery *adjective* blowy, gusty, rough, squally, stormy, wild, windy.

board *noun* **1** beam, plank, sheet, slat, timber. **2** committee, council, panel.

board *verb* **1** catch, embark, get on, go on board. **2** live, lodge, reside.

boast *verb* be conceited, blow your own trumpet, brag, congratulate yourself, crow, have tickets on yourself (*Australian informal*), show off, skite (*Australian informal*), swagger, swank (*informal*), talk big (*informal*). □ **boaster** *noun* braggart, show-off, skite (*Australian informal*). □ **boastful** *adjective* bragging, cocky (*informal*), conceited, egotistical, proud, swaggering, swanky (*informal*), vain.

boat *noun* craft, vessel; (*various boats*) barge, canoe, catamaran, cutter, dinghy, ferry, gondola, houseboat, hydrofoil, junk, kayak, ketch, launch, lifeboat, motor boat, pontoon, punt, raft, rowing boat, sailing boat, sampan, skiff, sloop, speedboat, trawler, tug, yacht, yawl; see also SHIP.

bob *verb* bounce, curtsy, duck, jerk, jig, jump, leap, nod.

□ **bob up** appear, come up, show up, turn up.

bobbin noun reel, spool.

bode verb augur, indicate, portend, presage, promise.

body noun **1** anatomy, figure, form, frame, physique, shape. **2** torso, trunk. **3** cadaver, carcass, corpse, remains. **4** fuselage, hull, shell. **5** see GROUP. **6** object, thing. □ **bodily** adjective corporal, physical.

bodyguard noun escort, guard, minder, protector.

bog noun fen, marsh, mire, morass, mudflat, quagmire, quicksand, slough, swamp, wetlands. □ **boggy** adjective marshy, miry, muddy, spongy, swampy, wet. □ **bogged down** immobilised, impeded, stuck, trapped.

bogus adjective counterfeit, fake, false, forged, imitation, phoney (informal), sham.

bogyman noun bogy, devil, evil spirit, goblin.

boil verb **1** bubble, heat, seethe, simmer. **2** cook, simmer, stew.

boil noun abscess, carbuncle, gumboil, inflammation, pustule.

boisterous adjective active, energetic, exuberant, high-spirited, lively, noisy, rough, rowdy, unruly, vivacious, wild.

bold adjective **1** brave, confident, courageous, daring, fearless, game, heroic, intrepid, unafraid, undaunted. **2** assertive, audacious, brazen, cheeky, forward, immodest, impudent, presumptuous, shameless. **3** bright, conspicuous, showy, striking, strong, vibrant, vivid.

bolster noun cushion, pillow, support.

bolster verb boost, encourage, prop up, reinforce, shore up, strengthen, support.

bolt noun **1** bar, catch, latch, lock, snib. **2** flash, shaft. □ **a bolt from the blue** bombshell, shock, surprise, thunderbolt. □ **bolt upright** erect, straight.

bolt verb **1** fasten, latch, lock, secure, snib. **2** dart off, dash off, escape, run away, run off, scarper, take off, tear off. **3** gobble, gulp, guzzle, shovel in, wolf.

bomb noun **1** device (euphemism), explosive, grenade, incendiary, missile. **2** heap (informal), jalopy (informal), rattletrap (informal), rust bucket (informal), wreck.

bomb verb attack, blitz, blow up, bombard, shell.

bombard verb **1** attack, besiege, blitz, bomb, fire at, pelt, shell. **2** assail, attack, besiege, hound.

bombastic *adjective* extravagant, grandiloquent, grandiose, high-flown, inflated, ostentatious, pompous.

bombshell *noun* bolt from the blue, jolt, shock, surprise.

bonanza *noun* bonus, godsend, windfall.

bond *noun* **1** attachment, connection, link, relationship, tie. **2** agreement, bargain, contract, deal, guarantee. ☐ **bonds** *plural noun* chains, fetters, handcuffs, manacles, ropes, shackles.

bond *verb* adhere, bind, cement, connect, fasten, fuse, join, link, stick, tie.

bondage *noun* captivity, enslavement, serfdom, servitude, slavery.

bone *verb* fillet.

bonnet *noun* **1** cap, hat. **2** hood (*American*).

bonus *noun* addition, bounty, extra, gratuity, perk (*informal*), plus, premium, reward, supplement, tip.

bony *adjective* angular, emaciated, gaunt, lean, rawboned, scrawny, skinny, thin.

boo *verb* heckle, hoot, jeer, scoff.

book *noun* publication, tome, volume, work; (*kinds of book*) almanac, annual, anthology, atlas, concordance, dictionary, digest, directory, encyclopedia, guidebook, handbook, hymnal, manual, missal, omnibus, primer, textbook, thesaurus, yearbook; (*a book for writing or drawing in*) account book, album, daybook, diary, exercise book, journal, ledger, logbook, memo book, notebook, passbook, pocketbook, scrapbook, sketchbook.

book *verb* **1** order, reserve. **2** charge, fine.

booklet *noun* brochure, handbook, handout, leaflet, pamphlet.

boom *verb* **1** echo, resonate, resound, reverberate. **2** expand, flourish, grow, prosper, thrive.

boom *noun* **1** bang, blast, reverberation, roar, rumble, thunder. **2** expansion, growth, improvement, upturn.

boomerang *verb* backfire, rebound, recoil.

boon *noun* advantage, asset, benefit, blessing, help.

boost *verb* **1** assist, bolster, encourage, heighten, improve, increase, lift, raise, strengthen. **2** hoist, lift, push, raise. ☐ **booster** *noun* immunisation, injection, inoculation, jab (*informal*), shot, vaccination.

boost *noun* assistance, encouragement, help, impetus, shot in the arm, stimulus.

boot *noun* **1** gumboot, wellington; see also SHOE. **2** trunk (*American*).

booth *noun* **1** kiosk, stall, stand. **2** box, compartment, cubicle, enclosure.

booty *noun* gains, haul, loot, pickings, plunder, spoils, swag (*informal*), takings.

booze *noun* alcohol, drink, grog (*Australian*), liquor.

border *noun* **1** boundary, frontier, limit. **2** brink, circumference, edge, margin, perimeter, periphery, rim, verge. **3** binding, edge, edging, frame, frieze, fringe, hem, margin, mount, strip, surround.

border *verb* abut on, adjoin, be next to, flank.

borderline *noun* boundary, dividing line, limit, threshold.

borderline *adjective* doubtful, line-ball (*Australian*), marginal, touch-and-go, uncertain.

bore *verb* drill, gouge, penetrate, perforate, pierce.

bore *noun* calibre, diameter, gauge.

bore *verb* send to sleep, tire, weary. □ **bored** *adjective* blasé, fed up, jack (*Australian slang*), jaded, tired. □ **boring** *adjective* dreary, dull, monotonous, repetitious, routine, soul-destroying, tedious, tiresome, unexciting, uninteresting.

boredom *noun* apathy, dreariness, dullness, monotony, tedium.

borrow *verb* be lent, have the loan of; see also CADGE.

bosom *noun* breasts, bust, chest.

boss *noun* administrator, chief, director, employer, foreman, governor (*slang*), head, leader, manager, master, overseer, proprietor, superintendent, supervisor.

boss *verb* control, give orders to, order about, push around, tell what to do.

bossy *adjective* autocratic, despotic, dictatorial, domineering, imperious, masterful, officious, overbearing, tyrannical.

botch *verb* bungle, make a hash of (*informal*), make a mess of, mess up, muck up (*informal*), muff (*informal*), ruin, spoil, wreck.

bother *verb* **1** annoy, concern, disconcert, distress, disturb, harass, hassle (*informal*), hound, irritate, nag, perturb, pester, plague, put out (*informal*), trouble, upset, worry. **2** care, concern yourself, take the time, take the trouble, trouble yourself.

bother noun difficulty, fuss, hassle (informal), inconvenience, irritation, nuisance, pest, problem, to-do, trouble, worry.

bottle noun carafe, container, cruet, decanter, flagon, flask, magnum, phial, vial.

bottle verb □ **bottle up** conceal, hide, keep back, suppress.

bottleneck noun blockage, hold-up, jam, obstruction.

bottom noun **1** base, bed, depths, floor, foot, foundation, pedestal, support, underneath, underside. **2** backside (informal), behind (informal), bum (slang), butt (slang), buttocks, posterior, rear (informal), rump, seat.

bottom adjective base, ground, lowest.

bottomless adjective deep, inexhaustible, infinite.

bough noun branch, limb.

boulder noun gibber (Australian), rock, stone.

boulevard noun avenue, parade, road, street.

bounce verb **1** rebound, recoil, ricochet. **2** bob, bound, hop, jump, leap, spring.

bouncy adjective elastic, resilient, springy.

bound verb bob, bounce, gallop, hurdle, jump, leap, lope, spring, vault.

bound noun bob, bounce, gallop, hurdle, jump, leap, lope, spring, vault.

bound adjective confined, restricted, tied. □ **bound to** certain to, destined to, sure to.

bound adjective (bound for) destined for, en route for, heading for, off to, travelling to.

bound verb border, circumscribe, enclose, limit, surround.

boundary noun border, borderline, bounds, circumference, confines, demarcation, edge, fringes, frontier, limit, margin, perimeter, threshold.

boundless adjective endless, infinite, limitless, unbounded, unlimited, vast.

bounds plural noun boundaries, limitations, limits. □ **out of bounds** off limits.

bountiful adjective **1** abundant, ample, copious, lavish, plentiful, prolific. **2** generous, lavish, liberal, munificent, open-handed, unstinting.

bounty noun **1** benevolence, charity, generosity, goodness, kindness, largesse, liberality, philanthropy. **2** gift, gratuity, premium, reward.

bouquet noun bunch, corsage, posy, spray.

bout noun **1** competition, contest, fight, match, round. **2** attack, fit, period, session, spell, stint, stretch, turn.

bow verb bend, bob, curtsy, genuflect, kneel, nod, salaam, stoop.

bow noun fore, front, prow.

bowel noun (bowels) entrails, guts, innards (informal), insides (informal), intestines, viscera.

bower noun arbour, gazebo, pavilion, pergola, shelter, summer house.

bowl noun basin, dish, tureen.

bowl verb deliver, fling, hurl, lob, pitch, throw, toss. ▫ **bowl over** flabbergast, floor, overwhelm, stun, surprise.

box noun **1** carton, case, chest, coffer, container, crate, pack, package, receptacle, trunk. **2** compartment, stall, stand. **3** booth, cabin, cubicle, hut, shelter.

box verb **box in** box up, confine, coop up, enclose, hem in, shut in, surround.

box verb **1** fight, spar. **2** clout (informal), cuff, punch, slap, thump; see also HIT.

boxer noun fighter, prize-fighter, pugilist, sparring partner.

boy noun child, fellow, guy (informal), kid (informal), lad, male, schoolboy, youngster, youth. ▫ **boyish** adjective childish, childlike, immature, juvenile, young, youthful.

boycott verb avoid, ban, blacklist, ostracise, shun, stay away from. ▫ **boycott** noun ban, blacklist, embargo, prohibition.

boyfriend noun admirer, beau, date (informal), escort, fellow, male companion, suitor, swain (poetical).

brace noun **1** bracket, buttress, calliper, prop, splint, stay, strut, support. **2** couple, pair.

brace verb reinforce, shore up, strengthen, support, tighten. ▫ **brace yourself** prepare yourself, steady yourself, steel yourself.

bracelet noun armlet, bangle, wristlet.

braces plural noun straps, suspenders (American).

bracing adjective invigorating, refreshing, stimulating.

bracket noun **1** brace, parenthesis. **2** shelf, support. **3** category, class, division, group, range, set.

brackish *adjective* briny, slightly saline, slightly salty.

brag *verb* blow your own trumpet (*informal*), boast, crow, show off, skite (*Australian informal*), swagger, swank (*informal*).

braid *noun* **1** plait. **2** ribbon, trimming.

brain *noun* intellect, intelligence, mind, reason, sense, wit.

brainwash *verb* condition, indoctrinate.

brainwave *noun* brainstorm, idea, inspiration, thought.

brainy *adjective* bright, brilliant, clever, gifted, intellectual, intelligent, smart, studious.

brake *verb* halt, pull up, slow down, stop.

branch *noun* **1** bough, limb, offshoot. **2** (*of a river*) anabranch, arm, billabong, distributary. **3** arm, department, division, office, part, section, subdivision.

branch *verb* divide, fork, split, subdivide. □ **branch out** diversify, expand, extend, open out, spread.

brand *noun* make, marque, sort, trade mark, type.

brand *verb* identify, label, mark, stamp.

brandish *verb* flourish, swing, wave.

brash *adjective* arrogant, audacious, bold, brazen, bumptious, cocky (*informal*), impertinent, impudent, self-assertive.

bravado *noun* boldness, daring, front, show, showing off.

brave *adjective* bold, courageous, daring, dauntless, fearless, gallant, game, heroic, intrepid, lion-hearted, plucky, undaunted, valiant. □ **bravery** *noun* boldness, courage, daring, fearlessness, fortitude, gallantry, grit (*informal*), guts (*informal*), heroism, intrepidity, mettle, nerve, pluck, prowess, valour.

brave *noun* fighter, warrior.

brave *verb* defy, endure, face, weather, withstand.

brawl *noun* clash, confrontation, fight, fisticuffs, free-for-all, mêlée, punch-up (*informal*), quarrel, row, scrap (*informal*), scuffle, set-to (*informal*), skirmish, stoush (*Australian slang*), struggle, tussle.

brawny *adjective* beefy, burly, hefty, muscular, nuggety (*Australian*), sinewy, stocky, strong, sturdy, thickset.

bray *noun* hee-haw, neigh, whinny.

brazen *adjective* audacious, bold, cheeky, forward, impertinent, impudent, insolent, saucy, shameless, unashamed.

breach *noun* **1** breaking, contravention, infringement, transgression, violation. **2** aperture, break, crack, fissure, gap, hole, opening, space, split.

breadth *noun* broadness, extent, magnitude, range, scope, span, spread, thickness, width.

break *verb* **1** burst, bust (*informal*), collapse, come apart, crack, crash, crumble, damage, demolish, destroy, disintegrate, fall apart, fracture, fragment, ruin, shatter, smash, snap, splinter, split, wreck; see also DIVIDE. **2** breach, contravene, disobey, flout, go back on, infringe, renege on, transgress, violate. **3** adjourn, discontinue, interrupt, pause, stop. **4** beat, exceed, outdo, outstrip, surpass. □ **break down 1** conk out (*informal*), fail, go bung (*Australian informal*), go on the blink (*informal*), malfunction, pack up (*informal*), seize up, stop working. **2** burst into tears, collapse, crack up (*informal*), cry, go to pieces (*informal*), weep. □ **break in 1** barge in, burst in, butt in, interrupt,

intrude. **2** discipline, tame, train. □ **break-in** *noun* burglary, forced entry, robbery. □ **break out 1** begin, commence, erupt, start. **2** bolt, escape, flee, get away, take flight. □ **break up** divorce, part, separate, split up. □ **break-up** *noun* breakdown, collapse, dissolution, failure, separation, split-up.

break *noun* **1** breach, breakage, burst, chink, cleft, crack, discontinuity, fissure, fracture, gap, gash, hole, leak, opening, rent, rift, rupture, slit, smash, space, split, tear. **2** bolt, dash, escape, run. **3** breather, hiatus, interlude, intermission, interruption, interval, let-up (*informal*), lull, pause, playtime, recess, respite, rest, smoko (*Australian informal*), spell (*Australian*); see also HOLIDAY. **4** chance, opening, opportunity.

breakable *adjective* brittle, delicate, flimsy, fragile, weak.

breakdown *noun* **1** collapse, crash (*Computing*), failure, hitch, malfunction, stoppage. **2** analysis, dissection, itemisation, run-down.

breakneck *adjective* dangerous, fast, headlong, reckless.

breakthrough *noun* advance, development, discovery, progress.

breakwater noun jetty, mole, pier.

breast noun bosom, bust, chest.

breath noun exhalation, gasp, inhalation, pant, puff, respiration.

breathe verb 1 exhale, inhale, pant, puff, respire. 2 let out, utter, whisper.

breather noun break, interval, pause, recess, rest, spell (*Australian*).

breathless adjective gasping, out of breath, panting, puffed, short of breath, winded.

breathtaking adjective amazing, astounding, awe-inspiring, exciting, overwhelming, spectacular, stupendous.

breed verb 1 bear young, multiply, procreate, produce young, reproduce. 2 propagate, raise, rear. 3 bring up, develop, educate, nurture, raise, rear, train. 4 create, engender, generate, give rise to, lead to, result in, yield.

breed noun kind, sort, strain, type, variety.

breeze noun draught, wind, zephyr. □ **breezy** adjective airy, blowy, draughty, fresh, windy.

brevity noun briefness, conciseness, curtness, succinctness, terseness.

brew verb 1 (*brew tea*) infuse, prepare; (*brew beer*) ferment, make. 2 develop, fester, gather force, hatch.

bribe noun backhander (*informal*), carrot, enticement, graft (*informal*), hush money, incentive, inducement, kickback (*informal*), pay-off (*informal*), sling (*Australian informal*), sweetener (*informal*).

bribe verb buy, buy off, corrupt, grease someone's palm (*slang*), influence, pervert, sling (*Australian informal*), tempt.

bridal adjective marriage, matrimonial, nuptial, wedding.

bridge noun 1 crossing, span; (*kinds of bridge*) aqueduct, drawbridge, flyover, footbridge, overpass, pontoon bridge, suspension bridge, swing bridge, viaduct. 2 bond, connection, link, tie.

bridge verb cross, extend across, span, straddle, traverse.

brief adjective (*a brief report*) abridged, concise, short, succinct, terse; (*brief happiness*) ephemeral, fleeting, momentary, passing, short-lived, temporary, transient, transitory. □ **in brief** briefly, concisely, in a nutshell, in short, in summary, succinctly.

brief noun directions, guidelines, instructions.

brief verb advise, fill in (*informal*), inform, instruct, prepare, put in the picture (*informal*).

briefs plural noun drawers (*old use*), jocks (*informal*), knickers, panties, pants, trunks, underpants.

brigade noun band, corps, crew, force, group, squad, team.

brigand noun bandit, buccaneer, bushranger, desperado, gangster, highwayman, outlaw, pirate, robber, thief.

bright adjective **1** beaming, blazing, dazzling, glaring, gleaming, glistening, glittering, glowing, incandescent, luminous, lustrous, radiant, resplendent, shining, sparkling. **2** bold, brilliant, flashy, gaudy, intense, showy, strong, vivid. **3** clear, cloudless, fair, fine, sunny. **4** able, astute, brainy, brilliant, clever, gifted, ingenious, intelligent, quick-witted, sharp, smart, talented. **5** animated, cheerful, gay, happy, jolly, light-hearted, lively, merry, sparkling, vivacious.

brighten verb **1** illuminate, lighten, light up. **2** animate, buck up (*informal*), buoy up, cheer up, enliven, liven up, perk up.

brilliant adjective **1** blazing, bright, dazzling, glaring, gleaming, radiant, resplendent, scintillating, shining, sparkling. **2** brainy, bright, clever, exceptional, gifted, ingenious, intelligent, outstanding, smart, talented.

brim noun brink, edge, lip, rim.

brim verb □ **brim over** overflow, pour over, run over, slop over, spill over.

bring verb **1** accompany, bear, carry, conduct, convey, deliver, escort, fetch, lead, take, transport, usher. **2** cause, create, generate, give rise to, lead to, produce, result in, yield □ **bring about** accomplish, achieve, cause, effect, produce. □ **bring in 1** initiate, institute, introduce, start. **2** earn, net, produce, realise, yield. □ **bring off** accomplish, achieve, carry off, pull off, succeed in. □ **bring out 1** draw attention to, emphasise, highlight, point out, point up, reveal, show. **2** issue, produce, publish, release. □ **bring up 1** care for, look after, nurture, raise, rear, train. **2** broach, introduce, mention, raise. **3** see VOMIT.

brink noun bank, border, brim, edge, margin, perimeter, threshold, verge.

brisk adjective bustling, energetic, fast, keen, lively, quick, rapid, snappy, spanking (informal), vigorous.

bristle noun hair, stubble, whisker.

brittle adjective breakable, crisp, fragile, hard.

broach verb bring up, introduce, mention, raise.

broad adjective **1** big, expansive, extensive, great, large, sweeping, vast, wide. **2** basic, general, overall, sweeping, vague. **3** clear, explicit, marked, obvious, strong, unmistakable.

broadcast noun programme, show, telecast, transmission.

broadcast verb air, relay, screen, send out, telecast, televise, transmit.

broaden verb enlarge, expand, extend, open out, spread out, widen.

broad-minded adjective flexible, liberal, open-minded, permissive, tolerant, understanding, unprejudiced.

brochure noun booklet, catalogue, flyer, handout, leaflet, pamphlet, prospectus.

brogue noun accent, dialect.

broke adjective bankrupt, destitute, penniless, skint (informal), stony-broke (slang), strapped for cash (informal); see also POOR.

broken-hearted adjective desolate, devastated, disconsolate, forlorn, grief-stricken, heartbroken, woebegone, wretched.

broker noun agent, dealer, intermediary, middleman, negotiator.

brooch noun badge, clasp, pin.

brood noun clutch, family, litter, offspring, young.

brood verb dwell (on), fret, meditate, mull, ponder, reflect, stew (informal), sulk, think, worry.

broody adjective depressed, gloomy, pensive, thoughtful.

brook noun creek (Australian), rill, rivulet, stream, watercourse.

brook verb allow, endure, permit, put up with, stand, tolerate.

broth noun bouillon, consommé, soup, stock.

brother noun **1** male sibling. **2** associate, colleague, comrade, fellow, fellow member, friend, mate. □ **brotherhood** noun association, community, fraternity, order, society. □ **brotherly** adjective fraternal; see also FRIENDLY.

brown adjective **1** auburn, bay, beige, biscuit, bronze, buff, camel, chestnut, chocolate, coffee, copper, fawn, hazel, khaki, mocha, ochre, rust, sepia, tan, tawny, umber, walnut. **2** bronzed, dark-skinned, suntanned, tanned. □ **brown-haired** adjective brunette, dark-haired.

brown verb (brown the meat etc.) cook, fry, grill, sauté, seal, sear, toast; (brown one's skin) bronze, suntan, tan.

browse verb **1** feed, graze. **2** flick through, flip through, glance through, leaf through, look through, scan, skim (through), thumb through.

bruise noun contusion, discoloration, shiner (informal).

bruise verb blacken, damage, discolour, injure, mark.

brumby noun bronco, mustang, warrigal (Australian), wild horse.

brunt noun force, impact, strain, stress.

brush noun clash, confrontation, dealings, encounter, skirmish.

brush verb **1** clean, dust, polish, scrub, smooth, sweep, tidy. **2** graze, touch. □ **brush aside** dismiss, disregard, ignore, reject, sweep aside. □ **brush up on** bone up on (informal), go over, revise, study.

brusque adjective abrupt, blunt, curt, offhand, short, terse.

brutal adjective atrocious, barbarous, beastly, bloodthirsty, callous, cruel, ferocious, inhuman, inhumane, merciless, ruthless, sadistic, savage, vicious.

brute noun **1** beast, bully, monster, ogre, sadist. **2** animal, beast, creature.

bubble verb boil, effervesce, fizz, foam, froth, seethe, simmer.

bubbly adjective **1** aerated, carbonated, effervescent, fizzy, foamy, frothy, sparkling. **2** animated, buoyant, exuberant, lively, sparkling, vivacious.

buccaneer noun adventurer, brigand, corsair (old use), marauder, pirate, privateer.

buck verb **1** jump, leap, start. **2** fight, oppose, resist. □ **buck up** get a move on (informal), hasten, hurry up, make haste, rush. **2** brighten, cheer up, liven up, perk up.

bucket noun pail, scuttle.

buckle noun catch, clasp, clip, fastening.

buckle *verb* **1** do up, fasten. **2** bend, cave in, collapse, contort, crumple, distort, give way, twist, warp.

Buckley's chance Buckley's (*Australian informal*), no chance, no hope, no show (*informal*).

bud *noun* shoot, sprout.

budding *adjective* burgeoning, developing, growing, promising, up-and-coming.

buddy *noun* chum (*informal*), cobber (*Australian informal*), companion, comrade, confidant, confidante, crony, friend, mate, pal (*informal*).

budge *verb* move, shift, stir.

budget *noun* **1** estimate, plan. **2** allocation, allowance.

budget *verb* allocate, allow, estimate, plan, set aside.

buffer *noun* cushion, damper, guard, pad, shield.

buffet *noun* café, cafeteria, counter, snack bar.

buffet *verb* batter, hit, knock, pound, strike.

buffoon *noun* clown, comic, fool, jester, wag.

bug *noun* **1** insect, mite. **2** bacterium, germ, infection, microbe, micro-organism, virus, wog (*Australian informal*).

bug *verb* **1** eavesdrop on, listen in on, tap. **2** annoy, bother, exasperate, irritate, trouble.

bugbear *noun* bogy, dread, nightmare, pet hate.

buggy *noun* carriage, gig, trap.

build *verb* assemble, construct, erect, fabricate, form, make, put together, put up, raise. □ **build up 1** develop, enlarge, establish, expand. **2** accrue, accumulate, amass, grow. **3** escalate, grow, increase, intensify, rise, strengthen.

build *noun* figure, frame, physique, shape.

building *noun* construction, edifice, premises, structure.

bulge *noun* bump, curve, hump, lump, protrusion, protuberance, swelling.

bulge *verb* bloat, distend, enlarge, expand, protrude, stick out, swell.

bulk *noun* **1** magnitude, mass, size, volume, weight. **2** best part, greater part, lion's share, majority, most. □ **in bulk** in quantity, in volume, wholesale.

bulky *adjective* big, cumbersome, heavy, huge, large, massive, unwieldy, voluminous.

bulldoze *verb* clear, demolish, flatten, level, raze.

bulletin *noun* announcement, broadcast, communiqué, dispatch, message, newsletter, notice, report, statement.

bullfighter *noun* matador, picador, toreador.

bull's-eye *noun* bull, centre, middle.

bully *verb* cow, frighten, harass, hector, intimidate, oppress, persecute, pick on, push around (*informal*), stand over, terrorise, threaten, torment, tyrannise.

bully *noun* intimidator, persecutor, ruffian, tormentor, tough, tyrant.

bulwark *noun* barrier, buffer, defence, earthwork, fortification, protection, rampart, wall.

bumble *verb* **1** blunder, flounder, lumber, lurch, stumble. **2** babble, mumble, mutter, ramble.

bump *verb* **1** hit, hurt, injure, knock. **2** bounce, bucket, jerk, jolt, shake. ◻ **bump into** come across, meet, run into, see. ◻ **bump off** see KILL.

bump *noun* **1** bang, collision, crash, knock, thud, thump. **2** bulge, hump, lump, protrusion, protuberance, swelling. ◻ **bumpy** *adjective* (*a bumpy road*) corrugated, potholed, rough, uneven; (*a bumpy ride*) bouncy, jarring, jolting, rough.

bumpkin *noun* hick (*informal*), hill-billy (*American informal*), peasant, rustic, yokel.

bumptious *adjective* arrogant, brash, cocky (*informal*), conceited, overbearing, self-assertive, self-important.

bunch *noun* **1** batch, bundle, cluster, collection, lot, pack, quantity, set, sheaf, wad; (*a bunch of flowers*) bouquet, corsage, nosegay, posy, spray. **2** band, crowd, gang, group, lot, mob, team.

bundle *noun* bale, bunch, collection, package, parcel, set, sheaf, swag (*Australian*).

bundle *verb* **1** pack, package, tie, wrap. **2** pack off, push, shove, thrust.

bung *noun* cork, plug, stopper.

bung *verb* put, shove, stick (*informal*), throw, toss ◻ **bunged up** blocked (up), clogged up, congested, stuffed up.

bung *adjective* ◻ **go bung** be on the blink (*informal*), be out of order, break down, conk out (*informal*), fail, go kaput (*informal*), pack up (*informal*), seize up.

bungle *verb* botch, fluff (*slang*), foul up (*informal*), goof (*slang*), mess up, mismanage, muff (*informal*), ruin, spoil, wreck.☐ **bungle** *noun* blunder, botch, mess, mistake, mix-up.

bunk *noun* bed, berth.

bunk *noun* ☐ **do a bunk** abscond, bolt, escape, flee, make off, nick off (*Australian slang*), run off, scarper (*informal*), shoot through (*Australian informal*), vanish.

buoy *noun* float, marker.

buoy *verb* (*buoy up*) boost, cheer, encourage, hearten, sustain, uplift.

buoyant *adjective* **1** floating, light. **2** bouncy, carefree, cheerful, light-hearted, lively, resilient.

burden *noun* **1** load, weight. **2** care, concern, problem, strain, trial, trouble, worry.

burden *verb* encumber, load, lumber, oppress, saddle, weigh down, worry.

bureau *noun* **1** desk, writing-desk. **2** agency, branch, department, division, office.

bureaucracy *noun* **1** administration, officialdom, public service. **2** formalities, paperwork, red tape, regulations.

bureaucrat *noun* administrator, functionary, official, public servant.

burglar *noun* housebreaker, intruder, robber, thief.

☐ **burglary** *noun* break-in, breaking and entering, larceny, robbery, stealing, theft.

burial *noun* entombment, funeral, interment. ☐ **burial ground** SEE CEMETERY.

burlesque *noun* caricature, imitation, mockery, parody, send-up (*informal*), spoof (*informal*), take-off (*informal*).

burly *adjective* beefy, brawny, hefty, husky, muscular, nuggety (*Australian*), stocky, stout, strapping, strong, sturdy, thickset, tough.

burn *verb* **1** be ablaze, be alight, be on fire, blaze, catch fire, flame, flare, smoulder. **2** blacken, brown, char, cremate (*a corpse*), ignite, incinerate, kindle, scald, scorch, sear, set alight, set fire to, set on fire, singe, toast. **3** feel hot, flush, redden.

burning *adjective* **1** ardent, deep, fervent, intense, passionate, strong. **2** crucial, important, pressing, urgent, vital.

burnish *verb* buff, polish, rub, shine.

burp *verb* belch, bring up wind.

burrow *noun* den, hole, lair, tunnel, warren.

burrow *verb* **1** dig, excavate, tunnel. **2** delve, fossick

(*Australian informal*), rummage, search.

bursar noun accountant, financial controller, treasurer.

bursary noun allowance, endowment, grant, scholarship.

burst verb **1** blow out, break, bust (*informal*), disintegrate, explode, pop, puncture, rip, rupture, split, tear. **2** (*burst into a room*) barge, fly, run, rush; (*burst into tears*) break, collapse, dissolve, erupt. □ **bursting** adjective see FULL.

burst noun blaze, explosion, fusillade, outbreak, outburst, round, rush, spurt, volley.

bury verb **1** entomb, inter, lay to rest. **2** conceal, cover up, hide, submerge.

bus noun coach, minibus, omnibus.

bush noun **1** plant, shrub. **2** brush, forest, scrub, woodland, woods. □ **bushy** adjective **1** scrubby, shrubby. **2** (*a bushy tail*) bristly, fluffy, fuzzy, hairy, shaggy, thick, woolly. □ **the bush** backblocks (*Australian*), country, donga (*Australian*), inland, interior, mallee (*Australian*), mulga (*Australian*), outback (*Australian*), sticks (*Australian informal*).

bushfire noun blaze, conflagration, fire.

bushranger noun bandit, brigand, escapee, highwayman, outlaw, robber.

bushwalker noun hiker, rambler, trekker, walker.

business noun **1** concern, duty, function, job, province, responsibility, task, work. **2** calling, career, employment, field, industry, job, line, occupation, profession, trade, vocation, work. **3** affair, concern, issue, matter, situation, subject, topic. **4** company, concern, corporation, enterprise, establishment, firm, outfit (*informal*), practice, undertaking, venture. **5** buying and selling, commerce, trade, trading.

businesslike adjective efficient, methodical, organised, practical, professional, systematic.

businessman, **businesswoman** noun entrepreneur, executive, industrialist, magnate, merchant, trader, tycoon.

busker noun street entertainer, street performer.

bust noun **1** sculpture. **2** bosom, breast, chest.

bust verb break, burst, collapse, crack. □ **go bust** fail, go bankrupt, go broke (*informal*).

bustle *verb* dash, hasten, hurry, hustle, rush, tear.

bustle *noun* activity, busyness, commotion, excitement, hurly-burly, hurry, hustle.

busy *adjective* **1** active, employed, engaged, industrious, involved, occupied, on the go (*informal*), snowed under (*informal*), working. **2** active, bustling, frenetic, frenzied, full, hectic, lively.

busybody *noun* interferer, meddler, mischief-maker, Nosy Parker (*informal*), snooper (*informal*), stickybeak (*Australian informal*).

but *conjunction* however, nevertheless, still, yet.

but *preposition* apart from, aside from, except, other than, save.

butcher *verb* kill, massacre, murder, slaughter, slay.

butt *noun* **1** handle, shaft, stock. **2** end, remnant, stub; (*cheque butt*) counterfoil.

butt *noun* barrel, cask, hogshead, tun.

butt *noun* object, subject, target, victim.

butt *verb* bump, knock, poke, prod, push, ram. □ **butt in** chip in (*informal*), interfere, interrupt, intervene, meddle, poke your nose in (*informal*).

buttocks *plural noun* backside (*informal*), behind (*informal*), bottom, bum (*slang*), butt (*slang*), haunches, posterior, rear (*informal*), rump, seat.

button *noun* control, knob, switch.

button *verb* do up, fasten.

buttonhole *verb* accost, bail up (*Australian*), corner, detain, waylay.

buttress *noun* prop, reinforcement, stay, support. □ **buttress** *verb* brace, prop up, reinforce, shore up, support.

buy *verb* acquire, come by, gain, get, obtain, pay for, procure, purchase. □ **buyer** *noun* client, consumer, customer, patron, purchaser, shopper.

buy *noun* acquisition, deal, purchase.

buzz *noun* burr, drone, hum, vibration, whirr.

buzz *verb* burr, drone, hum, throb, whirr.

by *preposition* **1** alongside, beside, close to, near, next to. **2** along, through, via. **3** at, during. □ **by yourself** alone, single-handed, unaccompanied, unaided, unassisted.

by *adverb* **1** past. **2** aside, away, in reserve. □ **by and by** before long, presently, soon. □ **by and large** all things considered, generally speaking, on the whole.

bygone *adjective* ancient, former, olden, past.

bypass *noun* detour, deviation, diversion, ring road, ring route.

bypass *verb* (*bypass a city*) avoid, go round; (*bypass a problem*) avoid, circumvent, dodge, evade, ignore, sidestep, skirt.

by-product *noun* consequence, offshoot, repercussion, side benefit, side effect, spin-off.

bystander *noun* eyewitness, observer, onlooker, passer-by, spectator, witness.

byword *noun* **1** example, model, symbol. **2** adage, catchphrase, maxim, motto, proverb, saying, slogan.

Cc

cabin *noun* **1** chalet, hut, lodge, shack, shanty, shelter. **2** berth, compartment, room.

cabinet *noun* buffet, case, chest, closet, console, cupboard, locker, sideboard, wall unit.

cable *noun* **1** chain, cord, flex, guy, hawser, lead, line, rope, wire. **2** telegram, wire (*informal*).

cache *noun* **1** hoard, reserve, stash (*informal*), stockpile, store, supply. **2** depot, hiding place, repository.

cackle *verb* **1** cluck, squawk. **2** see *LAUGH*.

cadet *noun* learner, novice, recruit, trainee.

cadge *verb* beg, bludge (*Australian informal*), bot (*Australian slang*), hum (*Australian slang*), put the bite on (*Australian informal*), scab (*Australian slang*), scrounge, sponge.

café *noun* bistro, brasserie, buffet, cafeteria, coffee shop, eatery (*informal*), milk bar, restaurant, snack bar, tea room.

cage *noun* aviary, coop, enclosure, hutch, pen. □ **caged** *adjective* confined, cooped up, locked up, penned, shut in.

cajole *verb* beguile, coax, entice, persuade, seduce, sweet-talk (*informal*), wheedle.

cake *noun* **1** baba, bun, cheesecake, cupcake, doughnut, éclair, flan, gateau, lamington, muffin, pastry, scone, sponge, tart, torte. **2** (*a cake of soap*) bar, block, hunk, lump, piece, slab; (*a fish cake*) croquette, patty.

caked *adjective* coated, covered, encrusted.

calamity *noun* accident, catastrophe, disaster, misadventure, misfortune, mishap, tragedy.

calculate *verb* 1 add up, assess, compute, count, determine, estimate, figure out, reckon, total, tot up (*informal*), work out. 2 aim, design, intend, mean, plan. □ **calculating** *adjective* crafty, cunning, designing, devious, plotting, scheming, shrewd, sly, wily. □ **calculation** *noun* answer, computation, estimate, forecast, result, sum.

calendar *noun* daybook, diary, programme, schedule, timetable.

calf *noun* heifer, mickey (*Australian*), poddy (*Australian*).

call *noun* 1 bellow, cooee (*informal*), cry, exclamation, roar, scream, shout, shriek, signal, yell. 2 stay, stop, visit. 3 appeal, invitation, plea, request, summons. 4 bell (*informal*), buzz (*informal*), phone call, ring, telephone call.

call *verb* 1 bellow, cooee (*informal*), cry, cry out, exclaim, roar, scream, shout, shriek, yell. 2 ask, bid, command, fetch, invite, order, page, send for, summon. 3 arouse, awaken, rouse, waken. 4 contact, phone, ring, telephone. 5 drop in, look in, pay a visit, visit. 6 address as, baptise, christen, describe as, designate, dub, label, name, nickname, term. □ **call for** 1 collect, fetch, get, pick up. 2 demand, deserve, justify, necessitate, occasion, require, warrant. □ **call up** conscript, draft (*American*), recruit, summon.

calling *noun* career, employment, job, mission, niche, occupation, profession, trade, vocation.

callous *adjective* cold-hearted, cruel, hard-hearted, harsh, heartless, insensitive, merciless, pitiless, ruthless, thick-skinned, uncaring, unfeeling, unsympathetic.

calm *adjective* 1 (*a calm day*) balmy, halcyon, mild, quiet, still; (*calm seas*) even, flat, motionless, quiet, smooth, steady, still. 2 collected, composed, cool, imperturbable, level-headed, nonchalant, peaceful, phlegmatic, placid, relaxed, sedate, self-possessed, serene, stoical, tranquil, unexcited, unfazed (*informal*), unflappable (*informal*), unruffled. □ **calm** *noun* calmness, lull, peace, quietness, repose, serenity, stillness, tranquillity. □ **calmness** noun calm, composure, coolness, equanimity, imperturbability, nonchalance, poise, presence of mind, serenity.

calm verb allay, alleviate, appease, lull, mollify, pacify, quell, quieten, relieve, soothe, still, subdue. □ **calm down** collect yourself, compose yourself, cool off, relax, settle, simmer down.

camouflage verb conceal, cover up, disguise, hide, mask, screen.

camp noun base, bivouac, encampment, tent.

camp verb encamp, pitch your tent.

campaign noun **1** action, battle, blitz, crusade, fight, manoeuvre, offensive, operation, war. **2** crusade, drive, offensive, strategy.

campaign verb agitate, battle, canvass, crusade, fight, lobby, press, push, strive, work.

campus noun grounds, property, site.

can noun caddy, canister, tin.

can verb preserve, tin.

canal noun **1** channel, watercourse, waterway. **2** duct, passage, tube.

cancel verb **1** abandon, call off, scrap, scrub (informal), stop, wash out (informal); see also DISCONTINUE. **2** abolish, annul, countermand, quash, repeal, rescind, retract, revoke. **3** cross out, delete, erase, obliterate, scratch out, wipe out. □ **cancel out** balance out, counteract, counterbalance, negate, neutralise, nullify, offset, undo.

cancer noun carcinoma, growth, malignancy, melanoma, tumour.

candid adjective blunt, direct, forthright, frank, honest, open, outspoken, plain, sincere, straight, straightforward, upfront (informal).

candidate noun **1** applicant, competitor, contender, contestant, entrant, interviewee, nominee, runner. **2** entrant, examinee.

cane noun rod, staff, stick, walking-stick.

cane verb beat, hit, flog, lash, strike, thrash, whack.

canister noun caddy, can, tin.

canoe noun dugout, kayak.

canopy noun awning, cover, covering, tester.

canteen noun cafeteria, dining room, refectory, restaurant, snack bar, tuckshop.

canvass *verb* campaign, electioneer, solicit votes.

canyon *noun* chasm, defile, gorge, gully, pass, ravine, valley.

cap *noun* **1** hat, head-covering, headgear; (*kinds of cap*) beanie, beret, bonnet, busby, deerstalker, fez, mob cap, mortarboard, nightcap, skullcap, yarmulke. **2** cover, lid, top.

capable *adjective* able, accomplished, adept, clever, competent, effective, efficient, expert, gifted, proficient, skilful, skilled, smart, talented. ☐ **capability** *noun* ability, aptitude, calibre, capacity, competence, potential, proficiency, prowess, skill, talent.

capacity *noun* **1** dimensions, magnitude, size, volume. **2** ability, aptitude, capability, competence, gift, potential, power, skill, talent. **3** duty, function, office, position, post, role.

cape *noun* cloak, cope, mantle, poncho, shawl, stole, wrap.

cape *noun* head, headland, point, promontory.

caper *verb* bound, cavort, dance, frisk, frolic, gambol, hop, jump, leap, play, prance, romp, scamper, skip.

capital *adjective* chief, foremost, important, leading, main, major, principal. ☐ **capital letter** block letter, upper-case letter.

capital *noun* assets, cash, finance, funds, means, money, principal, resources, stock, wealth.

capitalise *verb* **capitalise on** cash in on, exploit, make the most of, profit from, take advantage of.

capitalism *noun* free enterprise, private enterprise.

capitulate *verb* cave in, give in, give up, submit, succumb, surrender, throw in the towel, yield.

capricious *adjective* changeable, erratic, fickle, flighty, impulsive, inconstant, mercurial, temperamental, unpredictable, unreliable, variable, volatile, whimsical.

capsize *verb* flip over, invert, keel over, overturn, tip over, turn over, turn turtle.

capsule *noun* pill, tablet.

captain *noun* commander, master, skipper; see also *CHIEF*.

caption *noun* heading, headline, subtitle, surtitle, title.

captivate *verb* attract, beguile, bewitch, capture, charm, delight, enchant, enthral, entrance, fascinate, mesmerise, seduce.

captive noun convict, detainee, hostage, prisoner.

captivity noun bondage, confinement, custody, detention, imprisonment, incarceration, internment, servitude, slavery.

captor noun abductor, kidnapper.

capture verb **1** apprehend, arrest, catch, collar (informal), nab (informal), nail, nick (slang), seize. **2** catch, hold, take, win.

capture noun apprehension, arrest, seizure.

car noun auto (informal), automobile (American), motor, motor car, motor vehicle, vehicle, wheels (slang); (an old or dilapidated car) banger, bomb (Australian), heap, jalopy, rattletrap, rust bucket, wreck; (kinds of car) convertible, coupé, fastback, four-wheel drive, hatchback, hearse, hot rod, limousine, panel van (Australian), saloon, sedan, soft-top, sports car, station wagon (Australian), ute (Australian informal), utility (Australian), van, wagon (informal).

caravan noun camper, campervan, mobile home, trailer (American), van.

carcass noun body, cadaver, corpse, remains.

care noun **1** attention, carefulness, caution, circumspection, concentration, diligence, meticulousness, precision, thoroughness, thought. **2** charge, control, custody, guardianship, hands, keeping, protection, responsibility, supervision. **3** anxiety, bother, burden, concern, problem, trouble, woe, worry. □ **take care** be careful, be cautious, beware, be wary, look out, take heed, take pains, watch out. □ **take care of 1** keep an eye on, look after, mind, supervise, take charge of, watch over. **2** attend to, deal with, take charge of.

care verb be concerned, be interested, bother, concern yourself, mind, worry. □ **care for 1** attend to, look after, mind, mother, nurse, take care of, tend, watch over. **2** be fond of, be keen on, cherish, like, love.

career noun calling, employment, job, occupation, profession, trade, vocation, work.

career verb hurtle, run, rush, shoot, speed.

carefree adjective blithe, breezy, casual, cheerful, contented, easygoing, footloose, happy-go-lucky, laid-back (*informal*), light-hearted, nonchalant, relaxed, untroubled.

careful *adjective* **1** accurate, conscientious, diligent, fastidious, methodical, meticulous, neat, organised, painstaking, pernickety (*informal*), precise, punctilious, rigorous, scrupulous, systematic, thorough. **2** alert, attentive, cautious, chary, circumspect, guarded, mindful, on guard, prudent, vigilant, wary, watchful.

careless *adjective* **1** absent-minded, inattentive, incautious, irresponsible, lax, negligent, rash, reckless, slack. **2** cursory, disorganised, hasty, hit-or-miss, imprecise, inaccurate, inexact, lax, messy, perfunctory, shoddy, slapdash, slipshod, sloppy, slovenly, untidy. **3** imprudent, inconsiderate, indiscreet, insensitive, tactless, thoughtless, uncaring, unguarded, unthinking.

caress *verb* cuddle, embrace, fondle, hug, kiss, pat, pet, stroke, touch.

caretaker *noun* curator, custodian, janitor, keeper, sexton, steward, verger, warden.

cargo *noun* consignment, freight, goods, load, shipment.

caricature *noun* burlesque, cartoon, parody, satire, send-up (*informal*), spoof (*informal*), take-off (*informal*).

carnage *noun* bloodbath, bloodshed, butchery, holocaust, killing, massacre, murder, slaughter.

carnival *noun* celebration, fair, festival, fête, fiesta, gala, jamboree, Mardi Gras, pageant, show.

carol *noun* canticle, hymn, song.

carpentry *noun* cabinet-making, joinery, woodwork.

carpet *noun* floor covering, mat, rug, runner.

carriage *noun* **1** car, coach. **2** brougham, buggy, chaise, chariot, coach, curricle, gig, hansom, landau, phaeton, post-chaise, stagecoach, sulky, trap, wagon.

carrier *noun* **1** carter, courier, dispatch rider, haulier, messenger. **2** basket, container, holder, pannier, receptacle.

carry *verb* **1** bear, bring, cart, convey, ferry, fetch, freight, haul, lift, lug, move, remove, ship, take, transfer, transport. **2** bear, hold up, support, sustain, take. □ **carry on 1** continue, go on, keep on, persevere, persist, remain. **2**

conduct, manage, operate, run. **3** complain, go on, rant, rave, spout. □ **carry out** accomplish, complete, conduct, discharge, do, execute, finish, fulfil, perform, undertake.

cart noun barrow, billycart, dray, float, go-cart, handcart, trolley, tumbrel, wagon, wheelbarrow.

carton noun box, case, container, pack, package, packet.

cartoon noun **1** caricature, drawing. **2** comic, comic strip. **3** animated film, animation.

carve verb **1** chip, chisel, fashion, hew, sculpt (informal), sculpture, shape, whittle. **2** engrave, etch, inscribe. **3** cut, slice.

cascade noun cataract, falls, rapids, waterfall.

case noun **1** box, cabinet, canteen (of cutlery), capsule, carton, cartridge, casing, casket, chest, coffer, container, covering, crate, envelope, holder, holster, housing, jacket, pack, packaging, receptacle, sheath, shell, skin, sleeve, wrapper. **2** attaché case, bag, briefcase, holdall, port (Australian), portmanteau, suitcase, trunk; (cases) baggage, luggage.

case noun **1** example, illustration, instance, occasion,

occurrence, situation. **2** action, dispute, hearing, lawsuit, proceedings, suit, trial. **3** arguments, facts.

cash noun banknotes, change, coins, currency, dosh (slang), dough (slang), funds, money, notes, paper money, ready money, wherewithal (informal).

cash verb redeem, turn into cash. □ **cash in on** capitalise on, exploit, make the most of, profit from, take advantage of.

cask noun barrel, butt, hogshead, keg, tub, tun, vat.

casket noun box, case, chest, coffer, container.

casserole noun cassoulet, fricassee, goulash, hotpot, ragout, stew.

cast verb **1** chuck (informal), drop, eject, fling, heave, hurl, launch, pitch, shy, sling, throw, toss. **2** discard, get rid of, shed, slough, throw off. **3** fashion, form, model, mould, sculpt, shape.

cast noun **1** form, mould, shape. **2** actors, company, performers, players, troupe.

caste noun class, level, order, rank, standing, station, stratum.

castigate verb admonish, censure, chastise, chide (old use), criticise, haul over the coals, punish, rebuke, reprimand, reproach, reprove, scold, tear strips off (*informal*), tell off (*informal*), tick off (*informal*).

castle noun château, citadel, fort, fortress, mansion, palace, stronghold.

casual adjective **1** accidental, chance, fortuitous, random, serendipitous, unexpected, unforeseen, unintentional, unplanned. **2** apathetic, blasé, carefree, careless, easygoing, happy-go-lucky, lackadaisical, laid-back (*informal*), lax, light-hearted, nonchalant, offhand, relaxed, slap-happy (*informal*), unconcerned, unthinking. **3** informal, leisure, sports. **4** erratic, irregular, occasional, temporary.

casualty noun fatality, victim.

cat noun feline, kitten, moggie (*informal*), puss, pussy (*informal*), tom, tomcat.

catalogue noun directory, file, index, inventory, list, register.

catalogue verb index, list, record, register.

catapult noun ging (*Australian informal*), shanghai (*Australian*), sling, slingshot.

catapult verb fling, hurl, propel, throw.

cataract noun cascade, falls, waterfall.

catastrophe noun accident, blow, calamity, disaster, misadventure, misfortune, mishap, tragedy. ☐ **catastrophic** adjective calamitous, devastating, dire, disastrous.

catch verb **1** clutch, grab, grasp, grip, hang on to, hold on to, seize, snatch. **2** (*catch a thief*) apprehend, arrest, capture, collar (*informal*), cop (*informal*), corner, intercept, nab (*informal*), nail, nick (*slang*), pick up, seize; (*catch a fish, wild animal, etc.*) bag, capture, ensnare, gaff, hook, land, net, snare, trap. **3** catch up with, draw level with, overtake, reach. **4** become infected with, come down with, contract, get. **5** detect, discover, find, spot, surprise. **6** entangle, jam, snag, stick. ☐ **catch on 1** become fashionable, become popular, take off. **2** comprehend, cotton on (*informal*), get it (*informal*), latch on (*informal*), learn, understand.

catch noun **1** bag, booty, haul, prize, take. **2** difficulty, disadvantage, drawback, hitch, problem, snag, trap. **3** bolt, clasp, clip, fastener, hasp, hook, latch, lock.

catching *adjective* communicable, contagious, infectious, transmissible.

catchphrase *noun* byword, catchword, motto, proverb, slogan, watchword.

catchy *adjective* attractive, haunting, memorable, popular, tuneful.

categorical *adjective* absolute, definite, emphatic, explicit, express, unambiguous, unequivocal, unqualified, unreserved.

category *noun* class, classification, division, group, grouping, kind, rank, set, sort, type.

cater *verb* provide food, supply food. □ **cater to** indulge, pander to, satisfy.

catholic *adjective* all-embracing, broad, comprehensive, eclectic, liberal, universal, varied, wide.

cattle *plural noun* bullocks, bulls, calves, cows, heifers, livestock, oxen, steers, stock.

catty *adjective* bitchy (*informal*), malicious, mean, nasty, sly, spiteful, vicious.

cause *noun* **1** beginning, genesis, origin, root, source. **2** basis, call, grounds, justification, need, occasion, reason. **3** aim, end, goal, object, principle, purpose.

cause *verb* bring about, create, effect, generate, give rise to, induce, lead to, occasion, precipitate, produce, provoke, result in, spark off.

caustic *adjective* **1** burning, corrosive. **2** acrimonious, biting, bitter, cutting, sarcastic, scathing, sharp, stinging, virulent.

caution *noun* **1** alertness, attention, attentiveness, care, carefulness, circumspection, discretion, heed, prudence, vigilance, wariness. **2** admonition, warning.

caution *verb* admonish, advise, alert, counsel, forewarn, warn.

cautious *adjective* alert, attentive, careful, chary, circumspect, discreet, guarded, heedful, mindful, prudent, vigilant, wary, watchful.

cave *noun* cavern, cavity, den, dugout, grotto, hole, hollow, pothole.

cave *verb* □ **cave in 1** collapse, fall in, subside. **2** capitulate, give in, submit, surrender, yield.

cavity *noun* cave, crater, gap, hole, hollow, pit, pocket.

cease *verb* break off, conclude, cut out, desist, die away, discontinue, end, finish, halt, knock off (*informal*), leave off, peter out, quit, refrain from, stop, suspend, terminate.

ceasefire noun armistice, truce.

ceaseless adjective constant, continual, continuous, endless, eternal, everlasting, incessant, interminable, nonstop, permanent, perpetual, persistent, relentless.

cede verb give up, grant, hand over, relinquish, surrender, yield.

ceiling noun cap, limit, upper limit.

celebrate verb **1** commemorate, keep, mark, observe, remember. **2** make merry, party, rejoice, revel. **3** officiate at, perform, solemnise. □ **celebration** noun carnival, commemoration, festival, festivity, gala, jamboree, jollification, jubilee, merrymaking, observance, party, revelry, solemnisation.

celebrated adjective acclaimed, distinguished, eminent, famous, illustrious, notable, noted, popular, prominent, renowned, respected, wellknown.

celebrity noun **1** big name, identity (Australian informal), luminary, notable, personage, personality, star. **2** eminence, fame, popularity, prestige, prominence, renown, stardom.

celestial adjective **1** astral, heavenly, stellar. **2** angelic, beatific, divine, heavenly, spiritual, sublime.

celibate adjective chaste, single, unmarried, unwed, virginal.

cell noun **1** compartment, cubicle, den, dungeon, room. **2** cavity, compartment, hole.

cellar noun basement, crypt, dugout, vault.

cement verb bond, braze, fuse, glue, join, paste, solder, stick, unite, weld.

cemetery noun burial ground, churchyard, graveyard, necropolis.

censor verb ban, bowdlerise, cut out, delete, expurgate, remove.

censure noun condemnation, criticism, disapproval, rebuke, reprimand, reproach, reproof. □ **censure** verb castigate, chide (old use), condemn, criticise, rap over the knuckles, rebuke, reprimand, reproach, reprove, scold, upbraid.

central adjective **1** innermost, medial, median, mid, middle. **2** cardinal, chief, core, essential, foremost, fundamental, key, main, major, paramount, primary, principal.

centre noun **1** bull's-eye, core, heart, hub, middle, midpoint, nucleus. **2** focus, headquarters, heart, hub, nucleus.

centre verb concentrate, focus, home in on.

ceremonial adjective formal, ritual, ritualistic, solemn, stately.

ceremonious adjective dignified, formal, over-polite, pompous, prim, proper, punctilious, solemn, starchy, stiff.

ceremony noun **1** celebration, event, function, observance, occasion, rite, ritual, sacrament, service. **2** decorum, formality, pageantry, pomp, protocol, ritual.

certain adjective **1** assured, confident, convinced, definite, positive, sure. **2** definite, indisputable, indubitable, irrefutable, plain, undeniable, undoubted, unquestionable. **3** destined, fated, guaranteed, inescapable, inevitable, sure, unavoidable; (certain to) bound to, sure to. **4** dependable, failsafe, guaranteed, infallible, reliable, sure, sure-fire (informal), trustworthy, unfailing. **5** particular, specific.

certainly adverb **1** assuredly, clearly, definitely, indubitably, surely, undoubtedly, without doubt. **2** absolutely, by all means, of course, yes.

certainty noun **1** cert (slang), cinch (informal), foregone conclusion, moral certainty, sure thing (informal). **2** assurance, certitude, confidence, conviction.

certificate noun award, credentials, degree, diploma, document, licence, paper, qualification.

certify verb affirm, attest, bear witness, confirm, declare, endorse, guarantee, testify, verify, vouch, warrant. □ **certified** adjective accredited, authorised, chartered, licensed, official, qualified.

chafe verb abrade, fret, gall, rub.

chain noun **1** (chains) bonds, fetters, handcuffs, irons, manacles, shackles. **2** combination, line, progression, range (of mountains), row, sequence, series, set, string, succession, train.

chain verb bind, fasten, fetter, handcuff, join, link, secure, tie.

chair noun place, seat; (kinds of chair) armchair, banana chair, chaise longue, deckchair, dining chair, easy chair, high chair, recliner chair, rocking chair, throne, wheelchair.

chair verb conduct, direct, lead, preside over, run.

chairman *noun* chair, chairperson, chairwoman, moderator, president, speaker (*in a legislative assembly*).

challenge *noun* dare, invitation, provocation, summons, trial.

challenge *verb* **1** dare, defy, invite, provoke, summon. **2** contest, dispute, object to, protest against, query, question.

challenging *adjective* demanding, inspiring, stimulating, taxing, testing, thought-provoking.

chamber *noun* **1** bedroom, boudoir, hall, office, room. **2** assembly, council, house, legislative body.

champion *noun* **1** ace, conqueror, hero, title-holder, victor, winner. **2** advocate, backer, defender, guardian, patron, protector, supporter, upholder. □ **championship** *noun* competition, contest, match, tournament.

chance *noun* **1** likelihood, possibility, probability, prospect, risk. **2** break (*informal*), look-in (*informal*), occasion, opening, opportunity, turn. **3** accident, coincidence, destiny, fate, fluke, fortune, luck.

chance *adjective* accidental, casual, coincidental, fortuitous, lucky, unexpected, unintentional, unplanned.

chancy *adjective* dangerous, dicey (*slang*), hazardous, perilous, precarious, risky, uncertain.

change *verb* **1** adapt, adjust, affect, alter, amend, be transformed, chop and change, convert, develop, evolve, fluctuate, have an effect on, have an impact on, influence, metamorphose, modify, mutate, rearrange, reform, reorganise, revise, revolutionise, shift, swing, transfigure, transform, transmute, vary. **2** exchange, interchange, replace, substitute, swap, switch, trade.

change *noun* **1** about-turn, adaptation, adjustment, alteration, amendment, conversion, development, deviation, difference, fluctuation, innovation, metamorphosis, modification, mutation, rearrangement, reform, reorganisation, reversal, revision, revolution, shift, swing, transfiguration, transformation, transition, transmutation, U-turn, variation, variety. **2** coins, coppers, silver. **3** exchange, interchange, replacement, substitution, swap, switch.

changeable adjective capricious, erratic, fickle, fitful, flighty, inconsistent, inconstant, mercurial, moody, temperamental, unpredictable, unreliable, unsteady, variable, volatile.

channel noun **1** narrows, passage, strait. **2** aqueduct, canal, conduit, culvert, ditch, drain, duct, dyke, furrow, groove, gully, gutter, outlet, sluice, trench, trough, watercourse, waterway. **3** band, frequency, station, wavelength.

channel verb direct, guide, lead, steer.

chant noun canticle, psalm, song.

chant verb intone, recite, sing.

chaos noun anarchy, bedlam, confusion, disarray, disorder, havoc, mayhem, mess, muddle, pandemonium, tumult, turmoil, upheaval. □ **chaotic** adjective confused, disorderly, disorganised, haphazard, haywire (informal), jumbled, messy, muddled, out of control, topsy-turvy, uncontrolled, unruly.

chap noun bloke (informal), boy, fellow, guy (informal), lad (informal), man, person.

chaperone noun companion, escort, protector. □ **chaperone** verb accompany, escort, protect, watch over.

chaplain noun clergyman, clergywoman, minister, padre, pastor, priest.

chapter noun division, part, section, subdivision.

char verb blacken, brown, scorch, sear, singe, toast.

character noun **1** part, persona, role. **2** attributes, characteristics, disposition, features, flavour, make-up, manner, nature, peculiarities, personality, qualities, spirit, temperament, traits. **3** chap (informal), fellow, human being, individual, person, specimen, type (informal). **4** card (informal), eccentric, individual, oddball (informal), oddity, weirdo (informal). **5** figure, letter, sign, symbol.

characteristic noun aspect, attribute, feature, hallmark, mark, peculiarity, property, quality, trait.

characteristic adjective distinctive, idiosyncratic, individual, particular, peculiar, recognisable, singular, special, typical, unique.

charade noun farce, mockery, pretence, sham.

charge noun **1** cost, expense, fare, fee, levy, payment, price, rate, tariff, terms, toll. **2** accusation, allegation, complaint, imputation, indictment. **3** care, command, control, custody, keeping, protection, responsibility, supervision.

charge verb **1** ask, debit, demand, levy, require. **2** assault, attack, rush, storm. **3** accuse, blame, book, impeach, indict. **4** burden, encumber, entrust, give, saddle.

charity noun **1** fund, good cause, institution. **2** alms (old use), assistance, contributions, donations, financial assistance, handouts. **3** altruism, benevolence, compassion, generosity, goodwill, humanity, kindness, love, philanthropy, sympathy. □ **charitable** adjective see GENEROUS.

charlatan noun cheat, con man (informal), fake, fraud, humbug, impostor, phoney (informal), quack, swindler, trickster.

charm noun **1** allure, appeal, attractiveness, charisma, magnetism. **2** incantation, magic, sorcery, spell, witchcraft, witchery, wizardry. **3** amulet, mascot, talisman, trinket.

charm verb allure, attract, beguile, bewitch, captivate, delight, enchant, enthral, entrance, fascinate, hold spellbound, hypnotise, mesmerise, seduce. □ **charming** adjective appealing, attractive, beguiling, captivating, delightful, enchanting, enthralling, fascinating, likeable, pleasant, pleasing, sweet (informal).

chart noun **1** map, plan. **2** diagram, graph, histogram, table, tabulation.

chart verb graph, map, plot, record, register.

charter verb hire, lease, rent.

chase verb follow, hound, hunt, pursue, run after, track, trail.

chasm noun abyss, breach, canyon, cavity, cleft, crack, crevasse, fissure, gap, gorge, hole, opening, ravine, rift.

chassis noun frame, framework, skeleton, substructure.

chaste adjective celibate, pure, virginal, virtuous. □ **chastity** noun celibacy, purity, sexual abstinence, virginity, virtue.

chastise verb beat, castigate, censure, chasten, chide (old use), discipline, flog, lash, punish, rebuke, reprimand, reproach, reprove, scold, tell off (informal), thrash, upbraid.

chat noun chinwag (informal), conversation, gossip, natter (informal), talk, yabber (Australian informal), yak (informal).

chat *verb* chatter, converse, gossip, have a word, mag (*Australian informal*), natter (*informal*), prattle, talk, yabber (*Australian informal*), yak (*informal*).

chatter *verb* babble, chat, gabble, gossip, jabber, natter (*informal*), prattle, talk, yak (*informal*).

chatter *noun* chit-chat, gossip, talk, tattle, tittle-tattle.

chatterbox *noun* chatterer, gasbag (*informal*), magpie, windbag (*informal*).

cheap *adjective* **1** bargain, budget, competitive, cut-price, discount, economical, inexpensive, keen, low, reasonable, reduced, sale. **2** gimcrack, inferior, poor, rubbishy, second-rate, shoddy, tacky (*informal*), tinny, tinpot, trashy, worthless.

cheat *verb* **1** bamboozle (*informal*), bilk, bluff, con (*informal*), deceive, defraud, diddle (*informal*), double-cross, dupe, fleece, have on (*informal*), hoax, hoodwink, outwit, rip off (*informal*), rob, rook, rort (*Australian slang*), short-change, swindle, take for a ride (*informal*), trick, welsh on. **2** break the rules, copy, crib (*informal*).

cheat *noun* charlatan, con man (*informal*), crook (*informal*), embezzler, extortioner, fraud, racketeer, rogue, shark (*informal*), sharper, shicer (*Australian slang*), shyster (*informal*), swindler, trickster, welsher.

check *verb* **1** audit, check on, check out, check up, correct, double-check, examine, inspect, investigate, look over, mark, monitor, screen, scrutinise, suss out (*informal*), test, verify, vet. **2** curb, frustrate, hamper, hinder, hold back, impede, inhibit, limit, restrict, retard, slow down, stop, stunt, thwart.

check *noun* **1** check-up, examination, going-over (*informal*), inspection, investigation, once-over (*informal*), probe, scrutiny, search, test. **2** brake, constraint, control, curb, limitation, restraint, restriction.

cheek *noun* **1** chap, jowl. **2** audacity, boldness, effrontery, front, gall (*slang*), hide (*informal*), impertinence, impudence, insolence, nerve, presumption, temerity.

cheeky *adjective* arrogant, audacious, bold, brazen, discourteous, disrespectful, forward, fresh (*informal*), impertinent, impolite, impudent, insolent, pert, pre sumptuous, rude, saucy, shameless.

cheer *noun* cheerfulness, gaiety, gladness, glee, good spirits, happiness, jollity, joy, merriment, mirth, pleasure.

cheer *verb* **1** applaud, barrack for (*Australian*), clap, encourage, shout for, support. **2** brighten, buck up (*informal*), buoy up, comfort, console, divert, encourage, gladden, hearten, perk up, uplift.

cheerful *adjective* blithe, bright, buoyant, carefree, cheery, chirpy, contented, elated, exhilarated, exuberant, gay, glad, gleeful, good-humoured, happy, happy-go-lucky, jaunty, jolly, jovial, joyful, joyous, jubilant, light-hearted, lively, merry, optimistic, perky, positive, radiant, upbeat (*informal*).

chemist *noun* apothecary (*old use*), dispenser, druggist, pharmacist.

chequered *adjective* check, checked, chequerboard, criss-cross, plaid, tartan.

cherish *verb* **1** care for, foster, look after, nurse, nurture, protect. **2** adore, be fond of, dote on, hold dear, love, prize, treasure, value.

chest *noun* **1** bosom, breast, bust, ribcage, thorax. **2** ark, box, case, casket, coffer, crate, ottoman, strongbox, trunk. □ **chest of drawers** bureau, chest, dresser, lowboy, tallboy.

chew *verb* champ, chomp, crunch, gnaw, grind, masticate, munch, nibble.

chic *adjective* classy (*informal*), elegant, fashionable, smart, sophisticated, stylish.

chick *noun* fledgling, nestling.

chicken *noun* chook (*Australian informal*), fowl, hen, rooster.

chicken *verb* □ **chicken out** back out, opt out, pike out (*Australian informal*), pull out, withdraw.

chief *noun* boss, captain, chieftain, commander, director, employer, governor, head, leader, manager, master, overseer, president, principal, ruler, superintendent, supervisor.

chief *adjective* basic, cardinal, central, dominant, essential, first, foremost, fundamental, greatest, head, highest, key, leading, main, major, overriding, paramount, predominant, primary, prime, principal, supreme. □ **chiefly** *adverb* especially, for the most part, generally, in the main, mainly, mostly, particularly, primarily, principally.

child noun 1 babe, baby, bairn (Scottish), boy, girl, infant, juvenile, kid (informal), lad, lass, minor, piccaninny, toddler, tot, youngster, youth. 2 daughter, descendant, offspring, son.

childhood noun boyhood, girlhood, infancy, youth.

childish adjective babyish, immature, infantile, juvenile, naïve, puerile, silly.

childlike adjective artless, guileless, ingenuous, innocent, naïve, simple, trusting, youthful.

chill noun chilliness, coldness, crispness, iciness, nip.

chill verb cool, refrigerate.

chilly adjective 1 cold, crisp, freezing, frosty, icy, nippy (informal), raw, wintry. 2 aloof, cold, cool, frosty, hostile, icy, stony, unfriendly, unwelcoming.

chime verb ding, dong, peal, ring, sound, strike, toll.

china noun crockery, dinner service, porcelain, pottery, tableware.

chink noun aperture, breach, cleft, crack, cranny, fissure, gap, hole, opening, rift, slit, split.

chip verb 1 bit, flake, fragment, piece, shard, shaving, sliver, splinter. 2 crisp, French fry.

chip verb break, damage, nick, splinter.

chirp verb cheep, chirrup, peep, tweet, twitter.

chirpy adjective bright, cheerful, happy, light-hearted, lively, perky, vivacious.

chivalrous adjective considerate, courteous, courtly, gallant, gentlemanly, heroic, honourable, noble, polite.

chock noun block, wedge.

chock-a-block adjective chockers (informal), chockfull, crammed, crowded, full, jam-packed (informal), packed.

choice noun 1 alternative, option. 2 array, assortment, collection, range, selection, variety. 3 decision, election, pick, preference, selection.

choice adjective excellent, fine, first-class, first-rate, prime, prize, select, superior.

choir noun choral group, choristers, chorus, ensemble, singers.

choke verb 1 asphyxiate, smother, stifle, strangle, suffocate, throttle. 2 gag, gasp. 3 block, clog, congest, crowd, jam, obstruct, pack.

chook noun chicken, fowl, poultry.

choose verb adopt, appoint, decide on, draw lots for, elect, name, nominate, opt for, pick, plump for, prefer, select, settle on, single out, vote for. ☐ **choosy** adjective fastidious, finicky, fussy, particular, pernickety (informal), picky (informal), selective.

chop verb cleave, cut, fell, hack, hew, split; (chop up) chip, cube, cut, dice, mince.

chopper noun axe, cleaver, hatchet, tomahawk.

choppy adjective rough, stormy, turbulent.

chore noun duty, errand, job, task, work.

chorus noun **1** jingle, refrain. **2** choir, choral group, ensemble, singers.

christen verb **1** baptise. **2** call, dub, name, nickname. ☐ **christening** noun baptism.

Christmas noun Xmas, yule (old use), yuletide (old use).

chronic adjective ceaseless, constant, continuing, continuous, lifelong, lingering, long-standing, perennial, permanent, persistent, unending.

chubby adjective dumpy, fat, obese, overweight, plump, podgy, rotund, round, stout, tubby.

chuck verb cast, fling, heave, hurl, pitch, sling, throw, toss. ☐ **chuck in** give up, jack in (slang), leave, quit, resign, throw in, toss in (informal). ☐ **chuck out** boot out (slang), cast out, discard, ditch (informal), expel, get rid of, kick out (informal), throw away, throw out.

chuckle verb & noun chortle, giggle, laugh, snigger, titter.

chum noun buddy (informal), cobber (Australian informal), companion, comrade, confidant(e), crony, friend, mate, pal (informal).

chunk noun hunk, lump, mass, piece, slab, wedge, wodge.

church noun **1** abbey, basilica, cathedral, chapel, minster, sanctuary, shrine, tabernacle, temple. **2** devotions, divine service, service, worship.

churlish adjective bad-tempered, boorish, ill-bred, ill-mannered, impolite, mean, rude, surly, uncivil, unfriendly, unsociable.

churn verb **1** agitate, beat, stir, whip, whisk. **2** foam, heave, seethe, swirl, toss.

cigarette noun ciggy (informal), fag (slang), smoke (informal).

cinder noun (cinders) ashes, clinker, embers.

cinema noun films, flicks (informal), motion pictures,

movies (*informal*), pictures (*informal*), the screen.

circle noun **1** band, disc, halo, hoop, loop, ring, round. **2** circuit, circumnavigation, lap, loop, orbit, revolution. **3** clique, company, group, set, sphere, world.

circle verb circumnavigate, circumscribe, encircle, go round, orbit, ring, tour.

circuit noun **1** circle, lap, loop, orbit, revolution. **2** course, ring, track.

circular adjective discoid, round.

circular noun bulletin, flyer, leaflet, memorandum, newsletter, notice.

circulate verb **1** flow, go round, move round. **2** distribute, issue, pass round, release, send round.

circumference noun boundary, edge, limit, margin, perimeter.

circumstance noun background, condition, context, detail, event, fact, particular, position, situation.

citadel noun acropolis, bastion, castle, fort, fortress, garrison, stronghold.

cite verb adduce, mention, name, put forward, quote, refer to, specify.

citizen noun denizen, dweller, inhabitant, national, native, resident.

city noun big smoke (*slang*), metropolis, town.

civic adjective citizen's, communal, community, local, municipal, public.

civil adjective **1** citizen's, civic. **2** civilian, non-military. **3** cordial, courteous, obliging, polite, respectful, well-mannered.

civilised adjective cultivated, cultured, developed, educated, enlightened, refined, sophisticated.

clad adjective attired, clothed, dressed.

claim verb **1** ask for, bags (*informal*), demand, lay claim to, request, require. **2** allege, assert, contend, declare, insist, maintain, make out, pretend, profess, state.

claim noun **1** application, call, demand, request. **2** entitlement, right, title.

clairvoyance noun ESP, extrasensory perception, second sight, sixth sense.

clamber verb climb, crawl, scramble, shin.

clammy adjective damp, dank, humid, moist, sticky, sweaty, wet.

clamour *noun* commotion, din, hubbub, hullabaloo, noise, outcry, racket, row, rumpus, shouting, uproar.

clamour *verb* call, cry out, demand, protest, shout.

clamp *noun* brace, clasp, clip, fastener, grip, support, vice.

clamp *verb* clasp, clip, fasten, grip, secure.

clan *noun* family, group, line, tribe.

clang *noun* chime, clangour, clank, clash, clink, jangle, peal, ringing.

clank *noun* clang, clash, clatter, clunk, jangle, rattle.

clap *verb* applaud.

clap *noun* **1** bang, burst, crack, crash, explosion, peal. **2** applause, hand (*informal*).

clarify *verb* clear up, elucidate, explain, make clear, shed light on, spell out.

clarity *noun* clearness, limpidity, purity, transparency.

clash *verb* **1** bang, clang, clank, clatter, crash, jangle. **2** argue, battle, be opposed, conflict, contend, disagree, dispute, feud, fight, quarrel, squabble, wrangle. □ **clash** *noun* **1** bang, clang, clangour, clank, clatter, crash, jangle. **2** altercation, battle, combat, conflict, confrontation, contest, dis-

agreement, fight, skirmish. **3** discord, disharmony, incompatibility, mismatch.

clasp *noun* brooch, buckle, catch, clip, fastener, hook, lock.

clasp *verb* **1** clutch, embrace, enfold, grasp, grip, hold, hug, squeeze. **2** clip, fasten, join, secure.

class *noun* **1** form, grade, group, set, year. **2** category, classification, division, family, genre, genus, group, kind, league, order, set, sort, species, subset, type, variety. **3** caste, level, order, rank, station, stratum.

class *verb* arrange, categorise, classify, grade, group, label, rank, sort.

classic *adjective* **1** excellent, exemplary, first-class, firstrate, outstanding. **2** archetypal, characteristic, model, standard, typical. **3** abiding, ageless, enduring, established, immortal, lasting, time-honoured, traditional.

classical *adjective* **1** Greek, Latin, Roman. **2** ageless, conventional, enduring, serious, standard, traditional.

classify *verb* arrange, categorise, class, grade, group, label, order, organise, pigeonhole, rank, sort.

clatter *noun* banging, clack, clang, clangour, clank, jangle, rattle.

clause *noun* article, condition, paragraph, provision, proviso, section, stipulation.

claw *noun* nail, nipper, pincer, talon.

claw *verb* lacerate, maul, scratch, slash, tear.

clean *adjective* **1** cleansed, disinfected, fresh, hygienic, immaculate, laundered, sanitary, sanitised, scoured, scrubbed, spick and span, spotless, sterilised, unsoiled, washed. **2** (*clean air*) clear, fresh, pure, purified, uncontaminated, unpolluted; (*a clean page*) blank, fresh, new, unmarked, unused. **3** above board, fair, honest, honourable, sporting, sportsmanlike. **4** decent, innocent, inoffensive, respectable.

clean *verb* bath, bathe, brush, cleanse, decontaminate, disinfect, dry-clean, dust, groom, launder, mop, purge, purify, rinse, sanitise, scour, scrub, shampoo, shower, sponge, sterilise, swab, sweep, swill, tidy (up), vacuum, wash, wipe.

cleanser *noun* antiseptic, bactericide, detergent, disinfectant, germicide, sanitiser, soap, steriliser.

clear *adjective* **1** (*a clear liquid*) clean, crystal-clear, crystal line, limpid, pure, see-through, transparent; (*clear skies*) bright, cloudless, fair, starry sunny, unclouded. **2** apparent blatant, clear-cut, coherent comprehensible, crystal-clear definite, distinct, evident glaring, intelligible, lucid manifest, marked, noticeable obvious, palpable, patent plain, pronounced, straight forward, unambiguous, under standable, unequivocal unmistakable, visible. **3** empty free, open, passable, un impeded, unobstructed. **4** blameless, easy, guilt-free guiltless, untroubled.

clear *verb* **1** clean, empty evacuate, free, unblock unclog. **2** absolve, acquit exonerate, vindicate. **3** bound over, jump over, leap over spring over, vault. **4** approve authorise, OK (*informal*), pass sanction. □ **clear off** see *LEAVE*. □ **clear up 1** clean up sort out, straighten up, tidy up **2** clarify, explain, resolve settle, sort out.

clearing *noun* gap, glade opening, space.

cleaver *noun* chopper, hatchet meat-axe; see also *KNIFE*.

clench *verb* clamp together close, grit, set.

clergy *noun* ministry, priesthood; (*various members of the clergy*) archbishop, archdeacon, bishop, canon, cardinal, chaplain, churchman, churchwoman, clergyman, clergywoman, cleric, curate, deacon, deaconess, dean, minister, padre, parson, pastor, preacher, prelate, priest, primate, rector, vicar.

clerical *adjective* **1** book, bookkeeping, office, paper, secretarial, stenographic, white-collar. **2** ecclesiastical, priestly, sacerdotal.

clerk *noun* bookkeeper, office worker, record-keeper, secretary.

clever *adjective* able, accomplished, adept, adroit, artful, astute, brainy, bright, brilliant, canny, crafty, cunning, deft, dexterous, expert, gifted, ingenious, intelligent, inventive, nifty (*informal*), perceptive, quick-witted, resourceful, sharp-witted, shrewd, slick, sly, smart, talented, wily, wise, witty. □ **cleverness** *noun* ability, adroitness, astuteness, brains, brilliance, cunning, dexterity, expertise, ingenuity, intelligence, mastery, quickness, resourcefulness, shrewdness, skill, smartness, talent, wit, wizardry.

cliché *noun* banality, commonplace, hackneyed phrase, platitude.

click *noun* crack, snap, tick.

client *noun* consumer, customer, patron, shopper, user.

cliff *noun* bluff, crag, escarpment, precipice, rock face, scarp.

climate *noun* clime (*literary*), weather.

climax *noun* apex, crisis, culmination, highlight, peak, pinnacle, summit, zenith.

climb *verb* **1** clamber over, go over, mount, scale, shin. **2** ascend, go up, rise, soar.

clinch *verb* close, conclude, finalise, secure, settle, sew up (*informal*).

cling *verb* adhere, attach, stick; (*cling to*) clasp, cleave to (*old use*), clutch, embrace, grasp, grip, hang on to, hold on to, hug.

clinic *noun* health centre, hospital, infirmary, medical centre, surgery.

clink *verb* jangle, jingle, ring, tinkle.

clip *noun* clasp, fastener, grip, hook.

clip *verb* attach, fasten, fix, join, pin, secure, staple.

clip *verb* bob, crop, cut, prune, shear, shorten, snip, trim.

clip noun excerpt, extract, segment, snippet, trailer.

clippers plural noun cutters, scissors, secateurs, shears, snips.

clique noun circle, crowd, faction, group, mob, set.

cloak noun burnous, cape, coat, cope, mantle, poncho, shroud, wrap.

clock noun chronometer, timepiece.

clog verb block, bung up, choke, jam, obstruct, stop up.

close adjective **1** accessible, adjacent, at hand, near, neighbouring; see also *IMPENDING*. **2** affectionate, attached, dear, devoted, familiar, fond, inseparable, intimate. **3** alert, attentive, careful, concentrated, detailed, minute, searching, thorough. **4** cramped, narrow, tight. **5** even, level-pegging, narrow, neck and neck, tight. **6** airless, humid, muggy, oppressive, stale, stifling, stuffy, sultry.

close adverb alongside, close by, near, nigh (old use), within cooee (Australian informal).

close verb **1** bar, block, bolt, cork, fasten, latch, lock, plug, seal, secure, shut, slam, stop. **2** conclude, end, finish, stop, terminate, wind up.

close noun completion, conclusion, culmination, end, finale, finish, halt, stop, termination.

closet noun cupboard, wardrobe.

clot verb coagulate, solidify, thicken.

cloth noun fabric, material, stuff, textile.

clothe verb array, attire, deck, dress, garb, robe.

clothes plural noun apparel (formal), attire (formal), clobber (slang), clothing, costume, dress, finery, garb, garments, gear (informal), get-up (informal), kit, outfit, raiment (old use), rig (informal), togs (informal), uniform, vestments, wardrobe, wear.

cloud noun fog, haze, mist, vapour.

cloud verb blur, darken, dim, fog, grow overcast, muddy, obscure.

cloudless adjective blue, bright, clear, fair, starlit, starry, sunny, unclouded.

cloudy adjective **1** dull, gloomy, grey, heavy, leaden, louring, overcast. **2** hazy, milky, muddy, murky, opaque.

clown noun buffoon, comedian, comic, fool, jester, joker, wag, zany.

club *noun* **1** bat, baton, bludgeon, cudgel, nulla-nulla, stick, truncheon, waddy. **2** alliance, association, fellowship, group, guild, league, organisation, society, union.

club *verb* batter, beat, bludgeon, clobber, cudgel, hit, strike, wallop.

clue *noun* cue, guide, hint, idea, indication, inkling, key, lead, pointer, sign, suggestion, tip.

clump *noun* bunch, cluster, group, mass, tuft.

clumsy *adjective* awkward, blundering, bungling, fumbling, gawky, ham-fisted (*informal*), heavy-handed, inept, maladroit, unco (*informal*), uncoordinated, ungainly, unskilful.

cluster *noun* assembly, batch, bunch, collection, congregation, crowd, gathering, group, herd, hive, huddle, swarm, throng.

cluster *verb* assemble, bunch, collect, congregate, crowd, flock, gather, group, herd, huddle, throng.

clutch *verb* clasp, cling to, grasp, grip, hang on to, hold, hug.

clutter *noun* jumble, litter, mess, muddle.

clutter *verb* crowd, litter, mess up, scatter, strew.

coach *noun* **1** bus, omnibus (*formal*). **2** carriage, stagecoach. **3** instructor, teacher, trainer, tutor.

coach *verb* drill, instruct, teach, train, tutor.

coagulate *verb* clot, congeal, curdle, solidify, stiffen, thicken.

coalition *noun* alliance, amalgamation, association, bloc, partnership, union.

coarse *adjective* **1** harsh, looseweave, prickly, rough, scratchy. **2** boorish, common, crude, foul, impolite, improper, indecent, low, offensive, rough, rude, uncouth, unrefined, vulgar.

coast *noun* beach, coastline, foreshore, seaboard, seashore, seaside, shore.

coast *verb* cruise, drift, freewheel, glide.

coat *noun* **1** (*kinds of coat*) anorak, blazer, cagoule, dinner-jacket, doublet, duffel coat, greatcoat, jacket, mackintosh, overcoat, parka, raincoat, tailcoat, topcoat, trench coat, tuxedo, waistcoat, windcheater, wrap. **2** fleece, fur, hair, hide, pelt, skin. **3** coating, cover, film, layer, overlay. □ **coat of arms**

blazon, crest, emblem, heraldic device, shield.

coat *verb* cover, daub, encase, encrust, laminate, paint, plaster, protect, seal, smear, spread, veneer.

coating *noun* coat, cover, covering, film, glaze, layer, outside, overlay, sealant, skin, surface, veneer.

coax *verb* beguile, cajole, charm, entice, induce, inveigle, persuade, sweet-talk (*informal*), talk into, tempt.

cobber *noun* buddy (*informal*), chum (*informal*), companion, comrade, confidant, confidante, crony, friend, mate, pal (*informal*).

cobbler *noun* shoemaker, shoe repairer.

cock *noun* cockerel, rooster.

cock *verb* prick up, raise, tilt, tip.

cock-eyed *adjective* **1** askew, awry, crooked, lopsided. **2** absurd, crazy, foolish, harebrained, ludicrous, mad, stupid, wild.

cocky *adjective* arrogant, brash, bumptious, cocksure, conceited, impudent, opinionated, overconfident, self-assured, self-confident, vain.

code *noun* **1** cipher. **2** laws, principles, regulations, rules, system.

code *verb* encode, encrypt.

codicil *noun* addendum, appendix, postscript, rider, supplement.

coerce *verb* bludgeon, browbeat, bulldoze (*informal*), bully, compel, constrain, dragoon, force, intimidate, lean on (*informal*), press, pressure, railroad.

coffin *noun* box, casket, sarcophagus.

coherent *adjective* articulate, clear, connected, consistent, intelligible, logical, lucid, rational, structured, systematic, understandable.

coil *noun* circle, convolution, curl, helix, kink, loop, ring, spiral, twist, whorl.

coil *verb* bend, curl, entwine, kink, loop, roll, turn, twine, twirl, twist, wind, wrap.

coin *noun* cash, change, copper, money, silver.

coin *verb* **1** mint, strike. **2** create, devise, invent, make up, originate.

coincide *verb* **1** be concurrent, clash, happen simultaneously, happen together, synchronise. **2** accord, agree, be the same, concur, correspond, match, square, tally.

coincidence *noun* accident, chance, fluke, luck. □ **coincidental** *adjective* accidental, chance, fortuitous, unintentional, unplanned.

cold *adjective* **1** biting, bitter, bleak, chill, chilly, cool, crisp, freezing, frigid, frosty, glacial, icy, nippy (*informal*), raw, subzero, wintry. **2** aloof, callous, clinical, cold-hearted, cool, distant, frigid, frosty, hard-hearted, heartless, hostile, indifferent, inhuman, insensitive, severe, stand-offish, stony, uncaring, undemonstrative, unemotional, unenthusiastic, unfeeling, unfriendly, unkind, unsympathetic. □ **cold-shoulder** *verb* freeze out (*informal*), ostracise, rebuff, send to Coventry, snub.

cold-blooded *adjective* brutal, callous, cold-hearted, cruel, hard-hearted, heartless, inhuman, inhumane, merciless, pitiless, ruthless, savage, unemotional, unfeeling.

collaborate *verb* cooperate, join forces, team up, work together. □ **collaborator** *noun* **1** ally, assistant, associate, colleague, co-worker, fellow worker, helper, partner. **2** fraterniser, quisling, traitor.

collapse *verb* **1** break, buckle, cave in, crumble, crumple, disintegrate, drop, fall down, give way, subside, tumble down. **2** faint, fall down, flop, keel over, pass out, sink, slump, swoon. **3** break down, fail, fold, founder, go bung (*Australian informal*), go bust (*informal*).

collapse *noun* breakdown, cave-in, destruction, disintegration, downfall, failure, fall, ruin, subsidence.

collate *verb* arrange, collect, sort, systematise.

colleague *noun* associate, collaborator, co-worker, fellow worker, partner, workmate.

collect *verb* **1** accumulate, acquire, amass, garner, gather, heap up, hoard, pile up, save, stockpile, store. **2** assemble, cluster, come together, congregate, convene, flock, gather, group, herd, rally, swarm, throng. **3** obtain, raise, receive, solicit. **4** bring, fetch, get, obtain, pick up.

collection *noun* **1** (*of things*) accumulation, anthology, arrangement, array, assortment, batch, bundle, compendium, compilation, conglomeration, corpus, group, heap, hoard, jumble, library, mass, medley, miscellany, mixture, pile, selection, series, set, stack, stockpile, store, storehouse, swag (*Australian*), treasury, variety; (*of people*) assembly, band, bevy, body, bunch, cluster, company, congregation, crowd, flock, gathering, group, herd, horde, host, mass, mob, multitude, pack, swarm, throng. **2** alms (*old use*), contributions, donations, gifts, offering, offertory.

college *noun* academy, conservatorium, institute, school, seminary, university.

collide *verb* (*collide with*) bump into, cannon into, crash into, hit, knock into, ram into, run into, slam into, smash into, strike. □ **collision** *noun* bingle (*Australian informal*), crash, impact, pile-up (*informal*), prang (*informal*), smash.

colloquial *adjective* casual, chatty, conversational, everyday, familiar, informal, vernacular.

colonise *verb* occupy, people, populate, settle. □ **colonist** *noun* immigrant, pioneer, settler.

colony *noun* **1** dependency, dominion, possession, province, settlement, territory. **2** community, group.

colossal *adjective* big, enormous, extensive, gargantuan, giant, gigantic, ginormous (*slang*), great, huge, humungous (*slang*), immense, large, mammoth, massive, mighty, monstrous, monumental, prodigious, stupendous, towering, tremendous, vast, whopping (*slang*).

colour *noun* **1** hue, shade, tinge, tint, tone. **2** dye, paint, pigment, stain, tint.

colour *verb* **1** dye, paint, stain, tinge, tint. **2** blush, flush, glow, redden. **3** affect, bias, distort, influence, prejudice, taint.

colourful *adjective* **1** bright, brilliant, flashy, gaudy, gay, loud, multicoloured, showy, vibrant, vivid. **2** descriptive, graphic, interesting, lively, picturesque, vivid.

colourless *adjective* **1** anaemic, ashen, pale, pallid, pasty, sickly, wan, washed out, waxen, white. **2** boring, drab, dreary, dull, insipid, lacklustre, lifeless, monotonous, nondescript, ordinary, tame, unexciting, unimaginative, wishy-washy.

column *noun* **1** pile, pillar, pole, post, shaft, support, upright. **2** file, line, procession, queue, row, string, train. **3** article, feature, leader, piece.

comb *verb* **1** groom, tidy. **2** fossick through (*Australian informal*), ransack, rummage through, scour, search.

combat *noun* action, battle, clash, conflict, confrontation, contest, duel, engagement, fight, hostility, skirmish, struggle, war. □ **combat** *verb* battle, counter, fight, oppose, resist, tackle.

combination *noun* alliance, amalgam, amalgamation, association, blend, coalition, composite, conjunction, fusion, marriage, merger, mix, mixture, partnership, synthesis, union.

combine *verb* ally, amalgamate, associate, band together, bind, blend, coalesce, compound, consolidate, federate, fuse, incorporate, integrate, join forces, lump together, marry, merge, mix, put together, synthesise, team up, unite.

come *verb* 1 advance, approach, draw near. 2 appear, arrive, blow in (*informal*), drop in, lob in (*Australian slang*), materialise, reach, roll up (*informal*), show up, turn up. 3 happen, occur, take place. □ **come about** arise, come to pass, happen, occur, take place. □ **come across** chance upon, come upon, find, happen on, stumble on. □ **come back** reappear, recur, resurface, return. □ **come down** descend, drop, fall, land, nosedive, plunge. □ **come out** appear, become known, be published, be revealed, emerge, leak out. □ **come to**

1 add up to, amount to, equal, tot up to. 2 come round, rally, recover, regain consciousness, revive. □ **come up** 1 ascend, pop up, rise, surface. 2 arise, crop up, happen, occur. □ **come up with** contribute, produce, propose, put forward, submit, suggest.

comedian *noun* comic, humorist, jester, joker, wag, wit.

comedy *noun* farce, fun, hilarity, humour, joking, satire, slapstick.

comfort *noun* 1 contentment, ease, luxury, opulence, well-being. 2 commiseration, condolence, consolation, reassurance, relief, solace, support, sympathy.

comfort *verb* cheer, console, encourage, gladden, reassure, relieve, solace, soothe, sympathise with.

comfortable *adjective* 1 at ease, at home, contented, relaxed. 2 comfy (*informal*), cosy, easy, luxurious, pleasant, relaxing, restful, snug, soft.

comical *adjective* absurd, amusing, comic, droll, farcical, funny, hilarious, humorous, laughable, ludicrous, nonsensical, ridiculous, silly, zany.

command *noun* **1** bidding, commandment, decree, dictate, direction, directive, edict, injunction, instruction, order, precept, summons. **2** authority, charge, control, leadership, power, rule. **3** control, grasp, mastery, understanding.

command *verb* **1** bid, call upon, charge, decree, direct, instruct, order, prescribe, require, summon, tell. **2** be in charge of, control, direct, govern, head, lead, manage, rule, supervise. **3** compel, deserve, earn, get.

commandment *noun* command, law, order, precept, principle, rule.

commemorate *verb* celebrate, mark, observe, remember.

commence *verb* begin, embark on, enter upon, get going, get under way, inaugurate, initiate, kick off (*informal*), launch, open, start. □ **commencement** *noun* beginning, birth, dawn, founding, genesis, inauguration, inception, onset, opening, origin, outset, start.

commend *verb* acclaim, applaud, approve, extol, laud (*formal*), praise, recommend.

commendable *adjective* admirable, laudable, meritorious, praiseworthy, worthy.

comment *noun* annotation, note, observation, opinion, reference, reflection, remark, statement.

comment *verb* mention, observe, remark, say.

commentary *noun* account, description, narration, report, voice-over. □ **commentator** *noun* broadcaster, commenter, journalist, narrator, presenter, reporter.

commerce *noun* business, trade.

commercial *adjective* **1** business, mercantile, trade, trading. **2** economic, money-making, profitable, profit-making.

commercial *noun* ad (*informal*), advert (*informal*), advertisement, plug (*informal*).

commission *noun* **1** assignment, authority, duty, job, mission, order, task, warrant. **2** board, committee, council, panel. **3** brokerage, cut (*informal*), fee, percentage, share.

commit *verb* **1** carry out, do, perform, perpetrate. **2** commend, consign, entrust, hand over. **3** bind, pledge, promise.

commitment *noun* **1** duty, engagement, obligation, res ponsibility, task, tie. **2** pledge, promise, undertaking, vow, word. **3** allegiance, dedication, devotion, loyalty.

committee *noun* board, cabinet, council, panel, working party.

commodity *noun* article, item, product; (*commodities*) goods, merchandise, produce, wares.

common *adjective* **1** common or garden (*informal*), commonplace, conventional, customary, everyday, familiar, frequent, general, habitual, normal, ordinary, plain, prevalent, regular, routine, simple, standard, typical, universal, usual, well-known, widespread. **2** general, popular, public, universal. **3** communal, joint, mutual (*informal*), shared. **4** boorish, coarse, crude, ill-bred, low, plebeian, rude, uncouth, unrefined, vulgar. □ **common sense** gumption (*informal*), intelligence, judgement, nous (*informal*), sense.

commonplace *adjective* common, customary, everyday, familiar, mundane, normal, ordinary, regular, routine, usual.

commotion *noun* ado, ballyhoo, clamour, din, disturbance, fracas, furore, fuss, hubbub, hullabaloo,

kerfuffle (*informal*), noise, pandemonium, racket, riot, rumpus, shindy (*informal*), stir, to-do, tumult, turmoil, unrest, uproar.

communal *adjective* common, joint, public, shared.

communicate *verb* **1** announce, broadcast, convey, declare, disclose, disseminate, divulge, express, impart, indicate, make known, pass on, promulgate, relate, relay, report, reveal, say, show, signal, speak, state, voice. **2** commune, confer, converse, correspond, get in touch, make contact, speak, talk, write.

communication *noun* **1** contact, conversation, correspondence, dialogue, speaking, writing. **2** advice, announcement, bulletin, communiqué, dispatch, information, letter, memorandum, message, news, note, notice, notification, report, statement.

communicative *adjective* chatty, forthcoming, garrulous, informative, loquacious, open, talkative.

Communion *noun* Eucharist, Holy Communion, Lord's Supper, Mass.

communiqué *noun* announcement, bulletin, communication, dispatch, message, report, statement.

community noun **1** citizens, nation, people, populace, public, residents, society; see also *DISTRICT*. **2** group, people, sector, set.

compact adjective **1** little, neat, small. **2** brief, concise, condensed, laconic, pithy, succinct, terse.

companion noun assistant, associate, attendant, buddy (*informal*), chaperone, chum (*informal*), cobber (*Australian informal*), comrade, consort, crony, escort, friend, mate, pal (*informal*), partner, playmate, sidekick (*informal*).

company noun **1** assembly, audience, congregation, crew, crowd, gathering, group, mob, party, throng, troop, troupe (*of actors*). **2** business, concern, corporation, establishment, firm, institution, organisation. **3** companionship, fellowship, friendship, society. **4** callers, guests, visitors.

comparable adjective analogous, corresponding, equivalent, like, parallel, similar.

compare verb **1** contrast, juxtapose, weigh up. **2** liken. □ **compare with** approach, be on a par with, be similar to, compete with, match, rival.

comparison noun **1** contrast, juxtaposition. **2** analogy, likeness, parallel, resemblance, similarity.

compartment noun area, bay, booth, box, carrel, cell, chamber, cubby hole, cubicle, division, niche, part, pigeonhole, pocket, recess, section, slot, space, stall.

compassion noun concern, feeling, humanity, mercy, pity, sympathy, tenderness. □ **compassionate** adjective humane, kind-hearted, lenient, merciful, soft-hearted, sympathetic, tender-hearted, warm-hearted.

compatible adjective **1** harmonious, like-minded, well-matched, well-suited. **2** consistent, in accord, in agreement, reconcilable.

compel verb coerce, constrain, drive, force, impel, make, oblige, press, pressure, push, require.

compensate verb **1** indemnify, make amends, make up, recompense, reimburse, repay. **2** cancel out, counterbalance, make up for, neutralise, offset.

compensation noun compo (*Australian informal*), damages, indemnity, recompense, redress, reparation, restitution.

compère noun anchorperson, announcer, host, master of ceremonies, MC, presenter.

compete verb **1** enter, participate, take part. **2** contend, contest, fight, rival, strive, struggle, vie.

competent adjective able, adept, capable, effective, efficient, handy, practical, proficient, qualified, skilful, skilled, trained.

competition noun **1** challenge, championship, contest, game, match, meet, quiz, rally, tournament. **2** opposition, rivalry.

competitor noun adversary, candidate, challenger, contender, contestant, entrant, opponent, participant, player, rival.

compile verb accumulate, assemble, collate, collect, gather, organise, put together.

complacent adjective content, pleased with yourself, self-satisfied, smug.

complain verb beef (slang), bitch (informal), carp, gripe (informal), grizzle (informal), groan, grumble, moan, object, protest, rail, wail, whine, whinge (informal). □ **complainer** noun grizzler (informal), grouch (informal), grumbler, malcontent, moaner, objector, protester, whinger (informal).

complaint noun **1** beef (slang), criticism, grievance, gripe (informal), grizzle (informal), grumble, objection, protest. **2** affliction, ailment, disease, disorder, illness, malady, sickness.

complement verb complete, round off, set off.

complete adjective **1** comprehensive, entire, full, intact, total, unabridged, unbroken, uncut, whole. **2** accomplished, concluded, done, ended, finished. **3** absolute, downright, out-and-out, outright, perfect, positive, proper, pure, sheer, thorough, total, utter. □ **completely** adverb absolutely, altogether, entirely, fully, perfectly, quite, thoroughly, totally, utterly, wholly.

complete verb accomplish, achieve, carry out, conclude, end, finalise, finish, fulfil, round off, wind up, wrap up (informal); (complete a form) fill in, fill out.

complex adjective **1** composite, compound, multiple. **2** complicated, elaborate, intricate, involved, sophisticated.

complex noun fixation, hang-up (informal), obsession, preoccupation, thing (informal).

complexion noun colour, skin, tone.

compliant *adjective* biddable, deferential, docile, obedient, submissive, tractable, yielding.

complicated *adjective* **1** complex, elaborate, intricate, sophisticated. **2** complex, difficult, intricate, involved, knotty, messy, problematical, tricky.

complication *noun* difficulty, hitch, obstacle, problem, setback, snag, stumbling block.

compliment *noun* acclamation, accolade, bouquet, commendation, congratulations, flattery, honour, plaudits, praise, tribute.

compliment *verb* applaud, commend, congratulate, flatter, pay tribute to, praise.

complimentary *adjective* **1** admiring, approving, commendatory, congratulatory, favourable, flattering, positive. **2** free, free of charge, gratis, on the house (*informal*).

comply *verb* (*comply with*) accord with, conform to, follow, fulfil, meet, obey, satisfy.

component *noun* bit, constituent, element, ingredient, module, part, piece, unit.

compose *verb* **1** constitute, form, make up. **2** compile, concoct, construct, create, devise, fashion, formulate, invent, make up, produce, put together, write.

composed *adjective* calm, collected, controlled, cool, nonchalant, placid, sedate, self-controlled, serene, stoical, tranquil, unruffled.

composition *noun* **1** creation, opus, piece, work. **2** article, essay, paper, story. **3** constitution, make-up, structure.

composure *noun* calmness, control, cool (*informal*), coolness, equanimity, poise, self-control, serenity.

compound *adjective* complex, composite, multiple.

compound *noun* alloy, amalgam, blend, combination, composite, mixture, synthesis.

compound *noun* enclosure, pen, pound, yard.

comprehend *verb* appreciate, conceive, fathom, follow, grasp, perceive, realise, see, take in, understand. □ **comprehension** *noun* conception, grasp, insight, perception, realisation, understanding.

comprehensive *adjective* all-inclusive, broad, complete, detailed, exhaustive, extensive, full, inclusive, sweeping, thorough.

compress *verb* compact, condense, cram, crush, pack down, press, squash, squeeze.

comprise *verb* be composed of, be made up of, consist of, contain, include.

compromise *noun* bargain, deal, happy medium, middle course, trade-off.

compromise *verb* come to terms, give and take, make a deal, make concessions, meet halfway, strike a bargain.

compulsive *adjective* (*a compulsive gambler*) addicted, habitual, incorrigible, obsessive; (*a compulsive desire*) compelling, driving, irresistible, overpowering, uncontrollable.

compulsory *adjective* mandatory, necessary, obligatory, prescribed, required, unavoidable.

compute *verb* add up, calculate, reckon, total, tot up, work out.

comrade *noun* ally, associate, buddy (*informal*), chum (*informal*), cobber (*Australian informal*), colleague, companion, crony, fellow, friend, mate, pal (*informal*), partner.

con *noun* confidence trick, deception, hoax, swindle, swizz (*informal*), trick. □ **con man** charlatan, cheat, confidence man, fraud, humbug, illywhacker (*Australian informal*), impostor, phoney (*informal*), quack, swindler, trickster.

con *verb* cheat, deceive, have (*slang*), hoax, hoodwink, mislead, rip off (*informal*), swindle, trick.

conceal *verb* bury, camouflage, cover up, disguise, hide, keep secret, mask, obscure, plant, screen, secrete.

concede *verb* **1** accept, acknowledge, admit, confess. **2** allow, give, grant, yield. **3** admit defeat, give in, give up, resign, surrender.

conceit *noun* arrogance, boastfulness, egotism, pride, vanity. □ **conceited** *adjective* arrogant, boastful, bumptious, cocky, egotistical, haughty, immodest, proud, self-important, self-satisfied, smug, stuck-up (*informal*), swollen-headed (*informal*), vain.

conceive *verb* contrive, create, devise, dream up, envisage, formulate, hatch, imagine, plan, think up.

concentrate *verb* **1** (*concentrate on*) apply yourself to, attend to, be absorbed in, focus on, pay attention to, put your mind to. **2** boil down, condense, reduce.

concept *noun* belief, idea, notion, principle, thought.

conception *noun* **1** beginning, birth, creation, formulation, genesis, inception, origin, outset, start. **2** concept, idea, image, impression, notion, picture, understanding, vision.

concern *verb* **1** affect, apply to, be important to, interest, matter to, relate to, touch. **2** bother, disturb, perturb, trouble, worry. **3** be about, deal with, have to do with, involve, refer to, surround.

concern *noun* **1** affair, business, responsibility. **2** anxiety, burden, care, problem, trouble, worry. **3** business, company, corporation, enterprise, establishment, firm, organisation.

concerned *adjective* **1** anxious, caring, distressed, solicitous, troubled, uneasy, worried. **2** interested, involved.

concerning *preposition* about, re, regarding, relating to, with reference to, with regard to.

concert *noun* gig (*informal*), performance, recital, show.

concerted *adjective* collaborative, combined, cooperative, coordinated, joint, united.

concession *noun* discount, privilege, reduction, right.

concise *adjective* abridged, brief, compact, condensed, pithy, short, succinct, summary, terse.

conclude *verb* **1** bring to an end, cease, close, complete, come to an end, end, finish, round off, stop, terminate, wind up. **2** decide, deduce, gather, infer, judge, reason.

conclusion *noun* **1** close, completion, end, ending, finish, termination. **2** decision, deduction, finding, inference, judgement, verdict.

conclusive *adjective* absolute, convincing, decisive, definitive, incontrovertible, indisputable, unequivocal.

concoct *verb* **1** cook, make, prepare, put together. **2** cook up, create, devise, fabricate, invent, make up, put together, think up. □ **concoction** *noun* blend, confection, creation, mixture, preparation.

concord *noun* accord, agreement, harmony, peace, unity.

concrete *adjective* actual, definite, factual, material, objective, palpable, physical, real, solid, specific, substantial, tangible.

concur *verb* accord, agree, assent, be of the same mind, see eye to eye. □ **concurrent** *adjective* coexistent, coincident, parallel, simultaneous.

condemn *verb* **1** blame, censure, criticise, denounce, disapprove of, rebuke. **2** convict, declare guilty, sentence.

condense *verb* **1** boil down, concentrate, reduce, thicken. **2** abbreviate, abridge, compress, cut, précis, reduce, shorten, summarise.

condescending *adjective* disdainful, haughty, high and mighty, hoity-toity, patronising, snobbish, snooty (*informal*), supercilious, superior.

condition *noun* **1** fettle, fitness, form, health, nick (*informal*), order, repair, shape, state, trim. **2** (*conditions*) circumstances, environment, situation, surroundings. **3** prerequisite, provision, proviso, qualification, requirement, stipulation, term.

condition *verb* accustom, teach, train.

condolence *noun* commiseration, pity, sympathy.

condone *verb* connive at, disregard, forgive, ignore, overlook, tolerate, turn a blind eye to.

conduct *verb* **1** direct, escort, guide, lead, pilot, show, steer, take, usher. **2** administer, be in charge of, chair, control, direct, lead, manage, organise, preside over, run, supervise.

3 (*conduct yourself*) acquit yourself, act, behave.

conduct *noun* actions, behaviour, deportment, manners.

conductor *noun* director, maestro.

confer *verb* **1** award, bestow, give, grant, present. **2** consult, converse, discuss, speak, talk.

conference *noun* assembly, congress, convention, forum, gathering, convention, meeting, symposium.

confess *verb* acknowledge, admit, declare, disclose, own up.

confide *verb* confess, disclose, divulge, impart, tell, trust.

confidence *noun* **1** belief, faith, reliance, trust. **2** aplomb, assurance, boldness, certainty, conviction, coolness, courage, self-assurance, self-confidence, self-reliance. □ **confidence trick** con (*slang*), deception, hoax, swindle, swizz (*informal*), trick.

confident *adjective* **1** bold, cocksure, daring, fearless, self-assured, self-confident. **2** certain, convinced, positive, sure.

confidential *adjective* classified, hush-hush (*informal*), intimate, off the record, personal, private, secret.

confine verb **1** contain, keep, limit, localise, restrict. **2** box in, coop up, enclose, hold captive, imprison, intern, jail, keep, lock up, pen, shut in, shut up.

confirm verb attest to, authenticate, back up, bear out, corroborate, establish, prove, reinforce, substantiate, support, validate, verify, witness to.

confiscate verb appropriate, commandeer, impound, seize, take away.

conflict noun **1** action, battle, clash, combat, encounter, engagement, fight, fray, strife, struggle, war. **2** antagonism, confrontation, contention, difference, disagreement, discord, dispute, dissension, friction, hostility, opposition, strife.

conflict verb be at odds, be at variance, be incompatible, clash, contradict, differ, disagree.

conform verb comply, fit in, toe the line (*informal*); (*conform to*) abide by, accord with, comply with, correspond to, fit, follow, keep to, match, obey. □ **conformity** noun accord, accordance, agreement, compliance, harmony, keeping.

confound verb astonish, astound, baffle, bewilder,

confuse, disconcert, flummox (*informal*), mystify, nonplus, perplex, puzzle, surprise.

confront verb accost, brave, challenge, defy, encounter, face, face up to, meet, oppose, stand up to, take on.

confuse verb **1** baffle, bewilder, confound, disconcert, disorientate, flummox (*informal*), fluster, mislead, mix up, mystify, nonplus, perplex, puzzle, rattle (*informal*). **2** mistake, mix up, muddle. □ **confused** adjective **1** baffled, bemused, bewildered, bushed (*Australian informal*), disoriented, flummoxed (*informal*), flustered, hazy, mixed up, muddled, perplexed. **2** chaotic, disorganised, garbled, higgledy-piggledy, incoherent, jumbled, messy, muddled, topsy-turvy, unclear. □ **confusion** noun **1** anarchy, bedlam, chaos, commotion, disorder, disorganisation, havoc, jumble, mayhem, mess, muddle, pandemonium, riot, shambles, tumult, turmoil, upheaval, uproar. **2** misunderstanding, mix-up, muddle.

congeal adjective coagulate, set, solidify, thicken.

congenial adjective agreeable, amiable, compatible, friendly, genial, nice, pleasant, sympathetic.

congenital | conscientious

congenital *adjective* inborn, innate.

congested *adjective* blocked, chock-a-block, choked, clogged up, crowded, jammed, overcrowded, packed, stuffed up.

congratulate *verb* applaud, commend, compliment, praise.
□ **congratulations** *plural noun* compliments, felicitations, good wishes, greetings.

congregate *verb* assemble, cluster, collect, converge, crowd, flock, gather, group, herd, huddle, mass, meet, muster, rally, swarm, throng.

congregation *noun* flock, parishioners.

congress *noun* assembly, conference, convention, council, gathering, meeting, symposium, synod.

conjecture *noun* assumption, guess, hunch, hypothesis, speculation, supposition, surmise, suspicion, theory.
□ **conjecture** *verb* assume, guess, hypothesise, speculate, suppose, surmise, suspect, theorise.

conjure *verb* **conjure up** bring to mind, call up, evoke, produce.

conjuring *noun* legerdemain, magic, sleight of hand, tricks.

connect *verb* **1** attach, couple, fasten, hitch, interlock, join, link, secure, tie, unite. **2** associate, bracket together, correlate, link, relate.
□ **connection** *noun* **1** bond, hook-up, join, joint, junction, link. **2** association, correlation, correspondence, interconnection, link, relation, relationship, tie-up.

connive *verb* □ **connive at** condone, ignore, overlook, turn a blind eye to, wink at.

connoisseur *noun* authority, buff (*informal*), expert, specialist.

conquer *verb* beat, crush, defeat, get the better of, lick (*informal*), master, overcome, overpower, overthrow, prevail over, rout, stonker (*Australian slang*), subdue, subjugate, surmount, thrash, triumph over, trounce, vanquish.
□ **conqueror** *noun* champion, vanquisher, victor, winner.

conquest *noun* annexation, capture, defeat, invasion, occupation, subjugation, takeover.

conscience *noun* ethics, morals, principles, scruples.

conscientious *adjective* careful, dedicated, diligent, dutiful, hard-working, honest, meticulous, painstaking, particular, punctilious, responsible, rigorous, scrupulous, thorough.

conscious *adjective* alert, awake, aware.

conscript *verb* call up, draft (*American*).

consecrate *verb* bless, dedicate, hallow, sanctify.

consecutive *adjective* in a row, straight, successive, uninterrupted.

consensus *noun* agreement, harmony, unanimity.

consent *noun* acceptance, acquiescence, agreement, approval, assent, authorisation, concurrence, endorsement, go-ahead, leave, OK (*informal*), permission, sanction.

consent *verb* accede, acquiesce, agree, allow, approve, authorise, concur, permit.

consequence *noun* **1** aftermath, effect, outcome, ramification, repercussion, result, sequel, upshot. **2** account, gravity, import, importance, moment, seriousness, significance.

consequent *adjective* consequential, ensuing, following, resultant, resulting. □ **consequently** *adverb* accordingly, as a result, hence, so, therefore, thus.

conservation *noun* maintenance, preservation, protection, safe keeping, saving. □ **conservationist** *noun*

environmentalist, green (*informal*), greenie (*Australian informal*), preservationist.

conservative *adjective* **1** conventional, hidebound, middle-of-the-road, old-fashioned, orthodox, reactionary, traditional. **2** cautious, low, moderate, understated.

conservatory *noun* glasshouse, greenhouse, hothouse.

conserve *verb* hold on to, husband, keep, maintain, preserve, save.

consider *verb* **1** contemplate, deliberate over, examine, look at, meditate on, mull over, ponder, reflect on, ruminate over, study, think about, weigh. **2** allow for, bear in mind, pay heed to, respect, take into account. **3** believe, deem, judge, rate, reckon, regard, think.

considerable *adjective* appreciable, big, decent, extensive, fair, goodly, large, noticeable, respectable, significant, sizeable, substantial, tidy (*informal*).

considerate *adjective* attentive, helpful, kind, neighbourly, obliging, polite, sensitive, solicitous, thoughtful, unselfish.

consignment *noun* batch, cargo, delivery, load, shipment

consist *verb* (*consist of*) be composed of, comprise, contain, include.

consistency *noun* **1** agreement, compatibility, conformity, congruence, correspondence, uniformity. **2** density, firmness, solidity, stiffness, texture, thickness, viscosity.

consistent *adjective* **1** constant, dependable, invariable, predictable, reliable, stable, steady, unchanging, uniform. **2** compatible, corresponding, in accordance, in agreement, in keeping.

console *verb* cheer, comfort, encourage, relieve, solace, soothe.

consolidate *verb* **1** fortify, reinforce, strengthen. **2** amalgamate, combine, incorporate, join, merge, unite.

conspicuous *adjective* **1** apparent, blatant, clear, evident, flagrant, glaring, manifest, noticeable, obtrusive, obvious, ostentatious, patent, prominent, pronounced, showy, unconcealed, visible. **2** distinguished, impressive, notable, outstanding, remarkable, striking.

conspiracy *noun* collusion, intrigue, plot, scheme.

conspire *verb* collaborate, collude, connive, intrigue, plot, scheme.

constant *adjective* **1** even, fixed, invariable, level, stable, steady, unchanging, uniform, unvarying. **2** ceaseless, chronic, continual, continuous, endless, everlasting, incessant, never-ending, nonstop, perennial, permanent, perpetual, persistent, regular, repeated, unending. **3** dependable, devoted, faithful, firm, loyal, reliable, steadfast, true, trustworthy.

consternation *noun* alarm, anxiety, dismay, fear, panic, shock, terror.

constituent *noun* component, element, ingredient, material, part, unit.

constitute *verb* compose, form, make up.

constitution *noun* **1** charter, laws, principles, rules. **2** health, physique. **3** composition, make-up, structure.

constrain *verb* bind, compel, force, make, oblige, press, pressure, urge.

constraint *noun* **1** compulsion, force, obligation, pressure. **2** check, curb, limitation, restriction.

constrict *verb* compress, cramp, pinch, squeeze.

construct *verb* assemble, build, create, erect, fabricate, fashion, form, make, manufacture, produce, put together.

construction noun building, edifice, structure.

constructive adjective beneficial, helpful, positive, practical, productive, useful, valuable.

consult verb confer with, discuss with, refer to, speak to, talk with. □ **consultation** noun conference, discussion, hearing, interview, meeting, talk.

consultant noun adviser, expert, specialist.

consume verb 1 devour, eat up, gobble up, guzzle, knock back, swallow. 2 deplete, drain, eat into, exhaust, expend, take up, use up, utilise. 3 burn, demolish, destroy, devastate, gut, ravage, raze.

consumer noun buyer, client, customer, end-user, patron, purchaser, user.

contact noun communication, connection, touch.

contact verb communicate with, correspond with, get hold of, get in touch with, reach, speak to, talk to, write to.

contagious adjective catching, communicable, infectious, transmittable.

contain verb 1 enclose, hold, house. 2 be composed of, consist of, include, incorporate. 3 control, curb, hold back, keep in, repress, restrain, stifle, suppress.

container noun holder, receptacle, repository, vessel; (various containers) bag, barrel, basket, bin, bottle, box, bucket, caddy, can, canister, carton, cartridge, case, cask, casket, chest, coffer, crate, cup, dish, drum, jar, keg, packet, pot, pouch, punnet, sachet, sack, skip, tank, tin, trunk, tub, vat.

contaminate verb adulterate, defile, foul, infect, poison, pollute, spoil, taint.

contemplate verb 1 eye, gaze at, look at, observe, regard, stare at, study, survey, view, watch. 2 cogitate on, consider, deliberate over, meditate on, mull over, ponder, reflect on, ruminate on, think over; see also ENVISAGE.

contemporary adjective current, latest, modern, new, present-day, recent, trendy (informal), up to date, up to the minute.

contempt noun disdain, disgust, dislike, disrespect, hatred, loathing, scorn.

contemptible adjective abominable, base, dastardly,

despicable, detestable, hateful, loathsome, low, mean, miserable, odious, pitiful, shabby, shameful, vile, worthless.

contemptuous *adjective* derisive, disdainful, haughty, insolent, scornful, sneering, snooty (*informal*), supercilious.

contend *verb* **1** battle, clash, compete, contest, fight, grapple, strive, struggle, vie. **2** allege, argue, assert, claim, declare, insist, maintain.

content *adjective* contented, fulfilled, gratified, happy, pleased, satisfied.

content *verb* gratify, please, satisfy.

content *noun* **contents** components, constituents, elements, ingredients, parts.

contest *noun* battle, bout, challenge, championship, combat, competition, conflict, duel, fight, game, match, race, rally, struggle, tournament.

contest *verb* **1** battle for, compete for, contend for, fight for, struggle for, vie for. **2** argue, challenge, debate, dispute, question.

contestant *noun* candidate, challenger, competitor, contender, entrant, opponent, participant, player, rival.

context *noun* background, circumstances, environment, setting, situation, surroundings.

continual *adjective* constant, endless, everlasting, frequent, habitual, incessant, perpetual, persistent, recurrent, regular, repeated.

continue *verb* **1** carry on, endure, extend, go on, keep going, keep on, last, maintain, persevere, persist, proceed, prolong, protract, remain, stay, survive. **2** pick up, recommence, resume, take up. □ **continuation** *noun* extension, postscript, resumption, sequel, supplement.

continuous *adjective* ceaseless, constant, endless, everlasting, incessant, interminable, never-ending, non-stop, permanent, perpetual, persistent, relentless, solid, steady, unbroken, unceasing, uninterrupted, unrelieved.

contort *verb* bend, buckle, deform, distort, twist, warp. □ **contorted** *adjective* bent, buckled, deformed, distorted, misshapen, twisted, warped, wry.

contour *noun* form, lines, outline, profile, shape.

contract *noun* agreement, bargain, bond, charter, compact, covenant, deal, deed, pact, policy, treaty, under-standing, undertaking.

contract verb **1** become smaller, shrink, tighten. **2** agree, arrange, negotiate, undertake. **3** acquire, catch, come down with, develop, get, pick up.

contradict verb counter, deny, gainsay (formal), oppose. □ **contradictory** adjective conflicting, incompatible, inconsistent, irreconcilable, opposing.

contraption noun apparatus, appliance, device, gadget, gizmo (informal), implement, machine, tool.

contrary adjective **1** conflicting, contradictory, converse, opposing, opposite. **2** cantankerous, defiant, disobedient, headstrong, intractable, obstinate, perverse, pigheaded, rebellious, recalcitrant, refractory, stroppy (informal), stubborn, unreasonable, wayward, wilful.

contrary noun antithesis, converse, opposite, reverse.

contrast noun comparison, difference, disparity, dissimilarity, distinction.

contrast verb **1** compare, differentiate, distinguish, set against each other. **2** differ, disagree.

contribute verb **1** chip in (informal), donate, fork out (slang), give, pitch in (informal), provide, put in, subscribe, supply. **2** (contribute to) advance, have a hand in, lead to, play a part in, promote. □ **contribution** noun donation, gift, grant, handout, help, input, offering, offertory, subscription.

contrite adjective penitent, regretful, remorseful, repentant, sorry.

contrive verb arrange, engineer, manage, plan, plot, scheme, wangle (slang).

control verb (control an organisation) administer, command, direct, dominate, govern, head, lead, manage, oversee, preside over, regulate, rule, supervise; (control your temper) bridle, check, contain, curb, hold back, master, repress, restrain, subdue.

control noun authority, charge, command, direction, domination, influence, jurisdiction, leadership, management, mastery, power, rule, supervision, sway.

controversial adjective contentious, debatable, disputable, moot.

controversy noun argument, debate, disagreement, dispute, quarrel, row (*informal*), wrangle.

convalesce *verb* get better, improve, mend, recover, recuperate.

convenient *adjective* **1** handy, helpful, practical, suitable, timely, useful, well-timed. **2** accessible, handy, nearby.

convent *noun* abbey, cloister, nunnery, priory, religious community.

convention *noun* **1** custom, etiquette, formality, practice, protocol, rule, tradition. **2** assembly, conference, congress, council, gathering, jamboree, meeting, rally, synod.

conventional *adjective* accepted, accustomed, customary, established, mainstream, normal, ordinary, orthodox, regular, standard, traditional, usual.

converge *verb* come together, intersect, join, meet, merge.

conversation *noun* chat, chatter, chinwag (*informal*), confabulation, dialogue, discourse, discussion, gossip, natter (*informal*), talk, tête-à-tête, yabber (*Australian informal*), yak (*informal*).

converse *verb* chat, chatter, gossip, natter (*informal*), prattle, speak, talk, yabber

(*Australian informal*), yak (*informal*).

converse *noun* antithesis, contrary, opposite, reverse.

convert *verb* adapt, change, modify, switch, transform, turn.

convey *verb* **1** bear, bring, carry, conduct, deliver, fetch, haul, shift, take, transfer, transport. **2** communicate, impart, make known, put across, tell, transmit.

convict *verb* condemn, declare guilty.

convict *noun* criminal, felon, lag (*slang*), prisoner.

conviction *noun* **1** assurance, certainty, confidence, earnestness, fervour. **2** belief, creed, faith, opinion, persuasion, tenet, view.

convince *verb* assure, persuade, prove to, satisfy, sway, win over. □ **convinced** *adjective* certain, confident, definite, positive, sure. □ **convincing** *adjective* cogent, compelling, forceful, irresistible, persuasive, powerful, sound, strong, telling.

convoy *noun* armada, company, fleet, flotilla, group.

convulsion *noun* fit, paroxysm, seizure, spasm.

cook *verb* make, prepare, put together; (*various ways to cook*) bake, barbecue, boil, braise, broil, casserole, flambé, fry, grill, parboil, poach, roast, sauté, simmer, steam, stew, toast. □ **cook up** concoct, devise, fabricate, invent, make up, plan, plot.

cookery noun cooking, cuisine.

cool adjective **1** chilly, cold, nippy (informal). **2** calm, collected, composed, laid-back (informal), level-headed, nonchalant, relaxed, sedate, self-possessed, serene, unemotional, unexcited, unflappable (informal), unflustered, unruffled. **3** cold, frosty, half-hearted, hostile, icy, indifferent, lukewarm, offhand, unenthusiastic, unfriendly, unwelcoming. **4** see EXCELLENT, TRENDY.

cool verb chill, freeze, refrigerate.

coop noun cage, enclosure, pen.

coop verb □ **coop up** box in, cage in, confine, imprison, keep, lock up, pen in, shut up.

cooperate verb assist, collaborate, help, join forces, pull together, unite, work together. □ **cooperation** noun assistance, collaboration, contribution, help, involvement, participation, support, teamwork. □ **cooperative** adjective accommodating, helpful, obliging, willing.

coordinate verb integrate, orchestrate, organise, synchronise. □ **coordinator** noun controller, director, manager, organiser.

cope verb (cope with) contend with, deal with, endure, face, handle, manage, withstand.

copious adjective abundant, ample, bountiful, generous, lavish, liberal, plentiful, profuse.

copy noun carbon copy, counterfeit, double, duplicate, facsimile, fake, forgery, imitation, likeness, photocopy, print, replica, reproduction, twin.

copy verb **1** counterfeit, crib, duplicate, forge, photocopy, plagiarise, print, reproduce. **2** ape, imitate, mimic, parody, take off (informal).

cord noun cable, lace, line, rope, string, twine.

cordial adjective affable, amiable, amicable, friendly, genial, heartfelt, kind, sincere, warm.

cordon noun chain, circle, line, ring.

cordon verb □ **cordon off** close off, enclose, seal off, shut off, surround.

core noun **1** centre, heart, inside, middle. **2** centre, crux, essence, gist, heart, kernel nitty-gritty (*informal*), nub, nucleus.

cork noun bung, plug, stopper.

corkscrew noun helix, spiral.

corner noun angle, bend, crossroads, curve, intersection, junction, turn.

corner verb **1** bail up (*Australian*), buttonhole, capture, catch, trap. **2** control, dominate, monopolise.

corny adjective **1** banal, feeble, hackneyed, outworn, trite, weak. **2** mawkish, old-fashioned, over-sentimental, schmaltzy, soppy (*informal*).

corollary noun consequence, result, upshot.

coronation noun crowning, enthronement.

corporal adjective bodily, physical.

corporation noun **1** council. **2** company, firm, organisation.

corpse noun body, cadaver, carcass, remains.

correct adjective **1** accurate, exact, faultless, flawless, perfect, precise, proper, right, spot on (*informal*), true. **2** acceptable, appropriate, conventional, decent, decorous, fitting, impeccable, proper, right, seemly, suitable.

correct verb **1** adjust, alter, amend, cure, fix, improve, mend, put right, rectify, remedy, repair, revise. **2** assess, check, mark. **3** admonish, censure, chasten, chastise, discipline, rebuke, reprimand, reprove, scold.

correlation noun connection, correspondence, interdependence, link, relationship, tie-up.

correspond verb **1** communicate, exchange letters, keep in touch, send letters, write. **2** accord, agree, be consistent, coincide, concur, conform, fit, match, square, tally. ◻ **corresponding** adjective analogous, equivalent, homologous, like, matching, parallel, similar.

correspondence noun communications, letters, mail, messages.

corresponden noun journalist, reporter, writer.

corridor noun hall, hallway, lobby, passage, passageway.

corroborate verb back up, bear out, confirm, substantiate, support, validate, verify.

corrode verb consume, destroy, eat away, erode, oxidise, rot, rust, wear away.

corrugated adjective fluted, furrowed, grooved, ribbed, ridged, wrinkled.

corrupt adjective **1** bent (slang), crooked, dishonest, shady, shonky (Australian informal), unscrupulous, venal. **2** decadent, degenerate, depraved, dissolute, evil, immoral, iniquitous, perverted, sinful, wicked.

corrupt verb **1** bribe, buy off, influence, lead astray, pervert, tempt. **2** (corrupt a text) alter, spoil, tamper with. □ **corruption** noun bribery, decadence, degeneracy, depravity, dishonesty, fraud, graft, immorality, perversion, sinfulness, unscrupulousness, venality, vice, wickedness.

cortège noun procession, train.

cosmetic noun (cosmetics) beauty products, make-up.

cosmonaut noun astronaut, space traveller.

cosmopolitan adjective **1** international, multicultural, multiracial. **2** broad-minded, liberal, sophisticated, urbane, worldly.

cosmos noun universe, world.

cost noun charge, expenditure, expense, fare, fee, outlay, overheads, payment, price, rate, tariff, toll.

cost verb **1** be priced at, be worth, fetch, sell for. **2** estimate, price, value.

costly adjective dear, exorbitant, expensive, extravagant, precious, pricey (informal), valuable.

costume noun apparel (formal), attire (formal), clothes, clothing, dress, garb, garments, gear (informal), livery, outfit, raiment, regalia, uniform, vestments.

cosy adjective comfortable, comfy (informal), friendly, homely, relaxing, secure, snug, warm.

cot noun cradle, crib.

cottage noun cabin, chalet, hut, lodge, shack, weekender (Australian).

cotton noun thread, yarn.

couch noun chaise longue, chesterfield, divan, ottoman, settee, sofa.

council noun assembly, board, committee, conference, congress, corporation, synod.

counsel noun advice, direction, guidance, recommendation.

counsel verb advise, direct, guide, recommend.

counsellor noun adviser, guide, mentor.

count verb **1** add up, calculate, compute, enumerate, number, sum up, tally, total, to up (informal). **2** consider, include, reckon with, take into account. **3** be important, carry weight, matter, rate highly, signify. **4** consider, deem, judge, look upon, rate, reckon, regard, think. ☐ **count on** assume, bank on, depend on, expect, reckon on, rely on.

count noun **1** census, poll, stocktaking. **2** aggregate, amount, figure, number, reckoning, tally, total. **3** charge, point.

counter noun **1** bar, checkout, stand. **2** chip, disc, piece, token.

counter verb contradict, counter-attack, fight back, hit back, oppose, parry, rebut, retaliate.

counteract verb cancel out, counter, counterbalance, negate, neutralise, offset, oppose, undo.

counterfeit adjective bogus, dud (informal), fake, forged, imitation, phoney (informal), sham, spurious. ☐ **counterfeit** verb copy, fake, forge, imitate, reproduce.

counterpart noun equivalent, opposite number, parallel.

countless adjective endless, frequent, incalculable, innumerable, many, myriad, numerous.

country noun **1** commonwealth, democracy, duchy, emirate, kingdom, land, monarchy, nation, principality, realm, republic, state, territory. **2** citizens, community, inhabitants, nation, people, populace, population, public. **3** backblocks (Australian), backwoods, bush (Australian), inland, interior, outback (Australian), rural district, sticks (informal). **4** countryside, land, landscape, region, scenery, terrain, territory. ☐ **country** adjective agricultural, bucolic, farming, pastoral, provincial, rural, rustic.

countryman, **countrywoman** noun **1** bushie (Australian informal), farmer, rustic. **2** compatriot.

couple noun brace, duo, pair, twosome.

couple verb connect, fasten, hitch, join, link, tie, yoke.

coupon noun entry form, form, ticket, token, voucher.

courage noun boldness, bottle (slang), bravery, daring, determination, fearlessness, fortitude, gallantry, grit, guts (informal), heroism, mettle, nerve, pluck, prowess, spirit, spunk (informal), valour. ☐ **courageous** adjective bold, brave, daring, dauntless, determined, fearless, gallant, game, heroic, intrepid, lion-hearted, mettlesome, plucky, resolute, spirited, stoical, stout-hearted, unafraid, undaunted, valiant.

courier noun carrier, dispatch rider, messenger, runner.

course noun **1** development, flow, march, passage, progression, sequence, succession, unfolding. **2** direction, line, orbit, path, route, track. **3** classes, curriculum, lessons, programme, series. **4** circuit, racecourse, track. □ **of course** by all means, certainly, naturally, obviously, without a doubt.

court noun **1** attendants, courtiers (old use), entourage, household, retinue, train. **2** bar, bench, lawcourt, tribunal.

court verb date (informal), go out with, woo (old use).

courteous adjective chivalrous, civil, considerate, diplomatic, gallant, gracious, polite, proper, respectful, tactful, thoughtful, well-behaved, well-bred, well-mannered. □ **courtesy** noun chivalry, civility, consideration, deference, diplomacy, gallantry, good manners, politeness, respect, tact, thoughtfulness.

courtyard noun court, forecourt, patio, quad (informal), quadrangle, yard.

cove noun bay, inlet.

covenant noun agreement, bargain, compact, contract, deal, pact, pledge, promise, undertaking.

cover verb **1** bandage, bind, blot out, bury, camouflage, cloak, clothe, cloud, coat, conceal, drape, dress, encase, enclose, encrust, envelop, hide, mask, obscure, overlay, plaster, protect, screen, shield, shroud, surround, swaddle, swathe, veil, wrap. **2** travel, traverse. **3** indemnify, insure, protect. **4** deal with, encompass, include, survey, take in. □ **cover up** conceal, hide, hush up, suppress, whitewash.

cover noun **1** armour, binder, binding, canopy, cap, case, casing, cladding, coating, cocoon, covering, cowl, envelope, folder, hood, housing, jacket, lid, mantle, mask, outside, overlay, pall, roof, screen, sheath, shell, shield, shroud, skin, sleeve, slip, surface, top, veneer, wrapper, wrapping. **2** camouflage, disguise, façade, front, hiding place, protection, refuge, sanctuary, screen, shelter, smokescreen.

covert adjective clandestine, concealed, disguised, furtive, hidden, secret, secretive, surreptitious.

covet verb crave, desire, fancy, hanker after, long for, want, yearn for. □ **covetous** adjective avaricious, desirous, envious, grasping, greedy.

coward noun baby, chicken (informal), cry-baby, scaredy-cat (informal), sissy, sook (Australian informal), wimp (informal). □ **cowardly** adjective chicken-hearted, craven, dastardly, faint-hearted, fearful, gutless (informal), lily-livered, pusillanimous, spineless, timid, timorous, yellow (informal).

cower verb cringe, crouch, draw back, flinch, quail, recoil, shrink.

coy adjective bashful, demure, diffident, modest, self-conscious, sheepish, shy, timid, underconfident.

crack noun **1** breach, break, chink, cleft, cranny, crevasse, crevice, fissure, fracture, gap, opening, rift, rupture, slit, split. **2** crackle, pop, snap.

crack verb **1** break, chip, cleave, fracture, shatter, splinter, split. **2** clap, crackle, strike. **3** break down, collapse, crack up, fall apart, give way, go to pieces.

cradle noun basket, bassinet, cot, crib.

craft noun **1** handicraft, trade. **2** art, craftsmanship, skill, technique. **3** aircraft, boat, raft, ship, spacecraft, vessel.

craftsman, **craftswoman** noun artisan, artist, maker, smith, technician. □ **craftsmanship** noun artistry, expertise, handiwork, skill, workmanship.

crafty adjective artful, astute, calculating, canny, clever, cunning, deceitful, devious, foxy, guileful, knowing, machiavellian, shifty (informal), shrewd, sly, sneaky, subtle, tricky, underhand, wily.

crag noun bluff, cliff, precipice, rock, scarp.

cram verb **1** force, jam, pack, push, ram, squash, squeeze, stuff. **2** crowd, fill, overfill, pack.

cramp verb hamper, hinder, impede, inhibit, limit, restrict, stunt, thwart. □ **cramped** adjective confined, crowded, narrow, poky, tight.

crane noun cherry picker, davit, derrick, hoist.

crank noun eccentric, fanatic, freak (informal), maniac, nut (informal), weirdo (informal).

cranky *adjective* **1** bad-tempered, cantankerous, crabby, cross, crotchety, grouchy (*informal*), ill-tempered, irritable, peevish, snaky (*Australian informal*), surly. **2** bizarre, eccentric, odd, peculiar, quirky, strange, weird.

crash *noun* **1** bang, boom, clang, clangour, clank, clatter, smash, wham. **2** accident, bingle (*Australian informal*), collision, pile-up, prang (*slang*), smash. **3** collapse, failure.

crash *verb* fall, nosedive, plummet, plunge, shatter, smash, topple, tumble; (*crash into*) bang into, bump into, collide with, knock into, plough into, ram into, run into, slam into, smash into.

crate *noun* box, carton, case, packing case, tea chest.

crater *noun* cavity, hole, hollow, pit.

crave *verb* desire, hanker after, hunger for, long for, pine for, thirst for, want, wish for, yearn for.

craving *noun* desire, fancy, hankering, hunger, longing, thirst, wish, yearning, yen.

crawl *verb* **1** creep, move on all fours, slither, squirm, worm your way, wriggle, writhe. **2** edge forward, go at a snail's pace, inch forward, move slowly. **3** fawn, grovel, kowtow, lick someone's boots, suck up (*informal*), toady.

craze *noun* enthusiasm, fad, fashion, mania, passion, rage, thing (*informal*), vogue.

crazy *adjective* **1** barmy (*slang*), batty (*slang*), berserk, bonkers (*slang*), crackers (*slang*), crazed, cuckoo (*informal*), daft (*informal*), demented, deranged, dotty (*informal*), flaky (*slang*), insane, loony (*informal*), loopy (*informal*), mad, mental (*informal*), nuts (*informal*), nutty (*informal*), off your head, out of your mind, potty (*informal*), round the bend (*informal*), screwy (*informal*), troppo (*Australian slang*), unbalanced, unhinged, wacky (*slang*). **2** absurd, cock-eyed (*informal*), crackpot (*informal*), daft (*informal*), foolish, half-baked (*informal*), hare-brained, idiotic, impractical, imprudent, inane, lunatic, mad, outrageous, preposterous, ridiculous, senseless, silly, stupid, unwise, unworkable, zany.

cream *noun* emollient, lotion, ointment, salve.

crease *noun* corrugation, crinkle, crumple, fold, furrow, groove, line, pucker, ridge, ruck, wrinkle.

crease *verb* crimp, crinkle, crumple, fold, furrow, pleat, pucker, ruck, rumple, wrinkle.

create *verb* beget, bring into being, compose, conceive, construct, design, devise, engender, establish, fashion, form, found, generate, give rise to, initiate, institute, invent, lead to, make, originate, pioneer, produce, set up, think up. □ **creation** *noun* beginning, birth, formation, foundation, genesis, invention, making, origin. □ **creative** *adjective* fertile, imaginative, ingenious, inventive, original, productive, resourceful.

creator *noun* architect, author, designer, inventor, maker, originator, producer.

creature *noun* animal, beast, being, living thing, organism.

crèche *noun* child care centre, nursery, preschool.

credible *adjective* believable, conceivable, plausible, reasonable.

credit *noun* acclaim, acknowledgement, distinction, esteem, glory, honour, merit, praise, recognition, reputation. □ **on credit** by instalments, on hire purchase, on the never-never

(*informal*), on the slate (*informal*), on tick (*informal*).

creditable *adjective* admirable, commendable, honourable, laudable, meritorious, praiseworthy, respectable, worthy.

creed *noun* belief(s), conviction(s), doctrine, dogma, faith, principles, religion, tenets.

creek *noun* brook, rill, river, rivulet, stream, tributary, watercourse.

creep *verb* **1** crawl, move on all fours, slither, squirm, worm your way, wriggle, writhe. **2** edge, inch, slink, slip, sneak, steal, tiptoe.

creepy *adjective* disturbing, eerie, frightening, hair-raising, scary, sinister, spooky (*informal*), terrifying, uncanny, weird.

crest *noun* **1** comb, topknot, tuft. **2** apex, brow, crown, peak, pinnacle, summit, top. **3** badge, emblem, insignia, symbol.

crevice *noun* chink, cleft, crack, cranny, fissure, gap, opening, rift, split.

crew *noun* **1** company, corps, party, personnel, squad, staff, team, workforce. **2** band, bunch, crowd, gang, group, mob, troop.

crib *noun* cot, cradle.

crib verb cheat, copy, lift (informal), plagiarise.

crime noun felony (old use), misdeed, misdemeanour, offence, wrong, wrongdoing; see also SIN.

criminal noun baddy (informal), convict, crim (Australian informal), crook (informal), culprit, delinquent, desperado, felon, jailbird, lawbreaker, malefactor, miscreant, offender, outlaw, transgressor, villain, wrongdoer. □ **criminal** adjective corrupt, crooked, dishonest, illegal, illicit, lawless, shady, unlawful, wrong.

cringe verb cower, crouch, draw back, flinch, quail, recoil, shrink back, wince.

crinkle verb crease, crimp, crumple, furrow, pucker, rumple, wrinkle.

cripple verb **1** debilitate, disable, incapacitate, lame, maim, paralyse, weaken. **2** bring to a standstill, damage, hamstring, hurt, immobilise, paralyse.

crisis noun climax, crunch (informal), crux, danger period, emergency, height, turning point.

crisp adjective **1** brittle, crispy, crunchy, crusty. **2** bracing, chilly, cold, cool, fresh, nippy (informal). **3** abrupt, brisk, brusque, curt, sharp, snappy (informal), terse.

criterion noun benchmark, measure, principle, rule, standard, touchstone, yardstick.

critic noun **1** evaluator, judge, reviewer. **2** attacker, detractor, fault-finder, knocker (informal), objector, opponent.

critical adjective **1** captious, censorious, disapproving, disparaging, judgemental, nit-picking (informal), uncomplimentary. **2** (of critical importance) crucial, decisive, key, momentous, pivotal, vital (in a critical condition) dangerous, grave, perilous, precarious, risky, serious.

criticise verb bag (Australian informal), belittle, censure, condemn, decry, denounce, disparage, find fault with, knock (informal), object to, pan (informal), pick holes in, rebuke, reprimand, rubbish, slam (informal), slate (informal), tell off (informal), tick off (informal).

criticism noun **1** censure, condemnation, disapproval, disparagement, fault-finding, flak (informal), nit-picking (informal), reproach. **2** analysis, appraisal, commentary, critique, evaluation, review.

croaky adjective hoarse, husky, rasping, rough, throaty.

crockery noun china, dishes, earthenware, plates, pottery, tableware.

crook noun 1 crosier, staff, stick. 2 baddy (informal), cheat, criminal, knave (old use), lawbreaker, malefactor, rogue, scoundrel, swindler, thief, villain, wrongdoer.

crook adjective 1 bad, inferior, poor, shoddy, slipshod, unsatisfactory. 2 ailing, ill, indisposed, lousy (informal), poorly, rotten (informal), sick, unwell. □ **go crook** see BECOME ANGRY (at ANGRY).

crooked adjective 1 askew, awry, bent, bowed, cock-eyed (informal), contorted, crippled, curved, deformed, lopsided, off-centre, serpentine, sinuous, slanting, tortuous, twisted, uneven, winding, zigzag. 2 bent (slang), corrupt, criminal, dishonest, fraudulent, shady, shifty, shonky (Australian informal), underhand, unscrupulous, untrustworthy.

crop noun harvest, produce, vintage, yield.

crop verb 1 browse, eat, graze, nibble. 2 bob, clip, cut, shear, snip, trim. □ **crop up** appear, arise, come up, emerge, happen, occur, turn up.

cross noun 1 crucifix, rood. 2 bitser (Australian informal), blend, combination, crossbreed, hybrid, mixture, mongrel.

cross verb 1 cut across, extend across, go across, pass over, span, straddle, traverse. 2 criss-cross, intersect. 3 crossbreed, interbreed, mate. □ **cross out** cancel, delete, obliterate, scratch out, strike out.

cross adjective angry, annoyed, bad-tempered, cantankerous, crabby, cranky, crotchety, disagreeable, fractious, grouchy (informal), grumpy, ill-tempered, impatient, irascible, irate, irritable, maggoty (Australian informal), peevish, petulant, shirty (informal), snaky (Australian informal), surly, testy, tetchy.

cross-examine verb cross-question, examine, grill, interrogate, question. □ **cross-examination** noun examination, interrogation, questioning.

crosspatch noun curmudgeon, grouch (informal), grump, malcontent, sourpuss (informal).

crossroads noun crossing, interchange, intersection, junction.

crouch verb bend, cower, duck, huddle, hunch, squat, stoop.

crow verb blow your own trumpet, boast, brag, gloat, show off, skite (*Australian informal*), swagger, swank (*informal*).

crowd noun assembly, company, congregation, crush, flock, gathering, herd, horde, host, mass, mob, multitude, pack, rabble, swarm, throng.

crowd verb **1** assemble, cluster, collect, congregate, flock, gather, herd, mill, swarm, throng. **2** cram, huddle, jam, pack, pile, press, shove, squash, squeeze, stuff. ◻ **crowded** adjective congested, full, jam-packed, overflowing, over-populated, packed, populous.

crown noun **1** coronet, diadem, tiara. **2** apex, brow, crest, peak, pinnacle, summit, top.

crown verb **1** enthrone, install, invest. **2** cap, complete, consummate, round off, top off. ◻ **crowning** noun coronation, enthronement.

crucial adjective critical, decisive, important, key, momentous, pivotal, serious, significant, vital.

crude adjective **1** natural, raw, unprocessed, unrefined. **2** improvised, makeshift, primitive, rough, rudimentary, simple, unsophisticated. **3** blue, coarse, improper, indecent, lewd, obscene, ribald, rude, vulgar.

cruel adjective atrocious, barbaric, beastly, bloodthirsty, brutal, callous, cold-blooded, ferocious, fiendish, hardhearted, harsh, heartless, inhuman, inhumane, mean, merciless, monstrous, pitiless, ruthless, sadistic, savage, severe, tyrannical, unkind, vicious, violent. ◻ **cruelty** noun atrocity, barbarity, bestiality, brutality, callousness, ferocity, fiendishness, hard-heartedness, harshness, heartlessness, inhumanity, meanness, mercilessness, monstrousness, pitilessness, ruthlessness, sadism, savagery, severity, tyranny, unkindness, viciousness, violence.

cruise noun journey, sail, trip, voyage.

cruise verb sail, voyage.

crumb noun bit, fragment, morsel, particle, piece, scrap, speck.

crumble verb break up, crush, decompose, disintegrate, fall apart, go to pieces, grind, powder, pulverise. ◻ **crumbly** adjective friable.

crumple verb **1** crease, crinkle, crush, rumple, screw up, wrinkle. **2** collapse, fall down, flop.

crunch verb chew, chomp, gnaw, masticate, munch.

crunch noun **the crunch** acid test, moment of truth, showdown, test.

crusade noun campaign, drive, movement, push, struggle, war.

crush verb **1** compress, crumble, crunch, grind, mangle, mash, pound, press, pulp, pulverise, shatter, smash, squash, squeeze. **2** crease, crinkle, crumple, rumple, scrunch, wrinkle. **3** conquer, defeat, overcome, overpower, overthrow, overwhelm, rout, subdue, suppress, thrash, trounce, vanquish.

crust noun coating, incrustation, outside, rind, scab, skin.

crutch noun prop, support.

cry noun bellow, call, exclamation, howl, scream, screech, shout, shriek, squawk, squeak, squeal, wail, whimper, whine, whoop, yell, yelp, yowl.

cry verb **1** bawl, blubber, break down, grizzle, howl, shed tears, snivel, sob, wail, weep, whimper. **2** bellow, call out,

exclaim, roar, scream, shout, yell.

crypt noun undercroft, vault.

cryptic adjective baffling, coded, enigmatic, hidden, inscrutable, mysterious, obscure, perplexing, puzzling.

crystallise verb take form, take shape.

cubby hole carrel, compartment, cubicle, niche, nook, pigeon-hole.

cube verb chop, cut, dice.

cubicle noun booth, carrel, compartment, cubby hole, stall.

cuddle verb caress, clasp, embrace, fondle, hug, nurse, squeeze.

cue noun hint, prompt, reminder, sign, signal.

cul-de-sac noun blind alley, close, dead end.

culminate verb climax, close, conclude, end up, finish, terminate, wind up.

culprit noun lawbreaker, malefactor, miscreant, offender, troublemaker, wrongdoer.

cult noun religion, sect.

cultivate verb **1** farm, till, work. **2** grow, produce, raise, tend. **3** develop, foster, nurture, refine, work on.

culture noun **1** art, arts, civilisation, customs,

literature, music, society, traditions. **2** development, education, training.

cultured *adjective* civilised, cultivated, educated, enlightened, highbrow, intellectual, refined, sophisticated, well-bred.

cumbersome *adjective* awkward, bulky, clumsy, heavy, inconvenient, ponderous, unwieldy, weighty.

cumulative *adjective* accumulated, aggregate, combined.

cunning *adjective* artful, astute, calculating, clever, crafty, deceitful, devious, dodgy (*informal*), foxy, guileful, ingenious, knowing, machiavellian, scheming, sharp, shifty, shrewd, sly, sneaky, subtle, tricky, underhand, wily.

cunning *noun* cleverness, craftiness, deceitfulness, deviousness, guile, ingenuity, shrewdness, slyness, subtlety, trickery, wiliness.

cup *noun* **1** beaker, chalice, goblet, mug, tankard, teacup. **2** award, prize, trophy.

cupboard *noun* (*kinds of cupboard*) buffet, built-in, cabinet, chest, chiffonier, closet, dresser, larder, linen press, locker, pantry, safe, sideboard, wardrobe.

curator *noun* conservator, custodian, keeper, manager.

curb *verb* check, contain, control, curtail, hold back, limit, moderate, rein in, restrain, restrict, slow down.

cure *verb* **1** heal, make better, remedy. **2** correct, fix, mend, put right, rectify, remedy, repair.

cure *noun* antidote, corrective, medicine, remedy, restorative, therapy, treatment.

curiosity *noun* **1** inquisitiveness, interest, nosiness (*informal*), prying, snooping (*informal*). **2** curio, novelty, oddity, rarity.

curious *adjective* **1** inquiring, inquisitive, interested, nosy (*informal*), prying, snoopy (*informal*). **2** abnormal, bizarre, extraordinary, funny, mysterious, odd, peculiar, queer, strange, unusual, weird.

curl *noun* dreadlock, kink, ringlet, wave.

curl *verb* bend, coil, curve, loop, spiral, turn, twist, wind; (*curl hair*) crimp, frizz, perm, wave.

curly *adjective* crimped, frizzed, frizzy, permed, wavy.

currency *noun* cash, coinage, legal tender, money.

current *adjective* actual, contemporary, existing, latest, modern, present, present-day, prevailing, prevalent, up to date.

current *noun* flow, stream, tide.

curse *noun* **1** evil spell, hex, jinx (*informal*), malediction. **2** blasphemy, expletive, oath, obscenity, profanity, swear-word.

curse *verb* damn, revile, swear at. □ **be cursed with** be afflicted with, be blighted with, be plagued with, be troubled with, suffer from.

cursory *adjective* brief, hasty, hurried, perfunctory, quick, slapdash, superficial.

curt *adjective* abrupt, blunt, brief, brusque, gruff, offhand, short, snappy (*informal*), terse.

curtail *verb* **1** abbreviate, abridge, cut short, shorten, truncate. **2** curb, cut back, decrease, reduce, restrain, restrict, trim.

curtain *noun* drape, hanging, screen.

curtsy *noun* bob, bow, obeisance.

curtsy *verb* bob, bow, genuflect.

curve *verb* arc, arch, bend, bow, circle, coil, kink, loop, spiral, turn, twist, wind. □ **curved** *adjective* arched, bent, bowed, concave, convex, crescent-shaped, crooked, humped, looped, rounded, serpentine, sinuous, spiral, tortuous, twisting, winding.

curve *noun* arc, arch, bend, bow, crescent, crook, curl, curvature, kink, loop, spiral, turn, twist.

cushion *noun* bolster, hassock, kneeler, pad, pillow.

cushion *verb* absorb, buffer, damp, dampen, deaden, lessen, reduce, soften.

cushy *adjective* easy, pleasant, soft (*informal*), undemanding.

custodian *noun* caretaker, curator, guardian, keeper, steward, warden.

custody *noun* **1** care, charge, guardianship, hands, keeping. **2** detention, imprisonment, jail, prison.

custom *noun* **1** convention, habit, practice, routine, tradition, way, wont. **2** business, patronage, support, trade. □ **customs** *noun* duty, import tax, levy, tariff.

customary *adjective* accustomed, habitual, normal, ordinary, regular, routine, standard, traditional, typical, usual, wonted.

customer *noun* buyer, client, consumer, patron, purchaser, shopper.

cut *verb* **1** amputate, bisect, carve, chip, chisel, chop, cleave, clip, crop, cube, detach, dice, dissect, divide, dock, engrave, fell, gash, gouge, guillotine, hack, hew, incise, knife, lacerate, lance, lop, mangle, mince, mow, mutilate, nick, notch, pare, pierce, pink, prune, reap, remove, saw, score, scythe, sever, shave, shear, shred, slash, slice, slit, snick, snip, split, stab, trim, truncate, whittle, wound. **2** abbreviate, abridge, condense, curtail, reduce, shorten. **3** cross, go across, intersect. ◻ **cut back** downsize (*informal*), economise, rationalise, reduce, retrench. ◻ **cutback** *noun* cut, economy, rationalisation, reduction, retrenchment. ◻ **cut in** break in, butt in, interrupt, intervene. ◻ **cut off 1** disconnect, discontinue, halt, stop, suspend. **2** isolate, maroon, separate. ◻ **cut out** censor, delete, eliminate, excise, exclude, leave out, omit, remove.

cut *noun* **1** gash, groove, incision, indentation, laceration, nick, notch, slash, slit, snick, wound. **2** decline, decrease, fall, lowering, reduction. **3** commission, percentage, portion, share, slice.

cute *adjective* adorable, attractive, pretty, sweet (*informal*).

cutting *noun* **1** clipping, extract, piece, section. **2** slip.

cycle *noun* **1** bicycle, moped, motorcycle, motor scooter, penny farthing, scooter, tandem, tricycle. **2** repetition, revolution, rotation, round, sequence, series.

cycle *verb* pedal, ride.

cyclone *noun* hurricane, tropical cyclone, typhoon.

cynical *adjective* jaundiced, sardonic, sceptical, scoffing, sneering, suspicious.

Dd

dab *noun* pat, touch.

dab *verb* apply, daub, pat.

dabble *verb* **1** dip, paddle, splash. **2** play, potter, tinker.

dagger *noun* dirk, knife, kris, stiletto.

daily *adjective* day-to-day, diurnal, everyday.

dainty *adjective* delicate, dinky (*informal*), exquisite, fine, pretty, small.

dais *noun* platform, podium, rostrum, stage.

dally *verb* dawdle, delay, dilly-dally (*informal*), hang about, linger, loiter, take your time, tarry.

dam *noun* **1** bank, barrage, barrier, embankment, wall, weir. **2** pond, reservoir, tank (*Australian*).

damage *noun* destruction, devastation, harm, havoc, hurt, injury, loss, mutilation, ruin.

damage *verb* blemish, blight, break, bruise, bust (*informal*), chip, cripple, dent, destroy, devastate, flaw, harm, hurt, impair, injure, mangle, mar, mutilate, ravage, ruin, sabotage, scar, scratch, spoil, vandalise, wound, wreck.

damages *plural noun* compensation, costs, indemnity, reparations, restitution.

damnation *noun* eternal punishment, hell, perdition.

damp *adjective* clammy, dank, humid, moist, muggy, sodden, soggy, steamy, sticky, wet.

damp *verb* **1** dampen, moisten, sprinkle, wet. **2** cool, dampen, dash, discourage, dull, restrain.

dance *verb* bob, caper, cavort, frolic, gambol, jig, jump, leap, pirouette, prance, romp, skip, trip, twirl.

dance *noun* ball, disco (*informal*), formal, prom (*American*), social.

danger *noun* hazard, jeopardy, peril, pitfall, risk, snare, threat, trouble.

dangerous *adjective* (*a dangerous undertaking*) chancy, dicey (*slang*), dodgy (*informal*), hairy (*slang*), hazardous, perilous, precarious, risky, tricky, uncertain, unsafe; (*a dangerous criminal, animal, etc.*) desperate, destructive, ferocious, menacing, savage, threatening, treacherous, vicious, violent, wild.

dangle *verb* hang, sway, swing.

dapper *adjective* chic, natty (*informal*), neat, smart, snazzy (*informal*), spruce, trim, well-dressed.

dappled *adjective* mottled, piebald, pied, skewbald, spotted.

dare *verb* **1** be bold enough, be game, have the nerve, presume, venture. **2** challenge, defy, taunt.

daring *noun* boldness, bravery, courage, intrepidity, nerve, pluck, prowess, valour.

daring *adjective* adventurous, audacious, bold, brave, courageous, fearless, game, heroic, intrepid, plucky, reckless, valiant, venturesome.

dark adjective **1** black, dim, dingy, dull, dusky, gloomy, moonless, murky, overcast, pitch-dark, shadowy, shady, starless, unlit. **2** (*dark skin*) black, brown, dusky, swarthy, tanned. **3** black, brown, brunette. **4** confidential, hidden, hush-hush (*informal*), secret.

dark noun **1** blackness, darkness, dimness, gloom. **2** dusk, evening, gloaming, night, nightfall, night-time, sunset, twilight.

darken verb become overcast, blacken, cloud over.

darling noun beloved, dear, love, pet, sweet, sweetheart.

darn verb mend, repair, sew.

dart noun arrow, missile, projectile, shaft.

dart verb bolt, dash, jump, leap, race, run, scoot, shoot, spring, streak, tear, zip.

dash verb **1** bolt, dart, fly, gallop, hasten, hurry, hurtle, hustle, race, run, rush, scoot, shoot, speed, sprint, stampede, streak, sweep, tear, whiz, zip, zoom. **2** fling, hurl, knock, shatter, smash, strike, throw.

dash noun **1** bolt, run, rush, sprint, spurt. **2** energy, flair, gusto, liveliness, panache, pizazz (*informal*), spirit, style, verve, vigour, vivacity, zest.

3 drop, hint, splash, sprinkling, suggestion, touch.

dashing adjective bold, debonair, gallant, plucky, smart, spirited, stylish.

data plural noun evidence, facts, figures, information, material.

date noun **1** age, epoch, era, period, time, vintage. **2** appointment, arrangement, assignation, booking, commitment, engagement, meeting, rendezvous. **3** boyfriend, companion, escort, girlfriend, partner.

date verb (*date from*) come from, have existed from, originate in.

daub verb paint, plaster, slap, slop, smear.

daunt verb alarm, discourage, dishearten, dismay, frighten, intimidate, perturb, put off, scare, unnerve. □ **daunting** adjective awesome, fearsome, forbidding, formidable, frightening, overwhelming.

dauntless adjective bold, brave, courageous, fearless, gallant, game, heroic, intrepid, plucky, unafraid, undaunted, valiant.

dawdle verb dally, delay, dilly-dally (*informal*), hang about, lag behind, linger, loiter, straggle, take your time. □ **dawdler** noun laggard, slowcoach, sluggard, straggler

dawn noun **1** break of day, cock-crow, crack of dawn, daybreak, first light, sunrise, sun-up. **2** beginning, birth, inception, onset, origin, start, threshold.

dawn verb (dawn on) occur to, strike.

day noun **1** daylight, daytime. **2** age, epoch, era, period, time.

daydream noun castle in the air, dream, fantasy, illusion, pipe dream, reverie.

daydream verb dream, fantasise, muse.

daylight noun **1** daytime, light, sunlight, sunshine. **2** break of day, dawn, morning, sunrise.

dazed adjective bewildered, confused, stunned, stupefied. □ **daze** noun bewilderment, confusion, muddle, shock, stupor, trance.

dazzle verb **1** blind, daze. **2** amaze, awe, blind, confuse, impress, overawe, stun. □ **dazzling** adjective blinding, brilliant, radiant, resplendent, sparkling.

dead adjective **1** deceased, departed, late, lifeless. **2** dormant, inactive, inert, quiet, slow, sluggish, stagnant, static. **3** defunct, disused, extinct, obsolete. **4** absolute, complete, thorough, total, utter. □ **dead end** blind alley, close, cul-de-sac. □ **dead heat** draw, tie.

deaden verb (deaden pain) anaesthetise, dull, kill, numb, subdue; (deaden noise) damp, muffle, mute, quieten, soften, stifle, suppress.

deadline noun time limit.

deadlock noun halt, impasse, stalemate, stand-off, standstill.

deadly adjective fatal, lethal, mortal, terminal.

deaf adjective hard of hearing, hearing-impaired, stone-deaf.

deal verb **1** allocate, allot, apportion, distribute, divide, dole out, give out, hand out, share out. **2** do business, handle, market, sell, trade, traffic. □ **dealer** noun distributor, merchant, peddler (of drugs), retailer, salesperson, seller, shopkeeper, stockist, supplier, trader, trafficker, vendor, wholesaler. □ **deal with 1** be about, be concerned with, consider, cover, touch on, treat. **2** attend to, cope with, grapple with, handle, look after, manage, see to, sort out, tackle, take care of, treat.

deal noun agreement, arrangement, bargain, contract, pact, settlement, transaction. □ **a good deal** see LOT.

dear adjective **1** beloved, cherished, close, darling, loved, precious, treasured, valued. **2** costly, exorbitant, expensive, extortionate, pricey (informal).

dearth noun absence, deficiency, lack, paucity, scarcity, shortage, want.

death noun decease (formal), demise (formal), dying, end, passing. □ **put to death** execute, kill, slay.

deathly adjective ashen, cadaverous, deathlike, ghostly, pale.

debatable adjective arguable, contentious, controversial, disputable, dubious, moot, questionable.

debate noun argument, conference, controversy, discussion, dispute, wrangle.

debate verb argue, contest, discuss, dispute, wrangle over.

debilitate verb cripple, disable, enervate, enfeeble, incapacitate, weaken.

debris noun detritus, flotsam, fragments, litter, remains, rubbish, rubble, wreckage.

debt noun due, liability, obligation.

decadent adjective corrupt, debased, degenerate, depraved, immoral.

decapitate verb behead, guillotine.

decay verb break down, decompose, deteriorate, disintegrate, go bad, go off, go rotten, moulder, perish, putrefy, rot, spoil.

deceased adjective dead, departed, late.

deceit noun artifice, cheating, chicanery, cunning, deceitfulness, deception, dishonesty, double-dealing, duplicity, fraud, guile, humbug, hypocrisy, lies, misrepresentation, pretence, skulduggery (informal), treachery, trickery, untruthfulness, wiliness. □ **deceitful** adjective crafty, crooked, cunning, devious, dishonest, false, hypocritical, lying, machiavellian, phoney (informal), shifty, sneaky, treacherous, tricky, two-faced, underhand, unfaithful, untrustworthy.

deceive verb bamboozle (informal), beguile, bluff, cheat, con (informal), defraud, delude, diddle (informal), double-cross, dupe, fool, have (slang), have on (informal), hoax, hoodwink, kid (informal), mislead, rip off (informal), string along (informal), suck in (informal), swindle, take for a ride (informal), take in, trick.

decent adjective **1** acceptable, appropriate, becoming, com-

rect, decorous, honourable, law-abiding, polite, proper, respectable, seemly, suitable, upright. **2** civil, considerate, fair, generous, good, kind, obliging, sporting.

deception noun bluff, con (*informal*), fraud, hoax, lie, pretence, ruse, sham, subterfuge, swindle, swizz (*informal*), trick; see also *DECEIT*. ◻ **deceptive** adjective deceiving, false, illusory, misleading, specious, unreliable.

decide verb **1** choose, elect, opt for, pick, plump for, select. **2** adjudicate, conclude, determine, judge, resolve, rule, settle.

decided adjective **1** adamant, determined, firm, fixed, resolute. **2** clear, clear-cut, definite, distinct, marked, noticeable, obvious, pronounced, unmistakable.

decipher verb crack, decode, figure out, interpret, make out, read, translate, work out.

decision noun adjudication, conclusion, determination, finding, judgement, resolution, ruling, sentence, verdict; see also *CHOICE*.

decisive adjective **1** conclusive, critical, crucial, deciding, significant. **2** decided, determined, firm, resolute, unhesitating.

deck noun floor, level, platform, storey.

deck verb adorn, decorate, festoon, trim.

declare verb affirm, announce, assert, avow, confess, contend, disclose, make known, proclaim, profess, pronounce, reveal, state, testify, voice. ◻ **declaration** noun affirmation, announcement, assertion, attestation, avowal, confession, proclamation, profession, pronouncement, protestation, statement, testimony.

decline verb **1** pass up, refuse, reject, turn down. **2** decrease, deteriorate, diminish, dwindle, ebb, fall off, flag, go downhill, go to the pack (*Australian informal*), sink, slip, slump, wane, weaken, worsen.

decline noun decrease, deterioration, downturn, drop, falling off, recession, slump, wane.

decode verb crack, decipher, figure out, interpret, make out, read, translate.

decompose verb decay, disintegrate, go bad, go off, go rotten, moulder, perish, putrefy, rot, spoil.

decorate verb **1** adorn, deck, dress, embellish, festoon, ornament, tizzy (*Australian* *informal*), trim. **2** do up (*informal*), paint, paper, refurbish, renovate. □ **decoration** *noun* **1** adornment, ornament, trimming. **2** award, badge, medal, medallion. □ **decorative** *adjective* fancy, ornamental, ornate, pretty.

decorous *adjective* becoming, correct, decent, honourable, polite, proper, refined, respectable, seemly.

decorum *noun* correctness, decency, dignity, politeness, propriety, respectability, seemliness.

decoy *noun* bait, enticement, lure, stool-pigeon, trap.

decoy *verb* allure, bait, entice, lure, trap.

decrease *verb* abate, contract, cut, cut back, decline, diminish, drop (off), dwindle, ease off, ebb, fall, lessen, lower, reduce, shorten, shrink, slacken, subside, taper off, wane.

decrease *noun* contraction, cut, cutback, decline, drop, ebb, fall, reduction.

decree *noun* **1** command, commandment, dictate, direction, directive, edict, instruction, law, order, ordinance, proclamation, statute. **2** decision, judgement, ruling, verdict.

decree *verb* command, decide, declare, dictate, direct, enact, ordain, order, prescribe, proclaim, rule.

decrepit *adjective* battered, derelict, dilapidated, ramshackle, rickety, run-down, tumbledown.

dedicate *verb* **1** commit, consecrate, devote, give, pledge. **2** address, inscribe.

deduce *verb* conclude, gather, infer, reason, suss ou (*informal*), work out.

deduct *verb* knock of (*informal*), remove, subtract, take away, take off.

deduction *noun* **1** discount, rebate, removal, subtraction **2** conclusion, inference, reasoning.

deed *noun* **1** accomplishment, achievement, act, action, exploit, feat, work. **2** contract, document, paper.

deem *verb* consider, count, judge, rate, reckon, regard, think.

deep *adjective* **1** bottomless, cavernous, profound, un-fathomed. **2** (*deep colours*) dark, intense, rich, strong, vivid; (*deep feelings*) burning, earnest, extreme, fervent, heartfelt, intense, keer, profound, serious, strong. **3**

bass, booming, low, resonant, sonorous.

deer noun (*male deer*) buck, hart, stag; (*female deer*) doe, hind; (*young deer*) fawn.

deface verb damage, disfigure, mar, spoil.

defame verb blacken, denigrate, discredit, disparage, libel, malign, slander, smear, vilify.

defeat verb **1** beat, clobber (*slang*), conquer, crush, euchre, get the better of, lick (*informal*), outclass, outdo, outwit, overcome, overpower, overthrow, overwhelm, paste (*slang*), prevail over, pulverise (*informal*), rout, slaughter (*informal*), stonker (*Australian slang*), surpass, thrash, triumph over, trounce, vanquish. **2** baffle, beat, confound, frustrate, perplex, puzzle.

defeat noun beating, conquest, downfall, drubbing, failure, licking (*informal*), loss, overthrow, pasting (*informal*), reverse, thrashing.

defect noun blemish, bug (*informal*), fault, flaw, imperfection, mark, spot, stain; see also *DEFICIENCY*.

defect verb change sides, desert, go over. □ **defector** noun apostate, deserter, renegade, traitor, turncoat.

defective adjective crook (*Australian informal*), deficient, dud (*informal*), faulty, imperfect, malfunctioning, on the blink (*informal*), out of order.

defence noun **1** preservation, protection, security. **2** buffer, bulwark, cover, fortification, guard, protection, safeguard, shield. **3** excuse, explanation, justification, plea.

defenceless adjective helpless, powerless, vulnerable, weak.

defend verb **1** fortify, guard, preserve, protect, safeguard, secure, shelter, shield. **2** champion, justify, stand up for, support, uphold, vindicate.

defer verb adjourn, delay, hold over, postpone, put off, shelve.

defer verb bow, give in, give way, submit, yield.

deferential adjective courteous, dutiful, meek, obsequious, polite, respectful, submissive.

defiant adjective contrary, disobedient, insubordinate, mutinous, obstinate, rebellious, recalcitrant, refractory, truculent.

deficiency noun **1** absence, dearth, deficit, insufficiency, lack, shortage, want. **2** defect, failing, fault, flaw, imperfection, shortcoming, weakness. □ **deficient** adjective **1**

insufficient, lacking, light on (*Australian informal*), short, wanting. **2** defective, faulty, imperfect, inadequate, unsatisfactory.

deficit *noun* deficiency, shortfall.

defile *verb* **1** contaminate, dirty, poison, pollute, soil, taint. **2** corrupt, desecrate, dishonour, profane, violate.

define *verb* **1** clarify, explain. **2** delineate, describe, detail, set out, specify, spell out, state.

definite *adjective* **1** clear, defined, distinct, exact, explicit, fixed, particular, precise, specific. **2** assured, certain, decided, fixed, positive, settled, sure.

definition *noun* description, elucidation, explanation, interpretation.

deflect *verb* avert, divert, parry, turn aside.

deformed *adjective* contorted, crooked, disfigured, distorted, grotesque, lopsided, malformed, misshapen, twisted, warped. □ **deformity** *noun* contortion, disfigurement, distortion, malformation.

defraud *verb* bilk, cheat, con (*informal*), deceive, diddle (*informal*), dupe, fleece, have (*slang*), hoodwink, rip off (*informal*), rook, swindle, take for a ride (*informal*), trick.

defrost *verb* de-ice, melt, thaw, unfreeze.

deft *adjective* adept, adroit, agile, dexterous, expert, neat, nimble, proficient, skilful.

defunct *adjective* dead, extinct, obsolete.

defy *verb* **1** confront, disobey, flout, oppose, resist, stand up to. **2** challenge, dare.

degenerate *verb* decline, deteriorate, regress, retrogress, sink, worsen.

degrade *verb* abase, cheapen, debase, demean, disgrace, humiliate, lower. □ **degrading** *adjective* demeaning, humiliating, menial, undignified.

degree *noun* grade, level, order, rank, stage, step.

dehydrated *adjective* desiccated, dried.

deign *verb* condescend, lower yourself, stoop, vouchsafe.

deity *noun* divinity, god, goddess.

dejected *adjective* crestfallen, depressed, despondent, disconsolate, discouraged, disheartened, dispirited, doleful, downcast, down-hearted, forlorn, gloomy, glum, heavyhearted, melancholy, miserable, morose, sad, sorrowful.

delay *verb* **1** detain, hamper, hinder, hold up, impede, inhibit, obstruct, retard, slow. **2** defer, postpone, put off, shelve. **3** dilly-dally (*informal*), hang back, hesitate, linger, pause, procrastinate, stall, temporise, wait.

delay *noun* hold-up, interruption, lull, pause, postponement, setback, wait.

delegate *noun* agent, ambassador, deputy, emissary, envoy, proxy, representative, spokesperson.

delegate *verb* **1** appoint, authorise, commission, depute, designate, empower, nominate. **2** assign, depute, entrust, hand over, transfer.

delete *verb* cancel, cross out, cut out, edit out, efface, erase, expunge, obliterate, remove, rub out, strike out, take out, wipe out.

deliberate *adjective* **1** calculated, conscious, intended, intentional, planned, premeditated, studied, wilful. **2** careful, cautious, measured, painstaking, slow, unhurried.

deliberate *verb* cogitate, confer about, consider, debate, discuss, meditate, mull over, muse, ponder, reflect, ruminate, think.

delicate *adjective* **1** breakable, dainty, exquisite, filmy, fine, flimsy, fragile, intricate, lacy, light, sheer, thin. **2** faint, gentle, mild, muted, pale, pastel, soft, subdued, subtle. **3** feeble, frail, infirm, sickly, tender, unhealthy, weak. **4** awkward, hazardous, precarious, sensitive, ticklish, touchy, tricky. **5** careful, diplomatic, discreet, sensitive, skilful, tactful.

delicious *adjective* appetising, delectable, luscious, mouthwatering, palatable, scrumptious (*informal*), tasty, yummy (*informal*).

delight *verb* **1** amuse, captivate, charm, divert, enchant, enrapture, entertain, entrance, fascinate, please, thrill. **2** (*delight in*) adore, appreciate, be fond of, be keen on, enjoy, like, love, luxuriate in, relish, revel in, savour, take pleasure in.

delight *noun* bliss, ecstasy, enjoyment, gratification, happiness, joy, pleasure, satisfaction. □ **delightful** *adjective* adorable, agreeable, attractive, beautiful, charming, delectable, enchanting, enjoyable, heavenly, lovable, lovely, nice, pleasant, pleasurable, wonderful.

delinquent noun criminal, hooligan, lawbreaker, miscreant, offender, troublemaker, wrongdoer.

delirious adjective **1** demented, deranged, frantic, frenzied, hysterical, incoherent, light-headed, mad, raving. **2** ecstatic, euphoric, excited, wild.

deliver verb **1** bear, bring, carry, convey, distribute, give out, hand over, take, transport. **2** give, make, present, utter. **3** aim, deal, inflict, strike. **4** emancipate, free, liberate, release, rescue, save, set free. □ **delivery** noun **1** consignment, conveyance, dispatch, distribution, shipment, transport. **2** childbirth.

delude verb beguile, bluff, con (*informal*), deceive, dupe, fool, have on (*informal*), hoax, hoodwink, kid (*informal*), mislead, trick.

deluge noun **1** flood, inundation, spate. **2** cloudburst, downpour, rain, torrent. **3** flood, rush, shower, spate, stream, torrent.

deluge verb flood, inundate, overrun, overwhelm, swamp.

delusion noun fantasy, illusion, misbelief, misconception.

de luxe elegant, first-class, grand, luxurious, posh (*informal*), superior, upmarket.

delve verb dig, examine, investigate, probe, research, search.

demand verb **1** ask for, claim, clamour for, insist on, order, press for, request, require. **2** call for, need, require. □ **demanding** adjective arduous, challenging, difficult, exacting, hard, onerous, strenuous, taxing, tough.

demand noun **1** command, order, request, summons. **2** call, need, requirement, want.

demean verb debase, degrade, humble, humiliate, lower.

demeanour noun bearing, behaviour, conduct, deportment, manner, mien.

demented adjective berserk, bonkers (*slang*), crazy, deranged, insane, lunatic, mad, nutty (*informal*), out of your mind, potty (*informal*), screwy (*informal*), unbalanced, unhinged.

democratic adjective elected, popular, representative.

demolish verb destroy, dismantle, knock down, level, pull down, raze, tear down, wreck.

demon noun bogy, devil, evil spirit, fiend, goblin, hobgoblin, imp. □ **demonic** adjective devilish, diabolical, evil, fiendish, satanic, wicked.

demonstrate *verb* **1** display, establish, exhibit, present, prove, show. **2** describe, explain, illustrate, show, teach. **3** march, parade, protest, rally.

demonstration *noun* **1** display, exhibition, presentation, show. **2** demo (*informal*), march, parade, protest, rally, sit-in.

demoralise *verb* crush, depress, discourage, dishearten.

demure *adjective* bashful, coy, diffident, modest, prim, quiet, reserved, shy, unassuming.

den *noun* **1** burrow, hole, lair, nest. **2** hideaway, hide-out (*informal*), retreat, sanctum, study.

denial *noun* contradiction, disclaimer, negation, refusal, rejection, repudiation.

denomination *noun* church, persuasion, sect.

denote *verb* express, indicate, mean, represent, signal, signify, stand for, symbolise.

denounce *verb* **1** attack, censure, condemn, criticise, decry, object to. **2** accuse, betray, dob in (*Australian informal*), incriminate, inform against, report.

dense *adjective* **1** close, compact, heavy, impenetrable, packed, solid, thick. **2** bovine,

dim (*informal*), dull, dumb (*informal*), feeble-minded, foolish, obtuse, slow, stupid, thick, unintelligent.

dent *noun* depression, dimple, dint, hollow, indentation.

deny *verb* **1** contradict, disclaim, gainsay (*formal*), negate, reject, repudiate. **2** deprive of, disallow, refuse, withhold.

depart *verb* clear off (*informal*), decamp, embark, emigrate, escape, exit, go away, leave, make off, make tracks (*informal*), nick off (*Australian slang*), push off (*informal*), quit, retire, run away, run off, scarper (*informal*), scram (*informal*), set off, set out, shoot through (*Australian informal*), skedaddle (*informal*), take your leave, withdraw.

department *noun* branch, bureau, division, office, part, section, unit.

departure *noun* exit, exodus, going away, leaving, retreat, withdrawal.

depend *verb* □ **depend on 1** bank on, count on, need, reckon on, rely on. **2** hang on, hinge on, rest on, turn on.

dependable *adjective* consistent, constant, faithful, loyal, reliable, stalwart, steadfast, steady, true, trustworthy.

dependent *adjective* addicted, hooked (*slang*), reliant.

depict *verb* **1** draw, illustrate, paint, picture, portray, represent, show, sketch. **2** describe, narrate, outline, record, relate.

deplore *verb* **1** bewail, grieve over, lament, mourn, regret. **2** abhor, condemn, deprecate, disapprove of. □ **deplorable** *adjective* abominable, appalling, awful, bad, dire, disgraceful, dreadful, lamentable, pathetic, regrettable, reprehensible, shameful, shocking, wretched.

deploy *verb* arrange, dispose, organise, position, spread out.

deport *verb* banish, exile, expatriate, expel, send away, transport.

deportment *noun* bearing, behaviour, carriage, conduct, demeanour, manner, mien.

depose *verb* dethrone, get rid of, oust, remove.

deposit *noun* **1** down payment, first instalment. **2** alluvium, crust, dregs, lees, precipitate, sediment, silt.

deposit *verb* **1** drop, dump, lay, leave, park (*informal*), place, put down, set down. **2** bank, pay in, save.

depot *noun* **1** cache, repository, store, storehouse, warehouse. **2** base, headquarters. **3** garage, station, terminal, terminus.

depraved *adjective* base, corrupt, degenerate, dissolute, evil, immoral, perverted, vile, wicked.

depreciate *verb* decrease, devalue, drop, go down, lower, reduce.

depress *verb* **1** dishearten, oppress, sadden, weigh down. **2** lower, press down, push down. □ **depressed** *adjective* blue, dejected, desolate, despondent, disconsolate, disheartened, dismal, dispirited, down, downcast, downhearted, down in the dumps, gloomy, glum, heavy-hearted, hopeless, in the doldrums, low, melancholy, miserable, morose, out of sorts, pessimistic, sad, unhappy, woebegone, wretched.

depression *noun* **1** the blues, dejection, despair, despondency, gloom, hopelessness, low spirits, melancholy, pessimism, sadness, unhappiness, wretchedness. **2** decline, downturn, recession, slump. **3** basin, cavity, crabhole (*Australian*), crater, dent, dip, gilgai (*Australian*), hole, hollow, indentation, pit, trough. **4** cyclone, low, trough.

deprive verb (*deprive of*) deny, dispossess of, refuse, rob of, take away.

depth noun deepness, intensity, profundity, strength. ☐ **in depth** comprehensively, extensively, in detail, intensively, thoroughly.

deputise verb (*deputise for*) fill in for, hold the fort for, stand in for, substitute for, take the place of.

deputy noun assistant, delegate, lieutenant, locum, offsider (*Australian*), proxy, relief, replacement, representative, reserve, stand-in, substitute, surrogate, understudy.

deranged adjective berserk, crazy, demented, insane, irrational, lunatic, mad, unbalanced, unhinged.

derelict adjective abandoned, decrepit, deserted, dilapidated, forsaken, neglected, run-down, tumbledown.

deride verb jeer at, laugh at, make fun of, mock, poke fun at (*Australian informal*), poke fun at, ridicule, satirise, scoff at, sneer at, take the mickey out of (*informal*), taunt, tease.

derision noun contempt, disdain, mockery, ridicule, sarcasm, scorn.

derivation noun etymology, origin, root, source.

derive verb **1** draw, gain, get, glean, obtain, receive. **2** come, originate, stem.

derogatory adjective belittling, contemptuous, disparaging, insulting, pejorative, uncomplimentary.

descend verb climb down, come down, drop, fall, go down, nosedive, plummet, plunge, sink, swoop down. ☐ **descendant** noun child, heir, scion; (*descendants*) issue, offspring, progeny, seed (*old use*).

descent noun **1** coming down, dive, drop, fall, plunge. **2** ancestry, birth, blood, extraction, genealogy, lineage, origin, parentage, stock, strain.

describe verb characterise, depict, detail, elaborate, explain, express, narrate, outline, portray, recount, relate, represent, tell (about). ☐ **description** noun account, characterisation, commentary, depiction, explanation, outline, picture, portrait, portrayal, profile, record, report, representation, sketch, story.

desecrate verb debase, defile, degrade, profane, violate.

desert noun wasteland, wilderness. □ **desert** adjective arid, barren, desolate, dry, infertile, uncultivated, uninhabited, waste, wild.

desert verb **1** abandon, ditch (informal), dump (informal), forsake, jilt, leave, leave in the lurch, walk out on. **2** abscond, defect, run away. □ **deserter** noun absconder, defector, escapee, fugitive, runaway.

deserts plural noun comeuppance (informal), due, nemesis, punishment, retribution, reward.

deserve verb be entitled to, be worthy of, command, earn, justify, merit, warrant.

design noun **1** blueprint, diagram, draft, drawing, model, outline, pattern, plan, sketch. **2** arrangement, composition, configuration, form, layout, style. **3** motif, pattern.

design verb **1** conceive, draft, draw, lay out, plan, sketch, visualise. **2** aim, calculate, intend, mean, plan, tailor. □ **designer** noun architect, couturier, creator, inventor, originator, planner.

designate verb **1** identify, indicate, mark, specify, stipulate. **2** appoint, choose, name, nominate, select.

□ **designation** noun epithet, name, title.

desirable adjective **1** alluring, appealing, attractive, popular, sought-after, worthwhile. **2** advisable, preferable, recommended.

desire noun ambition, appetite, aspiration, craving, fancy, hunger, itch, longing, lust, passion, thirst, urge, wish, yen.

desire verb covet, crave, fancy, hanker after, hope for, hunger for, long for, lust after, set your heart on, thirst for, want, wish for, yearn for.

desist verb cease, discontinue, leave off, refrain, stop.

desolate adjective **1** dejected, depressed, despondent, disconsolate, forlorn, forsaken, glum, heavy-hearted, lonely, melancholy, miserable, unhappy, wretched. **2** barren, bleak, deserted, dismal, dreary, empty, inhospitable, isolated, lonely, remote, stark, uninhabited, wild, windswept.

despair noun depression, desperation, despondency, hopelessness.

despair verb give up, lose hope.

desperate adjective **1** acute, bad, critical, dire, grave, hopeless, serious, urgent. **2**

dangerous, daring, foolhardy, impetuous, rash, reckless, violent, wild.

despicable *adjective* abominable, bad, base, contemptible, detestable, evil, hateful, loathsome, low, mean, odious, outrageous, reprehensible, rotten, shameful, vile, wicked.

despise *verb* detest, disdain, dislike, feel contempt for, hate, loathe, look down on, scorn, spurn.

despondent *adjective* dejected, depressed, discouraged, disheartened, dispirited, doleful, down, downcast, downhearted, forlorn, gloomy, glum, heavy-hearted, melancholy, miserable, morose, sad, sorrowful, unhappy, wretched.

despot *noun* autocrat, dictator, tyrant. □ **despotic** *adjective* absolute, authoritarian, autocratic, dictatorial, domineering, imperious, oppressive, tyrannical.

dessert *noun* afters (*informal*), pudding, sweet.

destination *noun* end, goal, objective, target.

destined *adjective* doomed, fated, intended, meant, ordained, predestined.

destiny *noun* doom, fate, fortune, karma, kismet, lot, portion.

destitute *adjective* bankrupt, broke (*informal*), down and out, hard up (*informal*), impecunious, impoverished, insolvent, needy, penniless, penurious, poor, poverty-stricken.

destroy *verb* annihilate, blow up, break, bust (*informal*), crush, demolish, devastate, dismantle, eliminate, exterminate, extinguish, knock down, lay waste, mutilate, obliterate, pull down, pull to pieces, put an end to, ravage, raze, ruin, sabotage, shatter, smash, spoil, tear down, undermine, vandalise, wipe out, wreck, zap (*slang*); see also KILL. □ **destruction** *noun* annihilation, damage, demolition, devastation, elimination, extermination, extinction, havoc, holocaust, killing, massacre, ruin, sabotage, slaughter, vandalism, wreckage. □ **destructive** *adjective* adverse, baleful, damaging, dangerous, deleterious, detrimental, devastating, disastrous, harmful, injurious, malign, malignant, negative, pernicious, ruinous.

detach *verb* disconnect, disengage, part, pull off, release, remove, separate, slip off, take off, undo, unfasten.

detached adjective **1** free-standing, separate. **2** aloof, disinterested, impartial, neutral, objective, unbiased, uninvolved, unprejudiced.

detail noun aspect, circumstance, element, fact, factor, feature, item, particular, point, respect. □ **detailed** adjective blow-by-blow, comprehensive, elaborate, exact, exhaustive, full, graphic, in-depth, itemised, minute, rigorous, thorough.

detain verb **1** bail up (*Australian*), buttonhole, delay, hinder, hold up, impede, keep, waylay. **2** arrest, capture, confine, hold in custody, imprison, jail.

detect verb discern, discover, find, identify, locate, note, notice, observe, perceive, see, sense, spot, track down, uncover.

detective noun cop (*slang*), investigator, policeman, police officer, policewoman, private eye (*informal*), sleuth.

detention noun captivity, confinement, custody, imprisonment.

deter verb daunt, discourage, dissuade, hinder, impede, obstruct, prevent, put off, scare off.

deteriorate verb decline, degenerate, diminish, go backwards, go downhill, go to the dogs (*informal*), go to the pack (*Australian informal*), retrogress, sink, slip, wane, weaken, worsen.

determination noun backbone, courage, doggedness, fortitude, grit, guts (*informal*), perseverance, persistence, pertinacity, resolve, spirit, tenacity, will-power.

determine verb **1** agree on, decide, fix on, resolve, settle. **2** ascertain, calculate, discover, establish, find out, work out.

determined adjective adamant, dogged, firm, headstrong, intransigent, persistent, pertinacious, purposeful, resolute, single-minded, steadfast, strong-willed, stubborn, tenacious.

detest verb abhor, abominate, despise, dislike, hate, loathe. □ **detestable** adjective abhorrent, abominable, atrocious, contemptible, deplorable, despicable, disgusting, hateful, horrid, intolerable, loathsome, objectionable, obnoxious, odious, repugnant, repulsive, revolting, vile.

detonate verb discharge, explode, let off, set off.

detour noun bypass, deviation, diversion.

detract verb (detract from) diminish, lessen, reduce, take away from.

detrimental adjective adverse, damaging, deleterious, destructive, harmful, injurious, pernicious, prejudicial.

devastate verb damage, demolish, destroy, lay waste, level, ravage, ruin, wreck.

devastated adjective dismayed, overcome, overwhelmed, shattered, shocked, traumatised.

develop verb **1** advance, blossom, build up, cultivate, diversify, enlarge, evolve, expand, flourish, grow, improve, increase, mature, mushroom, progress. **2** acquire, contract, get, pick up. □ **development** noun advance, building, enlargement, evolution, expansion, growth, improvement, increase, progress, spread.

deviate verb depart, digress, diverge, stray, turn aside.

device noun apparatus, appliance, contraption (informal), gadget, implement, instrument, invention, machine, tool, utensil.

devil noun **1** bogy, demon, evil spirit, fiend. **2** monster, rascal, rogue, scamp, scoundrel. □ **the Devil** Lucifer, Old Nick, Satan. □ **devilish** adjective demonic, diabolical, evil, fiendish, hellish, infernal, satanic, ungodly, villainous, wicked.

devious adjective **1** circuitous, indirect, roundabout, tortuous, winding. **2** calculating, crafty, cunning, deceitful, dishonest, sly, sneaky, underhand, wily.

devise verb conceive, concoct, contrive, cook up (informal), create, design, dream up, formulate, hatch, invent, make up, plan, plot, produce, think up, work out.

devoid adjective (devoid of) bereft of, free from, lacking, without.

devote verb commit, consecrate, dedicate, give, set aside.

devoted adjective close, committed, constant, dedicated, enthusiastic, faithful, loving, loyal, reliable, staunch, true.

devotee noun aficionado, buff (informal), enthusiast, fan, fanatic, follower, lover, supporter.

devotion noun affection, allegiance, attachment, commitment, dedication, fervour, fondness, love, loyalty, zeal.

devotions plural noun prayers, worship.

devour *verb* bolt, consume, demolish (*informal*), eat, gobble, gorge, gulp down, guzzle, knock back, scoff (*informal*), swallow, wolf.

devout *adjective* ardent, committed, dedicated, devoted, earnest, fervent, genuine, godly, holy, pious, religious, sincere, staunch.

dexterous *adjective* adept, adroit, agile, deft, nimble, skilful.

diabolical *adjective* devilish, evil, fiendish, hellish, infernal, inhuman, satanic, ungodly, villainous, wicked.

diagnose *verb* detect, determine, identify, name, recognise.

diagonal *adjective* oblique, slanting, sloping.

diagram *noun* chart, drawing, figure, graph, illustration, outline, picture, plan, representation, sketch.

dial *verb* call, phone, ring, telephone.

dialect *noun* accent, brogue, idiom, lingo (*informal*), patois, variety, vernacular; see also *LANGUAGE*.

dialogue *noun* communication, conference, conversation, discourse, discussion, talk.

diameter *noun* bore, calibre, thickness, width.

diary *noun* chronicle, journal, log, record.

dictate *verb* command, decree, lay down the law, ordain, order, prescribe.

dictator *noun* autocrat, despot, tyrant. ☐ **dictatorial** *adjective* authoritarian, autocratic, bossy, despotic, domineering, imperious, overbearing, peremptory, totalitarian, tyrannical. ☐ **dictatorship** *noun* autocracy, despotism, tyranny.

dictionary *noun* glossary, lexicon, phrase book, thesaurus, vocabulary.

die *verb* **1** bite the dust (*slang*), breathe one's last, croak (*slang*), depart this world, expire, fall (*in war*), go to glory (*slang*), kick the bucket (*slang*), lose one's life, pass away, pass on, perish, snuff it (*slang*). **2** break down, conk out (*informal*), fail. ☐ **die down** decline, decrease, diminish, ebb, fade, fizzle out, lessen, peter out, subside, taper off, wane. ☐ **die out** cease, disappear, end, pass, vanish.

diet *noun* fare, food intake, nourishment, nutrition.

differ *verb* **1** be different, be dissimilar, be distinguishable, be poles apart, be unlike, contrast. **2** be at odds, clash, conflict, disagree, quarrel.

difference noun **1** contrast, deviation, disparity, dissimilarity, distinction, divergence, nuance, variation; see also *CHANGE*. **2** balance, deficit, gap. **3** argument, conflict, disagreement, dispute, quarrel, strife, tiff.

different adjective **1** altered, alternative, changed, conflicting, contradictory, contrary, contrasting, disparate, dissimilar, divergent, diverse, other, unlike. **2** discrete, distinct, individual, separate.

differentiate verb contrast, discriminate, distinguish, separate, set apart, tell apart.

difficult adjective **1** (*a difficult task*) arduous, demanding, exacting, exhausting, formidable, gruelling, hard, herculean, laborious, onerous, strenuous, taxing, tiring, tough, uphill; (*a difficult problem*) abstruse, baffling, challenging, complex, complicated, confusing, hard, knotty, perplexing, problematical, puzzling, thorny, ticklish, tough, tricky. **2** awkward, demanding, fussy, intractable, obstreperous, recalcitrant, refractory, stroppy (*informal*), stubborn,

troublesome, trying, uncooperative.

difficulty noun adversity, complication, hang-up (*informal*), hardship, hassle (*informal*), hindrance, hitch, hurdle, impediment, obstacle, ordeal, pitfall, pressure, problem, snag, stumbling block, trouble. □ **in difficulties** in a bind (*informal*), in a fix, in a jam (*informal*), in a mess, in a pickle (*informal*), in a plight, in a predicament, in a quandary, in a spot (*informal*), in dire straits, in hot water (*informal*), in strife (*Australian informal*), in the soup (*informal*), in trouble, up the creek (*informal*).

diffident adjective bashful, coy, hesitant, meek, modest, reserved, reticent, shy, tentative, timid, timorous, unassertive.

diffuse verb circulate, disperse, spread.

diffuse adjective **1** dispersed, scattered, spread out. **2** longwinded, rambling, verbose, wordy.

dig verb **1** burrow, delve (*old use*), excavate, gouge, hollow, scoop, tunnel. **2** jab, plunge, poke, prod, stab, thrust. **3** (*dig up*) discover, dredge up, ferret out, find, fossick out

(*Australian informal*), root out, seek, uncover, unearth.

dig noun **1** excavation. **2** nudge, poke, prod, thrust.

digest verb absorb, assimilate, comprehend, grasp, take in, understand.

digit noun figure, integer, number, numeral.

dignified adjective calm, decorous, elegant, formal, grand, honourable, imposing, majestic, noble, proper, sedate, serious, sober, solemn, staid, stately.

dignitary noun celebrity, luminary, personage, VIP, worthy.

dignity noun **1** decorum, formality, gravity, majesty, nobility, poise, propriety, self-respect, solemnity, stateliness. **2** position, rank, standing, station, status.

digress verb deviate, diverge, drift, ramble, stray, wander.

dilapidated adjective battered, broken down, decrepit, derelict, ramshackle, rickety, ruined, run-down, tumble-down.

dilate verb broaden, distend, enlarge, expand, swell, widen.

dilemma noun bind (*informal*), catch-22 (*informal*), difficulty, fix, hole (*informal*), jam

(*informal*), mess, plight, predicament, problem, quandary, spot (*informal*).

diligent adjective assiduous, attentive, careful, conscientious, earnest, hard-working, indefatigable, industrious, meticulous, painstaking, persevering, scrupulous, sedulous, steady, studious, thorough.

dilute verb adulterate, thin, water down, weaken.

dim adjective **1** blurred, cloudy, dark, dingy, dull, dusky, faint, fuzzy, gloomy, hazy, indistinct, murky, obscure, pale, shadowy, vague, weak. **2** see *STUPID*.

dimension noun **1** area, breadth, capacity, depth, height, length, measurement, proportion, thickness, volume, width. **2** extent, magnitude, scale, scope, size.

diminish verb abate, contract, decline, decrease, dwindle, fade, lessen, reduce, shrink, subside, wane.

din noun bedlam, clamour, clatter, commotion, hubbub, hullabaloo, noise, pandemonium, racket, row (*informal*), rumpus, shindy (*informal*), tumult, uproar.

dine verb eat, feast, have dinner, sup.

dingy *adjective* dark, dirty, dismal, drab, dreary, dull, gloomy, shabby.

dinkum *adjective* authentic, bona fide, dinky-di (*Australian informal*), genuine, honest-to-goodness (*informal*), real, true, veritable.

dinner *noun* banquet, feast, meal, repast (*formal*), supper, tea.

dip *verb* **1** dunk, immerse, plunge, sink, steep, submerge, wet. **2** decline, descend, drop, go down, slope downwards.

dip *noun* **1** depression, hollow. **2** bathe, bogey (*Australian*), plunge, swim.

diploma *noun* award, certificate, qualification.

diplomacy *noun* courtesy, delicacy, discretion, tact, tactfulness.

diplomat *noun* ambassador, attaché, consul, envoy, representative.

diplomatic *adjective* courteous, delicate, discreet, judicious, polite, politic, sensitive, tactful.

dire *adjective* (*dire consequences*) appalling, calamitous, catastrophic, disastrous, dreadful, gloomy, grave, grim, horrible, terrible; (*dire need*) critical, desperate, drastic,

extreme, pressing, serious, urgent.

direct *adjective* **1** straight, unswerving. **2** blunt, candid, explicit, forthright, frank, honest, open, outspoken, plain, straight, straightforward, to the point. **3** absolute, complete, diametrical, exact, polar.

direct *verb* **1** conduct, guide, lead, navigate, point, show, steer, usher. **2** aim, level, point, target, train, turn. **3** administer, command, control, govern, head, lead, manage, mastermind, oversee, preside over, regulate, run, superintend, supervise. **4** bid, command, instruct, order, tell. □ **director** *noun* administrator, boss, captain, chairperson, chief, commander, conductor, coordinator, executive, governor, head, leader, manager, superintendent, supervisor.

direction *noun* **1** administration, charge, command, control, guidance, leadership, management, supervision. **2** course, line, route, tack, way.

directions *plural noun* guidelines, instructions, orders, recipe, rules.

directory *noun* index, list, register.

dirge *noun* elegy, keen, lament.

dirt noun **1** clay, earth, loam, soil. **2** dust, filth, grime, mire, muck, mud, soot.

dirty adjective **1** blackened, dingy, dusty, filthy, foul, grimy, grotty (slang), grubby, insanitary, messy, muddy, soiled, sooty, sordid, squalid, stained, unclean, unwashed. **2** base, contemptible, despicable, dishonest, dishonourable, low, low-down, mean, nasty, shabby, underhand, unfair, unsporting. **3** bawdy, blue, coarse, crude, filthy, improper, indecent, lewd, obscene, offensive, pornographic, rude, smutty, tasteless, vulgar.

dirty verb blacken, foul, muddy, pollute, soil, stain, sully, tarnish.

disabled adjective crippled, handicapped, incapacitated, lame, maimed. □ **disability** noun handicap, impairment, incapacity.

disadvantage noun drawback, handicap, hindrance, impediment, inconvenience, liability, minus. □ **disadvantaged** adjective deprived, underprivileged.

disagree verb argue, be at loggerheads, be at odds, be at variance, be incompatible, clash, conflict, contrast, differ, dissent, diverge, quarrel, squabble, wrangle. □ **disagreement** noun altercation, argument, clash, conflict, controversy, difference, dispute, dissension, dissent, quarrel, row, squabble, tiff, wrangle.

disagreeable adjective **1** disgusting, distasteful, nasty, objectionable, obnoxious, offensive, repugnant, repulsive, revolting, unpleasant. **2** bad-tempered, crabby, cross, crotchety, fractious, grouchy (informal), grumpy, irritable, shirty (informal), snaky (Australian informal), stroppy (informal), surly, unfriendly.

disappear verb clear, dissipate, evaporate, fade, melt away, pass, vanish; see also RUN AWAY (at RUN).

disappoint verb dash the hopes of, discourage, disenchant, dishearten, disillusion, dissatisfy, frustrate, let down, sadden, thwart. □ **disappointment** noun **1** chagrin, discontent, disenchantment, disillusionment, dissatisfaction, frustration, regret, sadness, unhappiness. **2** anticlimax, comedown, damp squib, failure, fiasco, fizzer (Australian informal), flop (informal), let-down, non-event, swizz (informal), washout (informal).

disapprove verb (*disapprove of*) condemn, criticise, denounce, deplore, deprecate, frown on, object to, take a dim view of (*informal*). ☐ **disapproval** noun censure, condemnation, criticism, disapprobation, disfavour, dissatisfaction, objection, opposition.

disarray noun chaos, confusion, disorder, havoc, mess, muddle, shambles.

disaster noun **1** accident, adversity, calamity, cataclysm, catastrophe, misfortune, mishap, reverse, tragedy. **2** failure, fiasco, fizzer (*Australian informal*), flop (*informal*), wash-out (*informal*). ☐ **disastrous** adjective appalling, calamitous, cataclysmic, catastrophic, devastating, dire, dreadful, ruinous, terrible, tragic.

disband verb break up, disperse, dissolve, separate, split up.

disbelieve verb distrust, doubt, mistrust, question.

discard verb cast off, chuck out (*informal*), dice (*Australian informal*), dispose of, ditch (*informal*), dump, get rid of, jettison, reject, scrap, shed, throw away.

discern verb detect, make out, notice, observe, perceive, recognise, see, sense.

discerning adjective critical, discriminating, intelligent, judicious, perceptive, sharp, shrewd, wise.

discharge verb **1** free, liberate, release. **2** dismiss, fire, kick out (*informal*), sack (*informal*). **3** belch, eject, emit, empty out, expel, exude, give out, leak, ooze, pour out, release, secrete, send out, spurt. **4** detonate, explode, fire, let off, set off, shoot, trigger. **5** clear, meet, pay, settle, square.

disciple noun adherent, apprentice, devotee, follower, pupil, supporter.

disciplinarian noun authoritarian, hard-liner, martinet, stickler, taskmaster.

discipline noun control, order, routine, system.

discipline verb **1** coach, drill, educate, indoctrinate, instruct, train. **2** chastise, correct, penalise, punish, rebuke, reprimand.

disclaim verb deny, disown, refuse, reject, repudiate.

disclose verb air, betray, blab, blow (*slang*), bring to light, divulge, expose, give away, impart, leak, let out, let slip, make known, make public, publish, reveal, tell, uncover.

disco noun club, discothèque, nightclub.

discolour verb bleach, fade, scorch, stain, tarnish, tinge.

discomfort noun ache, affliction, distress, hardship, irritation, misery, pain, soreness, suffering, uneasiness.

disconcert verb agitate, confuse, discomfit, disturb, faze (*informal*), fluster, perturb, put off, rattle (*informal*), ruffle, throw (*informal*), trouble, unnerve, upset, worry.

disconnect verb cut off, detach, disengage, switch off, turn off, uncouple, undo, unplug.

disconnected adjective disjointed, disorganised, garbled, haphazard, incoherent, jumbled, rambling, random, unsystematic.

discontent noun disenchantment, displeasure, disquiet, dissatisfaction, misery, regret, resentment, restlessness, unhappiness. ☐ **discontented** adjective browned off (*slang*), cheesed off (*slang*), disenchanted, disgruntled, displeased, dissatisfied, fed up (*informal*), miserable, unhappy.

discontinue verb abandon, break off, cancel, cease, cut end, finish, interrupt, stop suspend, terminate.

discord noun argument conflict, disagreement, dis harmony, dissension, disunity friction, quarrelling, strife ☐ **discordant** adjective cacophonous, dissonant, grating harsh, jarring, strident.

discount noun concession, cut deduction, rebate, reduction.

discourage verb 1 daunt demoralise, depress, dis hearten, dismay, intimidate. 2 deter, dissuade, put off, talk out of.

discourse noun 1 address dissertation, essay, lecture monograph, oration, paper sermon, speech, talk, thesis treatise. 2 see *CONVERSATION*.

discourteous adjective bad mannered, boorish, cheeky disrespectful, ill-mannered impertinent, impolite, impudent, insolent, insulting, rude uncivil, uncouth.

discover verb come across come upon, detect, dig up ferret out, find, find out, hear of, hit on, identify, learn, light on, locate, perceive, read of realise, spot, stumble on, suss out (*informal*), track down uncover, unearth, work out

□ **discoverer** noun creator, explorer, inventor, pioneer.

discredit verb (discredit a person) blacken, defame, denigrate, disgrace, disparage, malign, slander, smear, sully, vilify; (discredit an idea) challenge, debunk (informal), disprove, explode, invalidate, question.

discreet adjective careful, cautious, chary, circumspect, diplomatic, guarded, judicious, prudent, tactful, wary.

discrepancy noun difference, disagreement, disparity, inconsistency.

discrete adjective disconnected, distinct, separate.

discretion noun care, discernment, judgement, prudence, sense, sensitivity, tact, wisdom.

discriminate verb differentiate, distinguish, tell apart. □ **discrimination** noun bias, favouritism, inequity, intolerance, prejudice, unfairness.

discuss verb argue, confer on, consider, converse about, debate, deliberate, examine, have out, speak about, talk about, thrash out. □ **discussion** noun argument, conference, consultation, conversation, debate, delibera-

tion, dialogue, examination, exchange, talk.

disdain noun contempt, derision, scorn. □ **disdainful** adjective arrogant, contemptuous, derisive, haughty, hoitytoity, proud, scornful, sneering, snobbish, snooty (informal), supercilious, superior.

disdain verb despise, look down on, rebuff, reject, scorn, sneer at, spurn.

disease noun affliction, ailment, bug (informal), complaint, condition, disorder, illness, infection, malady, plague, sickness.

disembark verb alight, get off, get out, go ashore, land.

disentangle verb detach, extricate, free, liberate, sort out, straighten out, unravel, untangle, untie, untwist.

disfigure verb damage, deface, deform, mar, mutilate, ruin, scar, spoil.

disgrace noun discredit, dishonour, disrepute, humiliation, ignominy, reproach, scandal, shame, stigma. □ **disgraceful** adjective contemptible, degrading, discreditable, dishonourable, ignominious, outrageous, scandalous, shameful, unbecoming, unseemly.

disgrace *verb* bring dishonour to, bring shame on, degrade, embarrass, humiliate, let down.

disgruntled *adjective* browned off (*slang*), cheesed off (*slang*), cross, discontented, displeased, dissatisfied, fed up (*informal*), unhappy.

disguise *verb* camouflage, conceal, cover up, dress up, hide, mask, masquerade, veil.

disguise *noun* camouflage, costume, cover, mask, masquerade.

disgust *noun* abhorrence, antipathy, aversion, contempt, dislike, distaste, hatred, loathing, nausea, repugnance, repulsion, revulsion.

disgust *verb* appal, horrify, nauseate, offend, repel, revolt, shock, sicken, turn someone's stomach. ◻ **disgusting** *adjective* appalling, detestable, distasteful, dreadful, filthy, foul, gross (*informal*), loathsome, nauseating, objectionable, obnoxious, offensive, off-putting, repellent, repugnant, repulsive, revolting, shocking, sickening, unpleasant, vile, yucky (*informal*).

dish *noun* basin, bowl, casserole, container, coolamon (*Australian*), plate, platter, ramekin,

receptacle, tureen; (*dishes*) crockery.

dishearten *verb* demoralise, depress, discourage, dismay, sadden.

dishevelled *adjective* bedraggled, messy, ruffled, scruffy, tangled, tousled, unkempt, untidy.

dishonest *adjective* bent (*slang*), corrupt, criminal, crooked, deceitful, deceptive, dodgy (*informal*), false, fraudulent, hypocritical, insincere, lying, mendacious, misleading, shady, shonky (*Australian, informal*), two-faced, underhand, unscrupulous, untrustworthy, untruthful.

dishonour *noun* discredit, disgrace, disrepute, humiliation, ignominy, reproach, scandal, shame, stigma. ◻ **dishonourable** *adjective* base, despicable, discreditable, disgraceful, disreputable, ignominious, improper, low, opprobrious, reprehensible, shabby, shameful, unprincipled.

disillusion *verb* disabuse, disappoint, disenchant, enlighten, undeceive.

disincentive *noun* deterrent, discouragement.

disinfect *verb* clean, cleanse, fumigate, purify, sanitise, sterilise.

disinfectant *noun* antiseptic, bactericide, germicide, sanitiser, steriliser.

disintegrate *verb* break up, collapse, crumble, decay, decompose, deteriorate, fall apart, perish, rot, shatter.

disinterested *adjective* detached, dispassionate, impartial, neutral, objective, unbiased, uninvolved, unprejudiced.

disjointed *adjective* desultory, disconnected, disorganised, fragmented, incoherent, jumbled, mixed up, rambling.

dislike *noun* abhorrence, animosity, antipathy, aversion, contempt, detestation, disgust, distaste, hatred, horror, hostility, loathing, repugnance, resentment, revulsion.

dislike *verb* abominate, despise, detest, hate, have an aversion to, loathe, object to, resent, take exception to.

disloyal *adjective* faithless, false, perfidious, treacherous, two-faced, unfaithful, untrue. □ **disloyalty** *noun* betrayal, infidelity, perfidy, treachery, treason, unfaithfulness.

dismal *adjective* black, bleak, cheerless, depressing, dreary, funereal, gloomy, grim, lugubrious, melancholy, miserable, mournful, sad, sombre.

dismantle *verb* demolish, knock down, pull to pieces, take apart, take down, undo.

dismay *noun* agitation, alarm, anxiety, apprehension, consternation, discouragement, dread, fear, horror, shock, terror, trepidation. □ **dismay** *verb* alarm, appal, daunt, depress, disconcert, discourage, dishearten, distress, frighten, horrify, scare, shock, terrify, unnerve.

dismiss *verb* **1** disband, let go, release, send away. **2** discharge, fire, get rid of, give notice to, give the boot to (*slang*), give the sack to (*informal*), kick out (*informal*), lay off, make redundant, pension off, remove, sack (*informal*). **3** discard, give up, pooh-pooh (*informal*), reject, set aside, spurn.

dismount *verb* alight, descend, get down, get off.

disobedient *adjective* contrary, defiant, insubordinate, intractable, mutinous, naughty, obstreperous, perverse, rebellious, recalcitrant, refractory, unmanageable, unruly, wayward.

disobey *verb* break, contravene, defy, disregard, flout, ignore, infringe, transgress, violate.

disorder *noun* **1** chaos, confusion, disarray, mess,

muddle, shambles, untidiness. **2** anarchy, bedlam, chaos, commotion, confusion, disturbance, havoc, lawlessness, mayhem, pandemonium, rioting, trouble, turmoil, unrest, uproar. **3** ailment, complaint, condition, disease, illness, malady, sickness. □ **disorderly** adjective **1** chaotic, confused, disorganised, higgledy-piggledy, jumbled, messy, muddled, topsy-turvy, unsystematic, untidy. **2** badly-behaved, boisterous, lawless, obstreperous, riotous, rowdy, turbulent, undisciplined, unruly, wild.

disorganised adjective careless, confused, disorderly, haphazard, messy, slipshod, sloppy, unmethodical, unsystematic.

disown verb cast off, deny, disclaim, ostracise, reject, renounce, repudiate.

disparage verb bag (Australian informal), belittle, criticise, depreciate, knock (informal), rubbish, run down, talk down. □ **disparaging** adjective critical, derogatory, insulting, pejorative, uncomplimentary.

disparity noun contrast, difference, discrepancy, gap, inequality.

dispassionate adjective calm, clinical, composed, disinterested, impartial, neutral, objective, unbiased, unemotional, uninvolved, unprejudiced.

dispatch verb **1** consign, convey, deliver, forward, mail, post, send, transmit. **2** see KILL

dispatch noun bulletin, communication, communiqué, letter, message, report.

dispel verb allay, banish, drive away, remove, scatter.

dispense verb **1** allocate, allot, apportion, deal out, dish out (informal), distribute, dole out, give out, hand out, issue, mete out. **2** make up, prepare, provide, supply. □ **dispense with** dispose of, do without, forgo, get rid of, relinquish.

disperse verb break up, disband, scatter, spread out.

displace verb oust, replace, supersede, supplant.

display verb demonstrate, exhibit, flaunt, manifest, parade, present, reveal, show.

display noun array, demonstration, exhibition, exposition, pageant, presentation, show, spectacle.

displease verb anger, annoy, exasperate, irk, irritate, offend, trouble, upset, vex.

worry. □ **displeasure** noun anger, annoyance, chagrin, disapproval, disfavour, exasperation, indignation, irritation, wrath.

disposable adjective discardable, throw-away.

dispose verb arrange, array, group, marshal, order, organise, place, set out. □ **dispose of** discard, dispatch, ditch (*informal*), dump, get rid of, give away, scrap, sell, throw away, throw out.

disposition noun attitude, character, make-up, nature, personality, spirit, temperament.

disprove verb confute, debunk (*informal*), discredit, explode, negate, rebut, refute.

dispute verb **1** argue, bicker, clash, debate, disagree, haggle, quarrel, squabble, wrangle. **2** challenge, contest, doubt, query, question.

dispute noun altercation, argument, battle, conflict, controversy, debate, disagreement, feud, quarrel, row, squabble, wrangle.

disqualify verb ban, bar, debar, outlaw, preclude, prohibit.

disregard verb brush aside, forget, ignore, neglect, overlook, pay no attention to; see also *DISOBEY*.

disrepair noun decay, dilapidation, neglect, ruin.

disreputable adjective (*a disreputable company*) discreditable, dishonourable, dodgy (*informal*), dubious, notorious, shady, shonky (*Australian informal*), suspect, untrustworthy; (*a disreputable appearance*) dirty, scruffy, seedy, shabby, sleazy, slovenly, unkempt, untidy.

disrespect noun contempt, impiety, impoliteness, insolence, irreverence, rudeness. □ **disrespectful** adjective cheeky, contemptuous, discourteous, impertinent, impolite, impudent, insolent, irreverent, offensive, rude, uncivil.

disrupt verb break up, cut into, disturb, interfere with, interrupt, obstruct, upset.

dissatisfied adjective browned off (*slang*), cheesed off (*slang*), disappointed, discontented, disenchanted, disgruntled, displeased, fed up (*informal*), frustrated, unhappy.

dissect verb cut up, dismember.

disseminate verb broadcast, circulate, distribute, promulgate, publicise, publish, spread.

dissent verb differ, disagree, object, protest.

disservice *noun* bad turn, injury, injustice, unkindness, wrong.

dissident *noun* apostate, dissenter, nonconformist, objector, protester, rebel.

dissipate *verb* **1** clear, disappear, dispel, disperse, evaporate, scatter. **2** blow (*slang*), fritter away, squander, waste.

dissociate *verb* cut off, detach, distance, divorce, isolate, separate.

dissolve *verb* **1** liquefy, melt. **2** annul, break up, cancel, end, sever, terminate, wind up.

dissuade *verb* (*dissuade from*) advise against, deter from, discourage from, put off.

distance *noun* gap, haul, interval, length, range, space, span, stretch.

distant *adjective* **1** far, far-away, far-flung, far-off, outlying, remote. **2** aloof, cold, cool, detached, estranged, formal, offhand, remote, reserved, stand-offish, unfriendly, withdrawn.

distasteful *adjective* detestable, disagreeable, disgusting, loathsome, nauseating, objectionable, offensive, off-putting, repugnant, repulsive, revolting, sickening, unpalatable, unpleasant, vile.

distend *verb* bloat, bulge, enlarge, expand, puff up, swell up.

distinct *adjective* **1** clear, clear-cut, definite, marked, noticeable, obvious, plain, pronounced, sharp, strong, unmistakable. **2** different, discrete, individual, separate, unconnected.

distinction *noun* **1** contrast, difference. **2** class, eminence, excellence, fame, merit, note, prestige, prominence, quality, renown, superiority, worth.

distinctive *adjective* characteristic, different, distinguishing, idiosyncratic, individual, peculiar, personal, singular, special, specific, unique.

distinguish *verb* **1** characterise, differentiate, discriminate, identify, mark, separate, set apart, single out, tell apart. **2** discern, identify, make out, perceive, pick out, recognise.

distinguished *adjective* celebrated, eminent, famed, famous, great, illustrious, important, legendary, notable, noted, outstanding, pre-eminent, prominent, renowned, respected, well-known.

distort *verb* **1** bend, buckle, contort, deform, skew, twist, warp. **2** colour, falsify, garble, misrepresent, pervert, slant, twist.

distract verb divert, draw away, sidetrack.

distraction noun amusement, diversion, entertainment, escape, pastime, recreation.

distraught adjective agitated, distressed, frantic, hysterical, overwrought, upset.

distress noun adversity, affliction, agony, anguish, danger, difficulty, discomfort, misery, pain, sorrow, suffering, torment, torture, trouble, woe.

distress verb afflict, bother, dismay, disturb, grieve, hurt, pain, perturb, sadden, shake, shock, torment, torture, trouble, upset, worry. □ **distressing** adjective appalling, disturbing, grievous, harrowing, heartbreaking, heart-rending, horrific, painful, pathetic, poignant, sad, terrible, tragic, traumatic, upsetting.

distribute verb allocate, allot, apportion, assign, circulate, deal out, deliver, dish out (informal), dispense, divide up, dole out, give out, hand out, issue, mete out, pass round, serve, share out.

district noun area, community, electorate (Australian), locality, municipality, neighbourhood, place, precinct, province, quarter, region, sector, shire, suburb, territory, vicinity, ward, zone.

distrust noun doubt, mistrust, scepticism, suspicion. □ **distrustful** adjective chary, mistrustful, paranoid, sceptical, suspicious, wary.

distrust verb be wary of, doubt, have misgivings about, mistrust, question, suspect.

disturb verb **1** annoy, bother, disrupt, hassle (informal), interrupt, pester. **2** agitate, alarm, churn up, discomfit, disconcert, distress, fluster, perturb, rattle (informal), ruffle, shake, startle, trouble, unsettle, upset, worry. □ **disturbance** noun commotion, fracas, hullabaloo, kerfuffle (informal), racket, riot, row, rumpus, stir, to-do, trouble, tumult, turmoil, unrest, uproar.

disused adjective abandoned, idle, neglected, obsolete.

ditch noun channel, drain, dyke, gutter, moat, trench.

ditch verb abandon, dice (Australian informal), discard, drop, dump (informal), get rid of, reject.

dither verb hesitate, hum and haw, shilly-shally, vacillate, waver.

dive verb **1** dip, plunge, submerge. **2** descend, drop, nosedive, pitch, plummet, plunge, swoop. □ **dive** noun header, nosedive, plunge.

diverge verb **1** branch, divide, fork, separate, split. **2** depart, deviate, digress, stray, turn aside.

diverse adjective assorted, different, heterogeneous, miscellaneous, mixed, motley, varied, various.

diversion noun **1** bypass, detour, deviation. **2** amusement, distraction, entertainment, escape, game, hobby, pastime, recreation, sport.

divert verb **1** deflect, redirect, shunt, sidetrack, switch, turn aside. **2** amuse, cheer up, distract, entertain, interest, occupy.

divide verb **1** bifurcate, branch, break up, carve up, cut up, diverge, fork, joint, part, partition, separate, split, subdivide. **2** allot, apportion, deal out, dish out (informal), distribute, dole out, parcel out, share. **3** arrange, categorise, class, classify, group, sort.

divine adjective celestial, godlike, heavenly, holy, sacred, spiritual, superhuman, supernatural.

division noun **1** allocation, distribution, partition, separa-

tion, sharing, splitting. **2** branch, compartment, department, part, section, sector, segment, subdivision.

divorce verb break up, part, separate, split up.

divulge verb betray, blab, blow (slang), disclose, expose, give away, impart, leak, let out, let slip, make known, publish, reveal, tell.

dizzy adjective faint, giddy, light-headed, reeling, unsteady, woozy (informal). □ **dizziness** noun faintness, giddiness, light-headedness, vertigo.

do verb **1** accomplish, carry out, complete, execute, fulfil, perform, undertake. **2** make, prepare, produce, turn out. **3** attend to, deal with, handle, look after, manage, see to. **4** answer, solve, work out. **5** act, behave, conduct yourself, practise. **6** fare, get on, make out. **7** be acceptable, be adequate, be enough, be satisfactory, be sufficient, be suitable, suffice. □ **do with** abolish, axe, discard, get rid of, scrap, stop. □ **do up 1** buckle, fasten, lace up, zip. **2** redecorate, refurbish, renovate, repair, restore. □ **do without** abstain from, dispense with, forgo, go without.

do noun event, function, occasion, party, reception.

dob verb □ **dob in** blow the whistle on, denounce, grass (on) (slang), inform on, report, shelf (Australian slang), shop (slang), split on (slang), tell on.

docile adjective biddable, compliant, gentle, manageable, meek, mild, obedient, passive, submissive, tame, tractable.

dock noun berth, jetty, landing stage, pier, quay, slipway, wharf; (docks) dockyard, harbour, marina, port, shipyard.

dock verb berth, moor, put in.

docker noun longshoreman, stevedore, watersider (Australian), waterside worker, wharfie (Australian informal), wharf labourer.

docket noun invoice, receipt.

doctor noun consultant, general practitioner, GP, intern, locum, medical practitioner, medico (informal), physician, quack (slang), registrar, specialist, surgeon.

doctrine noun belief, conviction, credo, creed, dogma, philosophy, precept, principle, teaching, tenet.

document noun certificate, charter, contract, deed, form, instrument, licence, paper, policy, record, report.

doddery adjective decrepit, frail, infirm, shaky, tottering, trembling, unsteady.

dodge verb avoid, bob, duck, escape, evade, sidestep, skirt round, swerve, veer.

dodge noun lurk (Australian informal), racket, rort (Australian slang), ruse, scam (slang), trick.

dog noun bitch (female), cur, hound, mongrel, mutt (informal), pooch (slang), pup, puppy, whelp.

dogged adjective determined, firm, obstinate, patient, persistent, pertinacious, resolute, single-minded, stubborn, tenacious, unwavering.

dogma noun belief, credo, creed, doctrine, principle, teaching, tenet.

dogmatic adjective assertive, authoritative, categorical, cocksure, dictatorial, opinionated, peremptory.

dole verb (dole out) allocate, allot, apportion, deal out, deliver, dish out (informal), dispense, distribute, give out, hand out, issue, mete out, share out.

dole noun benefit, social security, unemployment benefit.

doleful adjective dismal, down in the dumps (informal),

gloomy, glum, lugubrious, melancholy, mournful, rueful, sad, sorrowful, unhappy, woebegone.

domain *noun* dominion, empire, kingdom, land, province, realm, territory.

dome *noun* cupola.

domestic *adjective* **1** family, home, household. **2** domesticated, house-trained, pet, tame.

domicile *noun* abode (*old use*), accommodation, address, dwelling, habitation, home, house, residence.

dominate *verb* control, govern, monopolise, rule. □ **dominant** *adjective* chief, commanding, controlling, influential, leading, main, outstanding, paramount, predominant, prevailing, principal, ruling.

domineering *adjective* authoritarian, bossy, dictatorial, imperious, masterful, overbearing, peremptory, tyrannical.

dominion *noun* **1** ascendancy, authority, control, jurisdiction, power, rule, sovereignty, supremacy, sway. **2** domain, empire, kingdom, realm, state, territory.

donate *verb* bequeath, bestow, chip in (*informal*), contribute, fork out (*slang*), give, grant,

present, provide, subscribe □ **donation** *noun* alms (*old use*), bequest, contribution, gift, handout, offering, present, subscription.

donkey *noun* ass, jackass (*male*), jenny (*female*).

donor *noun* benefactor, contributor, giver, provider, sponsor.

doom *noun* death, destiny, destruction, end, fate, fortune, lot, ruin.

doom *verb* condemn, destine, fate, ordain, predestine.

door *noun* doorway, entrance, entry, exit, gate, hatch, portal, trapdoor.

doorstep *noun* step, threshold.

dope *noun* **1** drug, narcotic, opiate. **2** ass (*informal*), clot (*informal*), fool, idiot (*informal*), imbecile, mug (*informal*), nincompoop, twit (*slang*). □ **dopey** *adjective* **1** groggy, half asleep, sleepy, somnolent. **2** dumb (*informal*), foolish, idiotic, imprudent, reckless, senseless, silly, stupid, unwise.

dope *verb* anaesthetise, drug, sedate.

dormant *adjective* **1** asleep, comatose, hibernating, resting, sleeping. **2** inactive, inert, latent, quiescent.

dose *noun* amount, dosage, measure, portion, quantity.

dossier *noun* file, records.

dot *noun* fleck, mark, point, speck, speckle, spot.

dot *verb* fleck, speckle, spot, stipple.

dote *verb* □ **dote on** adore, cherish, idolise, love, treasure, worship.

double *adjective* dual, duplicate, paired, twin, twofold.

double *noun* clone, copy, dead spit, duplicate, look-alike, ringer (*informal*), spitting image, twin.

double *verb* dink (*Australian*), dinky (*Australian*), donkey (*Australian*), double-bank (*Australian*), double-dink (*Australian*).

double-cross *verb* betray, cheat, deceive, trick.

doubt *noun* disbelief, distrust, hesitation, incredulity, misgiving, mistrust, qualm, question, reservation, scepticism, suspicion, uncertainty.

doubt *verb* distrust, mistrust, question, suspect.

doubtful *adjective* distrustful, dubious, hesitant, mistrustful, sceptical, suspicious, uncertain, undecided, unsure.

dour *adjective* forbidding, gloomy, grim, harsh, morose, severe, stern, sullen, unfriendly.

douse *verb* drench, immerse, saturate, soak, submerge, wet.

dowdy *adjective* daggy (*Australian informal*), drab, dull, frumpish, old-fashioned, shabby, sloppy, unattractive, unfashionable.

down *noun* feathers, fluff, plumage.

downcast *adjective* blue, crestfallen, dejected, depressed, despondent, disconsolate, discouraged, disheartened, dispirited, down, downhearted, down in the dumps, gloomy, heavy-hearted, low, melancholy, miserable, sad, unhappy, wretched.

downfall *noun* collapse, destruction, fall, ruin, undoing.

downpour *noun* cloudburst, deluge, rainstorm, shower, storm.

downright *adjective* absolute, arrant, complete, out-and-out, outright, pure, sheer, thorough, utter.

doze *verb* drop off, kip (*slang*), nap, nod off, sleep, slumber, snooze.

drab *adjective* cheerless, colourless, dingy, dismal, dreary, dull, sombre, unattractive.

draft noun outline, plan, sketch.

draft verb **1** draw up, frame, outline, plan. **2** call up, conscript.

drag verb draw, haul, lug, pull, tow, tug. □ **drag out** draw out, extend, prolong, protract, spin out.

drag noun bind (informal), bore, nuisance, pain in the neck (informal), strain.

drain noun channel, conduit, culvert, ditch, gutter, outlet, pipe, sewer, trench.

drain verb **1** draw off, empty, pour off, remove, siphon off. **2** discharge, empty, flow out, seep out, trickle away. **3** consume, deplete, exhaust, sap, spend, use up.

drama noun **1** play, show. **2** acting, dramatics, stagecraft, theatre. **3** action, excitement, suspense.

dramatic adjective **1** stage, theatrical. **2** impressive, marked, noticeable, radical, spectacular, startling, striking.

dramatist noun playwright, screenwriter, scriptwriter.

drastic adjective desperate, dire, extreme, radical, severe, strong.

draught noun breeze, wind.

draw verb **1** delineate, depict, doodle, illustrate, outline, picture, portray, represent, scribble, sketch, trace. **2** drag, haul, lug, pull, tow, tug. **3** extract, remove, pull out, take out. **4** attract, bring in, entice, lure, pull. **5** be equal, tie. **6** deduce, gather, infer, make out, work out. □ **draw back** cringe, recoil, retreat, shrink back, withdraw. □ **draw out** drag out, extend, lengthen, prolong, protract, spin out. □ **draw up 1** come to a halt, come to a stop, halt, pull up, stop. **2** compose, draft, formulate, prepare, write out.

draw noun **1** attraction, drawcard, enticement, lure. **2** dead heat, deadlock, stalemate, tie.

drawback noun catch, disadvantage, handicap, hindrance, inconvenience, liability, minus, shortcoming.

drawing noun cartoon, chart, design, diagram, illustration, pattern, picture, plan, portrait, sketch.

drawing room parlour (old use), reception room, salon, sitting room.

dread noun alarm, anxiety, apprehension, consternation, dismay, fear, foreboding, horror, panic, terror, trepidation.

dread verb be afraid of, be scared of, fear.

dreadful *adjective* **1** appalling, awful, calamitous, catastrophic, dire, disastrous, fearful, frightful, ghastly, grisly, hideous, horrendous, horrible, horrific, shocking, terrible, tragic. **2** see *BAD*.

dream *noun* **1** daydream, fantasy, hallucination, illusion, nightmare, reverie, trance, vision. **2** ambition, aspiration, desire, goal, hope, wish.

dream *verb* daydream, fancy, fantasise, hallucinate, imagine. □ **dream up** conceive, concoct, create, devise, hatch, imagine, invent, think up.

dreary *adjective* **1** boring, deadly (*informal*), dull, humdrum, lacklustre, lifeless, monotonous, mundane, stodgy, tedious, tiresome, uninteresting. **2** bleak, cheerless, colourless, depressing, dingy, dismal, drab, dull, gloomy, miserable, sombre.

dregs *plural noun* deposit, grounds, lees, remains, residue, sediment.

drench *verb* douse, saturate, soak, souse, wet.

dress *noun* **1** frock, gown, kimono, robe, sari. **2** apparel (*formal*), attire (*formal*), clobber (*slang*), clothes, clothing, costume, garb, garments, gear (*informal*), getup (*informal*), outfit, raiment, rig (*informal*), togs (*informal*), vestments, wear.

dress *verb* **1** array, attire, clothe, deck out, doll up (*informal*), robe. **2** bandage, bind.

dresser *noun* buffet, cupboard, sideboard.

dressing *noun* **1** bandage, plaster, poultice. **2** mayonnaise, sauce, vinaigrette.

dressing gown bath robe, brunch coat, housecoat, negligée, robe, wrapper.

dressmaker *noun* couturier, couturière, seamstress, tailor.

dribble *verb* drool, salivate, slaver, slobber.

dried *adjective* dehydrated, desiccated.

drift *verb* **1** coast, float, waft. **2** meander, mosey (*slang*), ramble, roam, rove, saunter, stray, wander.

drift *noun* **1** movement, shift, tide. **2** gist, meaning, point, tenor, trend.

drill *noun* exercises, practice, training.

drill *verb* **1** bore, penetrate, pierce. **2** coach, instruct, teach, train.

drink *verb* down, drain, gulp, guzzle, lap, quaff, sip, swallow, swig (*informal*), swill.

drink *noun* **1** beverage, liquid, refreshment. **2** gulp, mouthful, sip, swallow, swig (*informal*). **3** alcohol, booze (*informal*), grog (*Australian*), liquor.

drip *verb* dribble, drizzle, filter, leak, sprinkle, trickle.

drip *noun* drop, droplet, splash.

drive *verb* **1** herd, propel, push, send, urge. **2** control, guide, handle, operate, pilot, steer. **3** compel, constrain, force, impel, motivate, oblige, pressure, push, spur. □ **driver** *noun* chauffeur, motorist.

drive *noun* **1** excursion, jaunt, journey, outing, run, spin, trip. **2** ambition, determination, energy, enterprise, enthusiasm, go, initiative, motivation, push, vigour, zeal. **3** campaign, crusade, push.

drizzly *adjective* damp, misty, rainy, showery, wet.

droll *adjective* see *FUNNY*.

drone *verb* buzz, hum, purr, whirr.

drool *verb* dribble, salivate, slaver, slobber.

droop *verb* dangle, flop, hang down, sag, wilt, wither.

drop *noun* **1** bead, drip, droplet, globule, spot, splash, sprinkling; see also *DASH*. **2** cut, decline, decrease, fall, reduction, slump. **3** descent, precipice, slope.

drop *verb* **1** collapse, descend, dive, fall, nosedive, plummet, plunge, sink, slump, tumble. **2** let fall, let go of, release. **3** decline, decrease, diminish, lower, reduce. **4** eliminate, exclude, leave out, omit. **5** abandon, desert, discard, ditch (*informal*), dump, forsake, give up, jilt, leave, reject, scrap. □ **drop in** call in, look in, pop in, visit. □ **drop off** doze, drowse, fall asleep, kip (*slang*), nap, nod off, sleep, snooze.

drove *noun* crowd, flock, herd, horde, mob, swarm.

drown *verb* drench, engulf, flood, inundate, submerge, swamp.

drowsy *adjective* dopey (*informal*), dozy, lethargic, sleepy, somnolent, tired, weary.

drudge *noun* dogsbody (*informal*), hack, labourer, menial, servant, worker.

drug *noun* medicament, medication, medicine, pill.

drug *verb* anaesthetise, dope, knock out (*informal*), sedate, stupefy.

drum *noun* **1** bongo, kettle drum, side drum, snare drum, tabor, tambour, timpano, tom

tom. **2** barrel, cask, container, cylinder, keg, tub. **3** bluey (*Australian*), matilda (*Australian*), shiralee (*Australian*), swag (*Australian*).

drum *verb* beat, pound, rap, tap, thump. □ **drummer** *noun* timpanist.

drunk *adjective* drunken, full (*slang*), full as a goog (*Australian slang*), happy (*informal*), inebriated, intoxicated, jolly (*informal*), legless (*slang*), merry (*informal*), paralytic (*informal*), pickled (*slang*), plastered (*slang*), shickered (*Australian slang*), sloshed (*slang*), smashed (*slang*), sozzled (*slang*), tanked (*slang*), tiddly (*informal*), tipsy, under the influence (*informal*), under the weather.

drunkard *noun* alcoholic, boozer (*informal*), dipsomaniac, drunk (*informal*), soak (*informal*), sot, tippler, wino (*informal*).

dry *adjective* **1** arid, bone-dry, dehydrated, desiccated, parched, scorched, waterless. **2** dehydrated, parched, thirsty. **3** boring, dull, prosaic, tedious, uninteresting. **4** ironic, laconic, subtle, wry.

dry *verb* dehydrate, desiccate, shrivel, wilt, wither.

dual *adjective* binary, double, twin, twofold.

dub *verb* christen, name, nickname, rename.

dubious *adjective* **1** disbelieving, distrustful, doubtful, mistrustful, sceptical, suspicious, uncertain, unsure. **2** dodgy (*informal*), fishy (*informal*), questionable, shady, suspect, suspicious, unreliable, untrustworthy.

duck *noun* drake (*male*), duckling (*young*).

duck *verb* **1** bend down, bob down, crouch, stoop. **2** bob, dip, dive, plunge, submerge. **3** avoid, dodge, evade, get out of, shirk, sidestep.

duct *noun* canal, channel, conduit, pipe, tube.

dud *adjective* bung (*Australian informal*), defective, inoperative, unusable, useless, worthless.

due *adjective* **1** expected, scheduled. **2** outstanding, owed, owing, payable, unpaid. **3** adequate, appropriate, deserved, fitting, merited, proper, rightful, suitable.

due *noun* **1** deserts, entitlement, right. **2** (*dues*) fee, levy, sub (*informal*), subscription.

duel *noun* combat, contest, fight.

duffer noun clot (*informal*), fool, goose (*informal*), idiot, mug (*informal*), muggins (*informal*), nincompoop, nitwit (*informal*), silly, twit (*slang*).

dull adjective **1** cloudy, dismal, gloomy, grey, overcast, sunless; (*dull colours*) dark, dingy, drab, dreary, faded, flat, matt, sombre, subdued, tarnished. **2** bovine, dense, dim, dumb (*informal*), obtuse, slow, stupid, thick. **3** bland, boring, dreary, dry, humdrum, lacklustre, lifeless, monotonous, mundane, ordinary, prosaic, routine, stodgy, tedious, tiresome, unimaginative, uninteresting, vapid. **4** (*a dull knife*) blunt, blunted; (*a dull sound*) deadened, indistinct, muffled, muted. □ **dull** verb deaden, numb, relieve, soothe, subdue.

dumb adjective **1** mute, silent, speechless, tongue-tied. **2** dense, dim (*informal*), foolish, obtuse, slow, stupid, thick, unintelligent.

dumbfounded adjective amazed, astonished, astounded, confounded, flabbergasted, nonplussed, speechless, staggered, stunned, surprised, thunderstruck.

dummy noun **1** lay figure, mannequin, model. **2** pacifier.

dump noun garbage dump, garbage tip, rubbish tip, scrap heap, tip.

dump verb **1** chuck ou (*informal*), discard, dispose of ditch (*informal*), get rid of offload, scrap, throw out. **2** deposit, drop, place, plonk, pu down, set down, throw down unload.

dumpy adjective chubby, fat plump, podgy, pudgy, rotund squat, stout, tubby.

dunce noun blockhead, bone head, clot (*informal*), dil (*Australian informal*), dimwi (*informal*), dolt, dop (*informal*), dullard, dumm (*informal*), dunderhead, fool half-wit, idiot, ignoramus imbecile, moron (*informal*) nincompoop, nitwit (*informal*, nong (*Australian informal*) simpleton, twit (*slang*).

dung noun droppings, excre ment, faeces, manure, muck.

dungeon noun cell, lock-up prison.

dunk verb dip, immerse, sop.

dupe verb bluff, cheat, co (*informal*), deceive, delude fool, hoax, hoodwink, ki (*informal*), mislead, strin along (*informal*), suck i (*informal*), swindle, take in trick.

duplicate *noun* clone, copy, double, facsimile, photocopy, replica, reproduction, twin.

duplicate *verb* copy, photocopy, replicate, reproduce.

durable *adjective* hard-wearing, indestructible, long-lasting, serviceable, solid, stout, strong, sturdy, tough.

duration *noun* length, period, span, term, time.

duress *noun* coercion, compulsion, force, pressure, threat.

dusk *noun* evening, gloaming, nightfall, sundown, sunset, twilight.

dust *noun* bulldust (*Australian*), dirt, grime, grit, powder, sawdust, soot.

dust *verb* **1** brush, clean, wipe. **2** dredge, sprinkle.

dust storm Darling shower (*Australian*), dust devil, sandstorm, willy willy (*Australian*).

dutiful *adjective* compliant, conscientious, devoted, diligent, faithful, loyal, obedient, reliable, responsible.

duty *noun* **1** allegiance, loyalty, obligation, responsibility. **2** assignment, charge, chore, function, job, office, role, task. **3** customs, excise, levy, tariff, tax, toll.

dwarf *noun* elf, gnome, leprechaun, midget, pygmy, troll.

dwarf *verb* dominate, overshadow, tower over.

dwell *verb* abide (*old use*), live, reside; see also *INHABIT*. □ **dwell on** concentrate on, focus on, harp on, linger over.

dwelling *noun* abode (*old use*), domicile, habitation, home, house, lodging, residence; see also *FLAT*, *HOUSE*.

dwindle *verb* contract, decline, decrease, diminish, lessen, reduce, shrink, wane.

dye *verb* colour, paint, stain, tint.

dye *noun* colour, colouring, pigment, stain, tint.

dyke *noun* **1** embankment, levee, stopbank, wall. **2** canal, channel, ditch, furrow, gutter, watercourse.

dynamic *adjective* active, energetic, forceful, go-ahead, high-powered, lively, powerful, progressive, vigorous.

dynasty *noun* family, house, line, lineage.

Ee

eager *adjective* ardent, avid, bursting, desirous, earnest, enthusiastic, fervent, impatient, interested, itching, keen, longing, motivated, passionate, raring (*informal*), willing, yearning, zealous. □ **eagerness** *noun* alacrity, ardour, desire, earnestness, enthusiasm, fervour, hunger, impatience, keenness, longing, readiness, yearning, zeal.

early *adjective* **1** premature. **2** beginning, first, initial, preliminary. □ **early** *adverb* ahead of time, prematurely, too soon.

earmark *verb* assign, designate, reserve, set aside, specify, tag.

earn *verb* **1** bring in, clear, collect, draw, get, gross, make, net, obtain, rake in (*informal*), receive, take home, work for. **2** be entitled to, be worthy of, deserve, gain, merit, win.

earnest *adjective* ardent, conscientious, determined, diligent, fervent, grave, heartfelt, impassioned, intense, passionate, serious, sincere, sober, solemn, staid, strong, thoughtful, wholehearted, zealous.

earnings *plural noun* income, pay, remuneration, salary, wages.

earth *noun* **1** globe, planet, world. **2** clay, dirt, ground, land, loam, soil.

earthenware *noun* ceramics, crockery, pottery, terracotta.

earthly *adjective* mortal, mundane, physical, secular, terrestrial, worldly.

earthquake *noun* quake (*informal*), shock, tremor.

ease *noun* **1** deftness, dexterity, effortlessness, facility, simplicity. **2** comfort, contentment, leisure, luxury, prosperity, relaxation, repose, rest.

ease *verb* **1** allay, alleviate, assuage, calm, lessen, lighten, mitigate, pacify, palliate, quell, quieten, reduce, relax, relieve, soothe, still, subdue. **2** abate, diminish, let up, moderate, slacken.

easy *adjective* **1** effortless, elementary, foolproof, light, painless, simple, straightforward, uncomplicated, undemanding, user-friendly. **2** carefree, comfortable, cosy, cushy (*informal*), leisurely, peaceful, relaxed, restful, soft (*informal*), tranquil, untroubled.

easygoing *adjective* calm, carefree, casual, even-tempered, happy-go-lucky, indulgent, laid-back (*informal*), lenient, liberal, nonchalant, open-minded, permissive, placid, relaxed, soft, tolerant, unflappable (*informal*).

eat *verb* **1** bite, bolt, chew, chomp, consume, devour, feast on, feed on, gnaw, gobble gorge, gulp, guzzle, ingest, knock back (*informal*), masticate, munch, nibble, partake of, peck, pick at, polish off, scoff, stuff, swallow, tuck in (*informal*), wolf. **2** breakfast, dine, lunch, snack, sup. **3** consume, corrode, destroy, erode, make a hole in, rot, use up, wear away.

eatable *adjective* digestible, edible.

eavesdrop *verb* bug (*informal*), listen in, monitor, overhear, tap.

ebb *verb* **1** flow back, go out, recede, retreat, subside. **2** decline, decrease, diminish, dwindle, fade, wane, weaken.

eccentric *adjective* abnormal, bizarre, cranky, dotty (*informal*), freakish, idiosyncratic, irregular, nutty (*informal*), odd, offbeat, outlandish, peculiar, queer, singular, strange, unconventional, unusual, way-out, weird, zany. □ **eccentric** *noun* character, crackpot (*informal*), crank, dag (*Australian informal*), dingbat (*informal*), freak, hard case (*Australian informal*), nonconformist, nut (*informal*), oddball (*informal*), oddity, screwball (*informal*), weirdo (*informal*).

echo *noun* resonance, reverberation.

echo *verb* **1** reflect, resound, reverberate. **2** ape, copy, imitate, mimic, parrot, repeat, reproduce.

eclipse *noun* blocking out, covering, darkening, obscuring, shadowing.

eclipse *verb* exceed, outshine, overshadow, surpass.

economic *adjective* **1** budgetary, financial, fiscal, monetary, trade. **2** cost-effective, profitable.

economical *adjective* careful, frugal, provident, sparing, thrifty.

economise *verb* be economical, conserve, cut back, cut costs, retrench, save, scrimp, skimp, stint, tighten your belt.

ecstasy *noun* bliss, delight, elation, euphoria, happiness, joy, rapture. □ **ecstatic** *adjective* blissful, delighted, elated, euphoric, exultant, happy, joyful, overjoyed, over the moon, rapt, rapturous.

eddy *noun* swirl, vortex, whirl, whirlpool.

edge *noun* border, boundary, brim, brink, circumference, end, extremity, fringe, kerb, limit, lip, margin, outskirts, perimeter, periphery, rim, selvedge, side, verge.

edge *verb* **1** bind, border, fringe, hem, trim. **2** crawl, creep, inch, sidle, slink, steal, worm.

edgy *adjective* anxious, irritable, jittery (*informal*), jumpy, nervous, nervy, on edge, on tenterhooks, tense, uptight (*informal*).

edible *adjective* digestible, eatable.

edifice *noun* building, construction, structure.

edify *verb* see EDUCATE.

edit *verb* adapt, adjust, alter, assemble, check, collate, compile, correct, modify, polish, put together, revise, rewrite.

edition *noun* **1** copy, form, version. **2** issue, number, publication.

educate *verb* bring up, coach, edify, enlighten, indoctrinate, inform, instruct, nurture, rear, school, teach, train, tutor. □ **educated** *adjective* cultivated, cultured, enlightened, erudite, informed, knowledgeable, learned, literate, scholarly.

education *noun* cultivation, development, edification, enlightenment, instruction, schooling, teaching, training, tuition, upbringing. □ **educational** *adjective* **1** academic, pedagogical, scholastic. **2** edifying, educative, enlightening, informative, instructive.

eerie *adjective* creepy, frightening, ghostly, mysterious, scary, spooky (*informal*), uncanny, weird.

efface *verb* delete, erase, expunge, obliterate, rub out, wipe out.

effect *noun* **1** consequence, impact, outcome, repercussion, result, upshot. **2** illusion, impression, sensation.

effect *verb* accomplish, achieve, bring about, cause, perform, produce.

effective *adjective* **1** capable, competent, effectual, efficient, productive, strong, successful. **2** compelling, convincing, forceful, impressive, persuasive, potent, powerful, striking, successful.

effeminate *adjective* camp, unmanly, womanish.

effervescent *adjective* aerated, bubbly, carbonated, fizzy, foaming, gassy, sparkling.

efficient *adjective* businesslike, capable, competent, effective, effectual, organised, productive, proficient, skilful.

effigy *noun* dummy, figure, guy, image, likeness, model, puppet, statue.

effort noun **1** elbow grease, energy, exertion, labour, pains, strain, struggle, toil, trouble, work. **2** attempt, endeavour, try.

effortless adjective cushy (informal), easy, painless, simple, undemanding.

egg verb (egg on) encourage, goad, incite, prompt, push, sool on (Australian informal), spur on, urge.

egotistic adjective conceited, egocentric, egotistical, narcissistic, proud, self-centred, self-important, vain.

eiderdown noun continental quilt, Doona (trade mark), duvet, quilt.

eject verb **1** discharge, emit, expel, send out, spew, spit out (informal). **2** banish, chuck out (informal), evict, expel, get rid of, kick out (informal), oust, remove, throw out, turf out (informal), turn out.

elaborate adjective busy, complex, complicated, detailed, fancy, fussy, intricate, involved, ornate, showy, sophisticated.

elaborate verb enlarge on, expand (on), flesh out, work out.

elapse verb go by, pass, roll by, slip by.

elastic adjective expandable, resilient, rubbery, springy, stretchy.

elated adjective chuffed (slang), delighted, ecstatic, enraptured, euphoric, exhilarated, exultant, happy, joyful, jubilant, overjoyed, over the moon, rapt, rapturous, thrilled.

elbow verb jostle, nudge, push, shove, thrust.

elder noun senior.

elderly adjective aged, ageing, old, oldish, retired, senior.

eldest adjective first-born, oldest.

elect verb appoint, choose, opt for, pick, select, vote for.

election noun ballot, poll, vote.

electorate noun **1** constituents, electors, people, voters. **2** constituency, seat.

elegant adjective chic, dignified, fashionable, graceful, gracious, grand, handsome, luxurious, opulent, plush, posh (informal), refined, smart, stately, stylish, sumptuous, tasteful.

elegy noun dirge, lament, requiem.

element noun **1** component, constituent, factor, ingredient, member, part, unit. **2** (elements) basics, essentials, fundamentals, principles, rudiments.

elementary *adjective* basic, fundamental, introductory, primary, rudimentary, simple.

elevate *verb* boost, exalt, lift, promote, raise, upgrade, uplift. □ **elevation** *noun* altitude, height.

elf *noun* fairy, gnome, goblin, gremlin (*informal*), hobgoblin, imp, leprechaun, pixie, spirit, sprite.

elicit *verb* call forth, draw out, evoke, extract, get, obtain.

eligible *adjective* acceptable, allowed, authorised, entitled, qualified, suitable.

eliminate *verb* abolish, cut out, delete, destroy, do away with, eradicate, exclude, exterminate, get rid of, omit, remove, root out, stamp out, weed out.

elite *noun* best, choice, chosen, cream, pick.

ellipse *noun* oval.

elocution *noun* articulation, delivery, diction, enunciation, oratory, public speaking, speech.

elongated *adjective* drawn out, extended, lengthened, protracted, stretched out.

eloquent *adjective* articulate, expressive, fluent, forceful, persuasive, powerful.

elude *verb* avoid, dodge, escape from, evade, give the slip to, shake off. □ **elusive** *adjective* fugitive, indefinable, intangible, subtle, transient.

emaciated *adjective* cadaverous, gaunt, scrawny, skinny, thin.

emanate *verb* come, flow, issue, originate, proceed, spring, stem.

emancipate *verb* deliver, free, liberate, release, set free.

embankment *noun* bank, levee, stopbank.

embark *verb* board ship, get on, go aboard. □ **embark on** begin, commence, enter on, start, undertake.

embarrass *verb* abash, chagrin, discomfit, disconcert, distress, humiliate, mortify, shame. □ **embarrassed** *adjective* abashed, ashamed, awkward, chagrined, discomfited, disconcerted, distressed, humiliated, mortified, self-conscious, shamefaced, sheepish, uncomfortable.

embed *verb* fix, implant, insert, lodge, set, stick.

embellish *verb* **1** adorn, beautify, decorate, dress up, enhance, ornament, prettify, tizzy (*Australian*). **2** embroider, enhance, exaggerate, improve upon.

embers *plural noun* cinders, coals.

embezzle *verb* misappropriate, steal.

emblem *noun* badge, coat of arms, crest, device, hallmark, insignia, logo, seal, sign, symbol.

embody *verb* **1** exemplify, express, represent. **2** contain, include, incorporate, integrate. □ **embodiment** *noun* epitome, model, personification, quintessence, soul.

embrace *verb* clasp, cuddle, enfold, hold, hug.

embroider *verb* **1** sew, stitch, work. **2** embellish, enhance, improve upon. □ **embroidery** *noun* needlework, sewing.

embroil *verb* entangle, involve, mix up.

embryonic *adjective* early, immature, incipient, rudimentary, undeveloped.

emerge *verb* **1** appear, come out, materialise, peep out, show up, surface. **2** become apparent, become known, be revealed, come out, come to light, transpire, turn out.

emergency *noun* crisis, danger, difficulty, predicament.

emigrate *verb* depart, leave, migrate, move, quit, relocate. □ **emigrant** *noun* émigré, expatriate, refugee, settler.

eminence *noun* celebrity, distinction, fame, importance, note, pre-eminence, prominence, renown, repute, standing, stature.

eminent *adjective* celebrated, distinguished, famous, great, illustrious, important, notable, noted, outstanding, pre-eminent, prominent, renowned, respected, well-known.

emit *verb* beam, discharge, expel, exude, give off, give out, issue, leak, ooze, pour forth, radiate, send out, shed, transmit.

emotion *noun* feeling, passion, sentiment. □ **emotional** *adjective* ardent, demonstrative, excitable, fervent, passionate, sensitive, sentimental, temperamental.

emotive *adjective* emotional, impassioned, moving, passionate, poignant, sentimental, stirring, touching.

emperor *noun* Caesar, czar, head of state, kaiser, mikado, monarch, ruler, sovereign, tsar.

emphasis *noun* accent, attention, importance, priority, prominence, stress, weight.

emphasise *verb* accent, accentuate, draw attention to, highlight, impress, insist on, point up, stress, underline.

emphatic *adjective* categorical, decisive, definite, forceful, strong, unequivocal, vigorous.

empire *noun* domain, dominion, kingdom, realm, territory.

employ *verb* **1** appoint, contract, engage, give work to, hire, sign up, take on. **2** apply, make use of, use, utilise. □ **employer** *noun* **1** boss, chief, manager, master, proprietor. **2** business, company, corporation, establishment, firm, organisation. □ **employment** *noun* business, calling, career, job, occupation, profession, pursuit, trade, vocation, work.

employee *noun* hand, wage-earner, worker; (*employees*) human resources, labour, personnel, staff, workforce.

empower *verb* authorise, commission, enable, equip, give power to, license.

empty *adjective* **1** bare, blank, clean, clear, hollow, unfilled, unfurnished, unused, void. **2** deserted, uninhabited, unoccupied, vacant. **3** hollow, idle, insincere, insubstantial, meaningless, vain.

empty *verb* clear, drain, evacuate, pour out, remove, tip out.

enable *verb* allow, assist, authorise, entitle, facilitate, let, license, permit, qualify.

enact *verb* **1** decree, legislate, ordain, pass. **2** act out, perform, play.

enchant *verb* bewitch, captivate, charm, delight, enrapture, enthral, entrance, fascinate, hold spellbound, hypnotise, mesmerise, thrill. □ **enchanter** *noun* magician, sorcerer, warlock, wizard. □ **enchantress** *noun* magician, siren, sorceress, witch.

encircle *verb* besiege, circle, enclose, encompass, hem in, ring, surround.

enclose *verb* **1** box in, circle, close in, confine, cordon off, encircle, encompass, fence in, pen, restrict, ring, shut in, surround, wall in. **2** include, insert, send with.

enclosure *noun* cage, compound, coop, corral, fold, hutch, paddock, pen, pound, run, stall, sty, yard.

encompass *verb* **1** circle, encircle, enclose, ring, surround. **2** contain, cover, embrace, include, incorporate.

encounter *verb* **1** bump into, (*informal*) chance upon, meet, run into. **2** be faced with, come up against, confront, contend with, experience, face, grapple with, meet with, run into.

encounter *noun* **1** meeting. **2** battle, brush, clash, conflict, confrontation, fight, run-in.

encourage verb **1** buck up (*informal*), build up, buoy up, cheer up, comfort, hearten, inspire, reassure. **2** egg on, exhort, persuade, spur, urge. **3** aid, assist, boost, foster, further, help, promote, stimulate. □ **encouragement** noun boost, incentive, inspiration, reassurance, shot in the arm, stimulus, support.

encroach verb impinge, infringe, intrude, invade, make inroads, poach, trespass.

encumber verb burden, hamper, load down, lumber, saddle, weigh down.

encyclopedic adjective comprehensive, extensive, vast, wide-ranging.

end noun **1** boundary, limit, terminus. **2** extremity, point, tip. **3** back, rear, tail. **4** butt, remains, remnant, stub. **5** breakup, cessation, close, completion, conclusion, culmination, ending, expiration, expiry, finale, finish, termination. **6** death, demise (*formal*), destruction, downfall, extinction, fall, passing, ruin. **7** aim, design, goal, intention, object, objective, purpose. □ **in the end** eventually, finally, in the long run, ultimately.

end verb abolish, break off, bring to an end, cease, close, come to an end, complete, conclude, cut off, discontinue, dissolve, eliminate, eradicate, expire, finish, get rid of, halt, peter out, put an end to, put a stop to, round off, run out, stamp out, stop, terminate, wind up, wipe out.

endanger verb imperil, jeopardise, put at risk, threaten.

endearing adjective appealing, attractive, charming, disarming, engaging, likeable, lovable, winsome.

endeavour verb aim, attempt, make an effort, strive, try.

endeavour noun attempt, effort, try.

ending noun conclusion, denouement, end, finale, finish, resolution, termination.

endless adjective abiding, boundless, ceaseless, constant, continual, continuous, eternal, everlasting, immeasurable, incessant, inexhaustible, infinite, interminable, limitless, never-ending, non-stop, ongoing, permanent, perpetual, persistent, unending.

endorse verb **1** countersign, sign. **2** agree with, approve, assent to, back, confirm, OK (*informal*), ratify, sanction, second, subscribe to, support, vouch for.

endow verb bestow, bless, favour, provide, supply.

endure verb **1** abide, bear, brave, brook, cope with, experience, put up with, stand, stomach, suffer, tolerate, undergo, weather, withstand. **2** carry on, continue, last, live on, persist, prevail, remain, stay, survive. □ **endurance** noun fortitude, hardiness, patience, perseverance, persistence, stamina, staying power, strength, tenacity.

enemy noun adversary, antagonist, foe, opponent, opposition, rival.

energetic adjective active, animated, brisk, dynamic, forceful, full of beans (informal), go-ahead, hard-working, high-powered, indefatigable, industrious, lively, perky, spirited, sprightly, spry, strenuous, tireless, vibrant, vigorous, zippy.

energy noun drive, enthusiasm, force, go, gusto, liveliness, oomph (informal), pep, power, stamina, steam, verve, vigour, vim (informal), vitality, vivacity, zeal, zest, zing (informal), zip.

enforce verb administer, apply, carry out, implement, impose, insist on.

engage verb **1** appoint, employ, hire, recruit, take on. **2** absorb, engross, involve, occupy.

engaged adjective **1** affianced (formal), betrothed (formal). **2** busy, in use, occupied.

engagement noun **1** betrothal. **2** appointment, arrangement, assignation, booking, commitment, date (informal), meeting, rendezvous.

engaging adjective appealing, attractive, charming, delightful, disarming, enchanting, endearing, likeable, lovable, winning, winsome.

engineer verb arrange, bring about, contrive, fix, mastermind, orchestrate, organise, plan, rig, wangle (slang).

engrave verb carve, chisel, cut, etch, incise, inscribe.

engrossed adjective absorbed, immersed, involved, lost, occupied, preoccupied.

engulf verb cover, flood, inundate, overrun, overwhelm, submerge, swallow up, swamp.

enhance verb boost, enrich, heighten, improve, increase, intensify, strengthen.

enigma noun conundrum, mystery, problem, puzzle, riddle, secret.

enigmatic adjective arcane, baffling, cryptic, inscrutable mysterious, obscure, perplexing, puzzling, unfathomable.

enjoy verb appreciate, bask in, be fond of, be keen on, delight in, fancy, lap up, like, love, luxuriate in, relish, revel in, savour, wallow in. □ **enjoy yourself** be happy, have a ball (informal), have a good time, have fun. □ **enjoyable** adjective agreeable, cool (informal), delightful, good, lovely (informal), nice, pleasant, pleasurable, satisfying. □ **enjoyment** noun amusement, delectation, delight, entertainment, fun, happiness, joy, kick (informal), pleasure, recreation, satisfaction, thrill, zest.

enlarge verb add to, blow up (informal), broaden, bulge, distend, expand, extend, fill out, grow, lengthen, magnify, stretch, swell, widen.

enlighten verb edify, educate, inform, instruct, teach.

enlist verb 1 call up, conscript, draft (American), enrol, join up, recruit, register, sign on, volunteer. 2 drum up, gather, get, mobilise, muster, obtain, secure.

enmity noun acrimony, animosity, antagonism, antipathy, bitterness, hatred, hostility, ill will, malevolence, opposition, rancour.

enormous adjective astronomical, big, colossal, gargantuan, giant, gigantic, ginormous (slang), great, huge, humungous (slang), immeasurable, immense, incalculable, jumbo, king-sized, large, mammoth, massive, mighty, monstrous, monumental, outsize, prodigious, spacious, staggering, stupendous, sweeping, tremendous, vast.

enough adjective adequate, ample, sufficient.

enquire verb ask, inquire, query, question. □ **enquiry** noun inquiry, query, question.

enrage verb anger, annoy, exasperate, incense, infuriate, irritate, madden, outrage, provoke, rile (informal).

enrol verb 1 enlist, join up, register, sign on. 2 accept, admit, enlist, recruit, take on.

ensemble noun band, group, orchestra.

ensign noun banner, flag, jack, standard.

ensue verb follow, result. □ **ensuing** adjective following, next, subsequent, succeeding.

ensure verb guarantee, make certain, make sure, secure.

entail verb call for, involve, mean, necessitate, require.

entangle verb catch up, ensnare, entwine, interlace,

intertwine, mat, mix up, ravel, snarl, tangle, trap, twist.

enter verb **1** come in, go in, infiltrate, intrude in, invade, penetrate. **2** inscribe, jot, list, note, record, register, write. **3** compete in, go in, participate in, register for, sign up for, take part in.

enterprise noun **1** drive, get-up-and-go, initiative, push, resourcefulness. **2** endeavour, mission, operation, project, undertaking, venture. **3** business, company, concern, corporation, establishment, firm, operation, organisation.

enterprising adjective adventurous, bold, daring, energetic, go-ahead, imaginative, industrious, intrepid, resourceful, venturesome.

entertain verb **1** amuse, delight, divert, please. **2** play host to, receive, regale, welcome, wine and dine. **3** consider, contemplate, harbour, think about. □ **entertainer** noun artist, artiste, performer, player; (various entertainers) actor, actress, busker, clown, comedian, comic, conjuror, dancer, instrumentalist, jester, juggler, magician, minstrel, musician, singer, vocalist.

entertainment noun **1** amusement, distraction, diversion, enjoyment, fun, pastime, pleasure, recreation, sport. **2** extravaganza, performance, presentation, production, show, spectacle.

enthral verb beguile, bewitch, captivate, charm, enchant, enrapture, entrance, fascinate, hold spellbound, hypnotise, mesmerise.

enthusiasm noun ardour, eagerness, excitement, exuberance, fervour, gusto, keenness, passion, relish, verve, zeal, zest. □ **enthusiast** noun addict, aficionado, buff (informal), devotee, fan, fanatic, follower, freak (informal), lover, nut (informal), supporter, zealot.

enthusiastic adjective ardent, avid, committed, eager, excited, exuberant, fervent, hearty, keen, passionate, warm, wholehearted, zealous.

entice verb allure, attract, bribe, cajole, coax, decoy, inveigle, lure, persuade, seduce, tempt.

entire adjective complete, full, intact, total, unbroken, whole. □ **entirely** adverb absolutely, altogether, completely, fully, one hundred per cent, perfectly, quite, totally, utterly, wholly.

entitle verb allow, authorise, permit, qualify. □ **entitlement**

noun claim, eligibility, prerogative, right.

entitled *adjective* called, named, titled.

entrance *noun* **1** access, door, doorway, entry, foyer, gate, gateway, opening, passage, porch, portal, postern, threshold, way in. **2** appearance, arrival, entry. **3** admission, admittance, entry.

entrance *verb* beguile, bewitch, captivate, charm, delight, enchant, enrapture, enthral, fascinate, hold spellbound, hypnotise, mesmerise, transport.

entrant *noun* applicant, candidate, competitor, contestant, participant.

entreat *verb* appeal to, beg, beseech, implore, plead with, pray, request, supplicate.

entrench *verb* establish, fix, root, settle.

entrust *verb* assign, charge, commend, commit, consign, delegate, hand over, trust.

entry *noun* **1** access, approach, door, doorway, entrance, gate, gateway, opening, way in. **2** item, jotting, note, record.

entwine *verb* entangle, intertwine, interweave, snarl, tangle, twine, twist, weave.

envelop *verb* cocoon, cover, shroud, surround, swaddle, swathe, wrap.

envelope *noun* case, cover, covering, holder, jacket, pocket, sheath, wrapper.

envious *adjective* covetous, green, grudging, jealous, resentful.

environment *noun* ambience, atmosphere, circumstances, conditions, context, ecosystem, element, environs, habitat, medium, milieu, setting, situation, surroundings.

environmentalist *noun* conservationist, ecologist, green, greenie (*Australian informal*).

environs *noun* district, neighbourhood, outskirts, surroundings, vicinity.

envisage *verb* conceive of, contemplate, foresee, imagine, picture, predict, visualise.

envoy *noun* agent, ambassador, delegate, diplomat, emissary, messenger, representative.

envy *noun* covetousness, jealousy, resentment.

envy *verb* begrudge, be jealous of, covet, grudge, resent.

ephemeral *adjective* brief, fleeting, impermanent, momentary, passing, short-lived, temporary, transient, transitory.

epidemic noun outbreak, pestilence, plague.

epigram noun aphorism, pun, quip, saying, witticism.

epilogue noun conclusion, postscript.

episode noun **1** affair (*informal*), event, happening, incident, occasion, occurrence. **2** chapter, instalment, part, scene, section.

epistle noun communication, letter, note.

epoch noun age, era, period, time.

equal adjective equivalent, even, identical, level, like, matching, parallel, same, uniform.

equal noun match, parallel, peer, rival.

equal verb add up to, amount to, be equivalent to, come up to, draw with, match, tie with.

equality noun egalitarianism, equivalence, evenness, parity, sameness, uniformity.

equilibrium noun balance, poise, stability, steadiness.

equip verb arm, fit out, furnish, kit out, prepare, provide, rig out, stock, supply.

equipment noun apparatus, appliances, gear, hardware, implements, instruments, kit, machinery, materials, outfit, paraphernalia, plant, rig, supplies, tackle, tools.

equity noun even-handedness, fairness, impartiality, justice.
□ **equitable** adjective even-handed, fair, impartial, just, open-minded, proper, reasonable, right, unbiased.

equivalent adjective commensurate, comparable, corresponding, equal, identical, interchangeable, matching, same, tantamount.

equivocal adjective ambiguous, imprecise, indefinite, obscure, uncertain, unclear, vague.

era noun age, day, epoch, period, time.

eradicate verb annihilate, destroy, eliminate, exterminate, get rid of, obliterate, remove, root out, uproot, weed out, wipe out.

erase verb blot out, cancel, delete, efface, expunge, obliterate, remove, rub out, wipe out.

erect adjective bolt upright, perpendicular, standing, upright, vertical.

erect verb build, construct, pitch (*a tent*), put up, raise, set up.

erode verb abrade, corrode, destroy, eat away, grind down, rub away, wear away, weather

□ **erosion** noun abrasion, corrosion, eating away, wearing away, weathering.

erotic adjective seductive, sensual, sexy, suggestive, titillating.

err verb 1 be incorrect, go wrong, make a mistake, miscalculate, slip up. 2 do wrong, go astray, sin, transgress, trespass (old use).

errand noun chore, job, mission, task.

erratic adjective capricious, changeable, fickle, inconsistent, irregular, spasmodic, uneven, unpredictable, variable.

error noun bloomer (slang), blue (Australian informal), blunder, booboo (slang), clanger (informal), fault, flaw, gaffe, howler (informal), inaccuracy, lapse, miscalculation, misprint, mistake, oversight, slip, slip-up (informal), typo (informal).

erupt verb belch, burst out, discharge, gush out, issue, pour out, shoot forth, spew, spurt out.

escalate verb blow up, heighten, increase, intensify, jump, mount, multiply, rise, skyrocket, soar, step up, worsen.

escapade noun adventure, caper, exploit, lark, prank, scrape.

escape verb 1 abscond, bolt, break free, break out, flee, get away, get out, run away, scarper, slip away, take flight. 2 avoid, dodge, elude, evade, get out of, wriggle out of.

escape noun 1 breakout, flight, getaway. 2 exit, outlet, way out.

escapee noun absconder, bolter, escaper, fugitive, runaway.

escort noun 1 bodyguard, chaperone, convoy, guard, minder, protector. 2 companion, date (informal), partner.

escort verb accompany, chaperone, conduct, guide, lead, take, usher.

especially adverb 1 chiefly, expressly, particularly, primarily, specially, specifically. 2 exceptionally, extraordinarily, outstandingly, particularly.

essay noun article, composition, critique, dissertation, paper, thesis.

essence noun 1 core, crux, gist, heart, kernel, nub, pith, quintessence, substance. 2 concentrate, extract.

essential *adjective* **1** imperative, indispensable, necessary, requisite, vital. **2** basic, central, chief, fundamental, inherent, intrinsic, key, main, primary, principal.

essential *noun* must, necessity, prerequisite, requirement, requisite.

establish *verb* **1** begin, build, construct, create, found, inaugurate, initiate, institute, introduce, originate, pioneer, set up, start. **2** confirm, demonstrate, prove, show, substantiate, verify.

establishment *noun* business, company, concern, corporation, enterprise, firm, institution, organisation, plant.

estate *noun* **1** area, development. **2** assets, fortune, money, property, wealth.

esteem *noun* admiration, appreciation, approval, estimation, regard, respect, reverence, veneration.

estimate *noun* appraisal, approximation, assessment, calculation, evaluation, guesstimate (*informal*), judgement, opinion, valuation.

estimate *verb* appraise, assess, calculate, evaluate, guess, judge, put, rate, reckon, size up, value.

estranged *adjective* alienated, driven apart.

estuary *noun* firth, inlet, mouth.

etch *verb* carve, engrave, impress, imprint, inscribe, stamp.

eternal *adjective* see EVERLASTING.

ethical *adjective* above board, correct, honourable, moral, principled, proper, right, righteous, upright, virtuous.

ethics *plural noun* moral code, morality, morals, principles, scruples.

ethnic *adjective* cultural, national, racial.

etiquette *noun* code of behaviour, conventions, decorum, form, manners, proprieties, protocol, rules.

Eucharist *noun* Holy Communion, Lord's Supper, Mass.

evacuate *verb* **1** move out, relocate, remove, send away. **2** clear, empty.

evade *verb* avoid, dodge, duck, elude, escape from, shirk, shun, sidestep, steer clear of.

evaluate *verb* appraise, assess, calculate, compute, judge, review, size up, value, weigh up.

evangelist *noun* missionary, preacher.

evaporate *verb* **1** dry up, vaporise. **2** disappear, fade away, melt away, vanish.

evasive *adjective* ambiguous, devious, equivocal, non-committal, oblique, round-about, shifty.

even *adjective* **1** flat, flush, level, plane, smooth, straight. **2** consistent, constant, regular, steady, unchanging, uniform, unvarying. **3** balanced, drawn, equal, identical, level, neck and neck, square, the same, tied. □ **even-tempered** *adjective* calm, easygoing, equable, imperturbable, placid, serene, steady, tranquil, unfazed (*informal*), unflappable (*informal*).

even *verb* balance, equalise, level, straighten, tie.

evening *noun* dusk, eventide (*old use*), gloaming, night, nightfall, sundown, sunset, twilight.

event *noun* **1** affair, circumstance, episode, eventuality, experience, happening, incident, occasion, occurrence. **2** competition, contest, item, race.

eventful *adjective* action-packed, busy, exciting, full, memorable, momentous, unforgettable.

eventuality *noun* contingency, possibility; see also *EVENT*.

eventually *adverb* at last, finally, in the end, ultimately.

everlasting *adjective* **1** endless, eternal, immortal, infinite, limitless, never-ending, timeless, unending, unlimited. **2** abiding, ceaseless, chronic, constant, continual, continuous, endless, eternal, incessant, interminable, non-stop, perennial, permanent, perpetual, persistent, recurrent, repeated.

everybody *pronoun* all, all and sundry, everyone, one and all, the world.

everyday *adjective* common, commonplace, customary, daily, day-to-day, familiar, mundane, normal, ordinary, regular, routine, usual.

everywhere *adverb* extensively, far and wide, globally, high and low, near and far, ubiquitously, universally.

evict *verb* chuck out (*informal*), drive out, eject, expel, get rid of, kick out (*informal*), remove, throw out, turf out (*informal*), turn out.

evidence *noun* **1** data, documentation, facts, grounds, indication, manifestation, proof, sign, symptom, token. **2** affidavit, deposition, statement, testimony.

evident *adjective* apparent, clear, manifest, noticeable, obvious, patent, plain, undeniable, unmistakable.

evil *adjective* abominable, atrocious, bad, base, beastly, corrupt, demonic, depraved, despicable, detestable, diabolical, foul, hateful, heinous, immoral, infamous, iniquitous, loathsome, malevolent, malicious, nefarious, satanic, sinful, sinister, ungodly, unrighteous, vicious, vile, villainous, wicked.

evil *noun* corruption, depravity, immorality, iniquity, sin, turpitude, ungodliness, vice, wickedness, wrong, wrongdoing.

evoke *verb* arouse, awaken, call up, conjure up, elicit, inspire, rouse, stimulate, stir up, suggest.

evolve *verb* develop, grow, unfold.

exact *adjective* **1** accurate, correct, literal, perfect, precise, right, spot-on (*informal*), true. **2** careful, detailed, explicit, fastidious, meticulous, minute, painstaking, particular, precise, punctilious, rigorous, scrupulous, specific, strict.

exact *verb* claim, demand, extort, extract, insist on.

exacting *adjective* arduous, demanding, difficult, hard, onerous, stiff, taxing, tough.

exaggerate *verb* inflate, lay on thick (*informal*), magnif, make a mountain out of molehill, overdo, overestimate overstate, pile it on (*informal* ☐ **exaggeration** *noun* hyperbole, magnification, over statement.

exalt *verb* **1** advance, elevate promote, raise, upgrade. adore, extol, glorify, hallow honour, laud (*formal*), magnif (*old use*), praise, revere venerate, worship.

examination *noun* **1** exar (*informal*), oral (*informal* quiz, test; see also *CROSS EXAMINATION* (at *CROS EXAMINE*). **2** analysis, audi check, inspection, investi gation, observation, perusa probe, review, scrutiny, stud survey.

examine *verb* **1** question, qui sound out, test; see also *CROSS EXAMINE*. **2** analyse, audi check, consider, go ove inquire into, inspect, ir vestigate, look at, look ove peruse, pore over, probe research, review, scar scrutinise, sift, study, survey vet.

example *noun* **1** cas illustration, instance, mode

precedent, prototype, sample, specimen. **2** model, paragon, pattern, standard.

exasperate *verb* anger, annoy, bug (*informal*), enrage, get on someone's nerves, infuriate, irk, irritate, madden, needle (*informal*), peeve (*informal*), provoke, rile (*informal*), vex.

excavate *verb* **1** burrow, dig, hollow out, mine, scoop out, shovel out, tunnel. **2** dig up, exhume, uncover, unearth.

exceed *verb* **1** beat, better, excel, outdo, outnumber, overtake, pass, surpass, top, transcend. **2** go beyond, go over, overstep.

excel *verb* be outstanding, shine, stand out.

excellent *adjective* ace (*informal*), admirable, awesome (*informal*), beaut (*Australian informal*), brilliant (*informal*), capital, choice, classic, cool (*informal*), exceptional, fabulous, fantastic, far-out (*informal*), fine, first-class, first-rate, great, groovy (*slang*), impressive, magnificent, marvellous, masterly, matchless, meritorious, model, out of the box (*Australian informal*), outstanding, peerless, perfect, prize, remarkable, select, sensational, splendid, sterling, super (*informal*), superb,

superior, superlative, supreme, swell (*informal*), terrific (*informal*), top-notch (*informal*), tremendous, wicked (*slang*), wizard (*informal*), wonderful. □ **excellence** *noun* greatness, merit, perfection, pre-eminence, quality, superiority.

except *preposition* apart from, bar, besides, but, excluding, other than, save.

exception *noun* **1** anomaly, departure, deviation, inconsistency, irregularity. **2** exclusion, omission.

exceptional *adjective* **1** abnormal, anomalous, atypical, extraordinary, odd, phenomenal, rare, remarkable, singular, special, uncommon, unusual. **2** see EXCELLENT.

excerpt *noun* citation, clip, extract, passage, quotation, selection, trailer.

excess *noun* glut, over-abundance, overflow, over-supply, superfluity, surfeit, surplus.

excessive *adjective* exaggerated, exorbitant, extortionate, extravagant, extreme, fulsome, immoderate, inordinate, intemperate, outrageous, overdone, profuse, steep, superfluous, unreasonable.

exchange verb barter, change, interchange, substitute, swap, trade.

excitable adjective emotional, highly-strung, hotheaded, mercurial, nervous, temperamental, volatile.

excite verb 1 agitate, animate, arouse, disturb, fluster, rouse, stir up, thrill, upset, wind up (*informal*), work up. 2 arouse, awaken, generate, incite, inspire, kindle, provoke, stimulate, whet. □ **exciting** adjective breathtaking, electrifying, exhilarating, gripping, heady, moving, riveting, rousing, sensational, spectacular, stimulating, stirring, suspenseful, thrilling.

excitement noun action, activity, ado, adventure, agitation, ferment, flurry, frenzy, furore, fuss, kerfuffle, kicks (*informal*), sensation, stir, thrill, to-do, unrest.

exclaim verb bawl, bellow, call out, cry out, shout, yell.

exclude verb 1 ban, bar, debar, expel, forbid, keep out, leave out, ostracise, oust, prohibit, shut out. 2 eliminate, omit, preclude, reject, rule out.

exclusive adjective 1 closed, private, restricted, select. 2 complete, full, sole, undivided, unique.

excrete verb defecate, urinate, void.

excruciating adjective acute, agonising, insufferable, intolerable, painful, severe, unbearable.

excursion noun drive, expedition, hike, holiday, jaunt, journey, outing, pleasure-trip, ramble, ride, run, tour, trek, trip, walk.

excusable adjective forgivable, pardonable, venial.

excuse verb 1 (*excuse a person*) exonerate, forgive, let off, make allowances for, pardon; (*excuse an action*) condone, explain, justify, mitigate, vindicate, warrant. 2 exempt, free, let off, release.

excuse noun defence, explanation, justification, plod (*Australian informal*), pretext, reason.

execute verb 1 kill, put to death, slay; (*various ways to execute*) behead, crucify, electrocute, garrotte, gas, guillotine, hang, lynch, shoot, stone. 2 accomplish, carry out, complete, do, effect, fulfil, implement, perform.

executive noun administrator, chief, director, manager.

exemplify verb embody, epitomise, illustrate, personify, represent, typify.

exempt *adjective* excused, freed, immune, released, relieved, spared.

exempt *verb* excuse, free, let off, release, relieve, spare. ☐ **exemption** *noun* dispensation, immunity, privilege.

exercise *noun* **1** activity, aerobics, callisthenics, exertion, games, gymnastics, PE, physical education, physical training, PT, sport. **2** drill, manoeuvres, movements, practice, training.

exercise *verb* **1** limber up, loosen up, practise, train, work out. **2** apply, employ, exert, use, utilise, wield.

exert *verb* apply, employ, exercise, use, utilise, wield. ☐ **exertion** *noun* effort, exercise, labour, strain, toil, work.

exhale *verb* blow, breathe out, expire, pant, puff.

exhaust *verb* **1** drain, fatigue, tire out, weaken, wear out, weary. **2** blow (*slang*), consume, deplete, dissipate, expend, spend, use up. ☐ **exhausted** *adjective* all in (*informal*), burnt out, bushed (*informal*), dog-tired, done in (*informal*), drained, fagged out (*informal*), fatigued, knackered (*slang*), played out, pooped (*informal*), run down, sapped, spent, tired out,

washed out, weak, weary, whacked (*informal*), worn out, zapped (*slang*), zonked (*slang*). ☐ **exhausting** *adjective* arduous, difficult, gruelling, hard, heavy, laborious, strenuous, tiring.

exhaust *noun* emissions, fumes, gases, smoke.

exhaustive *adjective* complete, comprehensive, detailed, full, in-depth, intensive, minute, thorough.

exhibit *verb* display, present, show.

exhibition *noun* demonstration, display, expo, exposition, fair, presentation, show.

exhilarated *adjective* cheerful, delighted, ecstatic, elated, euphoric, excited, happy, joyful, overjoyed, thrilled.

exhort *verb* advise, appeal to, beseech, encourage, entreat, implore, plead with, urge.

exile *verb* banish, deport, expatriate, expel, send away.

exile *noun* **1** deportee, expatriate, outcast, refugee. **2** banishment, deportation, expatriation, expulsion.

exist *verb* **1** be, be real, live, occur. **2** keep going, subsist, survive. ☐ **existence** *noun* being, life, subsistence, survival.

exit verb see LEAVE.

exit noun **1** door, outlet, way out. **2** departure, escape, retreat.

exonerate verb absolve, acquit, clear, free, pardon, vindicate.

exorbitant adjective excessive, expensive, extortionate, high, inordinate, outrageous, preposterous, steep, unreasonable.

exotic adjective **1** bizarre, curious, different, extraordinary, odd, outlandish, peculiar, rare, singular, strange, unfamiliar, unusual, weird. **2** alien, foreign, imported.

expand verb **1** bloat, broaden, build up, develop, distend, enlarge, extend, fatten, grow, increase, open out, spread (out), stretch (out), swell, unfurl, widen. **2** (expand on) amplify, elaborate upon, enlarge upon, expatiate on, flesh out, pad out.

expanse noun area, extent, sea, stretch, sweep, tract.

expect verb **1** anticipate, bargain for, contemplate, envisage, forecast, foresee, predict. **2** count on, demand, insist on, rely on, require.

expectant adjective eager, hopeful, ready, waiting, watchful.

expectation noun anticipation, hope, likelihood, outlook, probability, prospect.

expedition noun excursion, exploration, journey, mission, outing, safari, tour, trek, trip, voyage.

expel verb banish, chuck out (informal), deport, discharge, dismiss, drive out, eject, evict, exile, get rid of, kick out (informal), remove, send away, throw out, turf out (informal).

expenditure noun expenses, outgoings, outlay, overheads, spending.

expense noun charge, cost, fee, payment, price; see also EXPENDITURE.

expensive adjective costly, dear, exorbitant, extravagant, luxurious, precious, priceless, pricey (informal), valuable.

experience noun **1** background, familiarity, involvement, practice. **2** adventure, episode, event, happening, incident, occurrence, ordeal.

experience verb bear, encounter, endure, face, feel, go through, know, meet with, suffer, sustain, undergo.

experienced adjective accomplished, competent, expert, fully-fledged, practised, proficient, seasoned, skilled, veteran, well-versed.

experiment *noun* investigation, test, trial. □ **experimental** *adjective* pilot, test, trial.

experiment *verb* investigate, research, test, try.

expert *noun* ace, adept, authority, buff (*informal*), connoisseur, consultant, dab hand (*informal*), genius, know-all (*informal*), maestro, master, old hand, past master, pro (*informal*), professional, pundit, scholar, specialist, virtuoso, whiz (*informal*).

expert *adjective* accomplished, capable, competent, experienced, knowledgeable, practised, professional, proficient, qualified, skilful, skilled, talented.

expertise *noun* know-how, knowledge, mastery, proficiency, skill.

expire *verb* **1** cease, end, finish, lapse, run out, stop, terminate. **2** breathe your last, die, pass away, perish. **3** breathe out, exhale.

explain *verb* **1** clarify, clear up, decipher, define, demonstrate, describe, detail, elaborate, elucidate, expound, illustrate, interpret, show, spell out, teach, justify. □ **explanation** *noun* **1** account, clarification, commentary, definition, description, elucidation, interpretation, key. **2** excuse, justification, reason.

explicit *adjective* categorical, clear, definite, exact, express, particular, plain, positive, precise, specific, unambiguous, unequivocal.

explode *verb* **1** blast, blow up, burst, detonate, erupt, go off. **2** detonate, discharge, let off, set off.

exploit *noun* achievement, act, adventure, deed, escapade, feat.

exploit *verb* **1** capitalise on, cash in on, make the most of, profit from, take advantage of, use, utilise. **2** abuse, misuse, take advantage of, use.

explore *verb* **1** inspect, look around, prospect, reconnoitre, scout, survey, tour, travel about. **2** analyse, examine, inquire into, investigate, look into, probe, research, study, survey. □ **explorer** *noun* discoverer, pioneer, prospector, surveyor, trailblazer, traveller.

explosion *noun* bang, blast, boom, burst, detonation, discharge, eruption, outburst, pop, report, shot.

explosive *adjective* charged, dangerous, dicey (*slang*), precarious, tense, unstable, volatile.

explosive noun dynamite, gelignite, gunpowder, jelly (slang), nitroglycerine, TNT.

expose verb bare, betray, disclose, display, divulge, lay bare, leak, let out, make known, reveal, show, uncover.

express adjective **1** direct, expeditious, fast, hasty, high-speed, non-stop, prompt, quick, rapid, speedy, swift. **2** clear, definite, exact, explicit, particular, plain, precise, specific, unequivocal.

express verb air, communicate, convey, disclose, indicate, put into words, reveal, speak, state, utter, vent, verbalise, voice.

expression noun **1** air, appearance, aspect, countenance, face, look, mien. **2** idiom, phrase, saying, term, word. **3** eloquence, emotion, feeling, intonation, meaning, sensitivity. □ **expressionless** adjective blank, deadpan, empty, poker-faced, vacant, vacuous, wooden.

expressive adjective eloquent, meaningful, revealing, significant, telling.

expulsion noun banishment, eviction, exclusion, removal.

exquisite adjective beautiful, dainty, delicate, elegant, fine, lovely, perfect.

extend verb **1** hold out, reach out, stick out, straighten out, stretch out. **2** carry on, continue, drag out, elongate, enlarge, lengthen, prolong, protract, spin out, stretch. **3** accord, bestow, confer, give, grant, impart, offer, proffer.

extension noun addition, annexe, wing.

extensive adjective big, broad, comprehensive, far-reaching, huge, immense, large, spacious, sweeping, thorough, vast, wholesale, wide, wide-ranging, widespread.

extent noun **1** area, breadth, expanse, length, size, spread, stretch, width. **2** amount, degree, limit, range, scale, scope.

extenuating adjective mitigating.

exterior adjective external, outer, outside, outward, superficial.

exterior noun façade, face, outside, shell, surface.

exterminate verb annihilate, destroy, eliminate, eradicate, get rid of, kill, liquidate, murder, root out, slaughter, wipe out.

external adjective exterior, outer, outside, outward, superficial.

extinct adjective **1** dead, died out. **2** burnt out, extinguished, inactive.

extinguish verb douse, put out, quench, smother, snuff out.

extort verb exact, extract, squeeze, wring.

extortionate adjective excessive, exorbitant, immoderate, inordinate, outrageous, preposterous, steep, unreasonable.

extra adjective additional, auxiliary, excess, further, more, other, reserve, spare, superfluous, supplementary, surplus.

extra adverb especially, exceptionally, extremely, particularly, unusually.

extra noun accessory, addition, add-on, attachment, bonus, luxury, supplement.

extract verb draw out, pull out, remove, take out.

extract noun **1** citation, clip, clipping, cutting, excerpt, passage, quotation, snippet, trailer. **2** concentrate, distillate, essence.

extraordinary adjective abnormal, amazing, astonishing, bizarre, curious, exceptional, incredible, miraculous, odd, outstanding, peculiar, phenomenal, rare, remarkable, singular, special, strange, striking, uncommon, unusual, weird.

extravagant adjective improvident, lavish, munificent, overgenerous, prodigal, profligate, spendthrift, wasteful.

extreme adjective **1** acute, excessive, great, intense, severe. **2** farthest, furthermost, furthest, utmost, uttermost. **3** Draconian, drastic, fanatical, hard-line, harsh, immoderate, intemperate, radical, severe, stiff, stringent, uncompromising, unreasonable. □ **extremely** adverb awfully (informal), especially, exceedingly, exceptionally, extraordinarily, remarkably, terribly (informal), very.

extreme noun boundary, end, extremity, limit, maximum, minimum, pole.

extroverted adjective gregarious, outgoing, sociable.

exuberant adjective animated, boisterous, energetic, excited, exhilarated, full of beans (informal), high-spirited, irrepressible, lively, spirited, vivacious.

exude verb drip, emanate, ooze, secrete, seep.

exult verb crow, gloat, glory, rejoice, revel. □ **exultant** adjective delighted, ecstatic, elated, gleeful, jubilant, overjoyed, triumphant.

eye verb behold (old use), contemplate, gaze at, look at, observe, ogle, peer at, stare at, study, view, watch.

eyesight noun sight, vision.

eyesore noun blight, blot, monstrosity.

eyewitness noun bystander, looker-on, observer, onlooker, spectator, witness.

Ff

fable noun allegory, legend, myth, parable, story, tale.

fabric noun cloth, material, stuff, textile.

fabricate verb 1 assemble, build, construct, make, manufacture, produce. 2 concoct, devise, hatch, invent, make up, manufacture.

fabulous adjective 1 see EXCELLENT. 2 extraordinary, great, inconceivable, incredible, mind-boggling (informal), phenomenal, prodigious, stupendous, tremendous, unbelievable. 3 fabled, fanciful, fictional, fictitious, imaginary, legendary, mythical.

façade noun 1 exterior, face, front, frontage, outside. 2 appearance, exterior, front, mask, pretence, show, veneer.

face noun 1 air, countenance, expression, look, physiognomy, visage. 2 façade, front, side, surface.

face verb 1 front on, lie opposite, look out on, overlook. 2 brave, confront, cope with, deal with, encounter, experience, meet, weather, withstand.

facet noun aspect, face, feature, side.

facetious adjective amusing, comical, flippant, funny, humorous, jocular, joking, witty.

facilitate verb aid, assist, ease, expedite, help, simplify.

facility noun 1 amenity, convenience, resource. 2 competence, ease, effortlessness, fluency, proficiency, skill.

facsimile noun copy, duplicate, photocopy, replica, reproduction.

fact noun 1 actuality, certainty, reality, truth. 2 circumstance, detail, particular; (facts) data, evidence, information, low-down (slang).

faction noun camp, clique, division, group, lobby, set, wing.

factor noun aspect, circumstance, component, element, influence, ingredient, part.

factory noun forge, foundry, mill, plant, refinery, works, workshop.

factual adjective accurate, faithful, objective, strict, true, truthful.

faculty noun ability, aptitude, bent, capability, capacity, facility, flair, gift, knack, power, skill, talent.

fad noun craze, cult, fashion, mania, passion, rage, trend, vogue.

fade verb 1 bleach, dim, dull, lighten, pale, wash out, whiten. 2 decline, decrease, die away, diminish, disappear, dwindle, ebb, grow faint, peter out, trail away, vanish, wane, weaken. □ **fade away** die, shrivel, waste away, wither.

fail verb 1 abort, backfire, be unsuccessful, bomb out (informal), come unstuck (informal), fall through, flop (informal), flunk (informal), founder, miscarry, misfire. 2 break down, conk out (informal), decline, deteriorate, dwindle, ebb, fade, malfunction, pack up (informal), wane, weaken. 3 forget, neglect, omit.

failing noun fault, flaw, foible, imperfection, shortcoming, vice, weakness.

failure noun damp squib, disaster, fiasco, fizzer (Australian informal), flop (informal), non-event, washout (informal).

faint adjective 1 (a faint picture) blurred, dim, hazy, indistinct, misty, unclear; (faint colours) delicate, faded, light, pale, pastel, soft, subtle; (faint sounds) feeble, low, muffled, muted, slight, soft, subdued, weak. 2 dizzy, giddy, light-headed, unsteady, weak, woozy (informal).

faint verb black out, collapse, flake out (informal), keel over, lose consciousness, pass out (informal), swoon.

fair adjective 1 above board, disinterested, equitable, even-handed, honest, impartial, just, legitimate, objective, open-minded, proper, reasonable, right, sporting, sportsmanlike, unbiased, unprejudiced. 2 blond, flaxen, golden, light, tow-coloured. 3 bright, clear, cloudless, fine, sunny, unclouded. 4 all right, average, indifferent, mediocre, middling, OK (informal), passable, reasonable, satisfactory, so-so (informal), tolerable. □ **fairness** noun

disinterest, equity, even-
handedness, impartiality,
justice, neutrality, objectivity.

fair noun **1** carnival, funfair,
show. **2** exhibition, expo,
exposition, sale, show. **3**
bazaar, fête, gala, market.

fairly adverb **1** equitably,
honestly, impartially, justly,
objectively, properly, reasonably. **2** moderately, pretty,
quite, rather, reasonably,
somewhat.

fairy noun elf, imp, pixie, sprite.

faith noun **1** belief, confidence,
reliance, trust. **2** belief,
church, conviction, creed,
doctrine, persuasion, religion.

faithful adjective committed,
constant, dedicated, dependable, devoted, dutiful, loyal,
reliable, stalwart, staunch,
steadfast, true, trustworthy,
trusty. □ **faithfulness** noun see
FIDELITY.

fake noun (thing) copy,
counterfeit, duplicate, forgery,
fraud, hoax, imitation, phoney
(informal), replica, reproduction, sham; (person)
charlatan, cheat, con man
(informal), fraud, humbug,
impostor, phoney (informal),
quack. □ **fake** adjective
artificial, bogus, counterfeit,
false, forged, imitation,
phoney (informal), pretend

(informal), pseudo, sham,
synthetic.

fake verb **1** copy, counterfeit,
fabricate, forge, reproduce.
2 affect, feign, fudge, pretend,
simulate.

fall verb **1** cascade, collapse,
come a buster (Australian
informal), come a cropper (informal), come a gutser
(Australian slang), crash,
descend, founder, nosedive,
overbalance, plummet, plunge,
slide, slip, spill, stumble,
topple, trip, tumble. **2** decline,
decrease, diminish, drop,
dwindle, reduce, slump. **3** be
killed, die, perish. **4** happen,
occur, take place. □ **fall out**
argue, disagree, fight, quarrel,
squabble. □ **fall through** see
FAIL.

fall noun collapse, crash,
decline, decrease, descent, dip,
dive, downturn, drop, nosedive, plunge, reduction, slump.

fallacy noun delusion, error,
inconsistency, misconception,
mistake, myth.

falls plural noun cascade,
cataract, waterfall.

false adjective **1** erroneous,
fallacious, faulty, inaccurate,
incorrect, invalid, misleading,
spurious, unsound, untrue,
wrong. **2** artificial, assumed
(name), bogus, counterfeit,
fake, fictitious, imitation,

made-up, phoney (*informal*), pretend (*informal*), pseudo, sham, synthetic. **3** deceitful, dishonest, disloyal, duplicitous, faithless, hypocritical, insincere, lying, perfidious, treacherous, two-faced, unfaithful, untruthful.

falsehood noun fabrication, fairy story, fairy tale, fib, fiction, lie, myth, porky (*slang*), story, untruth.

falsify verb alter, cook (*informal*), doctor, fiddle (*slang*), tamper with.

falter verb **1** stagger, stumble, totter. **2** hesitate, pause, stammer, stutter.

fame noun celebrity, distinction, eminence, glory, honour, kudos (*informal*), prestige, prominence, recognition, renown, reputation, repute.

familiar adjective **1** common, commonplace, customary, everyday, habitual, normal, regular, routine, usual, well-known. **2** (*familiar with*) acquainted with, at home with, conversant with, knowledgeable about, used to, versed in. **3** chummy (*informal*), close, friendly, informal, intimate, matey, pally (*informal*). **4** disrespectful, forward, free and easy, impertinent, impudent, informal, presumptuous.

familiarise verb (*familiarise with*) accustom to, acquaint with, inform about, instruct in, teach.

family noun **1** clan, flesh and blood, folk, kin, kindred, kinsmen, kinswomen, kith and kin, people, relations, relatives, tribe. **2** brood, children, kids (*informal*), offspring, progeny. **3** ancestry, dynasty, forebears, genealogy, house, line, lineage, parentage, pedigree, roots, stock.

famished adjective hungry, peckish (*informal*), ravenous, starving.

famous adjective acclaimed, celebrated, distinguished, eminent, famed, great, illustrious, important, legendary, notable, noted, outstanding, pre-eminent, prominent, renowned, well-known.

fan noun addict, admirer, aficionado, buff (*informal*), devotee, enthusiast, fanatic, follower, lover, nut (*informal*), supporter.

fanatic noun enthusiast, extremist, maniac, zealot.

fanciful adjective curious, fabulous, fantastic, imaginative, romantic, unrealistic, visionary, whimsical, wild.

fancy noun **1** craving, desire, hunger, liking, longing. **2**

delusion, fantasy, illusion, imagination, make-believe, unreality.

fancy *adjective* complicated, decorated, decorative, detailed, elaborate, intricate, ornamental, ornate, showy.

fancy *verb* **1** believe, guess, reckon, suppose, suspect, think. **2** dream, fantasise, imagine, picture. **3** be attracted to, desire, hanker after, like, long for, prefer, want, wish for, yearn for.

fantasise *verb* daydream, dream, imagine.

fantastic *adjective* **1** see *EXCELLENT*. **2** absurd, amazing, bizarre, extraordinary, fanciful, far-fetched, implausible, incredible, outlandish, preposterous, strange, unbelievable, unreal, unrealistic, weird, whimsical, wild.

fantasy *noun* daydream, delusion, dream, fancy, hallucination, illusion, imagination, invention, make-believe, reverie.

far *adjective* distant, far-away, far-off, remote.

farce *noun* charade, joke, mockery, sham. □ **farcical** *adjective* absurd, comical, laughable, ludicrous, nonsensical, preposterous, ridiculous.

fare *noun* **1** charge, cost, fee, payment, price, rate. **2** food, meals, tucker (*Australian informal*).

fare *verb* do, get on, make out, manage.

farewell *interjection* adieu, au revoir, bye (*informal*), bye-bye (*informal*), cheerio (*informal*), cheers (*informal*), ciao (*informal*), goodbye, hooray (*Australian informal*), see you (*informal*), see you later (*informal*), so long (*informal*). □ **farewell** *noun* departure, goodbye, leave-taking, parting, send-off.

farm *noun* plantation, property, ranch, run (*Australian*), small-holding, station (*Australian*).

farm *verb* cultivate, till, work. □ **farming** *noun* agribusiness, agriculture, cultivation, husbandry.

farmer *noun* agriculturalist, cocky (*Australian informal*), grazier (*Australian*), pastoralist (*Australian*), peasant, sharefarmer (*Australian*), smallholder.

fascinate *verb* attract, beguile, bewitch, captivate, charm, enchant, enthral, entrance, hold spellbound, hypnotise, mesmerise, rivet.

fashion *noun* **1** craze, fad, mode, rage, style, trend, vogue.

2 manner, method, mode, way. □ **fashionable** *adjective* chic, classy (*informal*), contemporary, elegant, in, in fashion, latest, modern, smart, stylish, swish (*informal*), trendy (*informal*), up to date, with it (*informal*).

fashion *verb* carve, construct, create, devise, form, make, manufacture, model, mould, produce, shape, work.

fast *adjective* **1** breakneck, brisk, express, fleet, hasty, high-speed, nippy (*informal*), quick, rapid, rattling, speedy, swift, zippy. **2** fixed, indelible, permanent.

fast *adverb* **1** at full pelt, at full speed, at the double, briskly, hastily, hell for leather (*informal*), hurriedly, like lightning (*informal*), like mad (*informal*), like the clappers (*informal*), post-haste, quickly, rapidly, speedily, swiftly. **2** firmly, securely, solidly, tightly.

fast *verb* go without food, starve.

fasten *verb* adhere, affix, anchor, attach, bind, bolt, bond, buckle, button, chain, clamp, clasp, clip, close, connect, couple, do up, fix, hitch, hook, join, knot, lace, lash, latch, link, lock, moor, nail, peg, pin, rivet, screw, seal, secure, sew, shut, staple, stick, strap, tack, tape, tether, tie, truss, zip up.

fastidious *adjective* choosy (*informal*), finicky, fussy, particular, pernickety (*informal*), picky (*informal*), selective.

fat *noun* **1** blubber, corpulence, flab (*informal*). **2** butter, dripping, grease, lard, margarine, suet.

fat *adjective* **1** chubby, corpulent, dumpy, flabby, gross, heavy, large, obese, overweight, plump, podgy, portly, roly-poly, rotund, squat, stout, tubby. **2** bulky, thick, weighty.

fatal *adjective* deadly, lethal, mortal, terminal.

fatality *noun* casualty, death.

fate *noun* **1** chance, destiny, fortune, luck, predestination, providence. **2** destiny, doom, fortune, karma, kismet, lot, portion.

fated *adjective* destined, doomed, predestined, preordained.

fateful *adjective* decisive, important, momentous, significant; see also *DISASTROUS* (at *DISASTER*).

father *noun* patriarch; (*informal terms of address*) dad, daddy, pa, papa, pater, pop. □ **fatherly**

adjective fatherlike, kindly, paternal, protective, tender.

father *verb* beget, procreate, sire.

fathom *verb* **1** measure, plumb, sound. **2** comprehend, get to the bottom of, penetrate, understand, work out.

fatigue *noun* exhaustion, lassitude, lethargy, tiredness, weariness.

fatty *adjective* greasy, oily.

fault *noun* **1** blemish, bug (*informal*), defect, error, failing, flaw, foible, glitch (*informal*), imperfection, lapse, malfunction, misdeed, misdemeanour, mistake, offence, shortcoming, sin, slip-up (*informal*), transgression, trespass (*old use*), vice, weakness, wrongdoing. **2** blame, responsibility. □ **at fault** culpable, guilty, in the wrong, liable, responsible, to blame.

fault *verb* censure, criticise, find fault with, knock (*informal*), pick holes in.

faultless *adjective* consummate, correct, exemplary, flawless, ideal, immaculate, perfect, unblemished.

faulty *adjective* defective, imperfect, kaput (*informal*), malfunctioning, on the blink (*informal*), out of order.

fauna *noun* animals, wildlife.

favour *noun* **1** courtesy, good deed, good turn, kindness, service. **2** approval, goodwill, support, sympathy. **3** bias, favouritism, partiality, preference.

favour *verb* **1** advocate, approve, back, choose, endorse, espouse, opt for, prefer, recommend, select, support. **2** assist, benefit, give an advantage to, help.

favourable *adjective* **1** advantageous, auspicious, beneficial, conducive, helpful, promising, propitious. **2** approving, encouraging, good, positive, reassuring, supportive, sympathetic.

favourite *adjective* chosen, pet, preferred.

favouritism *noun* bias, nepotism (*towards relatives*), partiality, positive discrimination, preference, prejudice.

fawn *noun* beige, buff, camel, khaki, light brown, neutral.

faze *verb* daunt, discomfit, disconcert, fluster, perturb, rattle (*informal*), throw (*informal*), trouble, unnerve, upset, worry.

fear *noun* alarm, anxiety, apprehension, awe, conster

nation, dismay, dread, foreboding, fright, horror, panic, phobia, terror, trepidation, worry.

fear verb be afraid of, be frightened of, be scared of, dread, worry about.

fearful adjective **1** afraid, alarmed, anxious, apprehensive, cowardly, faint-hearted, frightened, nervous, panicky, pusillanimous, scared, terrified, timid, timorous, worried. **2** alarming, appalling, awful, dreadful, fearsome, frightening, frightful, ghastly, horrendous, horrific, scary, shocking, terrible, terrific, terrifying.

fearless adjective bold, brave, courageous, daring, dauntless, gallant, game, heroic, intrepid, lion-hearted, plucky, unafraid, undaunted, valiant, valorous. □ **fearlessness** noun boldness, bravery, courage, daring, grit, guts (informal), intrepidity, nerve, pluck, valour.

feasible adjective achievable, possible, practicable, viable, workable.

feast noun **1** banquet, dinner, meal, repast (formal), spread. **2** celebration, festival, fête, holiday. □ **feast** verb dine, eat, gorge, tuck in (informal).

feat noun achievement, act, action, deed, exploit, performance, stunt.

feather noun hackle, plume, quill; (feathers) down, plumage.

feature noun **1** (features) countenance, face, lineaments, physiognomy, visage. **2** aspect, attribute, characteristic, detail, facet, point, property, quality, respect, trait.

federation noun alliance, association, confederation, league, syndicate, union.

fee noun brokerage, charge, commission, cost, dues, levy, payment, price, rate, remuneration, subscription, sum, tariff, toll.

feeble adjective debilitated, decrepit, delicate, frail, helpless, infirm, listless, poorly, puny, sickly, weak, weedy.

feed verb **1** nourish, nurse, suckle. **2** browse, eat, graze; (feed on) dine on, live on, subsist on.

feedback noun reaction, response.

feel verb **1** finger, fumble, grope, handle, manipulate, maul, paw, stroke, touch. **2** be aware of, be conscious of, experience, notice, perceive, sense, suffer, undergo. **3** believe, consider, reckon, think.

feeler noun antenna, tentacle.

feeling noun **1** awareness, sensation. **2** compassion, concern, emotion, empathy, passion, sensitivity, sympathy, tenderness, understanding. **3** attitude, hunch, idea, impression, inkling, instinct, intuition, notion, opinion, premonition, sense, sentiment, suspicion, thought, view.

feign verb affect, fake, pretend, sham, simulate.

fell verb chop down, cut down, knock down.

fellow noun **1** associate, colleague, companion, comrade, mate, peer. **2** bloke (*informal*), boy, chap (*informal*), gentleman, guy (*informal*), lad, man.

fellowship noun **1** camaraderie, companionship, company, friendship, society. **2** association, brotherhood, club, fraternity, league, sisterhood, society, sorority.

felon noun criminal, culprit, lawbreaker, miscreant, offender, outlaw.

female adjective see *FEMININE*.

female noun see *GIRL, WOMAN*.

feminine adjective female, girlish, ladylike, womanly; see also *EFFEMINATE*.

fence noun barricade, barrier, hoarding, palings, palisade, railing, stockade, wall.

fence verb (*fence in*) box in, close in, confine, coop up, enclose, hedge in, hem in, surround, wall in.

fend verb □ **fend for** look after, shift for, support, take care of. □ **fend off** fight off, hold at bay, keep off, parry, repel, repulse, ward off.

ferocious adjective barbarous, bestial, bloodthirsty, brutal, cruel, fierce, ruthless, sadistic, savage, vicious, violent, wild.

ferret verb dig out, discover, forage, fossick (*Australian informal*), hunt, root out, rummage, search, unearth.

ferry verb carry, convey, ship, shuttle, take, transfer, transport.

fertile adjective **1** fruitful, productive, rich. **2** creative, imaginative, inventive, productive, prolific, rich.

fertilise verb **1** compost, dress, feed, manure, top-dress. **2** impregnate, inseminate, pollinate.

fervent or **fervid** adjective ardent, devout, eager, earnest, emotional, enthusiastic, fanatical, impassioned, keen, passionate, vehement, warm, zealous.

fester *verb* **1** become infected, discharge, gather, putrefy, suppurate. **2** grow, intensify, rankle, smoulder.

festival *noun* anniversary, carnival, celebration, eisteddfod, fair, fête, fiesta, gala, holiday, jamboree, jubilee, pageant, party, show.

festive *adjective* cheerful, gay, happy, jolly, jovial, joyous, light-hearted, merry.

festivity *noun* celebration, gaiety, jollification, merry-making, mirth, party, rejoicing, revelry, revels, roistering, wassailing (*old use*).

festoon *noun* garland, wreath.

fetch *verb* **1** bring, call for, carry, collect, get, pick up, retrieve. **2** bring in, go for, raise, sell for, yield.

fête *noun* bazaar, fair, gala, jumble sale; see also *FESTIVAL*.

fetter *noun* (*fetters*) bonds, chains, irons, manacles, shackles.

feud *noun* conflict, dispute, quarrel, row, vendetta.

feverish *adjective* **1** burning, febrile, hot. **2** agitated, excited, frantic, frenetic, frenzied, hectic, restless.

few *adjective* infrequent, rare, scarce, sparse, sporadic.

few *noun* handful, remnant, sprinkling.

fiancé, fiancée *noun* betrothed, husband-to-be, intended, wife-to-be.

fiasco *noun* catastrophe, disaster, failure, fizzer (*Australian informal*), flop (*informal*), non-event, wash-out (*informal*).

fib *noun* fabrication, fairy story, falsehood, fiction, lie, porky (*slang*), story, untruth, white lie (*informal*), prevaricate. □ **fib** *verb* lie, prevaricate.

fibre *noun* filament, strand, thread.

fickle *adjective* capricious, changeable, erratic, inconsistent, inconstant, mercurial, mutable, temperamental, unfaithful, unpredictable, unreliable, vacillating, variable.

fiction *noun* **1** fable, fairy story, fantasy, legend, myth, novel, romance, story, tale. **2** fabrication, fib, invention, lie, make-believe.

fictitious *adjective* apocryphal, bogus, fabled, false, fanciful, fictional, imaginary, invented, legendary, made-up, mythical, phoney (*informal*), spurious, untrue.

fiddle *noun* **1** violin. **2** fraud, racket, rort (*Australian slang*), scam (*slang*), swindle, swizz (*informal*).

fiddle verb **1** fidget, finger, jiggle, juggle, mess about, muck around, play, tamper, tinker, toy, twiddle. **2** alter, cook (*informal*), doctor, falsify, fix.

fiddly adjective awkward, intricate, messy, ticklish, tricky.

fidelity noun **1** allegiance, devotion, faithfulness, loyalty. **2** accuracy, faithfulness, honesty, integrity, truthfulness.

fidget verb fiddle, jiggle around, shuffle, squirm, twitch, wriggle. ☐ **fidgety** adjective jittery (*informal*), nervous, restive, restless, twitchy.

field noun **1** lea (*poetical*), meadow, paddock, paddy (*for rice*), pasture. **2** arena, ground, oval, pitch, stadium. **3** area, domain, province, sphere, subject.

fiend noun **1** demon, devil, evil spirit. **2** beast, brute, monster, ogre. **3** addict, crank, devotee, enthusiast, fanatic, freak (*informal*), maniac, nut (*informal*).

fierce adjective **1** bloodthirsty, bloody, brutal, cutthroat, ferocious, merciless, relentless, savage, vicious, violent,

wild. **2** extreme, great, intense, severe, strong.

fiery adjective **1** blazing, burning, flaming, hot, red-hot. **2** ardent, emotional, fervent, impassioned, intense, passionate, spirited, tempestuous, vehement. **3** hotheaded, impetuous, irascible, pugnacious, violent.

fight noun action, affray, aggression, altercation, argument, barney (*informal*), battle, blue (*Australian informal*), brawl, brush, campaign, clash, combat, conflict, confrontation, contest, dispute, duel, dust-up (*informal*), encounter, engagement, feud, fisticuffs, fracas, fray, free-for-all, hostilities, joust, mêlée, punch-up (*informal*), quarrel, row, scrap (*informal*), scrimmage, scuffle, set-to, skirmish, squabble, stoush (*Australian slang*), strife, struggle, tussle, war, wrestle, see also BOUT.

fight verb **1** argue, battle, be at loggerheads, bicker, box, brawl, clash, combat, contend, duel, feud, grapple, joust, quarrel, scrap (*informal*), scuffle, skirmish, spar, squabble, stoush (*Australian slang*), strive, struggle, tussle, war, wrestle. **2** campaign, crusade, strive, struggle, take a stand. **3** defy, oppose, resist. □ **fighter** noun aggressor, battler, boxer, campaigner, combatant, duellist, gladiator, guerrilla, marine, mercenary, partisan, pugilist, soldier, warrior, wrestler.

figure noun **1** digit, integer, number, numeral. **2** body, build, form, outline, physique, shape. **3** effigy, figurine, image, sculpture, statue.

figure verb **1** calculate, compute, work out. **2** appear, feature, play a part.

filament noun fibre, strand, thread, wire.

file verb rub, shape, smooth.

file noun **1** binder, folder, holder, portfolio. **2** dossier, papers, records. **3** column, line, queue, rank, row, string, train.

file verb **1** arrange, catalogue, organise, pigeon-hole, put away, store. **2** march, parade, troop.

fill verb **1** cram, jam, load up, occupy, pack, stuff. **2** block up, bung up, close, plug, seal, stop up.

filling noun contents, padding, stuffing, wadding.

film noun **1** feature, flick (informal), motion picture, movie, picture, video.

2 coating, covering, layer, sheet, skin.

film verb photograph, record, shoot, video.

filter noun colander, screen, sieve, strainer.

filter verb **1** clarify, purify, refine, sieve, strain. **2** leach, percolate, seep, trickle.

filth noun dirt, grime, gunge, gunk (informal), muck (informal), mud, slime, sludge.

filthy adjective **1** blackened, dirty, dusty, grimy, grubby, muddy, soiled, squalid. **2** blue, coarse, crude, dirty, foul, improper, indecent, obscene, offensive, rude, smutty, vile, vulgar.

final adjective **1** closing, concluding, end, finishing, last, ultimate. **2** conclusive, decisive, definitive, indisputable, irrevocable, unalterable. □ **finally** adverb at last, eventually, in the end, lastly, once and for all, ultimately.

finale noun see ENDING.

finalise verb clinch, complete, conclude, finish, settle, sew up (informal), wrap up (informal).

finance noun **finances** assets, capital, cash, funds, means, money, resources.

finance verb back, fund, pay for, sponsor, subsidise, underwrite.

financial adjective **1** budgetary, economic, fiscal, monetary, pecuniary. **2** in funds, solvent.

find verb **1** bring to light, chance upon, come across, come upon, detect, diagnose, dig up, discover, identify, light on, locate, recover, regain, retrieve, spot, stumble on, trace, track down, uncover, unearth. **2** discover, learn.

fine adjective **1** accomplished, brilliant, consummate, excellent, exceptional, exquisite, fantastic, first-class, first-rate, flawless, great, high-quality, impressive, magnificent, marvellous, masterly, meritorious, meticulous, outstanding, peerless, praiseworthy, prize, sensational, skilful, splendid, sterling, super (informal), superb, superior, superlative, top-notch (informal), wonderful. **2** balmy, bright, clear, fair, sunny. **3** (a fine line) narrow, slender, slim, thin; (fine material) delicate, diaphanous, filmy, flimsy, gauzy, gossamer, lacy, light, sheer, thin, transparent. **4** all right, comfortable, OK (informal), well.

fine noun charge, penalty, ticket.

fine verb book, charge, penalise.

finicky adjective choosy (informal), fastidious, fussy, particular, pernickety (informal), picky (informal).

finish verb accomplish, achieve, cease, close, come to an end, complete, conclude, discontinue, end, finalise, get through, halt, round off, stop, terminate, wind up, wrap up (informal); see also CONSUME.

finish noun **1** cessation, close, completion, conclusion, culmination, end, ending, finale, termination. **2** coating, exterior, surface, veneer.

finite adjective bounded, limited, measurable, restricted.

fire noun **1** burning, combustion, flames. **2** blaze, bonfire, bushfire (Australian), conflagration, holocaust, inferno. **3** flak, fusillade, gunfire, salvo, shelling, shooting, volley. □ **on fire** ablaze, aflame, alight, blazing, burning, in flames.

fire verb **1** ignite, kindle, light, set ablaze, set fire to, set on fire. **2** open fire, shoot, snipe; (fire a rocket) detonate, discharge, explode, launch, let off, set off. **3** discharge, dismiss, give someone notice, give someone the boot (informal), remove, sack (informal). **4** animate, excite, inspire, motivate, stimulate.

fireplace noun fire, grate, hearth, range.

fireworks plural noun crackers, pyrotechnics.

firm noun business, company, concern, corporation, enterprise, establishment, organisation, partnership.

firm adjective **1** compact, dense, hard, rigid, set, solid, stiff, unyielding. **2** fixed, secure, stable, steady, strong, sure, tight. **3** (a firm belief) adamant, definite, dogged, inflexible, obstinate, persistent, resolute, rigid, settled, staunch, steadfast, stubborn, unalterable, unchangeable, unshakeable, unwavering, unyielding; (firm friends) constant, dependable, faithful, loyal, reliable, steadfast.

firm verb compact, harden, jell, set, solidify, stiffen.

first adjective **1** earliest, initial, introductory, maiden (voyage), oldest, opening, original, preliminary. **2** basic, cardinal, chief, foremost, fundamental, greatest, highest, leading, main, major, premier, primary, prime, principal, supreme.

fish verb **1** angle, go fishing, trawl. **2** fossick (Australian informal), hunt, look, probe, search, seek.

fishy adjective doubtful, dubious, questionable, shady, strange, suspect, suspicious, suss (informal).

fissure noun cleft, crack, cranny, crevasse, crevice, opening, rift, slit, split.

fit adjective **1** appropriate, fitting, proper, right, suitable, worthy. **2** hardy, healthy, in condition, in fine fettle, in training, robust, well.

fit verb **1** belong, conform, correspond, dovetail, go, interlock, join, match, meet, satisfy, suit. **2** assemble, connect, install, join, put together. **3** adapt, adjust, alter, modify, shape.

fit noun **1** attack, convulsion, paroxysm, seizure, spasm. **2** bout, burst, outbreak, outburst, paroxysm, spell.

fitful adjective erratic, haphazard, intermittent, irregular, occasional, spasmodic, sporadic, variable.

fitting adjective apposite, appropriate, apt, fit, proper, right, suitable, timely.

fix verb **1** anchor, attach, cement, fasten, fit, glue, implant, install, mount, nail, peg, pin, plant, rivet, screw, secure, stick, tape. **2** agree on, appoint, arrange, decide on, establish, organise, set, settle on, specify. **3** correct, cure, mend, put right, rectify, remedy, repair, sort out.

fix noun bind (*informal*), catch-22 (*informal*), difficulty, dilemma, hole (*informal*), jam (*informal*), mess, pickle (*informal*), plight, predicament, quandary, spot (*informal*).

fixation noun infatuation, mania, obsession, preoccupation, thing (*informal*).

fixture noun **1** fitment, fitting. **2** engagement, event, match, meet, meeting.

fizz verb bubble, effervesce, fizzle, froth, hiss, sparkle, sputter. □ **fizzy** adjective aerated, bubbly, carbonated, effervescent, sparkling.

fizzer noun damp squib, disappointment, failure, fiasco, flop (*informal*), non-event.

flabbergasted adjective astonished, astounded, confounded, dumbfounded, nonplussed, overwhelmed, speechless, staggered, stunned, surprised, thunderstruck.

flabby adjective flaccid, limp, soft, weak.

flag noun banner, colours, ensign, jack, pennant, standard, streamer.

flag verb **1** decline, droop, fail, languish, tire, wane, weaken,

weary, wilt. **2** hail, signal, wave.

flagrant adjective barefaced, blatant, brazen, conspicuous, glaring, gross, obvious, open, patent, scandalous, shameless, undisguised.

flair noun ability, aptitude, faculty, gift, knack, talent.

flake noun bit, leaf, piece, scale, shaving, sliver.

flamboyant adjective bright, colourful, extravagant, flashy, gaudy, lairy (*Australian informal*), ostentatious, showy, theatrical.

flame verb blaze, burn, flare.

flammable adjective combustible, inflammable.

flan noun pie, quiche, tart.

flank noun face, side.

flank verb border, edge, line.

flap verb flutter, swing, wave.

flap noun bother, flat spin (*informal*), fluster, panic, state, stew (*informal*), tizzy (*informal*).

flare verb **1** blaze, burn, flame. **2** blow up, erupt, rage; see also *BECOME ANGRY* (at *ANGRY*). **3** broaden, widen.

flash noun **1** blaze, flare, gleam, ray, shaft. **2** burst, display, spark. **3** instant, jiffy (*informal*), moment, second split second, tick (*informal*), trice.

flash *verb* blink, flicker, gleam, glimmer, glint, sparkle, twinkle, wink.

flashy *adjective* flamboyant, garish, gaudy, jazzy, lairy (*Australian informal*), loud, ostentatious, pretentious, showy, snazzy (*informal*), tacky (*informal*), tasteless, tawdry.

flat *adjective* **1** even, horizontal, level, plane, smooth, unruffled. **2** absolute, categorical, definite, firm, unqualified. **3** boring, dull, lacklustre, lifeless, monotonous, unemotional, uninteresting.

flat *noun* apartment, bedsit (*British*), condominium (*American*), home unit (*Australian*), penthouse, tenement, unit (*Australian*).

flatten *verb* **1** compress, iron out, level, pat down, press, roll, smooth. **2** crush, demolish, destroy, knock down, level, raze, run over, squash, trample.

flatter *verb* **1** butter up (*informal*), compliment, crawl to, humour, play up to, praise, suck up to (*informal*), sweet-talk (*informal*). **2** become, do something for, suit. □ **flattery** *noun* adulation, blandish-ments, cajolery, compliments, obsequiousness, praise, smooth talk, soft soap (*informal*), sweet talk (*informal*), sycophancy.

flaunt *verb* display, exhibit, parade, show off, sport.

flavour *noun* piquancy, relish, savour, tang, taste.

flavour *verb* season, spice.

flaw *noun* blemish, bug, defect, error, failing, fault, foible, imperfection, mistake, shortcoming, weakness.

flawless *adjective* faultless, immaculate, impeccable, perfect, spotless, unblemished.

fleck *noun* dot, freckle, patch, speck, speckle, spot.

flee *verb* abscond, beat it (*slang*), bolt, decamp, disappear, do a bunk (*slang*), escape, leave, make tracks (*slang*), retreat, run away, scarper (*slang*), scram (*slang*), shoot through (*Australian informal*), skedaddle (*informal*), take flight, vanish.

fleece *noun* coat, wool.

fleece *verb* cheat, con (*informal*), defraud, diddle (*informal*), rip off (*informal*), rob, swindle.

fleet *noun* argosy (*poetical*), armada, convoy, flotilla, line, navy, squadron.

fleet *adjective* fast, nimble, quick, rapid, speedy, swift.

fleeting *adjective* brief, ephemeral, momentary, passing, short-lived, temporary, transient, transitory.

flex *noun* cable, cord, lead, wire.

flexible *adjective* **1** bendable, elastic, limber, lithe, pliable, resilient, springy, supple. **2** adaptable, adjustable, changeable, open, versatile.

flick *verb* brush, flip, sweep, whisk. ☐ **flick through** flip through, leaf through, skim (through), thumb through.

flicker *verb* **1** blink, glimmer, shimmer, twinkle, wink. **2** flutter, quiver, tremble, waver.

flight *noun* journey, trip.

flight *noun* departure, escape, exit, exodus, fleeing, getaway, retreat.

flighty *adjective* capricious, changeable, erratic, fickle, frivolous, scatterbrained, scatty (*informal*), temperamental, unpredictable.

flimsy *adjective* **1** delicate, diaphanous, filmy, fine, gossamer, lacy, see-through, sheer, thin. **2** breakable, fragile, frail, gimcrack, jerry-built, ramshackle, rickety, shaky, weak.

flinch *verb* cower, cringe, draw back, duck, quail, recoil, shrink, wince.

fling *verb* cast, catapult, chuck (*informal*), heave, hurl, launch, pitch, shy, sling, throw, toss.

flip *verb* flick, spin, throw, toss. ☐ **flip through** flick through, leaf through, skim (through), thumb through.

flippant *adjective* cheeky, disrespectful, frivolous, glib, impertinent, jocular, light hearted, offhand, pert.

flirt *verb* (*flirt with*) chat up, dally with, lead on, philander with, trifle with.

flirt *noun* coquette (*female*), philanderer (*male*), tease.

flit *verb* dart, flitter, flutter, fly.

float *verb* bob, drift, glide, hover, sail, waft.

flock *noun* assembly, band, bevy, brood, bunch, cluster, collection, colony, community, company, congregation, contingent, crowd, drove, flight, gaggle, gathering, herd, horde, mob, multitude, pack, swarm, throng, troop.

flock *verb* assemble, cluster, collect, congregate, converge, crowd, gather, herd, huddle, mass, mob, swarm, throng.

flog *verb* beat, belt (*slang*), birch, cane, chastise, lash, scourge, thrash, whip.

flood *noun* **1** deluge, inundation, spate, torrent. **2** deluge, outpouring, rush, shower, spate, stream, torrent, wave.

flood *verb* **1** cover, deluge, drown, engulf, inundate, overflow, run a banker (*Australian*), submerge, swamp. **2** flow, pour.

floor *noun* **1** deck, level, storey.

floor *verb* **1** bowl over, fell, knock down. **2** baffle, bamboozle (*informal*), confound, confuse, dumbfound, flummox (*informal*), nonplus, perplex, stump (*informal*), throw.

flop *verb* **1** collapse, drop, fall, loll, slump, tumble. **2** dangle, droop, hang down, sag.

flop *noun* disaster, failure, fiasco, fizzer (*Australian informal*), non-event, wash-out (*informal*).

floppy *adjective* baggy, drooping, flaccid, limp, loose, wilting.

flora *noun* botany, plants, vegetation.

flounce *verb* march, stamp, stomp, storm, strut.

flounce *noun* frill, furbelow, ruffle.

flounder *verb* bumble, fumble, stagger, struggle, stumble, wallow.

flourish *verb* **1** bloom, blossom, burgeon, flower, grow, thrive. **2** be successful, boom, grow, prosper, succeed, thrive. **3** brandish, display, flaunt, wave.

flow *verb* **1** circulate, course, move, proceed, run. **2** discharge, dribble, drip, gush, leak, ooze, pour, run, rush, seep, spill, spout, spurt, squirt, stream, trickle.

flow *noun* course, current, drift, flood, gush, influx, outflow, outpouring, spate, stream, tide, torrent.

flower *noun* **1** bloom, blossom, bud. **2** (*flowers*) bouquet, corsage, garland, nosegay, posy, spray, wreath.

flower *verb* bloom, blossom.

flowery *adjective* elaborate, embellished, florid, grandiloquent, high-flown, ornate.

fluctuate *verb* alternate, change, oscillate, see-saw, shift, swing, vacillate, vary, waver.

fluent *adjective* articulate, eloquent, smooth-spoken, voluble.

fluff *noun* down, fuzz, lint.

fluffy *adjective* downy, fleecy, furry, fuzzy, woolly.

fluid *noun* gas, liquid, solution.

fluid *adjective* flowing, gaseous, liquid, molten, runny, sloppy, watery.

fluke noun accident, chance, stroke of luck.

flush verb 1 blush, colour, glow, redden. 2 clean out, rinse out, wash out. □ **flushed** adjective florid, red, rosy, ruddy.

flush adjective 1 flat, level. 2 rich, wealthy, well in (*Australian informal*), well off.

flustered adjective agitated, bothered, confused, disconcerted, fazed (*informal*), in a dither, in a flap (*informal*), in a state, in a tizzy (*informal*), nervous, panicky, rattled (*informal*), ruffled, thrown (*informal*), upset.

flutter verb 1 flit, flitter. 2 bat, beat, flap, palpitate, quiver, shake, tremble, vibrate, wave.

flutter noun 1 dither, flap (*informal*), fluster, stir, tizzy (*informal*). 2 bet, gamble, punt, wager.

fly verb 1 flit, flitter, flutter, glide, hover, soar, swoop, wing. 2 flap, flutter, wave. 3 burst, dart, dash, hurry, hurtle, race, run, rush, scoot, shoot, speed, sweep, tear, whiz, zoom. □ **flying** noun aeronautics, aviation, flight.

foal noun colt (*male*), filly (*female*).

foam noun 1 bubbles, froth, lather, suds. 2 rubber, sponge.

foam verb bubble, effervesce, fizz, froth.

fob verb □ **fob off** get rid of, offload, palm off (*informal*), pass off, unload.

focus noun centre, core, hub.

focus verb centre, concentrate, fix, home in, zero in.

fodder noun feed, food, forage, provender, silage.

foe noun adversary, antagonist, enemy, opponent, rival.

fog noun cloud, haze, mist, murkiness, smog. □ **foggy** adjective hazy, misty, murky.

foible noun failing, flaw, idiosyncrasy, peculiarity, quirk, shortcoming, weakness.

foil verb baffle, baulk, frustrate, hamper, hinder, obstruct, stonker (*Australian slang*), thwart.

fold verb bend, crease, crimp, double over, pleat, wrinkle.

fold noun crease, crinkle, gather, pleat, pucker, tuck, wrinkle.

fold noun compound, enclosure, pen, yard.

folder noun binder, cover, file, portfolio, ringbinder.

folk noun family, kin, kinsfolk, parents, people, relations, relatives.

folklore noun beliefs, legends, lore, myths, traditions.

follow verb **1** chase, go after, hound, hunt, pursue, run after, shadow, stalk, tail (*informal*), track, trail. **2** come after, replace, succeed, supersede, supplant. **3** comply with, conform to, copy, emulate, heed, imitate, keep, obey, observe. **4** comprehend, cotton on to (*informal*), get (*informal*), grasp, latch on to (*informal*), take in, understand. **5** come next, ensue, result. □ **follower** noun adherent, admirer, devotee, disciple, fan, hanger-on, supporter.

folly noun foolishness, idiocy, imprudence, insanity, lunacy, madness, recklessness, silliness, stupidity.

fond adjective **1** adoring, affectionate, caring, devoted, doting, indulgent, loving, tender, warm. **2** absurd, foolish, naïve, silly, vain. □ **fondness** noun affection, attachment, devotion, love, tenderness, warmth.

fondle verb caress, cuddle, pat, pet, stroke, touch.

food noun chow (*slang*), delicacies, diet, eats (*informal*), fare, feed, fodder, foodstuff, forage, grub (*slang*), nosh (*slang*), nourishment, nutriment, produce, provender, provisions, rations, refreshments, sustenance,

tucker (*Australian informal*), victuals.

fool noun **1** ass (*informal*), blockhead, bonehead, boofhead (*Australian informal*), chump (*informal*), clot (*informal*), cretin, dill (*Australian informal*), dimwit (*informal*), dingbat (*informal*), dodo (*informal*), dolt, dope (*informal*), drongo (*Australian informal*), duffer, dummy (*informal*), dunce, fat-head (*informal*), galah (*Australian slang*), gig (*Australian informal*), git (*informal*), goof (*slang*), goon (*slang*), goose (*informal*), half-wit, idiot (*informal*), ignoramus, imbecile, jerk (*slang*), lunatic, moron (*informal*), mug (*informal*), muggins (*informal*), nincompoop, ninny, nitwit (*informal*), nong (*Australian informal*), numskull, nut (*informal*), sap (*informal*), silly (*informal*), silly billy (*informal*), simpleton, sucker (*informal*), thickhead (*informal*), tomfool, twerp (*slang*), twit (*slang*), wally (*slang*). **2** buffoon, clown, comic, entertainer, jester, zany.

fool verb **1** jest, joke, kid (*informal*), tease; (*fool around*) clown around, mess around, monkey about, play around, play the fool. **2** bluff, con (*informal*), deceive, delude, dupe, hoax, hoodwink, mislead, take in, trick.

foolhardy adjective bold, daredevil, daring, impetuous, imprudent, irresponsible, madcap, precipitate, rash, reckless, unwise.

foolish adjective absurd, barmy (*slang*), crazy, daft (*informal*), dopey (*informal*), fatuous, goofy (*slang*), half-witted, hare-brained, idiotic, illogical, imprudent, inane, insane, irrational, ludicrous, lunatic, mad, madcap, misguided, nonsensical, nutty (*informal*), potty (*informal*), ridiculous, senseless, short-sighted, silly, stupid, unintelligent, unwise, witless. □ **foolishness** noun see *FOLLY*.

foot noun **1** hoof, pad, paw, trotter. **2** base, bottom.

foothold noun footing, purchase, toehold.

footing noun basis, standing, status, terms.

footpath noun footway, path, pavement, sidewalk (*American*).

footprint noun footmark, footstep, track.

forage noun feed, fodder, food, provender.

forage verb fossick (*Australian informal*), hunt, poke around, ransack, rummage, scrounge, search.

foray noun assault, attack, incursion, invasion, offensive, raid.

forbearance noun indulgence, lenience, mercy, patience, self-control, tolerance.

forbid verb ban, bar, outlaw, prohibit, proscribe, veto.

forbidding adjective grim, harsh, hostile, inhospitable, menacing, off-putting, ominous, severe, stern, threatening, unfriendly, uninviting.

force noun **1** effort, energy, exertion, might, power, pressure, strength, vigour. **2** body, corps, posse, squad, team, unit. □ **into force** into effect, into operation, into play, into use.

force verb **1** bully, coerce, compel, constrain, dragoon, drive, make, oblige, order, pressure. **2** break open, burst open, prise open, push open, wrench open.

forceful adjective aggressive, assertive, dynamic, effective, energetic, masterful, potent, powerful, pushy, strong, vigorous, weighty.

forebears *plural noun* ancestors, forefathers, predecessors, progenitors.

foreboding *noun* apprehension, forewarning, intuition, misgiving, omen, portent, premonition, presentiment.

forecast *noun* outlook, prediction, prognosis, projection, prophecy.

forecast *verb* foretell, forewarn, predict, prophesy.

forefathers *plural noun* ancestors, forebears, predecessors, progenitors.

forefront *noun* cutting edge, fore, lead, van, vanguard.

forehead *noun* brow.

foreign *adjective* **1** alien, exotic, imported, overseas, strange, unfamiliar. **2** alien, outside, uncharacteristic, unnatural.

foreigner *noun* alien, immigrant, new chum (*Australian informal*), newcomer, outsider, stranger, visitor.

foreman *noun* **1** boss, overseer, superintendent, supervisor. **2** spokesman, spokesperson, spokeswoman.

foremost *adjective* best, chief, greatest, leading, main, major, pre-eminent, premier, principal, supreme, top.

forerunner *noun* ancestor, harbinger, herald, precursor, predecessor, prototype.

foresee *verb* anticipate, envisage, expect, forecast, foretell, predict, prophesy.

foresight *noun* far-sightedness, forethought, prescience, providence, vision.

forest *noun* brush, jungle, plantation, thicket, wood, woodland, woods.

forestall *verb* anticipate, foil, pre-empt, prevent, thwart.

foretaste *noun* preview, sample, token.

foretell *verb* forecast, foresee, predict, prophesy.

forethought *noun* foresight, planning, preparation.

forever *adverb* always, constantly, continually, eternally, everlastingly, incessantly, permanently, perpetually.

foreword *noun* introduction, preamble, preface, prologue.

forfeit *verb* cede, forgo, give up, relinquish, renounce, sacrifice, surrender, waive.

forfeit *noun* fine, penalty.

forge *noun* furnace, smithy, workshop.

forge *verb* **1** fashion, form, hammer out, mould, shape. **2** copy, counterfeit, fake, falsify. □ **forgery** *noun* copy, counterfeit, dud (*informal*), fake, fraud, imitation, phoney (*informal*), replica, reproduction, sham.

forget *verb* leave behind, leave out, miss, neglect, omit, overlook, pass over, skip.

forgetful *adjective* absent-minded, careless, inattentive, neglectful, negligent, oblivious, remiss, scatterbrained, vague.

forgive *verb* absolve, excuse, exonerate, let off, overlook, pardon, remit. □ **forgivable** *adjective* excusable, pardonable, venial. □ **forgiveness** *noun* absolution, amnesty, exoneration, pardon, remission.

forgo *verb* abandon, abstain from, give up, go without, renounce.

fork *noun* bifurcation, Y-junction.

fork *verb* bifurcate, branch, divide, separate, split.

forlorn *adjective* dejected, depressed, desolate, disconsolate, forsaken, heavy-hearted, lonely, melancholy, miserable, sad, unhappy, woebegone, wretched.

form *noun* **1** appearance, arrangement, composition, configuration, construction, contour, design, figure, format, formation, layout, mould, organisation, outline, pattern, profile, shape, silhouette, structure. **2** brand, breed, class, edition, genre, genus, kind, model, sort, species, style, type, variety, version. **3** class, grade, year. **4** bench, seat. **5** application, coupon, document, paper, questionnaire. **6** condition, fettle, fitness, health, shape, trim.

form *verb* **1** build, carve, cast, construct, create, establish, fabricate, fashion, forge, found, make, model, mould, produce, sculpt, set up, shape. **2** appear, develop, grow, materialise, take shape.

formal *adjective* (*a formal occasion*) ceremonial, official, solemn, stately; (*a formal manner*) ceremonious, conventional, dignified, pompous, prim, proper, punctilious, reserved, starchy, stiff, stilted, strait-laced.

formality *noun* **1** ceremoniousness, ceremony, conventionality, decorum, punctiliousness, stiffness. **2** convention, custom, form, procedure, regulation, rite, ritual, rule.

format *noun* arrangement, design, form, layout, organisation, shape, size, structure.

former *adjective* ancient, bygone, earlier, old, olden, past, previous. □ **formerly** *adverb* in the past, once, previously.

ormidable *adjective* arduous, challenging, daunting, difficult, herculean, mammoth, onerous, overwhelming, tough.

ormula *noun* **1** algorithm, rule, statement, theorem. **2** prescription, recipe.

ormulate *verb* articulate, compose, express, form, frame, phrase, work out.

orsake *verb* abandon, desert, leave, reject.

ort *noun* see *FORTRESS*.

orte *noun* speciality, specialty, strength, strong point.

orthcoming *adjective* **1** coming, future, imminent, impending, prospective, upcoming. **2** communicative, expansive, responsive, talkative.

orthright *adjective* blunt, candid, direct, frank, open, outspoken, plain-spoken, straightforward, truthful, upfront (*informal*).

ortification *noun* bastion, battlement, bulwark, parapet, rampart, stronghold.

ortify *verb* **1** defend, garrison, protect, reinforce, secure, strengthen. **2** boost, invigorate, strengthen, sustain.

ortitude *noun* boldness, bravery, courage, determination, endurance, grit, guts

(*informal*), pluck, resoluteness, stoicism.

fortress *noun* acropolis, castle, citadel, fort, fortification, garrison, stronghold.

fortuitous *adjective* accidental, casual, chance, coincidental, random, serendipitous, unexpected, unintentional, unplanned.

fortunate *adjective* **1** blessed, favoured, happy, lucky, prosperous. **2** auspicious, favourable, lucky, opportune, propitious, providential, timely.

fortune *noun* **1** chance, destiny, fate, luck, providence. **2** big bickies (*Australian informal*), bundle (*informal*), heaps (*informal*), megabucks (*informal*), mint, packet (*informal*), pile (*informal*), pots (*informal*), riches, wealth. □ **fortune-teller** *noun* astrologer, clairvoyant, crystal-gazer, diviner, palmist, prophet, seer, sibyl (*female*), soothsayer.

forward *adjective* **1** advanced, developed, early, precocious, quick. **2** assertive, audacious, bold, brazen, cheeky, fresh (*informal*), impertinent, impudent, pert, presumptuous, pushy, saucy.

forward *verb* **1** deliver, dispatch, readdress, redirect, send on. **2** advance, assist, foster, further, help, promote, support.

forwards adverb ahead, forward, frontwards, onwards.

fossick verb ferret, fish, forage, hunt, poke around, rake through, rummage, scavenge, scrounge, search.

fossil noun relic, remains.

foster verb advance, cultivate, encourage, further, nurture, promote.

foul adjective 1 bad, disgusting, horrible, nauseating, noisome (literary), objectionable, obnoxious, off (informal), offensive, on the nose (Australian informal), putrid, rank, revolting, rotten, smelly, stinking, vile. 2 atrocious (informal), crook (Australian informal), dreadful (informal), lousy (informal), rough, shocking (informal), stormy, terrible (informal), wild. 3 (a foul crime) abhorrent, abominable, appalling, atrocious, beastly, contemptible, despicable, detestable, evil, loathsome, monstrous, shocking, terrible, vicious, vile, villainous, violent, wicked; (foul language) abusive, bad, blasphemous, coarse, crude, dirty, disgusting, filthy, impolite, indecent, obscene, offensive, rude, smutty, vulgar.

foul verb 1 contaminate, pollute, taint. 2 entangle, snarl, tangle.

found verb 1 begin, create, establish, inaugurate, initiate, institute, originate, pioneer, set up, start. 2 base, build, ground, root.

foundation noun 1 establishment, institution, organisation. 2 base, basis, grounds, justification, support. 3 base, footing, substructure.

fountain noun fount, jet, shower, spout, spray, spring.

fox noun cub (young), kit (young), vixen (female). □ **fox** adjective see CUNNING.

fox verb baffle, bamboozle (informal), confound, flummox (informal), perplex, puzzle, stump, trick.

foyer noun entrance hall, lobby, vestibule.

fraction noun bit, fragment, part, piece, portion, section.

fracture noun break, cleft, crack, fissure, rift, rupture, split.

fracture verb break, crack, rupture, split.

fragile noun breakable, brittle, delicate, flimsy, frail, weak.

fragment noun bit, chip, crumb, morsel, part, particle, piece, remnant, scrap, shred, sliver, snatch, snippet, speck, splinter; (*fragments*) smith-ereens.

fragrance *noun* aroma, balm, bouquet, odour, perfume, redolence, scent, smell.

frail *adjective* **1** delicate, flimsy, fragile, rickety, unsound, weak. **2** ailing, decrepit, feeble, infirm, sickly, weak.

frame *noun* **1** border, case, edge, margin, mount, mounting, surround. **2** chassis, framework, shell, skeleton, structure, substructure. **3** body, build, figure, physique, skeleton. □ **frame of mind** attitude, disposition, humour, mood, outlook, state, temper.

frame *verb* **1** enclose, mount, surround. **2** compose, construct, devise, draft, formulate.

framework *noun* **1** chassis, frame, shell, skeleton, structure, substructure. **2** outline, plan, structure, system.

franchise *noun* suffrage, right to vote, vote.

frank *adjective* blunt, candid, direct, forthright, honest, open, outspoken, plain-spoken, straightforward, truthful, upfront (*informal*).

frantic *adjective* agitated, anxious, berserk, beside yourself, crazy, desperate, distraught, frenzied, hysteri-cal, overwrought, panic-stricken, worried.

fraternise *verb* associate, consort, hobnob, mingle, mix, socialise.

fraud *noun* **1** cheating, deceit, deception, dishonesty, duplicity, fraudulence, rorting (*Australian slang*), swindling, trickery. **2** charlatan, cheat, con man (*informal*), fake, humbug, impostor, phoney (*informal*), quack, sham, swindler, trickster. □ **fraudulent** *adjective* crooked, deceitful, dishonest, false, phoney (*informal*), shady, shonky (*Australian informal*), unscrupulous.

frayed *adjective* ragged, shabby, tattered, tatty (*informal*), threadbare, unravelled, worn.

freak *noun* monster, monstrosity, mutant, oddity, weirdo (*informal*). □ **freakish** *adjective* abnormal, atypical, bizarre, eccentric, exceptional, extraordinary, freak, odd, outlandish, peculiar, queer, strange, unusual, weird.

free *adjective* **1** at liberty, emancipated, liberated, released. **2** complimentary, gratis, on the house (*informal*), unpaid. **3** detached, loose, unattached, untied. **4** exempt (from), immune (from), rid (of), without. **5** available, spare, uncommitted, unoccupied, vacant. **6** bountiful, generous, lavish, liberal, open-handed, unstinting.

free *verb* **1** deliver, emancipate, excuse, exempt, let loose, let off, let out, liberate, release, relieve, rescue, save, set free, spare, uncage, unchain, unleash. **2** clear, detach, disengage, disentangle, extricate, loosen, untangle.

freedom *noun* **1** autonomy, deliverance, emancipation, independence, liberation, liberty, release, self-determination, self-government. **2** discretion, free hand, free rein, latitude, licence, scope.

freeway *noun* expressway, highway, motorway.

freewheel *verb* coast, drift, glide.

freeze *verb* **1** ice over, turn to ice. **2** chill, cool, refrigerate. **3** fix, hold, peg. **4** halt, petrify, stop. □ **freezing** *adjective* arctic, bitter, chilly, cold, frigid, frosty, ice-cold, icy, nippy (*informal*), perishing (*informal*), subzero.

freight *noun* **1** carriage, cartage, conveyance, haulage, shipment, shipping, transport. **2** cargo, consignment, goods, lading, load. □ **freight** *verb* carry, cart, dispatch, forward, move, send, ship, transport.

frenzy *noun* agitation, excitement, fever, hysteria, insanity, madness, mania. □ **frenzied** *adjective* agitated, berserk, crazy, delirious, demented, distraught, excited, feverish, frantic, frenetic, hectic, hysterical, mad, wild.

frequent *adjective* common, constant, continual, eternal, familiar, habitual, incessant, perpetual, persistent, recurrent, regular, repeated. □ **frequently** *adverb* again and again, commonly, constantly, continually, habitually, often, regularly, repeatedly.

frequent *verb* haunt, patronise, visit.

fresh *adjective* **1** latest, new, recent, up to date, up to the minute. **2** alternative, different, innovative, new, newfangled (*derogatory*), novel, original, untried. **3** clean, cool, crisp, pure, refreshing, unpolluted. **4** alert, energetic, invigorated, lively, perky, refreshed, revived.

freshen *verb* air, clean, deodorise, ventilate.

fret *verb* brood, distress yourself, grieve, mope, pine, worry. □ **fretful** *adjective* anxious, distressed, miserable, peevish, restless, troubled, upset.

friar noun brother, monk, religious.

friction noun **1** abrasion, chafing, fretting, rubbing. **2** antagonism, conflict, contention, disagreement, discord, dissension, quarrelling, strife.

friend noun **1** acquaintance, ally, boyfriend, buddy (*informal*), chum (*informal*), cobber (*Australian informal*), companion, comrade, confidant, confidante, crony, girlfriend, mate, pal (*informal*), partner, penfriend, playmate, steady. **2** backer, benefactor, helper, patron, supporter, sympathiser.

friendly adjective affable, affectionate, amiable, amicable, approachable, brotherly, chummy (*informal*), companionable, convivial, cordial, familiar, genial, good-natured, gracious, hospitable, intimate, kind, kind-hearted, kindly, loving, matey, neighbourly, outgoing, pally (*informal*), sisterly, sociable, sympathetic, tender, warm-hearted, welcoming. □ **friendliness** noun affability, affection, amiability, amicability, approachability, camaraderie, conviviality, cordiality, geniality, goodwill, hospitality, kindness, neighbourliness, sociability, warmth.

friendship noun alliance, amity, association, camaraderie, companionship, comradeship, cordiality, friendliness, harmony, mateship, partnership, relationship.

fright noun alarm, anxiety, apprehension, consternation, dismay, dread, fear, horror, panic, scare, shock, start, terror, trepidation.

frighten verb alarm, cow, daunt, dismay, freak out (*informal*), horrify, intimidate, menace, perturb, petrify, put the wind up (*informal*), rattle (*informal*), scare, shock, startle, terrify, terrorise, unnerve. □ **frightened** adjective afraid, alarmed, anxious, apprehensive, chicken (*informal*), faint-hearted, fearful, nervous, panic-stricken, petrified, scared, terrified, terror-stricken. □ **frightening** adjective alarming, chilling, creepy, daunting, dreadful, eerie, fearful, fearsome, frightful, hair-raising, horrifying, nightmarish, scary, sinister, spine-chilling, spooky, terrifying.

frightful adjective appalling, awful, bad, dreadful, fearful, fearsome, ghastly, grisly, gruesome, hideous, horrendous, horrible, horrid, horrific, shocking, terrible.

frill noun **1** flounce, ruff, ruffle. **2** addition, extra, supplement, trimming.

fringe noun **1** border, edge, edging, tassels. **2** borders, edge, limits, margin, outskirts, perimeter, periphery.

frisk verb **1** caper, cavort, dance, frolic, gambol, jump, leap, play, prance, romp, skip. **2** check, inspect, search. □ **frisky** adjective active, frolicsome, lively, perky, playful, skittish, spirited.

fritter verb (fritter away) dissipate, misspend, squander, waste.

frivolous adjective facetious, flighty, flippant, giddy, inane, irresponsible, light-hearted, petty, ridiculous, shallow, silly, superficial, trivial, unimportant.

frizzy adjective Afro, bushy, curly, fuzzy.

frock noun dress, gown, robe.

frolic verb caper, cavort, frisk, gambol, let off steam, play, romp, skip.

front noun beginning, bow (of a ship), façade, face, fore, forefront, frontage, head, start, van, vanguard.

front adjective anterior, first, fore, initial, leading.

frontier noun border, boundary, limits.

frost noun hoar-frost, rime.

froth noun bubbles, foam, lather, scum, suds.

frown verb glare, glower, grimace, knit your brow, lour, scowl.

frugal adjective **1** economical, parsimonious, pennypinching, provident, sparing, thrifty. **2** meagre, paltry, scanty, skimpy.

fruit noun consequence, harvest, outcome, product, result, reward, upshot.

fruitful adjective fertile, productive, profitable, rewarding, successful, useful, valuable, worthwhile.

fruitless adjective abortive, barren, futile, ineffective, pointless, unproductive, unsuccessful, useless, vain.

frustrate verb baffle, baulk, block, check, foil, hamper, hamstring, hinder, impede, prevent, stonker (Australian slang), stop, stymie, thwart.

fry verb brown, sauté.

fugitive noun deserter, escapee, renegade, runaway.

fulfil verb accomplish, achieve, carry out, complete, comply with, conform to, discharge, execute, keep, live up to, meet, perform, satisfy.

full adjective **1** brimming, bursting, chock-a-block

chockers (*Australian informal*), chock-full, congested, crammed, crowded, filled, jam-packed, overcrowded, overflowing, packed, stuffed. **2** abounding (in), rich (in), teeming (with). **3** complete, comprehensive, detailed, entire, exhaustive, thorough, total, unabridged, whole.

fumbling *adjective* awkward, bumbling, bungling, clumsy, inept.

fume *noun* □ **fumes** exhaust, gas, smoke, vapour.

fume *verb* **1** smoke, smoulder. **2** blow up (*informal*), blow your stack (*informal*), blow your top (*informal*), explode, flare up, lose your temper, rage, seethe, smoulder.

fun *noun* amusement, diversion, enjoyment, entertainment, frivolity, frolic, gaiety, hilarity, joking, jollity, kicks (*informal*), laughter, merriment, merry-making, mirth, play, pleasure, recreation, relaxation, sport. □ **make fun of** chiack (*Australian informal*), deride, jeer at, joke about, laugh at, mock, parody, poke borak at (*Australian informal*), poke fun at, rib (*informal*), ridicule, satirise, send up (*informal*), sling off at (*Australian informal*), take the mickey out of (*informal*), taunt, tease.

function *noun* **1** activity, duty, job, purpose, role, task, use. **2** affair (*informal*), ceremony, do (*informal*), event, gathering, occasion, party, reception.

function *verb* act, behave, go, operate, perform, run, serve, work.

functional *adjective* **1** functioning, going, operational, running, working. **2** practical, serviceable, useful, utilitarian.

fund *noun* **1** kitty, nest egg, pool, reserve. **2** hoard, mine, reserve, reservoir, stock, store, supply. □ **funds** *plural noun* capital, cash, finances, means, money, resources, savings, wealth.

fund *verb* back, finance, pay for, sponsor, subsidise.

fundamental *adjective* basic, cardinal, central, crucial, elementary, essential, important, key, primary, principal, underlying, vital.

funeral *noun* burial, cremation, interment.

funnel *noun* chimney, smokestack.

funny *adjective* **1** amusing, comical, crazy, droll, entertaining, facetious, farcical, hilarious, humorous, laughable, ludicrous, priceless (*informal*), ridiculous, witty, zany. **2** abnormal, bizarre, curious, extraordinary, odd, peculiar, queer, strange, unusual, weird.

fur noun **1** coat, down, fleece, hair. **2** hide, pelt, skin.

furious adjective **1** angry, cross, enraged, hopping mad (*informal*), incensed, indignant, infuriated, irate, livid, mad, rabid, ropeable (*Australian informal*), wrathful. **2** fierce, intense, raging, savage, tempestuous, violent, wild.

furnace noun boiler, forge, incinerator, kiln, oven.

furnish verb arm, equip, fit out, provide, supply.

furniture noun effects, furnishings, movables.

furore noun commotion, hullabaloo, rumpus, stir, storm, to-do, uproar.

furrow noun **1** channel, ditch, drill, rut, trench. **2** channel, corrugation, groove, hollow, rut. **3** crease, line, wrinkle.

furry adjective downy, fleecy, fluffy, fuzzy, hairy, woolly.

further adjective additional, extra, fresh, more, new, other, supplementary.

further verb advance, aid, assist, boost, champion, forward, help, promote.

furthermore adverb also, besides, in addition, moreover, too.

furthest adjective extreme, farthest, furthermost, outermost, ultimate, uttermost.

furtive adjective clandestine, covert, secretive, shifty, sly, sneaky, stealthy, surreptitious, wily.

fury noun anger, exasperation, frenzy, ire, paddy (*informal*), rage, temper, wrath.

fuse verb amalgamate, blend, bond, coalesce, combine, consolidate, incorporate, merge, stick, synthesise, unite, weld.

fuss noun ado, bother, bustle, commotion, excitement, flurry, fluster, furore, hue and cry, hullabaloo, kerfuffle (*informal*), palaver (*informal*), rumpus, stir, to-do, uproar.

fuss verb carry on, complain, create (*slang*), flap (*informal*), fret, niggle, quibble, worry.

fussy adjective **1** choosy (*informal*), faddy, fastidious, finicky, hard to please, particular, pernickety (*informal*), picky (*informal*), selective. **2** busy, cluttered, detailed, elaborate, fancy, intricate, ornate.

futile adjective fruitless, ineffective, ineffectual, pointless senseless, unproductive, unsuccessful, useless, vain, worthless.

future *noun* hereafter, outlook, prospect.

future *adjective* approaching, coming, forthcoming, prospective, subsequent.

fuzzy *adjective* **1** downy, fleecy, fluffy, frizzy, furry, woolly. **2** blurred, dim, hazy, imprecise, indistinct, unclear, vague, woolly.

Gg

gabble *verb* babble, chatter, jabber, prattle, yabber (*Australian informal*).

gadget *noun* apparatus, appliance, contraption (*informal*), device, gizmo (*informal*), implement, instrument, machine, tool, utensil.

gag *noun* jest, joke, quip, wisecrack, witticism.

gag *verb* **1** muzzle. **2** keep quiet, muzzle, silence, stifle. **3** choke, gasp, retch.

gaiety *noun* celebration, cheer, cheerfulness, festivity, fun, glee, happiness, hilarity, jollity, joy, merriment, merrymaking, mirth, revelry.

gain *verb* **1** achieve, acquire, attain, earn, get, obtain, procure, profit, receive, score, secure, win. **2** arrive at, get to, reach.

gain *noun* advantage, benefit, dividend, improvement, income, increase, jump, profit, return, reward, rise, yield. □ **gains** *plural noun* booty, earnings, income, loot, proceeds, profits, takings, winnings.

gait *noun* carriage, pace, step, stride, tread, walk.

gala *noun* carnival, fair, festival, fête, pageant.

gale *noun* blast, cyclone, gust, hurricane, storm, tempest, tornado, typhoon, wind.

gall *noun* audacity, boldness, cheek, effrontery, hide, impertinence, impudence, nerve, temerity.

gall *verb* abrade, chafe, fret, rub.

gallant *adjective* attentive, brave, chivalrous, considerate, courageous, courteous, daring, dauntless, fearless, gentlemanly, gracious, heroic, intrepid, kind, lion-hearted, manly, noble, polite, suave, valiant.

gallery *noun* **1** balcony, gods (*informal*). **2** arcade, cloister, colonnade, loggia, portico, veranda. **3** hall, museum.

gallop *verb* bolt, bound, dash, fly, hurry, hurtle, race, run, rush, shoot, speed, sprint, tear, whiz.

gallows *noun* gibbet, scaffold.

gamble *verb* bet, chance, have a flutter (*informal*), punt, risk, stake, venture, wager. □ **gambler** *noun* better, punter, speculator.

gamble *noun* chance, lottery, punt, risk, speculation, uncertainty.

game *noun* **1** amusement, diversion, entertainment, pastime, playing, recreation, sport. **2** bout, competition, contest, event, match, round.

game *adjective* **1** eager, keen, prepared, ready, willing. **2** bold, brave, courageous, daring, fearless, intrepid, plucky.

gang *noun* band, bunch, crew, group, mob (*informal*), pack, push (*Australian old use*), relay, set, squad, team, troop.

gangling *adjective* gawky, lanky, lean, skinny, tall, thin, ungainly.

gangster *noun* bandit, brigand, criminal, crook (*informal*), desperado, robber, ruffian, thug, tough.

gangway *noun* aisle, gap, passage.

gap *noun* **1** aisle, aperture, breach, break, chasm, crack, cranny, crevice, discontinuity, fissure, gangway, hole, opening, space. **2** break, hiatus, interlude, intermission, interval, lull, pause, recess. **3** chasm, difference, disparity, divergence, gulf.

gape *verb* **1** gawp (*informal*), gaze, goggle, stare. **2** come apart, open up, part, split open.

garage *noun* **1** shed. **2** filling station, petrol station, service station.

garbage *noun* debris, junk, litter, refuse, rubbish, scraps, trash, waste.

garbled *adjective* confused, incoherent, jumbled, mixed up, unclear.

garden *noun* allotment, grounds, lawn, patch, plot, yard.

garish *adjective* bright, flashy, gaudy, lairy (*Australian informal*), loud, showy, vivid.

garland *noun* festoon, lei, wreath.

garment *noun* (*garments*) apparel (*formal*), attire (*formal*), clothes, clothing, costume, dress, garb, gear (*informal*), outfit, raiment (*old use*), vestments, wear.

garnish verb decorate, embellish.

garrison noun citadel, fort, fortress, stronghold. □ **garrison** verb defend, guard, occupy, protect.

garrulous adjective chatty, long-winded, loquacious, talkative, verbose, voluble, wordy.

gas noun exhaust, fumes, vapour.

gash noun cut, laceration, slash, slit, tear, wound.

gash verb cut, lacerate, slash, slit, tear, wound.

gasp verb choke, pant, puff, wheeze.

gate noun 1 barrier, door, portcullis, turnstile. 2 entrance, entry, exit, gateway, portal.

gather verb 1 assemble, cluster, concentrate, congregate, convene, crowd, flock, herd, marshal, mass, meet, mobilise, muster, rally, rendezvous, round up, swarm, throng. 2 accumulate, amass, collect, hoard, pile up, stack up, stockpile, store. 3 collect, garner, glean, harvest, pick, pluck, reap. 4 conclude, infer, learn, surmise, take it, understand. 5 ruffle, shirr.

gathering noun assembly, collection, congregation, congress, convention, crowd, flock, get-together (informal), group, meeting, mob, muster, party, rally, reunion, social, swarm, throng.

gaudy adjective bright, colourful, flamboyant, flashy, garish, jazzy, lairy (Australian informal), loud, lurid, showy, tawdry, vivid.

gauge noun guide, indicator, measure, meter, rule, yardstick.

gauge verb 1 calculate, compute, determine, measure, quantify, weigh. 2 assess, estimate, judge.

gaunt adjective bony, cadaverous, emaciated, haggard, lanky, lean, scraggy, scrawny, skeletal, skinny, thin.

gauzy adjective diaphanous, fine, flimsy, light, see-through, sheer, thin, transparent.

gay adjective 1 blithe, bright, carefree, cheerful, happy, jolly, jovial, light-hearted, lively, merry. 2 bright, colourful, gaudy, showy, vivid. 3 homosexual, lesbian (female).

gaze verb (gaze at) behold (old use), contemplate, eye, gape at, gawp at (informal), look at, observe, peer at, stare at, study, survey, view, watch.

gaze noun look, stare.

gear noun 1 apparatus, appliances, equipment, implements, instruments, kit, materials, outfit, paraphernalia, rig, stuff, tackle, things, tools. **2** apparel (*formal*), attire (*formal*), clothes, clothing, dress, garments, get-up (*informal*), outfit, rig (*informal*), wear.

geld verb castrate, de-sex, doctor, neuter, spay, sterilise.

gem noun gemstone, jewel, precious stone.

genealogy noun ancestry, family history, lineage, pedigree.

general adjective **1** all-round, broad, common, comprehensive, extensive, global, overall, popular, public, sweeping, universal, wholesale, widespread, worldwide. **2** customary, everyday, familiar, habitual, normal, ordinary, regular, standard, typical, usual. **3** broad, imprecise, indefinite, vague. **4** chief, head, principal.

generally adverb by and large, for the most part, in general, largely, mainly, mostly, normally, on the whole, usually.

generate verb bring about, create, drum up, give rise to, inspire, produce, whip up.

generous adjective **1** benevolent, big-hearted, bountiful, charitable, kind-hearted, lavish, magnanimous, munificent, open-handed, philanthropic, selfless, unselfish, unstinting. **2** abundant, ample, copious, lavish, liberal, plentiful, sizeable. □ **generosity** noun benevolence, bounty, charity, largesse, liberality, magnanimity, munificence, philanthropy.

genesis noun beginning, birth, commencement, creation, inception, origin, start.

genial adjective affable, amiable, convivial, cordial, easygoing, friendly, hospitable, kind, outgoing, pleasant, sociable, warm-hearted.

genius noun **1** brain (*informal*), expert, know-all, mastermind, prodigy, virtuoso, whiz-kid (*informal*). **2** ability, aptitude, brains, brilliance, intellect, intelligence, talent.

genteel adjective civil, courteous, courtly, gentlemanly, ladylike, mannerly, polite, posh (*informal*), refined, well-bred, well-mannered.

gentle adjective **1** benign, compassionate, docile, harmless, humane, kind, kindhearted, kindly, lenient, meek, merciful, mild, peaceful, placid, quiet, serene, softhearted, sympathetic, tame, tender-hearted. **2** (*a gentle voice*) calm, mild, pleasant, quiet, soft, soothing, sweet, tender; (*a gentle breeze*) balmy, faint, light, mild, moderate, soft; (*a gentle slope*) easy, gradual, moderate, slight.

genuine *adjective* actual, authentic, bona fide, dinkum (*Australian informal*), dinky-di (*Australian informal*), honest, honest-to-goodness (*informal*), kosher (*informal*), real, ridgy-didge (*Australian informal*), sincere, true.

germ *noun* bacterium, bug (*informal*), microbe, micro-organism, virus.

germinate *verb* come up, grow, shoot, spring up, sprout.

gesture *noun* action, gesticulation, motion, movement, sign, signal. ☐ **gesture** *verb* beckon, gesticulate, motion, nod, point, signal, wave.

get *verb* **1** acquire, be given, buy, come by, earn, gain, get hold of, land, obtain, procure, purchase, receive, score, take, win; see also *FETCH*. **2** become, grow, turn. **3** arrive at, reach. **4** fix, make ready, prepare. **5** cause, convince, induce, influence, make, persuade. **6** be afflicted with, catch, come down with, contract, develop, pick up, suffer from. **7** comprehend, cotton on to (*informal*), fathom, follow, grasp, realise, understand.

☐ **get away** abscond, bolt, break free, decamp, depart, do a bunk (*slang*), escape, flee, leave, nick off (*Australian slang*), push off (*informal*), scarper, shoot through (*Australian informal*), slip away. ☐ **get on** cope, fare, get along, make out (*informal*), manage. ☐ **get out of** avoid, dodge, escape, evade, shirk, wriggle out of. ☐ **get over** overcome, pull through, recover from, survive. ☐ **get up** arise (*old use*), rise, surface. ☐ **get your own back** get even, have your revenge, pay back, retaliate.

getaway *noun* escape, flight, retreat.

get-together *noun* function, gathering, meeting, party, rendezvous, reunion, social.

ghastly *adjective* **1** appalling, awful, dreadful, frightful, gruesome, hideous, horrendous, horrible, repulsive, shocking, terrible. **2** ashen, deathly, ghostly, pale, pallid, pasty, sickly, wan, washed out.

ghost *noun* apparition, phantom, poltergeist, shade, spectre, spirit, spook (*informal*), vision, wraith. ☐ **ghostly** *adjective* creepy, eerie, sinister, spooky (*informal*), uncanny, unearthly, weird.

ghoulish adjective gruesome, macabre, morbid.

giant noun monster, ogre, Titan.

gibberish noun babble, double Dutch, drivel, gobbledegook (informal), jabber, mumbo-jumbo, nonsense, poppycock (slang), rubbish, twaddle.

gibe verb (gibe at) chiack (Australian informal), jeer at, make fun of, mock, poke borak at (Australian informal), ridicule, scoff at, sling off at (Australian informal), sneer at, taunt, tease.

giddy adjective dizzy, faint, light-headed, unsteady.
□ **giddiness** noun dizziness, light-headedness, unsteadiness, vertigo.

gift noun **1** alms, bequest, bonus, contribution, donation, endowment, freebie (informal), give-away (informal), gratuity, handout, legacy, offering, offertory, present, tip. **2** ability, aptitude, facility, flair, genius, head, knack, talent.

gifted adjective able, accomplished, bright, brilliant, capable, clever, intelligent, skilful, skilled, talented.

gig noun performance, show.

gigantic adjective big, boomer (Australian informal), colossal, enormous, extensive, gargantuan, giant, ginormous (slang), huge, humungous (slang), immeasurable, immense, jumbo-sized, king-sized, large, mammoth, massive, mighty, monstrous, monumental, prodigious, stupendous, tremendous, vast, whopping (slang).

giggle verb chuckle, laugh, snicker, snigger, titter.

giggle noun chuckle, laugh, snicker, snigger, titter.

gimmick noun device, ploy, stratagem, trick.

gingerly adverb carefully, cautiously, charily, timidly, warily.

gird verb **1** brace, prepare, ready, steel. **2** encircle, enclose, encompass, ring, surround.

girl noun babe (informal), bird (informal), chick (slang), damsel (old use), female, gal (informal), lass, lassie (informal), maid (old use), maiden (old use), miss, schoolgirl, sheila (Australia slang); see also CHILD, WOMAN.

girlfriend noun date (informal), female friend, fiancée, steady, sweetheart.

girth noun circumference, perimeter.

gist noun content, core, drift, essence, meaning, pith, point, substance.

give verb **1** allot, allow, award, bestow, confer, contribute, deal out, dish out (*informal*), distribute, dole out, donate, endow with, entrust with, equip with, furnish with, grant, hand out, hand over, offer, pay, present, proffer, provide with, ration out, supply with. **2** communicate, convey, deliver, impart, pass on, report, tell, transmit. **3** emit, let out, utter. **4** break, buckle, collapse, crack, fold up, give way, yield. □ **give away** betray, blab, divulge, leak, let out, make known, reveal. □ **give back** pay back, refund, reimburse, repay, return. □ **give in** capitulate, cave in, concede, give up, submit, succumb, surrender, yield. □ **give off** discharge, emit, exude, give out, release. □ **give up 1** abandon, cease, chuck in (*informal*), discontinue, give away (*Australian*), leave, quit, resign, retire, stop. **2** cede, forfeit, forgo, part with, relinquish, renounce, sacrifice, waive. **3** capitulate, concede, give in, surrender, throw in the towel, throw up the sponge, yield.

glad adjective **1** delighted, gratified, happy, joyful, pleased, thrilled. **2** cheerful, good, happy, joyful, pleasing, welcome.

gladden verb brighten, cheer, delight, please.

glamorous adjective attractive, beautiful, bewitching, charming, elegant, exciting, fascinating.

glance verb look, peek, peep, scan, skim. □ **glance** noun glimpse, look, peek, peep, squiz (*Australian slang*).

glare verb frown, glower, lour, scowl, stare. □ **glare** noun **1** brightness, dazzle, radiance. **2** black look, frown, glower, lour, scowl, stare.

glaring adjective **1** blazing, blinding, bright, dazzling, harsh, strong. **2** blatant, conspicuous, flagrant, obvious, patent, plain, unmistakable.

glass noun **1** crystal, pane, plate glass. **2** beaker, goblet, tumbler, wineglass. **3** looking-glass, mirror. □ **glassy** adjective glazed, reflective, shiny, smooth, vitreous.

glasses plural noun **1** eyeglasses, goggles, lorgnette, pince-nez, specs (*informal*), spectacles, sunglasses. **2** binoculars, field glasses, opera glasses.

glaze noun enamel, finish, lustre.

gleam noun beam, flash, glimmer, glint, ray, shaft, shimmer, spark.

gleam verb flash, glimmer, glisten, shimmer, shine, sparkle.

glean verb collect, garner, gather, harvest, obtain, pick up.

glee noun cheerfulness, delight, ecstasy, elation, excitement, exhilaration, happiness, joy, jubilation, mirth. □ **gleeful** adjective cheerful, chuffed (slang), delighted, ecstatic, elated, excited, exhilarated, exuberant, exultant, glad, happy, joyful, jubilant, merry, pleased.

glib adjective facile, offhand, pat, ready, slick, smooth.

glide verb 1 aquaplane, coast, glissade, skate, skid, skim, slide, slip. 2 drift, float, fly, sail, soar.

glimmer noun flash, flicker, gleam, glint, glow, ray, shimmer, sparkle.

glimmer verb flicker, gleam, glint, glow, shimmer, shine, twinkle.

glimpse noun glance, look, peek, peep, squiz (Australian slang), view.

glimpse verb catch sight of, discern, espy, notice, peep at, see, sight, spot.

glint noun flash, gleam, sparkle.

glint verb flash, gleam, glimmer, glisten, glitter, shine, sparkle, twinkle.

glisten verb gleam, shimmer, shine, sparkle.

glitter verb glimmer, scintillate, shimmer, shine, sparkle, twinkle.

gloat verb crow, delight, exult, glory, rejoice, revel; see also BOAST.

global adjective general, international, universal, widespread, worldwide.

globe noun 1 ball, bulb, sphere. 2 earth, world.

gloom noun 1 darkness, dimness, dusk, gloaming, semi-darkness, shadows, twilight. 2 dejection, depression, despair, glumness, melancholy, misery, pessimism, sadness, unhappiness, woe.

gloomy adjective 1 black, bleak, cheerless, cloudy, dark, depressing, dismal, dreary, dull, murky, overcast. 2 depressed, desolate, dismal, doleful, down-hearted, funereal, glum, heavy-hearted, lugubrious, melancholy, moody, morbid, morose, mournful, pessimistic, sad, saturnine, sombre, sullen, unhappy.

glorify verb adore, exalt, extol, hallow, honour, laud (formal), magnify (old use), praise, revere, venerate, worship.

glorious adjective **1** famous, grand, heroic, illustrious, noble. **2** beautiful, brilliant, excellent, fine, gorgeous, grand, impressive, magnificent, majestic, marvellous, spectacular, splendid, stunning, sublime, superb, terrific (informal), wonderful.

glory noun **1** credit, distinction, esteem, fame, honour, kudos (informal), prestige, renown. **2** adoration, exaltation, honour, praise, reverence, veneration, worship. **3** beauty, grandeur, greatness, magnificence, majesty, splendour.

glory verb delight, exult, pride yourself, rejoice, revel, take pride.

gloss noun brightness, gleam, lustre, polish, sheen, shine, sparkle.

gloss verb □ **gloss over** conceal, cover up, hide, make light of, whitewash.

glossy adjective gleaming, glistening, lustrous, shining, shiny, sleek.

glove noun gauntlet, mitt, mitten.

glow noun **1** brightness, gleam, heat, incandescence, light, luminosity, radiance, warmth. **2** blush, colour, flush, radiance, redness, rosiness, ruddiness.

glow verb **1** gleam, radiate, shine, smoulder. **2** blush, colour, flush, redden, shine.

glower verb frown, glare, lour, scowl, stare.

glue noun adhesive, cement, gum, paste. □ **gluey** adjective adhesive, gluggy (informal), glutinous, sticky, tacky, viscous.

glue verb affix, attach, cement, fasten, gum, paste, stick.

glum adjective cheerless, crestfallen, depressed, despondent, doleful, down-hearted, down in the mouth, forlorn, gloomy, melancholy, miserable, moody, morose, mournful, sad, unhappy, woebegone.

glut verb **1** flood, inundate, oversupply, saturate, swamp. **2** cram, gorge, overfill, satiate, stuff.

glut noun excess, overabundance, oversupply, superfluity, surfeit, surplus.

glutton noun gormandiser, gourmand, greedy-guts (informal), guts (informal), guzzler, hog (informal), pig (informal).

☐ **gluttonous** adjective greedy, gutsy (slang), insatiable, voracious.

gnarled adjective distorted, knobbly, knotty, lumpy, misshapen, rough, twisted.

gnash verb grate, grind.

gnaw verb bite, chew, chomp, crunch, eat, munch, nibble.

gnome noun dwarf, elf, goblin, troll.

go verb **1** head for, journey, make for, nip (informal), pop, proceed, set out for, start for, travel, visit, wend your way, zip off; see also ADVANCE. **2** beat it (slang), be off, buzz off (slang), clear off (informal), decamp, depart, disappear, exit, get away, go away, hop it (slang), leave, make tracks (informal), make yourself scarce, nick off (Australian slang), push off (informal), retire, retreat, run off, scarper (informal), scoot, scram (informal), set off, shoot through (Australian informal), shove off (informal), skedaddle (informal), take your leave, take yourself off, vanish, withdraw. **3** extend, lead, reach, run, stretch. **4** function, move, operate, perform, run, work. **5** become, turn. **6** belong, fit. **7** fare, proceed, progress, turn out, work out. **8** elapse, pass, slip by. **9** be spent, be used, dry up, run out. ☐ **go after** chase, follow, pursue, tail (informal), track, trail. ☐ **go along with** agree with, be in sympathy with, concur with, subscribe to. ☐ **go back on** break, recant, renege on, repudiate. ☐ **go before** lead, precede. ☐ **go off 1** blow up, detonate, explode. **2** decay, deteriorate, go bad, go rotten, perish, rot, spoil. **3** go on carry on, continue, keep on, persevere, persist, proceed. ☐ **go round** circle, gyrate, orbit, revolve, rotate, spin, swirl, swivel, turn, twirl, whirl. ☐ **go through 1** enter, penetrate, pierce, puncture. **2** bear, endure, experience, suffer, undergo. **3** check, inspect, look through, search, sift through. ☐ **go up** ascend, climb, escalate, increase, mount, rise, rocket, soar. ☐ **go with** accompany, escort. ☐ **go without** be deprived of, deny yourself, do without, forgo, give up, sacrifice.

go noun **1** attempt, bash (informal), crack (informal), shot, stab (informal), try, turn. **2** dash, drive, dynamism, energy, get-up-and-go (informal), oomph (informal), pep, vigour, vim (informal), vivacity, zip.

goad verb drive, egg on, incite, prod, prompt, provoke, spur

(*Australian informal*), spur, stimulate, urge.

go-ahead *adjective* ambitious, dynamic, energetic, enterprising, forward-looking, progressive.

goal *noun* aim, ambition, end, object, objective, purpose, target.

goat *noun* billy goat, he-goat, kid, nanny goat.

gobble *verb* bolt, devour, gulp, guzzle, scoff (*informal*), wolf.

gobbledegook *noun* double Dutch, gibberish, humbug, jargon, mumbo-jumbo, nonsense.

go-between *noun* agent, broker, intermediary, liaison, mediator, messenger, middleman, negotiator.

goblin *noun* bogy, elf, gnome, hobgoblin, imp, leprechaun, sprite.

go-cart *noun* billycart, hill trolley.

God *noun* Allah, the Almighty, the Creator, the Father, Jehovah, the Lord, our Maker, Yahweh.

god *noun* deity, divinity.

goddess *noun* deity, divinity.

godly *adjective* devout, God-fearing, holy, pious, religious, saintly.

godsend *noun* blessing, bonanza, boon, windfall.

goggles *plural noun* glasses, spectacles.

gold *adjective* gilded, gilt, golden, gold-plated.

golden *adjective* **1** blond, flaxen, gold, yellow. **2** excellent, favourable, precious, priceless, valuable, wonderful.

good *adjective* **1** acceptable, adequate, admirable, appropriate, commendable, desirable, meritorious, praiseworthy, proper, right, satisfactory, suitable, worthy. **2** benevolent, benign, blameless, considerate, decent, ethical, godly, holy, honest, honourable, innocent, just, kind, law-abiding, moral, noble, righteous, upright, virtuous, well-intentioned, well-meaning, worthy. **3** biddable, courteous, dutiful, helpful, obedient, polite, well-behaved, well-mannered. **4** beneficial, healthy, nutritious, wholesome. **5** able, accomplished, adept, capable, competent, conscientious, dependable, diligent, effective, efficient, expert, first-rate, professional, proficient, reliable, skilful, skilled, sound, thorough. **6** agreeable, cool (*informal*), delightful, enjoyable, excellent, fabulous (*informal*), fantastic (*informal*), fine, great (*informal*), happy, lovely, marvellous, nice, outstanding, pleasant, satisfying, superb, swell (*informal*), terrific (*informal*), tremendous (*informal*), wonderful.

good noun **1** goodness, merit, virtue. **2** advantage, benefit, interest, profit, welfare, well-being.

goodbye interjection adieu, au revoir, bon voyage, bye-bye (*informal*), cheerio (*informal*), cheers (*informal*), ciao (*informal*), farewell, hooray (*Australian informal*), see you (*informal*), see you later (*informal*), so long (*informal*), ta-ta (*informal*).

good-looking adjective attractive, beautiful, bonny (*Scottish*), comely, fair (*old use*), fetching, handsome, lovely, personable, pretty.

good-natured adjective benevolent, big-hearted, compassionate, easygoing, forgiving, friendly, generous, genial, gracious, helpful, kind, kind-hearted, kindly, obliging, sympathetic, tender-hearted, thoughtful, tolerant, unselfish.

goodness noun benevolence, generosity, honour, integrity, kindness, merit, morality, probity, rectitude, righteousness, virtue.

goods plural noun **1** articles, commodities, merchandise, products, wares. **2** cargo, freight.

good-tempered adjective affable, amiable, amicable, cheerful, easygoing, even-tempered, gentle, good-humoured, happy, happy-go-lucky, jovial, mild, pleasant.

goodwill noun benevolence, charity, favour, friendliness, grace, kindness.

goose noun gander (*male*), gosling (*young*).

gore verb pierce, poke, puncture, wound.

gorge noun canyon, chasm, gully, pass, ravine, valley.

gorge verb feast, fill, glut, overeat, satiate, stuff.

gorgeous adjective beautiful, colourful, exquisite, magnificent, rich, splendid, stunning (*informal*), sumptuous.

gory adjective bloody, grisly, gruesome, macabre, sanguinary, violent.

gossip verb blab, chat, natter (*informal*), prattle, tattle, tell tales, tittle-tattle.

gossip noun **1** backbiting, chit-chat, hearsay, rumour, scandal, talk, tittle-tattle. **2** busy-body, gossip-monger, rumour-monger, scandal-monger, tattler.

gouge *verb* bore, chisel, cut, dig, groove, hollow, incise, scoop.

gourmet *noun* connoisseur, epicure, foodie (*informal*), gastronome.

govern *verb* administer, be in charge of, command, control, direct, guide, head, lead, manage, reign over, rule, run, superintend, supervise.

government *noun* administration, command, control, leadership, management, regime, rule.

governor *noun* **1** chief, head, ruler. **2** viceroy.

gown *noun* dress, frock, habit, kimono, robe, vestment.

grab *verb* clasp, clutch, grasp, hold, nab (*informal*), pluck, seize, snatch, swipe (*informal*).

grace *noun* **1** beauty, elegance, gracefulness, smoothness. **2** favour, forbearance, forgiveness, goodness, goodwill, lenience, mercy. **3** benediction, blessing, prayer, thanksgiving.

graceful *adjective* agile, elegant, limber, lissom, lithe, nimble, supple.

gracious *adjective* amiable, benevolent, benign, courteous, friendly, good-natured, hospitable, kind, kindly, merciful, polite, tactful.

grade *noun* **1** category, class, level, quality, rank, rating, standard; (*exam grade*) mark, result, score. **2** class, form, year.

grade *verb* class, classify, mark, rank, rate, sort.

gradient *noun* grade, hill, incline, slope.

gradual *adjective* gentle, piecemeal, progressive, slow, steady. □ **gradually** *adverb* bit by bit, by degrees, little by little, progressively, slowly, steadily, step by step.

grain *noun* granule, grist, kernel, seed.

grand *adjective* **1** elegant, glorious, imposing, impressive, large, luxurious, magnificent, majestic, opulent, palatial, posh (*informal*), splendid, stately, sumptuous, superb. **2** all-inclusive, complete, comprehensive, full.

grandeur *noun* dignity, magnificence, majesty, pomp, splendour.

grandiose *adjective* ambitious, grand, impressive, ostentatious, pretentious.

grant *verb* **1** accord, allocate, allow, award, bestow, donate, give, pay, provide. **2** acknowledge, admit, agree, concede.

grant *noun* allowance, award, bursary, endowment, scholarship, subsidy.

grapevine *noun* bush telegraph, mulga wire, network.

graphic *adjective* **1** diagrammatic, drawn, illustrated, pictorial, visual. **2** colourful, descriptive, detailed, explicit, vivid.

grapple *verb* fight, struggle, tackle, tussle, wrestle.

grasp *verb* **1** clasp, clench, cling to, clutch, grab, grip, hang on to, hold, seize, snatch, take, take hold of. **2** apprehend, comprehend, cotton on to (*informal*), fathom, follow, get (*informal*), latch on to (*informal*), see, understand. ☐ **grasp** *noun* **1** clasp, clutch, grip, hold. **2** command, comprehension, mastery, understanding.

grasping *adjective* acquisitive, avaricious, covetous, greedy, mercenary.

grass *noun* green, lawn, pasture, sward, turf.

grassland *noun* field, meadow, pampas, pasture, plain, prairie, range, savannah, steppe.

grate *noun* fireplace, hearth.

grate *verb* **1** grind, mince, shred. **2** grind, rasp, rub, scrape, scratch.

grateful *adjective* appreciative, thankful.

gratify *verb* **1** content, delight, gladden, please. **2** fulfil, indulge, pander to, satisfy.

grating *noun* grate, grid, grille.

grating *adjective* discordant, harsh, jarring, rasping, raucous, shrill, strident.

gratitude *noun* appreciation, thankfulness, thanks.

gratuity *noun* bonus, gift, present, tip.

grave *noun* burial place, crypt, mausoleum, sepulchre, tomb, vault.

grave *adjective* **1** earnest, funereal, gloomy, grim, pensive, serious, sober, solemn, sombre, staid, thoughtful. **2** critical, crucial, important, momentous, serious, weighty.

gravel *noun* pebbles, road metal, shingle, stones.

gravestone *noun* headstone, monument, tombstone.

graveyard *noun* burial ground, cemetery, churchyard, necropolis.

graze *verb* **1** browse, feed. **2** bark, scrape, scratch, skin.

graze *noun* abrasion, scrape, scratch.

grazier *noun* cattle farmer, pastoralist (*Australian*), sheep farmer.

grease *noun* dripping, fat, lard, lubricant, oil, suet, tallow. □ **greasy** *adjective* fatty, oily, slick.

grease *verb* lubricate, oil.

great *adjective* **1** big, colossal, considerable, enormous, extensive, gigantic, huge, humungous (*slang*), immense, immeasurable, large, massive, monumental, phenomenal, prodigious, stupendous, sweeping, vast. **2** acute, deep, extreme, intense, profound, severe, strong. **3** brilliant, celebrated, distinguished, eminent, first-class, gifted, illustrious, important, leading, noted, outstanding, pre-eminent, prominent, remarkable, renowned, superior, talented, well-known. **4** brilliant (*informal*), cool (*informal*), delightful, enjoyable, excellent, fabulous (*informal*), fantastic (*informal*), fine, first-rate, good, grand (*informal*), lovely, magnificent, marvellous, outstanding, pleasant, splendid, super (*informal*), superb, swell (*informal*), terrific (*informal*), tremendous (*informal*), wonderful. □ **greatest** *adjective* best, chief, highest, main, maximum, paramount, supreme, top, utmost. □ **greatness** *noun* distinction,

eminence, grandeur, importance, pre-eminence, stature.

greed *noun* avarice, covetousness, cupidity, gluttony, rapacity, voraciousness.

greedy *adjective* (*for food*) gluttonous, ravenous, voracious; (*for money etc.*) avaricious, covetous, grasping, miserly, money-hungry, on the make (*informal*), rapacious.

green *adjective* **1** apple green, aquamarine, beryl, bottle green, chartreuse, emerald, jade, lime, olive, pea green, sea green. **2** callow, immature, inexperienced, naïve, raw.

greenhouse *noun* conservatory, glasshouse, hothouse.

greet *verb* **1** address, receive, welcome. **2** appear to, meet, present itself to.

greeting *noun* **1** reception, salutation, welcome. **2** compliments, congratulations, regards, wishes.

gregarious *adjective* extroverted, friendly, outgoing, sociable, social.

grey *adjective* **1** charcoal grey, dun, grizzled, grizzly, gunmetal, hoary, mousy, silver, slate, smoky, steely. **2** cloudy, dark, dull, gloomy, heavy, leaden, louring, overcast.

grid *noun* **1** grating, grille. **2** lattice, network.

grief *noun* anguish, desolation, distress, heartache, heartbreak, misery, regret, remorse, sadness, sorrow, suffering, unhappiness, woe.

grievance *noun* beef (*slang*), complaint, gripe (*informal*), objection.

grieve *verb* **1** distress, hurt, pain, sadden, upset. **2** fret, lament, mope, mourn, pine, weep.

grill *verb* **1** barbecue, broil, brown, toast. **2** cross-examine, interrogate, question.

grim *adjective* **1** dour, forbidding, gloomy, glum, harsh, severe, stern. **2** bleak, desolate, dire, dismal, dreadful, forbidding, frightful, ghastly, gloomy, horrible, unpleasant.

grimace *verb* frown, pull a face, scowl, wince.

grimy *adjective* blackened, dirty, filthy, grubby, soiled, sooty.

grin *verb* beam, smile, smirk.

grind *verb* **1** crush, granulate, mill, pound, pulverise. **2** file, polish, rub, sharpen, smooth, whet. **3** gnash, grate.

grip *verb* **1** clasp, clutch, grab, grasp, hang on to, hold, seize, snatch, take hold of. **2** absorb, captivate, engross, enthral, hold spellbound, rivet.

grip *noun* **1** clasp, clutch, grasp, hold. **2** command, comprehension, grasp, hold, mastery, understanding.

gripe *verb* beef (*slang*), bitch (*informal*), complain, find fault, grizzle (*informal*), groan, grumble, moan, protest, whine, whinge (*informal*). □ **gripe** *noun* beef (*slang*), complaint, grievance, grizzle (*informal*), grumble, objection, protest, whine, whinge (*informal*).

grisly *adjective* appalling, dreadful, frightful, ghastly, gory, grim, gruesome, hideous, horrendous, horrible, horrid, macabre, repugnant, repulsive, shocking, vile.

gristly *adjective* leathery, tough.

grit *noun* **1** dirt, dust, sand. **2** backbone, courage, determination, endurance, fortitude, guts (*informal*), mettle, pluck, spirit, spunk (*informal*).

grit *verb* clench, set.

grizzle *verb* cry, fret, moan, whimper, whine, whinge (*informal*); see also *COMPLAIN*.

groan *verb* bellow, cry, howl, moan, wail.

grog *noun* alcohol, liquor.

groggy *adjective* dazed, dopey (*informal*), shaky, unsteady, wonky (*informal*), woozy (*informal*).

groom *noun* bridegroom, husband.

groom *verb* **1** brush, comb, curry. **2** clean up, preen, spruce up, tidy, wash. **3** prepare, prime, train.

groove *noun* channel, cut, furrow, rut, score, slot.

grope *verb* feel about, fish, fossick (*Australian informal*), fumble, rummage, scrabble, search.

gross *adjective* **1** corpulent, enormous, fat, flabby, huge, obese, overweight, rotund. **2** boorish, coarse, crass, crude, rude, unrefined, vulgar. **3** blatant, clear, flagrant, glaring, manifest, obvious, outrageous. **4** entire, pre-tax, total, whole. **5** see DISGUSTING (at *DISGUST*).

grotesque *adjective* absurd, bizarre, deformed, distorted, fantastic, freakish, hideous, misshapen, monstrous, odd, ugly, weird.

grotto *noun* cave, cavern.

grouch *noun* crosspatch, grumbler, grump (*informal*), killjoy, malcontent, misery (*informal*), sourpuss (*informal*), spoilsport, wet blanket, whinger (*informal*).
□ **grouchy** *adjective* bad-tempered, cantankerous, churlish, crabby, cranky, cross, crotchety, crusty, discontented, disgruntled, fractious, grumpy, irritable, peevish, shirty (*informal*), snaky (*Australian informal*), stroppy (*informal*), sullen, surly, testy, tetchy.

ground *noun* **1** dirt, earth, land, loam, soil. **2** arena, field, oval, pitch, stadium.

ground *verb* **1** beach, run aground, shipwreck, strand. **2** drill, educate, instruct, teach, train. **3** base, establish, found, root.

groundless *adjective* baseless, irrational, unfounded, unjustified, unwarranted.

grounds *plural noun* **1** campus, estate, garden(s), lawn(s), surroundings. **2** deposit, dregs, lees, sediment. **3** basis, cause, evidence, justification, reason.

groundwork *noun* preparation, spadework.

group *noun* alliance, assembly, association, assortment, band, batch, battery, bevy, body, bracket, brigade, brood, bunch, category, circle, clan, class, classification, clique, club, cluster, cohort, collection, colony, combination, community, company, congregation, consortium, constellation (*of stars*), contingent, convoy, corps, crew, crop, crowd, drove, ensemble, faction, family, federation, fleet, flock, flotilla, force, gaggle (*of geese*), galaxy (*of stars*), gang, gathering, genus, herd, horde, host, league, legion, litter, lot, mass, mob, movement, order, organisation, pack, panel, party, phalanx, platoon, pod (*of seals, dolphins, or whales*), posse, pride (*of lions*), rabble, ring, school (*of fish, dolphins, or whales*), series, set, shoal (*of fish*), society, species, squad, subset, swarm (*of bees*), syndicate, team, throng, tribe, troop, troupe (*of actors*), union.

group verb **1** associate, band, cluster, collect, congregate, gather. **2** arrange, class, classify, organise, sort.

grove noun orchard, plantation.

grovel verb crawl (*informal*), fawn (on), ingratiate yourself (with), kowtow, suck up (*informal*), toady.

grow verb **1** become bigger, boom, build up, develop, enlarge, evolve, expand, extend, fill out, flourish, grow up, increase, lengthen, mature, multiply, mushroom, progress, prosper, shoot up, snowball, spread, thrive. **2** burgeon, develop, flourish, germinate,

live, shoot, spring up, sprout, thrive. **3** cultivate, produce, propagate, raise. **4** become, get, turn.

growl verb snarl.

growth noun **1** advancement, development, enlargement, expansion, improvement, increase, progress, proliferation. **2** cancer, cyst, lump, polyp, tumour.

grub noun caterpillar, larva, maggot.

grubby adjective blackened, dirty, dusty, filthy, grimy, soiled.

grudge noun animosity, bitterness, grievance, hard feelings, ill will, rancour, resentment. □ **hold a grudge against** have a derry on (*Australian informal*), have a down on (*informal*), have a set on (*Australian informal*).

grudging adjective reluctant, resentful, sparing, unwilling.

gruelling adjective arduous, demanding, exhausting, hard, laborious, strenuous, tiring, tough.

gruesome adjective ghastly, ghoulish, gory, grisly, hideous, horrible, macabre, repulsive, revolting, shocking, sickening.

gruff adjective **1** gravelly, guttural, harsh, hoarse, husky, rough, throaty. **2** abrupt, bad-tempered, blunt, brusque, crabby, crusty, curt, grouchy (*informal*), grumpy, sullen, surly, unfriendly.

grumble *verb* beef (*slang*), bitch (*informal*), carp, cavil, complain, find fault with, gripe (*informal*), grizzle (*informal*), groan, moan, object, protest, whine, whinge (*informal*).

grumpy *adjective* bad-tempered, cantankerous, churlish, crabby, cranky, cross, crotchety, grouchy, irritable, peevish, petulant, shirty (*informal*), snaky (*Australian informal*), sullen, surly, testy, tetchy.

guarantee *noun* assurance, pledge, promise, undertaking, warranty, word.

guarantee *verb* certify, ensure, pledge, promise, secure, swear, vow.

guard *verb* defend, keep an eye on, look after, mind, preserve, protect, safeguard, shelter, shield, supervise, watch over.

guard *noun* **1** bodyguard, chaperone, escort, garrison, guardian, guardsman, lookout, minder, patrol, picket, security officer, sentinel, sentry, warder, watchman. **2** protector, screen, shield. □ **on (your) guard** alert, careful, on the watch, prepared, ready, vigilant, wary, watchful. □ **stand guard** guard, keep a lookout, keep nit (*slang*), keep watch, patrol.

guardian *noun* custodian, defender, keeper, preserver, protector, trustee, warden, watchdog. □ **guardianship** *noun* care, charge, custody, keeping, protection.

guess *noun* assumption, conjecture, estimate, guesstimate (*informal*), hunch, hypothesis, prediction, shot in the dark, supposition, surmise, suspicion, theory.

guess *verb* assume, conjecture, estimate, have a stab at (*informal*), imagine, predict, reckon, speculate, suppose, surmise, suspect, think.

guest *noun* billet, caller, company, visitor.

guidance *noun* advice, counselling, direction, help, information, instruction.

guide *noun* **1** conductor, courier, director, escort, leader, pilot, usher. **2** adviser, counsellor, guru, mentor, teacher.

guide *verb* conduct, direct, escort, lead, manoeuvre, navigate, pilot, show the way, steer, usher.

guidebook *noun* directory, guide, handbook, manual.

guidelines *plural noun* instructions, principles, regulations, requirements, rules, standards.

guild *noun* association, federation, league, organisation, society, union.

guile *noun* artifice, craftiness, cunning, deceit, duplicity, slyness, trickery.

guilt *noun* **1** blame, fault, responsibility. **2** compunction, contrition, disgrace, remorse, self-reproach, shame.

guilty *adjective* **1** blameworthy, culpable, responsible. **2** ashamed, contrite, hangdog, remorseful, shamefaced, sheepish.

guise *noun* cover, disguise, masquerade, pretence, show.

gulf *noun* **1** bay, cove, inlet. **2** chasm, gap, rift.

gullet *noun* craw, oesophagus, throat.

gullible *adjective* believing, credulous, green, naïve, trusting, unsuspecting.

gully *noun* **1** gorge, ravine, valley. **2** channel, ditch, drain, gutter.

gulp *verb* bolt, devour, gobble, guzzle, wolf.

gulp *noun* draught, mouthful, swallow, swig (*informal*).

gum *noun* adhesive, glue, paste.

gum *verb* glue, paste, stick.

gumption *noun* common sense, enterprise, initiative, nous (*informal*), sense, wit.

gun *noun* arm, firearm; (*various guns*) airgun, automatic, blunderbuss, cannon, carbine, flintlock, handgun, howitzer, machine-gun, mortar, musket, pistol, revolver, rifle, semiautomatic, shotgun, submachine-gun, tommy-gun. □ **gunfire** *noun* broadside, cannonade, fire, flak, fusillade, salvo, shooting.

gunman *noun* assassin, gunslinger, marksman, sniper.

gurgle *verb* & *noun* babble, burble.

gush *verb* **1** flow, pour, run, rush, spout, spurt, stream, surge. **2** babble on, get carried away (*informal*), go overboard (*informal*), rave (*informal*). □ **gush** *noun* cascade, flood, jet, outflow, outpouring, rush, spurt, stream, torrent.

gust *noun* blast, puff, rush, squall. □ **gusty** *adjective* blowy, blustery, squally, stormy, windy.

gusto *noun* enjoyment, enthusiasm, relish, spirit, verve, vigour, zeal, zest.

gut noun abdomen, bowel, insides (*informal*), intestine.

gut verb destroy, devastate, ravage.

guts plural noun boldness, courage, determination, grit (*informal*), nerve, pluck, spunk (*informal*).

gutter noun channel, culvert, ditch, drain, gully, sewer, trench, trough.

guy noun bloke (*informal*), boy, chap (*informal*), fellow (*informal*), gentleman, lad, male, man.

guzzle verb bolt, devour, gobble, gulp, scoff (*informal*), wolf.

gymnastics plural noun acrobatics, callisthenics.

gypsy noun nomad, Romany, traveller, vagabond, wanderer.

gyrate verb circle, pirouette, revolve, rotate, spin, spiral, turn, twirl, wheel, whirl.

Hh

habit noun **1** custom, inclination, practice, predisposition, propensity, routine, tendency, way, wont. **2** costume, dress, garb, robe.

habitat noun domain, environment, habitation, home, setting, surroundings, territory.

habitual adjective **1** accustomed, customary, established, familiar, fixed, normal, regular, routine, set, standard, traditional, usual. **2** addicted, chronic, confirmed, hardened, inveterate.

hack verb chop, cut, hew, mutilate, slash.

hackneyed adjective banal, clichéd, common, commonplace, conventional, overused, pedestrian, stale, stereotyped, stock, trite.

hag noun bag (*slang*), battleaxe (*informal*), crone, witch.

haggard adjective careworn, drawn, emaciated, exhausted, gaunt, thin, worn.

haggle verb argue, bargain, dispute, negotiate, quarrel, quibble, wrangle.

hail verb call to, flag down, signal to, wave to. □ **hail from** be born in, come from, originate from.

hair noun **1** curls, locks, ringlets, tresses; (*facial hair*) beard, bristles, fuzz, moustache, sideburns, whiskers; (*an animal's hair*) coat, down, fleece, fur, mane, pelt, wool. **2** bristle, filament, strand.

hairdresser noun barber, haircutter, hair stylist.

hair-raising adjective frightening, hairy (slang), nerve-racking, scary, spine-chilling, terrifying.

hairy adjective **1** bristly, bushy, downy, fleecy, furry, fuzzy, hirsute, shaggy, stubbly, unshaven, whiskery, woolly. **2** dangerous, dicey (slang), difficult, frightening, hair-raising, nerve-racking, scary, terrifying.

hale adjective fit, healthy, lively, robust, sprightly, spry, strong, vigorous, well.

half adverb partially, partly, slightly.

half-hearted adjective apathetic, feeble, indifferent, lackadaisical, lukewarm, unenthusiastic.

halfway adjective intermediate, median, mid, middle, midway.

hall noun **1** corridor, entrance hall, foyer, lobby, passage, vestibule. **2** assembly hall, auditorium, chamber, concert hall, room, theatre.

hallmark noun badge, brand, characteristic, mark, stamp, trade mark.

hallow verb **1** bless, consecrate, make holy, make sacred, sanctify. **2** honour, respect, revere, venerate.

hallucination noun apparition, dream, fantasy, illusion, mirage, nightmare, phantasm, vision.

halo noun aureole, nimbus.

halt verb arrest, block, check, come to a stop, pull up, stem, stop.

halt noun break, close, delay, hiatus, intermission, interruption, pause, recess, shutdown, standstill, stop, stoppage, suspension, termination.

halve verb **1** bisect, divide in two. **2** cut by half, reduce to half.

hammer noun claw hammer, gavel, mallet, sledgehammer.

hammer verb **1** bang, drive, hit, knock, nail, tack. **2** bash, batter, beat, hit, knock, pound, strike, thump.

hamper noun basket, pannier.

hamper verb check, curb, hinder, impede, inhibit, interfere with, limit, obstruct, restrict.

hand noun **1** fist, mitt (slang), palm, paw (informal). **2** assistant, employee, labourer, worker. **3** authority, care, charge, control, custody, jurisdiction, keeping, possession, power, responsibility. **4** aid, assistance, help, support.
□ **at hand 1** accessible, close,

handy, near, nearby. **2** approaching, close, coming, imminent, near, soon. □ **by hand** manually. □ **hands down** easily, effortlessly. □ **on hand** accessible, available, handy, present. □ **out of hand** chaotic, out of control, out of order.

hand *verb* give, pass. □ **hand in** deliver, give, present, submit. □ **hand out** deal out, dish out (*informal*), dispense, distribute, dole out, give out, share out. □ **hand over** deliver, give, pass, present, surrender, turn over.

handbag *noun* bag, purse (*American*).

handbook *noun* guidebook, manual.

handcuffs *plural noun* manacles, shackles.

handful *noun* few, remnant, sprinkling.

handicap *noun* **1** barrier, disadvantage, drawback, hindrance, impediment, limitation, obstacle, stumbling block. **2** disability, impairment. □ **handicap** *verb* disadvantage, hamper, hinder, impede, limit, restrict.

handle *noun* grip, haft, helve, hilt, knob, shaft, stock.

handle *verb* **1** feel, finger, pick up, poke, touch. **2** control,

drive, manage, manoeuvre, operate, steer. **3** cope with, deal with, look after, manage, tackle, take care of.

handsome *adjective* **1** attractive, beautiful, comely, elegant, fine-looking, good-looking, smart. **2** ample, considerable, generous, large, lavish, liberal, sizeable.

handwriting *noun* calligraphy, copperplate, hand, longhand, scrawl, scribble, script, writing.

handy *adjective* **1** convenient, helpful, practical, useful. **2** accessible, at hand, available, convenient, near, on hand, to hand. **3** adept, adroit, capable, competent, deft, dexterous, expert, good, proficient, skilful.

hang *verb* **1** dangle, drape, string, suspend. **2** bend, bow, dangle, droop, drop, flop, incline, lean. □ **hang about** hang around, hover, linger, loiter, lurk, remain, stay, wait. □ **hang back** hesitate, hold back, wait. □ **hang on 1** cling, clutch, grasp, grip, hold on. **2** (*informal*) hold on, hold the line, wait.

hang *noun* □ **get the hang of** come to grips with, comprehend, figure out, get the knack of, grasp, master, understand.

hanker *verb* (*hanker after*) covet, crave, desire, have a yen for, hunger for, long for, thirst for, want, yearn for.

haphazard *adjective* arbitrary, careless, casual, chaotic, disorganised, hit-or-miss, indiscriminate, random, slapdash, unorganised, unplanned, unsystematic.

happen *verb* arise, come about, come to pass, crop up, ensue, eventuate, occur, result, take place.

happening *noun* episode, event, incident, occasion, occurrence, proceeding.

happy *adjective* **1** blissful, blithe, cheerful, contented, delighted, ecstatic, elated, enraptured, euphoric, exhilarated, glad, gleeful, gratified, joyful, joyous, jubilant, lighthearted, merry, overjoyed, pleased, rapturous, satisfied, thrilled. **2** auspicious, convenient, favourable, fortunate, lucky, opportune, propitious, timely. □ **happiness** *noun* bliss, cheerfulness, contentment, delight, ecstasy, elation, enjoyment, euphoria, exhilaration, exuberance, felicity, gladness, glee, joy, jubilation, light-heartedness, merriment, mirth, pleasure, rapture, satisfaction.

harangue *verb* berate, earbash (*Australian informal*), lecture nag, scold. □ **harangue** *noun* diatribe, earbashing (*Australian informal*), lecture sermon, speech, tirade.

harass *verb* annoy, badger bother, bug (*informal*), disturb harry, hassle (*informal*), hound, importune, pester plague, stand over (*Australian*), trouble, worry.

harbour *noun* anchorage, dock haven, marina, port, shelter.

harbour *verb* **1** conceal, hide house, protect, shelter, shield **2** cling to, foster, hold maintain, nurse, nurture retain.

hard *adjective* **1** dense, firm inflexible, rigid, solid, stiff tough. **2** (*a hard question*) awkward, baffling, complex complicated, confusing cryptic, difficult, knotty puzzling, thorny, ticklish tricky; (*a hard job*) arduous back-breaking, demanding difficult, exacting, gruelling heavy, herculean, laborious onerous, rigorous, strenuous taxing, tiring, tough. **3** severe stern, strict, unbending, uncompromising. **4** bad, difficult grim, harsh, oppressive painful, rough, severe, tough unbearable, unpleasant. **5** assiduous, conscientious, dilig gent, earnest, energetic, indefatigable, industrious, painstaking, sedulous, unflagging, untiring. □ **hard up** broke (informal), impecunious, impoverished, penniless, poor, poverty-stricken, skint (informal).

hard adverb (work hard) assiduously, conscientiously, diligently, doggedly, energetically, indefatigably, industriously, sedulously, strenuously, untiringly, vigorously; (press hard) firmly, forcefully, forcibly, heavily, intensely, powerfully, strongly, violently.

harden verb firm, set, solidify, stiffen, strengthen, toughen.

hard-hearted adjective callous, cold, cruel, hard, harsh, heartless, indifferent, inhuman, insensitive, mean, merciless, pitiless, remorseless, ruthless, stony-hearted, uncaring, unfeeling, unforgiving, unkind, unrepentant, unsympathetic.

hardly adverb barely, scarcely.

hardship noun adversity, affliction, deprivation, difficulty, distress, misery, misfortune, need, poverty, privation, strain, suffering, trials, tribulation, woe.

hardware noun equipment, implements, instruments, ironmongery, machinery, tools.

hard-wearing adjective durable, heavy-duty, long-lasting, stout, strong, tough.

hardy adjective drought-resistant, frost-resistant, resilient, robust, strong, sturdy, tough, vigorous.

hare noun buck (male), doe (female), leveret (young).

hark verb □ **hark back** go back, return, revert.

harlequin adjective motley, multicoloured, variegated.

harm verb abuse, damage, destroy, hurt, ill-treat, impair, injure, maltreat, mistreat, molest, ruin, spoil, undermine, wound.

harm noun damage, destruction, detriment, hurt, injury, pain, suffering. □ **harmful** adjective adverse, bad, damaging, dangerous, deleterious, destructive, detrimental, hurtful, injurious, noxious, pernicious, ruinous, unhealthy. □ **harmless** adjective gentle, innocent, innocuous, inoffensive, mild, non-toxic, safe.

harmony noun **1** euphony, melodiousness, tunefulness. **2** accord, agreement, compatibility, concord, friendliness, peace, sympathy, unanimity, unity. □ **harmonious** adjective **1** dulcet, euphonious, melodious, musical, sweet, tuneful. **2** amicable, compatible, congenial, friendly, pleasant.

harness verb **1** bridle, hitch up, yoke. **2** capture, control, exploit, use.

harp verb □ **harp on** dwell on, get on your hobby-horse, go on (*informal*), keep on, nag.

harrowing adjective alarming, chilling, distressing, disturbing, horrifying, spine-chilling, terrifying.

harsh adjective **1** (*a harsh voice*) cacophonous, discordant, grating, gravelly, gruff, guttural, jarring, rasping, raucous, rough, shrill, stern, strident; (*harsh light*) bright, brilliant, dazzling, glaring. **2** (*harsh conditions*) austere, hard, inhospitable, rough, severe, stark, tough, unpleasant; (*harsh treatment*) bitter, brutal, cruel, hard, hostile, hurtful, malicious, mean, merciless, nasty, severe, spiteful, stern, unfeeling, unfriendly, unkind, unsympathetic, vicious, vindictive.

harvest noun crop, produce, vintage, yield.

harvest verb collect, garner, gather, glean, pick, reap.

hash noun □ **make a hash of** botch, bungle, make a mess of,

mess up, muff (*informal*), ruin, spoil.

hassle noun bother, difficulty, inconvenience, problem, trouble, worry.

hassle verb annoy, badger, bother, bug (*informal*), harass, hound, nag, pester, worry.

haste noun alacrity, dispatch, promptness, rapidity, speed, swiftness, urgency.

hasten verb **1** dash, fly, hurry, make haste, race, rush, scurry, scuttle, speed. **2** accelerate, bring forward, expedite, precipitate, quicken, speed up.

hasty adjective **1** fast, hurried, prompt, quick, rapid, speedy, sudden, swift. **2** careless, headlong, hurried, impetuous, impulsive, precipitate, quick, rash, rushed, snap.

hat noun (*kinds of hat*) Akubra (*trade mark*), beanie, bearskin, beret, boater, bonnet, bowler hat, busby, cabbage-tree hat (*Australian*), cap, deerstalker, fez, mortarboard, panama, slouch hat, sombrero, sou'wester, stetson, sunhat, tam o'shanter, top hat, trilby.

hatch noun aperture, manhole, opening.

hatch verb **1** brood, incubate. **2** conceive, concoct, cook up (*informal*), design, devise, dream up, invent, plan, think up.

hatchet noun axe, mogo (Australian), tomahawk.

hate verb abhor, abominate, despise, detest, dislike, loathe.

hateful adjective abhorrent, abominable, atrocious, contemptible, despicable, detestable, disgusting, execrable, horrid, loathsome, nasty, objectionable, obnoxious, odious, offensive, repugnant, repulsive, revolting, vile.

hatred noun abhorrence, abomination, animosity, antagonism, antipathy, aversion, bitterness, contempt, detestation, disgust, dislike, enmity, hate, hostility, loathing, malevolence, odium, repugnance, resentment, revulsion.

naughty adjective arrogant, conceited, condescending, contemptuous, disdainful, high and mighty, hoity-toity, lofty, lordly, patronising, proud, scornful, self-important, snobbish, snooty (informal), stuck-up (informal), supercilious, superior.

haul verb drag, draw, heave, hoick (slang), lug, pull, tow, tug, wrench, yank (informal).

haul noun **1** booty, profit, swag (informal), takings. **2** distance, stretch.

haunt verb **1** frequent, hang around, loiter around, patronise. **2** linger with, obsess, plague, prey on, stay with.

have verb **1** keep, own, possess. **2** contain, hold, include. **3** endure, experience, go through, suffer, undergo. **4** (have to) be forced to, be obliged to, must, need to. **5** accept, allow, permit, put up with, stand for (informal), take, tolerate. **6** cheat, con (informal), deceive, swindle, take for a ride (informal), trick. □ **have on** fool, hoax, kid (informal), pull someone's leg, tease.

haven noun asylum, hide-out, refuge, retreat, sanctuary, shelter; see also HARBOUR.

haversack noun backpack, knapsack, pack, rucksack, satchel.

havoc noun chaos, confusion, destruction, devastation, disorder, mayhem, ruin, upheaval.

hawker noun huckster, pedlar, travelling salesman.

haywire adjective awry, chaotic, confused, disorganised, out of control, wrong.

hazard noun danger, peril, pitfall, risk, threat. □ **hazardous** adjective chancy, dangerous, dicey (*slang*), hairy (*slang*), perilous, precarious, risky, tricky, uncertain.

haze *noun* cloud, fog, mist, smog.

hazy *adjective* **1** foggy, misty, smoggy. **2** blurred, confused, faint, fuzzy, imprecise, indefinite, indistinct, nebulous, sketchy, unclear, vague.

head *noun* **1** cranium, pate (*old use*), scone (*Australian informal*), skull. **2** brain, intellect, intelligence, loaf (*slang*), mind, nut (*informal*). **3** ability, aptitude, capacity, faculty, gift, intellect, mind, talent. **4** beginning, front, origin, source, top. **5** boss, captain, CEO, chairman, chief, commander, director, governor, headmaster, headmistress, head teacher, leader, manager, president, principal, superintendent, supervisor; see also *RULER*. **6** climax, crisis.

head *verb* **1** be in charge of, command, control, direct, govern, lead, manage, rule, superintend, supervise. **2** aim for, go, make for, make tracks for (*informal*), proceed, set off for, start for, steer for, turn for. □ **head off** block, cut off, deflect, divert, intercept, turn aside.

headache *noun* bugbear, difficulty, nightmare (*infor-*

mal), nuisance, pain (*informal*), problem, worry.

heading *noun* caption, headline, title.

headland *noun* cape, head, promontory.

headline *noun* caption, heading, title.

headlong *adverb* **1** head first, head-on. **2** hastily, impetuously, impulsively, precipitately, rashly, recklessly.

headquarters *plural noun* base, central office, depot, head office.

headstrong *adjective* determined, intractable, obstinate, pigheaded, recalcitrant, refractory, self-willed, strong-willed, stubborn, uncontrollable, wilful.

headteacher *noun* head, headmaster, headmistress, principal.

headway *noun* □ **make headway** advance, get ahead, get on, have a breakthrough, make inroads, progress.

heal *verb* **1** be better, improve, knit, mend. **2** cure, restore, treat.

health *noun* **1** condition, constitution, fettle, form, shape, state. **2** fitness, healthiness, robustness, vitality, wellbeing.

healthy *adjective* **1** fit, flourishing, hale, hearty, robust, sound, strapping, strong, thriving, well. **2** beneficial, bracing, health-giving, invigorating, salubrious, wholesome.

heap *noun* accumulation, bundle, mass, mound, mountain, pile, stack, stockpile. □ **heaps** *plural noun* loads (*informal*), lots (*informal*), masses, mountains, oodles (*informal*), piles (*informal*), plenty, stacks (*informal*), tons (*informal*), whips (*Australian informal*).

heap *verb* **1** accumulate, bank, collect, gather, pile, stack. **2** fill, load, pile.

hear *verb* **1** catch, listen to, overhear, pick up. **2** discover, find out, gather, learn.

hearing *noun* inquiry, investigation, trial.

hearsay *noun* gossip, rumour, tittle-tattle.

heart *noun* **1** ticker (*informal*). **2** compassion, consideration, emotions, feelings, humanity, love, pity, sympathy, tenderness. **3** courage, determination, enthusiasm, guts (*informal*), nerve, pluck, spirit, spunk (*informal*). **4** centre, core, crux, essence, hub, middle, nitty-gritty (*informal*), nub, nucleus. □ **heartbroken**
adjective broken-hearted, desolate, devastated, disconsolate, forlorn, grief-stricken, woebegone, wretched. □ **by heart** by memory, by rote, parrot-fashion.

hearten *verb* buck up (*informal*), buoy up, cheer, comfort, encourage, please.

heartfelt *adjective* deep, earnest, fervent, genuine, profound, sincere, warm.

hearth *noun* fireplace, fireside.

heartless *adjective* callous, cold, cruel, hard-hearted, harsh, merciless, pitiless, ruthless, unfeeling, unkind, unsympathetic.

heart-warming *adjective* cheering, encouraging, heartening, inspiring, pleasing, touching.

hearty *adjective* **1** energetic, hardy, healthy, robust, sprightly, spry, strong, vigorous. **2** effusive, enthusiastic, exuberant, heartfelt, lively, sincere, vigorous, warm, wholehearted. **3** big, large, solid, substantial.

heat *noun* **1** hotness, temperature, warmth. **2** preliminary, round.

heat *verb* reheat, warm up.

heathen *noun* infidel, non-believer, pagan, unbeliever.

heave verb **1** drag, draw, haul, hoick (*slang*), hoist, lift, pull, raise, yank (*informal*). **2** cast, chuck (*informal*), fling, hurl, pitch, sling, throw, toss.

heaven noun **1** Elysium, hereafter, next world, paradise. **2** bliss, delight, ecstasy, happiness, joy, paradise. □ **the heavens** firmament, sky.

heavenly adjective **1** angelic, celestial, divine. **2** beautiful, blissful, delightful, divine (*informal*), exquisite, glorious, sublime, wonderful.

heavy adjective **1** (*a heavy person*) big, burly, fat, hefty, hulking, large, overweight, solid, stocky, stout, sturdy, thickset; (*a heavy object*) bulky, cumbersome, massive, ponderous, unwieldy, weighty. **2** (*heavy rain*) copious, hard, pouring, profuse, torrential; (*heavy drinking*) excessive, immoderate, intemperate, unrestrained; (*heavy fighting*) concentrated, extensive, intense, relentless, severe, unrelenting. **3** arduous, exhausting, hard, laborious, onerous, strenuous, tiring. **4** depressed, downcast, forlorn, gloomy, melancholy, miserable, sad, sorrowful, unhappy.

heckle verb harass, harry,

interrupt, jeer at, shout down, taunt.

hectic adjective active, busy, exciting, frantic, frenzied, lively, wild.

hedge noun hedgerow, screen, windbreak.

hedge verb beat about the bush, dodge, equivocate, play for time, stall, temporise.

heed verb bear in mind, listen to, mark, mind, pay attention to, take notice of.

heed noun attention, notice, regard, thought. □ **heedless** adjective careless, inattentive, negligent, oblivious, rash, reckless, unthinking, unwary.

hefty adjective beefy, big, brawny, burly, heavy, huge, husky, large, massive, mighty, muscular, powerful, sizeable, solid, strong, sturdy, substantial, tough, vigorous.

height noun **1** altitude, elevation, stature, tallness. **2** cliff, highland, hill, hilltop, peak, pinnacle, rise, summit, top. **3** acme, apex, climax, heyday, peak, pinnacle, zenith.

heighten verb grow, increase, intensify.

heir, heiress noun beneficiary, inheritor, legatee, successor.

hell noun **1** Hades, inferno, underworld. **2** agony, misery, torment, torture.

help verb **1** abet, aid, assist, back, collaborate, cooperate, lend a hand, serve, support. **2** alleviate, cure, ease, improve, relieve, remedy, soothe. **3** avoid, keep from, prevent, refrain from, resist. □ **helper** noun abetter, accessory, accomplice, aid, aide, assistant, auxiliary, collaborator, helpmate, off-sider (*Australian*), partner, sidekick (*informal*), supporter. □ **helpful** adjective (*a helpful person*) accommodating, considerate, cooperative, kind, neighbourly, obliging, supportive, willing; (*a helpful thing*) constructive, handy, instructive, practical, useful, valuable, worthwhile.

help noun **1** advice, aid, assistance, backing, backup, collaboration, contribution, cooperation, encouragement, succour, support. **2** advantage, asset, benefit, boon.

helping noun portion, ration, serving.

helpless adjective defenceless, dependent, feeble, impotent, incapable, powerless, vulnerable.

hem verb □ **hem in** beset, besiege, box in, encircle, enclose, fence in, hedge in, restrict, surround.

hence adverb accordingly, consequently, so, therefore, thus.

henchman noun attendant, follower, hanger-on, lackey, retainer (*old use*), stooge (*informal*), supporter, yes-man.

herald noun **1** announcer, messenger, town crier. **2** forerunner, harbinger, portent, precursor, sign.

herald verb announce, foretell, proclaim, signal, usher in.

herb noun flavouring, seasoning, spice.

herd noun **1** drove, flock, mob (*Australian*), pack. **2** army, company, crowd, drove, flock, group, horde, host, mass, mob, multitude, swarm, throng.

herd verb **1** assemble, congregate, crowd, flock, gather, group, huddle, mob, muster, throng. **2** drive, guide, lead, round up, shepherd.

hereditary adjective genetic, inbred, inherited.

heretic noun apostate, dissenter, iconoclast, nonconformist, rebel, renegade.

heritage noun background, history, inheritance, legacy, past, tradition.

hermit noun loner, recluse, solitary.

hero, heroine noun **1** celebrity, champion, idol, legend (*informal*), star, superstar. **2** protagonist. □ **heroic** *adjective* bold, brave, chivalrous, courageous, daring, dauntless, doughty, fearless, gallant, intrepid, lion-hearted, plucky, valiant.

hesitant *adjective* diffident, dubious, faltering, halting, indecisive, in two minds, irresolute, reluctant, uncertain, unsure.

hesitate *verb* delay, dilly-dally (*informal*), dither, falter, hang back, hum and haw, pause, shilly-shally, vacillate, waver.

hew *verb* chop, cut, fell, hack, saw; see also *CARVE*.

heyday *noun* height, peak, pinnacle, prime, zenith.

hibernate *verb* be dormant, be inactive, sleep.

hide *verb* **1** bury, conceal, put away, secrete, stash (*informal*). **2** conceal yourself, go into hiding, go underground, hole up (*informal*), lie low, take cover. **3** bottle up, conceal, cover up, disguise, mask, repress, suppress.

hide *noun* fell, pelt, skin.

hideous *adjective* abominable, appalling, atrocious, dreadful, frightful, ghastly, grim, grisly, grotesque, gruesome, horrendous, horrible, horrid, monstrous, objectionable, odious, repulsive, revolting, shocking, sickening, ugly, unsightly, vile.

hideout *noun* den, hidey-hole (*informal*), hiding place, lair, refuge, sanctuary.

hiding *noun* beating, caning, flogging, spanking, thrashing, whipping.

higgledy-piggledy *adjective* chaotic, confused, disorderly, jumbled, mixed-up, muddled, topsy-turvy.

high *adjective* **1** elevated, high-rise, lofty, soaring, tall, towering. **2** (*high rank*) exalted, important, powerful, prominent, senior, top; (*high quality*) best, first, superior, supreme, top; (*high temperature*) above average, extreme, great, intense; (*high prices*) dear, excessive, exorbitant, expensive, steep (*informal*), stiff (*informal*). **3** high-pitched, piercing, sharp, shrill, soprano, treble. **4** delirious, euphoric, high as a kite (*slang*), spaced out (*slang*); see also *INTOXICATED*.

highbrow *adjective* cultured, erudite, intellectual, learned, scholarly, sophisticated.

highlands *plural noun* heights, hills, mountains, plateau, ranges, tableland, uplands.

highlight noun climax, feature, high point, high spot.

highlight verb accent, accentuate, emphasise, point up, spotlight, stress, underline.

highway noun expressway, freeway, main road, motorway, tollway.

highwayman noun bandit, brigand, bushranger, robber, thief.

hike noun bushwalk, ramble, tramp, trek, walk. □ **hike** verb backpack, ramble, roam, rove, tramp, trek, walk. □ **hiker** noun backpacker, bushwalker, rambler, trekker, walker.

hilarious adjective 1 amusing, comical, funny, humorous, witty. 2 boisterous, exuberant, jolly, lively, merry, noisy, riotous, rollicking.

hill noun bluff, dune, elevation, fell, foothill, headland, hillock, mesa, mountain, peak, promontory, rise, summit, tor; (hills) downs, heights, highlands, ranges, tiers (Tasmania & early South Australia). □ **hillside** noun bank, brae (Scottish), slope.

hillock noun hummock, knoll, mound, rise.

hind adjective back, hinder, posterior, rear.

hinder verb block, curb, delay, frustrate, hamper, handicap, hold back, hold up, impede, inhibit, obstruct, prevent, restrict, slow, stonker (Australian slang), stop, thwart. □ **hindrance** noun barrier, handicap, impediment, obstacle, obstruction, restriction, snag, stumbling block.

hinge noun joint, pivot.

hinge verb depend, hang, pivot, rest, revolve (around), turn.

hint noun 1 allusion, clue, implication, indication, inkling, innuendo, insinuation, intimation, lead, suggestion. 2 pointer, suggestion, tip, wrinkle (informal).

hint verb imply, indicate, insinuate, intimate, suggest.

hire verb 1 charter, lease, rent. 2 appoint, employ, engage, take on.

hiss verb boo, deride, heckle, hoot, jeer.

historic adjective celebrated, famous, important, memorable, momentous, significant.

history noun 1 background, past. 2 account, annals, biography, chronicle, memoirs, record, saga, story. □ **historical** adjective actual, authentic, documented, factual, real, recorded, true.

hit verb **1** bash, batter, beat, belt (*slang*), box, buffet, butt, clip (*informal*), clobber (*slang*), clout (*informal*), club, cuff, dong (*Australian informal*), flog, hammer, job (*informal*), knock, lash, lay into (*informal*), pound, pummel, punch, quilt (*Australian slang*), rap, slap, slog, slug, smack, smite, sock (*slang*), spank, stoush (*Australian slang*), strike, swat, swipe (*informal*), tap, thrash, thump, thwack, trounce, wallop (*slang*), whack, whip; (*of a vehicle, etc.*) bang into, bump into, collide with, crash into, knock, ram into, run into, slam into, smash into, strike. **2** affect, attack, strike, touch. □ **hit back** see RETALIATE. □ **hit on** chance on, come up with, discover, stumble on.

hit noun **1** bash, blow, buffet, bump, clip (*informal*), clout (*informal*), dong (*Australian informal*), king-hit (*Australian informal*), knock, knock-out, punch, slap, slog, slug, smack, stroke, swipe (*informal*), thump, thwack, wallop (*slang*), whack. **2** sell-out, sensation, smash hit (*informal*), success, triumph, winner.

hitch verb **1** jerk, pull, tug, yank (*informal*). **2** attach, connect, couple, fasten, harness, join, tie, yoke. **3** hitchhike, thumb a lift.

hitch noun catch, complication, difficulty, hiccup, hold-up, interruption, obstacle, problem, snag, stumbling block.

hitchhike verb hitch, thumb a lift.

hive noun apiary, beehive.

hoard noun cache, fund, reserve, stash (*informal*), stock, stockpile, store, supply, treasure trove.

hoard verb accumulate, amass, collect, gather, hang on to, hold on to, keep, lay up, save, stash away (*informal*), stockpile, store.

hoarding noun billboard, fence.

hoarse adjective croaky, gravelly, gruff, harsh, husky, rasping, rough, scratchy.

hoax verb bluff, con (*informal*), deceive, delude, dupe, fool, have on (*informal*), hoodwink, pull someone's leg, swindle, take in (*informal*), trick. □ **hoax** noun con (*informal*), confidence trick, deception, fraud, prank, scam (*slang*), spoof (*informal*), swindle, trick.

hobble verb limp, shamble, shuffle, stumble.

hobby noun diversion, interest, leisure activity, pastime, recreation, relaxation, side-line.

hobby-horse noun fixation, obsession, pet subject, pre-occupation.

hobgoblin noun bogy, goblin, imp, spirit, sprite.

hog noun glutton, greedy-guts (slang), pig (informal).

hoist verb haul, heave, hoick (slang), lift, pull up, raise, winch.

hold verb 1 carry, clasp, clutch, grasp, grip, hang on to, have, keep, maintain, possess, retain, seize, take. 2 accommodate, contain, have a capacity of, house, seat, take. 3 bear, carry, support, sustain, take. 4 carry on, continue, endure, last, persist, stay. 5 believe, consider, deem, judge, regard, think. 6 call, conduct, convene, run. 7 check, control, curb, restrain, stop. □ **hold back** block, check, control, curb, halt, keep back, repress, restrain, stop, suppress, withhold. □ **hold forth** harangue, lecture, preach, sermonise, sound off (informal), speak, spout. □ **hold off** defer, delay, postpone, put off, stall. □ **hold out 1** extend, put out, reach out, stretch out. 2 continue, hang on (informal), last,

persevere, persist, stick it out (informal). □ **hold up 1** delay, hinder, obstruct, slow down. 2 bail up (Australian), mug, rob, stick up (informal), waylay.

hold noun clasp, clutch, grasp, grip.

holder noun see CONTAINER.

hold-up noun 1 delay, jam, snarl, stoppage. 2 burglary, robbery, stick-up (informal).

hole noun 1 aperture, breach, break, cavity, chink, crabhole (Australian), crack, crater, depression, fissure, gap, gash, gilgai (Australian), hollow, leak, opening, orifice, perforation, pit, pocket, pothole, puncture, slit, slot, space, split, tear, tunnel. 2 burrow, den, hideout (informal), lair, warren.

holiday noun 1 feast day, festival. 2 furlough, break, leave, rest, time off, vacation.

hollow adjective empty, unfilled, void.

hollow noun 1 basin, bunker (Golf), cave, cavern, cavity, crabhole (Australian), crater, depression, ditch, gilgai (Australian), hole, pit, pothole, trough. 2 dell, glen, gully (Australian), valley.

hollow verb dig, excavate, gouge, scoop.

holocaust noun annihilation, carnage, conflagration, destruction, devastation, genocide, massacre, mass murder.

holy adjective **1** blameless, devout, godly, pious, religious, righteous, saintly, virtuous. **2** blessed, consecrated, divine, hallowed, heavenly, sacred, sacrosanct.

homage noun honour, obeisance, respect, tribute.

home noun **1** abode (old use), domicile, dwelling, habitation, house, place, residence; see also FLAT, HOUSE. **2** birthplace, fatherland, homeland, mother country, native land. **3** hospice, hostel, institution, nursing home, rest home, retirement home.

home verb ◻ **home in on** aim at, concentrate on, focus on, zero in on, zoom in on.

homeless adjective abandoned, displaced, evicted, exiled, itinerant, nomadic, outcast, stray, vagabond, vagrant, wandering.

homely adjective comfortable, cosy, friendly, informal, liveable, ordinary, plain, simple, unpretentious, welcoming.

homestead noun farmhouse, home, house, residence.

home unit apartment, condominium (American), flat, unit.

homework noun assignment, prep, preparation, study, work.

homicide noun assassination, killing, manslaughter, murder, slaying.

homily noun address, lecture, sermon, speech.

homogeneous adjective consistent, uniform, unvarying.

homosexual adjective gay, (informal), lesbian (female).

honest adjective **1** honourable, law-abiding, principled, scrupulous, straight, trustworthy, truthful, upright, upstanding, veracious. **2** blunt, candid, direct, forthright, frank, genuine, open, sincere, straightforward, truthful. **3** above board, ethical, fair, lawful, legal, legitimate, proper. ◻ **honesty** noun frankness, genuineness, integrity, openness, probity, rectitude, sincerity, trustworthiness, truthfulness, uprightness, veracity.

honour noun **1** acclaim, admiration, credit, distinction, esteem, fame, glory, homage, prestige, recognition, renown, repute, respect, reverence, veneration, worship. **2** decency, fairness, honesty, integrity, morality, principle, probity, rectitude, scruples, virtue.

honour verb **1** admire, esteem, glorify, hallow, pay homage to, pay tribute to, pay your respects to, praise, respect, revere, salute, value, venerate, worship. **2** abide by, keep, stand by, stick to.

honourable adjective above board, decent, ethical, high-minded, honest, principled, reputable, respectable, scrupulous, upright.

hoodwink verb bamboozle (informal), bluff, cheat, con (informal), deceive, defraud, dupe, fool, hoax, swindle, trick.

hook noun hanger, nail, peg.

hook verb **1** capture, catch, take. **2** fasten, hitch, latch, secure. ☐ **be hooked on** be addicted to, be dependent on.

hooked adjective aquiline (nose).

hooligan noun delinquent, hoodlum, hoon (Australian informal), larrikin (Australian informal), lout, ruffian, tearaway, thug, tough, troublemaker, vandal, yob (informal).

hoop noun band, circle, ring.

hoot noun **1** (an owl's hoot) cry, scream, screech, shriek, whoop. **2** boo, catcall, hiss, jeer. ☐ **hoot** verb **1** (hoot a horn) blast, blow, honk, sound, toot. **2** boo, deride, heckle, hiss, jeer,

mock. ☐ **hooter** noun horn, siren, whistle.

hop verb bob, bounce, bound, jump, leap, skip, spring.

hope noun ambition, aspiration, confidence, desire, dream, expectation, faith, longing, optimism, trust, wish.

hope verb aspire, desire, dream, expect, hanker, long, trust, want, wish.

hopeful adjective **1** confident, expectant, optimistic, sanguine, trusting. **2** auspicious, encouraging, favourable, heartening, positive, promising, propitious, reassuring.

hopeless adjective **1** dejected, demoralised, depressed, despairing, desperate, despondent, downcast, forlorn, pessimistic, wretched. **2** incurable, irredeemable, irreparable, irretrievable, irrevocable. **3** bad, feeble, inadequate, incompetent, poor, useless.

horde noun crowd, drove, mass, mob, multitude, swarm, throng.

horizon noun skyline.

horizontal adjective flat, level, prone, prostrate, supine.

horrible adjective **1** abhorrent, abominable, appalling, atrocious, awful, despicable, detestable, dreadful, foul, frightful, ghastly, grisly, gruesome, hideous, horrendous, horrid, horrific, loathsome, monstrous, odious, repugnant, repulsive, revolting, shocking, sickening, terrible, vile. **2** awful, disagreeable, horrid, mean, nasty, objectionable, obnoxious, offensive, unbearable, unkind, unpleasant.

horrify *verb* alarm, appal, disgust, frighten, revolt, scare, shock, terrify.

horror *noun* abhorrence, alarm, antipathy, aversion, consternation, dislike, dismay, dread, fear, hatred, loathing, panic, revulsion, terror, trepidation.

horse *noun* bronco, brumby (*Australian*), carthorse, charger, draughthorse, gee-gee (*informal*), hack, moke (*Australian*), mount, mustang, nag (*informal*), nanto (*Australian old use*), neddy (*informal*), pacer, palfrey (*old use*), pony, racehorse, steed (*poetical*), trotter, yarraman (*Australian*); (*male horses*) colt, gelding, sire, stallion; (*female horses*) filly, mare; (*young horses*) colt, filly, foal.

horseman, horsewoman *noun* equestrian, horse-rider, jockey, rider.

hospice *noun* home, hospital institution, nursing home.

hospitable *adjective* amiable, cordial, friendly, generous, genial, gracious, kind, sociable, warm, welcoming.

hospital *noun* clinic, hospice, infirmary, medical centre, nursing home, sanatorium.

host *noun* anchorperson, announcer, compère, disc jockey, DJ, Master of Ceremonies, MC, presenter.

host *noun* army, crowd, horde, lot, mass, mob, multitude, myriad, swarm, throng; see also *GROUP*.

hostage *noun* captive, prisoner.

hostel *noun* boarding house, guest house, home.

hostile *adjective* **1** attacking, enemy, opposing, warring. **2** aggressive, angry, belligerent, chilly, cold, frosty, icy, spiteful, unfriendly, unkind, vicious. ▢ **hostility** *noun* aggression, animosity, antagonism, antipathy, belligerence, enmity, friction, opposition, rancour, resentment, unfriendliness. (*hostilities*) see *WAR*.

hot *adjective* **1** baking, blazing, boiling, burning, fiery, flaming, glowing, piping hot, red-hot, roasting, scalding, scorching, searing, sizzling, steaming, sultry, summery, sweltering, torrid, warm. **2** burning, peppery, piquant, pungent, sharp, spicy. **3** animated, ardent, emotional, excited, fervent, fiery, heated, intense, lively, passionate, stormy.

hot verb □ **hot up** heat up, reheat, warm up.

hotel noun guest house, inn, local (informal), motel, pub (informal), public house, tavern.

hotheaded adjective excitable, fiery, impetuous, impulsive, rash, reckless, wild.

hothouse noun conservatory, glasshouse, greenhouse.

hotpot noun casserole, goulash, ragout, stew.

hound noun beagle, bloodhound, dog, foxhound, greyhound, hunting dog, wolfhound.

hound verb badger, chase, dog, harass, hunt, keep at, nag, pester, pursue.

house noun **1** abode (old use), accommodation, domicile, dwelling, habitation, home, place, residence; (kinds of house) bungalow, chalet, cottage, farmhouse, homestead, hut, igloo, maisonette, manor, manse, mansion, presbytery, rectory, shack, shanty, terrace house, town house, vicarage, villa. **2** auditorium, hall, theatre. **3** assembly, chamber, council, legislative body. **4** dynasty, family, line, lineage.

house verb accommodate, billet, put up, shelter.

householder noun occupant, owner, resident, tenant.

housework noun cleaning, cooking, home duties, housekeeping.

housing noun **1** accommodation, dwellings, homes, houses, lodging(s), quarters, residences, shelter. **2** case, casing, container, cover.

hovel noun dump (informal), hole (informal), hut, shack, shanty, shed.

hover verb **1** float, flutter. **2** hang about, linger, wait near.

however adverb nevertheless, none the less, though.

howl noun bay, bellow, cry, groan, scream, shout, shriek, wail, whine, yell, yelp, yowl.

howl verb **1** bawl, bellow, cry, roar, scream, shout, shriek, wail, whine, yell, yelp, yowl. **2** see WEEP.

hub noun centre, core, focus, heart, middle.

hubbub noun babble, clamour, din, hullabaloo, noise, racket.

huddle verb **1** cluster, cram, crowd, flock, herd, jam, pile, press, squash, squeeze, throng. **2** curl up, nestle, snuggle.

hue noun colour, shade, tinge, tint, tone.

hue noun □ **hue and cry** clamour, commotion, furore, fuss, hullabaloo, outcry, protest, to-do, uproar.

huffy adjective annoyed, grumpy, in a huff, miffed (informal), offended, peevish, petulant, piqued, resentful, shirty (informal), sulky, testy, touchy.

hug verb clasp, cuddle, embrace, hold, squeeze.

huge adjective astronomical, big, colossal, enormous, exorbitant, gargantuan, giant, gigantic, great, humungous (slang), immense, jumbo, large, mammoth, massive, mighty, monstrous, staggering, stupendous, sweeping, vast.

hulking adjective bulky, burly, heavy, hefty, husky, large, massive.

hull noun body, frame, framework, skeleton.

hullabaloo noun clamour, commotion, din, fracas, fuss, hubbub, racket, rumpus, uproar.

hum verb buzz, drone, purr, vibrate, whirr.

hum noun buzz, drone, purr, vibration, whirr.

human adjective □ **human being** child, human, individual, man, mortal, person, woman.

humane adjective benevolent, compassionate, humanitarian, kind, kind-hearted, merciful, sympathetic, understanding.

humanitarian adjective benevolent, humane, philanthropic.

humanity noun **1** humankind, human race, man, mankind, people, society. **2** benevolence, compassion, goodness, humaneness, kindness, mercy, sympathy, understanding.

humble adjective **1** meek, modest, ordinary, plain, self-effacing, simple, unassertive, unassuming, unpretentious. **2** insignificant, low, lowly, unimportant.

humble verb abase, chasten, disgrace, humiliate, mortify, shame, subdue, take down a peg (informal).

humbug noun **1** blarney, boloney (informal), bull (slang), bunkum, claptrap, deceit, deception, fraud, hocus-pocus, lies, mumbo-jumbo, nonsense, pretence, rubbish, rot (slang), sham, trickery.

charlatan, cheat, con man (*informal*), fake, fraud, phoney (*informal*), quack, sham, swindler, trickster.

humdrum *adjective* boring, commonplace, dreary, dull, monotonous, mundane, ordinary, repetitive, routine, tedious, unexciting, uninteresting, wearisome.

humid *adjective* clammy, close, damp, dank, moist, muggy, steamy, sticky, sultry.

humiliate *verb* abase, chasten, demean, disgrace, embarrass, humble, mortify, put down, shame, take down a peg (*informal*). □ **humiliation** *noun* abasement, disgrace, embarrassment, indignity, mortification, shame.

humility *noun* deference, humbleness, lowliness, meekness, modesty, unpretentiousness.

humorous *adjective* amusing, comic, comical, droll, facetious, farcical, funny, hilarious, laughable, ridiculous, witty.

humour *noun* **1** absurdity, comedy, farcicalness, funniness, ludicrousness, ridiculousness, wittiness. **2** disposition, mood, spirits, temper.

humour *verb* go along with, indulge, pamper, pander to, play up to.

hump *noun* bulge, bump, hunch, lump, swelling.

hump *verb* arch, curve, hunch.

hunch *noun* feeling, idea, inkling, intuition, premonition, suspicion.

hunch *verb* arch, bend, crouch, hump.

hunger *noun* appetite, emptiness, malnutrition, ravenousness, starvation.

hungry *adjective* famished, peckish (*informal*), ravenous, starved, starving.

hunk *noun* block, chunk, lump, piece, slab, wedge.

hunt *verb* **1** chase, pursue, stalk, track, trail. **2** ferret out, forage for, fossick for (*Australian informal*), look for, rummage for, search for, seek. □ **hunter** *noun* huntsman, predator, tracker.

hunt *noun* chase, pursuit, quest, search.

hurdle *noun* **1** barricade, barrier, fence. **2** barrier, difficulty, impediment, obstacle, problem, snag, stumbling block.

hurl *verb* cast, chuck (*informal*), fling, heave, pitch, propel, sling (*informal*), throw, toss.

hurly-burly *noun* activity, bustle, commotion, hubbub, hustle and bustle, tumult.

hurricane noun cyclone, tropical cyclone, typhoon; see also STORM, WIND.

hurry verb **1** be quick, bolt, dash, fly, get a move on (*informal*), get cracking (*informal*), get your skates on (*informal*), hasten, hurtle, hustle, make haste, make it snappy (*informal*), race, run, rush, scoot, scurry, scuttle, speed, step on it (*informal*), whiz, zip, zoom. **2** accelerate, expedite, fast-track (*informal*), hasten, push, quicken, speed up.

hurry noun bustle, haste, hurry-scurry, hustle, rush, scurry, urgency.

hurt verb **1** bruise, cripple, cut, damage, disable, distress, grieve, harm, impair, injure, maim, mutilate, offend, pain, scratch, spoil, sprain, trouble, upset, wound. **2** ache, be painful, be sore, smart, sting, throb.

hurt noun ache, affliction, agony, anguish, damage, discomfort, distress, grief, harm, injury, misery, pain, sadness, soreness, sorrow, suffering, torment, torture. □ **hurtful** adjective brutal, cruel, cutting, distressing, malicious, mean, nasty, unkind, upsetting.

hurtle verb fly, race, shoot, speed, tear, whiz, zip, zoom.

husband noun bridegroom, groom, mate, partner, spouse.

husband verb conserve, hoard, preserve, save.

hush verb calm, lull, quieten, shush (*informal*), silence, soothe. □ **hushed** adjective low, quiet, soft, subdued.

hush noun quietness, silence, stillness.

husk noun case, hull, pod, shell.

husky adjective **1** croaking, dry, gravelly, gruff, guttural, harsh, hoarse, rasping, rough, throaty. **2** beefy, brawny, burly, hefty, hulking, muscular, nuggety (*Australian*), solid, stocky, strapping, strong, sturdy, thickset, tough.

hustle verb bustle, hasten, hurry, jostle, pressure, push, rush, shove, thrust. □ **hustle** noun activity, bustle, haste, hurly-burly, hurry, hurry, scurry, rush, tumult.

hut noun cabin, chalet, gunya (*Australian*), house, hovel, humpy (*Australian*), lean-to, mia mia (*Australian*), shack, shanty, shed, shelter, skillion (*Australian*), wurley (*Australian*).

hutch noun box, cage, coop, enclosure, pen.

hybrid *noun* blend, cross, crossbreed, half-breed, mixture.

hygienic *adjective* aseptic, clean, disinfected, germ-free, healthy, sanitary, sterile, sterilised.

hymn *noun* anthem, canticle, carol, chorus, introit, psalm, song.

hyperbole *noun* exaggeration, overstatement.

hypnotise *verb* bewitch, enthral, entrance, fascinate, mesmerise. □ **hypnotic** *adjective* mesmerising, soporific, spellbinding.

hypocrite *noun* deceiver, dissembler, phoney (*informal*), pretender. □ **hypocrisy** *noun* deceit, dishonesty, dissembling, falseness, insincerity. □ **hypocritical** *adjective* false, inconsistent, insincere, pharisaical, two-faced.

hypothesis *noun* assumption, conjecture, idea, proposition, speculation, supposition, theory, thesis. □ **hypothetical** *adjective* academic, conjectural, imaginary, speculative, theoretical.

hysterical *adjective* berserk, crazed, distraught, frantic, frenzied, overwrought, raving, uncontrollable.

Ii

ice *noun* black ice, floe, frost, glacier, iceberg, icicle, pack ice, rime.

icing *noun* frosting, glaze.

icon *noun* idol, image, statue.

icy *adjective* biting, bitter, chilly, cold, freezing, frigid, frosty, glacial, nippy (*informal*), subzero; (*icy roads*) frozen, glassy, slippery.

idea *noun* **1** brainwave, concept, hunch, hypothesis, impression, notion, plan, proposal, scheme, suggestion, suspicion, theory, thought. **2** attitude, belief, conviction, notion, opinion, thought, view.

ideal *adjective* excellent, exemplary, faultless, model, optimal, optimum, perfect.

idealistic *adjective* impractical, optimistic, romantic, unrealistic, Utopian, visionary.

identical *adjective* alike, duplicate, indistinguishable, matching, same, twin.

identify *verb* **1** diagnose, discover, distinguish, name, pick out, pinpoint, recognise, single out, spot. **2** (*identify with*) empathise with, relate to, respond to, sympathise with.

identity noun distinctiveness, individuality, personality, uniqueness.

ideology noun beliefs, creed, doctrine, ideas, philosophy, principles, tenets.

idiom noun expression, phrase.

idiosyncrasy noun characteristic, eccentricity, foible, habit, mannerism, peculiarity, quirk, trait.

idiot noun ass (informal), blockhead, bonehead, chump (informal), clot (informal), cretin, dill (Australian informal), dimwit (informal), dodo (informal), dolt, dope (informal), drongo (Australian informal), dummy (informal), dunce, fat-head (informal), fool, galah (Australian slang), half-wit, ignoramus, imbecile, jerk (slang), lunatic, moron (informal), nincompoop, ninny, nitwit (informal), nong (Australian informal), numskull, nut (informal), simpleton, thickhead (informal), twerp (slang), twit (slang). □ **idiotic** adjective absurd, crazy, dumb (informal), foolhardy, foolish, inane, irrational, lunatic, mad, nutty (informal), reckless, ridiculous, senseless, silly, stupid, unintelligent, unwise.

idle adjective **1** indolent, lazy, shiftless, slothful, sluggish. **2** inactive, out of action, unused. **3** empty, frivolous, pointless, superficial, trivial, useless, worthless.

idle verb laze, loaf, potter, slack, take it easy, vegetate. □ **idler** noun bludger (Australian informal), good-for-nothing, layabout, lazybones (in-formal), loafer, malingerer, shirker, skiver (informal), slacker, slouch (informal).

idol noun **1** effigy, graven image, icon, image, statue. **2** celebrity, heart-throb (slang), hero, heroine, star, superstar.

idolise verb adore, deify, dote on, glorify, lionise, look up to, love, revere, venerate, worship.

ignite verb **1** fire, kindle, light, set fire to. **2** burn, catch fire, kindle.

ignominious adjective degrading, disgraceful, dishonourable, humiliating, infamous, inglorious, shameful.

ignorant adjective **1** oblivious (of), unaware (of), unfamiliar (with), uninformed (about). **2** illiterate, uneducated, uninformed, unschooled, untaught.

ignore verb brush aside, close your eyes to, cold-shoulder, disregard, neglect, overlook, pass over, send a person to Coventry, shrug off, slight, snub, take no notice of.

ill *adjective* **1** ailing, crook (*Australian informal*), diseased, indisposed, infirm, nauseous, off colour, out of sorts, poorly, queasy, rotten, seedy (*informal*), sick, sickly, under the weather, unhealthy, unwell. **2** adverse, bad, damaging, destructive, detrimental, evil, harmful, unfavourable. □ **ill will** animosity, antipathy, hostility, malevolence, malice, rancour, resentment, spite.

illegal *adjective* banned, criminal, forbidden, illegitimate, illicit, outlawed, prohibited, proscribed, unauthorised, unlawful.

illegible *adjective* indecipherable, unreadable.

illegitimate *adjective* illegal, improper, inadmissible, wrong.

illicit *adjective* see ILLEGAL.

illiterate *adjective* ignorant, uneducated, uninformed, unknowledgeable.

illness *noun* affliction, ailment, bug (*informal*), complaint, condition, disease, disorder, indisposition, infection, infirmity, malady, sickness, trouble, wog (*Australian informal*).

illogical *adjective* absurd, irrational, unreasonable, unsound.

illuminate *verb* **1** brighten up, floodlight, light up. **2** clarify, elucidate, explain, shed light on, throw light on.

illusion *noun* deception, hallucination, mirage, trick. □ **illusory** *adjective* deceptive, fancied, illusive, imaginary, imagined, unreal.

illustrate *verb* clarify, demonstrate, depict, draw, elucidate, exemplify, explain, picture, portray, represent, show.

illustration *noun* **1** diagram, drawing, figure, picture, plate. **2** example, instance, sample, specimen.

illustrious *adjective* celebrated, distinguished, eminent, famous, notable, prominent, renowned, well-known.

image *noun* **1** carving, effigy, figure, icon, idol, picture, representation, statue. **2** appearance, likeness, reflection. **3** copy, dead ringer (*informal*), duplicate, replica, spit, spitting image.

imaginary *adjective* fancied, fanciful, fictitious, hypothetical, illusory, invented, legendary, made-up, mythical, mythological, non-existent, pretend (*informal*), unreal.

imagination noun creativity, fancy, fantasy, ingenuity, innovation, inspiration, inventiveness, vision. ◻ **imaginative** adjective creative, ingenious, innovative, inspired, inventive, visionary.

imagine verb conceive, dream up, envisage, fancy, fantasise, picture, speculate, think up, visualise.

imbalance noun disproportion, inequality, unevenness.

imitate verb ape, copy, duplicate, echo, emulate, impersonate, mimic, parody, replicate, reproduce, send up (*informal*), simulate, take off.

imitation noun 1 burlesque, impersonation, impression, mimicry, parody, send-up (*informal*), spoof (*informal*), take-off. 2 copy, counterfeit, duplicate, fake, forgery, replica, reproduction. ◻ **imitation** adjective artificial, fake, mock, phoney (*informal*), sham, synthetic.

immaculate adjective 1 clean, neat, spick and span, spotless, tidy. 2 faultless, flawless, impeccable, perfect, unblemished.

immature adjective babyish, callow, spick, childish, green,

inexperienced, infantile, juvenile, naïve, puerile, youthful.

immediate adjective 1 direct, instant, instantaneous, prompt, speedy, swift, unhesitating. 2 adjacent, closest, nearest, next. ◻ **immediately** adverb at once, directly, forthwith, instantly, on the knocker (*Australian informal*), on the spot, promptly, right away, straight away, then and there.

immense adjective astronomical, big, colossal, considerable, enormous, excessive, exorbitant, extensive, gigantic, great, hefty, huge, immeasurable, large, mammoth, massive, monstrous, prodigious, staggering, stupendous, terrific, tremendous, vast.

immerse verb 1 dip, drench, dunk, plunge, soak, steep, submerge, wet. 2 absorb, bury, engross, occupy, preoccupy.

immigrant noun migrant, newcomer, settler.

imminent adjective approaching, close, impending, looming, near, nigh, threatening.

immobile adjective fixed, immobilised, immovable, motionless, paralysed, stationary, still, stuck.

immodest adjective **1** brazen, forward, improper, indecent, shameless, wanton. **2** see CONCEITED (at CONCEIT).

immoral adjective bad, base, corrupt, degenerate, depraved, evil, iniquitous, shameless, sinful, unethical, unprincipled, unscrupulous, wicked.

immortal adjective abiding, enduring, eternal, everlasting, undying.

immovable adjective fast, fixed, immobile, immobilised, jammed, stationary, stuck.

immune adjective exempt (from), free (from), impervious (to), invulnerable (to), protected (from), resistant (to), safe (from).

immunisation noun inoculation, vaccination.

imp noun **1** demon, devil, elf, fairy, goblin, hobgoblin, pixie, spirit, sprite. **2** devil, monkey, rascal, scallywag, scamp.

impact noun **1** bump, collision, crash, knock, smash. **2** consequence, effect, impression, influence, repercussions.

impair verb damage, harm, hurt, injure, ruin, spoil, undermine, weaken.

impart verb **1** communicate, convey, disclose, divulge, make known, pass on, report, reveal, tell, transmit. **2** contribute, give.

impartial adjective disinterested, even-handed, fair, just, neutral, non-aligned, nonpartisan, objective, unbiased.

impasse noun deadlock, stalemate, standstill.

impassive adjective apathetic, cool, dispassionate, indifferent, phlegmatic, stolid, stony, unemotional, unmoved, unresponsive, wooden.

impatient adjective edgy, fidgety, nervous, nervy, restive, restless, toey (Australian informal); (impatient to) anxious to, eager to, itching to, keen to, raring to.

impeccable adjective blameless, exemplary, faultless, flawless, irreproachable, perfect, unimpeachable.

impede verb block, check, curb, delay, hamper, handicap, hinder, hold up, inhibit, obstruct, prevent, restrict, retard, slow, stonker (Australian slang), thwart.

impediment noun **1** bar, barrier, hindrance, hitch, hurdle, obstacle, obstruction, snag, stumbling block. **2** defect, handicap, lisp, stammer, stutter.

impel verb compel, drive, force, make, prompt, urge.

impending adjective approaching, coming, forthcoming, imminent, looming, threatening.

impenetrable adjective dense, impassable, impervious, inaccessible, thick.

impenitent adjective hardened, remorseless, unrepentant.

imperative adjective compulsory, essential, mandatory, necessary, obligatory.

imperceptible adjective indiscernible, minuscule, minute, negligible, slight, subtle, tiny, unnoticeable.

imperfect adjective defective, deficient, faulty, flawed, incomplete, shoddy, substandard, unfinished. □ **imperfection** noun blemish, defect, deficiency, fault, flaw, shortcoming, weakness.

imperious verb bossy, commanding, dictatorial, domineering, lordly, magisterial, masterful, overbearing, peremptory.

impersonate verb ape, imitate, masquerade as, mimic, portray, pose as, pretend to be, take off.

impertinent adjective cheeky, disrespectful, forward, impolite, impudent, insolent, presumptuous, rude. □ **impertinence** noun cheek,

effrontery, gall, hide, impudence, insolence, nerve, presumptuousness, rudeness.

impervious adjective **1** impenetrable, impermeable, resistant, waterproof. **2** immune, invulnerable, unaffected (by), unresponsive.

impetuous adjective **1** hasty, headlong, impulsive, precipitate, quick, rash, reckless, spontaneous, spur-of-the-moment, sudden, wild. **2** eager, foolhardy, headstrong, hotheaded, impulsive, rash, reckless, spontaneous.

impetus noun boost, drive, impulse, incentive, momentum, motivation, push, spur, stimulus.

impinge verb **1** affect, have an effect, have an impact, touch. **2** encroach, infringe, intrude, trespass.

implant verb fix, insert, introduce, plant, put, sow.

implement noun appliance, device, gadget, instrument, tool, utensil.

implement verb accomplish, carry out, effect, enforce, execute, put into effect.

implicate verb dob in (Australian informal), embroil, grass on (slang), incriminate, inform on, involve.

implication *noun* innuendo, insinuation, intimation, overtone, significance.

implicit *adjective* implied, tacit, understood, unsaid, unspoken.

implore *verb* appeal to, ask, beg, beseech, entreat, plead with, request.

imply *verb* hint, indicate, insinuate, intimate, suggest.

impolite *adjective* bad-mannered, boorish, cheeky, churlish, coarse, discourteous, disrespectful, impudent, insolent, insulting, loutish, rude, tactless, uncivil, vulgar.

important *adjective* **1** big, consequential, critical, crucial, fateful, grave, historic, key, life and death, major, momentous, newsworthy, noteworthy, pivotal, pressing, primary, serious, significant, urgent, vital, weighty. **2** celebrated, distinguished, eminent, famed, famous, great, high-ranking, influential, leading, notable, outstanding, powerful, pre-eminent, prominent, renowned, well-known.
□ **importance** *noun* **1** account, consequence, import, moment, significance, weight. **2** distinction, eminence, influence, note, prominence, renown, standing, stature, status.

impose *verb* enforce, exact, inflict, lay, levy, prescribe, put.
□ **impose on** abuse, exploit, presume on, take advantage of.

imposing *adjective* big, grand, impressive, magnificent, majestic, ostentatious, splendid, stately, striking.

impossible *adjective* hopeless, impracticable, inconceivable, insoluble, out of the question, unachievable, unattainable, unthinkable, unworkable.

impostor *noun* charlatan, con man (*informal*), fraud, impersonator, phoney (*informal*), pretender.

impotent *adjective* feeble, helpless, ineffective, ineffectual, powerless, unable, weak.

impound *verb* confiscate, seize, take, take possession of.

impoverished *adjective* destitute, down and out, hard up (*informal*), impecunious, needy, penniless, penurious, poor, poverty-stricken.

impractical *adjective* airy-fairy, idealistic, starry-eyed, unrealistic, visionary.

imprecise *adjective* approximate, fuzzy, general, hazy, indefinite, inexact, nebulous, rough, sketchy, vague.

impregnable *adjective* invincible, invulnerable, safe,

secure, unassailable, unconquerable.

impregnate verb **1** fertilise,
inseminate. **2** fill, imbue,
permeate, saturate, soak,
steep.

impress verb **1** affect, influence,
move, stir, strike, touch.
2 emphasise, stress, underline.

impression noun **1** effect,
impact, mark. **2** belief, feeling,
hunch, idea, notion, opinion,
sense, suspicion. **3** imitation,
impersonation, parody, send-
up (informal), take-off.

impressive adjective august,
awe-inspiring, grand, great,
imposing, magnificent, majestic, memorable, moving,
outstanding, remarkable, sensational, spectacular, splendid,
stately, striking, superb.

imprint noun impression,
indentation, mark, print, seal,
stamp. □ **imprint** verb
engrave, etch, impress, stamp.

imprison verb confine, detain,
incarcerate, intern, jail, lock
up, place in custody, shut up.
□ **imprisonment** noun confinement, custody, detention,
incarceration, internment,
jail.

improbable adjective far-
fetched, implausible, incredible, unbelievable, unlikely.

impromptu adjective ad lib
extempore, off the cuff
spontaneous, unprepared
unrehearsed, unscripted.

improper adjective coarse
crude, inappropriate, in
decent, irreverent, obscene
offensive, rude, unbecoming
unseemly, unsuitable, vulgar.

improve verb advance
ameliorate, amend, be on the
mend, develop, enhance, fix up
get better, lift, look up, perk up
pick up, polish, progress, rally
recover, recuperate, refine
reform, revamp, revise, raise a
turn for the better, touch up
upgrade. □ **improvement**
noun advance, amelioration
amendment, development
enhancement, lift, progress
rally, recovery, refinement
reform, revamp, revision
touch-up, upgrade, upturn.

improvise verb ad lib (infor
mal), extemporise, invent
make up, play by ear.

imprudent adjective foolhardy
foolish, ill-advised, impolitic
inadvisable, indiscreet, reck
less, short-sighted, unintel
ligent, unwise.

impudent adjective brazen
cheeky, discourteous, dis
respectful, fresh (informal)
impertinent, impolite, in
solent, pert, presumptuous
rude, saucy.

impulsive adjective (an impulsive person) capricious, hotheaded, impetuous, rash, reckless; (an impulsive action) automatic, hasty, headlong, impetuous, instinctive, precipitate, rash, reckless, spontaneous, spur-of-the-moment, unplanned.

impure adjective adulterated, contaminated, dirty, filthy, foul, polluted, tainted, unclean.

inability noun helplessness, impotence, incapacity, powerlessness.

inaccessible adjective cut off, isolated, out of reach, remote, unreachable.

inaccurate adjective careless, false, imprecise, incorrect, inexact, sloppy, untruthful, wrong.

inactive adjective asleep, dormant, hibernating, idle, indolent, inert, lazy, lethargic, listless, passive, resting, sedentary, sleepy, slothful, sluggish, torpid.

inadequate adjective deficient, insufficient, scanty, sketchy, skimpy, sparse.

inadvertent adjective accidental, involuntary, unconscious, unintentional, unwitting.

inadvisable adjective foolish, ill-advised, impolitic, imprudent, unwise.

inane adjective see SILLY.

inanimate adjective lifeless.

inappropriate adjective improper, incongruous, irrelevant, unbecoming, unsatisfactory, unsuitable, wrong.

inattentive adjective absent-minded, careless, distracted, heedless, incautious, negligent.

inborn adjective congenital, hereditary, inbred, inherent, innate, native, natural.

incalculable adjective countless, enormous, immeasurable, inestimable, infinite, innumerable.

incapable adjective incompetent, ineffective, ineffectual, inept, useless.

incapacitate verb cripple, disable, immobilise, lay up, maim.

incense verb anger, enrage, exasperate, infuriate, madden, outrage, provoke, rile (informal), vex.

incentive noun carrot, encouragement, goad, inducement, lure, reward, spur, stimulus.

incessant adjective ceaseless, chronic, constant, continual, continuous, endless, eternal, everlasting, interminable, non-stop, permanent, perpetual, persistent, relentless.

incidence noun frequency, occurrence, prevalence, rate.

incident noun affair, episode, event, experience, happening, occasion, occurrence.

incidental adjective ancillary, minor, secondary, subsidiary.

incision noun cut, slit.

incite verb arouse, egg on, encourage, excite, goad, provoke, rouse, spur, stimulate, stir up, urge.

inclement adjective bad, foul, rough, stormy, wet.

inclination noun **1** habit, predisposition, propensity, tendency. **2** fondness, liking, partiality, penchant, predilection, preference. **3** angle, gradient, incline, slant, slope.

incline verb **1** cant, pitch, slant, slope. **2** bend, bow, lean, tilt, tip. □ **be inclined** be apt, be liable, be prone, be wont (old use), tend.

incline noun grade, gradient, hill, inclination, pitch, rise, slant, slope.

include verb comprise, consist of, contain, count, cover, embrace, encompass, incorporate, subsume, take in.

incoherent adjective confused, garbled, illogical, inarticulate, incomprehensible, jumbled, muddled, rambling, unclear, unintelligible.

income noun earnings, livelihood, pay, receipts, revenue, salary, stipend, takings, wages.

incomparable adjective inimitable, matchless, peerless, superlative, supreme, unequalled, unparalleled, unrivalled, unsurpassed.

incompatible adjective conflicting, contradictory, incongruous, inconsistent, irreconcilable, mismatched, unsuited.

incompetent adjective clueless (informal), hopeless, inadequate, incapable, ineffectual, inefficient, inept, inexpert, unskilful, useless.

incomplete adjective abridged, fragmentary, imperfect, partial, sketchy, unfinished.

incomprehensible adjective abstruse, bewildering, complicated, inexplicable, inscrutable, unfathomable, unintelligible.

inconceivable adjective impossible, improbable, incredible, unbelievable, unimaginable, unthinkable.

incongruous adjective absurd, inappropriate, odd, out of keeping, out of place.

nconsiderate *adjective* careless, insensitive, rude, selfish, tactless, thoughtless, uncaring, unthinking.

nconsistent *adjective* **1** capricious, changeable, erratic, fickle, patchy, temperamental, unpredictable, unreliable, variable. **2** at odds, conflicting, contradictory, incompatible, irreconcilable.

nconspicuous *adjective* unnoticeable, unobtrusive, unostentatious.

nconvenience *noun* bother, disruption, disturbance, hassle (*informal*), irritation, nuisance, trouble.

nconvenience *verb* bother, disrupt, disturb, hassle (*informal*), impose on, put out (*informal*), trouble.

nconvenient *adjective* awkward, bothersome, ill-timed, inopportune, troublesome, unsuitable, untimely.

ncorporate *verb* amalgamate, blend, combine, consolidate, integrate, merge, mix, unite; see also *INCLUDE*.

ncorrect *adjective* erroneous, false, inaccurate, mistaken, untrue, wrong.

ncorrigible *adjective* hardened, hopeless, incurable, inveterate, unreformable.

increase *verb* add to, advance, appreciate, augment, boost, build up, develop, enlarge, escalate, expand, extend, gain, go up, grow, heighten, improve, intensify, jump, lengthen, lift, magnify, multiply, prolong, protract, raise, skyrocket, soar, step up, strengthen, supplement, swell.

increase *noun* addition, advance, boost, build-up, development, enlargement, escalation, expansion, explosion, extension, gain, growth, increment, inflation, jump, rise, upsurge.

incredible *adjective* amazing, extraordinary, far-fetched, implausible, improbable, inconceivable, miraculous, unbelievable, unlikely.

incredulous *adjective* disbelieving, distrustful, doubtful, dubious, sceptical, unbelieving.

incriminate *verb* accuse, blame, implicate, inculpate.

incubate *verb* brood, hatch.

incurable *adjective* hopeless, inoperable, uncorrectable, untreatable; see also *INCORRIGIBLE*.

indebted *adjective* beholden, grateful, obliged, thankful.

indecent *adjective* blue, coarse, crude, dirty, filthy, foul, improper, indelicate, lewd, obscene, offensive, pornographic, risqué, rude, suggestive, tasteless, unprintable, unseemly, vulgar.

indecisive *adjective* hesitant, in two minds, irresolute, tentative, uncertain, undecided, unsure.

indefinable *adjective* elusive, indescribable, obscure, vague.

indefinite *adjective* confused, equivocal, evasive, fuzzy, general, hazy, imprecise, indeterminate, inexact, noncommittal, obscure, openended, tentative, uncertain, unspecified, unsure, vague.

indelible *adjective* fast, fixed, lasting, permanent.

indentation *noun* cut, groove, nick, notch, recess, score.

independent *adjective* **1** selfreliant, self-sufficient, selfsupporting; see also *NEUTRAL*. **2** autonomous, free, selfdetermining, self-governing, self-ruling, sovereign. **3** nongovernment, private.

indescribable *adjective* ineffable, inexpressible, unspeakable, unutterable.

indestructible *adjective* durable, enduring, eternal, everlasting, lasting, permanent, strong, sturdy, tough, unbreakable, undying.

index *noun* catalogue, concordance, directory, gazetteer, inventory, list, register.

indicate *verb* **1** make known, point out, reveal, show, signal, specify, tell. **2** be a sign of, denote, imply, mean, show, signify, spell, suggest. □ **indication** *noun* clue, evidence, hint, mark, sign, signal, symptom, token, warning.

indicator *noun* dial, display, gauge, guide, index, meter.

indifferent *adjective* **1** apathetic, blasé, cold, cool, dispassionate, half-hearted, lukewarm, neutral, nonchalant, uncaring, unconcerned, uninterested. **2** fair, mediocre, middling, ordinary, passable, so-so, unexciting, uninspired.

indigenous *adjective* Aboriginal, native, original.

indignant *adjective* angry, cross, disgruntled, infuriated, irate, irritated, livid (*informal*), riled (*informal*), ropeable (*Australian informal*), up in arms (*informal*), vexed. □ **indignation** *noun* anger, displeasure, dudgeon, fury, ire, irritation, outrage, umbrage, wrath.

indirect *adjective* circuitous, devious, meandering, rambling, roundabout, tortuous.

indiscreet *adjective* impolitic, imprudent, injudicious, tactless, thoughtless, untactful, unwise.

indispensable *adjective* essential, key, necessary, required, requisite, vital.

indisposed *adjective* ailing, crook (*Australian informal*), ill, off colour, poorly, sick, unwell.

indisputable *adjective* certain, conclusive, incontestable, incontrovertible, indubitable, irrefutable, undeniable, unquestionable.

indistinct *adjective* blurred, confused, dim, faint, fuzzy, hazy, indefinite, nebulous, obscure, unclear, vague.

individual *adjective* **1** characteristic, distinct, distinctive, exclusive, idiosyncratic, own, particular, peculiar, personal, special, specific, unique. **2** separate, single.

individual *noun* character, fellow, human being, man, person, woman.

indoctrinate *verb* brainwash; see also *TEACH*.

indolent *adjective* idle, inactive, inert, lazy, lethargic, slothful, sluggish.

indubitable *adjective* certain, definite, indisputable, unde-

niable, undoubted, unquestionable.

induce *verb* **1** coax, influence, inspire, motivate, move, persuade, prompt, sway, tempt. **2** bring about, cause, give rise to, lead to, produce, provoke.

inducement *noun* attraction, carrot, enticement, goad, incentive, spur, stimulus.

indulge *verb* (*indulge a person*) cosset, mollycoddle, pamper, pander to, spoil; (*indulge a craving*) cater to, give in to, gratify, satisfy. ☐ **indulgent** *adjective* easygoing, forbearing, forgiving, kind, lenient, liberal, merciful, permissive, soft, tolerant.

industrious *adjective* assiduous, conscientious, diligent, energetic, hard-working, indefatigable, tireless, unflagging, zealous.

industry *noun* business, commerce, manufacturing, trade.

inedible *adjective* uneatable, unpalatable.

ineffective *adjective* **1** futile, unavailing, unproductive, unsuccessful, useless. **2** feckless, incapable, incompetent, ineffectual, inefficient, useless.

ineffectual *adjective* feckless, feeble, hopeless, impotent, incapable, incompetent, ineffective, weak.

inefficient *adjective* **1** ineffective, uneconomic, unproductive, wasteful. **2** disorganised, incapable, incompetent, ineffective, ineffectual.

inept *adjective* **1** absurd, inappropriate, unsuitable. **2** bungling, clumsy, incompetent, inefficient, inexpert, unskilful.

inequality *noun* bias, difference, discrimination, disparity, imbalance, prejudice.

inertia *noun* inactivity, indolence, languor, laziness, lethargy, listlessness, passivity, sluggishness, torpor.

inevitable *adjective* certain, fated, inescapable, sure, unavoidable.

inexact *adjective* approximate, imprecise, inaccurate, loose, rough.

inexcusable *adjective* indefensible, unforgivable, unjustifiable, unpardonable.

inexhaustible *adjective* boundless, endless, everlasting, infinite, never-ending, unending, unlimited.

inexpensive *adjective* budget-priced, cheap, economical, low-priced, reasonable.

inexperienced *adjective* callow, green, immature, naïve, raw, unsophisticated, unworldly.

inexplicable *adjective* baffling, enigmatic, incomprehensible, insoluble, mysterious, puzzling, unaccountable, unexplainable, unfathomable.

infallible *adjective* certain, dependable, foolproof, guaranteed, perfect, reliable, sure, unfailing.

infamous *adjective* disgraceful, dishonourable, disreputable, evil, nefarious, notorious, outrageous, scandalous, wicked.

infancy *noun* babyhood, childhood.

infant *noun* babe, baby, bairn (*Scottish*), child, piccaninny, toddler, tot.

infantile *adjective* babyish, childish, immature, juvenile, puerile.

infatuated *adjective* (*infatuated with*) besotted with, crazy about, enamoured of, in love with, keen on, mad about, rapt in. □ **infatuation** *noun* crush (*informal*), obsession, passion.

infect *verb* contaminate, poison, pollute, taint.

infection *noun* ailment, bug (*informal*), disease, illness, virus, wog (*Australia, informal*).

infectious *adjective* catching, communicable, contagious, transmittable.

infer *verb* conclude, deduce, gather, reason, surmise, work out.

inferior *adjective* (*inferior rank*) junior, lower, subordinate; (*inferior quality*) cheap, crook (*Australian informal*), faulty, imperfect, inadequate, indifferent, mediocre, poor, second-rate, shoddy, substandard, third-rate.

infertile *adjective* barren, poor, sterile, unproductive.

infest *verb* invade, overrun, swarm, take over.

infidelity *noun* adultery, disloyalty, unfaithfulness.

infinite *adjective* **1** boundless, endless, inexhaustible, interminable, limitless, never-ending, unbounded, unending, unlimited. **2** countless, immeasurable, immense, incalculable, innumerable, myriad.

infinitesimal *adjective* little, microscopic, miniature, minuscule, minute, small, teeny, tiny.

infirm *adjective* ailing, decrepit, feeble, frail, ill, poorly, senile, unwell, weak.

inflame *verb* anger, arouse, enrage, fire up, incense, incite, infuriate, provoke, rouse, stir up. □ **inflamed** *adjective*

festering, infected, red, sore, swollen.

inflammable *adjective* combustible, flammable.

inflate *verb* **1** blow up, fill, pump up. **2** increase, raise.

inflexible *adjective* **1** firm, hard, rigid, solid, stiff. **2** adamant, firm, immutable, intractable, intransigent, obstinate, pigheaded, rigid, stubborn, unbending, uncompromising, unyielding.

inflict *verb* administer, deal out, impose, wreak.

influence *noun* authority, clout (*informal*), control, leverage, muscle, power, pressure, sway, weight.

influence *verb* affect, bias, change, control, lead, manipulate, motivate, move, persuade, predispose, prejudice, sway.

influential *adjective* authoritative, important, persuasive, powerful, strong.

influx *noun* flood, inflow, inrush, rush, stream.

inform *verb* acquaint, advise, apprise (*formal*), brief, enlighten, fill in (*informal*), instruct, keep posted, notify, tell, warn. □ **inform on** betray, blow the whistle on (*informal*), denounce, dob in (*Australian informal*), grass (on) (*slang*), rat on (*informal*), report, shelf (*Australian* slang), shop (*slang*), sneak on (*informal*), split on (*slang*), tell on.

informal adjective casual, easygoing, free and easy, homely, natural, relaxed, unofficial; (*informal language*) colloquial, everyday, slangy, vernacular.

information noun advice, communication, data, evidence, facts, info (*informal*), intelligence, knowledge, low-down (*informal*), material, message, news, notice, notification, particulars, report, tidings.

informer noun dobber (*Australian informal*), dog (*slang*), grass (*slang*), informant, source, stool-pigeon, tell-tale, whistle-blower (*informal*).

infrequent adjective irregular, occasional, rare, sporadic, uncommon.

infringe verb breach, break, contravene, disobey, transgress, violate. □ **infringement** noun breach, contravention, transgression, violation.

infuriate verb anger, enrage, exasperate, gall, incense, irritate, madden, needle (*informal*), outrage, rile (*informal*), vex.

ingenious adjective artful, brilliant, clever, crafty, cunning, imaginative, inventive, neat, nifty (*informal*), resourceful, shrewd, skilful, smart.

ingenuous adjective artless, guileless, innocent, naïve, simple, unaffected, unsophisticated.

ingrained adjective confirmed, deep-rooted, deep-seated.

ingratiate verb □ **ingratiate yourself with** crawl to, curry favour with, fawn on, grovel to, kowtow to, play up to, suck up to (*informal*), toady to.

ingratitude noun thanklessness, unappreciativeness, ungratefulness.

ingredient noun component, constituent, element, part.

inhabit verb abide in (*old use*), dwell in, live in, occupy, people, populate, reside in, settle in. □ **inhabitant** noun citizen, denizen, dweller, inmate, native, occupant, resident, tenant.

inhale verb breathe in, draw in, suck in.

inherent adjective essential, inborn, inbred, innate, intrinsic, native, natural.

inheritance noun bequest, birthright, estate, heritage, legacy.

inheritor noun beneficiary, heir, heiress.

inhibit verb block, check, curb, hamper, hinder, hold back, impede, limit, obstruct, prevent, restrain, restrict, retard, stunt. □ **inhibition** noun hang-up (informal), mental block, reserve, self-consciousness, shyness.

inhospitable adjective **1** cool, unfriendly, unsociable, unwelcoming. **2** bleak, desolate, forbidding, uninviting.

inhuman adjective barbarous, brutal, cold-hearted, cruel, heartless, inhumane, merciless, ruthless, savage, unfeeling, vicious.

inimitable adjective incomparable, matchless, singular, unique.

iniquity noun crime, evil, injustice, offence, sin, transgression, trespass, wickedness, wrong, wrongdoing.

initial adjective beginning, early, first, introductory, opening, original, preliminary, starting.

initiate verb begin, commence, embark on, inaugurate, instigate, institute, kick off (informal), launch, open, originate, set in motion, start.

initiative noun drive, dynamism, enterprise, resourceful-

ness. □ **take the initiative** begin, commence, make the first move, start, take the lead.

inject verb bring in, infuse, instil, introduce. □ **injection** noun booster, immunisation, inoculation, jab (informal), shot, vaccination.

injure verb bruise, cripple, cut, damage, disable, fracture, harm, hurt, impair, lacerate, maim, mangle, mutilate, scar, sprain, strain, wound. □ **injurious** adjective adverse, damaging, deleterious, destructive, detrimental, harmful, hurtful. □ **injury** noun abrasion, bruise, contusion, cut, damage, fracture, harm, hurt, laceration, lesion, scrape, scratch, wound.

injustice noun **1** bias, discrimination, inequity, prejudice, unfairness, unjustness. **2** abuse, injury, offence, wrong.

inkling noun clue, hint, idea, knowledge, suspicion.

inland noun backblocks (Australian), back of beyond, bush, interior, never-never (Australian), outback (Australian), sticks (informal).

inlet noun bay, cove, creek (British), estuary, fiord, firth, harbour, sound.

inn noun hotel, pub (informal), public house, tavern.

□ **innkeeper** noun hotelier, hotel-keeper, landlady, landlord, proprietor, publican.

innate adjective congenital, hereditary, inborn, inbred, inherent, inherited, intrinsic, native, natural.

inner adjective central, inside, interior, internal.

innocent adjective 1 blameless, guiltless. 2 angelic, moral, pure, righteous, sinless, virtuous. 3 harmless, innocuous, inoffensive. 4 green, gullible, inexperienced, ingenuous, naïve, trusting, unworldly.

innocuous adjective harmless, inoffensive, safe.

innovative adjective creative, imaginative, new, novel, original.

innuendo noun hint, insinuation, intimation, overtone, suggestion.

innumerable adjective countless, infinite, myriad, numberless, numerous.

inoculate verb immunise, vaccinate.

inoffensive adjective bland, harmless, innocuous, safe, unobjectionable, unoffending.

inordinate adjective disproportionate, excessive, exorbitant, undue, unreasonable.

inquire verb ask, enquire, query, question; (inquire into) examine, explore, inspect, investigate, look into, probe, research, study. □ **inquiry** noun 1 hearing, inquest, inquisition, investigation, post-mortem, probe, review, study. 2 enquiry, query, question.

inquisitive adjective curious, nosy (informal), prying, snoopy (informal).

insane adjective berserk, crazy, demented, deranged, irrational, lunatic, mad, mental (informal), nutty (informal), unbalanced, unhinged.

insatiable adjective greedy, ravenous, unquenchable, voracious.

inscribe verb carve, engrave, etch, write.

inscription noun engraving, epitaph, words, writing.

inscrutable adjective arcane, baffling, cryptic, enigmatic, impenetrable, incomprehensible, mysterious, puzzling, unfathomable.

insect noun bug (informal), creepy-crawly (informal).

insecure adjective dangerous, precarious, rickety, rocky, shaky, unsafe, unsteady, wobbly.

insensible adjective **1** comatose, knocked out, senseless, unconscious. **2** oblivious, unaware, unconscious.

insensitive adjective callous, cold-hearted, hard-hearted, heartless, indifferent, tactless, thick-skinned, thoughtless, uncaring, unfeeling, unsympathetic.

inseparable adjective attached, close, thick as thieves (informal).

insert verb add, implant, interject, interpolate, interpose, introduce, put in, slip in, stick in, tuck in.

inside noun centre, core, heart, interior, middle. □ **insides** plural noun bowels, entrails, guts, innards (informal), intestines, stomach, viscera.

inside adjective inmost, inner, innermost, interior, internal.

insight noun acumen, discernment, intuition, judgement, perception, perspicacity, understanding.

insignificant adjective inconsequential, little, minor, minute, negligible, paltry, petty, slight, tiny, trifling, trivial, unimportant, useless, worthless.

insincere adjective deceitful, dishonest, false, hypocritical, phoney (informal), two-faced.

insinuation noun hint, implication, innuendo, intimation, suggestion.

insipid adjective **1** bland, tasteless, watery, weak, wishy-washy. **2** characterless, colourless, dull, uninteresting, vapid, wishy-washy.

insist verb assert, claim, command, contend, declare, demand, emphasise, maintain, put your foot down, require, stipulate, stress.

insolent adjective arrogant, brazen, cheeky, contemptuous, disrespectful, impertinent, impolite, impudent, insubordinate, presumptuous, rude. □ **insolence** noun arrogance, audacity, backchat (informal), cheek, effrontery, impertinence, impudence, insubordination, lip (slang), rudeness.

insoluble adjective baffling, inexplicable, mysterious, perplexing, puzzling, unanswerable, unfathomable, unsolvable.

inspect verb check, examine, investigate, look over, scrutinise, survey, suss out (informal), view. □ **inspection** noun check, check-up, examination, going-over (informal), investigation, once-over (informal), review, scrutiny.

inspire verb animate, drive, encourage, motivate, move,

prompt, provoke, spur, stimulate, stir.

install verb **1** establish, fit, fix, mount, place, put, set up. **2** inaugurate, induct, invest, ordain.

instalment noun chapter, episode, part, section.

instance noun case, example, illustration, sample.

instant adjective immediate, instantaneous, prompt, quick, ready, speedy, unhesitating.

instant noun flash, jiffy (informal), moment, split second, trice, twinkling of an eye.

instantaneous adjective immediate, instant, quick, swift.

instead adverb **instead of** in place of, in lieu of.

instigate verb bring about, initiate, prompt, set up, start.

instil verb implant, inculcate, infuse.

instinct noun aptitude, flair, gift, intuition, knack, sixth sense, skill, talent. □ **instinctive** adjective automatic, inborn, innate, intuitive, natural, reflex, spontaneous, subconscious, unlearned.

institute noun academy, college, establishment, institution, organisation, school, society.

institute verb begin, create, establish, found, inaugurate, initiate, originate, start.

institution noun **1** establishment, foundation, institute, organisation, society. **2** convention, custom, habit, practice, ritual, routine, tradition.

instruct verb **1** coach, drill, educate, ground, lecture, school, teach, train, tutor. **2** acquaint, advise, apprise (formal), brief, enlighten, inform, notify, tell. **3** bid, charge, command, direct, enjoin, order, tell. □ **instructor** noun coach, educator, lecturer, mentor, teacher, trainer, tutor.

instruction noun **1** education, guidance, lessons, schooling, teaching, training, tuition. **2** command, direction, guideline, order, prescription, recipe.

instructive adjective edifying, educational, enlightening, helpful, illuminating, informative.

instrument noun apparatus, appliance, device, gadget, implement, machine, tool, utensil; see also EQUIPMENT.

instrumentalist noun musician, performer, player.

insubordinate *adjective* contrary, defiant, disobedient, insurgent, mutinous, rebellious, recalcitrant.

insufferable *adjective* intolerable, obnoxious, unbearable, unendurable.

insufficient *adjective* deficient, inadequate, meagre, scant, scanty, scarce, wanting.

insulate *verb* clad, cover, encase, lag, protect, shield, wrap.

insult *verb* abuse, affront, be rude to, disparage, malign, offend, put down, slight, snub. □ **insulting** *adjective* abusive, derogatory, disparaging, offensive, rude, uncomplimentary.

insult *noun* abuse, affront, insolence, put-down (*informal*), rudeness, slight, snub.

insuperable *adjective* insurmountable, unconquerable.

insurance *noun* assurance, cover, indemnity, protection.

insurgent *noun* dissident, insurrectionist, mutineer, rebel, revolutionary. □ **insurgent** *adjective* dissident, insubordinate, mutinous, rebellious, revolutionary, seditious.

insurmountable *adjective* insuperable, overwhelming, unconquerable.

insurrection *noun* mutiny, rebellion, revolt, revolution, riot, rising, uprising.

intact *adjective* complete, entire, perfect, sound, unbroken, undamaged, whole.

intangible *adjective* abstract, elusive, impalpable, subtle.

integral *adjective* basic, constituent, essential, indispensable, necessary, vital.

integrate *verb* amalgamate, blend, combine, consolidate, incorporate, join, merge, mix, unite.

integrity *noun* honesty, honour, morality, probity, rectitude, scrupulousness, trustworthiness, truthfulness, uprightness, veracity, virtue.

intellect *noun* brains, intelligence, mental ability, mind, nous (*informal*), reason, sense, understanding, wits.

intellectual *adjective* **1** academic, mental. **2** academic, bookish, brainy, erudite, highbrow, intelligent, learned, scholarly, studious, thinking.

intellectual *noun* academic, brain (*informal*), highbrow, scholar, thinker.

intelligence *noun* **1** acumen, brains, cleverness, intellect, mental ability, nous (*informal*), reason, sense, understanding, wisdom, wits. **2** advice, information, knowledge, low-down (*informal*), news, notification, report, tidings, word.

intelligent *adjective* astute, brainy, bright, clever, discerning, intellectual, perceptive, perspicacious, quick, reasoning, sagacious, sensible, sharp, shrewd, smart, thinking, wise.

intelligible *adjective* clear, coherent, comprehensible, lucid, plain, understandable.

intend *verb* aim, mean, plan, propose.

intense *adjective* (*intense pain*) acute, concentrated, excruciating, extreme, great, piercing, raging, severe, sharp, strong, violent; (*intense feeling*) ardent, burning, deep, earnest, fervent, keen, passionate, powerful, profound, strong, vehement.

intensify *verb* aggravate, boost, compound, escalate, exacerbate, heighten, increase, magnify, mount, multiply, reinforce, strengthen.

intensive *adjective* comprehensive, concentrated, in-depth, thorough.

intent *noun* intention, object, objective, plan, purpose.

intent *adjective* absorbed, concentrated, engrossed, fixed, intense, keen, steadfast, steady, watchful.

intention *noun* aim, ambition, design, end, goal, intent, object, objective, plan, purpose.

intentional *adjective* conscious, deliberate, intended, planned, premeditated, purposeful, wilful. □ **intentionally** *adverb* consciously, deliberately, on purpose, wilfully, wittingly.

inter *verb* bury, entomb, lay to rest.

intercept *verb* ambush, block, cut off, head off, obstruct, stop, waylay.

interchange *verb* exchange, substitute, swap, transpose.

interchange *noun* crossroads, intersection, junction.

interest *noun* **1** concern, curiosity, enthusiasm, fascination, diversion **2** activity, diversion, hobby, pastime, preoccupation, pursuit. **3** advantage, benefit, gain, good.

interest *verb* absorb, appeal to, attract, concern, engage, engross, excite, fascinate, intrigue, preoccupy. □ **interested** *adjective* absorbed, attentive, concerned, curious, engrossed, enthusiastic, inquisitive, keen. □ **interesting**

adjective absorbing, engrossing, exciting, fascinating, gripping, intriguing, readable, riveting, stimulating.

interfere *verb* **1** butt in, intervene, intrude, meddle, poke your nose in, pry. **2** conflict, get in the way, hamper, hinder, impede, obstruct.

interim *noun* interval, meantime, meanwhile.

interim *adjective* provisional, stopgap, temporary.

interior *adjective* inner, inside, internal.

interior *noun* backblocks (*Australian*), centre, inland, outback (*Australian*).

interlude *noun* break, gap, intermission, interval, pause, recess, rest.

intermediary *noun* agent, go-between, intercessor, mediator, middleman.

intermediate *adjective* halfway, medial, middle, midway, neutral.

interminable *adjective* ceaseless, endless, everlasting, lengthy, long, never-ending, unending.

intermission *noun* break, interlude, interruption, interval, lull, pause, recess, respite, rest.

intermittent *adjective* fitful, occasional, on and off, periodic, spasmodic, sporadic.

intern *verb* confine, detain, imprison, jail, lock up.

internal *adjective* inner, inside, interior.

international *adjective* cosmopolitan, global, universal, worldwide.

interpret *verb* construe, decipher, decode, explain, read, take, translate, understand.

interrogate *verb* cross-examine, examine, grill, question, quiz. □ **interrogation** *noun* cross-examination, examination, inquisition, questioning, third degree.

interrupt *verb* barge in, break in, butt in, chip in, cut in, discontinue, disrupt, disturb, halt, hold up, interfere (with), interject, stop, suspend. □ **interruption** *noun* break, disruption, gap, halt, hiatus, pause, stop, stoppage, suspension.

intersect *verb* converge, cross, cut. □ **intersection** *noun* corner, crossing, crossroads, interchange, junction.

interval *noun* **1** break, gap, hiatus, interlude, intermission, interruption, lapse, lull, pause, recess, respite, rest, space, spell. **2** gap, opening, space.

intervene *verb* butt in, intercede, interfere, intrude, meddle, mediate, step in.

interview *noun* conversation, dialogue, discussion, meeting.

intestines *plural noun* bowels, entrails, guts, innards (*informal*), insides (*informal*), viscera.

intimate *adjective* **1** affectionate, bosom, close, familiar. **2** confidential, heart-to-heart, personal, private. **3** deep, detailed, firsthand, in-depth, thorough.

intimate *verb* hint, imply, indicate, insinuate, make known, suggest.

intimidate *verb* browbeat, bully, coerce, cow, frighten, hector, menace, scare, stand over (*Australian*), terrorise, threaten.

intolerable *adjective* agonising, excruciating, insufferable, insupportable, unbearable.

intolerant *adjective* bigoted, illiberal, narrow-minded, prejudiced.

intoxicated *adjective* drunk, drunken, fuddled, full (*slang*), happy (*informal*), high (*informal*), high as a kite (*informal*), inebriated, merry

(*informal*), off one's face (*Australian slang*), plastered (*slang*), shickered (*Australian slang*), smashed (*slang*), sozzled (*slang*), stoned (*slang*), tiddly (*informal*), tipsy, under the influence, under the weather.

intoxicating *adjective* alcoholic, heady, spirituous, strong.

intractable *adjective* headstrong, mulish, obstinate, perverse, rebellious, recalcitrant, refractory, stubborn, uncontrollable, unmanageable, unruly, wayward, wilful.

intrepid *adjective* bold, brave, courageous, daring, fearless, gallant, game, heroic, plucky, valiant.

intricate *adjective* complex, complicated, detailed, elaborate, fancy, involved, ornate.

intrigue *verb* appeal to, fascinate, interest.

intrigue *noun* conspiracy, machination, plot, scheme.

intrinsic *adjective* basic, essential, inherent, natural.

introduce *verb* **1** acquaint (with), make known, present. **2** announce, present. **3** begin, bring in, establish, inaugurate, initiate, institute, launch, phase in, pioneer, set up, start

introduction noun beginning, foreword, opening, preamble, preface, prelude, prologue. □ **introductory** adjective opening, prefatory, preliminary, preparatory.

introverted adjective introspective, inward-looking, reserved, shy, unsociable, withdrawn.

intrude verb barge in, break in, butt in, encroach, gatecrash, interfere, intervene, muscle in (slang), trespass.

intruder noun burglar, gatecrasher, housebreaker, interloper, invader, robber, thief, trespasser.

intuition noun feeling, hunch, instinct, sixth sense. □ **intuitive** adjective automatic, inborn, innate, instinctive, spontaneous, subconscious, unlearned.

inundate verb deluge, drown, engulf, flood, overflow, overwhelm, submerge, swamp.

invade verb **1** attack, enter, infiltrate, occupy, overrun, penetrate, raid. **2** encroach on, impinge on, infringe upon, intrude on, trespass on, violate.

invalid noun patient, sufferer.

invalid adjective expired, illegal, out of date, unusable, useless, void, worthless.

invalidate verb annul, cancel, nullify, rescind, revoke, void.

invaluable adjective inestimable, precious, useful, valuable.

invariable adjective consistent, constant, immutable, predictable, regular, set, unchanging, unchanging, unfailing, uniform.

invasion noun attack, foray, incursion, infiltration, inroad, onslaught, raid.

invent verb **1** coin, conceive, contrive, create, design, devise, make, manufacture, mint, originate. **2** concoct, cook up (informal), dream up, fabricate, make up, think up. □ **invention** noun coinage, contraption, contrivance, creation, device, innovation. □ **inventive** adjective clever, creative, enterprising, imaginative, ingenious, innovative, resourceful. □ **inventor** noun architect, creator, designer, discoverer, innovator, maker, originator.

invest verb devote, expend, lay out, put in, spend.

investigate verb check on, examine, explore, go into, inquire into, look into, probe, research, study, suss out (informal). □ **investigation** noun examination, exploration, inquest, inquiry, inspection, research, review, scrutiny, study, survey.

inveterate *adjective* chronic, confirmed, established, habitual, incorrigible.

invigorate *verb* enliven, pep up (*informal*), perk up, refresh, rejuvenate, stimulate, strengthen.

invincible *adjective* strong, unbeatable, unconquerable, undefeatable, unstoppable.

invisible *adjective* concealed, hidden, imperceptible, inconspicuous, undetectable, unnoticeable, unseen.

invite *verb* **1** ask, bid, call on, request, summon, urge. **2** ask for, attract, court, provoke, tempt.

inviting *adjective* appealing, attractive, enticing, tempting.

invoice *noun* account, bill, statement.

involuntary *adjective* automatic, impulsive, instinctive, mechanical, reflex, spontaneous, unconscious, unintentional.

involve *verb* **1** entail, mean, necessitate, require. **2** embroil, entangle, implicate, include, incriminate, mix up.

involved *adjective* **1** complex, complicated, convoluted, elaborate, intricate. **2** caught up, concerned, embroiled, implicated, interested, mixed up.

inward *adjective* inner, mental, personal, spiritual.

irate *adjective* angry, annoyed, cross, enraged, furious, indignant, infuriated, livid (*informal*), mad, ropeable (*Australian informal*).

irk *verb* annoy, exasperate, gall, irritate, pique, rile (*informal*), vex.

iron *noun* **irons** bonds, chains, fetters, manacles, shackles.

iron *verb* press, smooth.

ironic *adjective* derisory, mocking, sarcastic, satirical, wry.

irrational *adjective* crazy, illogical, insane, mad, nonsensical, senseless, unreasonable.

irrefutable *adjective* incontrovertible, indisputable, undeniable, watertight.

irregular *adjective* **1** asymmetric, bumpy, lopsided, lumpy, pitted, rough, rugged, uneven. **2** erratic, haphazard, infrequent, intermittent, occasional, random, spasmodic, sporadic. **3** aberrant, anomalous, deviant, eccentric, extraordinary, odd, peculiar, strange, unconventional, unusual.

rrelevant *adjective* beside the point, extraneous, immaterial, inapplicable, neither here nor there, unconnected.

rrepressible *adjective* boisterous, buoyant, ebullient, exuberant, lively, spirited, unrestrained.

rreproachable *adjective* beyond reproach, blameless, faultless, impeccable, unimpeachable.

cresistible *adjective* compelling, overpowering, overwhelming, powerful; see also *TEMPTING* (at *TEMPT*).

cresolute *adjective* hesitant, indecisive, spineless, tentative, uncertain, undecided, unsure, vacillating, wavering.

crespective *adjective* □ **irrespective of** disregarding, ignoring, regardless of.

cresponsible *adjective* careless, negligent, reckless, thoughtless, unthinking, untrustworthy.

creverent *adjective* blasphemous, disrespectful, impious, irreligious, profane, sacrilegious, ungodly.

crevocable *adjective* binding, final, immutable, irreversible, settled, unalterable.

critable *adjective* bad-tempered, cantankerous, crabby, cranky, cross,

crotchety, fractious, grouchy (*informal*), grumpy, irascible, peevish, petulant, prickly, ratty (*informal*), shirty (*informal*), short-tempered, snaky (*Australian informal*), snappy, stroppy (*informal*), surly, testy, tetchy.

irritate *verb* anger, annoy, bother, bug (*informal*), drive someone mad (*informal*), drive someone up the wall (*informal*), exasperate, get on someone's nerves, give someone the pip (*informal*), harass, infuriate, irk, nark (*informal*), needle (*informal*), pester, plague, provoke, rankle, rile (*informal*), rub someone up the wrong way (*informal*), trouble, upset, vex. □ **irritating** *adjective* annoying, bothersome, exasperating, irksome, tiresome, trying, upsetting. □ **irritation** *noun* anger, annoyance, chagrin, displeasure, exasperation, impatience, vexation.

island *noun* isle, islet; (*group of islands*) archipelago.

isolate *verb* cut off, detach, insulate, quarantine, seclude, segregate, separate, set apart, shut off.

issue *verb* **1** come out, discharge, emanate, emerge, erupt, escape, flow out, gush, pour, stream. **2** distribute, give

out, provide, supply. **3**
circulate, distribute, publish,
put out, release, send out.

issue noun **1** affair, matter,
point, question, subject, topic.
2 conclusion, consequence,
outcome, result. **3** edition,
number, publication.

itch verb **1** prickle, tickle, tingle.
2 be desperate, be eager,
hanker, long, thirst, yearn.

itch noun **1** irritation, prickling,
tickle, tingling. **2** desire,
longing, urge, yearning, yen.

item noun **1** article, detail,
entry, object, piece, point,
product, thing. **2** article,
feature, piece, report, story.

itemise verb detail, enumerate,
list, specify, spell out.

itinerant adjective nomadic,
peripatetic, roving, travelling,
wandering.

Jj

jab verb poke, prod, stab, thrust.

jab noun **1** dig, nudge, poke,
prod, stab, thrust. **2** immunisation, injection, shot,
vaccination.

jabber verb babble, blather,
chatter, gabble, gibber, prattle,

yabber (*Australian informal*)
see also TALK.

jack verb hoist, lift, raise.

jacket noun **1** anorak, blazer,
bolero, cagoule, coat, parka,
tuxedo, windcheater. **2** cover,
dust cover, dust jacket,
wrapper.

jaded adjective done in
(*informal*), fatigued, spent,
tired, weary, worn out.

jagged adjective broken,
chipped, indented, notched,
ragged, rough, serrated,
uneven.

jail noun detention centre, lock-
up, nick (*slang*), penitentiary
(*American*), prison, remand
centre, watch-house. □ **jail**
verb imprison, incarcerate,
intern, lock up, put away, put
behind bars, send down.
□ **jailer** noun keeper, prison
officer, warder.

jam noun **1** conserve, jelly,
marmalade, preserve. **2**
bottleneck, build-up, con-
gestion, hold-up, snarl. **3** bind
(*informal*), difficulty, fix
(*informal*), hole (*informal*),
mess, pickle (*informal*), plight,
predicament, quandary, spot
(*informal*).

jam verb **1** cram, crowd, fill,
jam-pack, pack, push, ram,
squash, squeeze, stick, stuff,

wedge. **2** block, choke, clog, obstruct.

jamboree noun carnival, celebration, convention, festival, gathering, rally.

jangle verb clang, clank, clink, jingle, rattle. ☐ **jangle** noun clang, clangour, clank, clink, jingle, rattle.

janitor noun caretaker, concierge, doorkeeper, doorman.

jar noun bottle, container, crock, jug, pot, receptacle, vase, vessel.

jar verb **1** jerk, jolt, shake. **2** grate, irritate, jangle. ☐ **jarring** adjective discordant, grating, harsh, irritating, raucous.

jargon noun cant, gobbledegook (*informal*), idiom, lingo (*informal*), slang.

jaunt noun drive, excursion, expedition, outing, trip.

jaunty adjective breezy, bright, cheerful, energetic, lively, perky, sprightly.

jaw noun jowl, mandible, maxilla.

jazzy adjective flash (*informal*), flashy, gaudy, showy, smart, snazzy (*informal*).

jealous adjective **1** covetous, envious, grudging, resentful. **2** protective, vigilant, watchful.

jeer verb boo, chiack (*Australian informal*), deride, gibe, heckle, hiss, laugh at, make fun of, mock, poke borak at (*Australian informal*), ridicule, scoff at, sneer at, taunt. ☐ **jeer** noun boo, catcall, gibe, hiss, scoff, sneer, taunt.

jeopardise verb endanger, imperil, put on the line, risk, threaten.

jeopardy noun danger, peril, risk, threat.

jerk verb bump, jig, jiggle, jolt, lurch, pull, shake, tug, tweak, twist, twitch, wrench, yank.

jerk noun bump, jig, jiggle, jolt, lurch, pull, shake, tug, tweak, twist, twitch, wrench, yank. ☐ **jerky** adjective bumpy, disconnected, rough, spasmodic, twitchy, uncoordinated, uneven.

jersey noun jumper, pullover, sweater, top.

jest noun gag, joke, quip, wisecrack (*informal*), witticism.

jest verb joke, kid (*informal*), pull someone's leg (*informal*), tease.

jester noun buffoon, clown, comedian, comic, entertainer, fool, joker, wag, zany.

jet noun **1** fountain, gush, spray, spurt, stream. **2** nozzle, spout, sprinkler. **3** jumbo, jumbo jet, plane; see also *AIRCRAFT*.

jettison verb discard, dump, eject, get rid of, throw away, throw overboard, toss out.

jetty noun landing stage, pier, quay, wharf.

jewel noun gem, gemstone, precious stone.

jewellery noun adornments, jewels, ornaments, trinkets; (*kinds of jewellery*) anklet, bangle, beads, bracelet, brooch, chain, charm, cuff link, earring, locket, necklace, pendant, ring, stud, tiepin.

jib verb (*jib at*) baulk at, recoil from, refuse, shrink from.

jiffy noun flash, instant, minute, moment, second (*informal*), tick (*informal*), trice.

jig verb bob, bounce, dance, hop, jump.

jiggle verb jerk, rock, shake, wiggle.

jilt verb abandon, drop (*informal*), dump (*informal*), forsake, reject.

jingle verb clink, jangle, rattle, ring, tinkle.

jingle noun **1** clink, jangle, rattle, ring, tinkle. **2** chorus, poem, rhyme, song, tune, verse.

jinx noun curse, hex, spell. □ **jinxed** adjective see *UNLUCKY*.

jitters plural noun butterflies (*informal*), collywobbles (*informal*), heebie-jeebies (*informal*), jim-jams (*informal*), nerves, shakes, willies (*informal*). □ **jittery** adjective anxious, apprehensive, frightened, jumpy, nervous, nervy, quaking, quivering, shaky, uneasy.

job noun **1** appointment, career, employment, occupation, position, post, profession, situation, trade, vocation, work. **2** activity, assignment, chore, duty, errand, function, piece of work, project, responsibility, role, task.

jobless adjective out of work, unemployed.

jockey noun hoop (*Australian informal*), horseman, horse-rider, horsewoman, rider.

jocular adjective amusing, funny, humorous, jesting, joking, playful, witty.

jog verb **1** run, trot. **2** jerk, jolt, knock, nudge, prod, push, shake. □ **jog someone's memory** prompt, remind; see also *STIMULATE*.

join verb **1** add, attach, bind, bracket, cement, combine, come together, connect, converge, couple, dovetail, fasten, fit, fuse, glue, knit, link, meet, merge, put together, solder, splice, stick, tack, tie, unite, weld, yoke. **2** partake, participate, share, take part. **3** enlist in, enrol in, enter, register for, sign up for, volunteer for.

oin noun connection, joint, knot, link, seam.

oint adjective collective, combined, common, concerted, cooperative, shared, united. □ **jointly** adverb as a team, cooperatively, in partnership, together.

oke noun gag, jest, pun, quip, wisecrack (informal), witticism; see also *PRACTICAL JOKE* (at *PRACTICAL*).

oke verb crack jokes, jest, kid (informal), pun, quip, tease.

oker noun buffoon, clown, comedian, comic, jester, prankster, wag, wit, zany.

olly adjective bright, cheerful, cheery, exuberant, goodhumoured, happy, highspirited, jocular, jovial, joyful, merry.

olt verb **1** bump, dislodge, jerk, shake. **2** bounce, bump, jerk, judder, kangaroo, kangaroohop, lurch.

olt noun **1** bounce, bump, jerk, lurch. **2** shock, start, surprise.

ostle verb bump, elbow, knock, push, shove.

jot verb □ **jot down** note, record, scribble, take down, write down.

jotter noun notebook, notepad, pad, writing pad.

journal noun **1** gazette, magazine, newspaper, paper, periodical. **2** chronicle, diary, logbook, record.

journalist noun columnist, commentator, correspondent, editor, journo (Australian informal), reporter, roundsman (Australian), writer.

journey noun cruise, drive, excursion, expedition, flight, jaunt, mission, outing, pilgrimage, ride, safari, tour, trek, trip, voyage, walk.

journey verb commute, cruise, fly, go, roam, rove, tour, travel, trek, voyage, wander.

jovial adjective breezy, bright, cheerful, convivial, goodhumoured, happy, jolly, joyful, lively, merry.

joy noun bliss, contentment, delight, ecstasy, elation, euphoria, exultation, gladness, happiness, jubilation, pleasure, rapture. □ **joyful** adjective blithe, cheerful, content, delighted, ecstatic, elated, euphoric, exultant, glad, happy, jolly, jovial, joyous, jubilant, merry, overjoyed.

jubilant *adjective* delighted, elated, exultant, gleeful, happy, joyful, overjoyed, rejoicing, triumphant. □ **jubilation** *noun* delight, elation, exultation, glee, happiness, joy, rejoicing, triumph.

jubilee *noun* anniversary, celebration, commemoration, festival.

judge *noun* **1** justice, magistrate. **2** adjudicator, arbiter, arbitrator, referee, umpire. **3** authority, connoisseur, expert.

judge *verb* **1** adjudicate, arbitrate, referee, umpire; (*judge a case*) decide, hear, try. **2** appraise, assess, estimate, evaluate, gauge, guess, rate, size up (*informal*).

judgement *noun* **1** adjudication, decision, decree, finding, ruling, sentence, verdict. **2** assessment, belief, mind, opinion, view. **3** acumen, discernment, discretion, discrimination, good sense, insight, sagacity, shrewdness, wisdom.

judicial *adjective* legal.

judicious *adjective* discerning, politic, prudent, sensible, shrewd, sound, wise.

jug *noun* carafe, decanter, ewer, pitcher, vessel.

juggle *verb* cook (*informal*), doctor, falsify, fiddle (*slang*), fix, manipulate, rearrange, rig, tamper with.

juice *noun* **1** drink, extract, liquid, nectar, sap. **2** fluid, secretion. □ **juicy** *adjective* moist, ripe, succulent.

jumble *verb* confuse, disorganise, mix, mix up, muddle.

jumble *noun* confusion, hotchpotch, mess, mixture, muddle. □ **jumble sale** bazaar, boot sale, bring-and-buy-sale, garage sale, rummage sale.

jump *verb* **1** bounce, bound, hop, leap, pounce, spring. **2** clear, go over, hurdle, pass over, vault. **3** leave out, miss, omit, overlook, pass over, skip. **4** buck, flinch, rear, recoil, shy, start. **5** escalate, increase, rise, shoot up. □ **jump at** grab, leap at, seize, snatch.

jump *noun* **1** bounce, bound, hop, leap, pounce, spring, vault. **2** fence, gate, hurdle, obstacle. **3** boost, escalation, increase, rise, upturn.

jumper *noun* guernsey, jersey, pullover, skivvy, sweater, top.

jumpy *adjective* anxious, edgy, jittery (*informal*), nervous, nervy, tense, twitchy (*informal*), uneasy, uptight (*informal*).

junction noun corner, cross-roads, interchange, intersection, meeting point, T-junction, Y-junction.

juncture noun point, point in time, stage, time.

jungle noun forest, rainforest.

junior adjective **1** younger. **2** inferior, lower, subordinate.

junk noun cast-offs, clutter, garbage, odds and ends, rubbish, scrap, trash.

jurisdiction noun authority, control, dominion, power, rule.

just adjective **1** equitable, even-handed, fair, impartial, neutral, reasonable, unbiased, unprejudiced. **2** appropriate, deserved, due, fair, fitting, merited, right, rightful.

just adverb **1** exactly, precisely, right. **2** merely, no more than, only, simply.

justice noun **1** equity, even-handedness, fairness, fair play, impartiality, right. **2** judge, magistrate.

justify verb defend, excuse, explain, rationalise, vindicate, warrant. □ **justifiable** adjective fair, legitimate, reasonable, valid. □ **justification** noun defence, excuse, explanation, grounds, reason.

jut verb poke out, project, protrude, stick out.

juvenile adjective **1** adolescent, junior, teenage, young, youthful. **2** childish, immature, infantile, puerile.

Kk

kangaroo noun boomer (male), doe (female), joey (young), old man (male), roo (informal).

keel noun base, bottom, underside. □ **on an even keel** balanced, calm, level, stable, steady.

keel verb □ **keel over** capsize, collapse, fall over, heel over, overturn, tilt, turn over, upset.

keen adjective **1** ardent, avid, eager, enthusiastic, fervent, intense, zealous; (keen on) fond of, interested in, mad about, nuts about (informal). **2** sharp. **3** biting, bitter, cold, penetrating, piercing, severe.

keep verb **1** conserve, hang on to, hold on to, maintain, preserve, put aside, put away, reserve, retain, save, store, withhold. **2** hold, remain, stay. **3** carry on, continue, go on, persevere in, persist in. **4** abide by, comply with, conform to, fulfil, honour, obey, respect, stick to. **5** celebrate, commemorate, honour, observe. **6** delay, detain, hinder, hold up, impede, obstruct, prevent. **7** defend, guard, protect, shield. **8** care for, look after, own, tend. **9** be usable, last, stay fresh. □ **keep up** carry on with, continue, maintain, sustain.

keep noun **1** board, food, maintenance, subsistence. **2** donjon, stronghold, tower. □ **for keeps** forever, for good, permanently.

keeper noun caretaker, curator, custodian, guard, guardian, jailer, ranger, warden, warder, watchman.

keeping noun care, charge, custody, guardianship, hands. □ **in keeping with** conforming with, fitting, in harmony with, in line with, in step with, in tune with, suiting.

keepsake noun memento, reminder, souvenir.

keg noun barrel, cask, hogshead.

kerb noun edge, roadside, verge.

kernel noun nut, seed.

key noun **1** latchkey, master key, passkey, skeleton key. **2** answer, clue, explanation, guide, interpretation, secret, solution.

kick verb **1** boot, punt. **2** recoil, spring back. □ **kick out**

kick noun **1** boot, punt. **2** buzz (informal), enjoyment, excitement, fun, pleasure, satisfaction, thrill.

kid noun child, youngster.

kid verb bluff, deceive, fool, have on (informal), hoax, hoodwink, jest, joke, pull someone's leg (informal), tease, trick.

kidnap verb abduct, carry off, seize, snatch.

kill verb **1** annihilate, assassinate, bump off (slang), butcher, cull, destroy, dispatch, do in (slang), eliminate, execute, exterminate, finish off, knock off (informal), liquidate, martyr, massacre, mow down, murder, put down, put to death, put to sleep, slaughter, slay, take someone's life, wipe out, zap (slang) (various ways to kill asphyxiate, behead, choke, crucify, decapitate, drown, electrocute, gas, guillotine, gun down, hang, knife, poison, shoot, stab, starve, stifle, stone, strangle, suffocate, throttle. **2** destroy, do away with, end, put an end to, ruin, stop. □ **killer** noun assassin, executioner, hit man (slang), murderer, slayer. □ **killing** noun annihilation, assassination, bloodshed, butchery, carnage, destruction, euthanasia, execution, extermination, genocide, homicide, manslaughter, massacre, murder, pogrom, slaughter, slaying, suicide.

kin *noun* family, kindred, kinsfolk, kith and kin, relations, relatives.

kind *noun* brand, breed, category, class, classification, form, genre, genus, ilk (*informal*), make, nature, order, set, sort, species, strain, style, type, variety.

kind *adjective* affectionate, altruistic, amiable, attentive, avuncular, benevolent, benign, big-hearted, caring, charitable, compassionate, considerate, fatherly, friendly, generous, genial, gentle, good, good-natured, gracious, helpful, hospitable, humane, kind-hearted, kindly, lenient, loving, merciful, motherly, neighbourly, nice, obliging, philanthropic, soft-hearted, sympathetic, tender-hearted, thoughtful, understanding, unselfish, warm-hearted, well-meaning.

kindergarten *noun* nursery school, preschool.

kindle *verb* **1** fire, ignite, light, set alight, set fire to. **2** arouse, awaken, excite, inspire, spark off, stimulate, stir.

kindred *adjective* allied, associated, related, similar.

king *noun* monarch, ruler, sovereign; see also *RULER*.
□ **kingly** *adjective* regal, royal.

kingdom *noun* country, domain, dominion, empire, land, monarchy, nation, realm, state, territory.

kink *noun* **1** bend, coil, crinkle, curve, loop, tangle, twist. **2** eccentricity, foible, idiosyncrasy, peculiarity, quirk.
□ **kinky** *adjective* abnormal, depraved, deviant, perverted, unnatural, warped.

kiosk *noun* **1** booth, stall, stand. **2** café, snack bar, tea room.

kiss *noun* caress, peck, smack, smooch (*informal*).

kit *noun* clothing, equipment, gear, outfit, paraphernalia, rig, tackle, things.

kitchen *noun* galley, kitchenette, scullery.

kitty *noun* fund, pool, reserve.

knack *noun* ability, aptitude, art, expertise, flair, gift, skill, talent, trick.

knapsack *noun* backpack, haversack, pack, rucksack; see also *BAG*.

knave *noun* baddy (*informal*), blackguard, miscreant, rascal, rogue, scoundrel, villain.

kneel verb bend, bow, crouch, genuflect, stoop.

knickers plural noun briefs, drawers, panties (informal), pants (informal), underpants, underwear, undies (informal).

knick-knack noun bagatelle, curio, ornament, trifle, trinket.

knife noun blade, cutter; (kinds of knife) bowie knife, carving knife, chopper, clasp-knife, cleaver, flick knife, jackknife, lancet, machete, paperknife, penknife, pocket knife, scalpel, sheath knife, switchblade.

knife verb cut, slash, slit, stab.

knit verb grow together, heal, join, mend.

knob noun **1** handle. **2** bulge, bump, knot, lump, node, nodule, nub, projection, swelling. □ **knobbly** adjective gnarled, knotty, lumpy, rough, uneven.

knock verb **1** bang, bash, batter, beat, belt, clip (informal), clout (informal), dong (Australian informal), hammer, hit, kick, pound, pummel, punch, rap, smite, sock (slang), strike, tap, thrash, thud, thump, wallop (slang), whack. **2** bag (Australian informal), belittle, bucket (Australian informal), criticise, disparage, find fault with, insult, pan (informal), pick holes in, rubbish

(Australian informal), run down, slam (informal), tear to pieces. □ **knock back** see REFUSE. □ **knock down 1** demolish, destroy, pull down, raze. **2** bring down, decrease, lower, reduce. □ **knock off 1** cease, finish, quit, stop. **2** deduct, subtract, take off. **3** nick (slang), pinch (informal), steal, thieve.

knock noun bang, blow, bump, clip (informal), clout (informal), dong (Australian informal), hit, kick, punch, rap, slap, smack, tap, thud, thump, thwack, wallop (slang), whack, wham (informal).

knot noun **1** bow, hitch, loop, twist. **2** snarl, tangle. **3** knob, lump, node, nodule.

knot verb **1** bind, fasten, hitch, join, lash, loop, tie. **2** entangle, snarl up, tangle.

knotty adjective **1** gnarled, knobbly, uneven. **2** baffling, complex, complicated, difficult, intricate, perplexing, puzzling, thorny, tricky.

know verb **1** be aware of, be in on (informal), comprehend, have learnt, have memorised, perceive, realise, remember, understand. **2** be acquainted with, be a friend of, be familiar with, recognise. **3** discern, discriminate, distinguish, identify, recognise.

know-all noun expert, genius, smart alec (informal), wise guy (informal).

know-how noun ability, competence, expertise, knack, knowledge, skill.

knowing adjective artful, astute, aware, crafty, cunning, meaningful, perceptive, shrewd, sly, wily.

knowledge noun 1 awareness, consciousness, experience, expertise, familiarity, grasp, know-how, perception, realisation, understanding. 2 education, learning, scholarship, science; see also INFORMATION.

knowledgeable adjective educated, enlightened, erudite, intelligent, learned, well-informed.

kudos noun acclaim, fame, glory, honour, prestige, renown, respect.

Ll

label noun sticker, tag, ticket.

label verb brand, identify, mark, name, stamp, tag.

laborious adjective 1 arduous, difficult, exhausting, hard, onerous, strenuous, taxing, tiring. 2 forced, laboured, ponderous, strained, studied.

labour noun 1 effort, exertion, industry, slog, toil, work, yakka (Australian informal). 2 childbirth, contractions, travail (old use).

labour verb 1 exert oneself, grind away, slave, sweat, toil, work. 2 dwell on, elaborate, emphasise, harp on, impress, stress.

labourer noun blue-collar worker, hand, manual worker, navvy, unskilled worker, worker, workman.

labyrinth noun maze, network, warren.

lace verb 1 do up, fasten, tie. 2 entwine, intertwine, weave. 3 fortify, spike (informal).

lacerate verb cut, gash, injure, mangle, rip, slash, tear, wound.

lack noun absence, dearth, deficiency, insufficiency, need, paucity, scarcity, shortage, want.

lack verb be deficient in, be short of, be without, miss, need, want.

lackadaisical adjective apathetic, blasé, careless, casual, half-hearted, indifferent, listless, lukewarm, unconcerned, unenthusiastic.

laconic *adjective* brief, concise, economical, succinct, terse.

lacquer *noun* gloss, varnish.

lacy *adjective* delicate, fine, flimsy, net.

lad *noun* boy, child, kid (*informal*), young man, youngster, youth.

ladder *noun* stepladder, steps.

laden *adjective* burdened, encumbered, loaded, weighed down.

ladle *verb* dish out, serve.

lady *noun* see WOMAN.
□ **ladylike** *adjective* dignified, genteel, polite, posh (*informal*), proper, refined, respectable.

lag *verb* dawdle, drag the chain (*Australian*), drop back, drop behind, fall behind, go slow, straggle, trail.

lag *verb* encase, insulate, wrap.

lagoon *noun* billabong, lake, pond, pool.

lair *noun* burrow, den, hideout (*informal*), hidey-hole (*informal*), hiding place, hole, home, shelter.

lair *noun* see LARRIKIN, SHOW-OFF (at SHOW). □ **lairy** *adjective* bright, flash (*informal*), flashy, garish, gaudy, loud, showy.

lake *noun* lagoon, loch (*Scottish*), mere (*poetical*), pond, reservoir, sea, tarn.

lame *adjective* **1** crippled, disabled, maimed, paralysed, paraplegic. **2** feeble, flimsy, unconvincing, unsatisfactory, weak.

lament *noun* dirge, elegy, keen, lamentation, requiem.

lament *verb* bewail, grieve over, mourn, regret, wail over, weep over.

lamentable *adjective* deplorable, regrettable, sad, sorry, terrible, unfortunate.

lamp *noun* see LIGHT.

lance *noun* harpoon, javelin, pike, shaft, spear.

lance *verb* cut open, incise, jab, pierce, prick.

land *noun* **1** ground. **2** earth, ground, soil. **3** area, country, region, terrain, tract. **4** country, empire, nation, state, territory.

land *verb* **1** alight, arrive, berth, disembark, dock, go ashore, put into port, touch down. **2** clinch, get, obtain, secure, win. **3** end up, fetch up (*informal*), find yourself, finish up, wind up. **4** give, present.

landing *noun* **1** arrival, touch down. **2** jetty, landing stage, pier, quay, wharf.

landlady, **landlord** *noun* owner, proprietor.

landmark *noun* **1** feature. **2** milestone, turning point, watershed.

landowner *noun* grazier (*Australian*), laird (*Scottish*), landholder, pastoralist (*Australian*), squire.

landscape *noun* panorama, scene, scenery, view, vista.

landslide *noun* avalanche, landslip.

lane *noun* alley, path, road, track.

language *noun* dialect, idiom, jargon, lingo (*informal*), slang, speech, terminology, tongue, vocabulary, words.

languid *adjective* apathetic, drained, inert, lazy, lethargic, listless, sluggish, torpid, weak, weary.

languish *verb* **1** droop, faint, wilt, wither. **2** decline, deteriorate, fail, go downhill, stagnate.

lank *adjective* lifeless, limp, long, straight, thin.

lanky *adjective* gangling, gawky, lank, lean, skinny, thin.

lantern *noun* lamp, light.

lap *noun* **1** circuit, orbit, tour. **2** part, section, stage.

lap *verb* **1** drink, lick, sip. **2** splash, wash.

lapse *noun* **1** error, fault, mistake, omission, oversight, slip, slip-up. **2** backsliding, decline, deterioration, drop, regression, slip. **3** break, gap, hiatus, interlude, interruption, interval, passage.

lapse *verb* **1** degenerate, fall, regress, relapse, slip. **2** expire, run out, stop, terminate.

larceny *noun* robbery, stealing, theft.

larder *noun* food cupboard, pantry.

large *adjective* ample, big, broad, bulky, capacious, colossal, commodious, considerable, copious, enormous, extensive, fat, gargantuan, generous, giant, gigantic, ginormous (*slang*), grand, great, handsome, hefty, huge, hulking (*informal*), humungous (*slang*), immeasurable, immense, infinite, jumbo-sized, king-sized, mammoth, massive, monstrous, outsize, oversized, overweight, prodigious, roomy, sizeable, spacious, stupendous, substantial, tremendous, unlimited, vast, whopping (*slang*), wide. □ **at large** free, loose, unconfined, unrestrained.

largely *adverb* chiefly, in the main, mainly, mostly, primarily, principally.

largesse noun benevolence, bounty, generosity, liberality, munificence, philanthropy.

lark noun game, joke, prank, tease, trick.

larrikin noun hooligan, hoon (Australian informal), lair (Australian informal), rowdy, ruffian, tearaway.

larva noun caterpillar, grub, maggot.

lash noun blow, cut, stroke.

lash verb **1** beat, belt, cane, flog, hit, lay into (informal), strike, thrash, whip. **2** fasten, secure, tie.

lass noun damsel (old use), girl, lassie (informal), maid (old use), maiden (old use), young woman.

lassitude noun languor, lethargy, listlessness, tiredness, weariness.

lasso noun lariat, rope.

last adjective **1** closing, concluding, final, ultimate. **2** latest, most recent.

last noun □ **at last** eventually, finally, in the end, ultimately.

last verb **1** carry on, continue, endure, go on, keep on, persist. **2** suffice.

lasting adjective abiding, enduring, everlasting, long-lasting, long-lived, long-term, permanent.

lastly adverb finally, in conclusion.

latch noun bar, bolt, catch, lock, snib.

latch verb bar, bolt, fasten, lock, secure, snib.

late adjective **1** belated, delayed, held up, overdue, tardy. **2** (latest) current, freshest, most recent, newest, up to date, up to the minute. **3** dead, deceased, departed.

lately adverb latterly, nowadays, of late, recently.

latent adjective concealed, dormant, hidden, invisible, potential, undeveloped.

lather noun bubbles, foam, froth, suds.

latitude noun freedom, independence, leeway, liberty, scope.

lattice noun framework, trellis.

laudable adjective admirable, commendable, creditable, meritorious, praiseworthy.

laugh verb **1** be in stitches (informal), cackle, chortle, chuckle, crack up (informal), giggle, guffaw, snicker, snigger, split your sides, titter. **2** (laugh at) deride, jeer at, joke about, make fun of, mock, poke borak at (Australian informal), poke fun at, ridicule, satirise, slime off at (Australian informal), take the mickey out of (*informal*), taunt, tease.

laugh noun cackle, chortle, chuckle, giggle, guffaw, snicker, snigger, titter.

laughable adjective absurd, derisory, farcical, ludicrous, nonsensical, outrageous, preposterous, ridiculous.

laughter noun cackling, chuckling, giggling, glee, hilarity, hysterics, laughing, merriment, mirth, sniggering.

launch verb **1** float, set afloat. **2** fire, project, propel, send forth, send off. **3** begin, embark upon, introduce, open, set going, start.

launch noun blast-off, lift-off, take-off.

launder verb clean, wash.

lavatory noun bathroom, convenience, dunny (*Australian slang*), Gents (*informal*), Ladies, latrine, loo (*informal*), men's, powder room, privy, rest room, toilet, toot (*Australian informal*), urinal, washroom, water closet, WC, women's.

lavish adjective **1** extravagant, generous, liberal, unstinting. **2** abundant, bountiful, copious, plentiful, profuse.

lavish verb bestow, heap, pour, shower.

law noun **1** act, by-law, commandment, decree, edict, regulation, rule, statute. **2** axiom, formula, principle, rule, theorem.

law-abiding adjective honest, obedient, orderly, upstanding.

lawbreaker noun criminal, delinquent, felon, miscreant, offender, transgressor, wrongdoer.

lawful adjective allowable, authorised, constitutional, legal, legitimate, permissible, permitted, sanctioned, valid.

lawless adjective **1** disorderly, insubordinate, rebellious, riotous, rowdy, uncontrolled, unruly, wild. **2** anarchic, chaotic, ungoverned.

lawn noun grass, sward, turf.

lawsuit noun action, case, legal proceedings, litigation, suit, trial.

lawyer noun advocate, attorney, barrister, counsel, legal adviser, QC, Queen's Counsel, solicitor.

lax adjective careless, casual, easygoing, indulgent, lenient, permissive, relaxed, remiss, slack.

lay verb **1** deposit, leave, place, put, rest, set down. **2** arrange, set, spread. **3** ascribe, assign, attribute, impute, place. **4** concoct, design, devise, formulate, hatch, make. □ **lay off** stand down, suspend; see also *DISMISS*. □ **lay on** provide, supply. □ **lay out** arrange, design, plan, prepare, set out.

lay *adjective* **1** non-clerical, non-ordained. **2** non-professional, non-specialist.

layabout *noun* bludger (*Australian informal*), bum (*slang*), good-for-nothing, idler, lazybones (*informal*), loafer, malingerer, shirker, skiver (*informal*), slacker.

layer *noun* coating, film, level, ply, sheet, stratum, thickness, tier.

layman *noun* amateur, layperson, non-professional, non-specialist.

layout *noun* arrangement, composition, design, organisation, plan, structure.

laze *verb* loaf, lounge, put your feet up, relax, rest, take it easy.

lazy *adjective* idle, inactive, indolent, inert, languid, lethargic, listless, shiftless, slack, slothful, sluggish, torpid.

lazybones *noun* couch potato (*informal*), good-for-nothing, idler, layabout, loafer, slacker, sluggard.

lead *verb* **1** conduct, escort, guide, pilot, steer, usher. **2** cause, induce, influence, persuade, prompt. **3** be in charge of, command, control, direct, head, spearhead, supervise.

lead *noun* **1** direction, example, guidance, leadership. **2** leash.

leader *noun* boss, captain, chief, chieftain, commander, conductor, director, governor, head, manager, overseer, premier, president, prime minister, principal, ringleader, ruler, supervisor.

leaf *noun* **1** blade, frond, needle (*leaves*) foliage, greenery. **2** folio, page, sheet.

leaflet *noun* booklet, brochure, flyer, handout, pamphlet.

league *noun* alliance, association, group, organisation, society, union.

leak *noun* **1** crack, fissure, gash, hole, puncture, split. **2** disclosure, revelation.

leak *verb* **1** discharge, drip, escape, ooze, seep, trickle. **2** disclose, divulge, let out, reveal.

lean *adjective* angular, bony, emaciated, gaunt, lanky, scraggy, scrawny, skinny, slender, slim, thin, weedy, wiry.

lean *verb* **1** incline, list, slant, slope, tilt, tip. **2** prop yourself, rest, support yourself.

leaning *noun* bent, inclination, partiality, penchant, predilection,

tion, preference, proclivity, tendency.

leap *verb* & *noun* bounce, bound, jump, pounce, spring, vault.

learn *verb* **1** assimilate, grasp, master, memorise, pick up, study. **2** ascertain, become aware, discover, find out, gather, hear.

learned *adjective* clever, educated, erudite, informed, intellectual, knowledgeable, scholarly, well-informed, well-read.

learner *noun* apprentice, beginner, cadet, novice, pupil, rookie (*informal*), student, trainee.

learning *noun* education, erudition, knowledge, scholarship.

lease *verb* hire, let, rent.

least *adjective* barest, faintest, littlest, lowest, minimum, scantiest, slightest, smallest, tiniest.

leather *noun* hide, skin, suede. □ **leathery** *adjective* hard, hardened, rugged, tough, weather-beaten.

leave *verb* **1** abscond, beat it (*slang*), buzz off (*slang*), clear off (*informal*), decamp, depart, disappear, exit, flee, get away, go away, head off, make off, make

yourself scarce, nick off (*Australian slang*), push off (*informal*), quit, rack off (*Australian slang*), retire, retreat, run away, run off, scarper (*informal*), scram (*informal*), set off, shoot through (*Australian informal*), shove off (*informal*), skedaddle (*informal*), slope off (*informal*), take off, take your leave, vanish, withdraw. **2** chuck in (*informal*), give up, quit, resign, retire from, walk out of. **3** abandon, desert, forsake, leave in the lurch, part from, separate from. **4** bequeath, give, hand down, will. □ **leave off** cease, desist, lay off (*informal*), quit, refrain from, stop. □ **leave out** drop, exclude, miss out, omit, skip.

leave *noun* **1** consent, permission. **2** break, exeat, furlough, holiday, sabbatical, vacation.

lecherous *adjective* lascivious, lewd, lustful, randy.

lecture *noun* **1** address, discourse, lesson, speech, talk. **2** dressing down (*informal*), earbashing (*Australian informal*), reprimand, reproof, scolding, sermon, serve (*Australian informal*), talking-to (*informal*), telling-off (*informal*).

ledge *noun* mantelpiece, projection, shelf, sill.

leer *verb* goggle, ogle, smirk, stare.

leeway *noun* freedom, latitude, margin, play, room, scope.

left *noun* larboard (*old use*), port.

leftovers *plural noun* dregs, excess, remainder(s), residue, scraps, surplus.

leg *noun* **1** limb, pin (*informal*), shank. **2** lap, part, section, stage.

legacy *noun* bequest, inheritance.

legal *adjective* allowed, authorised, lawful, legitimate, permissible, permitted, proper, rightful.

legalise *verb* allow, authorise, decriminalise, permit.

legend *noun* folk tale, myth, saga, story, tale. □ **legendary** *adjective* fabled, fictional, fictitious, mythical, traditional; see also *FAMOUS*.

legible *adjective* clear, neat, plain, readable, tidy.

legislation *noun* act, bill, law, statute.

legislative *adjective* lawmaking, parliamentary.

legitimate *adjective* lawful, legal, permissible.

leisure *noun* free time, recreation, relaxation, spare time, time off. □ **leisurely** *adjective* calm, easy, gentle, relaxed, restful, slow, unhurried.

lend *verb* advance, loan.

length *noun* **1** distance, extent, measurement, size, span. **2** duration, period, span, term, time. □ **at length 1** at last, eventually, finally, in the end. **2** fully, in depth, in detail.

lengthen *verb* draw out, elongate, extend, increase, prolong, protract, spin out, stretch out.

lengthways *adverb* lengthwise, longitudinally, longways, longwise.

lengthy *adjective* drawn-out, extended, interminable, long, long-winded, prolonged, protracted, verbose, wordy.

lenient *adjective* compassionate, easygoing, forbearing, indulgent, merciful, mild, soft, sparing.

leprechaun *noun* elf, fairy, sprite.

lesbian *adjective* gay (*informal*), homosexual.

less *adjective* slighter, smaller.

less *preposition* deducting, minus, subtracting, taking away.

lessen verb abate, cut down, deaden, decrease, die down, diminish, dwindle, ease, let up, minimise, moderate, reduce, subside, weaken.

lesser adjective minor, secondary, slighter, smaller, subsidiary.

lesson noun 1 class, period, session. 2 message, moral, principle, rule, warning. 3 passage, reading.

let verb 1 agree to, allow, consent to, enable, permit. 2 lease, rent. □ **let down** 1 deflate. 2 disappoint, fail, leave high and dry, leave in the lurch. □ **let-down** noun anticlimax, comedown, disappointment, disillusionment. □ **let off** 1 detonate, discharge, explode, set off. 2 excuse, exempt, pardon, release, reprieve, spare. □ **let on** admit, confess, disclose, divulge, give away, let slip, reveal. □ **let out** 1 free, let go, let loose, liberate, release, set free. 2 enlarge, loosen. □ **let up** abate, ease, lessen, relax, slacken, subside.

lethal adjective deadly, fatal, mortal, poisonous, toxic.

lethargy noun indolence, inertia, languor, lassitude, listlessness, sluggishness, torpor, weariness.

letter noun 1 character, symbol. 2 communication, dispatch, epistle, message, missive, note; (letters) correspondence, mail, post.

letterbox noun mailbox, pillar box (old use), postbox.

level adjective 1 even, flat, horizontal, plane, smooth. 2 equal, even, neck and neck, tied. 3 constant, steady, unchanging, uniform.

level noun 1 altitude, amount, degree, depth, grade, elevation, height, measure, position, rank, rung, stage, standard, value. 2 deck, floor, storey, tier.

level verb 1 even out, tie. 2 aim, direct, point, train. 3 demolish, flatten, knock down, raze, tear down, topple.

lever noun control, handle.

lever verb prise, wrench.

levy verb charge, collect, exact, impose. □ **levy** noun charge, duty, excise, impost, tariff, tax, toll.

lewd adjective bawdy, blue, crude, dirty, indecent, obscene, ribald, salacious, vulgar.

liability noun 1 accountability, answerability, responsibility. 2 debt, obligation, responsibility. 3 burden, disadvantage, drawback, encumbrance, handicap, millstone.

liable *adjective* **1** (*liable to colds*) prone, subject, susceptible, vulnerable; (*liable to cry*) apt, inclined, likely, prone. **2** accountable, answerable, responsible.

liaison *noun* **1** communication, contact, cooperation. **2** contact, coordinator, go-between, link, mediator.

liar *noun* fibber, storyteller (*informal*).

libel *noun* calumny, defamation, denigration, false statement, slander, slur, smear, vilification.

libel *verb* defame, denigrate, discredit, malign, slander, smear, vilify.

liberal *adjective* **1** abundant, ample, copious, extravagant, generous, lavish, plentiful. **2** broad-minded, enlightened, flexible, lax, open-minded, permissive, tolerant, unbiased, unprejudiced.

liberate *verb* deliver, emancipate, free, let go, release, set free. □ **liberation** *noun* deliverance, emancipation, freedom, liberty, release.

liberty *noun* autonomy, freedom, independence, self-determination, self-rule.

licence *noun* authorisation, franchise, permit, warrant.

license *verb* allow, authorise, permit.

lick *verb* lap, tongue.

lid *noun* cap, cover, top.

lie *noun* falsehood, fib, porky (*slang*), story (*informal*), untruth, whopper (*slang*).

lie *verb* bluff, deceive, dissemble, fib, perjure yourself, prevaricate.

lie *verb* **1** recline, rest, sprawl. **2** be, be found, be located, be situated. **3** be, remain, stay. □ **lie low** go into hiding, go to ground, hide, keep a low profile (*informal*), take cover.

lieu *noun* □ **in lieu of** instead of, in the place of.

lieutenant *noun* assistant, deputy.

life *noun* **1** being, existence, survival. **2** flora and fauna, living things. **3** animation, energy, exuberance, go, liveliness, vigour, vitality, vivacity. **4** autobiography, biography.

lifeless *adjective* **1** dead, deceased, inanimate, inert, non-living. **2** blacked out, comatose, insensible, knocked out, senseless, unconscious.

lifelike *adjective* accurate, authentic, realistic, true to life.

lifelong *adjective* abiding, enduring, lasting, permanent,

lifetime noun existence, life, life span.

lift verb **1** boost, elevate, hoist, jack up, pick up, push up, raise. **2** ascend, climb, go upwards, mount, rise, soar. **3** see *STEAL*. **4** cancel, remove, revoke, withdraw.

lift noun elevator.

lift-off noun blast-off, launch, take-off.

light noun **1** blaze, brightness, brilliance, flash, glare, glow, illumination, incandescence, radiance, reflection. **2** beacon, candle, floodlight, headlight, lamp, lantern, spotlight, torch. □ **bring to light** disclose, expose, reveal, uncover. □ **come to light** appear, become apparent, come out, emerge, transpire.

light adjective **1** bright, illuminated, well-lit. **2** delicate, pale, pastel, soft.

light verb ignite, kindle, set alight, start. □ **light up** brighten, illuminate, lighten.

light adjective **1** delicate, flimsy, lightweight, portable, thin. **2** faint, fine, gentle, low, moderate, slight. **3** easy, effortless, simple, undemanding. **4** entertaining, frivolous, superficial.

lighten verb brighten, illuminate, light up.

lighten verb alleviate, ease, lessen, mitigate, reduce, relieve.

light-headed adjective dizzy, faint, giddy, woozy (*informal*).

light-hearted adjective blithe, bright, carefree, cheerful, gay, happy, jolly, merry.

lighthouse noun beacon.

like verb **1** admire, appreciate, approve of, be fond of, be keen on, delight in, enjoy, fancy, relish; see also *LOVE*. **2** care, desire, have a mind to, want, wish.

like adjective corresponding, identical, matching, similar, the same.

likeable adjective agreeable, amiable, attractive, charming, congenial, friendly, genial, pleasant, pleasing, winsome.

likelihood noun chance, possibility, probability, prospect.

likely adjective **1** believable, credible, expected, plausible, probable. **2** appropriate, fitting, promising, qualified, suitable.

liken verb compare, draw an analogy between, equate.

likeness noun **1** resemblance, sameness, similarity. **2** copy, picture, portrait, replica, representation.

liking noun affinity, appetite, appreciation, fondness, partiality, penchant, preference, taste.

limb noun **1** appendage, arm, leg, wing. **2** bough, branch. □ **out on a limb** alone, isolated, stranded.

limber verb □ **limber up** exercise, loosen up, prepare, warm up.

limbo noun □ **in limbo** half-finished, in abeyance, suspended, unfinished, up in the air.

limelight noun prominence, public eye, publicity, spotlight.

limit noun **1** border, boundary, bounds, confines, edge, end, extent, frontier, perimeter. **2** ceiling, cut-off, limitation, maximum, restriction.

limit verb check, confine, contain, control, curb, restrain, restrict. □ **limitation** noun deficiency, shortcoming, weakness.

limited adjective minimal, restricted, scanty, small.

limp verb falter, hobble, shuffle.

limp adjective droopy, flaccid, floppy, lifeless, wilted.

line noun **1** band, dash, mark, score, slash, streak, strip, stripe, stroke. **2** crease, crow's-foot, furrow, wrinkle. **3** border,

borderline, boundary, limit **4** chain, column, cordon, crocodile, file, procession, queue, row, series. **5** cable, cord, hawser, lead, rope, string, wire. **6** branch, route, track. **7** company, fleet. **8** course, direction, path, tack, tendency, track, trend, way. □ **in line with** conforming with, in accordance with, in agreement with, in keeping with, in step with.

line verb **1** rule. **2** align, form a line, queue up, straighten.

lineage noun ancestry, descent, extraction, family, genealogy, line, origins, pedigree.

linen noun manchester, napery.

linger verb dally, dawdle, delay, dilly-dally, hang about, hang around, loiter, remain, stay, take your time, tarry.

lingerie noun corsetry, underclothes, undergarments, underwear, undies (informal).

liniment noun balm, embrocation, ointment, salve.

lining noun backing, facing, interfacing.

link noun **1** loop, ring. **2** association, bond, connection, relationship, tie, tie-up.

link verb associate, connect, identify, join, relate, unite.

lion noun cub (*young*), king of beasts, lioness (*female*).

lip noun brim, edge, rim.

liquid noun fluid, juice, liquor, solution.

liquid adjective flowing, fluid, molten, runny, watery.

liquidate verb **1** clear, discharge, pay, settle. **2** close down, dissolve, wind up. **3** do away with, eliminate, exterminate, get rid of, remove; see also *KILL*.

liquidise verb crush, liquefy, pulp, purée.

liquor noun alcohol, drink, grog (*Australian*), spirits.

list noun catalogue, directory, index, inventory, register, roll, schedule, series, table.

list verb catalogue, enter, enumerate, index, itemise, note, record, register, write down.

list verb heel, lean, tilt, tip over.

listen verb lend an ear, pay attention, pay heed, take notice, tune in. □ **listen in** bug (*informal*), eavesdrop, overhear, tap. □ **listener** noun auditor, hearer; (*listeners*) audience.

listless adjective apathetic, languid, lethargic, lifeless, sluggish, tired, torpid, unenthusiastic.

literal adjective exact, precise, strict, true, verbatim, word for word.

literate adjective educated, well-read.

literature noun **1** letters, writings, written works. **2** booklets, brochures, handouts, information, leaflets, material, pamphlets.

lithe adjective agile, flexible, limber, lissom, nimble, pliant, supple.

litter noun **1** debris, garbage, mess, refuse, rubbish, trash, waste. **2** brood, family, group.

litter verb clutter, mess up, scatter, strew.

little adjective **1** baby, brief, compact, concise, diminutive, dwarf, microscopic, midget, miniature, minuscule, minute, petite, pocket-sized, puny, short, slight, small, stunted, tiny, undersized, wee; (*little in amount*) inadequate, meagre, measly (*informal*), scanty, skimpy, small, stingy. **2** insignificant, marginal, minimal, minor, negligible, petty, slight, trivial, unimportant. □ **little by little** bit by bit, by degrees, gradually, progressively, slowly.

live verb **1** be, be alive, breathe, continue, endure, exist, keep going, last, persist, remain,

stay alive, subsist, survive.
2 abide (*old use*), dwell, reside;
see also INHABIT.

live *adjective* **1** alive, animate,
breathing, living, surviving.
2 burning, glowing, hot.

livelihood *noun* crust (*Australian informal*), income, living,
means of support.

lively *adjective* active, animated,
boisterous, cheerful, chirpy,
energetic, enthusiastic, full of
beans (*informal*), irrepressible, perky, spirited,
sprightly, spry, vigorous,
vivacious.

liven *verb* brighten up, buck up
(*informal*), cheer up, perk up.

livestock *noun* animals, stock.

livid *adjective* see ANGRY.

living *adjective* alive, animate,
breathing, live, quick (*old use*).

living *noun* **1** being alive,
existence, life. **2** crust
(*Australian informal*), income,
livelihood, means of support;
see also JOB.

living room drawing room,
family room, lounge, lounge
room, parlour (*old use*), sitting
room.

load *noun* **1** burden, cargo,
consignment, freight, shipment; see also WEIGHT. **2** see
LOT.

load *verb* fill, pack, pile up.

loading *noun* allowance,
margin.

loaf *verb* idle, laze, lounge, take
it easy, veg out (*slang*).
□ **loafer** *noun* bludger
(*Australian informal*), bum
(*slang*), couch potato
(*informal*), good-for-nothing,
idler, layabout, lazybones (*informal*), shirker, skiver
(*informal*), slacker.

loan *noun* advance, credit,
mortgage.

loan *verb* advance, lend.

loath *adjective* disinclined,
reluctant, unwilling.

loathe *verb* abhor, abominate,
despise, detest, dislike, hate.

loathsome *adjective* abhorrent,
abominable, despicable, detestable, disgusting, hateful,
odious, offensive, repugnant,
repulsive.

lob *verb* see THROW.

lobby *noun* **1** corridor, entrance
hall, foyer, hall, porch,
vestibule. **2** force, pressure
group.

lobby *verb* campaign, petition,
push.

local *adjective* **1** area, community, district, neighbourhood, provincial, regional. **2**
confined, localised, restricted.

local *noun* inhabitant, native,
resident.

localise verb confine, contain, limit, restrict.

locality noun area, community, district, neighbourhood, region, suburb, vicinity.

locate verb **1** detect, discover, find, identify, pinpoint. **2** place, position, put, site, situate.

location noun area, locality, place, position, setting, site, spot, whereabouts.

lock noun bar, bolt, catch, latch, padlock, snib.

lock verb bar, bolt, fasten, secure, snib. □ **lock up** imprison, incarcerate, intern, jail, put away.

lock noun tress, tuft.

locker noun cabinet, compartment, cupboard.

locomotion noun mobility, motion, movement, moving, transport, travel.

locum noun deputy, replacement, stand-in, substitute.

lodge noun **1** cottage, gatehouse, home, house, residence. **2** cabin, chalet, hostel, hotel, motel, resort.

lodge verb **1** board, live, reside, stay. **2** become embedded, get stuck, stick. **3** file, lay, make, register, submit.

lodger noun boarder, guest, tenant.

lodgings plural noun accommodation, billet, digs (informal), quarters, residence, room(s).

loft noun attic, garret.

lofty adjective **1** high, soaring, tall, towering. **2** exalted, high-minded, noble, sublime. **3** arrogant, disdainful, haughty, high and mighty, hoity-toity, proud, scornful, snooty (informal), supercilious.

log noun **1** block, piece, stump. **2** diary, journal, logbook, record.

logical adjective coherent, intelligent, rational, reasonable, reasoned, sensible, sound, valid.

logo noun emblem, symbol, trade mark.

loiter verb dally, dawdle, hang around, linger, lurk, skulk.

loll verb lie, lounge, recline, relax, slump, sprawl.

lolly noun candy (American), confection, sweet, toffee.

lone adjective alone, lonely, single, sole, solitary, unaccompanied.

lonely adjective **1** forlorn, forsaken, friendless, lonesome. **2** companionless, isolated, solitary. **3** deserted, isolated, remote, secluded, unfrequented, uninhabited.

long *adjective* **1** big, drawn-out, elongated, endless, extended, interminable, lengthy, prolonged, protracted, sustained, unending. **2** abiding, enduring, lasting, long-lasting, long-lived, long-standing, long-term, permanent.

long *verb* (*long for*) crave, desire, hanker after, hunger for, pine for, thirst for, want, wish for, yearn for.

longing *noun* appetite, craving, desire, hunger, thirst, urge, wish, yearning, yen.

long-suffering *adjective* forbearing, patient, tolerant.

long-winded *adjective* garrulous, loquacious, rambling, tedious, verbose, wordy.

look *verb* **1** gape, gawp (*informal*), gaze, glance, glare, goggle, leer, ogle, peek, peep, peer, squint, stare; (*look at*) behold (*old use*), consider, contemplate, examine, eye, glimpse, inspect, observe, scrutinise, see, study, survey, view, watch, witness; (*look for*) check for, fossick for (*Australian informal*), hunt for, search for, seek. **2** face. **3** appear, seem. ☐ **look after** attend to, care for, guard, mind, protect, take care of. ☐ **look down on** despise, disdain, look down your nose at, patronise, scorn. ☐ **look forward to** anticipate, await, long for. ☐ **look in** call in, drop in, visit. ☐ **look into** check on, examine, explore, go into, inquire into, investigate, probe, research. ☐ **look out** beware, keep your eyes open, pay attention, take care, watch out. ☐ **look up 1** check, hunt for, search for, seek. **2** get better, improve, pick up. ☐ **look up to** admire, esteem, idolise, respect, revere, worship.

look *noun* **1** gaze, glance, glare, glimpse, peek, peep, squint (*informal*), squiz (*Australian slang*), stare, stickybeak (*Australian informal*); see also SEARCH. **2** appearance, countenance, expression, face.

looker-on *noun* bystander, observer, onlooker, spectator, viewer, witness.

lookout *noun* **1** guard, picket, sentinel, sentry, watchman. **2** future, outlook, prospect.

loom *verb* appear, menace, rise, soar, stand out, threaten, tower.

loop *noun* circle, circuit, coil, curl, knot, noose, ring, twirl, twist.

loop *verb* coil, curl, entwine, kink, twist, wind.

loophole *noun* **1** escape, get out, let-out, way out. **2** aperture, gap, opening, slit.

loose *adjective* **1** detached, rickety, shaky, unattached, unfastened, unsteady, unstuck, wobbly; (*of clothing*) baggy, floppy, slack. **2** at large, free, uncaged, unconfined, unleashed, unrestrained, untethered, untied. **3** bulk, unpackaged. **4** broad, imprecise, inexact, rough, sloppy, vague.

loose *verb* **1** ease, loosen, relax, slacken, undo, unfasten, untie. **2** free, let go, let loose, liberate, release, set free, untie.

loosen *verb* ease, free, loose, relax, release, slacken, undo, unfasten, untie.

loot *noun* booty, goods, pillage, plunder, spoils, swag (*informal*), takings.

loot *verb* pillage, plunder, raid, ransack, rob, sack.

lop *verb* chop, cut, prune.

lopsided *adjective* askew, asymmetrical, awry, crooked, unbalanced, uneven.

lord *noun* **1** aristocrat, noble, nobleman, peer. **2** king, master, monarch, ruler, sovereign. □ **lordly** *adjective* arrogant, bossy, disdainful, haughty, high and mighty, imperious, lofty, overbearing, snobbish, stuck-up (*informal*). □ **the Lord** God, Jehovah, Jesus Christ, Yahweh.

lore *noun* folklore, legends, myths, traditions.

lorry *noun* pick-up, road train (*Australian*), semi (*Australian informal*), semitrailer, transport, truck, van.

lose *verb* **1** mislay, misplace; (*lost*) gone, mislaid, misplaced, missing, strayed, vanished. **2** forfeit, let slip, miss, pass up (*informal*), waste. **3** be defeated, get beaten. □ **lose your way** miss the way, stray from the way, wander from the way.

loss *noun* **1** bereavement, deprivation, disappearance, forfeiture, impairment, reduction. **2** casualty, death, fatality. □ **at a loss** baffled, mystified, nonplussed, perplexed, puzzled.

lot *noun* **1** allocation, allotment, part, portion, quota, ration, share. **2** destiny, fate, fortune, portion, set. **3** batch, collection, group, set. **4** allotment, block, plot. □ **a lot**, **lots** dozens (*informal*), a good deal, a great deal, heaps (*informal*), loads (*informal*), many, masses, oodles (*informal*), piles (*informal*), plenty, scores, stacks (*informal*), a swag (*Australian informal*), tons (*informal*).

lotion *noun* balm, cream, liniment, moisturiser, ointment, salve.

loud adjective **1** amplified, blaring, booming, deafening, noisy, penetrating, piercing, raucous, resounding, rowdy, sonorous, stentorian, strident, thundering. **2** bold, bright, flashy, garish, gaudy, lurid, obtrusive, showy. □ **loudness** noun volume.

lounge noun drawing room, living room, lounge room, parlour (old use), sitting room.

lounge verb laze, lie, loaf, loll, recline, relax, sprawl, veg out (slang).

louring adjective black, cloudy, dark, gloomy, grey, heavy, leaden, overcast.

lousy adjective awful (informal), bad, dreadful (informal), miserable, nasty, rotten (informal), terrible (informal); see also BAD.

loutish djective boorish, churlish, discourteous, ill-mannered, impolite, rough, rude, uncouth.

lovable adjective adorable, appealing, charming, darling, dear, delightful, endearing, likeable, lovely, sweet.

love noun **1** adoration, affection, devotion, fondness, tenderness, warmth. **2** ardour, desire, fervour, infatuation, lust, passion. **3** delight, enjoyment, fondness, liking, pleasure, taste. **4** beloved, darling, lover, sweetheart; □ **in love** besotted, devoted, enamoured, infatuated, smitten.

love verb **1** adore, be devoted to, be fond of, care for, cherish, dote on, hold dear, idolise, revere, treasure. **2** appreciate, be fond of, delight in, enjoy, like, relish, treasure. □ **lover** noun admirer, beloved, boyfriend, girlfriend, suitor, sweetheart; see also ENTHUSIAST (at ENTHUSIASM). □ **loving** adjective adoring, affectionate, amorous, ardent, caring, close, devoted, doting, fond, friendly, kind, kind-hearted, passionate, sympathetic, tender, warm, warm-hearted.

lovely adjective **1** adorable, attractive, beautiful, charming, good-looking, gorgeous, pretty, winsome. **2** cool (informal), delightful, enjoyable, excellent, fantastic (informal), good, great (informal), nice, pleasant, terrific (informal), wonderful.

low adjective **1** dwarf, little, miniature, short, small, squat, stunted. **2** humble, inferior, junior, lowly, unimportant. **3** budget, cheap, cut-price, inexpensive, modest, reduced **4** faint, gentle, hushed muffled, quiet, soft, subdued; (*low-pitched*) bass, deep. **5** blue, dejected, depressed, despondent, down, downcast, forlorn, gloomy, glum, listless, melancholy, miserable, sad.

lower verb **1** (*lower the volume*) quieten, soften, subdue, tone down, turn down; (*lower the price*) cut, decrease, discount, drop, mark down, reduce. **2** bring down, drop, let down, pull down, take down.

lowly adjective humble, modest, unassuming, unpretentious.

loyal adjective constant, dedicated, dependable, devoted, faithful, patriotic, staunch, steadfast, true, true-blue, trustworthy. □ **loyalty** noun allegiance, constancy, devotion, faithfulness, fidelity, steadfastness, trustworthiness.

lozenge noun drop, lolly, pastille, sweet, tablet.

lubricate verb grease, oil.

lucid adjective **1** clear, comprehensible, intelligible, straightforward, understandable. **2** all there, rational, sane, sensible.

luck noun **1** accident, chance, coincidence, destiny, fate, fluke, fortune, serendipity. **2** good fortune, prosperity, success.

luckless adjective doomed, fated, hapless, ill-fated, jinxed, unfortunate, unlucky.

lucky adjective **1** blessed, charmed, favoured, fortunate. **2** accidental, chance, fluky, fortuitous, serendipitous.

lucrative adjective profitable, remunerative, well-paid.

ludicrous adjective absurd, crazy, derisory, farcical, laughable, nonsensical, preposterous, ridiculous.

lug verb carry, drag, haul, heave, pull.

luggage noun baggage, bags, cases, gear, ports (*Australian*), suitcases, trunks; see also BELONGINGS.

lukewarm adjective **1** tepid, warm. **2** apathetic, cool, half-hearted, indifferent, unenthusiastic.

lull verb calm, hush, pacify, quieten, relax, soothe.

lull noun break, gap, hiatus, interval, let-up (*informal*), pause, silence.

lumber verb **1** burden, encumber, land, load, saddle. **2** clump, plod, shuffle, trudge, waddle.

luminous adjective bright, glowing, luminescent, phosphorescent, radiant, shining.

lump *noun* **1** ball, bit, chunk, cube, hunk, piece, wedge. **2** bulge, bump, growth, protrusion, swelling, tumour. □ **lumpy** *adjective* bumpy, chunky, uneven.

lump *verb* combine, group, mix.

lump *verb* accept, endure, put up with, suffer, tolerate, wear (*informal*).

lunacy *noun* **1** insanity, madness, mania, mental illness. **2** folly, foolhardiness, foolishness, idiocy, imprudence, madness, recklessness, stupidity.

lunatic *noun* crackpot (*informal*), loony (*informal*), madman, madwoman, maniac, nut (*informal*), nutter (*informal*), psychopath.

lunch *noun* dinner, luncheon (*formal*), midday meal.

lunge *verb* charge, dive, plunge, pounce, rush, thrust.

lurch *verb* flounder, reel, stagger, stumble, sway, totter.

lurch *noun* □ **leave in the lurch** abandon, desert, forsake, leave high and dry, leave stranded.

lure *verb* attract, draw, entice, seduce, tempt. □ **lure** *noun* attraction, bait, decoy, draw, drawcard, enticement.

lurid *adjective* **1** bright, flashy, garish, gaudy, loud, showy. **2** explicit, gory, graphic, horrifying, sensational, shocking, vivid.

lurk *verb* hide, lie in wait, linger, skulk.

lurk *noun* dodge (*informal*), racket, rort (*Australian slang*), scam (*slang*), scheme, stratagem.

luscious *adjective* delectable, delicious, juicy, rich, succulent, sweet.

lush *adjective* green, luxuriant, profuse, prolific, strong, thick.

lust *noun* appetite, craving, desire, greed, hunger, longing, passion. □ **lustful** *adjective* lascivious, lecherous, lewd, randy.

lustre *noun* brightness, brilliance, gleam, gloss, sheen, shine, sparkle.

luxuriant *adjective* abundant, dense, lush, profuse, strong, thick.

luxuriate *verb* bask, delight, enjoy yourself, indulge yourself, relax, wallow.

luxury *noun* **1** extra, extravagance, indulgence, treat. **2** affluence, comfort, ease, opulence, self-indulgence. □ **luxurious** *adjective* de luxe, elegant, expensive, first-class, grand, opulent, plush, posh (*informal*), sumptuous, swish (*informal*), upmarket.

lying noun deception, dishonesty, fibbing, mendacity, perjury, prevarication. ☐ **lying** adjective deceitful, dishonest, mendacious, untruthful.

lynch verb execute, put to death.

lyric noun libretto, text, words. ☐ **lyrical** adjective melodic, melodious, musical, poetic, songlike.

M m

macabre adjective eerie, frightening, ghastly, ghoulish, gory, grim, grisly, gruesome, hideous, horrific, morbid, spooky (*informal*), weird.

machine noun apparatus, appliance, computer, contraption, device, engine, gadget, instrument, mechanism, robot, tool.

machinery noun equipment, gear, machines, plant.

macho adjective manly, masculine, tough, virile.

mad adjective **1** bananas (*slang*), barmy (*slang*), batty (*slang*), berserk, bonkers (*slang*),
crackers (*slang*), crazy, demented, deranged, dotty (*informal*), flaky (*slang*), frenzied, insane, irrational, loony (*informal*), lunatic, manic, mental (*informal*), nuts (*informal*), nutty (*informal*), off your head, out of your mind, potty (*informal*), psychotic, round the bend (*informal*), screwy (*informal*), troppo (*Australian slang*), unbalanced, unhinged. **2** absurd, crazy, daft (*informal*), foolhardy, foolish, harebrained, idiotic, illogical, insane, lunatic, nonsensical, preposterous, rash, reckless, silly, stupid, unwise, wild. **3** crazy, enthusiastic, fanatical, infatuated, keen, nuts (*informal*), obsessed, passionate, wild. **4** angry, annoyed, cross, enraged, furious, incensed, infuriated, irate, livid, riled (*informal*), ropeable (*Australian informal*), wild. ☐ **madman, madwoman** noun crackpot (*informal*), loony (*slang*), lunatic, maniac, nut (*informal*), nutcase (*informal*), nutter (*informal*), psychopath. ☐ **madness** noun **1** dementia, derangement, insanity, lunacy, mania, mental illness, psychosis. **2** folly, foolishness, idiocy, lunacy, stupidity.

madden verb anger, annoy, bug (*informal*), drive someone mad, enrage, exasperate, incense, infuriate, irritate, needle (*informal*), rile (*informal*), vex, wind up (*informal*).

maelstrom noun eddy, swirl, vortex, whirlpool.

maestro noun ace (*informal*), adept, expert, genius, master, virtuoso, whiz (*informal*), wizard; see also *MUSICIAN*.

magazine noun bulletin, journal, newsletter, pamphlet, periodical.

maggot noun grub, larva.

magic noun black magic, conjuring, divination, illusion, sleight of hand, sorcery, spells, trickery, voodoo, witchcraft, wizardry.

magician noun conjuror, enchanter, enchantress, illusionist, medicine man, sorcerer, sorceress, warlock (*old use*), witch, witchdoctor, wizard.

magisterial adjective assertive, authoritative, bossy (*informal*), domineering, high-handed, imperious, lordly, masterful, overbearing, peremptory.

magistrate noun beak (*slang*), justice, stipendiary magistrate.

magnanimous adjective benevolent, big-hearted, bountiful, charitable, gener-ous, kind, noble.

magnate noun baron, big shot (*informal*), bigwig (*informal*), leader, mogul (*informal*), tycoon; see also *BUSINESSMAN*.

magnetic adjective alluring, attractive, captivating, charismatic, charming, enchanting, enthralling, fascinating, irresistible, seductive.

magnificent adjective 1 beautiful, brilliant, exquisite, extraordinary, fine, glorious, gorgeous, grand, great, imposing, impressive, majestic, opulent, spectacular, splendid, stately, striking, stunning, sumptuous, superb. 2 see *EXCELLENT*.

magnify verb amplify, blow up (*informal*), enlarge, exaggerate, overstate.

magnitude noun 1 extent, largeness, size. 2 consequence, importance, significance.

maid noun chambermaid, domestic, help, housemaid, lady's maid, maidservant, parlourmaid, servant.

maiden noun damsel (*old use*), girl, lass, lassie (*informal*), maid (*old use*).

maiden adjective 1 spinster, unmarried, unwed. 2 first, inaugural, initial.

mail noun correspondence, letters, packages, parcels, post.

mail verb dispatch, post, send.

maim verb cripple, disable, incapacitate, injure, lame, mutilate, wound.

main adjective biggest, central, chief, critical, crucial, essential, first, foremost, greatest, head, largest, leading, major, most important, outstanding, paramount, predominant, primary, prime, principal, vital.

mainly adverb chiefly, especially, generally, in the main, largely, mostly, predominantly, primarily, principally.

mainstay noun anchor, backbone, foundation, linchpin, pillar, support.

maintain verb **1** carry on, continue, keep, keep up, perpetuate, preserve, prolong, uphold. **2** care for, keep in good repair, look after, preserve, service, take care of. **3** finance, keep, provide for, support. **4** assert, claim, contend, declare, hold, insist.

maintenance noun **1** care, preservation, repairs, running, servicing, upkeep. **2** alimony, allowance.

majestic adjective august, dignified, glorious, grand, imperial, imposing, impressive, kingly, lordly, magnificent, noble, regal, royal, splendid, stately.

majesty noun dignity, glory, grandeur, magnificence, nobility, pomp, royalty, splendour, stateliness.

major adjective bigger, chief, crucial, greater, important, key, larger, main, paramount, primary, prime, principal, significant.

majority noun **1** bulk, greater part, lion's share, most. **2** margin.

make verb **1** assemble, build, carve, concoct, construct, create, erect, fabricate, fashion, forge, form, invent, manufacture, model, mould, produce, put together, sculpture, sew, shape. **2** acquire, earn, gain, get, obtain, realise, win. **3** cause, coerce, compel, force, oblige, order, pressure. **4** accomplish, achieve, arrive at, attain, reach. **5** (make a bow) do, execute, perform; (make a speech) deliver, give, present, utter. **6** arrange, prepare, straighten, tidy. **7** compile, compose, devise, draw up, establish, formulate, frame, invent, think up, write. **8** add up to, amount to, come to, equal, total. **9** agree on, arrange, choose, decide on, fix, organise, settle on. □ **make do** get by, improvise, manage. □ **make for** aim for, go towards, head for, proceed towards. □ **make out 1** discern, distinguish, espy, perceive, see. **2** decipher, figure out, read, understand, work out. **3** allege, assert, claim, imply, pretend. □ **make up 1** compose, constitute, form. **2** concoct, cook up (*informal*), dream up, fabricate, invent, manufacture, think up. **3** (*make up for*) atone for, compensate for, offset, recompense, redeem. □ **make up your mind** choose, come to a decision, decide, resolve, settle.

make *noun* brand, kind, sort, type.

make-believe *noun* daydreaming, dreaming, fantasy, imagination, play-acting, pretence.

maker *noun* builder, constructor, creator, inventor, manufacturer, producer.

makeshift *adjective* improvised, provisional, stopgap, temporary.

make-up *noun* **1** cosmetics, face paint, greasepaint. **2** character, nature, personality, temperament.

maladjusted *adjective* disturbed, mixed-up (*informal*), neurotic, screwed-up (*informal*).

malady *noun* affliction, ailment, complaint, condition, disease, disorder, illness, infirmity, sickness.

malcontent *noun* agitator, complainer, dissenter, grouch (*informal*), grumbler, moaner, rebel, stirrer (*Australian informal*), troublemaker, whinger (*informal*).

male *adjective* masculine.

male *noun* see BOY, MAN.

malefactor *noun* baddy (*informal*), criminal, crook (*informal*), delinquent, evildoer, felon, lawbreaker, miscreant, offender, outlaw, sinner, villain, wrongdoer.

malevolent *adjective* hostile, malicious, malignant, nasty, sinister, spiteful, vicious, vindictive.

malformed *adjective* crooked, deformed, distorted, misshapen, twisted.

malfunction *noun* breakdown, failure, fault, glitch (*informal*), hiccup, hitch. □ **malfunction** *verb* break down, conk out (*informal*), fail, go bung (*Australian slang*), stop working.

malice *noun* animosity, bitterness, enmity, hostility, ill will, malevolence, maliciousness, spite, spitefulness, vindictiveness. □ **malicious** *adjective* bitchy (*informal*), hostile, malevolent, malignant, mean, mischievous, nasty, spiteful, unkind, vicious, vindictive.

malign *adjective* bad, baleful, damaging, deleterious, destructive, evil, harmful, injurious, noxious, pernicious, sinister.

malign *verb* defame, denigrate, disparage, knock (*informal*), libel, revile, run down, slander, smear, vilify.

malignant *adjective* **1** cancerous, deadly, fatal. **2** destructive, evil, harmful, hostile, malevolent, malicious, pernicious, spiteful, venomous, vicious, vindictive.

malingerer *noun* see *SHIRKER* (at *SHIRK*).

mall *noun* arcade, centre, complex, plaza, precinct.

malleable *adjective* **1** plastic, soft, workable. **2** adaptable, biddable, docile, impressionable, manageable, pliable, suggestible, tractable.

malnutrition *noun* emaciation, hunger, starvation, undernourishment.

malpractice *noun* dereliction, misconduct, negligence, wrongdoing.

maltreat *verb* abuse, bully, harm, ill-treat, ill-use, mistreat, oppress.

mammoth *adjective* colossal, enormous, gargantuan, giant, gigantic, herculean, huge, immense, large, massive, mighty, stupendous, tremendous.

man *noun* **1** bloke (*informal*), chap (*informal*), fellow (*informal*), gentleman, guy (*informal*), lad (*informal*), male. **2** human, human being, individual, mortal, person. **3** human beings, humanity, humankind, human race, humans, mankind, people.

man *verb* attend, operate, staff.

manage *verb* **1** accomplish, carry out, do, perform, succeed in, undertake. **2** control, deal with, handle, manipulate, operate, use, wield. **3** administer, be in charge of, command, conduct, control, direct, govern, head, oversee, run, superintend, supervise. **4** cope, get along, get by, make do, make ends meet, survive. □ **manageable** *adjective* biddable, compliant, controllable, docile, governable, pliable, tractable.

management *noun* **1** administration, control, direction, handling, organisation, running, supervision. **2**

administrators, bosses, directors, employers, executives, managers.

manager noun administrator, boss, chief, director, foreman, head, organiser, overseer, proprietor, superintendent, supervisor.

manchester noun bedlinen, linen, napery, table linen.

mandate noun approval, authorisation, authority, direction, permission.

mangle verb crush, cut, damage, disfigure, injure, lacerate, maim, mutilate.

manhole noun hatch, opening, trapdoor.

manhood noun 1 adulthood, majority, maturity. 2 bravery, courage, machismo, manliness, masculinity, strength, valour, virility.

mania noun 1 dementia, derangement, insanity, lunacy, madness, mental illness. 2 craze, enthusiasm, fad, obsession, passion.

maniac noun crackpot (informal), loony (slang), lunatic, madman, madwoman, nut (informal), nutcase (informal), nutter (informal), psychopath.

manifest adjective apparent, blatant, clear, conspicuous, evident, obvious, patent, plain,

transparent, undisguised, un mistakable, visible.

manifest verb declare, demon strate, display, exhibit express, indicate, make known, reveal, show.

manifesto noun declaration platform, policy statement programme.

manipulate verb 1 control handle, manage, operate, use wield, work. 2 (manipulat figures, etc.) cook (informal) falsify, fiddle (slang), juggle massage, rig.

mankind noun human beings humanity, humankind, human race, man, people, society.

manly adjective 1 male mannish, masculine. 2 brave chivalrous, courageous, fear less, gallant, heroic, macho manful, valiant.

man-made adjective artificial made, manufactured, syn thetic.

manner noun 1 fashion method, procedure, style technique, way. 2 air, attitude bearing, demeanour, disposi tion, mien. 3 category, class kind, sort, type, variety □ **manners** plural noun behaviour, conduct, form. 2 courtesy, decorum, etiquette politeness, social graces, tact

mannerism noun habit, idiosyncrasy, peculiarity, quirk, trait.

mannish adjective butch (slang), masculine.

manoeuvre noun device, dodge (informal), move, ploy, ruse, scheme, stratagem, tactic, trick.

manoeuvre verb guide, jockey, manipulate, move, negotiate, position, steer.

manpower noun employees, hands, human resources, labour, personnel, staff, workers, workforce.

manse noun house, rectory, residence.

mansion noun castle, château, manor, manor house, palace.

manslaughter noun homicide, killing.

mantle noun cape, cloak, shawl.

manual adjective (a manual device) hand-operated; (manual work) blue-collar, hand, physical.

manual noun handbook, primer, reference book, textbook.

manufacture verb assemble, build, construct, fabricate, make, process, produce. □ **manufacture** noun assembly, building, construction, fabrication, making, production.

manure noun compost, dung, fertiliser, muck.

manuscript noun document, script.

many adjective a lot of (informal), copious, countless, dozens of (informal), heaps of (informal), innumerable, lots of (informal), myriad, numbers of, numerous, oodles of (informal), piles of (informal), plenty of, scores of, umpteen (informal).

map noun chart, diagram, plan, projection.

map verb chart, survey. □ **map out** arrange, devise, organise, plan, plot, prepare.

mar verb blemish, damage, deface, disfigure, flaw, ruin, scar, spoil, stain, tarnish.

marauder noun bandit, buccaneer, looter, pillager, pirate, plunderer, robber.

march verb file, parade, stride, tramp, troop, walk.

march noun demo (informal), demonstration, parade, procession.

margin noun **1** border, boundary, edge, frame, fringe. **2** difference, gap.

marginal adjective little, minimal, minor, negligible, slight.

marine adjective **1** oceanic, salt-water, sea. **2** maritime, nautical, naval, ocean-going, seafaring, seagoing.

mariner *noun* sailor, seafarer, seaman.

marital *adjective* conjugal, married, matrimonial, nuptial, wedded.

maritime *adjective* marine, nautical, naval, seafaring, seagoing, shipping.

mark *noun* **1** blemish, blotch, dot, impression, line, patch, scar, scratch, smear, smudge, spatter, speck, speckle, splash, splotch, spot, stain, streak, trace. **2** assessment, grade, rating, result, score. **3** badge, brand, emblem, hallmark, imprint, label, logo, seal, sign, stamp, symbol, token, trade mark. **4** bull's-eye, goal, objective, target.

mark *verb* **1** blemish, brand, deface, disfigure, label, mar, scar, score, scratch, scuff, smudge, spot, stain. **2** assess, correct, evaluate, grade, judge, rate, score. **3** heed, mind, note, pay attention to, take notice of.

marked *adjective* clear, definite, distinct, noticeable, obvious, pronounced, strong, unmistakable.

market *noun* bazaar, fair, mart, sale.

market *verb* see *SELL*.

marksman, markswoma *noun* gunman, sharpshoote shooter, shot, sniper.

maroon *verb* abandon, deser forsake, isolate, leave, stranc

marriage *noun* **1** matrimon wedlock. **2** marriag ceremony, wedding.

marry *verb* become husbar and wife, become man ar wife, get hitched (*informal*), t the knot (*informal*), wed.

marsh *noun* bog, fen, mir morass, quagmire, sloug swamp. □ **marshy** *adjecti* boggy, spongy, swamp waterlogged.

marshal *noun* controlle officer, official, organiser.

marshal *verb* **1** align, arrang array, assemble, collect, deplc dispose, gather, mobilis muster, organise. **2** conduc escort, lead, usher.

martial *adjective* **1** militar **2** belligerent, combativ fighting, militant, pugnaciou warlike.

martyr *noun* sufferer, victim

martyr *verb* kill, put to deat torment, torture.

marvel *noun* miracle, wonde

marvel *verb* (*marvel* admire, be amazed by, astonished by, be staggered I be surprised by, wonder at.

marvellous *adjective* amazing, astonishing, astounding, breathtaking, brilliant (*informal*), cool (*informal*), excellent, extraordinary, fabulous (*informal*), fantastic (*informal*), fine, first-rate, glorious, grand, great, magnificent, miraculous, outstanding, phenomenal, prodigious, remarkable, sensational, spectacular, splendid, staggering, stunning (*informal*), stupendous, superb, terrific (*informal*), tremendous (*informal*), wonderful.

mascot *noun* charm, emblem, symbol, talisman.

masculine *adjective* macho, male, manly, virile; (*of a woman*) butch (*slang*), mannish.

mash *verb* crush, pound, pulp, purée, squash.

mask *noun* covering, cover-up, disguise, goggles, shield, visor.

mask *verb* camouflage, conceal, cover up, disguise, hide, obscure, screen.

mass *noun* **1** congregation, crowd, flock, gathering, herd, horde, mob, mob, multitude, sea, swarm, throng. **2** blob, block, body, bundle, chunk, collection, heap, hunk, lump, mound, mountain, pile, quantity, stack.

mass *verb* assemble, collect, congregate, flock, gather, herd, muster, rally.

Mass *noun* Communion, Eucharist, Holy Communion, Lord's Supper.

massacre *noun* bloodbath, carnage, extermination, killing, murder, pogrom, slaughter, slaying. □ **massacre** *verb* butcher, execute, exterminate, kill, murder, slaughter, slay.

massage *noun* kneading, manipulation, rubbing.

massive *adjective* colossal, enormous, extensive, giant, gigantic, heavy, hefty, huge, hulking, immense, large, mammoth, monumental, solid, substantial, vast.

mast *noun* pole, post, spar.

master *noun* **1** boss (*informal*), captain, chief, employer, governor (*slang*), head, leader, lord, overseer, owner, ruler, skipper. **2** schoolmaster, teacher. **3** ace, expert, genius, maestro, past master, professional, virtuoso, wizard. **4** original.

master *verb* **1** get the hang of (*informal*), get the knack of, grasp, learn, understand. **2** conquer, control, overcome, subdue, tame, vanquish.

masterful adjective author-itative, bossy, commanding, controlling, dictatorial, dom-ineering, forceful, imperious, magisterial, overbearing, powerful.

masterly adjective accom-plished, adept, brilliant, consummate, deft, excellent, expert, skilful, virtuoso.

mastermind noun 1 ace, brain (informal), expert, genius, master, wizard. 2 architect, creator, designer, engineer, originator, planner.

mastermind verb conceive, devise, direct, engineer, lead, orchestrate, organise, plan.

masterpiece noun chef-d'œuvre, classic, treasure.

mastery noun 1 authority, control, domination, domin-ion, power, rule, supremacy, sway, the upper hand. 2 ability, command, competence, exper-tise, grasp, proficiency, skill, understanding.

mat noun carpet, doormat, matting, rug.

matador noun bullfighter, toreador.

match noun 1 bout, com-petition, contest, game, rubber, tournament. 2 equal, equivalent, peer, rival.

match verb 1 agree with, coincide with, coordinate with, correspond with, equal, fit, go with, harmonise with, suit, team with, tone with. 2 connect, couple, fit, join, link, pair, put together, unite.

mate noun buddy (informal), chum (informal), cobber (Australian informal), com-panion, comrade, crony, friend, pal (informal).

mate verb breed, copulate, couple, pair up.

material noun 1 constituent, element, ingredient, matter, stuff, substance. 2 cloth, fabric, textile.

materialise verb 1 appear, emerge, show up (informal), turn up. 2 come to pass, eventuate, happen, occur, take place.

materialistic adjective acqui-sitive, greedy, mercenary, worldly.

maternity noun 1 mother-hood, motherliness. 2 see BIRTH.

mateship noun camaraderie, comradeship, friendship.

matey adjective chummy (informal), familiar, friendly, pally (informal), sociable.

matrimony noun marriage, wedlock.

matt adjective dull, flat.

matted adjective knotted, knotty, tangled, unkempt.

matter noun **1** material, stuff, substance, thing. **2** affair, business, concern, issue, question, situation, subject, topic.

matter verb be important, count, signify.

matter-of-fact adjective down-to-earth, factual, unemotional.

mature adjective **1** adult, developed, fully-fledged, grown, grown-up. **2** aged, mellow, ripe, ripened. □ **maturity** noun adulthood, coming of age, majority, manhood, womanhood.

mature verb age, develop, grow up, mellow, ripen.

maudlin adjective mawkish, sentimental, soppy (*informal*), tearful, weepy (*informal*).

maul verb claw, lacerate, mutilate, savage, tear to pieces.

maverick noun dissenter, dissident, eccentric, individualist, law unto yourself, nonconformist, rebel.

maxim noun adage, aphorism, axiom, motto, principle, proverb, rule, saying, slogan.

maximise verb boost, build up, enhance, improve, increase.

maximum noun ceiling, peak, top, upper limit. □ **maximum** adjective extreme, full, greatest, highest, most, top, utmost.

maybe adverb perchance (*old use*), perhaps, possibly.

mayhem noun bedlam, chaos, commotion, confusion, disorder, havoc, pandemonium, tumult, uproar, violence.

maze noun labyrinth, network, warren.

meadow noun field, grassland, lea (*poetical*), paddock, pasture.

meagre adjective mean, measly (*informal*), mingy (*informal*), paltry, scanty, skimpy, small, stingy.

meal noun banquet, breakfast, brunch, dinner, feast, lunch, luncheon, repast (*formal*), spread, supper, tea.

mean verb **1** communicate, connote, convey, denote, express, imply, indicate, say, signify, stand for, symbolise. **2** aim, intend, plan.

mean adjective **1** miserly, niggardly, parsimonious, penny-pinching, stingy, tight-fisted. **2** base, beastly (*informal*), contemptible, cruel, despicable, hard-hearted, lousy (*informal*), low-down, malicious, nasty, spiteful, unkind. **3** humble, inferior, lowly, miserable, poor, shabby, sordid, squalid.

meander verb **1** loop, snake, twist, wind, zigzag. **2** ramble, roam, rove, wander.

meaning noun drift, gist, implication, import, importance, point, purpose, purport, sense, significance, value. □ **meaningful** adjective deep, eloquent, expressive, pointed, significant, telling. □ **meaningless** adjective absurd, aimless, empty, hollow, incomprehensible, nonsensical, pointless, senseless, unintelligible, useless, worthless.

means noun agency, manner, medium, method, mode, process, way.

means plural noun assets, funds, income, money, property, resources, riches, wealth.

meanwhile adverb **1** for now, in the interim, in the interval, in the meantime, in the meanwhile, meantime. **2** at the same time, concurrently, simultaneously.

measly adjective meagre, mean, mingy (informal), miserable, paltry, stingy.

measure verb assess, calculate, compute, determine, estimate, gauge, quantify, weigh; (measure depth) fathom, plumb, sound. □ **measure out** apportion, deal out, dispense, distribute, dole out, mete out, ration out. □ **measure up to** come up to, fulfil, meet, pass, reach, satisfy. □ **measurable** adjective appreciable, calculable, considerable, determinable, discernible, mensurable, noticeable, perceptible, quantifiable, significant. □ **measurement** noun area, breadth, capacity, depth, dimension, extent, height, length, magnitude, mass, size, volume, weight, width.

measure noun **1** standard, unit. **2** callipers, gauge, rule, ruler, scale, tape-measure, yardstick. **3** amount, capacity, dimensions, extent, magnitude, mass, measurement, proportions, quantity, size. **4** action, course, law, means, method, procedure, process, step, way.

meat noun flesh. □ **meateating** adjective carnivorous, flesh-eating.

mechanic noun repairman, technician, workman.

mechanical adjective **1** automated, mechanised. **2** automatic, instinctive, involuntary, reflex, unconscious, unthinking.

mechanism noun action, machinery, movement, workings, works.

medal noun award, decoration, gong (slang), medallion, prize.

medallist noun champion, prizewinner, winner.

meddle verb butt in, interfere, intervene, intrude, poke your nose in, pry. □ **meddler** noun busybody, interloper, intruder, Nosy Parker, stickybeak (Australian informal).

median adjective mid, middle.

mediate verb arbitrate, conciliate, intercede, intervene, liaise, negotiate. □ **mediator** noun arbitrator, broker, conciliator, go-between, intercessor, intermediary, middleman, negotiator, referee, umpire.

medication noun drug, medicament, medicine.

medicine noun capsule, cure, drug, elixir, linctus, medicament, medication, pill, remedy, tablet, treatment. □ **medicinal** adjective curative, healing, restorative, therapeutic.

mediocre adjective average, fair, indifferent, middling, ordinary, passable, run-of-the-mill, second-rate, so-so (informal).

meditate verb cogitate, contemplate, deliberate, muse, ponder, reflect, ruminate, think.

medium adjective average, intermediate, middle, middling, moderate.

medium noun **1** average, compromise, mean, middle ground. **2** agency, channel, instrument, means, vehicle.

medley noun anthology, assortment, collection, miscellany, mixture, pot-pourri.

meek adjective compliant, deferential, docile, gentle, humble, mild, obedient, submissive, tame, unassuming.

meet verb **1** assemble, come together, congregate, convene, gather, get together, join up, muster, rally, rendezvous; (meet by chance) bump into (informal), come across, encounter, run into, see. **2** be introduced to, make the acquaintance of. **3** abut, butt, connect, converge, cross, intersect, join, touch. **4** cover, pay, take care of. **5** come up against, confront, deal with, encounter, experience, face, run into.

meeting noun **1** appointment, date (informal), encounter, engagement, get-together (informal), rendezvous. **2** assembly, conference, congregation, congress, convention, council, forum, gathering, rally, summit, synod.

melancholy *adjective* dejected, depressed, despondent, dismal, doleful, down, down in the dumps (*informal*), forlorn, gloomy, glum, heavy-hearted, in the doldrums, in low spirits, miserable, sad.

melancholy *noun* blues, dejection, depression, despondency, gloom, misery, sadness, woe.

mellow *adjective* **1** (*mellow fruit*) juicy, luscious, mature, ripe, sweet; (*mellow sounds*) dulcet, rich, smooth, velvety. **2** affable, amiable, easygoing, genial, gentle, kindly, pleasant, sympathetic.

mellow *verb* develop, mature, soften.

melodious *adjective* dulcet, euphonious, harmonious, lyrical, musical, sweet, tuneful.

melodramatic *adjective* exaggerated, histrionic, overdone, sensational, theatrical.

melody *noun* air, strain, theme, tune.

melt *verb* **1** dissolve, liquefy, thaw. **2** (*melt away*) disappear, disperse, evaporate, fade away, vanish. **3** disarm, mollify, soften, touch.

member *noun* **1** associate, fellow, subscriber. **2** component, constituent, element.

membrane *noun* film, integument, lining, sheet, skin, tissue.

memento *noun* keepsake, remembrance, reminder, souvenir.

memoirs *plural noun* autobiography, diary, life story, memories, recollections, reminiscences.

memorable *adjective* historic, impressive, momentous, noteworthy, outstanding, remarkable, significant, striking, unforgettable.

memorial *noun* see MONUMENT.

memorise *verb* commit to memory, learn by heart, learn by rote, remember.

memory *noun* **1** recall, retention. **2** recollection, remembrance, reminder, reminiscence, souvenir.

menace *noun* **1** danger, hazard, risk, threat. **2** nuisance, pest.

menace *verb* bully, frighten, intimidate, terrify, terrorise, threaten. □ **menacing** *adjective* baleful, black, forbidding, hostile, intimidating, malignant, ominous, sinister, threatening.

mend *verb* **1** fix, patch up, put right, repair, restore. **2** ameliorate, correct, improve, rectify, reform.

menial *adjective* degrading, demeaning, humble, lowly, servile, unskilled.

menial *noun* dogsbody (*informal*), domestic, drudge, lackey, minion, servant, underling.

mental *adjective* **1** cerebral, intellectual, psychological. **2** see MAD.

mentality *noun* **1** ability, brains, intellect, intelligence, IQ. **2** attitude, disposition, mindset, outlook.

mention *verb* allude to, bring up, comment on, hint at, refer to, speak of, touch on.

mention *noun* allusion, hint, indication, reference, remark.

mentor *noun* adviser, counsellor, guide, guru, instructor, supervisor, teacher, tutor.

mercenary *adjective* avaricious, grasping, greedy, money-grubbing.

merchandise *noun* commodities, goods, produce, stock, wares.

merchant *noun* dealer, distributor, exporter, importer, salesman, supplier, trader, wholesaler.

merciful *adjective* compassionate, forbearing, forgiving, gentle, humane, kind, lenient, mild, sympathetic, tenderhearted, tolerant.

merciless *adjective* callous, cruel, hard-hearted, harsh, heartless, implacable, inhuman, inhumane, pitiless, relentless, remorseless, ruthless, severe, strict, unforgiving, unsympathetic.

mercy *noun* clemency, compassion, forbearance, forgiveness, grace, kindness, lenience, pity, sympathy, tolerance.

merge *verb* amalgamate, blend, combine, consolidate, converge, join, meet, unite.

merit *noun* **1** excellence, goodness, quality, value, worth. **2** advantage, good point, strength, virtue. □ **meritorious** *adjective* commendable, creditable, excellent, good, honourable, laudable, praiseworthy.

merit *verb* be entitled to, be worthy of, deserve, justify, warrant.

merry *adjective* cheerful, convivial, gleeful, happy, high-spirited, jolly, jovial, joyous, light-hearted, lively. □ **merriment** *noun* see MIRTH.

merry-go-round *noun* carousel, roundabout, whirligig.

mesh *noun* lacework, net, netting, network.

mesmerise *verb* bewitch, captivate, enthral, fascinate, hypnotise, magnetise.

mess *noun* **1** chaos, clutter, confusion, disarray, jumble, litter, muddle, shambles, shemozzle (*informal*), untidiness. **2** difficulty, fix (*informal*), hot water (*informal*), pickle (*informal*), plight, predicament, spot (*informal*), trouble. **3** canteen, dining room, refectory. □ **make a mess of** botch, bungle, make a hash of (*informal*), mess up, muddle, muff (*informal*), ruin, spoil.

mess *verb* **1** clutter up, jumble, litter, muck up, untidy. **2** botch, bungle, muck up (*informal*), ruin, spoil. □ **mess with** fiddle with, interfere with, meddle with, play with, tamper with, tinker with.

message *noun* **1** announcement, bulletin, communication, communiqué, dispatch, letter, memo (*informal*), missive, news, note, notice, report, statement, tidings, word. **2** meaning, moral, point, teaching, theme. □ **get the message** catch on, comprehend, cotton on (*informal*), get it (*informal*), grasp it, latch on (*informal*), twig (*informal*), understand.

messenger *noun* ambassador courier, envoy, go-between herald.

messy *adjective* **1** bedraggled chaotic, cluttered, dirty dishevelled, disorderly, jumbled, littered, mucked-up muddled, sloppy, slovenly topsy-turvy, unkempt, untidy **2** awkward, complicated difficult, embarrassing, problematical, sticky (*informal* ticklish, tricky.

metallic *adjective* (*metallic paint*) gleaming, glistening lustrous, shiny; (*metallic sounds*) brassy, clanging clanking, clinking, jangling ringing, tinny.

metamorphosis *noun* change conversion, mutation, transfiguration, transformation transmutation.

metaphorical *adjective* figurative, non-literal.

mete *verb* □ **mete out** allocate allot, apportion, deal ou dispense, distribute, dole ou measure out.

meteoric *adjective* brilliant fast, overnight, quick, rapid speedy, sudden, swift.

meter *noun* clock, dial, gauge indicator.

method *noun* **1** approach knack, manner, mean procedure, process, routine system, technique, way. **2** design, order, orderliness, pattern, plan, structure, system.

methodical *adjective* careful, disciplined, logical, meticulous, orderly, organised, structured, systematic, tidy.

meticulous *adjective* accurate, careful, exact, fastidious, fussy, methodical, orderly, painstaking, precise, punctilious, scrupulous, thorough.

metropolis *noun* capital, city.

mettle *noun* boldness, bravery, courage, gameness, grit, guts (*informal*), intrepidity, nerve, pluck, spirit.

microbe *noun* bacterium, bug (*informal*), germ, microorganism, virus.

microphone *noun* bug (*informal*), mike (*informal*).

microscopic *adjective* little, minuscule, minute, small, tiny.

middle *noun* **1** centre, core, heart, hub, nucleus. **2** midriff, stomach, waist.

middle *adjective* **1** central, halfway, medial, median, mid, midway. **2** average, intermediate, medium, moderate.

middleman *noun* agent, broker, distributor, go-between, intermediary.

middling *adjective* average, fair, indifferent, mediocre, medium, ordinary, so-so (*informal*), unremarkable.

midget *noun* dwarf, lilliputian, pygmy. □ **midget** *adjective* diminutive, little, miniature, minuscule, minute, small, tiny.

midst *noun* □ **in the midst of 1** amid, amidst, among, amongst, surrounded by. **2** during, halfway through, in the middle of.

mien *noun* air, appearance, bearing, demeanour, expression, look, manner.

might *noun* energy, force, power, strength.

mighty *adjective* indomitable, invincible, powerful, robust, strong, sturdy; see also *HUGE*.

migrant *noun* emigrant, immigrant, newcomer.

migrate *verb* emigrate, go overseas, immigrate, move, relocate, travel.

mild *adjective* **1** calm, docile, easygoing, gentle, kind, placid, serene, unassuming. **2** balmy, moderate, temperate, warm. **3** bland, delicate, faint, subtle.

mildew *noun* mould.

milestone *noun* **1** distance marker, milepost. **2** landmark, red-letter day, turning point, watershed.

militant *adjective* aggressive, assertive, belligerent, defiant, pugnacious, pushy (*informal*), uncompromising.

military *adjective* armed, army, defence, service.

milky *adjective* cloudy, opaque, white, whitish.

mill *noun* grinder.

mill *verb* **1** crush, granulate, grind, pulverise. **2** congregate, crowd, hover, mass, swarm, throng.

millstone *noun* burden, load, responsibility, trouble, worry.

mimic *verb* ape, caricature, copy, imitate, impersonate, parody, send up (*informal*), take off. □ **mimicry** *noun* burlesque, caricature, imitation, impersonation, parody, send-up (*informal*), spoof (*informal*), take-off.

mince *verb* chop, cut, grind, hash.

mind *noun* **1** brain, common sense, head, imagination, intellect, intelligence, mentality, reasoning, sense, understanding, wits. **2** attitude, intention, judgement, opinion, outlook, point of view, position, thoughts, view. □ **mind-boggling** *adjective* amazing, astonishing, astounding, incredible, staggering, startling, unbelievable.

□ **bring to mind** recall, recollect, remember.

mind *verb* **1** babysit, keep an eye on, look after, take care of, tend. **2** be careful of, beware of, look out for, take care with, watch out for. **3** be bothered by, dislike, object to, resent, take exception to. □ **minder** *noun* babysitter, bodyguard, carer, child-minder.

mindful *adjective* alert, attentive, aware, careful, conscious, considerate, heedful, thoughtful, wary, watchful.

mindless *adjective* boring, mechanical, routine, tedious.

mine *noun* colliery, excavation, pit, quarry, workings.

mine *verb* dig for, excavate, extract.

mingle *verb* **1** blend, combine, intermingle, merge, mix. **2** circulate, mix, socialise.

mingy *adjective* meagre, mean, measly (*informal*), niggardly, paltry, stingy.

miniature *adjective* diminutive, dwarf, little, microscopic, minuscule, minute, pocket, size, small, small-scale, tiny.

minimise *verb* cut, decrease, diminish, keep down, lessen, reduce.

minimum *noun* least, lowest. □ **minimal** *adjective* imperceptible, least, littlest, lowest.

marginal, minuscule, minutest, negligible, slightest, smallest, subtle, token.

minister noun archbishop, archdeacon, bishop, chaplain, clergyman, clergywoman, cleric, curate, deacon, dean, evangelist, father, padre, parson, pastor, preacher, priest, rector, vicar.

minister verb (minister to) attend to, care for, cater to, help, tend.

minor adjective inconsequential, insignificant, lesser, petty, slight, small, subordinate, trivial, unimportant.

minor noun adolescent, child, juvenile, teenager, youngster, youth.

minstrel noun bard, entertainer, musician, performer, singer, troubadour.

mint verb cast, coin, make, produce, strike.

minute noun flash, instant, jiffy (informal), moment, tick (informal), trice. □ **minutes** plural noun account, notes, proceedings, record, summary.

minute adjective **1** little, microscopic, minuscule, small, tiny. **2** close, detailed, exhaustive, meticulous, thorough.

miracle noun marvel, wonder. □ **miraculous** adjective amazing, astonishing, astounding, extraordinary, incredible, marvellous, mysterious, phenomenal, remarkable, supernatural, unbelievable, wonderful.

mirage noun hallucination, illusion, phantasm, vision.

mirror noun glass, looking-glass.

mirror verb reflect.

mirth noun amusement, cheerfulness, festivity, fun, gaiety, glee, happiness, hilarity, jollity, joviality, laughter, merriment, merrymaking, rejoicing, revelry.

misappropriate verb embezzle, misuse, steal, take.

misbehaviour noun bad manners, delinquency, disobedience, misconduct, naughtiness, playing up (informal), rebelliousness, unruliness.

miscalculate verb misjudge, overestimate, overvalue, underestimate, undervalue.

miscarriage noun **1** spontaneous abortion. **2** breakdown, collapse, error, failure.

miscellaneous adjective assorted, different, diverse, mixed, motley, varied, various.

mischief noun **1** high jinks, misbehaviour, misconduct, naughtiness, playfulness, playing up (*informal*), pranks, shenanigans (*informal*). **2** damage, harm, hurt, injury, trouble. □ **mischievous** *adjective* devilish, impish, naughty, playful, roguish.

misconduct *noun* **1** misbehaviour, naughtiness, playing up (*informal*), unruliness. **2** impropriety, malpractice, mishandling, mismanagement.

misconstrue *verb* misapprehend, misinterpret, misread, misunderstand.

miscreant *noun* baddy (*informal*), criminal, evildoer, rascal, scoundrel, villain, wretch, wrongdoer.

misdemeanour *noun* crime, misdeed, offence, sin, transgression, wrongdoing.

miser *noun* cheapskate (*informal*), hoarder, Scrooge, skinflint, tightwad (*informal*). □ **miserly** *adjective* closefisted, mean, mingy (*informal*), niggardly, parsimonious, penny-pinching, stingy, tightfisted.

miserable *adjective* **1** crestfallen, dejected, depressed, desolate, despondent, disconsolate, doleful, downcast, down-hearted, forlorn, gloomy, glum, heavy-hearted, melancholy, sad, sorrowful, unhappy, woebegone, wretched. **2** abysmal (*informal*), appalling (*informal*), atrocious (*informal*), depressing, dismal, dreadful (*informal*), dreary, inclement, lousy (*informal*), terrible (*informal*), unpleasant.

misery *noun* **1** blues, depression, despair, discomfort, distress, gloom, grief, melancholy, sadness, sorrow, suffering, torment, unhappiness, woe, wretchedness. **2** adversity, affliction, deprivation, hardship, misfortune, suffering, trouble. **3** complainer, grouch (*informal*), grumbler, malcontent, moaner, wet blanket, whinger (*informal*).

misfit *noun* fish out of water, maverick, nonconformist, square peg in a round hole.

misfortune *noun* **1** adversity, bad luck, mischance. **2** accident, affliction, blow, calamity, catastrophe, disaster, misadventure, mishap, reverse, setback, trial, tribulation, trouble.

misgiving *noun* anxiety, apprehension, doubt, fear, hesitation, qualm, question, reservation, second thoughts, uncertainty, worry.

misguided *adjective* foolish, misdirected, misinformed, misled, mistaken, unwise.

mishap *noun* see MISFORTUNE.

misinterpret *verb* misapprehend, misconstrue, misread, misunderstand.

misjudge *verb* exaggerate, get wrong, miscalculate, overestimate, underestimate.

mislay *verb* lose, misplace.

mislead *verb* bluff, con (*informal*), deceive, delude, dupe, fool, hoax, hoodwink, kid (*informal*), lead astray, lie, misguide, misinform, take for a ride (*informal*), take in, trick. □ **misleading** *adjective* ambiguous, confusing, deceptive, equivocal.

mismanagement *noun* bungling, maladministration, mishandling.

misplace *verb* lose, mislay.

misrepresent *verb* distort, falsify, misquote, misreport, twist.

miss *verb* **1** absent yourself from, be absent from, forgo, give up, skip. **2** let go, let pass, let slip, lose, pass up. **3** crave for, long for, pine for, want, yearn for. **4** avoid, bypass, dodge, steer clear of. □ **miss out** forget, leave out, omit, overlook, pass over, skip.

misshapen *adjective* contorted, crooked, deformed, distorted, malformed, twisted, warped.

missile *noun* projectile; (*kinds of missile*) arrow, ballistic missile, bomb, boomerang, bullet, dart, grenade, guided missile, harpoon, javelin, rocket, shell, spear, torpedo.

missing *adjective* **1** gone, lost, mislaid, misplaced, removed. **2** absent, disappeared, gone, lost.

mission *noun* assignment, campaign, exercise, expedition, operation, quest, undertaking; (*a mission in life*) calling, purpose, vocation.

missionary *noun* apostle, evangelist, preacher.

mist *noun* cloud, fog, haze, smog, steam, vapour.

mistake *noun* blooper (*informal*), blue (*Australian informal*), blunder, booboo (*slang*), clanger (*informal*), error, faux pas, gaffe, howler (*informal*), miscalculation, misjudgement, misprint, mix-up, oversight, slip, slip-up (*informal*), typo (*informal*).

mistake *verb* **1** confuse, get wrong, misapprehend, misconstrue, misinterpret, misunderstand. **2** confuse with, mix up with, take for.

mistreat verb abuse, harm, hurt, ill-treat, maltreat, manhandle, molest, torment.

mistress noun **1** keeper, owner. **2** schoolmistress, teacher. **3** girlfriend, lover.

mistrust verb distrust, doubt, have misgivings about, question, suspect. □ **mistrust** noun distrust, scepticism, suspicion, wariness.

misty adjective foggy, hazy.

misunderstand verb get wrong, misapprehend, misconstrue, misinterpret, misjudge, misread, mistake. □ **misunderstanding** noun confusion, misapprehension, misconception, misinterpretation, misjudgement, misreading, mistake, mix-up.

misuse noun abuse, misappropriation, squandering, waste.

mitigate verb alleviate, appease, assuage, diminish, ease, lessen, lighten, moderate, mollify, palliate, reduce, relieve, soften, soothe, subdue, weaken.

mix verb **1** blend, combine, incorporate, integrate, join, merge, mingle, unite. **2** be sociable, fraternise, mingle, socialise. □ **mix up** confuse, jumble up, muddle up, rearrange, shuffle.

mix noun see MIXTURE.

mixed adjective (a mixed group) assorted, diverse, miscellaneous, motley, varied; (a mixed breed) cross-bred, hybrid, mongrel.

mixture noun alloy, amalgam, assortment, blend, collection, combination, compound, concoction, cross, hash, hotchpotch, hybrid, jumble, medley, mix, patchwork, potpourri, rag-bag, variety.

moan noun **1** groan, wail, whimper, whine. **2** beef (slang), complaint, grievance, gripe (informal), grizzle (informal), grumble, whine, whinge (informal). □ **moan** verb **1** groan, wail, whimper, whine. **2** beef (slang), complain, gripe (informal), grizzle (informal), grumble, whine, whinge (informal).

mob noun **1** bunch, crowd, crush, gathering, herd, horde, lot, mass, multitude, pack, rabble, throng. **2** flock, group, herd.

mob verb besiege, crowd round, gather round, surround, swarm round.

mobile adjective movable, portable, transportable, travelling.

mobilise verb assemble, gather, marshal, muster, organise, rally.

mock verb **1** chiack (*Australian informal*), deride, jeer at, make fun of, pay out (*informal*), poke fun at, ridicule, scoff at, scorn, sling off at (*Australian informal*), sneer at, take the mickey out of (*informal*), taunt. **2** ape, caricature, copy, imitate, impersonate, mimic, parody, send up (*informal*), take off.

mock adjective fake, imitation, pretend (*informal*), pretended, sham, simulated.

mockery noun **1** derision, disdain, jeering, ridicule, scorn. **2** farce, joke, pretence, travesty.

mode noun **1** approach, fashion, form, manner, means, method, practice, procedure, system, technique, way. **2** custom, fashion, style, trend, vogue.

model noun **1** archetype, copy, dummy, miniature, mock-up, prototype, replica, representation. **2** design, style, type, version. **3** mannequin. **4** archetype, epitome, exemplar, ideal, paragon.

model adjective excellent, exemplary, ideal, perfect.

model verb **1** cast, form, make, mould, sculpt (*informal*), shape. **2** (*model on*) base on, copy on, follow.

moderate adjective average, fair, intermediate, medium, middling, modest, reasonable; (*of climate*) mild, temperate. □ **moderately** adverb fairly, pretty, quite, rather, reasonably, slightly, somewhat.

moderate verb abate, calm down, check, curb, die down, ease, quieten down, restrain, soften, subdue, subside, tame, temper, tone down.

modern adjective contemporary, current, fashionable, innovative, new, newfangled (*derogatory*), present, progressive, recent, trendy (*informal*), up to date, with it (*informal*).

modernise verb rejuvenate, renovate, update.

modest adjective **1** humble, quiet, unassertive, unassuming. **2** moderate, slight, small. **3** humble, lowly, ordinary, simple, unpretentious. **4** bashful, coy, self-conscious, shy.

modify verb **1** adapt, adjust, alter, change, refine, revise, transform, vary. **2** limit, qualify, restrict.

modulate verb adjust, alter, change, moderate, regulate, temper, tone down, vary.

module noun component, part, piece, unit.

moist adjective clammy, damp, dank, dewy, humid, muggy, steamy, wet.

moisten verb damp, dampen, irrigate, soak, spray, water, wet.

moisture noun condensation, damp, dampness, dew, humidity, liquid, steam, vapour, water, wetness.

molest verb abuse, annoy, bother, harass, ill-treat, maltreat, mistreat, persecute, pester, tease, torment.

mollify verb appease, calm, pacify, placate, quiet, soothe, subdue.

molten adjective liquefied, liquid, melted.

moment noun 1 flash, instant, jiffy (informal), minute, second, tick (informal), trice, two shakes (informal). 2 instant, juncture, point, stage. 3 consequence, gravity, import, importance, significance.

momentary adjective brief, ephemeral, fleeting, passing, short, short-lived, temporary, transient.

momentous adjective crucial, fateful, grave, historic, important, significant, weighty.

momentum noun force, impetus, strength.

monarch noun emperor, empress, head, king, queen, ruler, sovereign.

monarchy noun empire, kingdom, realm. □ **monarchist** noun royalist.

monastery noun abbey, cloister, friary, lamasery (Buddhism), priory, religious house. □ **monastic** adjective ascetic, austere, cloistered, reclusive, secluded, solitary, spartan.

money noun 1 banknotes, cash, coins, currency, dosh (slang), dough (slang), lucre (derogatory), notes, paper money, ready money. 2 assets, capital, finance, funds, means, resources, riches, wealth.

mongrel noun bitser (Australian informal), cross-breed, hybrid.

monitor noun 1 display, terminal, screen, VDU, visual display unit. 2 prefect.

monitor verb check, keep an eye on, keep track of, observe, record, watch.

monk noun abbot, brother, friar, lama (Buddhism), prior, religious.

monkey noun 1 simian, devil, imp, rascal, rogue, scallywag, scamp.

monolithic *adjective* colossal, enormous, gigantic, huge, large, massive, monumental.

monologue *noun* address, lecture, oration, sermon, soliloquy, speech.

monopolise *verb* dominate, preoccupy, take over.

monotonous *adjective* (*monotonous work*) boring, dreary, dull, humdrum, mechanical, repetitive, routine, soporific, tedious, unvarying; (*a monotonous voice*) droning, expressionless, flat, singsong, unexpressive.

monster *noun* beast, bogyman, brute, bunyip (*Australian*), demon, devil, dragon, fiend, giant, ogre.

monstrosity *noun* eyesore, horror, monster.

monstrous *adjective* **1** abnormal, freakish, grotesque, misshapen, odd, ugly, unnatural, weird. **2** colossal, enormous, gigantic, huge, immense, massive. **3** abhorrent, appalling, atrocious, brutal, cruel, despicable, detestable, fiendish, ghastly, heinous, hideous, horrible, horrid, outrageous, repulsive, savage, shocking, vile, wicked.

monument *noun* cairn, cenotaph, gravestone, headstone, mausoleum, memorial, obelisk, plaque, shrine, statue, tombstone.

monumental *adjective* **1** colossal, enormous, great, huge, immense, large, massive, monstrous, stupendous, terrific (*informal*), tremendous. **2** classic, enduring, great, impressive, lasting, major.

mood *noun* attitude, disposition, feeling, frame of mind, humour, spirits, state of mind, temper.

moody *adjective* **1** blue, depressed, dismal, gloomy, glum, irritable, melancholy, morose, peevish, sulky, sullen, testy, tetchy, unhappy. **2** changeable, erratic, inconsistent, mercurial, temperamental, unpredictable, volatile.

moor *noun* fell, heath.

moor *verb* anchor, berth, dock, secure, tie up.

moorings *plural noun* anchorage, berth.

moot *adjective* arguable, controversial, debatable, disputable, undecided, unresolved.

mop *verb* clean, sponge, wash, wipe.

mope *verb* brood, fret, languish, mooch (*informal*), moon, pine.

moral *adjective* **1** ethical. **2** above board, blameless, decent, ethical, good, honourable, principled, proper, right, righteous, upright, virtuous. □ **morality** *noun* decency, ethics, fairness, goodness, honour, integrity, morals, principles, rectitude, scruples, standards, virtue.

moral *noun* lesson, message, principle, teaching.

morale *noun* confidence, self-confidence, spirit.

morbid *adjective* **1** ghoulish, grim, gruesome, macabre, sick, unwholesome. **2** diseased, pathological, unhealthy.

more *adjective* additional, extra, further, other, reserve, spare, supplementary.

moreover *adverb* also, besides, further, furthermore, in addition.

moron *noun* see IDIOT.

morose *adjective* bad-tempered, churlish, depressed, dismal, dour, gloomy, glum, lugubrious, moody, sour, sulky, sullen, surly, taciturn, unsociable.

morsel *noun* bit, bite, fragment, mouthful, nibble, piece, scrap, sliver, taste, titbit.

mortal *adjective* **1** earthly, ephemeral, human, transient, worldly. **2** deadly, fatal, lethal.

mortal *noun* human being, man, person, woman.

mortify *verb* abase, abash, chagrin, discomfit, embarrass, humble, humiliate, shame.

mortuary *noun* morgue.

most *noun* bulk, lion's share, majority. □ **make the most of** capitalise on, exploit, profit by, take advantage of.

most *adverb* exceedingly, extremely, highly, very.

mostly *adverb* chiefly, for the most part, generally, in general, largely, mainly, on the whole, predominantly, primarily, principally, usually.

motel *noun* hotel, inn, motor inn.

mother *noun* matriarch (*informal terms of address*) ma, mama, mamma, mammy, mom (*American*), mum, mummy.

mother *verb* care for, fuss over, look after, nurse, nurture, protect, raise, rear, tend.

motherly *adjective* caring, gentle, kind, loving, maternal, protective, tender.

motif *noun* decoration, design, feature, idea, leitmotif, pattern, subject, theme.

motion *noun* **1** locomotion, mobility, movement. **2** proposal, recommendation, suggestion.

motion verb beckon, gesticulate, gesture, indicate, nod, signal, wave.

motionless adjective at rest, immobile, inert, paralysed, static, stationary, still, stock-still, transfixed.

motivate verb actuate, drive, galvanise, induce, influence, inspire, prompt, provoke, stimulate. □ **motivation** noun ambition, drive, impetus, inspiration, stimulus.

motive noun grounds, motivation, purpose, reason.

motley adjective **1** harlequin, mottled, multicoloured, variegated. **2** assorted, disparate, diverse, heterogeneous, miscellaneous, mixed, varied.

motorcycle noun bike (informal), motor bike (informal). □ **motorcyclist** noun biker, bikie (Australian informal).

mottled adjective blotchy, dappled, flecked, marbled, motley, speckled, spotty, variegated.

motto noun adage, maxim, proverb, saying, slogan, watchword.

mould verb (mould a statue) cast, fashion, forge, form, model, sculpt, shape; (mould character) develop, form, influence, make, shape.

mould noun fungus, mildew. □ **mouldy** adjective bad, mildewed, musty, rotten, stale.

mound noun **1** cairn, heap, pile, pyramid, stack. **2** hill, hillock, hummock, knoll.

mount verb **1** ascend, clamber up, climb, go up. **2** climb on, get astride, get on, straddle. **3** escalate, grow, heighten, increase, rise. **4** fix, install, place, position, put.

mountain noun **1** alp, ben (Scottish), bluff, elevation, hill, mount, peak, pinnacle, range, tier (Tasmania & early South Australia). **2** heap (informal), load (informal), lot (informal), pile (informal), stack (informal), swag (Australian informal), ton (informal).

mourn verb grieve, lament, sorrow, weep.

mournful adjective dismal, doleful, funereal, gloomy, lugubrious, melancholy, sad, sombre, sorrowful.

mouth noun **1** gob (slang), jaws, lips, trap (slang). **2** entrance, opening, outlet, portal. □ **mouthful** noun bit, bite, gulp, morsel, nibble, sip, spoonful, sup, swallow, swig (informal).

movable adjective mobile, portable, transportable.

move *verb* **1** budge, relocate, remove, shift, swap, switch, transfer, transplant, transport, transpose. **2** advance, go, go on, make headway, proceed, progress. **3** affect, disturb, stir, touch, upset. **4** propose, put forward, recommend, suggest. □ **moving** *adjective* emotional, inspiring, poignant, rousing, stirring, touching.

move *noun* **1** gesture, motion, movement. **2** chance, go, opportunity, shot (*informal*), turn. **3** act, action, initiative, measure, step, tactic.

movement *noun* **1** action, activity, gesture, manoeuvre, motion, move, step, stroke. **2** faction, group, lobby, organisation, party; see also *CAMPAIGN*. **3** division, part, section. **4** evolution, progress, shift, swing, tendency, trend.

movie *noun* film, flick (*informal*), motion picture, moving picture, picture, video.

mow *verb* clip, cut, trim.

much *adjective* abundant, a lot of (*informal*), ample, copious, plentiful.

much *noun* a great deal, heaps (*informal*), loads (*informal*), lots (*informal*), plenty, stacks (*informal*), volumes.

much *adverb* **1** a great deal, a lot, considerably, decidedly, far,

greatly. **2** about, almost, approximately, nearly, virtually.

muck *noun* **1** droppings, dung, manure. **2** dirt, filth, mud.

muck *verb* □ **muck up 1** disorganise, jumble, mess up, muddle, turn upside down. **2** botch, bungle, mess up, ruin, spoil.

mud *noun* dirt, filth, mire, muck (*informal*), silt, slime, sludge. □ **muddy** *adjective* boggy, dirty, filthy, mucky, slimy, waterlogged; (*muddy liquid*) cloudy, impure, murky, turbid.

muddle *verb* **1** disorganise, jumble, mess up, mix up, muck up. **2** bewilder, confuse, disorient, fluster, mix up.

muddle *noun* chaos, clutter, confusion, disarray, jumble, mess, shambles.

muff *verb* blow (*slang*), botch, bungle, fluff (*slang*), mess up, spoil.

muffle *verb* **1** cover, wrap. **2** dampen, deaden, dull, mute, quieten, silence, soften, stifle, suppress.

mug *noun* **1** beaker, cup, tankard. **2** bunny (*Australian informal*), duffer, dupe, fool, muggins (*informal*), simpleton, soft touch, sucker (*informal*).

mug *verb* assault, attack, rob.

muggy *adjective* close, humid, oppressive, steamy, sticky, stuffy, sultry.

mulga *noun* backblocks (*Australian*), bush, country, donga (*Australian*), mallee (*Australian*), never-never, outback (*Australian*), scrub, sticks (*informal*).

mull *verb* (*mull over*) consider, contemplate, deliberate on, dwell on, meditate on, ponder, reflect on, review, think over.

multicoloured *adjective* harlequin, motley, particoloured, pied, variegated.

multicultural *adjective* cosmopolitan, multiracial, pluralist.

multinational *adjective* international, worldwide.

multiple *adjective* manifold, many, numerous, several, sundry, various.

multiply *verb* breed, increase, proliferate, propagate, reproduce.

multitude *noun* crowd, horde, host, lot, mass, mob, myriad, swag (*Australian informal*), swarm, throng.

mumble *verb & noun* babble, murmur, mutter.

mumbo-jumbo *noun* bunkum, double Dutch, gibberish, gobbledegook (*informal*), hocus-pocus, humbug, nonsense, poppycock (*informal*).

munch *verb* bite, chew, chomp, crunch, eat, gnaw.

mundane *adjective* commonplace, dreary, dull, everyday, ordinary, prosaic, routine, unexciting, uninspiring, uninteresting.

municipal *adjective* civic, community, council, district, local.

munificent *adjective* bountiful, generous, lavish, liberal, philanthropic.

munitions *plural noun* ammunition, arms, ordnance, weapons.

mural *noun* fresco, wall-painting.

murder *verb* assassinate, bump off (*slang*), do in (*slang*), exterminate, kill, massacre, slaughter, slay. □ **murderer** *noun* assassin, cutthroat, hit man (*slang*), killer, murderess.

murder *noun* assassination, extermination, genocide, homicide, killing, massacre, slaughter, slaying. □ **murderous** *adjective* bloodthirsty, brutal, deadly, homicidal, savage, vicious.

murky *adjective* **1** dark, dim, dull, dusky, foggy, gloomy, shadowy. **2** cloudy, dirty, impure, muddy, turbid.

murmur *verb* **1** babble, burble, drone, hum, rumble, sigh. **2**

mumble, mutter, whisper. □ **murmur** *noun* babble, burble, drone, hum, mumble, mutter, rumble, sigh, undercurrent, whisper.

muscle *noun* brawn, might, muscularity, power, strength. □ **muscular** *adjective* athletic, beefy, brawny, burly, hefty, nuggety (*Australian*), robust, sinewy, strapping, strong, sturdy, thickset.

muse *verb* contemplate, meditate, ponder, reflect, ruminate, speculate, think.

mush *noun* mash, pap, pulp, purée. □ **mushy** *adjective* mashed, puréed, sloppy, soft, squidgy (*informal*), squishy (*informal*).

mushroom *verb* burgeon, develop, expand, grow, pop up, proliferate, shoot up, spring up, sprout.

music *noun* **1** harmony, melody. **2** score, soundtrack.

musical *adjective* dulcet, euphonious, harmonious, lyrical, melodic, melodious, sweet, tuneful.

musician *noun* artist, busker, composer, entertainer, instrumentalist, maestro, muso (*slang*), performer, player, soloist, virtuoso, vocalist.

must *noun* essential, necessity, requirement.

muster *verb* assemble, collect, gather, marshal, mobilise, rally, round up, summon.

musty *adjective* damp, fusty, mildewed, mouldy, stale, stuffy.

mutation *noun* alteration, change, metamorphosis, transformation, variation.

mute *adjective* dumb, mum (*informal*), quiet, silent, speechless, tight-lipped, tongue-tied, uncommunicative.

mute *verb* damp, deaden, dull, muffle, quieten, soften, subdue, suppress, tone down. □ **muted** *adjective* pale, pastel, soft, subdued, toned down.

mutilate *verb* damage, destroy, disfigure, dismember, injure, maim, mangle.

mutiny *noun* insurrection, rebellion, revolt, riot, rising, uprising. □ **mutinous** *adjective* defiant, disobedient, insubordinate, rebellious.

mutiny *verb* rebel, revolt, riot, rise up.

mutter *verb* **1** mumble, murmur. **2** complain, gripe (*informal*), grumble, moan, whine, whinge (*informal*).

mutual *adjective* reciprocal, reciprocated, requited.

muzzle *noun* jaws, mouth, nose, snout.

muzzle verb bridle, control, gag, restrain.

myriad adjective countless, incalculable, infinite, innumerable, manifold, numerous, untold.

myriads plural noun army, horde, host, millions, multitude, scores, swarm, thousands, throng.

mysterious adjective arcane, baffling, bizarre, cryptic, curious, enigmatic, incomprehensible, inexplicable, inscrutable, mystical, mystifying, puzzling, strange, supernatural, uncanny, weird; see also SECRETIVE.

mystery noun conundrum, enigma, problem, puzzle, riddle, secret.

mystical adjective allegorical, arcane, cryptic, esoteric, hidden, mysterious, mystic, occult, spiritual, supernatural, symbolic, transcendental.

mystify verb baffle, bamboozle (informal), bewilder, confound, confuse, perplex, puzzle.

myth noun **1** fable, legend, narrative, story, tale. **2** delusion, fallacy, falsehood, fantasy, fiction, lie, untruth.

mythical adjective **1** fictitious, imaginary, invented, made-up, non-existent. **2** fabled, legendary, mythological.

Nn

nab verb apprehend, arrest, capture, catch, collar (informal), nail, nick (slang), seize.

nag verb badger, harass, harp on at, hassle (informal), henpeck, hound, keep on at, pester, scold. □ **nagging** adjective continuous, niggling, persistent.

nail verb attach, fasten, fix, hammer, join, pin, tack.

naïve adjective artless, credulous, green, gullible, inexperienced, ingenuous, innocent, simple, unaffected, unsophisticated, unsuspecting, unworldly.

naked adjective bare, in the altogether (informal), in your birthday suit (informal), nude, starkers (slang), unclothed, uncovered, undressed.

name noun **1** alias, appellation, assumed name, Christian name, false name, family name, first name, given name, label, last name, maiden name, nickname, nom de plume, penname, pet name, pseudonym, surname, term, title. **2** see REPUTATION.

name verb **1** baptise, call, christen, dub, entitle, nickname, title. **2** appoint, choose, designate, identify, mention, nominate, pick, select, specify.

nameless adjective anonymous, unidentified, unnamed.

nanny noun nurse, nursemaid.

nap noun catnap, doze, forty winks, kip (slang), lie-down, rest, shut-eye (informal), siesta, sleep, slumber, snooze.

napkin noun serviette.

nappy noun diaper (American), napkin.

narcotic adjective anaesthetic, dulling, hypnotic, numbing, sedative, soporific.

narrate verb describe, recount, relate, tell.

narrative noun account, chronicle, report, saga, story, tale, yarn.

narrow adjective **1** fine, slender, slim, thin. **2** close, confined, constricted, cramped, limited, restricted, strait (old use), tight.

narrow verb close up, diminish, lessen, reduce.

narrow-minded adjective biased, bigoted, blinkered, hidebound, illiberal, inflexible, intolerant, parochial, petty, prejudiced, rigid, small-minded.

nasty adjective **1** awful, bad, disagreeable, disgusting, dreadful (informal), foul, horrible (informal), lousy (informal), nauseating, objectionable, obnoxious, offensive, repulsive, revolting, rotten (informal), shocking (informal), sickening, unpalatable, unpleasant, vile, yucky (informal). **2** beastly, ill-tempered, malevolent, malicious, malignant, mean, spiteful, unkind, vicious, vindictive.

nation noun community, country, land, people, race, society, state. □ **national** adjective countrywide, general, nationwide. □ **national** noun citizen, native, resident, subject.

nationalism noun chauvinism, jingoism, patriotism.

native noun inhabitant, local, resident.

native adjective **1** aboriginal, indigenous, original. **2** inborn, inherent, innate, natural.

natural adjective **1** crude, raw, unprocessed, unrefined. normal, ordinary, predictable, reasonable, understandable. inborn, inherent, innate, instinctive, intuitive, native. artless, authentic, down-to-earth, genuine, spontaneous, unaffected, unpretentious, unsophisticated.

nature noun **1** character, characteristics, disposition, features, make-up, personality, properties, qualities, spirit, temperament. **2** kind, sort, type, variety.

naughty adjective bad, contrary, disobedient, impish, incorrigible, mischievous, perverse, undisciplined, unruly, wayward, wilful.

nausea noun biliousness, motion-sickness, queasiness, seasickness, sickness, travel-sickness. □ **nauseous** adjective bilious, carsick, queasy, seasick, sick. □ **nauseating** adjective disgusting, foul, objectionable, offensive, repulsive, revolting, sickening.

nautical adjective marine, maritime, naval, seafaring, seagoing.

navel noun belly button (informal), umbilicus.

navigate verb **1** cross, sail, traverse. **2** direct, guide, manoeuvre, pilot, sail, steer.

navy noun armada, fleet, flotilla.

near adverb & adjective (near in space) alongside, at close quarters, close, nigh, within close range, within cooee (Australian informal); (near in time) approaching, at hand, close, imminent, impending, in sight, looming.

near preposition adjacent to, around, close to, in the vicinity of.

near verb approach, draw near to.

nearby adjective adjacent, adjoining, close, neighbouring.

nearly adverb about, almost, approaching, approximately, around, close to, in the region of, in the vicinity of, nigh on, practically, roughly, virtually.

neat adjective **1** clean, dapper, natty (informal), orderly, organised, shipshape, smart, spruce, straight, tidy, trim. **2** clever, deft, dexterous, elegant, nifty (informal), simple, skilful. **3** pure, straight, unadulterated, undiluted.

nebulous adjective fuzzy, hazy, imprecise, indefinite, obscure, uncertain, unclear, vague, woolly.

necessary adjective **1** compulsory, essential, indispensable, needed, obligatory, required, requisite, vital. **2** inevitable, inexorable, unavoidable. □ **necessarily** adverb automatically, inevitably, naturally, of necessity, perforce.

necessitate verb call for, entail, involve, mean, require.

necessity noun 1 destitution, hardship, need, poverty, straits, want. 2 essential, must (informal), need, prerequisite, requirement, requisite.

necklace noun beads, chain, choker, necklet.

need verb 1 be short of, lack, require, want; see also DEPEND ON (at DEPEND). 2 be compelled to, be obliged to, be required to, have to, must.

need noun 1 demand, desire, necessity, requirement, want. 2 call, cause, necessity, reason. 3 crisis, destitution, hardship, poverty, want. □ **needless** adjective inessential, pointless, uncalled-for, unjustifiable, unnecessary, useless.

needle noun bodkin, crewel, sharp.

needlework noun embroidery, sewing.

needy adjective deprived, destitute, disadvantaged, down and out, hard up (informal), impecunious, impoverished, indigent, penniless, poor, poverty-stricken, skint (informal).

nefarious adjective abominable, atrocious, base, criminal, despicable, diabolical, evil, heinous, immoral, infamous, iniquitous, odious, vile, villainous, wicked.

negate verb 1 annul, cancel, invalidate, nullify, void. 2 contradict, deny, disprove, refute.

negative adjective 1 contradictory, dissenting, objecting, opposing, refusing, rejecting. 2 antagonistic, defeatist, gloomy, pessimistic, reluctant, uncooperative, unenthusiastic, unwilling.

neglect verb 1 disregard, forget, ignore, let go, let slide, let slip, overlook, shirk. 2 fail, forget, omit.

negligence noun carelessness, forgetfulness, inattention, laxity, slackness, thoughtlessness. □ **negligent** adjective careless, heedless, inattentive, neglectful, remiss, slack, thoughtless, unthinking.

negligible adjective imperceptible, insignificant, minuscule, minute, small, tiny, trifling, unimportant.

negotiate verb 1 bargain, discuss, haggle, talk. 2 agree on, arrange, settle, transact, work out. 3 clear, cross, get over. □ **negotiator** noun broker, facilitator, go-between, intermediary, mediator, peacemaker.

neighbourhood noun area, community, district, locality, quarter, spot, suburb.

neighbouring adjective adjacent, adjoining, close, contiguous, nearby.

neighbourly adjective affable, considerate, friendly, helpful, hospitable, kind, kindly, obliging, sociable, thoughtful.

nerve noun **1** bravery, coolness, courage, daring, fearlessness, grit, guts (informal), intrepidity, mettle, pluck, spunk (informal). **2** audacity, boldness, cheek, effrontery, gall (slang), hide (informal), impertinence, impudence, insolence, presumption, temerity.

nerve-racking adjective stressful, tense, testing, trying, unnerving, worrying.

nervous adjective afraid, agitated, alarmed, anxious, apprehensive, edgy, fidgety, flustered, frightened, highly-strung, jittery (informal), jumpy, nervy, neurotic, restive, shaky, tense, timid, timorous, twitchy, uneasy, uptight (informal), worried. □ **nervousness** noun agitation, anxiety, apprehension, butterflies (informal), heebie-jeebies (informal), jitters (informal), nerves, stage fright, tension, trembling, uneasiness.

nest noun eyrie, perch, roost.

nestle verb cuddle, curl up, huddle, snuggle.

net noun **1** mesh, netting, network, web. **2** dragnet, driftnet, trawl.

net verb capture, catch, ensnare, snare, trap.

net adjective (net income) clear, disposable, take-home.

net verb clear, earn, gain, make, realise.

network noun complex, grid, system.

neurotic adjective anxious, obsessive, unbalanced.

neuter verb castrate, de-sex, doctor, geld, spay, sterilise.

neutral adjective **1** detached, disinterested, impartial, independent, non-aligned, non-partisan, unbiased, uninvolved. **2** beige, buff, colourless, dull, grey, indefinite, wishy-washy.

neutralise verb cancel (out), counteract, counterbalance, offset.

never-ending adjective constant, continuous, endless, everlasting, inexhaustible, infinite, limitless, unlimited.

nevertheless adverb but, however, none the less, still, yet.

new adjective **1** brand-new, fresh, hot, innovative, latest, modern, newfangled (*derogatory*), novel, original, recent, red-hot, trendy (*informal*), unused, up to date. **2** strange, unfamiliar, unheard-of, unknown. **3** additional, another, extra. **4** altered, changed, different, rejuvenated, renovated, restored, transformed.

newcomer noun **1** immigrant, migrant, new chum (*Australian informal*), stranger. **2** beginner, novice, probationer, tiro, trainee.

newly adverb freshly, just, lately, recently.

news noun announcement, bulletin, communication, communiqué, dispatch, information, intelligence, message, press release, report, statement, story, tidings, word.

newsletter noun bulletin, magazine, report.

newspaper noun broadsheet, daily, gazette, journal, paper, rag (*derogatory*), tabloid, weekly.

newsy adjective gossipy, informative, interesting.

next adjective **1** adjacent, adjoining, closest, nearest, neighbouring, next-door. **2** following, subsequent, succeeding.

next adverb afterwards, subsequently, then.

nibble verb bite, gnaw, munch, peck at, pick at; see also EAT □ **nibble** noun bite, morsel, mouthful, taste, titbit.

nice adjective **1** agreeable, delightful, enjoyable, fabulous (*informal*), fantastic (*informal*), fine, good, great (*informal*), lovely, marvellous, pleasant, satisfactory, splendid, wonderful; see also EXCELLENT, GOOD. **2** agreeable, amiable, amicable, attractive, benevolent, benign, caring, charming, compassionate, congenial, considerate, delightful, friendly, good, good-natured, gracious, kind, kindly, likeable, pleasant, polite, sweet, sympathetic, thoughtful, understanding, winsome. **3** careful, delicate, fine, minute, precise, subtle.

nicety noun detail, finer point, refinement, subtlety.

niche noun **1** alcove, bay, nook, recess. **2** calling, place, slot, vocation.

nick noun **1** cut, gouge, notch, score, scratch, snick. **2** condition, health, trim.

nick verb **1** cut, gash, scratch, snick. **2** knock off (*slang*), lift, pilfer, pinch (*informal*), snatch, snitch (*slang*), steal, swipe (*informal*), take. **3** arrest, catch, nab (*informal*), pick up.

nickname noun alias, pet name, sobriquet.

niggardly adjective mean, miserly, parsimonious, penny-pinching, stingy, tight-fisted.

niggle verb carp, fuss, nag, nit-pick (*informal*), quibble. □ **niggling** adjective annoying, lurking, nagging, persistent, worrying.

night noun dark, darkness, dusk, evening, nightfall, night-time.

nightly adjective after-dark, evening, night-time, nocturnal.

nightmarish adjective dreadful, frightening, horrible, horrifying, scary, terrible, terrifying.

nil noun love, none, nothing, nought, zero.

nimble adjective active, agile, lithe, lively, nippy (*informal*), quick, sprightly, spry, swift.

nip verb bite, nibble, pinch, squeeze, tweak.

nipple noun teat.

nippy adjective biting, bitter, chilly, cold, freezing, icy.

nit-picking noun carping, cavilling, fault-finding, niggling, quibbling.

noble adjective **1** aristocratic, blue-blooded, lordly, titled. **2** exalted, generous, high-minded, honourable, lofty, selfless, virtuous, worthy. **3** fine, grand, imposing, impressive, magnificent, majestic, splendid, stately. □ **nobility** noun aristocracy, peerage, upper class, upper crust (*informal*).

noble noun aristocrat, grandee, lady, lord, peer, peeress; (*kinds of nobleman*) baron, count, duke, earl, marquess, marquis, viscount; (*kinds of noble-woman*) baroness, countess, duchess, marchioness, marquise, viscountess.

nobody pronoun none, no one.

nocturnal adjective after-dark, evening, nightly, night-time.

nod verb **1** bob, bow, incline; see also SIGNAL. **2** (*nod off*) doze off, drop off, drowse, fall asleep.

node noun bump, knob, knot, lump, nodule, protuberance, swelling.

noise noun bedlam, clamour, clatter, commotion, din, hubbub, hullabaloo, outcry, pandemonium, racket, row, rumpus, sound, tumult, uproar. □ **noisy** adjective (*a noisy crowd*) boisterous, lively, rowdy, tumultuous, turbulent, uproarious, vociferous; (*noisy music*) blaring, booming, deafening, discordant, grating, jarring, loud, piercing, raucous, shrill, strident, thundering.

nomad noun gypsy, itinerant, rover, traveller, vagabond, wanderer. □ **nomadic** adjective itinerant, migratory, peripatetic, roving, travelling, vagabond, vagrant, wandering.

nominal adjective **1** in name only, ostensible, professed, socalled, theoretical. **2** minimal, small, token.

nominate verb appoint, choose, designate, elect, name, pick, propose, put forward, recommend, select, submit, suggest.

non-believer noun agnostic, atheist, freethinker, heathen, infidel, pagan, sceptic, unbeliever.

nonchalant adjective apathetic, blasé, calm, carefree, careless, casual, composed, cool, imperturbable, indifferent, laid-back (informal), unconcerned, unemotional, unexcited, unflappable (informal).

non-committal adjective cagey (informal), cautious, circumspect, evasive, guarded, indefinite, reserved, temporising, tentative, wary.

nonconformist noun dissenter, eccentric, heretic, iconoclast, individualist, maverick, misfit, radical, rebel.

nondescript adjective bland, characterless, ordinary, plain, unexceptional, uninteresting, unremarkable.

nonentity noun lightweight, nobody, small fry, unknown.

non-existent adjective fictitious, hypothetical, imaginary, make-believe, mythical, pretend (informal), pretended, unreal.

nonplus verb amaze, baffle, bamboozle (informal), bewilder, confound, confuse, dumbfound, flummox (informal), perplex, puzzle, stun, surprise.

nonsense noun balderdash, boloney (informal), boral (Australian), bunkum, claptrap, codswallop (slang), drivel, folly, foolishness, garbage, gibberish, gobbledegook (informal), guff (slang), hogwash (informal), hooey (informal), humbug, inanity, kidstakes (Australian informal), mumbo-jumbo, piffle (informal), poppycock (slang), rot (slang), rubbish, silliness, stupidity, tommyrot (slang), trash, tripe (informal), twaddle. □ **nonsensical** adjec-

tive absurd, crazy, fatuous, foolish, idiotic, inane, laughable, ludicrous, meaningless, preposterous, ridiculous, senseless, silly, stupid.

on-stop *adjective* **1** ceaseless, constant, continuous, endless, incessant, persistent, steady. **2** direct, express, through.

ook *noun* alcove, corner, cubby hole, niche, recess.

oon *noun* midday, noonday, twelve o'clock.

orm *noun* average, benchmark, criterion, mean, par, pattern, rule, standard, usual, yardstick.

ormal *adjective* **1** average, conventional, customary, habitual, ordinary, regular, routine, standard, typical, usual. **2** balanced, rational, reasonable, sane.

ose *noun* beak (*informal*), conk (*slang*), muzzle, proboscis, snout.

ose *verb* **1** nudge, nuzzle. **2** poke, prowl, pry, search, snoop (*informal*), stickybeak (*Australian informal*). **3** ease, edge, inch.

osedive *noun* descent, dive, drop, fall, plunge, swoop. □ **nosedive** *verb* crash, drop, fall, plummet, plunge.

ostalgia *noun* longing, pining, yearning. □ **nostalgic**

adjective homesick, maudlin, sentimental, wistful.

nosy *adjective* curious, inquisitive, meddlesome, prying, snoopy (*informal*).

notable *adjective* **1** conspicuous, important, noticeable, obvious, outstanding, remarkable, significant, striking. **2** celebrated, distinguished, eminent, famous, noted, prominent, renowned, well-known.

notation *noun* code, signs, symbols, system.

notch *noun* blaze, cut, nick, score, snick.

notch *verb* cut, gouge, nick, score, snick. □ **notch up** achieve, gain, score.

note *noun* **1** annotation, comment, endnote, explanation, footnote, jotting, minute, record. **2** communication, epistle, letter, memo (*informal*), memorandum, message, missive. **3** banknote, bill. **4** air, element, feeling, sound, tone. **5** attention, heed, notice.

note *verb* **1** enter, jot down, record, register, write down. **2** heed, mark, mind, notice, observe, pay attention to, perceive, see.

notebook *noun* exercise book, jotter, journal, logbook, memo book, pocketbook.

noted *adjective* celebrated, distinguished, eminent, famous, notable, prominent, renowned, well-known.

nothing *noun* nil, nought, zero, zilch (*informal*). □ **nothingness** *noun* emptiness, non-existence, nothing, oblivion, vacuum, void.

notice *noun* **1** advertisement, announcement, circular, flyer, leaflet, letter, memo (*informal*), message, note, pamphlet, placard, poster, sign. **2** attention, consideration. **3** advice, notification, warning.

notice *verb* be aware of, catch sight of, detect, discern, note, observe, perceive, see, spot.

noticeable *adjective* clear, conspicuous, definite, discernible, distinct, manifest, marked, obvious, perceptible, pronounced, striking, visible.

notify *verb* **1** advise, alert, inform, tell, warn. **2** announce, declare, make known, proclaim, publish, report. □ **notification** *noun* advice, announcement, communication, information, notice, warning.

notion *noun* belief, concept, fancy, idea, opinion, thought.

notorious *adjective* disreputable, infamous, scandalous, well-known.

nought *noun* **1** cipher, zero, nil, nothing, zero, zilc (*informal*).

nourish *verb* feed, nurtur, provide for. □ **nourishin** *adjective* healthy, nutritiou, nutritive, wholesome.

novel *noun* fiction, saga, stor, tale.

novel *adjective* differen, innovative, new, origina, strange, unfamiliar, unusua, □ **novelty** *noun* newnes, originality, strangeness, u, familiarity, uniqueness; se also *TRINKET*.

novice *noun* apprentic, beginner, learner, new chu, (*Australian informal*), rook, (*informal*), tiro, trainee.

now *adverb* at present, at th, moment, at this moment, a, this point, at this stage, in th, time, currently, nowadays.

noxious *adjective* damagin, deleterious, destructive, harr, ful, pernicious, poisonous, toxic.

nuance *noun* difference, distin, tion, nicety, refinement, shad, subtlety.

nub *noun* core, crux, essenc, gist, heart, kernel, nitty-grit, (*informal*), substance.

nucleus *noun* basis, centr, core, heart, kernel.

nude adjective bare, exposed, naked, stripped, unclothed, undressed. □ **in the nude** in the altogether (informal), in the raw, in your birthday suit (informal), starkers (slang).

nudge verb bump, dig in the ribs, elbow, jog, poke, prod, push, shove, touch.

nuggety adjective beefy, burly, hefty, husky, stocky, sturdy, thickset.

nuisance noun annoyance, bother, drag, hassle (informal), inconvenience, irritation, menace, pain (informal), pest, problem, trouble.

null adjective annulled, invalid, nullified, worthless.

nullify verb abolish, annul, cancel, invalidate, negate, neutralise, repeal, rescind, revoke, undo, void.

numb adjective asleep, deadened, insensible, paralysed.

numb verb anaesthetise, deaden, dull, paralyse.

number noun **1** digit, figure, integer, numeral. **2** amount, quantity, sum, total; (a number of) see SEVERAL; (numbers of) see MANY. **3** copy, edition, issue, publication. **4** item, piece, song.

number verb **1** calculate, count, enumerate, reckon, tally, tot up. **2** add up to, amount to, come to, total.

numeral noun digit, figure, integer, number.

numerous adjective abundant, copious, countless, innumerable, many, myriad, numberless, numbers of, untold.

nun noun abbess, prioress, religious, sister.

nunnery noun abbey, cloister, convent, priory, religious house.

nurse verb **1** care for, look after, minister to, tend. **2** breastfeed, feed, suckle. □ **nursing home** convalescent home, hospice, hospital, hostel, institution, rest home, sanatorium.

nurture verb **1** care for, feed, look after, nourish, provide for. **2** bring up, develop, discipline, educate, instruct, raise, rear, school, train.

nurture noun care, development, discipline, education, instruction, rearing, training, upbringing.

nut noun **1** kernel, seed. **2** crackpot (informal), crank, eccentric, fruitcake (informal), loony (informal), lunatic, madman, madwoman, maniac, nutcase (informal), nutter (informal), psychopath, weirdo (*informal*). □ **nutty** *adjective* see *CRAZY*.

nutritious *adjective* healthy, nourishing, nutritive, wholesome.

Oo

oath *noun* **1** pledge, promise, vow. **2** blasphemy, curse, expletive, obscenity, profanity, swear-word.

obedient *adjective* biddable, compliant, disciplined, docile, dutiful, meek, submissive, tractable.

obese *adjective* see *FAT*.

obey *verb* abide by, adhere to, comply with, follow, heed, keep to, observe, respect, stick to, submit to.

object *noun* **1** article, body, contraption (*informal*), device, entity, item, thing. **2** aim, goal, intention, objective, point, purpose.

object *verb* (*object to*) complain about, criticise, disapprove of, dislike, find fault with, grumble at, knock (*informal*), mind, oppose, protest at, take exception to.

objection *noun* **1** disagreement, disapproval, opposition, protest. **2** complaint, criticism demur, grievance, quibble reservation.

objectionable *adjective* abhorrent, disagreeable, disgusting foul, insufferable, intolerable nasty, nauseating, obnoxious offensive, on the nose (*Australian informal*), repugnant, repulsive, revolting unacceptable, unbearable unpleasant, vile.

objective *noun* aim, design, goal, intention, mission object, purpose, target.

objective *adjective* **1** actual concrete, factual, observable real. **2** detached, dispassionate, fair, impartial, just unbiased, unprejudiced.

obligation *noun* **1** compulsion constraint, liability, requirement. **2** commitment, duty onus, requirement, responsibility.

obligatory *adjective* compulsory, mandatory, necessary required.

oblige *verb* bind, compel constrain, force, require.

obliging *adjective* accommodating, considerate, cooperative, courteous, helpful kind, neighbourly.

oblique *adjective* angled diagonal, slanting, sloping.

obliterate *verb* annihilate, blot out, cancel, destroy, efface, erase, expunge, rub out, wipe out.

oblivious *adjective* forgetful, heedless, insensible, unaware, unconscious, unmindful.

oblong *noun* rectangle.

obnoxious *adjective* abhorrent, despicable, detestable, disagreeable, disgusting, hateful, horrible, insufferable, loathsome, nasty, objectionable, odious, offensive, repugnant, repulsive, unpleasant, vile.

obscene *adjective* blue, crude, dirty, filthy, foul, improper, indecent, lewd, offensive, pornographic, rude, smutty, unprintable, vulgar. ☐ **obscenity** *noun* **1** immorality, indecency, lewdness, pornography, smuttiness, vulgarity. **2** curse, expletive, profanity, swear-word.

obscure *adjective* **1** dark, dim, faint, fuzzy, hazy, indistinct, misty, murky, shadowy. **2** abstruse, arcane, cryptic, enigmatic, esoteric, hidden, inscrutable, mysterious, uncertain, unclear, vague. **3** forgotten, little-known, unheard-of, unimportant, unknown.

obscure *verb* block out, blot out, blur, cloud, conceal, cover, darken, eclipse, envelop, hide, mask, screen, shroud.

obsequious *adjective* crawling (*informal*), deferential, fawning, grovelling, kowtowing, servile, slimy, smarmy (*informal*), subservient, sycophantic, toadying, truckling.

observant *adjective* alert, attentive, aware, perceptive, sharp-eyed, shrewd, vigilant, watchful, wide awake (*informal*).

observation *noun* **1** surveillance, viewing, watching. **2** comment, remark, statement.

observe *verb* **1** contemplate, detect, discover, look at, monitor, note, notice, perceive, see, spot, study, survey, view, watch, witness. **2** abide by, adhere to, comply with, follow, heed, keep, obey. **3** celebrate, commemorate, honour, keep, mark. **4** comment, remark, say, state. ☐ **observer** *noun* bystander, eyewitness, onlooker, spectator, viewer, witness.

obsess *verb* consume, dominate, grip, haunt, possess, preoccupy. ☐ **obsession** *noun* fetish, fixation, hobby-horse, infatuation, mania, passion, preoccupation.

obsolescent *adjective* declining, disappearing, dying out, moribund, on the way out (*informal*), waning.

obsolete *adjective* antiquated, archaic, dead, defunct, disused, old-fashioned, outdated, out of date.

obstacle *noun* bar, barrier, blockage, difficulty, hindrance, hurdle, impediment, obstruction, snag, stumbling block.

obstinate *adjective* defiant, dogged, headstrong, inflexible, intractable, intransigent, mulish, perverse, pigheaded, recalcitrant, refractory, resolute, self-willed, stiff-necked, strong-willed, stubborn, uncompromising, unyielding, wilful.

obstreperous *adjective* boisterous, disorderly, irrepressible, noisy, rowdy, stroppy (*informal*), uncontrollable, unmanageable, unruly, wild.

obstruct *verb* **1** block, bung up, choke, clog, jam, plug up, stop up. **2** block, delay, deter, frustrate, halt, hamper, hinder, hold up, impede, inhibit, prevent, retard, slow down, stall, stop, thwart. □ **obstruction** *noun* barricade, barrier, blockage, obstacle.

obtain *verb* achieve, acquire, attain, buy, come by, earn, elicit, extract, gain, gather, get, get hold of, glean, pick up, procure, purchase, receive, secure.

obtrusive *adjective* **1** forward, importunate, interfering, intrusive, meddlesome, nosy (*informal*), pushy. **2** blatant, conspicuous, glaring, noticeable, obvious, prominent.

obtuse *adjective* dense, dimwitted, dopey (*informal*), dumb (*informal*), slow, stupid, thick

obvious *adjective* apparent, blatant, clear, conspicuous, distinct, evident, glaring, manifest, noticeable, palpable, patent, plain, prominent, pronounced, self-evident, unconcealed, unmistakable, visible.

occasion *noun* **1** ceremony, episode, event, function, happening, incident, occurrence. **2** chance, moment, opportunity, time.

occasional *adjective* fitful, infrequent, intermittent, irregular, odd, random, rare, scattered, spasmodic, sporadic. □ **occasionally** *adverb* at times, every so often, from time to time, now and then, once in a while, on occasion, sometimes.

occult *adjective* arcane, esoteric, hidden, magic, mysterious, mystic, mystical, secret, supernatural.

occupant *noun* dweller, householder, inhabitant, lessee, occupier, resident, tenant.

occupation *noun* **1** business, calling, career, employment, job, profession, trade, vocation, work. **2** capture, conquest, invasion, possession, seizure, takeover.

occupy *verb* **1** dwell in, inhabit, live in, reside in. **2** fill, hold, hold down, take up, use. **3** capture, conquer, invade, seize, take over, take possession of. **4** absorb, employ, engage, engross, involve, keep busy, preoccupy.

occur *verb* **1** befall, come about, come off, come to pass, eventuate, happen, take place. **2** appear, arise, be found, crop up, emerge, exist, manifest itself, show up, surface. **3** (*occur to*) come to, dawn on, enter a person's head, strike, suggest itself to.

occurrence *noun* bout, episode, event, happening, incident, instance, occasion, phenomenon.

ocean *noun* the blue, the briny (*humorous*), the deep, sea.

odd *adjective* **1** aberrant, abnormal, anomalous, bizarre, curious, deviant, eccentric, extraordinary, freakish, funny, incongruous, irregular, offbeat, peculiar, queer, quirky, singular, strange, uncommon, unconventional, unnatural, unusual, weird. **2** leftover,

lone, remaining, single, spare, surplus, unpaired. **3** casual, miscellaneous, occasional, random, sporadic, sundry, various.

oddments *plural noun* leftovers, odds and ends, odds and sods (*informal*), remainders, remnants, sundries.

odious *adjective* abhorrent, abominable, contemptible, despicable, detestable, hateful, heinous, horrible, loathsome, monstrous, obnoxious, repugnant, repulsive, vile.

odour *noun* aroma, bouquet, fragrance, perfume, scent, smell; (*a bad odour*) pong (*informal*), reek, stench, stink.

offbeat *adjective* bizarre, eccentric, odd, strange, unconventional, unusual, wayout, weird.

offcuts *plural noun* leftovers, remnants, scraps.

offence *noun* **1** crime, felony (*old use*), misdeed, misdemeanour, sin, transgression, trespass (*old use*), wickedness, wrongdoing. **2** annoyance, indignation, irritation, resentment, umbrage, upset. □ **take offence** be affronted, be offended, resent, take umbrage.

offend *verb* **1** affront, anger, disgust, displease, hurt someone's feelings, insult, outrage, upset. **2** do wrong, sin, transgress, trespass (*old use*). □ **offender** *noun* criminal, culprit, felon, lawbreaker, malefactor, miscreant, sinner, transgressor, trespasser (*old use*), wrongdoer.

offensive *adjective* **1** abusive, disrespectful, improper, indecent, insolent, insulting, nasty, objectionable, obscene, odious, rude. **2** bad, disgusting, foul, nasty, nauseating, obnoxious, off-putting (*informal*), on the nose (*Australian informal*), repulsive, revolting, sickening, unsavoury, yucky (*informal*). **3** aggressive, attacking.

offensive *noun* assault, attack, blitz, drive, invasion, onslaught, raid.

offer *verb* **1** give, hand, present, proffer. **2** propose, put forward, submit, suggest, tender, volunteer.

offer *noun* bid, proposal, proposition, suggestion, tender.

offering *noun* contribution, donation, gift, offertory, present, sacrifice.

offhand *adjective* **1** ad lib, extempore, impromptu, off the cuff, spontaneous, unprepared. **2** brusque, casual, curt,

perfunctory, rude, terse, unceremonious, unconcerned.

office *noun* **1** den, study, workroom. **2** agency, bureau, department, secretariat. **3** appointment, duty, function, job, position, post, role.

officer *noun* **1** functionary, official. **2** see *POLICE*.

official *adjective* accredited, approved, authorised, certified, endorsed, formal, legitimate, proper.

official *noun* bureaucrat, functionary, office-bearer, officer.

officious *adjective* bossy, bumptious, cocky, interfering, intrusive, meddlesome, overbearing, self-important.

off-putting *adjective* disconcerting, disgusting, offensive, repellent, repugnant, repulsive, unpleasant.

offset *verb* balance, cancel out, compensate for, counteract, counterbalance, neutralise, nullify.

offshoot *noun* **1** branch, side shoot. **2** by-product, derivative, development, spin-off.

offsider *noun* assistant, associate, helper, partner, sidekick (*informal*).

offspring *noun* **1** child(ren), descendant(s), family, heir(s), kid(s) (*informal*), progeny. **2** brood, litter, young.

often *adverb* constantly, continually, frequently, regularly, repeatedly.

ogle *verb* eye, gawp at (*informal*), gaze at, leer at, stare at.

ogre *noun* **1** bogyman, giant, monster. **2** beast, brute, bully, fiend, monster, tyrant.

oil *verb* grease, lubricate.

oily *adjective* fatty, greasy.

ointment *noun* balm, cream, embrocation, liniment, lotion, oil, salve.

OK *adjective* adequate, all right, fine, passable, reasonable, satisfactory, so-so (*informal*), tolerable.

old *adjective* **1** (*an old person*) aged, elderly, geriatric, mature, retired, senior; (*an old car*) antiquated, antique, archaic, obsolescent, obsolete, outdated, primitive, veteran, vintage; (*an old custom*) age-old, ancient, early, long-standing, time-honoured, traditional. **2** decrepit, dilapidated, ragged, shabby, tatty (*informal*), worn, worn-out. **3** earlier, former, original, previous, prior.

olden *adjective* bygone, earlier, early, former, old.

old-fashioned *adjective* antediluvian (*informal*), antiquated, archaic, behind the times, conservative, conventional, fuddy-duddy (*informal*), obsolete, old hat (*informal*), outdated, outmoded, out-of-date, traditional, unfashionable.

omen *noun* indication, portent, sign, warning.

ominous *adjective* inauspicious, menacing, portentous, sinister, threatening.

omission *noun* **1** exclusion, neglect, negligence, non-inclusion. **2** exclusion, gap, oversight.

omit *verb* **1** drop, exclude, ignore, leave out, miss, overlook, pass over, skip. **2** fail, forget, neglect.

omnipotent *adjective* all-powerful, almighty, sovereign, supreme.

omniscient *adjective* all-knowing, all-seeing, all-wise.

once *adverb* formerly, hitherto, in days gone by, in the past, previously.

oncoming *adjective* advancing, approaching.

onerous *adjective* arduous, burdensome, difficult, exacting, hard, heavy, herculean, oppressive, taxing, tiring.

one-sided *adjective* biased, unbalanced, unequal, uneven, unfair, prejudiced.

onlooker noun bystander, eye-witness, looker-on, observer, spectator, viewer, witness.

only adjective lone, one, single, sole, solitary.

only adverb just, merely, purely, simply.

onset noun beginning, commencement, inception, outbreak, outset, start.

onslaught noun aggression, assault, attack, blitz, bombardment, charge, incursion, offensive, raid.

onus noun burden, duty, obligation, responsibility.

ooze verb discharge, dribble, drip, exude, leak, seep, trickle.

opaque adjective cloudy, milky, muddy, murky, turbid, unclear.

open adjective 1 (an open door) ajar, gaping, unbolted, undone, unfastened, unlatched, unlocked; (open spaces) broad, clear, empty, exposed, extensive, unbounded, uncluttered, uncrowded, unfenced, unobstructed. 2 outspread, outstretched, spread out, unfolded, unfurled. 3 general, public, unrestricted. 4 candid, communicative, direct, forthright, frank, honest, outspoken, straightforward. 5 blatant, flagrant, obvious, overt, patent, unconcealed, undisguised. 6 undecided, un-

resolved, unsettled. □ **open air** adjective alfresco, outdoor, outside. □ **open-minded** adjective fair, impartial, just objective, tolerant, unbiased unprejudiced.

open verb 1 unbolt, unclasp uncork, undo, unfasten unhook, unlatch, unlock unroll, unseal, untie, unwrap unzip. 2 begin, commence initiate, kick off (informal launch, start.

opening noun 1 aperture breach, break, chink, clef crack, cut, fissure, gap, hatch hole, leak, manhole, mouth orifice, outlet, passage, rif slit, slot, space, vent. beginning, commencemen inception, launch, outse start. 3 break (informal chance, opportunity, positior vacancy.

operate verb 1 control, driv handle, manage, manipulate use, wield, work. 2 function go, perform, run, work.

operation noun 1 actior business, exercise, jok procedure, process, tasl undertaking. 2 op (informa surgery. 3 action, campaigr exercise, manoeuvre.

opinion noun belief, commen conclusion, conviction, cree feeling, idea, impression judgement, notion, point c view, sentiment, standpoint, thought, view, viewpoint. □ **opinion poll** Gallup poll, straw poll, poll, survey.

opinionated *adjective* bigoted, cocksure, dogmatic, headstrong, obstinate, self-assertive, stubborn.

opponent *noun* adversary, challenger, competitor, contender, enemy, foe, opposition, rival.

opportune *adjective* **1** advantageous, appropriate, apt, auspicious, convenient, expedient, favourable, fitting, fortunate, good, lucky, propitious. **2** convenient, timely, well-timed.

opportunity *noun* break (*informal*), chance, moment, occasion, opening, time.

oppose *verb* argue against, buck (*informal*), contest, counter, defy, fight, object to, resist, withstand.

opposite *adjective* **1** facing. **2** conflicting, contradictory, contrary, contrasting, incompatible, opposing.

opposite *noun* antithesis, contrary, converse, reverse.

opposition *noun* **1** antagonism, disagreement, disapproval, hostility, objection, resistance. **2** competitor, enemy, opponent, rival.

oppress *verb* **1** abuse, bully, crush, exploit, maltreat, persecute, subjugate, tyrannise. **2** afflict, burden, depress, overwhelm, torment, trouble, weigh down, worry.

oppressive *adjective* **1** cruel, despotic, hard, harsh, repressive, severe, tyrannical, unjust. **2** close, humid, muggy, stifling, stuffy, sultry, uncomfortable.

opt *verb* (*opt for*) choose, decide on, go for, pick, select, settle on, vote for.

optical *adjective* see VISUAL.

optimistic *adjective* cheerful, confident, expectant, hopeful, positive, sanguine, upbeat (*informal*).

optimum *adjective* best, ideal, optimal, peak, perfect.

option *noun* alternative, choice, possibility.

optional *adjective* elective, non-essential, voluntary.

opulent *adjective* **1** affluent, moneyed, prosperous, rich, wealthy, well off. **2** luxurious, plush (*informal*), splendid, sumptuous.

oral *adjective* spoken.

orange *adjective* amber, apricot, carroty, coral, ginger, saffron, salmon, tangerine.

oration *noun* address, discourse, eulogy, homily, lecture, speech.

orbit *noun* circuit, course, path, revolution, track, trajectory.

orbit *verb* circle, circumnavigate, revolve around.

orchestra *noun* band, ensemble.

orchestrate *verb* **1** arrange, score. **2** coordinate, mastermind, organise, stage-manage.

ordain *verb* **1** appoint, consecrate, induct, install, invest. **2** command, decree, dictate, order, prescribe, rule.

ordeal *noun* affliction, distress, hardship, nightmare, suffering, test, trial, tribulation, trouble.

order *noun* **1** command, decree, dictate, direction, directive, edict, injunction, instruction. **2** arrangement, classification, grouping, layout, organisation, sequence, series, system. **3** neatness, orderliness, tidiness. **4** condition, nick (*informal*), repair, shape, state. **5** calm, control, discipline, harmony, peace, quiet. **6** degree, kind, level, quality, sort, type. **7** association, brotherhood, community, fraternity, group, sisterhood, society. □ **out of order** broken, bung (*Australian informal*),

damaged, inoperative, kaput (*informal*), on the blink (*informal*).

order *verb* **1** bid, charge, command, decree, direct, enjoin, instruct, prescribe, tell. **2** apply for, book, request, reserve. **3** arrange, classify, dispose, group, lay out, organise, sort. □ **order about** boss around, bully, control, push around, tell someone what to do.

orderly *adjective* **1** methodical, neat, ordered, organised, shipshape, spick and span, straight, systematic, tidy. **2** controlled, disciplined, law-abiding, quiet, well-behaved.

ordinary *adjective* average, common, commonplace, conventional, customary, everyday, familiar, humble, humdrum, mediocre, middling, mundane, nondescript, normal, orthodox, plain, regular, routine, run-of-the-mill, simple, so-so (*informal*), standard, typical, undistinguished, unexceptional, unexciting, unimpressive, uninspired, uninteresting, unremarkable, usual.

organisation *noun* **1** alliance, association, body, business, club, company, corporation, corps, enterprise, establishment, federation, fellowship, firm, fraternity, group, institution, league, movement, order, party, society, union. **2** administration, arrangement, coordination, management, orchestration, planning, running. **3** arrangement, design, form, format, layout, presentation, structure, system.

organise verb **1** arrange, control, coordinate, manage, orchestrate, plan, run, stage-manage. **2** assemble, establish, form, mobilise, put together, set up. **3** arrange, catalogue, classify, group, order, put in order, sort, structure, systematise, tidy.

organism noun being, creature, living thing.

orgy noun **1** binge (*slang*), party, revelry, spree (*informal*). **2** frenzy, splurge (*informal*), spree (*informal*).

orientate verb □ **orientate yourself 1** find your position, get your bearings, orient yourself. **2** acclimatise, adapt, adjust, familiarise yourself, orient yourself.

origin noun **1** basis, beginning, birth, cause, commencement, creation, derivation, emergence, foundation, genesis, inception, root, source, start, starting point. **2** ancestry,

birth, descent, extraction, lineage, parentage, pedigree.

original adjective **1** Aboriginal, earliest, first, initial, native, primeval. **2** firsthand, fresh, new, novel, unique. **3** creative, imaginative, innovative, inventive, unconventional. □ **original** noun archetype, master, prototype.

originate verb arise, begin, commence, date from, emerge, spring up, start.

ornament noun adornment, bauble, decoration, embellishment, jewellery, knick-knack, trimming, trinket.

ornate adjective baroque, decorated, elaborate, fancy, flamboyant, ornamented, rococo, showy.

orthodox adjective accepted, conventional, established, mainstream, official, ordinary, standard, traditional.

oscillate verb **1** sway, swing. **2** fluctuate, see-saw, swing, vacillate, vary, waver.

ostensible adjective alleged, apparent, declared, outward, pretended, professed, seeming.

ostentatious adjective conspicuous, extravagant, flamboyant, flash (*informal*), flashy, grandiose, imposing, pretentious, showy, swanky (*informal*).

ostracise verb avoid, banish, blackball, blacklist, boycott, cold-shoulder, disown, exclude, reject, send to Coventry, shun, snub.

other adjective **1** alternative, different. **2** additional, extra, further, more, supplementary. □ **other than** apart from, aside from, besides, except.

oust verb banish, dismiss, drive out, eject, expel, fire, give the boot (slang), kick out (informal), sack (informal), throw out.

out-and-out adjective absolute, arrant, complete, downright, thorough, total, utter.

outback noun backblocks (Australian), back of beyond, bush, inland, interior, never-never (Australian), sticks (informal).

outbreak noun epidemic, eruption, outburst.

outburst noun blaze, burst, eruption, explosion, fit, flood, outbreak, spasm.

outcast noun deportee, exile, outlaw, pariah, refugee.

outcome noun consequence, effect, end, fruit, result, sequel, upshot.

outcry noun clamour, hue and cry, hullabaloo, objection, outburst, protest, uproar.

outdated adjective antiquated, archaic, obsolete, old, old-fashioned, outmoded, out-of-date, unfashionable.

outdo verb beat, defeat, eclipse, exceed, excel, get the better of, outclass, outshine, outstrip, overshadow, surpass, top.

outdoors adverb al fresco, in the open air, out of doors, outside.

outer adjective exterior, external, outside, superficial, surface; see also OUTLYING.

outfit noun **1** clothes, clothing, costume, gear (informal), get-up (informal). **2** apparatus, equipment, gear, kit.

outgoing adjective **1** departing, ex-, former, past, retiring. **2** extroverted, friendly, gregarious, sociable, warm. □ **outgoings** plural noun costs, expenditure, expenses.

outgrowth noun **1** knob, lump, node, nodule, offshoot, shoot, sprout. **2** by-product, consequence, development, offshoot, outcome, product, result, spin-off, upshot.

outhouse noun barn, outbuilding, shed.

outing noun drive, excursion, expedition, hike, jaunt, tour, trip.

outlandish adjective bizarre, exotic, freakish, odd, ou

rageous, peculiar, preposterous, strange, unusual, way-out, weird.

outlaw *noun* bandit, brigand, criminal, desperado, fugitive, marauder, outcast.

outlaw *verb* ban, forbid, prohibit, proscribe.

outlay *noun* charge, cost, expenditure, expense.

outlet *noun* **1** channel, duct, escape, exit, hole, opening, overflow, release, vent, way out. **2** shop, store.

outline *noun* **1** contour, profile, shadow, shape, silhouette, tracing. **2** abstract, draft, framework, plan, précis, résumé, run-down, sketch, summary, synopsis.

outlive *verb* outlast, survive.

outlook *noun* **1** aspect, panorama, prospect, scene, sight, view, vista. **2** attitude, frame of mind, perspective, view, viewpoint. **3** forecast, prediction, prognosis, prospect.

outlying *adjective* distant, far-flung, outer, remote.

outnumber *verb* exceed.

output *noun* production, yield.

outrage *noun* **1** affront, atrocity, crime, evil, insult, offence, scandal. **2** anger, disgust, fury, indignation, ire, rage, shock. □ **outrageous**

adjective (*outrageous prices*) absurd, excessive, exorbitant, immoderate, preposterous, shocking, unreasonable; (*outrageous crimes*) atrocious, barbarous, despicable, disgraceful, heinous, infamous, monstrous, notorious, offensive, scandalous, shocking, unspeakable, vile, wicked.

outrage *verb* affront, anger, enrage, incense, infuriate, insult, offend, scandalise, shock.

outright *adverb* **1** absolutely, altogether, categorically, completely, entirely, utterly. **2** at once, immediately, instantly. **3** directly, frankly, openly, straight.

outright *adjective* absolute, complete, downright, out-and-out, sheer, thorough, utter.

outset *noun* beginning, commencement, inception, start.

outside *noun* case, coating, cover, covering, crust, exterior, façade, face, shell, skin, surface.

outside *adjective* **1** exterior, external, outer. **2** distant, faint, remote, slender, slight, slim.

outside *adverb* al fresco, in the open air, outdoors, out of doors.

outsider *noun* alien, foreigner, immigrant, intruder,

newcomer, odd man out, ring-in (*Australian informal*), stranger, visitor.

outskirts *plural noun* edge, fringe, limits, periphery.

outspoken *adjective* blunt, candid, forthright, frank, open, straightforward, un-reserved.

outstanding *adjective* **1** distinguished, eminent, excellent, exceptional, exemplary, extraordinary, great, impressive, memorable, notable, pre-eminent, remarkable, sensational, singular, special, splendid, superior. **2** due, overdue, owing, unpaid.

outstrip *verb* **1** beat, outdistance, outpace, outrun. **2** eclipse, exceed, excel, outclass, outdo, outshine, overshadow, surpass, top.

outward *adjective* exterior, external, observable, outer, outside, superficial, visible.

outweigh *verb* exceed, override, predominate over, surpass.

outwit *verb* dupe, hoodwink, outfox (*informal*), outsmart, trick.

oval *adjective* egg-shaped, elliptical, ovoid.

oval *noun* **1** ellipse. **2** playing field, sports field, sports-ground.

ovation *noun* applause, clap, hand (*informal*).

oven *noun* cooker, furnace, kiln, microwave, range, stove.

overall *adjective* all-inclusive, broad, complete, general, total.

overalls *plural noun* boiler suit, dungarees.

overbearing *adjective* arrogant, autocratic, bossy, domineering, high-handed, imperious, officious, per-emptory.

overcast *adjective* cloudy, dull, foggy, gloomy, grey, heavy, leaden, louring, misty.

overcoat *noun* greatcoat, topcoat; see also *COAT*.

overcome *verb* **1** beat, conquer, crush, defeat, lick (*informal*), master, overpower, overthrow, quell, subdue, thrash, triumph over, trounce, vanquish. **2** conquer, rise above, surmount, triumph over.

overdo *verb* exaggerate, lay (it) on a bit thick (*informal*), overstate, pile (it) on (*informal*).

overdue *adjective* in arrears, late, outstanding, owing.

overeat *verb* binge (*informal*), gorge yourself, overindulge, pig out (*informal*), stuff yourself.

overestimate *verb* exaggerate, overrate, overstate.

overflow *verb* brim over, flood, flow over, pour over, run over, slop over, spill over. □ **overflow** *noun* excess, spillage, surplus.

overgrown *adjective* tangled, uncut, unkempt, untidy, wild.

overhang *verb* jut out over, project out over, protrude over, stick out over.

overhaul *verb* recondition, repair, restore, service.

overhear *verb* eavesdrop on, hear, listen in on.

overjoyed *adjective* delighted, ecstatic, elated, euphoric, exuberant, exultant, happy, joyful, joyous, jubilant, over the moon (*informal*), rapt, rapturous, thrilled.

overload *verb* overburden, overtax, weigh down.

overlook *verb* **1** disregard, forget, ignore, leave out, miss, neglect, omit, pass over, skip. **2** condone, disregard, excuse, forgive, ignore, pardon, turn a blind eye to. **3** face, front on to, look out on, look over.

overpower *verb* beat, conquer, defeat, get the better of, overcome, overwhelm, subdue.

overpowering *adjective* irresistible, overwhelming, powerful, uncontrollable.

overrate *verb* exaggerate, overestimate.

override *verb* **1** see *OVERRULE*. **2** have precedence over, outweigh, prevail over. □ **overriding** *adjective* chief, foremost, main, major, paramount, primary, principal, supreme.

overrule *verb* disallow, invalidate, override, overturn, reject, reverse, revoke, set aside, veto.

overrun *verb* cover, infest, invade, occupy, spread over, swarm over, take over.

overseas *adverb* abroad. □ **overseas** *adjective* foreign, offshore.

oversee *verb* be in charge of, direct, manage, run, superintend, supervise. □ **overseer** *noun* boss, foreman, forewoman, manager, superintendent, supervisor.

overshadow *verb* dwarf, eclipse, outshine, put in the shade, surpass, tower over.

oversight *noun* blunder, carelessness, error, lapse, mistake, omission, slip-up (*informal*).

overstate *verb* blow up, exaggerate, inflate, magnify. □ **overstatement** *noun* exaggeration, hyperbole.

overt *adjective* blatant, evident, manifest, obvious, open, patent, plain, unconcealed, visible.

overtake *verb* catch up with, go past, outpace, outstrip, overhaul, pass.

overtax *verb* overburden, overload, overwork, strain, stretch.

overthrow *verb* bring down, defeat, depose, oust, overturn, topple, unseat.

overthrow *noun* collapse, defeat, downfall, fall.

overtone *noun* connotation, hint, implication, innuendo, insinuation, suggestion, undercurrent.

overture *noun* beginning, introduction, opening, prelude.

overturn *verb* **1** capsize, invert, keel over, knock over, spill, tip over, topple over, turn over, turn turtle, up-end, upset, upturn. **2** see *OVERTHROW*.

overview *noun* outline, sketch, survey.

overweight *adjective* chubby, corpulent, dumpy, fat, gross, heavy, obese, plump, podgy, portly, rotund, stout, tubby.

overwhelm *verb* **1** bury, cove deluge, drown, engulf, flooo inundate, submerge, swamp **2** beat, conquer, crush, defea overcome, overpower, rou vanquish. □ **overwhelmin** *adjective* irresistible, ove powering, uncontrollable.

overwrought *adjective* ag tated, beside yoursel distressed, frantic, hysterica nervous, nervy, on edg overexcited, uptight (*in formal*), worked up.

owe *verb* be beholden to, b indebted to, be in debt to, b under an obligation t □ **owing** *adjective* du outstanding, overdue, unpai □ **owing to** because of, cause by, on account of, thanks to.

own *adjective* individua personal, private. □ **on you own** alone, by yourse independently, single-hande solo, unaccompanied, unaide unassisted, unescorted.

own *verb* be the owner of, hav hold, keep, possess. □ **own** admit, come clean (*informa* confess.

owner *noun* holder, landlad landlord, master, mistres possessor, proprietor, pr prietress.

ox *noun* bull, bullock, steer.

Pp

pace noun **1** step, stride. **2** rate, speed, velocity.

pace verb see WALK.

pacifist noun conscientious objector, dove, peace lover.

pacify verb appease, calm, placate, quieten, settle, soothe.

pack noun **1** bag, box, bundle, carton, package, packet, parcel. **2** backpack, haversack, kitbag, knapsack, rucksack, satchel; see also SWAG. **3** band, gang, group, mob, push (*Australian*), set. **4** heap, load, lot. □ **go to the pack** see DETERIORATE.

pack verb **1** load, package, parcel, place, put, store, stow, wrap up. **2** compact, compress, cram, crowd, fill, jam, press, ram, squash, squeeze, stuff, tamp. □ **pack off** bundle off, dispatch, send away, send off.

package noun bag, bale, box, bundle, carton, container, pack, packet, parcel.

packet noun bag, envelope, pack, package, parcel, sachet.

pact noun accord, agreement, bargain, compact, contract, covenant, deal, treaty, understanding.

pad noun **1** buffer, cushion, padding, pillow, wad. **2** jotter, notepad.

pad verb cushion, fill, line, protect, stuff, upholster. □ **pad out** bulk out, expand, fill out, lengthen, protract, spin out, stretch out.

padding noun cushioning, filling, stuffing, wadding.

paddle verb dabble, splash about, wade.

paddle noun oar, scull.

paddle verb row, scull.

paddock noun field, lea (*poetical*), meadow, pasture.

pagan noun heathen, infidel, non-believer, unbeliever.

page noun folio, leaf, sheet.

pageant noun display, parade, procession, show, spectacle, tableau.

pain noun **1** ache, affliction, agony, discomfort, distress, hurt, pang, soreness, sting, suffering, throb, torture, twinge. **2** affliction, agony, anguish, distress, grief, heartache, hurt, sadness, sorrow, suffering, torment, torture, woe. □ **painful** adjective aching, agonising, distressing, excruciating, hurting, raw, sensitive, smarting, sore, splitting, stabbing, stinging, tender, throbbing, upsetting. □ **pain-less** *adjective* comfortable, easy, effortless, pain-free, simple.

□ **painstaking** *adjective* assiduous, careful, conscientious, diligent, hard-working, meticulous, precise, punctilious, scrupulous, thorough.

pain *verb* distress, grieve, hurt, sadden, trouble.

paint *noun* colour, colouring, dye, pigment, stain, tint.

paint *verb* **1** coat, colour, daub, decorate. **2** depict, portray, represent.

painter *noun* artist, decorator.

painting *noun* picture, work of art; (*kinds of painting*) abstract, fresco, landscape, mural, oil painting, portrait, seascape, still life, watercolour.

pair *noun* brace, couple, duo, partnership, twosome.

pair *verb* match, pair up, put together.

pal *noun* buddy (*informal*), chum (*informal*), cobber (*Australian informal*), comrade, crony, friend, mate.

palace *noun* castle, château, mansion.

pale *adjective* **1** anaemic, ashen, colourless, deathly, ghostly, pallid, pasty, peaky, wan, washed out, white. **2** bleached, dim, faint, light, misty, muted, pastel, soft, subdued.

□ **paleness** *noun* pallor, pastiness, whiteness.

palpable *adjective* apparent, blatant, clear, distinct, evident, manifest, obvious, patent, plain, tangible, unmistakable.

paltry *adjective* beggarly, meagre, mean, measly (*informal*), minor, negligible, niggardly, pathetic, petty, puny, trifling, trivial, worthless.

pamper *verb* cosset, humour, indulge, mollycoddle, spoil.

pamphlet *noun* booklet, brochure, flyer, handout, leaflet, notice, tract.

pan *noun* billy (*Australian*), casserole, cauldron, Dutch oven, frying pan, frypan, griddle, pot, pressure cooker, saucepan, skillet, wok.

pancake *noun* crêpe, flapjack, pikelet.

pandemonium *noun* bedlam, chaos, commotion, confusion, disorder, hubbub, hullabaloo, racket, rumpus, tumult, turmoil, uproar.

pander *verb* □ **pander to** cater for, gratify, indulge.

panel *noun* **1** insert, piece, section, strip. **2** body, committee, group, jury, team.

pang *noun* ache, pain, spasm, stab, sting, twinge; see also QUALM.

panic noun alarm, anxiety, consternation, dismay, dread, fear, fright, horror, hysteria, terror, trepidation. □ **panicky** adjective agitated, flustered, frantic, frightened, jittery (informal), nervous, nervy, panic-stricken, petrified, scared, terrified, terror-stricken.

panic verb drop your bundle (Australian informal), freak out (informal), get into a flap (informal), get into a state, get into a tizzy (informal), get the jitters (informal), go to pieces, lose your cool (informal).

panorama noun landscape, prospect, scene, view, vista.

pant verb gasp, huff, puff, wheeze.

pantry noun cupboard, larder, storeroom.

pants plural noun 1 slacks, trousers. 2 boxer shorts, briefs, drawers, jocks (slang), knickers, panties (informal), trunks, underpants, undies (informal).

paper noun 1 card, letterhead, notepaper, papyrus, parchment, stationery, writing paper. 2 broadsheet, daily, gazette, journal, newspaper, rag (derogatory), tabloid, weekly. 3 certificate, deed, document, form, record.

par noun average, mean, norm, normal, standard.

parable noun allegory, fable, story, tale.

parade noun 1 cavalcade, march, march-past, motorcade, pageant, procession. 2 avenue, boulevard, road, street.

parade verb file past, march.

paradise noun 1 heaven. 2 Eden, Garden of Eden.

paradoxical adjective absurd, anomalous, illogical, incongruous, inconsistent, self-contradictory.

paragon noun example, exemplar, ideal, model, pattern, quintessence.

parallel adjective analogous, comparable, corresponding, like, similar.

parallel noun 1 counterpart, equal, equivalent. 2 analogy, comparison, correspondence, likeness, similarity.

parallel verb equal, match, rival.

paralysed adjective crippled, disabled, immobile, incapacitated, lame, numb, paraplegic, quadriplegic.

paramount adjective chief, foremost, greatest, highest, main, major, primary, prime, supreme, utmost.

parapet noun battlements, rampart.

paraphernalia noun accessories, belongings, effects, equipment, gear, materials, odds and ends, possessions, stuff, tackle, things.

paraphrase verb rephrase, reword, rewrite.

parasol noun sunshade, umbrella.

parcel noun bale, bundle, pack, package, packet.

parched adjective (parched earth) arid, baked, bone-dry, dried out, dry, scorched, seared, waterless; (parched walkers) dehydrated, dry, thirsty.

pardon noun absolution, amnesty, exoneration, forbearance, forgiveness, mercy, remission, reprieve.

pardon verb **1** absolve, acquit, exonerate, forgive, let off, reprieve. **2** condone, excuse, forgive, overlook.

parent noun father, mother.

parentage noun ancestry, birth, descent, extraction, lineage, origin.

park noun garden(s), parkland(s), playground, recreation ground, reserve.

parka noun anorak; see also JACKET.

parlour noun drawing room, living room, lounge, salon, sitting room.

parochial adjective hidebound, insular, narrow, narrow-minded, petty, provincial, small-minded.

parody noun burlesque, imitation, satire, send-up (informal), spoof (informal), take-off.

parry verb **1** avert, beat off, block, deflect, fend off, repel, repulse, ward off. **2** avoid, circumvent, dodge, duck, elude, evade, side-step.

parson noun chaplain, clergyman, clergywoman, minister, padre, pastor, preacher, priest, rector, vicar.

part noun **1** bit, chunk, division, fraction, fragment, percentage, piece, portion, proportion, section, sector, segment, share, slice, subdivision; (parts of a serial) chapter, episode, instalment, issue, section, volume; (spare parts) component, constituent, element, ingredient, module, unit. **2** area, district, neighbourhood, region. **3** character, role. □ **take part** be involved, compete, enter, join in, partake, participate, play a part.

part verb break up, divorce, separate, split up. □ **part with**

give away, give up, hand over, relinquish, spare, surrender.

partial *adjective* **1** imperfect, incomplete, limited. **2** biased, partisan, prejudiced, unfair. ☐ **be partial to** be fond of, be keen on, enjoy, like, love.

participate *verb* be active, be involved, join, partake, play a part, share, take part. ☐ **participant** *noun* contributor, party, player.

particle *noun* atom, bit, crumb, fragment, grain, iota, jot, morsel, scrap, shred, skerrick (*Australian informal*), speck, trace.

particular *adjective* **1** distinct, exact, individual, precise, special, specific. **2** especial, exceptional, special. **3** choosy (*informal*), fastidious, finicky, fussy, pernickety (*informal*), selective.

particular *noun* (*particulars*) circumstances, details, facts, information.

partisan *noun* **1** adherent, backer, champion, fan, follower, supporter, zealot. **2** freedom fighter, guerrilla.

partition *noun* barrier, divider, panel, room divider, screen, wall.

partition *verb* break up, divide, separate, split up, subdivide.

partly *adverb* half, in part, partially, semi-.

partner *noun* **1** accessory, accomplice, ally, associate, collaborator, colleague, helper, offsider (*Australian informal*), sidekick (*informal*). **2** companion, consort, husband, mate, spouse, wife. ☐ **partnership** *noun* alliance, association, collaboration, marriage, relationship, union.

party *noun* **1** at-home, ball, banquet, bash (*informal*), celebration, do (*informal*), feast, festivity, formal, function, gathering, get-together (*informal*), orgy, rave (*informal*), reception, shindig (*informal*), shivoo (*Australian informal*), social. **2** band, body, crew, force, group, squad, team. **3** camp, faction, league, side.

pass *verb* **1** get ahead of, go by, go past, outstrip, overhaul, overtake. **2** go on, move on, proceed, progress. **3** give, hand over, transfer. **4** get through, qualify, succeed. **5** adopt, approve, authorise, decree, enact, ratify. **6** employ, fill, kill, occupy, spend, take up, use up, while away. **7** elapse, fly, go by, roll by, slip away. **8** blow over, die away, disappear, evaporate, fade, peter out, vanish. ☐ **pass away** see *DIE*. ☐ **pass out** black out, collapse, faint, keel over, swoon.

pass noun **1** permit, ticket. **2** canyon, defile, gap, gorge, ravine.

passable adjective **1** clear, open, traversable. **2** acceptable, adequate, all right, fair, mediocre, middling, OK (informal), reasonable, satisfactory, so-so (informal), tolerable.

passage noun **1** aisle, alley, arcade, corridor, gangway, hall, opening, passageway, shaft, tunnel. **2** crossing, journey, trip, voyage. **3** episode, excerpt, extract, paragraph, piece, portion, quotation, section.

passenger noun commuter, traveller.

passing adjective brief, casual, cursory, fleeting, hasty, momentary, quick, short, superficial, transient.

passion noun **1** ardour, earnestness, emotion, feeling, fervour, fire, intensity, vehemence, zeal. **2** craze, enthusiasm, infatuation, mania, obsession.

passionate adjective ardent, burning, eager, earnest, emotional, enthusiastic, fervent, heartfelt, heated, impassioned, intense, vehement, zealous.

passive adjective apathetic, compliant, docile, inactive, inert, resigned, submissive, unassertive, unresisting, unresponsive.

password noun countersign, sign, signal, watchword.

past adjective bygone, earlier, former, previous, prior.

past noun antiquity, history, old days, olden days, yesterday, yesteryear.

past preposition beyond, by, in front of.

paste noun adhesive, glue, gum.

paste verb glue, gum, stick.

pastel adjective delicate, faint, light, muted, pale, soft, subdued.

pastime noun activity, amusement, diversion, entertainment, game, hobby, interest, leisure pursuit, recreation, sport.

pastor noun chaplain, clergyman, clergywoman, minister, padre, parson, preacher, priest, rector, vicar.

pastoral adjective **1** bucolic, country, rural, rustic. **2** agricultural, farming, grazing, stock-raising.

pastoralist noun cattle farmer, grazier (Australian), sheep farmer, squatter (Australian).

pasture noun field, meadow, paddock, run (Australian).

pasty noun pastry, turnover.

pasty adjective anaemic, colourless, pale, pallid, sallow, unhealthy, wan.

pat verb caress, dab, slap, stroke, tap, touch.

pat noun caress, dab, slap, stroke, tap, touch.

patch noun 1 mend, reinforcement, repair. 2 bandage, cover, dressing, pad, plaster. 3 area, blob, blotch, mark, speck, speckle, splash, splotch, spot. 4 area, garden, lot, plot.

patch verb mend, reinforce, repair. □ **patch up** make up, resolve, set right, settle.

patchy adjective blotchy, dappled, inconsistent, mottled, speckled, uneven, variable.

patent adjective apparent, blatant, clear, conspicuous, evident, manifest, obvious, plain, unconcealed.

paternal adjective fatherlike, fatherly, kindly, protective.

paternity noun fatherhood, fathership.

path noun 1 aisle, alley, footpath, footway, lane, passage, pathway, pavement, sidewalk (American), track, trail, walkway, way. 2 course, line, orbit, route, trajectory, way.

pathetic adjective 1 distressing, heartbreaking, heart-rending, moving, piteous, pitiable, pitiful, poignant, sad, touching, tragic, wretched. 2 meagre, measly (informal), miserable, paltry, stingy, woeful.

patience noun 1 calmness, endurance, forbearance, restraint, self-control, tolerance. 2 determination, diligence, doggedness, perseverance, persistence, staying power, tenacity.

patient adjective 1 calm, forbearing, long-suffering, resigned, stoical, tolerant. 2 determined, diligent, dogged, indefatigable, persistent, tenacious, tireless, unflagging.

patient noun case, client, invalid, sufferer.

patio noun courtyard, terrace.

patriotic adjective chauvinistic, jingoistic, loyal, nationalistic.

patrol verb guard, police, watch.

patrol noun guard, lookout, sentinel, sentry, watch, watchman.

patron noun 1 backer, benefactor, champion, promoter, sponsor, supporter. 2 client, customer, regular. □ **patronage** noun 1 aid, backing, help, promotion, sponsorship, support. **2** business, custom.

patronise *verb* look down on, put down, talk down to. □ **patronising** *adjective* condescending, contemptuous, disdainful, haughty, lofty, supercilious, superior.

patter *noun* **1** beating, pit-a-pat, pitter-patter, tapping. **2** pitch, spiel (*slang*).

patter *verb* beat, rap, tap.

pattern *noun* **1** decoration, design, figure, marking, motif, ornament. **2** design, guide, model, template. **3** example, exemplar, guide, ideal, model, standard. **4** consistency, formula, order, regularity, system.

patty *noun* cake, croquette, rissole.

paunch *noun* abdomen, belly, pot-belly, stomach, tummy (*informal*).

pause *noun* break, breather, gap, halt, hesitation, hiatus, interlude, interruption, let-up, lull, rest, spell, stop.

pause *verb* break off, delay, halt, hesitate, rest, stop, wait.

pavement *noun* footpath, path, pathway, sidewalk (*American*).

paw *noun* foot, pad.

pawn *noun* instrument, puppet, stooge (*informal*), tool.

pawn *verb* hock (*slang*), pledge

pay *verb* **1** (*pay a person*) compensate, indemnify, recom pense, reimburse, remunerate repay; (*pay an amount* advance, contribute, cough up (*informal*), expend, fork ou (*slang*), give, hand over, outlay part with, refund, remit, shel out (*informal*), spend. **2** (*pa one's debts*) clear, discharge honour, meet, pay off, pay up settle, square. **3** be ad vantageous, be profitable, b worthwhile, pay off. **4** bestov extend, give, grant, present. be punished, pay a penalty, pa the price, suffer. □ **pay back** see *REPAY, RETALIATE*.

pay *noun* earnings, emolument fee, income, remuneration salary, stipend, wages.

payment *noun* advanc allowance, award, benefi bonus, commission, comper sation, contribution, donation fee, instalment, outlay, pa pay-off (*informal*), payou premium, recompense, refund reimbursement, remittance remuneration, repaymen reward, royalty, salary, settl ment, subscription, surcharg tip, toll, wage(s).

peace *noun* **1** accord, concor harmony, order. **2** caln calmness, quiet, quietnes repose, serenity, silence, stil ness, tranquillity. □ **peaceful** *adjective* balmy, calm, quiet, restful, serene, still, tranquil, undisturbed, unruffled, untroubled; see also *PEACEABLE*. □ **peacemaker** *noun* conciliator, intercessor, mediator, negotiator.

peaceable *adjective* amicable, friendly, gentle, harmonious, mild, non-violent, pacific, peaceful, peace-loving, placid.

peak *noun* **1** apex, crest, pinnacle, summit, tip, top, zenith. **2** acme, apex, climax, culmination, height, heyday, pinnacle, summit, top, zenith.

peal *noun* **1** carillon, chime, knell, ringing, toll. **2** blast, burst, clap, crash, roar, rumble.

peal *verb* chime, resound, ring, sound, toll.

pebble *noun* (*pebbles*) cobbles, gravel, shingle, stones.

peck *verb* bite, nibble, nip, pick at.

peculiar *adjective* **1** abnormal, bizarre, crazy, curious, eccentric, extraordinary, freakish, funny, odd, offbeat, outlandish, quaint, queer, strange, unconventional, unusual, weird. **2** particular, special. **3** characteristic, distinctive, exclusive, idiosyncratic, individual, particular, personal, special, specific, unique.

□ **peculiarity** *noun* characteristic, eccentricity, foible, idiosyncrasy, mannerism, quirk, trait.

pedant *noun* dogmatist, pedagogue, purist, stickler.

pedantic *adjective* exact, fussy, hair-splitting, meticulous, nitpicking, particular, pernickety (*informal*), precise.

pedestrian *noun* hiker, rambler, walker.

pedigree *noun* ancestry, background, family, genealogy, line, lineage, stock.

pedlar *noun* door-to-door salesman, hawker, huckster.

peel *noun* rind, skin, zest.

peel *verb* flake, pare, remove, scale, skin, strip.

peep *verb* **1** glance, look, peek, peer. **2** appear, come into view, emerge, show. □ **peep** *noun* glance, glimpse, look, peek.

peer *verb* gaze, look, peek, peep, stare.

peer *noun* **1** aristocrat, lord, noble, nobleman; (*kinds of peer*) baron, duke, earl, marquess, viscount. **2** contemporary, equal, fellow. □ **peeress** *noun* aristocrat, lady, noblewoman; (*kinds of peeress*) baroness, countess, duchess, marchioness, viscountess.

peerless adjective incomparable, inimitable, matchless, superlative, supreme, unequalled, unparalleled, unrivalled, unsurpassed.

peeve verb annoy, bug (informal), irritate, miff (informal), needle, pique, provoke, rile, upset, vex.

peevish adjective bad-tempered, crabby, cranky, cross, fractious, grouchy, grumpy, irritable, petulant, querulous, snaky (Australian informal), sulky, surly, testy.

peg noun hook, pin, spike.

peg verb 1 attach, fasten, pin, secure. 2 control, fix, freeze, limit, set.

pejorative adjective derogatory, disparaging, uncomplimentary.

pellet noun ball, bead, pill.

pelt verb 1 assail, batter, bombard, pepper, shower. 2 bucket, teem.

pelt noun coat, fleece, hide, skin.

pen noun ballpoint, Biro (trade mark), felt-tipped pen, fountain pen, marker, quill, Texta (trade mark).

pen noun cage, compound, coop, corral, enclosure, fold, hutch, pound, run, stall, sty.

pen verb close in, confine, coop up, enclose, fence in, impound, restrict, shut in.

penalise verb fine, handicap, punish.

penalty noun fine, forfeit, price, punishment.

penetrate verb 1 break through, drill through, enter, perforate, pierce, prick, probe, puncture, spike. 2 permeate, saturate, seep through, soak through. □ **penetrating** adjective (a penetrating voice) harsh, loud, piercing, sharp, shrill; (a penetrating mind) astute, discerning, incisive, intelligent, keen, perceptive, sharp, shrewd.

penitent adjective apologetic, contrite, regretful, remorseful, repentant, sorry.

pen-name noun alias, assumed name, nom de plume, pseudonym.

pennant noun banner, ensign, flag, standard.

penniless adjective broke, destitute, hard up (informal), impecunious, impoverished, needy, poor, poverty-stricken, skint (informal).

pension noun annuity, benefit, super (informal), superannuation.

pensive adjective day-dreaming, dreamy, introspective, meditative, reflective, serious, thoughtful.

pent adjective (*pent up*) bottled up, held in, repressed, restrained, stifled, suppressed.

people plural noun **1** human beings, humanity, humans, mankind, men and women, persons. **2** citizens, community, electorate, inhabitants, nation, populace, population, public, residents, society.

people verb colonise, inhabit, occupy, populate, settle.

pep noun dash, energy, go, life, liveliness, spirit, verve, vigour, vim (*informal*), vitality, vivacity.

pepper noun capsicum.

pepper verb bombard, pelt, riddle, shower, spray.

perceive verb **1** become aware of, detect, discern, notice, observe, recognise, see. **2** apprehend, deduce, feel, gather, grasp, realise, sense, understand.

perceptible adjective appreciable, discernible, evident, noticeable, observable, obvious, palpable, tangible, visible.

perceptive adjective astute, clever, discerning, keen, observant, percipient, perspicacious, quick, sensitive, sharp, shrewd, understanding.

perch noun roost.

perch verb alight, land, rest, roost, settle, sit.

percolate verb filter, leach, ooze, permeate, seep, trickle.

perennial adjective chronic, constant, continuous, eternal, everlasting, lasting, never-ending, permanent, perpetual, persistent, recurring.

perfect adjective **1** complete, excellent, exemplary, faultless, flawless, ideal, immaculate, impeccable, in mint condition, model, optimum, spotless, unblemished, undamaged. **2** accurate, correct, exact, precise. **3** absolute, complete, out-and-out, pure, sheer, thorough, total, utter.

perfect verb polish, refine.

perforate verb penetrate, pierce, prick, puncture.

perform verb **1** act, appear, enact, play, present, put on, stage, star. **2** accomplish, achieve, carry out, complete, discharge, do, execute, fulfil. **3** behave, function, go, operate, run, work. □ **performance** noun concert, enactment, gig (*informal*), play, presentation, production, show, showing, staging. □ **performer** noun actor, actress, artist, artiste, busker, dancer, entertainer, instrumentalist, musician, player, singer, star, vocalist.

perfume noun aroma, bouquet, fragrance, odour, scent, smell.

perfunctory adjective brief, careless, casual, cursory, half-hearted, hasty, mechanical, offhand, routine, slapdash, superficial.

perhaps adverb maybe, perchance (old use), possibly.

peril noun danger, hazard, jeopardy, risk, threat. □ **perilous** adjective chancy, dangerous, dicey (slang), hairy (slang), hazardous, precarious, risky, unsafe.

perimeter noun border, boundary, circumference, edge, fringe, limits, margin.

period noun **1** age, bout, duration, epoch, era, interval, patch, phase, season, space, span, spell, stage, stint, stretch, term, time, while. **2** class, lesson, session. □ **periodic** adjective cyclical, periodical, recurrent, regular, seasonal.

periodical noun journal, magazine, newspaper, paper, serial.

peripatetic adjective itinerant, mobile, travelling.

periphery noun boundary, edge, fringe, limits, outskirts, perimeter. □ **peripheral** adjective incidental, marginal,

minor, secondary, subsidiary tangential.

perish verb **1** die, expire, los your life, pass away. **2** disintegrate, give way, go, rot

perjure verb □ **perjur yourself** bear false witness give false testimony, lie.

perk verb □ **perk up** brighter up, buck up, liven up, pep up revive.

perk noun bonus, extra, fring benefit, perquisite.

perky adjective animated bright, cheerful, energetic frisky, lively, sprightly, spr vivacious.

permanent adjective chronic constant, continual, con tinuous, durable, enduring everlasting, fixed, indelible indestructible, ingrained lasting, lifelong, long-lasting never-ending, ongoing, peren nial, perpetual, persistent stable. □ **permanently** adver always, constantly, con tinuously, eternally, forever, fo good, for keeps (informal perpetually, persistently.

permeate verb flow through penetrate, pervade, saturate soak through, spread through

permissible adjective accep able, admissible, allowable authorised, lawful, lega legitimate, permitted, proper, right, sanctioned, valid.

permission noun approval, authorisation, authority, clearance, consent, go-ahead, leave, licence.

permissive adjective broadminded, easygoing, indulgent, lenient, liberal, tolerant.

permit verb agree to, allow, approve of, authorise, consent to, legalise, license, put up with, sanction, tolerate.

permit noun authorisation, licence, pass, warrant.

perpendicular adjective upright, vertical.

perpetual adjective **1** abiding, endless, enduring, eternal, everlasting, lasting, never-ending, permanent, unending. **2** ceaseless, constant, continual, endless, incessant, interminable, non-stop, persistent, recurrent, repeated, unceasing.

perplex verb baffle, bamboozle (informal), bewilder, confuse, mystify, nonplus, puzzle, stump (informal), throw (informal).

persecute verb bully, harass, hassle, intimidate, maltreat, mistreat, oppress, terrorise, torment, torture, tyrannise, victimise.

persevere verb battle on, carry on, continue, endure, keep on, persist, plug away, stick at (informal). □ **perseverance** noun determination, diligence, doggedness, endurance, patience, persistence, pertinacity, stamina, staying power, sticking power, tenacity.

persist verb **1** carry on, continue, go on, keep on, persevere, stick at (informal). **2** continue, hold, last, live on, remain, survive. □ **persistent** adjective (a persistent person) assiduous, determined, diligent, dogged, firm, indefatigable, obstinate, patient, pertinacious, relentless, resolute, steadfast, stubborn, tenacious, tireless, unwavering; (a persistent problem) chronic, constant, continuous, endless, eternal, everlasting, incessant, interminable, nagging, permanent, perpetual, recurrent, unceasing, unrelenting, unremitting.

person noun chap (informal), character, creature, fellow (informal), human, human being, individual, mortal, sort (informal), soul, type (informal); see also CHILD, MAN, WOMAN.

personal adjective **1** characteristic, distinctive, idiosyncratic, individual, special, unique. **2** confidential, intimate, private, secret.

personality noun **1** character, disposition, make-up, nature, temperament. **2** celebrity, identity (*Australian informal*), luminary, star.

personify verb embody, epitomise, exemplify, represent, symbolise, typify.

personnel noun employees, human resources, staff, workers, workforce.

perspective noun angle, outlook, point of view, standpoint, viewpoint.

persuade verb cajole, coax, convert, convince, entice, induce, influence, lead, move, prevail on, sway, talk into, tempt, win over. □ **persuasion** noun argument, cajolery, coaxing, convincing, influence. □ **persuasive** adjective cogent, compelling, convincing, eloquent, forceful, plausible, powerful, strong, telling, weighty.

pertinent adjective applicable, apposite, appropriate, apt, germane, material, relevant, suitable.

perturb verb agitate, alarm, bother, disconcert, distress, disturb, frighten, scare, trouble, upset, worry.

peruse verb examine, inspect, look over, read, scan, scrutinise, study. □ **perusal** noun examination, inspection, reading, scanning, scrutiny, study.

pervade verb diffuse through, fill, permeate, spread through.

perverse adjective contrary, disobedient, headstrong, intractable, obstinate, pigheaded (*informal*), rebellious, recalcitrant, refractory, stroppy (*informal*), stubborn, unreasonable, wayward, wilful.

pervert verb bribe, corrupt, lead astray. □ **perverted** adjective corrupt, depraved, deviant, kinky (*informal*), sick, twisted, warped.

pervert noun deviant, weirdo (*informal*).

pessimistic adjective cynical, defeatist, despairing, despondent, fatalistic, gloomy, hopeless, morbid, negative, resigned, unhappy.

pest noun annoyance, bother, curse, inconvenience, menace, nuisance, pain (*informal*).

pester verb annoy, badger, bother, harass, hassle (*informal*), hound, irritate, keep on at, nag, plague, torment, trouble, worry.

pet noun apple of someone's eye, darling, favourite.

et *adjective* **1** domestic, domesticated, tame. **2** favourite, special.

et *verb* caress, cuddle, fondle, pat, stroke.

eter *verb* □ **peter out** diminish, end, fail, give out, run out, stop, taper off.

etition *noun* appeal, entreaty, plea, request, supplication.

etition *verb* appeal to, ask, beseech, call upon, entreat, plead, pray, request.

etrify *verb* appal, frighten, numb, paralyse, scare stiff (*informal*), terrify.

etrol *noun* fuel, gas (*American informal*), gasoline (*American*). □ **petrol station** filling station, garage, roadhouse, service station, servo (*Australian informal*).

etticoat *noun* slip, underskirt.

etty *adjective* insignificant, minor, paltry, piffling (*informal*), small, trifling, trivial, unimportant.

etulant *adjective* bad-tempered, crabby, cross, grouchy, grumpy, huffy, irritable, peevish, snappy, sulky, sullen, testy, tetchy.

hantom *noun* apparition, ghost, hallucination, phantasm, poltergeist, spectre,

spirit, spook (*informal*), vision, wraith.

pharmacist *noun* apothecary (*old use*), chemist, dispenser, druggist, pharmaceutical chemist.

pharmacy *noun* dispensary, drugstore (*American*).

phase *noun* period, point, stage, step, time.

phenomenal *adjective* amazing, exceptional, extraordinary, fabulous (*informal*), fantastic (*informal*), great, incredible (*informal*), marvellous, miraculous, noteworthy, outstanding, prodigious, rare, remarkable, sensational, singular, stupendous, uncommon, wonderful.

phenomenon *noun* event, experience, happening, occurrence.

philanthropic *adjective* benevolent, charitable, generous, humane, humanitarian, kind-hearted, magnanimous, munificent.

philistine *adjective* boorish, ignorant, lowbrow, uncultivated, uncultured, unrefined.

philosophical *adjective* calm, fatalistic, logical, rational, reasonable, resigned, serene, stoical, unemotional.

philosophy *noun* belief system, convictions, doctrine,

ideology, principles, values, view.

phlegmatic *adjective* apathetic, calm, cool, impassive, indifferent, lethargic, nonchalant, placid, serene, sluggish, stolid, unemotional, unexcitable, unflappable (*informal*).

phobia *noun* aversion, dislike, dread, fear, hang-up (*informal*), horror.

phone *noun* blower (*informal*), telephone.

phone *verb* call, dial, ring (up), telephone.

phoney *adjective* artificial, bogus, counterfeit, fake, false, forged, imitation, pretend (*informal*), pseudo, sham, synthetic.

photocopy *noun* copy, duplicate. □ **photocopy** *verb* copy, duplicate, reproduce.

photograph *noun* photo, picture, print, shot, snap, snapshot.

photograph *verb* shoot, snap.

phrase *noun* expression, idiom, term; see also *SAYING*.

phrase *verb* couch, express, formulate, frame, put, word.

phraseology *noun* idiom, language, parlance, terminology, vocabulary, wording.

physical *adjective* **1** bodily, corporal. **2** actual, concrete, material, real, solid, tangible.

physician *noun* doctor, medic, practitioner.

physique *noun* body, buil, figure, shape.

pick *verb* **1** collect, cut, gathe harvest, pluck, pull off. choose, decide on, elect, nam nominate, opt for, select, sett on, single out, vote for. □ **pic on** bully, criticise, find fau with, get at (*informal*), haras nag. □ **pick up 1** call fc collect, fetch, get. **2** get bette improve, rally, recover.

pick *noun* **1** choice, optio, preference, selection. **2** bes choice, cream, elite.

picket *noun* **1** guard, lookou patrol, sentinel, sentry, watc **2** pale, paling, post, stake.

pickle *noun* fix (*informal*), ja (*informal*), mess, pligh predicament, spot (*informal*

pickle *verb* preserve, souse.

picture *noun* **1** cartoo, collage, design, diagrar drawing, engraving, etchin illustration, image, landscap likeness, mosaic, mura painting, photo, photograp plate, portrait, prir representation, reproductio sketch, snapshot; (*pictur* graphics. **2** film, flic (*informal*), motion pictur movie (*informal*), movi, picture, video.

picture verb **1** depict, draw, illustrate, paint, portray, represent, reproduce, sketch. **2** conceive, dream up, envisage, fancy, imagine, see, visualise.

picturesque adjective **1** attractive, beautiful, charming, pretty, quaint, scenic. **2** colourful, descriptive, expressive, graphic, imaginative, striking, vivid.

pie noun flan, quiche, tart.

piebald adjective dappled, mottled, pied, skewbald.

piece noun **1** amount, bar, bit, bite, block, chip, chunk, component, division, element, fraction, fragment, hunk, length, lump, module, morsel, part, portion, quantity, remnant, scrap, section, segment, share, shred, slab, slice, sliver, snippet, stick, titbit, unit, wedge. **2** example, instance, item, object, sample, specimen, thing. **3** article, composition, creation, item, number, opus, work.

piece verb (piece together) assemble, join together, mend, patch up, put together, reassemble.

pier noun breakwater, jetty, landing stage, quay, wharf.

pierce verb bore through, enter, gore, impale, jab, lance, penetrate, perforate, prick, puncture, skewer, spear, spike, stab, wound.

piercing adjective **1** deafening, loud, noisy, penetrating, screeching, sharp, shrill, strident. **2** biting, bitter, cutting, keen.

piety noun devotion, devoutness, faith, godliness, holiness, piousness, reverence, saintliness, sanctity.

pig noun **1** boar, hog, piglet, porker, sow (female), swine. **2** see GLUTTON.

pigeon-hole noun compartment, cubby hole, niche.

pigheaded adjective headstrong, intractable, mulish, obstinate, refractory, selfwilled, stiff-necked, stubborn, wilful.

pigment noun colour, colouring, dye, tint.

pikelet noun drop scone, flapjack, pancake.

pile noun **1** batch, collection, heap, hoard, mass, mound, mountain, pyramid, stack, stockpile. **2** heap (informal), load (informal), lot (informal), mountain, oodles (informal), plenty, stack (informal), ton (informal).

pile verb accumulate, assemble, collect, gather, heap (up), load, mass, stack (up), stockpile.

pile *noun* column, pillar, post, stilt, support, upright.

pile *noun* nap, surface.

pilfer *verb* filch, help yourself to, lift (*informal*), nick (*slang*), pinch (*informal*), snitch (*slang*), souvenir (*slang*), steal, take.

pill *noun* capsule, lozenge, pellet, tablet.

pillage *verb* loot, maraud, plunder, raid, ransack, ravage, rob, sack.

pillar *noun* column, obelisk, pile, post, prop, shaft, stanchion, standard, support, upright.

pillow *noun* bolster, cushion.

pilot *noun* **1** airman, airwoman, aviator, captain. **2** coxswain, helmsman, navigator, steersman.

pilot *verb* conduct, escort, fly, guide, lead, navigate, steer.

pilot *adjective* experimental, preliminary, test, trial.

pimple *noun* blackhead, pustule, spot, whitehead, zit (*slang*); (*pimples*) acne.

pin *noun* brooch, drawing pin, hairpin, hatpin, nappy pin, safety pin, skewer, spike, split pin, staple, tack, tiepin.

pin *verb* **1** affix, attach, fasten, fix, nail, secure, spike, staple, stick, tack. **2** hold down, hold fast, immobilise, pinion.

pinch *verb* **1** nip, squeeze, tweak. **2** lift (*informal*), nick (*slang*), pilfer, purloin, snatch, snavel (*Australian informal*), snitch (*slang*), steal, swipe (*informal*), take.

pinch *noun* **1** nip, squeeze, tweak. **2** bit, smidgen, speck, touch, trace.

pine *verb* **1** crave for, hanker after, hunger for, long for, thirst for, yearn for. **2** grieve, languish, mope, mourn, waste away.

pink *adjective* coral, flesh-coloured, peach, rose, rosy, salmon-pink, shell-pink, skin-coloured.

pinnacle *noun* **1** apex, cap, crest, peak, summit, tip, top. **2** acme, apex, climax, culmination, height, heyday, peak, summit, top, zenith.

pinpoint *verb* discover, find, identify, locate, spot.

pioneer *noun* **1** colonist, discoverer, explorer, settler, trailblazer. **2** founder, innovator, trailblazer. □ **pioneer** *verb* create, develop, discover, establish, found, introduce, initiate, originate, start.

pious *adjective* devout, faithful, God-fearing, godly, holy, religious, reverent, saintly. □ **piousness** *noun* see PIETY.

pipe noun channel, conduit, drainpipe, duct, hose, main, pipeline, tube.

piquant adjective appetising, flavoursome, pungent, sharp, spicy, tangy, tart.

pique noun annoyance, displeasure, humiliation, irritation, mortification, resentment, umbrage. □ **pique** verb affront, annoy, gall, humiliate, hurt, irk, irritate, mortify, needle, nettle, offend, peeve (*informal*), vex, wound.

pirate noun buccaneer, corsair, marauder, privateer.

pit noun 1 abyss, bunker, cavity, crater, depression, ditch, gully, hole, hollow, trench. 2 coalmine, colliery, mine, quarry, shaft, working.

pit verb 1 dent, gouge, nick, pock-mark, scar. 2 match, oppose, set against.

pitch noun 1 highness, lowness. 2 degree, height, intensity, level, point. 3 angle, cant, grade, gradient, incline, slope.

pitch verb 1 bowl, cast, chuck (*informal*), fling, heave, hurl, lob, sling, throw, toss. 2 erect, put up, raise, set up. 3 lurch, plunge, rock, roll, toss about.

pitcher noun ewer, jug.

pitfall noun danger, difficulty, hazard, peril, snag, snare, trap.

pithy adjective brief, concise, meaningful, succinct, terse.

pitiful adjective 1 forlorn, heartbreaking, heart-rending, moving, pathetic, poignant, sad, touching, wretched. 2 contemptible, hopeless, miserable, pathetic, poor, sorry, useless, woeful.

pitiless adjective brutal, callous, cruel, hard-hearted, heartless, inhuman, merciless, relentless, remorseless, ruthless.

pittance noun chicken-feed (*informal*), peanuts (*informal*), trifle.

pity noun 1 commiseration, compassion, condolence, fellow-feeling, regret, sympathy. 2 shame.

pity verb commiserate with, feel for, feel sorry for, sympathise with.

pivot noun axis, fulcrum, shaft, spindle.

pivot verb revolve, rotate, spin, swivel, turn, twirl.

placard noun advertisement, bill, notice, poster, sign.

placate verb appease, calm, conciliate, mollify, pacify, propitiate, soothe.

place noun 1 address, area, locality, location, scene, setting, site, situation, spot, venue. 2 area, city, country, district, locality, neighbourhood, region, town, township, village. **3** chair, position, seat, space, spot. **4** dwelling, home, house, premises, residence. □ **in place of** in lieu of, instead of.

place verb arrange, deposit, dump, lay, leave, locate, plant, plonk, position, put, rest, set, situate, stand, station, stick (informal).

placid adjective calm, easygoing, equable, even-tempered, level-headed, mild, peaceable, peaceful, quiet, sedate, serene, tranquil, unexcitable, un-ruffled.

plagiarise verb appropriate, copy, crib, lift (informal), pirate.

plague noun **1** epidemic, pandemic, pestilence. **2** infestation, invasion, scourge.

plague verb annoy, bother, bug (informal), disturb, harass, hassle (informal), irritate, pester, torment, trouble, vex, worry.

plain adjective **1** austere, basic, bland, homely, insipid, ordinary, simple, unadorned, uncomplicated, undecorated, unembellished, uninteresting, unpatterned. **2** homely (American), unattractive, unprepossessing. **3** apparent, certain, clear, comprehensible, evident, explicit, intelligible, manifest, obvious, patent, transparent, unambiguous, understandable, unmistakable. **4** blunt, candid, direct, forthright, frank, honest, open, outspoken, straightforward, unambiguous.

plain noun flat, grassland, pampas, prairie, savannah, steppe, tundra, veld.

plaintive adjective doleful, melancholy, mournful, pitiful, sad, sorrowful.

plait verb braid, interlace, intertwine, interweave.

plan noun **1** aim, formula, intention, method, outline, plot, policy, procedure, programme, project, proposal, schedule, scheme, strategy. **2** blueprint, chart, design, diagram, drawing, layout, map, sketch.

plan verb **1** arrange, contrive, design, devise, draft, draw up, formulate, map out, organise, plot, premeditate, prepare, scheme, think up. **2** aim, intend, mean, propose.

plane noun **1** aeroplane, aircraft, jet, jumbo. **2** flat, level.

plane adjective even, flat, flush, level, smooth.

plank noun board, slab, timber.

plant noun **1** (plants) flora, greenery, vegetation. **2** factory, foundry, mill, works, workshop; see also *EQUIPMENT*.

plant *verb* **1** set out, sow, transplant. **2** fix, implant, put. **3** conceal, hide, secrete.

plaster *noun* bandage, dressing.

plaster *verb* coat, cover, daub, smear, spread.

plate *noun* **1** dish, platter. **2** layer, pane, panel, plaque, sheet.

plateau *noun* highland, tableland.

platform *noun* **1** dais, podium, pulpit, rostrum, stage, stand. **2** manifesto, policy, programme.

platitude *noun* banality, cliché, commonplace, truism.

platter *noun* dish, plate, salver, tray.

platypus *noun* duckbill, water mole (*old use*).

plausible *adjective* believable, conceivable, credible, likely, reasonable.

play *verb* **1** amuse yourself, cavort, enjoy yourself, entertain yourself, fool about, frisk, frolic, gambol, have fun, mess about, romp, skylark; (*play a game or sport*) join in, participate in, take part in; (*play the other team*) challenge, compete against, meet, oppose, take on, vie with. **2** perform

on. **3** act as, impersonate, perform as, portray, pretend to be, represent, star as. □ **player** *noun* **1** competitor, contestant, participant, sportsperson. **2** artist, artiste, entertainer, musician, performer. **3** actor, actress, performer. □ **play down** downplay, gloss over, make light of, minimise. □ **play for time** delay, hedge, procrastinate, stall, stonewall, temporise. □ **play up** be disobedient, be mischievous, be naughty, misbehave, muck up (*informal*).

play *noun* **1** drama, entertainment, production, show. **2** amusement, diversion, entertainment, fun, leisure, pleasure, recreation, sport.

playful *adjective* **1** active, frisky, high-spirited, lively, mischievous, skittish, spirited, sprightly, vivacious. **2** arch, facetious, humorous, jesting, jocular, light-hearted, teasing, tongue-in-cheek.

playground *noun* park, recreation ground.

plea *noun* **1** appeal, entreaty, petition, request, supplication. **2** excuse, grounds, pretext.

plead *verb* allege, assert, claim. □ **plead with** appeal to, ask, beg, beseech, entreat, implore, petition, request, urge.

pleasant noun 1 agreeable, attractive, beautiful, delightful, enjoyable, fine, good, inviting, lovely, mild, nice, peaceful, pleasing, pleasurable, relaxing, satisfying, soothing. 2 affable, agreeable, amiable, amicable, charming, cheerful, congenial, cordial, friendly, genial, good-humoured, hospitable, jolly, jovial, kindly, likeable, nice, sweet, sympathetic, winsome.

please verb 1 content, delight, gratify, satisfy, suit. 2 choose, desire, like, prefer, think fit, want, wish. □ **pleased** adjective content, contented, delighted, elated, glad, grateful, gratified, happy, joyful, satisfied, thankful.

pleasure noun 1 amusement, bliss, contentment, delight, diversion, enjoyment, entertainment, fulfilment, fun, gratification, happiness, joy, kick(s) (informal), recreation, satisfaction, thrill. 2 amusement, delight, diversion, entertainment, joy, recreation.

pleat noun crease, fold, tuck.

plebiscite noun ballot, poll, referendum, vote.

pledge noun assurance, commitment, guarantee, oath, promise, vow, word.

pledge verb guarantee, plight (old use), promise, swear, vow.

plentiful adjective abundant, ample, bountiful, copious, generous, large, lavish, liberal, profuse, prolific.

plenty noun abundance, heaps (informal), lashings (informal), loads (informal), lots (informal), masses, much, oodles (informal), piles (informal), stacks (informal), tons (informal).

pliable adjective 1 bendable, flexible, malleable, plastic, pliant, springy, supple. 2 adaptable, amenable, compliant, flexible, malleable, suggestible, tractable, yielding.

plight noun difficulty, dire straits, jam (informal), mess, pickle (informal), predicament, situation, state.

plod verb 1 lumber, plough, slog, traipse (informal), tramp, trudge. 2 beaver on, grind away, peg away, persevere, plug away, soldier on.

plot noun 1 conspiracy, intrigue, plan, scheme. 2 outline, scenario, story, storyline, synopsis. 3 allotment, block (Australian), field, garden, lot, patch.

plot verb **1** conspire, plan, scheme. **2** chart, draw, map out, outline, sketch.

ploy noun dodge, manoeuvre, ruse, scheme, stratagem, tactic, trick.

pluck verb **1** gather, harvest, pick, pull off. **2** pull out, pull up, remove. **3** clutch, grab, pull at, snatch, tug, yank (informal).

pluck noun bravery, courage, daring, grit, guts (informal), mettle, nerve, spunk (informal), valour.

plucky adjective bold, brave, courageous, daring, fearless, game, hardy, heroic, intrepid, mettlesome, spirited, valiant.

plug noun **1** bung, cork, stopper. **2** advertisement, boost, commercial, promotion, publicity.

plug verb block up, close up, fill, seal, stop up.

plummet verb crash, drop, fall, nosedive, plunge, take a dive, tumble.

plump adjective chubby, corpulent, dumpy, fat, obese, overweight, podgy, portly, roly-poly, rotund, squat, stout, tubby.

plunder verb loot, maraud, pillage, raid, ransack, ravage, rob, sack.

plunder noun booty, loot, pillage, spoils, swag (informal), takings.

plunge verb **1** force, jab, push, stick, thrust. **2** descend, dip, dive, drop, duck, fall, jump, leap, nosedive, plummet, sink, throw yourself, tumble. **3** dip, douse, immerse, lower, submerge.

plunge noun dive, drop, fall, header, jump, leap, nosedive, tumble.

poach verb **1** simmer. **2** hunt, steal.

pocket noun bag, compartment, envelope, pouch. ☐ **pocket knife** clasp-knife, jackknife, penknife. ☐ **pocket money** allowance.

pocket verb appropriate, misappropriate, pilfer, steal, take.

pod noun case, hull, husk, shell.

podgy adjective chubby, dumpy, fat, overweight, plump, portly, roly-poly, pudgy, rotund, squat, stout, tubby.

podiatry noun chiropody.

poem noun ballad, clerihew, doggerel, elegy, epic, haiku, idyll, jingle, lay, limerick, lyric, ode, rhyme, sonnet, verse.

poet noun bard.

poetry noun poems, verse. ☐ **poetic** adjective lyrical, metrical, poetical, rhythmic.

poignant *adjective* distressing, heartbreaking, heart-rending, moving, pathetic, pitiful, stirring, touching.

point *noun* **1** apex, extremity, nib, prong, spike, tine, tip, vertex. **2** dot, spot. **3** location, place, position, site, situation, spot. **4** instant, juncture, moment, stage, time. **5** aspect, attribute, characteristic, detail, feature, item, particular, property, quality, trait. **6** argument, drift, essence, gist, meaning, message, pith, substance, thrust. **7** aim, goal, intention, object, purpose, reason, sense, use, value. □ **point of view** opinion, outlook, perspective, stance, standpoint, viewpoint. □ **to the point** apposite, apropos, apt, germane, pertinent, relevant.

point *verb* **1** aim, direct, level, train. **2** indicate, show, signal. □ **point out** draw attention to, indicate, show.

pointed *adjective* **1** pointy, sharp, tapering. **2** barbed, cutting, incisive, penetrating, sharp, trenchant.

pointer *noun* clue, hint, indication, indicator, lead, recommendation, sign, suggestion, tip, wrinkle (*informal*).

pointless *adjective* aimless[...] fatuous, futile, irrelevant[...] meaningless, needless, sense[...] less, unnecessary, unpro[...] ductive, useless, worthless.

poise *verb* balance, steady.

poise *noun* **1** balance[...] equilibrium, steadiness. [...] aplomb, calmness, composure[...] confidence, coolness, equa[...] nimity, self-assurance, sel[...] confidence, self-control.

poison *noun* toxin, venom[...] □ **poisonous** *adjective* deadl[...] fatal, harmful, lethal, toxi[...] venomous.

poison *verb* **1** kill. **2** cor[...] taminate, infect, pollute, tain[...] **3** corrupt, defile, perver[...] pollute, warp.

poke *verb* **1** butt, dig, elbow, jab[...] nudge, prod, push, stab, stick[...] thrust. **2** (*poke out*) jut ou[...] project, protrude, stick out. [...] (*poke about*) forage, fossic[...] (*Australian informal*), run[...] mage, search, snoo[...] (*informal*). □ **poke fun a[...]** chiack (*Australian informa[...]*) deride, jeer at, laugh at, mak[...] fun of, mock, poke borak a[...] (*Australian informal*), ri[...] (*informal*), ridicule, satiris[...] sling off at (*Australia[...] informal*), take the mickey ou[...] of (*informal*), tease.

pole *noun* bar, boom, colum[...] mast, post, rod, shaft, spa[...]

staff, stanchion, standard, stick, stilt, upright.

police noun constabulary, cops (slang), fuzz (slang), law (informal). ☐ **police officer** constable, cop (slang), copper (slang), detective, inspector, officer, policeman, policewoman, sergeant, superintendent.

police verb control, patrol, supervise.

policy noun code, guidelines, line, manifesto, plan, platform, principles, procedure, rules, strategy, system, tactics.

polish verb **1** buff, burnish, rub, shine, smooth. **2** brush up, improve, perfect, refine, smarten up, touch up.

polish noun brilliance, gloss, lustre, sheen, shine, smoothness, sparkle.

polite adjective attentive, chivalrous, civil, civilised, considerate, courteous, diplomatic, gallant, genteel, gentlemanly, ladylike, refined, respectful, suave, tactful, thoughtful, urbane, well-behaved, well-bred, well-mannered.

politic adjective advisable, expedient, judicious, prudent, sensible, wise.

politician noun Member of Parliament, MP, parliamentarian, polly (slang), senator, statesman.

poll noun **1** ballot, election, vote. **2** Gallup poll, opinion poll, straw poll, survey.

poll verb gain, get, receive, win.

pollute verb contaminate, defile, dirty, foul, infect, poison, soil, taint.

pomp noun ceremony, display, glory, grandeur, magnificence, ostentation, pageantry, show, solemnity, spectacle, splendour, style.

pompous adjective arrogant, bombastic, grandiose, haughty, high and mighty, high-falutin (informal), hoity-toity, imperious, overbearing, pretentious, self-important, snobbish, stuck-up (informal), supercilious, superior.

pond noun dam (Australian), lake, pool, waterhole.

ponder verb brood, cogitate, consider, contemplate, deliberate, meditate, mull over, muse, reflect, ruminate, study, think.

ponderous adjective **1** bulky, cumbersome, heavy, massive, unwieldy, weighty. **2** dull, laborious, laboured, long-winded, stilted, stodgy, tedious, turgid, verbose, wordy.

pool noun **1** bogey hole (*Australian*), lagoon, lake, mere (*poetical*), pond, swimming hole, waterhole. **2** puddle. **3** aquatic centre, baths, swimming pool.

pool noun **1** bank, fund, jackpot, kitty. **2** reserve, supply.

pool verb amalgamate, combine, consolidate, merge, share.

poor adjective **1** bankrupt, broke (*informal*), destitute, hard up (*informal*), impecunious, impoverished, indigent, needy, penniless, penurious, poverty-stricken, skint (*informal*), stony-broke (*informal*). **2** bad, crummy (*informal*), defective, deficient, faulty, imperfect, inadequate, insufficient, inferior, lacking, mediocre, rotten, rubbishy, second-rate, shoddy, slipshod, substandard, unsatisfactory, useless, wanting. **3** hapless, miserable, pathetic, pitiable, pitiful, sorry, unfortunate, unlucky, wretched.

poorly adjective ill, indisposed, off colour, seedy (*informal*), sick, under the weather (*informal*), unwell.

pop noun bang, burst, crack, explosion, snap.

pop verb **1** bang, burst, crackle, explode. **2** (*pop in*) call in, drop in, nip in (*informal*), stop by, visit; (*pop up*) appear, come up, crop up, emerge, surface.

pope noun Bishop of Rome, Holy Father, pontiff.

populace noun masses, mob, multitude, people, population, public.

popular adjective **1** admired, celebrated, famous, favourite, renowned, sought-after, well known, well-liked. **2** common, general, mainstream, prevalent, universal, widely-held, widespread.

populate verb colonise, inhabit, occupy, people, settle.

population noun citizens, inhabitants, occupants, people, populace, public, residents.

porch noun entrance, lobby, portico, vestibule.

pore noun hole, opening, orifice.

pore verb **pore over** examine, go over, peruse, read, scrutinise, study.

pornographic adjective blue, dirty, erotic, indecent, lewd, obscene, smutty.

porous adjective absorbent, permeable, pervious, spongy.

port noun anchorage, dock, dockyard, harbour, marina, seaport.

portable adjective compact, light, movable, transportable.

portent noun harbinger, omen, presage, sign, warning.
□ **portentous** adjective menacing, ominous, threatening, warning.

porter noun attendant, carrier.

porter noun commissionaire, concierge, doorkeeper, doorman, gatekeeper, janitor.

portion noun allocation, allotment, bit, cut (informal), division, fraction, helping, part, percentage, piece, quantity, quota, ration, section, segment, serving, share, slice.

portion verb (portion out) allocate, allot, apportion, distribute, divide out, dole out, mete out, parcel out, share.

portly noun bulky, corpulent, fat, obese, overweight, rotund, stocky, stout, tubby.

portrait noun drawing, image, likeness, painting, photograph, picture, representation, sketch.

portray verb 1 depict, picture, represent, show. 2 characterise, depict, describe, represent, show. 3 act as, impersonate, perform as, play, represent.

pose noun attitude, position, posture, stance.

pose verb 1 model, sit. 2 (pose as) act as, impersonate, masquerade as, pass yourself off as, pretend to be. 3 ask, present, put forward, raise.

posh adjective elegant, grand, luxurious, opulent, smart, stylish, sumptuous, swanky (informal), swish (informal), upmarket.

position noun 1 locality, location, niche, place, point, possie (Australian informal), setting, site, situation, slot, spot, whereabouts. 2 pose, posture, stance. 3 circumstances, condition, situation, state. 4 appointment, job, occupation, office, post, situation.

position verb arrange, array, dispose, lay out, line up, mount, place, put, set.

positive adjective 1 absolute, categorical, certain, conclusive, definite, firm, incontrovertible, indisputable, irrefutable, sure, unmistakable, unequivocal. 2 assured, certain, confident, convinced, definite, sure. 3 affirmative. 4 beneficial, constructive, helpful, practical, useful.

possess verb 1 be blessed with, be endowed with, be gifted with, have, hold, own. 2 control, dominate, govern, influence, rule.

possession noun (possessions) assets, belongings, chattels, effects, gear, goods, property, stuff, things.

possessive adjective clinging, domineering, jealous, proprietorial.

possibility noun chance, contingency, likelihood, probability, prospect, risk.

possible adjective achievable, admissible, attainable, conceivable, credible, feasible, manageable, potential, practicable, reasonable, viable, workable.

possibly adverb maybe, perchance, perhaps.

post noun bollard, column, newel, pale, paling, picket, pier, pile, pillar, pole, prop, shaft, stake, stanchion, standard, stilt, support, upright.

post verb display, paste up, pin up, put up, stick up.

post noun correspondence, letters, mail, packets.

post verb dispatch, mail, send.
□ **keep someone posted** advise, brief, inform, notify.

post noun **1** appointment, employment, job, occupation, office, position, situation, work. **2** place, point, position, station.

post verb install, place, position, put, set, station.

postbox noun letterbox, mailbox, pillar box (old use).

poster noun advertisement announcement, bill, notice placard, sign.

post-mortem noun autopsy necropsy.

postpone verb adjourn, defer delay, hold over, put off, put on ice, shelve.

postscript noun addendum addition, afterthought, epi logue, PS, supplement.

postulate verb assume hypothesise, posit, propose suppose, theorise.

posture noun attitude, bearing carriage, deportment, pose position, stance.

posture verb pose, put on airs show off.

posy noun bouquet, bunch corsage, nosegay, spray.

pot noun billy, casserole cauldron, crockpot, dixie, pan quartpot, saucepan, urn vessel.

potent adjective effective efficacious, forceful, might overpowering, powerful strong. □ **potency** nou effectiveness, efficacy, force might, power, strength.

potential adjective budding future, likely, possible promising.

potential noun ability, aptitude capability, possibility, promise

potion noun brew, concoction, drink, liquid, mixture, philtre.

pottery noun ceramics, china, crockery, earthenware, porcelain, stoneware, terracotta.

pouch noun bag, dillybag (*Australian*), holder, pocket, purse, sack, wallet.

poultry noun domestic fowls.

pounce verb (**pounce on**) ambush, attack, fall upon, jump on, leap on, seize, spring on, swoop down on. □ **pounce** noun jump, leap, spring, swoop.

pound noun compound, enclosure, pen, yard.

pound verb **1** bang, batter, beat, clobber (*slang*), crush, grind, hammer, hit, knock, mash, pulp, pulverise, pummel, squash, thump. **2** beat, palpitate, pulsate, throb, thump.

pour verb **1** cascade, discharge, flow, gush, issue, run, spew, spill, spout, spurt, stream. **2** bucket, deluge, pelt, rain cats and dogs (*informal*), teem. **3** flood, rush, stream, swarm, throng.

poverty noun beggary, deprivation, destitution, hardship, impoverishment, indigence, need, penury, want.

power noun **1** energy, force, might, muscle, potency, strength, vigour. **2** ability,

capability, capacity, competence, faculty, skill, talent. **3** authority, clout (*informal*), control, dominance, dominion, influence, leverage, licence, mandate, muscle, right, sway, warrant. □ **powerless** adjective defenceless, feeble, helpless, impotent, incapable, weak.

powerful adjective **1** dynamic, energetic, hefty, invincible, mighty, potent, robust, strong, sturdy. **2** authoritative, cogent, compelling, convincing, effective, forceful, influential, persuasive, potent, sound, strong, weighty.

practicable adjective achievable, feasible, manageable, possible, practical, realistic, viable, workable.

practical adjective **1** businesslike, capable, competent, down-to-earth, hard-headed, pragmatic, proficient, realistic, sensible, skilled. **2** functional, handy, usable, useful, utilitarian. **3** applied, hands-on. □ **practical joke** gag, hoax, prank, trick.

practically adverb almost, close to, essentially, nearly, virtually.

practice noun **1** drill, exercise, preparation, rehearsal, training. **2** action, effect, operation, use. **3** convention, custom, habit, procedure, ritual, routine, tradition, way, wont.

practise verb 1 brush up, drill, exercise, rehearse, train. 2 apply, carry out, do, perform. 3 engage in, pursue, work at.

praise verb 1 acclaim, applaud, commend, compliment, congratulate, honour, pay homage to, pay tribute to. 2 adore, exalt, glorify, hallow, honour, laud (formal), magnify (old use), revere, venerate, worship.

praise noun acclaim, accolade, applause, bouquet, commendation, compliment, congratulations, eulogy, homage, honour, ovation, tribute. □ **praiseworthy** adjective admirable, commendable, creditable, deserving, exemplary, honourable, laudable, meritorious, worthy.

pram noun baby buggy, baby carriage, perambulator, pushchair, pusher (Australian), stroller.

prance verb caper, cavort, dance, frisk, frolic, gambol, jump, leap, romp, skip.

prank noun antic, caper, escapade, hoax, lark, practical joke, trick.

prattle verb babble, chatter, gabble, natter (informal), rabbit on (informal), yabber (Australian informal).

pray verb appeal to, ask, beg, beseech, entreat, implore, plead with, urge.

prayer noun benediction, blessing, collect, devotion, entreaty, intercession, litany, petition, request, supplication, thanksgiving.

preach verb deliver a sermon, expound, lecture, moralise, pontificate, proclaim, sermonise, teach. □ **preacher** noun chaplain, clergyman, clergywoman, curate, evangelist, minister, missionary, padre, parson, pastor, priest, rector, vicar.

prearranged adjective fixed, planned, predetermined.

precarious adjective chancy, dangerous, delicate, dicey (slang), dodgy (informal), hazardous, insecure, perilous, risky, rocky, shaky, ticklish, touch-and-go, uncertain, unsafe, unstable, unsteady, vulnerable.

precaution noun defence, preventive measure, protection, safeguard, safety measure.

precede verb come before, go before, herald, lead into, pave the way for, usher in.

precedent noun example, model, pattern, standard, yardstick.

precious adjective **1** costly, dear, expensive, invaluable, priceless, valuable. **2** beloved, cherished, dear, prized, treasured, valuable.

precipice noun bluff, cliff, crag, escarpment, rockface, scarp.

precipitate verb **1** accelerate, bring on, expedite, hasten, speed up. **2** fling down, hurl down, throw down.

precipitate adjective abrupt, hasty, headlong, hurried, impetuous, impulsive, rapid, rash, reckless, speedy, sudden, swift.

precipitation noun dew, hail, rain, rainfall, sleet, snow, snowfall.

precipitous adjective perpendicular, sheer, steep, vertical.

précis noun abstract, outline, résumé, summary, synopsis.

precise adjective **1** accurate, clear, correct, definite, exact, explicit, express, minute, particular, specific. **2** careful, fastidious, finicky, meticulous, painstaking, particular, particular, pernickety (*informal*), punctilious, scrupulous.

preclude verb bar, block, debar, exclude, prevent, prohibit, rule out.

precocious adjective advanced, bright, forward, gifted, mature, quick.

preconception noun assumption, expectation, prejudgement, prejudice, presumption, presupposition.

precursor noun ancestor, antecedent, forerunner, predecessor.

predator noun hunter, marauder.

predecessor noun ancestor, forebear, forefather, progenitor.

predestine verb destine, fate, foreordain, intend, mean, preordain.

predicament noun difficulty, dilemma, emergency, fix (*informal*), jam (*informal*), mess, pickle (*informal*), plight, quandary, spot (*informal*), trouble.

predict verb forecast, foretell, prophesy. □ **predictable** adjective expected, foreseeable, on the cards, unsurprising. □ **prediction** noun forecast, prognosis, prophecy.

predisposition noun inclination, proneness, propensity, susceptibility, tendency, vulnerability.

predominate verb dominate, preponderate, prevail. □ **predominant** adjective chief, dominant, main, major, paramount, prevailing, primary.

pre-eminent adjective distinguished, excellent, foremost, leading, outstanding, peerless, superior, supreme, unrivalled, unsurpassed.

preen verb clean, groom, neaten, plume, primp, smarten, spruce, tidy.

preface noun foreword, introduction, preamble, prologue.

prefer verb choose, fancy, favour, like better, opt for, pick out, select.

preference noun 1 inclination, leaning, liking, partiality, predilection. 2 choice, option, pick, selection.

pregnant adjective expectant, expecting, with child (*literary*).

prehistoric adjective ancient, antediluvian, earliest, olden (*old use*), primeval, primitive, primordial.

prejudice noun bias, bigotry, discrimination, intolerance, partiality, unfairness. □ **prejudiced** adjective biased, bigoted, discriminatory, intolerant, narrow-minded, one-sided, partisan, unfair.

preliminary adjective early, first, initial, introductory, opening, prefatory, preparatory.

prelude noun beginning, curtain-raiser, introduction, opening, overture, preamble, precursor, preface, prologue, start.

premature adjective hasty, precipitate, too early, too soon, untimely.

premeditated adjective calculated, deliberate, intended, intentional, planned, wilful.

premises plural noun accommodation, building, campus, house, property, site.

premiss or **premise** noun assumption, basis, ground, hypothesis, postulate, presupposition, proposition, supposition.

premonition noun feeling, foreboding, hunch, intuition, presentiment, suspicion.

preoccupied adjective absent-minded, absorbed, abstracted, engrossed, faraway, immersed, lost in thought, pensive, wrapped up.

preparation noun groundwork, homework, organisation, plan, planning, practice, setting up, spadework.

preparatory adjective introductory, preliminary.

prepare verb (*prepare a lesson*) arrange, design, develop, devise, get ready, lay out, make out, organise, plan, set up. (*prepare someone for a job*) brief, coach, equip, fit, groom.

prime, train; (*prepare a meal*) assemble, concoct, cook, make, mix, produce, put together, whip up. □ **be prepared to** be minded to, be ready to, be willing to.

preposterous *adjective* absurd, crazy, farcical, laughable, ludicrous, monstrous, nonsensical, outrageous, ridiculous, unthinkable, weird.

prerequisite *noun* condition, essential, must (*informal*), necessity, pre-condition, requirement, requisite.

prerogative *noun* authority, power, privilege, right.

preschool *noun* kindergarten, nursery school.

prescribe *verb* 1 advise, order, recommend, suggest. 2 dictate, impose, lay down, ordain, order, specify, stipulate.

presence *noun* attendance, company, society.

present *adjective* 1 about, at hand, here, in attendance, on the scene, on the spot. 2 contemporary, current, existing, immediate.

present *noun* here and now, now, today.

present *noun* contribution, donation, gift, handout, offering, tip.

present *verb* 1 award, bestow, confer, distribute, donate, give,

hand out, hand over. 2 announce, introduce, make known. 3 act, mount, perform, put on, stage. 4 demonstrate, display, exhibit, reveal, show. □ **present yourself** appear, arrive, attend, front up (*informal*), turn up.

presentable *adjective* acceptable, all right, decent, neat, OK (*informal*), passable, respectable, satisfactory, suitable, tidy.

presently *adverb* 1 anon, before long, by and by, directly, in a moment, shortly, soon. 2 at present, currently, now.

preserve *verb* 1 conserve, defend, guard, keep, keep safe, look after, maintain, perpetuate, protect, retain, safeguard, save, secure. 2 bottle, can, corn, cure, dry, freeze, pickle, salt, smoke, tin.

preserve *noun* conserve, jam, jelly.

preside *verb* (*preside over*) be in charge of, chair, conduct, control, direct, officiate at, run.

president *noun* chairman, chairperson, chairwoman, chief, director, head, leader.

press *verb* 1 compress, crush, depress, mash, push, squash, squeeze. 2 flatten, iron, smooth. 3 beg, entreat, implore, lean on (*informal*), persuade, pressure, request, urge. **4** (*press for*) call for, campaign for, demand, insist on, push for. □ **pressing** *adjective* critical, crucial, important, insistent, urgent, vital.

press *noun* newspapers, papers, print media; see also *JOURNALIST*.

pressure *noun* **1** compression, force. **2** burden, constraint, demand, difficulty, hardship, load, oppression, strain, stress, tension.

pressure *verb* browbeat, bulldoze (*informal*), bully, coerce, compel, constrain, drive, force, lean on (*informal*), persuade, press, pressurise, put pressure on, put the acid on (*Australian slang*), put the screws on (*informal*), railroad.

prestige *noun* celebrity, distinction, fame, glamour, glory, honour, kudos, renown, reputation, respect, status.

presume *verb* **1** assume, believe, guess, imagine, presuppose, suppose, surmise, take for granted, take it. **2** be so bold as, dare, have the audacity, take the liberty, venture.

presumptuous *adjective* arrogant, audacious, bold, cheeky, cocky, forward, impertinent, impudent, overconfident, pushy (*informal*).

presuppose *verb* assume, presume, suppose, take for granted.

pretence *noun* **1** acting, affectation, deception, fabrication, faking, hypocrisy, invention, lying, make-believe, pretending. **2** act, charade, cover, front, hoax, masquerade, pretext, put-on (*informal*), ruse, sham, show, trick.

pretend *verb* act, affect, bluff, deceive, fake, feign, kid (*informal*), make believe, make out, profess, put on an act, sham; (*pretend to be someone*) act as, impersonate, masquerade, pass yourself off as, pose as.

pretentious *adjective* affected, arty (*informal*), la-di-da (*informal*), ostentatious, pompous, self-important, showy, snobbish, stuck-up (*informal*), toffee-nosed (*informal*).

pretext *noun* excuse, pretence, ruse.

pretty *adjective* appealing, attractive, beautiful, bonny (*Scottish*), captivating, charming, dainty, fair (*old use*), fetching, good-looking, handsome, lovely, nice, pleasing, sweet (*informal*), winsome.

pretty *adverb* fairly, moderately, quite, rather, reasonably, somewhat.

prevail *verb* be victorious, rule, triumph, win the day. □ **prevailing** *adjective* chief, common, dominant, main, predominant, usual.

prevalent *adjective* common, current, dominant, general, popular, predominant, prevailing, usual, widespread.

prevent *verb* avert, avoid, bar, block, curb, deter, fend off, foil, forestall, halt, hamper, hinder, impede, inhibit, obstruct, preclude, prohibit, stave off, stop, thwart, ward off.

previous *adjective* earlier, former, one-time, past, preceding, prior. □ **previously** *adverb* above (*in a book*), before, earlier, formerly, hitherto, in the past, once.

prey *noun* quarry, victim.

prey *verb* □ **prey on** 1 devour, eat, feed on, hunt, kill, live off. 2 haunt, oppress, trouble, weigh on, worry.

price *noun* 1 amount, charge, cost, expense, fare, fee, payment, rate, sum, terms, toll, value, worth. 2 consequence, cost, penalty, punishment, sacrifice.

priceless *adjective* 1 costly, dear, expensive, invaluable, irreplaceable, precious, pricey (*informal*), valuable. 2 absurd, amusing, funny, hilarious.

prick *verb* jab, lance, perforate, pierce, puncture, stab. □ **prick** *noun* jab, pinprick, prickle, stab, sting.

prickle *noun* barb, needle, spike, spine, thorn.

prickle *verb* itch, smart, sting, tingle.

pride *noun* 1 delight, enjoyment, gratification, happiness, joy, pleasure, satisfaction. 2 delight, joy, pleasure. 3 dignity, honour, self-esteem, self-respect. 4 arrogance, conceit, egotism, hubris, self-importance, self-love, self-satisfaction, smugness, vanity.

pride *verb* □ **pride yourself on** be proud of, boast about, congratulate yourself on, flatter yourself on.

priest *noun* archdeacon, chaplain, chief priest, clergyman, clergywoman, cleric, father, high priest, minister, padre, parson, pastor, rector, vicar. □ **priestly** *adjective* clerical, ecclesiastical, ministerial, pastoral.

prim *adjective* demure, formal, old-fashioned, precise, prissy, proper, prudish, starchy, straitlaced, stuffy.

primary *adjective* basic, chief, essential, first, fundamental, key, main, major, paramount, prime, principal. □ **primarily** *adverb* basically, chiefly, essentially, firstly, fundamentally, generally, largely, mainly, mostly, predominantly, principally.

prime *adjective* **1** chief, key, leading, main, major, primary, principal. **2** best, excellent, first-class, superior, top-quality.

prime *noun* best, heyday, peak, zenith.

prime *verb* **1** make ready, prepare. **2** brief, coach, equip, fill in (*informal*), forearm, inform, instruct, prepare, train.

primeval *adjective* ancient, early, prehistoric, primal, primitive, primordial.

primitive *adjective* (*primitive tribes*) ancient, barbarian, prehistoric, primeval, primordial, savage, uncivilised; (*primitive methods*) archaic, basic, crude, elementary, obsolete, rough, rudimentary, simple, unsophisticated.

principal *adjective* basic, capital, cardinal, chief, dominant, essential, foremost, fundamental, leading, main, major, outstanding, pre-dominant, primary, prime, supreme.

principal *noun* **1** head, headmaster, headmistress, head teacher. **2** capital.

principle *noun* **1** assumption, axiom, belief, guideline, law, precept, rule, standard, tenet, truth. **2** conscience, ethics, honesty, honour, integrity, morality, morals, probity, scruples, standards, virtue.

print *verb* **1** produce, reproduce, run off; see also *PUBLISH*. **2** impress, imprint, stamp.

print *noun* **1** font, letters, type, typeface. **2** impression, imprint, indentation, mark, stamp. **3** copy, duplicate, facsimile, replica, re-production.

printout *noun* hard copy, output.

prior *adjective* anterior, earlier, pre-existing, previous. □ **prior** *adverb* **prior to** see *BEFORE*.

priority *noun* precedence, preference.

priory *noun* abbey, cloister, convent, friary, monastery, nunnery, religious house.

prise *verb* force, lever, wrench.

prison *noun* detention centre, dungeon, jail, lock-up, nick (*slang*), penitentiary (*American*), remand centre.

prisoner *noun* captive, convict, detainee, hostage, inmate, internee, jailbird, lag (*slang*).

private *adjective* **1** individual, own, personal. **2** classified, confidential, hush-hush (*informal*), quiet, secret. **3** hidden, isolated, off-limits, quiet, remote, secluded. **4** independent, non-government.

privilege *noun* advantage, benefit, concession, entitlement, exemption, perk (*informal*), prerogative, right.

prize *noun* award, crown, cup, jackpot, laurels, medal, reward, trophy.

prize *verb* appreciate, cherish, esteem, treasure, value.

probable *adjective* expected, likely, on the cards, predictable. □ **probability** *noun* chance, likelihood, possibility, prospect.

probationary *adjective* test, testing, trial.

probe *noun* examination, exploration, inquiry, inspection, investigation, study.

probe *verb* **1** examine, explore, feel around, poke, prod. **2** examine, inquire into, investigate, look into, question, scrutinise, sound out.

problem *noun* **1** burden, complication, concern, difficulty, dilemma, hassle (*informal*), headache, hitch, predicament, setback, snag, strife (*Australian informal*), trouble, worry. **2** conundrum, enigma, mystery, poser, puzzle, question, riddle, sum, teaser. □ **problematic**, **problematical** *adjective* **1** complicated, difficult, messy, ticklish, tricky, troublesome. **2** debatable, disputable, doubtful, questionable, uncertain.

procedure *noun* approach, method, operation, practice, process, routine, system, technique, way.

proceed *verb* **1** advance, go on, head, make your way, move on, press on, progress, push on. **2** carry on, continue, go on, keep going.

proceedings *plural noun* **1** actions, activities, business, events, goings-on, happenings. **2** action, lawsuit, legal action, litigation.

proceeds *plural noun* earnings, gain, income, profit(s), revenue, takings.

process *noun* course of action, means, method, operation, procedure, system, technique, way.

process *verb* (*process food*) change, convert, refine, transform, treat; (*process an application*) deal with, handle, take care of.

procession noun cavalcade, column, cortège, line, march, motorcade, pageant, parade.

proclaim verb advertise, announce, broadcast, circulate, declare, make known, pronounce, publicise, publish, tell, trumpet.

procrastinate verb dally, delay, dilly-dally (*informal*), dither, drag your feet, hesitate, hold off, play for time, stall.

procure verb acquire, buy, come by, find, get, get hold of, lay your hands on, obtain, pick up, secure.

prod verb **1** butt, elbow, jab, nudge, poke, push. **2** goad, prompt, push, rouse, spur, stimulate, stir, urge. □ **prod** noun **1** butt, elbow, jab, nudge, poke, push. **2** prompt, reminder, spur, stimulus.

prodigal adjective extravagant, improvident, profligate, spendthrift, wasteful.

prodigious adjective **1** amazing, astonishing, astounding, exceptional, extraordinary, great, marvellous, miraculous, phenomenal, rare, remarkable, stupendous, terrific (*informal*), wonderful. **2** colossal, enormous, gigantic, great, immense, massive, monumental, tremendous, vast.

prodigy noun genius, marvel, sensation, virtuoso, whiz-kid (*informal*), wizard.

produce verb **1** assemble, build, compose, construct, create, devise, fabricate, form, invent, make, manufacture, think up, write; (*produce offspring*) bear, beget, breed, bring forth, give birth to, raise, rear, reproduce; (*produce crops*) bear, bring forth, grow, yield; (*produce a sensation*) bring about, cause, create, generate, give rise to, provoke, raise. **2** bring forward, bring out, come up with, disclose, display, exhibit, furnish, offer, present, provide, reveal, show, supply.

produce noun crops, foodstuffs, harvest, products, yield.

product noun artefact, article, commodity, creation, item, object, production, thing; (*products*) goods, merchandise, output, produce, wares.

productive adjective **1** fertile, fruitful, prolific, rich. **2** beneficial, constructive, effective, profitable, rewarding, useful, valuable, worthwhile.

profane adjective blasphemous, disrespectful, impious, irreligious, irreverent, sacrilegious.

profane verb abuse, debase, defile, desecrate, misuse, violate.

profess verb **1** assert, avow, claim, confess, declare, proclaim, pronounce, state. **2** allege, claim, make out, pretend, purport.

profession noun calling, career, employment, job, occupation, vocation.

professional adjective adept, competent, expert, knowledgeable, proficient, qualified, skilful, skilled, trained. □ **professional** noun authority, expert, master, pro (informal), specialist.

proficient adjective able, accomplished, adept, adroit, capable, competent, deft, dexterous, expert, skilful, skilled, trained. □ **proficiency** noun ability, aptitude, capability, competence, expertise, mastery, skill.

profile noun **1** contour, outline, shape, silhouette. **2** account, biography, character sketch, description.

profit noun **1** gain, proceeds, return, surplus. **2** advantage, avail, benefit, gain, good, use, value. □ **profitable** adjective advantageous, beneficial, commercial, fruitful, helpful, lucrative, moneymaking, paying, productive, remunera-tive, rewarding, useful, valuable, worthwhile.

profit verb (profit from) be helped by, benefit from, capitalise on, exploit, gain from, make the most of.

profound adjective **1** deep, great, heartfelt, intense, sincere. **2** deep, erudite, intellectual, learned, penetrating, serious, thoughtful, wise.

profuse adjective abundant, ample, copious, extravagant, lavish, plentiful.

progeny noun children, descendants, family, offspring.

prognosis noun forecast, prediction.

programme noun **1** agenda, calendar, plan, schedule, timetable. **2** broadcast, performance, presentation, production, show, telecast.

progress noun **1** advance, headway, march, strides. **2** advance, advancement, development, evolution, expansion, growth, improvement, progression. □ **in progress** going on, happening, proceeding, taking place, under way.

progress verb advance, come along, come on, continue, develop, go ahead, improve, make headway, move ahead, move forward, move on, proceed. □ **progression** noun sequence, series, string, succession.

progressive adjective **1** continuous, gradual, ongoing, steady. **2** avant-garde, enlightened, enterprising, forward-thinking, go-ahead, innovative, modern, up-and-coming (informal).

prohibit verb ban, bar, forbid, outlaw, proscribe, veto.

project noun **1** enterprise, plan, proposal, scheme, undertaking, venture. **2** assignment, exercise, task.

project verb **1** extend, jut out, overhang, protrude, stand out, stick out. **2** cast, fling, hurl, launch, propel, shoot, throw. □ **projection** noun **1** ledge, overhang, ridge, shelf. **2** estimate, estimation, extrapolation, forecast, prediction.

projectile noun bullet, grenade, missile, rocket, shell, shot.

proletariat noun commoners, masses, plebs (informal), rank and file, wage earners, workers, working class.

proliferate verb burgeon, increase, multiply, mushroom.

prolific adjective fertile, fruitful, productive.

prologue noun foreword, introduction, preamble, preface, prelude.

prolong verb drag out, draw out, extend, lengthen, protract, spin out, stretch out, string out.

promenade noun **1** boulevard, esplanade, mall, parade. amble, saunter, stroll, walk.

prominent adjective **1** jutting out, projecting, protruding, sticking out. **2** conspicuous, noticeable, obtrusive, obvious, pronounced, salient, striking. **3** celebrated, distinguished, eminent, famous, illustrious, important, notable, outstanding, pre-eminent, renowned, well-known.

promiscuous adjective fast, immoral, licentious, loose, wanton.

promise noun **1** assurance, commitment, contract, covenant, guarantee, oath, pledge, vow, word, word of honour. aptitude, capability, potential, talent.

promise verb agree, assure, commit yourself, give you word, guarantee, pledge, swear, undertake, vow.

promising adjective (a promising start) auspicious, encouraging, favourable, propitious, reassuring; (a promising actor able, gifted, talented, up-and-coming (*informal*).

promontory noun cape, head, headland, point.

promote verb **1** advance, elevate, move up, raise, upgrade. **2** advance, boost, encourage, facilitate, foster, further, help, sponsor, support. **3** advertise, hype up (*slang*), make known, market, plug (*informal*), publicise, push.

prompt adjective **1** early, expeditious, immediate, instant, instantaneous, quick, speedy, swift. **2** on time, punctual. □ **promptly** adverb **1** at once, expeditiously, immediately, instantly, quickly, readily, right away, speedily, straight away, swiftly, without delay. **2** on the dot, on the knocker (*Australian informal*), on time, punctually.

prompt verb **1** egg on, encourage, incite, induce, influence, inspire, motivate, move, spur, stimulate. **2** cue, jog the memory of, remind.

prone adjective face down, flat, horizontal, prostrate. □ **be prone to** be inclined to, be liable to, be predisposed to, be subject to, be susceptible to.

prong noun point, spike, tine.

pronounce verb **1** articulate, enunciate, say, sound, speak,

utter, voice. **2** announce, declare, proclaim.

pronounced adjective apparent, clear, clear-cut, conspicuous, definite, distinct, evident, marked, noticeable, obvious, prominent, striking, strong, unmistakable.

proof noun confirmation, corroboration, demonstration, documentation, evidence, facts, grounds, substantiation, testimony, verification.

prop noun brace, buttress, post, reinforcement, stake, stay, strut, support.

prop verb lean, rest, stand. □ **prop up** brace, buttress, hold up, reinforce, shore up, stake, strengthen, support.

prop verb baulk, jib, pull up, stop.

propel verb catapult, drive, eject, fling, impel, push, send, shoot, throw, thrust.

propensity noun inclination, leaning, penchant, predisposition, proclivity, proneness, tendency.

proper adjective **1** accepted, appropriate, apt, conventional, correct, established, fitting, orthodox, right, standard, suitable. **2** courteous, decent, decorous, dignified, formal, polite, prim, respectable, seemly. **3** absolute, complete, real, thorough, utter.

property noun **1** assets, belongings, chattels, effects, fortune, gear, goods, possessions, riches, things, wealth. **2** building(s), land, real estate. **3** characteristic, feature, quality, trait.

prophecy noun forecast, prediction.

prophesy verb forecast, foresee, foretell, predict.

prophet noun augur, forecaster, fortune-teller, oracle, prophetess (female), seer, sibyl (female), soothsayer.

propitious adjective advantageous, auspicious, favourable, fortunate, lucky, opportune, timely.

proportion noun **1** cut (informal), division, fraction, part, percentage, piece, portion, quota, section, share. **2** balance, ratio, relationship. ☐ **proportions** plural noun dimensions, extent, magnitude, measurements, size.

propose verb advance, offer, present, proffer, propound, put forward, recommend, submit, suggest, tender. ☐ **proposal** noun bid, offer, plan, project, proposition, recommendation, scheme, submission, suggestion.

proprietor noun landlady, landlord, manager, owner, proprietress.

propriety noun correctness, courtesy, decency, decorum, politeness, respectability, seemliness.

prosaic adjective banal, boring, commonplace, dull, humdrum, monotonous, mundane, ordinary, pedestrian, routine, uninspiring, uninteresting, workaday.

proscribe verb ban, bar, forbid, outlaw, prohibit.

prosecute verb accuse, bring to trial, charge, indict, sue, take to court, try.

prospect noun **1** chance, hope, likelihood, odds, outlook, possibility, probability. **2** outlook, panorama, scene, sight, view, vista.

prospect verb explore, fossick (Australian informal), look, search.

prospective adjective future, likely, possible, potential, would-be.

prosper verb boom, do well, flourish, grow, make money, succeed, thrive.

prosperous adjective affluent, flourishing, moneyed, rich, successful, thriving, wealthy, well-heeled (informal), well off, well-to-do. ☐ **prosperity** noun affluence, fortune, plenty, riches, success, wealth.

prostitute noun call-girl, courtesan (old use), harlot (old use), hooker (slang), sex worker, whore.

prostrate adjective face down, flat, horizontal, procumbent, prone.

prostrate verb (prostrate yourself) bow, kneel, kowtow, throw yourself down.

protect verb care for, cherish, cover, defend, guard, insulate, keep safe, look after, mind, preserve, safeguard, screen, secure, shelter, shield, take care of, tend, watch over. □ **protection** noun armour, barrier, buffer, cover, defence, immunity, refuge, safeguard, screen, security, shelter, shield. □ **protective** adjective (a protective person) possessive, solicitous, vigilant, watchful; (protective clothing) covering, fireproof, insulating, protecting, waterproof.

protest noun beef (slang), complaint, demur, grumble, hue and cry, objection, outcry; see also DEMONSTRATION.

protest verb 1 beef (slang), be up in arms, complain, demonstrate, demur, grumble, moan, object, remonstrate, squeal (informal). 2 affirm, assert, avow, declare, insist on,

maintain, profess. □ **protester** noun agitator, complainer, demonstrator, dissident, objector.

prototype noun archetype, original, sample, trial model.

protract verb drag out, draw out, extend, lengthen, prolong, spin out, stretch out.

protrude verb bulge, jut out, poke out, project, stand out, stick out.

proud adjective 1 delighted, gratified, happy, pleased, satisfied. 2 dignified, independent, self-respecting. 3 arrogant, boastful, cocky, conceited, disdainful, egotistic(al), haughty, high and mighty, hoity-toity, self-satisfied, smug, snobbish, snooty (informal), stuck-up (informal), supercilious, superior, vain.

prove verb 1 bear out, confirm, corroborate, demonstrate, document, establish, show, substantiate, verify. 2 be found, turn out.

proverb noun adage, axiom, catchphrase, dictum, maxim, motto, saying, slogan.

provide verb 1 allot, arm, contribute, donate, endow, equip, furnish, give, grant, offer, present, supply. 2 (provide for) allow for, anticipate, cater for, make provision for, plan for, prepare for.

providential adjective fortunate, heaven-sent, lucky, opportune, timely.

province noun 1 area, district, region, state, territory. 2 area, domain, field, responsibility, sphere. □ **provincial** adjective country, district, local, regional, rural.

provision noun 1 arrangement, plan, preparation. 2 clause, condition, proviso, requirement, specification, stipulation, term. □ **provisions** plural noun food, groceries, rations, stores, supplies.

provisional adjective interim, stopgap, temporary.

proviso noun condition, provision, qualification, requirement, rider, stipulation.

provoke verb 1 anger, annoy, enrage, exasperate, incense, infuriate, irritate, madden, needle (informal), outrage, rile (informal), upset, vex, wind up (informal). 2 arouse, cause, draw, elicit, evoke, generate, inspire, produce, prompt, spark, stimulate, trigger. □ **provocative** adjective (a provocative dress) alluring, inviting, seductive, sexy, tantalising, tempting; (a provocative comment) annoying, exasperating, infuriating, irritating, maddening.

prow noun bow, front, nose.

prowess noun 1 ability, aptitude, competence, expertise, genius, proficiency, skill, talent. 2 boldness, bravery, courage, daring, grit, guts (informal), heroism, mettle, valour.

prowl verb lurk, roam, skulk, slink, sneak, steal.

prudent adjective careful, cautious, far-sighted, judicious, politic, sage, sensible, shrewd, smart, wise.

prudish adjective demure, narrow-minded, old-fashioned, prim, prissy, puritanical, strait-laced.

prune verb chop, cut back, lop, remove, snip off, trim.

pry verb delve, inquire, interfere, intrude, meddle, poke about, probe, snoop (informal), stickybeak (Australian informal).

pseudonym noun alias, assumed name, false name, nom de plume, pen-name.

psychic adjective clairvoyant, extrasensory, occult, paranormal, supernatural, telepathic.

psychological adjective emotional, mental.

pub noun bar, hotel (*Australian*), inn, local (*informal*), public house, saloon (*American*), tavern.

puberty noun adolescence, pubescence, teens.

public adjective civic, civil, common, community, council, general, government, municipal, national, popular, state; (*public information*) disclosed, familiar, known, open, published, unconcealed. □ **public servant** bureaucrat, civil servant (*British & American*), functionary, government employee, official.

public noun citizens, community, country, electorate, nation, people, populace, population, society, voters. □ **in public** openly, publicly.

publican noun hotelier, hotelkeeper, innkeeper, landlady, landlord, licensee, proprietor, proprietress.

publicise verb advertise, announce, hype up (*slang*), make known, plug (*informal*), promote, publish, push.

publicity noun 1 attention, fame, limelight, notice. 2 advertising, build-up, hype (*slang*), marketing, plug (*informal*), promotion, propaganda.

publish verb 1 bring out, issue, release; see also *PRINT*. 2

advertise, announce, broadcast, disclose, disseminate, make known, make public, proclaim, promulgate, publicise, report, reveal.

pucker verb contract, crinkle, furrow, gather, screw up, wrinkle. □ **pucker** noun crease, crinkle, fold, gather, pleat, tuck, wrinkle.

puddle noun pool.

puerile adjective childish, foolish, immature, infantile, juvenile, silly.

puff noun blast, breath, draught, gust.

puff verb 1 blow, exhale, gasp, heave, huff, pant, wheeze. 2 (*puff up*) bloat, blow up, distend, expand, inflate, swell.

puffy adjective puffed up, swollen.

pugnacious adjective aggressive, argumentative, bellicose, belligerent, combative, hostile, hot-tempered, militant, quarrelsome.

pull verb 1 drag, draw, haul, heave, jerk, lug, tow, trail, tug, wrench, yank (*informal*). 2 sprain, strain, stretch, tear, wrench. □ **pull down** demolish, destroy, dismantle, knock down, level, raze, remove, take down, tear down. □ **pull off** accomplish, achieve, carry off, do, manage,

pullover noun jersey, jumper, sweater.

pulp noun **1** flesh. **2** mash, mush, purée.

pulsate verb beat, palpitate, pound, pulse, quiver, throb, thump, vibrate.

pulse noun beat, pulsation, rhythm, throb, vibration.

pulverise verb crush, grind, mill, pound.

pummel verb hit, pound, punch.

pump verb **1** (pump out) drain, empty; (pump up) blow up, fill, inflate. **2** grill, interrogate, probe, question, quiz.

pun noun play on words.

punch verb bash, box, clout (informal), cuff, dong (Australian informal), hit, pummel, quilt (Australian slang), slog, slug, sock (slang), stoush (Australian slang), strike, thump.

punch noun **1** blow, box, clout (informal), hit, slog, slug, sock (slang), thump. **2** force, forcefulness, power, vigour.

succeed in. □ **pull out** draw, extract, remove, take out, withdraw. □ **pull somebody's leg** have on (informal), kid (informal), tease, trick. □ **pull through** get better, rally, recover, survive. □ **pull up** draw up, halt, stop.

punctual adjective on schedule, on the dot, on the knocker (Australian informal), on time, prompt.

punctuate verb break, dot, interrupt, intersperse, pepper.

puncture noun hole, leak, perforation, rupture, slit, tear.

puncture verb penetrate, perforate, pierce, prick.

pundit noun authority, expert, sage.

pungent adjective acid, acrid, aromatic, hot, piquant, sharp, spicy, strong, tangy, tart.

punish verb castigate, chastise, discipline, make to suffer, penalise, scold, sentence. □ **punishment** noun castigation, chastisement, discipline, fine, imposition, penalty, sentence.

punt verb bet, gamble, risk, speculate, stake, wager.

puny adjective feeble, frail, sickly, skinny, small, tiny, undersized, weak, weedy.

pup noun puppy, whelp.

pupil noun apprentice, disciple, learner, scholar, schoolboy, schoolchild, schoolgirl, student.

puppet noun doll, finger puppet, glove puppet, marionette, string puppet.

purchase verb acquire, buy, get, obtain, pay for

□ **purchaser** noun buyer, customer.

purchase noun acquisition, buy.

pure adjective **1** clean, clear, fresh, solid, straight, unadulterated, unalloyed, uncontaminated, undiluted, unmixed, unpolluted, untainted. **2** blameless, chaste, decent, good, guiltless, innocent, modest, moral, sinless, uncorrupted, upright, virtuous. **3** absolute, complete, downright, perfect, sheer, thorough, total, utter.

purée noun mash, mush, pulp.

purgative noun enema, laxative, purge.

purge verb clear out, dismiss, eliminate, eradicate, expel, get rid of, remove, weed out.

purify verb clean, disinfect, distil, filter, refine, sterilise.

purist noun dogmatist, pedant, stickler.

puritanical adjective ascetic, austere, moralistic, prim, prudish, strait-laced, strict, wowserish (*Australian*).

purple adjective amethyst, hyacinth, jacaranda, lavender, lilac, mauve, mulberry, plum, violet.

purport verb allege, claim, pretend, profess.

purport noun drift, gist, meaning, substance, thrust.

purpose noun **1** aim, function, goal, intent, intention, justification, motivation, motive, object, objective, point, use, value. **2** determination, resolution, resolve, single-mindedness. □ **purposeless** adjective aimless, meaningless, pointless, senseless, useless. □ **on purpose** consciously, deliberately, intentionally, knowingly, purposely, wittingly.

purse noun pouch, wallet.

purse verb press together, pucker, squeeze.

pursue verb **1** chase, follow, go after, hound, hunt, run after, shadow, stalk, tail (*informal*), track down, trail. **2** carry on, conduct, continue, engage in, follow, work at.

pursuit noun **1** chase, hunt, stalking, tracking. **2** activity, hobby, interest, occupation, pastime, recreation.

push verb **1** drive, move, propel, shove, thrust. **2** advance, butt, elbow, force, forge, jostle, nudge, press, ram, shoulder, shove, squeeze, thrust. **3** bully, coerce, compel, dragoon, drive, egg on, encourage, force, goad, hound, press, pressure, spur, urge.

pusher noun **1** dealer, peddler, seller. **2** pushchair, stroller.

pushover noun **1** bludge (*Australian informal*), breeze (*informal*), child's play, cinch (*informal*), doddle (*informal*), piece of cake (*informal*), snack (*Australian informal*), snap (*informal*), walkover. **2** dupe, easy prey, mug (*informal*), sitter (*informal*), sitting duck (*informal*), soft touch, sucker (*informal*).

pushy adjective aggressive, assertive, bumptious, forceful, forward, self-assertive.

put verb **1** arrange, bung (*informal*), deposit, dump, fit, hang, implant, insert, install, lay, leave, locate, mount, place, plant, plonk, pop, position, rest, set down, settle, situate, slap, stand, station, stick. **2** express, formulate, phrase, say, state, word. □ **put by** put aside, reserve, save, set aside, stash (*informal*). □ **put down 1** crush, quash, quell, stop, subdue, suppress. **2** belittle, denigrate, disparage, humiliate, slight, snub. **3** destroy, kill, put to sleep. □ **put forward** advance, nominate, offer, present, propose, propound, put up, recommend, submit, suggest. □ **put off 1** defer, delay, hold off, postpone, reschedule, shelve.

2 deter from, discourage from, dissuade from, talk out of. **3** disgust, repel, revolt, sicken. □ **put on 1** change into, don, dress in, slip into, wear. **2** adopt, affect, assume, fake, feign, pretend. **3** gain, increase. **4** mount, perform, present, produce, stage. □ **put out 1** douse, extinguish, quench, snuff out. **2** annoy, bother, inconvenience, irritate, trouble. □ **put together** assemble, build, construct, join, make. □ **put up 1** build, construct, erect, pitch (*a tent*), set up. **2** boost, bump up (*informal*), increase, jack up (*informal*), raise. **3** accommodate, billet, house, lodge, take in. **4** contribute, donate, pay, provide, supply. □ **put up with** abide, accept, bear, brook, endure, stand for, suffer, take, tolerate.

putrid adjective **1** bad, decayed, decomposed, rotten. **2** foul, rank, smelly, stinking.

puzzle noun brainteaser, conundrum, dilemma, enigma, mystery, paradox, problem, question, riddle.

puzzle verb **1** baffle, bamboozle (*informal*), bewilder, confound, confuse, flummox (*informal*), mystify, nonplus, perplex, stump (*informal*), throw (*informal*). **2** brood, muse ponder, rack your brains, wonder. □ **puzzling** *adjective* abstruse, baffling, difficult, enigmatic, inexplicable, inscrutable, insoluble, mysterious, perplexing, strange, unfathomable.

pygmy *noun* dwarf, lilliputian, midget. □ **pygmy** *adjective* dwarf, miniature, small, tiny, undersized.

Qq

quack *noun* **1** charlatan, fake, impostor, phoney (*informal*). **2** see *DOCTOR*.

quadrangle *noun* courtyard, quad.

quaff *verb* drink, gulp, guzzle, swallow, swig (*informal*).

quagmire *noun* bog, fen, marsh, mire, morass, slough, swamp.

quail *verb* cower, cringe, flinch, recoil, shrink, wince.

quaint *adjective* attractive, charming, curious, odd, old-fashioned, picturesque, twee, unusual.

quake *verb* quaver, quiver, shake, shiver, shudder, tremble.

qualify *verb* **1** allow, authorise, entitle, equip, fit, licence, make eligible, permit, prepare, train. **2** limit, modify, restrict. □ **qualification** *noun* **1** ability, aptitude, attribute, competence, competency, credentials, eligibility, experience, knowledge, prerequisite, quality, skill, training. **2** condition, limitation, modification, proviso, reservation, restriction, stipulation.

quality *noun* **1** calibre, class, grade, level, standard, value, worth. **2** excellence, merit, value, worth. **3** attribute, characteristic, feature, trait.

qualm *noun* compunction, misgiving, pang of conscience, scruple.

quandary *noun* difficulty, dilemma, predicament. □ **in a quandary** confused, perplexed, uncertain, unsure.

quantity *noun* amount, dose, extent, load, lot, mass, measure, number, portion, quantum, sum, volume, weight.

quarantine *noun* isolation, segregation.

quarrel *noun* altercation, argument, barney (*informal*), clash, conflict, controversy, difference, disagreement, dispute, feud, fight, row, spat (*informal*), squabble, tiff, wrangle.

quarrel verb argue, be at loggerheads, bicker, brawl, differ, fall out, fight, row (*informal*), scrap, squabble, wrangle. □ **quarrelsome** adjective argumentative, belligerent, cantankerous, contentious, contrary, cross, disputatious, irritable, petulant, pugnacious, truculent.

quarry noun excavation, mine, pit, working.

quarry noun prey, victim.

quarter noun area, district, locality, neighbourhood, region. □ **quarters** plural noun accommodation, barracks, billet, digs (*informal*), housing, lodgings.

quarter verb accommodate, billet, house, lodge, put up, station.

quash verb annul, invalidate, nullify, overrule, overturn, rescind, reverse, revoke.

quaver verb quiver, shake, tremble, vibrate, waver.

quaver noun quiver, shaking, trembling, tremor, vibration, wavering.

quay noun berth, dock, jetty, landing stage, pier, wharf.

queasy adjective bilious, ill, nauseous, off colour, sick, unwell.

queen noun monarch, ruler, sovereign. □ **queenly** adjective majestic, regal, royal.

queer adjective **1** abnormal, bizarre, curious, eccentric, funny, odd, offbeat, peculiar, singular, strange, unconventional, unusual, weird. **2** dizzy, faint, giddy, ill, off colour, out of sorts, poorly, queasy, unwell.

quell verb (*quell a rebellion*) crush, defeat, overcome, put down, quash, subdue, suppress; (*quell fears*) allay, alleviate, assuage, calm, quieten, soothe, subdue.

quench verb **1** satisfy, slake. **2** douse, extinguish, put out, smother.

query noun enquiry, inquiry, question.

query verb challenge, dispute, doubt, question.

quest noun hunt, pursuit, search.

question noun **1** issue, matter, point, problem. **2** conundrum, enquiry, inquiry, poser, problem, puzzle, query, riddle. **3** argument, controversy, debate, dispute, doubt, uncertainty. □ **out of the question** impossible, inconceivable, unthinkable.

question verb **1** ask, cross-examine, enquire of, examine, grill, inquire of, interrogate, interview, probe, pump, quiz, sound out. **2** call into question, cast doubt on, challenge, dispute, doubt, query.

questionable *adjective* doubtful, dubious, suspect, suss (*informal*), uncertain.

questionnaire *noun* set of questions, survey.

queue *noun* chain, column, file, line, line-up, row, string.

queue *verb* line up.

quibble *noun* complaint, objection, protest.

quibble *verb* argue, carp, cavil, find fault, niggle, nit-pick (*informal*), object, protest, quarrel, split hairs.

quiche *noun* flan, pie, tart.

quick *adjective* **1** brisk, express, fast, fleet, rapid, speedy, swift, zippy. **2** (*a quick look*) brief, cursory, fleeting, hasty, hurried, perfunctory, short; (*a quick response*) expeditious, immediate, instant, instantaneous, prompt, speedy, swift. **3** able, alert, astute, bright, clever, intelligent, perceptive, sharp, shrewd, smart. **4** agile, lively, nimble, nippy (*informal*), sprightly, spry. □ **quickly** *adverb* apace, at full pelt, at speed, at the double, briskly, expeditiously, fast, hastily, hell for leather

(*informal*), hurriedly, immediately, in a flash, in a jiffy (*informal*), in no time, instantly, like greased lightning (*informal*), posthaste, promptly, rapidly, speedily, swiftly.

quicken *verb* **1** accelerate, hasten, hurry, speed up. **2** arouse, enliven, inspire, kindle, stimulate.

quiet *adjective* **1** noiseless, silent, soundless, still. **2** gentle, hushed, inaudible, low, soft. **3** calm, gentle, mild, peaceful, placid, restful, sedate, serene, tranquil, undisturbed. **4** introverted, reserved, reticent, retiring, shy, silent, taciturn, uncommunicative. **5** muted, soft, subdued, subtle, unobtrusive. □ **quietness** *noun* calm, hush, peace, quiet, serenity, silence, stillness, tranquillity.

quieten *verb* calm, hush, pacify, quiet, restrain, shush (*informal*), silence, soothe, subdue.

quilt *noun* continental quilt, coverlet, Doona (*trade mark*), duvet, eiderdown.

quip *noun* jest, joke, sally, wisecrack, witticism.

quirk *noun* **1** eccentricity, foible, idiosyncrasy, oddity, peculiarity. **2** aberration, fluke, trick, twist, vagary.

quit *verb* **1** depart from, desert, go away from, leave, vacate. **2** abandon, abdicate, chuck in (*informal*), forsake, give up, jack in (*slang*), leave, pack in (*informal*), relinquish, resign, retire, toss in (*informal*). **3** cease, desist from, discontinue, leave off, stop.

quite *adverb* **1** absolutely, altogether, completely, entirely, fully, perfectly, positively, totally, utterly. **2** comparatively, fairly, moderately, pretty, rather, reasonably, relatively, somewhat.

quiver *verb* pulsate, quake, quaver, shake, shiver, shudder, tremble, vibrate.

quiz *noun* competition, exam, examination, questionnaire, test.

quiz *verb* ask, examine, grill, interrogate, question, test.

quota *noun* allocation, allowance, cut (*informal*), lot, part, portion, proportion, ration, share.

quotation *noun* **1** citation, excerpt, extract, passage, quote (*informal*), reference. **2** estimate, quote (*informal*), tender.

quote *verb* **1** recite, repeat. **2** call up, cite, instance, mention, name, refer to. **3** estimate, tender.

Rr

rabbit *noun* buck (*male*), bunny (*informal*), doe (*female*), kitten (*young*).

rabble *noun* crowd, horde, mob, swarm, throng.

race *noun* chase, competition, contest, heat, marathon, rally, relay.

race *verb* **1** compete. **2** career, dart, dash, fly, hurry, hurtle, run, rush, shoot, speed, sprint, sweep, tear, whiz, zip, zoom.

race *noun* ethnic group, nation, people, tribe. □ **racial** *adjective* ethnic, national, tribal.

racetrack *noun* circuit, course, racecourse, speedway, track.

racism *noun* racial discrimination, racial intolerance, racialism, racial prejudice.

rack *noun* framework, holder, shelf, stand, support.

racket *noun* **1** clamour, commotion, din, disturbance, hubbub, hullabaloo, noise, pandemonium, row, ruckus, rumpus, tumult, uproar. **2** dodge (*informal*), lurk (*Australian informal*), rort (*Australian slang*), scam (*slang*), scheme, swindle.

racy *adjective* animated, exciting, juicy (*informal*), lively, spicy, spirited, stimulating.

radiant *adjective* **1** bright, brilliant, dazzling, gleaming, glowing, incandescent, luminous, shining. **2** beaming, beautiful, blissful, ecstatic, glowing, happy, joyful, overjoyed.

radiate *verb* **1** diffuse, emit, give off, give out, send out, shed, transmit. **2** branch out, diverge, issue, spread out.

radical *adjective* **1** basic, complete, drastic, far-reaching, fundamental, profound, sweeping, thorough. **2** extreme, extremist, immoderate, revolutionary.

radio *noun* receiver, set, transistor, tuner, wireless.

raffle *noun* art union (*Australian*), draw, lottery, sweep, sweepstake.

rag *noun* cloth, fragment, remnant, scrap.

ragamuffin *noun* guttersnipe, urchin, waif.

rage *noun* **1** anger, exasperation, frenzy, fury, ire, paddy (*informal*), tantrum, temper, wrath. **2** craze, fashion, mode, trend, vogue.

rage *verb* be angry, be beside yourself, be furious, blow your stack (*informal*), blow your top (*informal*), do your block (*Australian informal*), flare up, fly off the handle (*informal*), fume, go off the deep end (*informal*), let off steam, lose your cool (*informal*), lose your temper, rail, rant, rave, seethe.

ragged *adjective* **1** dilapidated, frayed, holey, scruffy, shabby, tattered, tatty (*informal*), threadbare, torn, worn-out. **2** irregular, jagged, rough, uneven.

raid *noun* **1** assault, attack, blitz, foray, incursion, invasion, offensive, onslaught, sortie, swoop. **2** bust (*informal*), search.

raid *verb* **1** attack, descend on, invade, storm, swoop on. **2** loot, pillage, plunder, ransack, rifle, rob.

rail *noun* banisters, bar, handrail, railing.

rail *verb* complain, declaim, inveigh, lash out, protest, rage, vociferate.

railings *plural noun* balustrade, barrier, fence, rails.

railway *noun* rail, railroad (*American*), train.

rain *noun* cloudburst, deluge, downpour, drizzle, precipitation, rainfall, shower, storm, thunderstorm. □ **rainy**

adjective damp, drizzly, showery, wet.

rain *verb* bucket down, drizzle, pelt, pour, rain cats and dogs (*informal*), spit, sprinkle, teem.

raincoat *noun* anorak, mac (*informal*), mackintosh, oilskin, trench coat, waterproof.

rainfall *noun* precipitation.

raise *verb* **1** elevate, heave, hoist, jack, lift, pick up. **2** boost, build up, bump up (*informal*), heighten, increase, inflate, jack up (*informal*), mark up, put up. **3** accumulate, amass, collect, gather, get, obtain. **4** (*raise children*) bring up, educate, nurture, rear; (*raise crops*) breed, cultivate, farm, grow, produce, propagate. **5** arouse, awaken, cause, encourage, kindle, provoke, rouse, stimulate. **6** bring up, broach, initiate, introduce, pose, put forward.
□ **raise from the dead** restore to life, resurrect, resuscitate, revive.

raise *noun* increase, rise.

rake *verb* **1** collect, gather, sweep up. **2** comb, forage, fossick (*Australian informal*), rummage, scour, search.

rally *noun* **1** assembly, convention, demo (*informal*), demonstration, jamboree, gathering, meeting. **2** competition, race.

rally *verb* **1** assemble, come together, convene, gather, marshal, mobilise, muster, round up, summon, unite. **2** get better, improve, pull through, recover, revive.

ram *verb* **1** compress, cram, drive, force, hammer, jam, pack, push, squeeze, stuff, tamp. **2** bump into, collide with, crash into, hit, run into, slam into, smash into.

ramble *noun* hike, roam, stroll, trek, walk.

ramble *verb* **1** amble, hike, roam, rove, saunter, stroll, traipse, tramp, trek, walk, wander. **2** digress, go off at a tangent, waffle (*informal*), wander, witter on (*informal*).

ramification *noun* complication, consequence, implication, offshoot.

ramp *noun* incline, slope.

rampage *verb* go berserk, go wild, run amok, run riot.

rampant *adjective* epidemic, flourishing, out of control, prevalent, rife, unchecked, uncurbed, unrestrained, widespread.

rampart *noun* bulwark, earthwork, embankment, fortification, parapet, wall.

ramshackle *adjective* decrepit, derelict, dilapidated, rickety, run-down, tumbledown.

ranch *noun* farm, stud.

rancid *adjective* bad, high, off, on the nose (*Australian informal*), rank, rotten, sour, stale.

rancour *noun* acrimony, animosity, bitterness, grudge, hatred, hostility, ill will, malice, resentment, spite, venom.

random *adjective* accidental, arbitrary, chance, fortuitous, haphazard, hit-or-miss, indiscriminate, unplanned.

range *noun* **1** chain, line, row, series. **2** area, bounds, compass, domain, extent, field, gamut, limits, orbit, scope, span, spectrum, sphere, spread; see also *ASSORTMENT* (at *ASSORTED*). **3** cooker, fireplace, oven, stove.

range *verb* **1** differ, extend, fluctuate, go, vary. **2** ramble, roam, rove, stray, travel, wander.

ranger *noun* curator, keeper, warden.

rank *noun* **1** column, file, line, queue, row. **2** class, degree, grade, level, position, standing, station, status.

rank *verb* arrange, class, grade, order, place, rate.

rank *adjective* **1** dense, lush, luxuriant, overgrown, profuse, thick. **2** bad, foul, off, offensive, on the nose (*Australian informal*), rancid, smelly, stinking, strong. **3** absolute, complete, downright, flagrant, glaring, gross, obvious, out-and-out, sheer, total, utter.

ransack *verb* **1** comb, fossick in (*Australian informal*), rake through, rummage in, scour, search. **2** loot, pillage, plunder, raid, rob, sack.

rant *verb* bluster, declaim, hold forth, rave, sound off (*informal*), spout, vociferate.

rap *verb* hit, knock, strike, tap.

rap *noun* **1** blow, hit, knock, tap, whack. **2** blame, censure, punishment.

rape *verb* assault sexually, ravish, violate.

rapid *adjective* brisk, expeditious, fast, hasty, high-speed, meteoric, precipitate, prompt, quick, speedy, sudden, swift, whirlwind. ◻ **rapidity** *noun* alacrity, dispatch, haste, promptness, quickness, speed, swiftness. ◻ **rapidly** *adverb* see *QUICKLY* (at *QUICK*).

rapt *adjective* absorbed, captivated, engrossed, enraptured, enthralled, entranced, intent, spellbound.

rapture *noun* bliss, delight, ecstasy, elation, euphoria, happiness, joy.

rare *adjective* abnormal, infrequent, occasional, odd, scarce, strange, uncommon, unfamiliar, unusual. □ **rarely** *adverb* infrequently, occasionally, once in a blue moon, seldom.

rare *adjective* undercooked, underdone.

rarefied *adjective* rare, thin.

rascal *noun* **1** blackguard, knave (*old use*), miscreant, rogue, scoundrel, villain, wretch. **2** devil, imp, monkey, scallywag, scamp.

rash *adjective* foolhardy, harebrained, hasty, headlong, heedless, hotheaded, impetuous, imprudent, impulsive, madcap, precipitate, reckless.

rash *noun* dermatitis, eczema, eruption, hives, spots.

rate *noun* **1** pace, speed, velocity. **2** charge, cost, fare, fee, price, tariff. **3** levy, tax, taxation.

rate *verb* **1** assess, class, estimate, evaluate, gauge, judge, measure, rank, reckon, value. **2** class, consider, count, deem, reckon, regard.

rather *adverb* comparatively, fairly, moderately, pretty, quite, relatively, slightly, somewhat.

ratify *verb* agree to, approve, assent to, confirm, consent to, countersign, endorse, sign, validate.

ratio *noun* proportion, relationship.

ration *noun* allocation, allowance, helping, portion, quota, share.

ration *verb* (*ration out*) allocate, apportion, distribute, dole out, mete out, share out.

rational *adjective* intelligent, logical, lucid, normal, reasonable, sane, sensible, sound, well-balanced.

rationalise *verb* **1** account for, excuse, explain away, justify. **2** make efficient, reorganise, restructure, streamline.

rattle *verb* **1** clank, clatter, clink, jangle, shake. **2** (*rattle off*) recite, recount, reel off, relate. **3** agitate, alarm, disconcert, disturb, faze (*informal*), fluster, frighten, perturb, shake, throw, unnerve, upset, worry.

raucous *adjective* grating, harsh, hoarse, jarring, loud, noisy, piercing, rasping, shrill, strident.

ravage *verb* damage, destroy, devastate, lay waste, loot, pillage, plunder, raid, ransack, raze, ruin, sack, wreck. □ **ravages** *plural noun* damage, depredation, destruction, devastation.

rave verb **1** carry on (informal), go on (informal), rant, sound off (informal); see also BE ANGRY (at ANGRY). **2** be effusive, be enthusiastic, go overboard (informal), go wild, gush, wax lyrical (informal).

ravenous adjective famished, hungry, starving.

ravine noun canyon, defile, gorge, gully, valley.

raw adjective **1** uncooked. **2** crude, natural, unprocessed, unrefined, untreated. **3** callow, fresh, green, inexperienced, new, untrained. **4** grazed, scratched, skinned.

ray noun beam, shaft, streak, stream.

raze verb bulldoze, demolish, destroy, flatten, knock down, level, tear down, wreck.

reach verb **1** achieve, arrive at, attain, come to, get to, go as far as, hit, make. **2** extend, hold out, put out, stick out, stretch out.

reach noun **1** capability, capacity, compass, grasp, range, scope. **2** part, section, stretch.

react verb act, behave, respond.

reaction noun answer, feedback, reply, response.

read verb **1** (read a book) browse through, dip into, glance at, peruse, pore through, scan, skim, study, wade through; (read someone's writing) decipher, interpret, make out, understand. **2** indicate, register, show. □ **readable** adjective (a readable book) absorbing, enjoyable, entertaining, interesting; (readable handwriting) clear, decipherable, legible, neat, plain, understandable.

ready adjective **1** equipped, fit, geared up, organised, prepared, primed, set. **2** disposed, eager, game, glad, happy, inclined, keen, willing. **3** immediate, instant, pat, prompt, quick, rapid, speedy. **4** accessible, available, convenient, handy, on hand.

real adjective **1** actual, existent, factual, historical, true. **2** authentic, dinkum (Australian informal), dinky-di (Australian informal), genuine, honest-to-goodness (informal), natural, proper, true; (of feelings) heartfelt, honest, sincere, unaffected.

realise verb **1** appreciate, apprehend, become aware of, catch on to (informal), comprehend, cotton on to (informal), grasp, jerry to

(*Australian informal*), know, latch on to (*informal*), perceive, sense, suss out (*informal*), twig (*informal*), understand, wake up to. **2** accomplish, achieve, attain, fulfil. □ **realisation** *noun* appreciation, awareness, consciousness, knowledge, perception, recognition, understanding.

realistic *adjective* **1** accurate, authentic, faithful, lifelike, natural, true-to-life. **2** feasible, practicable, practical, pragmatic, viable, workable.

really *adverb* actually, certainly, definitely, genuinely, honestly, indeed, in fact, positively, sincerely, surely, truly.

realm *noun* **1** country, domain, dominion, empire, kingdom, monarchy, territory. **2** area, domain, field, province, sphere, world.

reap *verb* **1** cut, gather in, harvest. **2** gain, obtain, realise, receive.

rear *noun* back, end, stern, tail.

rear *adjective* back, hind.

rear *verb* (*rear children*) bring up, care for, look after, nurture, raise; (*rear animals*) breed, keep, produce, raise.

rearrange *verb* change, interchange, juggle, reorder, reorganise, reshuffle, shift,

shuffle, swap, switch, transpose.

reason *noun* **1** cause, excuse, explanation, grounds, justification, motive, pretext, rationale. **2** common sense, good sense, logic, reasoning, sense, wisdom.

reason *verb* **1** conclude, deduce, figure out, infer, solve, think through, work out, work through. **2** argue, debate, discuss, plead, remonstrate.

reasonable *adjective* **1** (*a reasonable person*) intelligent, logical, rational, sane, sensible, thinking; (*a reasonable explanation*) logical, plausible, rational, reasoned, sensible, sound, tenable, valid. **2** equitable, fair, just, justifiable, moderate.

reassure *verb* assure, comfort, encourage, set someone's mind at rest. □ **reassuring** *adjective* comforting, encouraging, favourable, hopeful, promising.

rebel *verb* buck (*informal*), disobey, mutiny, resist, revolt, rise up.

rebel *noun* dissenter, insurgent, malcontent, mutineer, nonconformist, revolutionary. □ **rebellion** *noun* insurgence, insurrection, mutiny, resistance, revolt, revolution, rising, uprising. □ **rebellious**

adjective defiant, disobedient, insubordinate, insurgent, intractable, mutinous, recalcitrant, refractory, unmanageable, unruly, wild.

rebound *verb* bounce back, ricochet, spring back.

rebuff *noun* brush-off, knock-back (*informal*), refusal, rejection, snub. □ **rebuff** *verb* brush off, decline, knock back (*informal*), refuse, reject, snub, spurn, turn down.

rebuild *verb* reconstruct, remake, renew, restore.

rebuke *verb* admonish, berate, castigate, censure, chide (*old use*), reprimand, reproach, reprove, scold, tell off (*informal*), tick off (*informal*), upbraid. □ **rebuke** *noun* admonition, censure, dressing down (*informal*), lecture, rap over the knuckles, reprimand, reproach, reproof, scolding, serve (*Australian informal*).

rebut *verb* counter, disprove, invalidate, negate, refute.

recalcitrant *adjective* defiant, disobedient, headstrong, intractable, obstinate, perverse, refractory, stubborn, wayward, wilful.

recall *verb* call to mind, recollect, remember.

recap *verb* go over, recapitulate, reiterate, repeat, restate,

summarise, sum up. □ **recap** *noun* recapitulation, résumé, summary, summing up.

recede *verb* ebb, go back, move back, retreat, subside.

receipt *noun* docket, proof of purchase.

receive *verb* **1** accept, acquire, collect, earn, gain, get, land, obtain, take, win. **2** greet, meet, welcome.

recent *adjective* contemporary, current, fresh, latest, new, up to date.

receptacle *noun* carrier, container, holder, repository, vessel.

reception *noun* **1** greeting, welcome. **2** do (*informal*), function, gathering, party.

receptive *adjective* amenable, open, open-minded, responsive.

recess *noun* **1** alcove, bay, niche, nook. **2** break, little lunch, morning tea, playlunch, playtime.

recession *noun* decline, depression, downturn, slump.

recipe *noun* directions, formula, instructions.

reciprocal *adjective* mutual, reciprocated, requited, returned.

recital *noun* concert, performance.

recite *verb* deliver, narrate, perform, rattle off, reel off, repeat, say, tell.

reckless *adjective* careless, daredevil, foolhardy, harebrained, heedless, hotheaded, impetuous, imprudent, impulsive, incautious, irresponsible, mad, madcap, negligent, rash, unthinking, wild.

reckon *verb* 1 add up, assess, calculate, compute, count, figure out, tally, total, tot up (*informal*), work out. 2 believe, consider, fancy, judge, think.

recline *verb* lean back, lie, loll, lounge, repose, rest, sprawl, stretch out. □ **reclining** *adjective* horizontal, leaning, lying, recumbent.

recluse *noun* hermit, loner, solitary.

recognise *verb* 1 identify, know, pick out, place, recall, recollect, remember. 2 accept, acknowledge, admit, appreciate, be aware of, concede, grant, perceive, realise, see, understand.

recoil *verb* 1 kick, kick back, spring back. 2 cower, cringe, draw back, flinch, jump back, quail, shrink, shy away, start, wince.

recollect *verb* call to mind, recall, remember.

recommend *verb* 1 approve of, commend, endorse, laud (*formal*), praise, speak well of. 2 advise, advocate, counsel, prescribe, propose, suggest, urge.

reconcile *verb* bring together, conciliate, placate, reunite.

recondition *verb* overhaul, rebuild, renovate, repair, restore.

reconnaissance *noun* exploration, inspection, investigation, observation, recce (*informal*), spying, survey.

reconsider *verb* consider again, reassess, rethink, review, think again.

reconstruct *verb* 1 reassemble, rebuild, remake, repair, restore. 2 re-create, re-enact.

record *noun* 1 account, annals, archives, chronicle, diary, document, dossier, history, journal, log, memorandum, minutes, narrative, note, register, report, transcription. 2 album, disc, recording, release. 3 background, curriculum vitae, CV, experience, history.

record *verb* 1 chronicle, document, enter, jot down, list, log, minute, note, register, take down, transcribe, write down. 2 film, tape, tape-record, video.

recount verb describe, detail, narrate, recite, relate, report, tell.

recoup verb get back, recover, redeem, regain, retrieve, win back.

recover verb **1** find, get back, reclaim, recoup, redeem, regain, retrieve, salvage, track down. **2** convalesce, get better, heal, improve, mend, pick up, pull through, rally, recuperate.

recreation noun **1** amusement, diversion, enjoyment, entertainment, fun, leisure, play, pleasure, relaxation. **2** game, hobby, pastime, sport.

recruit noun apprentice, beginner, newcomer, novice, rookie (informal), tiro, trainee.

recruit verb engage, enlist, sign on, take on.

rectangle noun oblong, square.

rectify verb correct, cure, fix, mend, put right, redress, remedy, repair.

recuperate verb convalesce, get better, improve, mend, recover, regain health.

recur verb be repeated, happen again, reappear, repeat itself, resurface, return. □ **recurrent** adjective continual, cyclical, frequent, perennial, periodic, perpetual, recurring, regular, repeated.

recycle verb reprocess, reuse, salvage, use again.

red adjective blood-red, brick-red, burgundy, cardinal, carmine, cerise, cherry, claret, cochineal, crimson, flame, garnet, maroon, ruby, russet, scarlet, vermilion; (of hair) auburn, carroty, ginger, sandy; (of the face) florid, flushed, rubicund, ruddy; (of the eyes) bloodshot.

redden verb blush, colour, flush, glow.

redeem verb **1** buy back, reclaim, recover, repurchase. **2** atone for, ransom, rescue, save, set free.

redress verb compensate for, make amends for, make up for, put right, rectify, remedy, repair.

redress noun compensation, recompense, reparation, restitution.

reduce verb abbreviate, abridge, condense, contract, curtail, cut, cut back, cut down, decline, decrease, diminish, dwindle, ease, lessen, lighten, lower, minimise, moderate, pare down, prune, scale down, shorten, shrink, slash, trim, whittle down.

redundant adjective excess, superfluous, surplus, unnecessary, unwanted.

reek verb pong (informal), smell, stink.

reel noun bobbin, spindle, spool.

reel verb lurch, rock, stagger, stumble, sway, teeter, totter, wobble. ◻ **reel off** rattle off, recite.

refer verb direct, pass, send. ◻ **refer to 1** allude to, bring up, cite, comment on, mention, speak of, touch on. **2** consult, look up in, turn to.

referee noun adjudicator, ref (informal), umpire.

reference noun **1** allusion, hint, mention. **2** citation, example, quotation. **3** testimonial.

referendum noun ballot, plebiscite, poll, vote.

refill verb replenish, restock, top up.

refine verb clarify, distil, filter, process, purify.

refined adjective civilised, cultivated, cultured, dignified, elegant, genteel, gentlemanly, ladylike, polished, polite, sophisticated, urbane, well-bred, well-mannered.

reflect verb **1** mirror. **2** brood, cogitate, consider, contemplate, deliberate, meditate, mull over, muse, ponder, ruminate, think. **3** demonstrate, display, exhibit, indicate, reveal, show. ◻ **reflection** noun image, likeness.

reform verb **1** ameliorate, amend, change, correct, improve, mend, rectify, revise, revolutionise, transform. **2** go straight, mend your ways, turn over a new leaf.

refractory adjective disobedient, headstrong, intractable, obstinate, perverse, pigheaded, rebellious, recalcitrant, stubborn, uncontrollable, unmanageable, wayward, wilful.

refrain verb (refrain from) abstain from, avoid, desist from, forbear from, stop.

refrain noun chorus.

refresh verb freshen, invigorate, perk up (informal), rejuvenate, restore, revive.

refreshments plural noun drinks, eats (informal), food, nibbles (informal), snacks.

refrigerate verb chill, cool, freeze.

refuge noun **1** asylum, cover, protection, safety, sanctuary, shelter. **2** haven, hideout (informal), hidey-hole (informal), hiding place, retreat, sanctuary, shelter.

refugee noun asylum seeker, displaced person, exile, fugitive, runaway.

efund verb give back, pay back, reimburse, repay, return.

efund noun reimbursement, repayment.

efurbish verb clean up, do up (*informal*), redecorate, remodel, renovate, restore, revamp, spruce up.

efuse verb (*refuse an offer*) decline, knock back (*informal*), pass up (*informal*), rebuff, reject, scorn, spurn, turn down; (*refuse permission*) deny, withhold. □ **refusal** noun knock-back (*informal*), rebuff, rejection, veto.

efuse noun debris, garbage, junk, litter, rubbish, scrap, trash, waste.

efute verb disprove, negate, rebut.

egain verb get back, recoup, recover, retrieve, win back.

egal adjective kingly, lordly, majestic, princely, queenly, royal, stately.

egard verb 1 behold (*old use*), contemplate, eye, gaze at, look at, observe, scrutinise, stare at, view, watch. 2 consider, deem, judge, look upon, reckon, view.

egard noun 1 attention, care, concern, consideration, heed, notice, thought. 2 admiration, approval, esteem, favour, honour, respect.

regarding preposition about, apropos, concerning, in regard to, with reference to, with regard to, with respect to.

regardless adverb anyhow, anyway, heedlessly, nevertheless, nonetheless. □ **regardless of** despite, disregarding, in spite of, irrespective of, notwithstanding.

region noun area, district, land, locality, neighbourhood, part, place, province, spot, territory, tract, vicinity, zone. □ **regional** adjective district, local, provincial. □ **in the region of** about, approximately, around, in the neighbourhood of, in the vicinity of, nearly, roughly.

register noun catalogue, directory, index, list, record, roll.

register verb 1 catalogue, enter, file, list, place on record, record, write down; see also *ENROL*. 2 indicate, read, record, show.

regret noun compunction, disappointment, penitence, remorse, repentance, sorrow. □ **regretful** adjective apologetic, contrite, penitent, remorseful, repentant, rueful, sorry.

regret verb bemoan, be sad about, be sorry about, deplore, lament, repent, rue.

☐ **regrettable** *adjective* deplorable, lamentable, reprehensible, sad, shameful, unfortunate.

regular *adjective* **1** consistent, fixed, periodic, predictable, repeated, routine, set, systematic, unchanging, unvarying. **2** (*regular footsteps*) even, measured, rhythmic, steady, uniform; (*a regular shape*) even, symmetrical. **3** conventional, correct, customary, established, habitual, normal, official, ordinary, orthodox, proper, routine, standard, traditional, typical, usual.

regulate *verb* **1** adjust, alter, change, moderate, modulate, vary. **2** control, direct, govern, manage, oversee, supervise.

regulation *noun* by-law, decree, directive, law, ordinance, rule, statute.

rehearse *verb* go over, practise, prepare, run through.

reign *verb* be on the throne, govern, rule.

reign *noun* kingship, rule, sovereignty.

reimburse *verb* indemnify, pay back, recompense, refund, repay.

reinforce *verb* bolster, brace, buttress, fortify, prop up, shore up, strengthen, suppor toughen.

reject *verb* **1** (*reject a person* brush off, disown, ditc (*informal*), drop, dump forsake, jilt, rebuff, renounce repudiate, snub; (*reject a offer*) decline, dismiss, knoc back (*informal*), pass u (*informal*), refuse, spurn, tur down, turn your nose up at. discard, get rid of, jettiso scrap, send back, throw awa throw out. ☐ **rejection** *nou* brush-off, knock-back (*i formal*), rebuff, refusal, snu thumbs down, veto.

rejoice *verb* be happy, be joyfu be overjoyed, celebrate, crow delight, exult, revel.

rejuvenate *verb* refresh reinvigorate, renew, restore revitalise, revive.

relapse *verb* backslid degenerate, fall back, lapse regress, retrogress, revert, sli back. ☐ **relapse** *noun* deter oration, regression, setback.

relate *verb* **1** describe, narrat recite, recount, report, spir tell. **2** (*relate to*) apply t belong to, be relevant t concern, connect with, have bearing on, pertain to, refer t **3** (*relate to*) empathise wit get on with, identify wit interact with, understand.

related *adjective* allied, associated, connected, inter-connected, interrelated.

relation *noun* **1** see *RELATIVE*. **2** association, connection, correlation, correspondence, link, relationship, tie-in.

relationship *noun* affinity, association, attachment, bond, connection, link, rapport, tie.

relative *noun* kinsman, kins-woman, relation; (*relatives*) clan, family, flesh and blood, folk, kin, kindred, kith and kin.

relative *adjective* comparative.

relax *verb* **1** ease off, loosen, slacken, weaken. **2** ease, liberalise, moderate, soften, stretch. **3** calm down, laze, lounge, rest, take it easy, unwind, veg out (*slang*). □ **relaxation** *noun* diversion, enjoyment, fun, hobby, leisure, pastime, pleasure, recreation, rest. □ **relaxed** *adjective* calm, carefree, casual, easygoing, informal, laid-back (*informal*), nonchalant, serene, slack.

relay *verb* communicate, pass on, send on, transmit.

release *verb* **1** deliver, discharge, emancipate, free, let go, let loose, let out, liberate, set free, unbuckle, undo, unfasten, untie. **2** circulate, distribute, issue, launch, publish.

relent *verb* be merciful, capitulate, give in, have pity, soften, yield.

relentless *adjective* **1** cruel, harsh, implacable, inexorable, merciless, pitiless, remorse-less, ruthless, severe, unyielding. **2** constant, con-tinuous, endless, incessant, persistent, unceasing, un-relenting, unremitting.

relevant *adjective* applicable, apposite, appropriate, apropos, apt, connected, germane, pertinent, related, to the point.

reliable *adjective* constant, dependable, faithful, loyal, staunch, steadfast, steady, sure, true, trusted, trust-worthy, trusty (*old use*).

relic *noun* antique, heirloom, keepsake, memento, reminder, remnant, souvenir, survival, vestige.

relief *noun* **1** alleviation, comfort, ease, let-up, pallia-tion, remission, respite, rest, solace. **2** aid, assistance, help, succour, support.

relieve *verb* **1** alleviate, assuage, ease, help, lessen, lighten, mitigate, palliate, reduce, soothe, subdue. **2** cover for, fill in for, replace, stand in for, substitute for, take the place of.

religion *noun* belief, creed, cult, denomination, faith, sect.

religious *adjective* **1** devotional, divine, doctrinal, holy, sacred, scriptural, spiritual, theological. **2** devout, God-fearing, godly, pious, spiritual.

relinquish *verb* abandon, abdicate, cede, forgo, forsake, give up, renounce, resign, surrender, waive.

relish *noun* delight, enthusiasm, gusto, keenness, pleasure, zest.

relish *verb* delight in, enjoy, fancy, like, love, revel in, savour.

reluctant *adjective* averse, disinclined, hesitant, loath, unwilling.

rely *verb* □ **rely on** bank on, count on, depend on, reckon on, trust.

remain *verb* **1** be left (over). **2** continue, endure, hang around, keep on, linger, live on, persist, prevail, stay, stick around (*informal*), survive, tarry, wait.

remainder *noun* balance, excess, leftovers, remnant, residue, rest, surplus.

remains *plural noun* **1** dregs, leftovers, remnants, scraps. **2** relics, ruins, wreckage. **3** body, carcass, corpse.

remark *noun* comment, observation, opinion, statement, word.

remark *verb* comment, mention, note, observe, reflect, say.

remarkable *adjective* amazing, astounding, conspicuous, exceptional, extraordinary, impressive, marvellous, memorable, notable, noteworthy, outstanding, phenomenal, sensational, signal, significant, singular, special, startling, striking, surprising, uncommon, unusual, wonderful.

remedial *adjective* corrective, curative, therapeutic.

remedy *noun* **1** antidote, cure, medication, medicine, panacea, therapy, treatment. **2** answer, corrective, cure, solution.

remedy *verb* correct, cure, fix mend, put right, rectify, redress, repair, solve.

remember *verb* **1** keep in mind, memorise, recall, recollect, retain. **2** call to mind, look back on, recall, recollect, reflect on, reminisce about, think back on. □ **remembrance** *noun* commemoration, memory, recollection.

remind *verb* jog someone's memory, prompt, refresh someone's memory. □ **reminder** *noun* keepsake, memento, remembrance, souvenir.

reminiscences *plural noun* memoirs, memories, recollections.

remiss *adjective* careless, forgetful, lax, neglectful, negligent, slack, slipshod, sloppy.

remnant *noun* fragment, leftover, offcut, piece, remainder, remains, residue, scrap.

remorse *noun* compunction, contrition, guilt, penitence, regret, repentance, shame, sorrow.

remote *adjective* **1** distant, faraway, far-flung, inaccessible, isolated, lonely, outlying, out of the way, secluded, solitary. **2** faint, outside, slender, slight, slim, unlikely.

remove *verb* **1** (*remove clothing*) doff (*a hat*), peel off, pull off, shed, strip off, take off; (*remove a branch*) chop off, cut off, lop off, prune; (*remove a tooth*) extract, pull out, take out. **2** carry away, cart off, convey, move, relocate, shift, take away, transfer, transport. **3** depose, dismiss, drive out, eject, evict, expel, fire, get rid of, kick out (*informal*), oust, sack (*informal*), throw out, turn out. **4** delete, efface, eliminate, eradicate, erase, expunge, get rid of, obliterate, rub out, wash off, wipe out.

remuneration *noun* pay, payment, recompense, reward, salary, wages.

render *verb* **1** do, give, perform, provide, supply. **2** make.

rendezvous *noun* appointment, assignation, date (*informal*), engagement, meeting.

renegade *noun* apostate, defector, deserter, traitor, turncoat.

renew *verb* **1** change, refresh, reinvigorate, rejuvenate, renovate, replace, restore, revive. **2** (*renew their requests*) begin again, begin anew, reiterate, repeat, restate; (*renew a friendship*) pick up again, re-establish, resume, resurrect, revive.

renounce *verb* abandon, abdicate, discard, disown, forgo, forsake, forswear, give up, reject, relinquish, repudiate, surrender, waive.

renovate *verb* do up (*informal*), modernise, redecorate, refurbish, rejuvenate, remodel, restore, revamp, update.

renown *noun* distinction, fame, importance, note, prestige, reputation, repute. □ **renowned** *adjective* celebrated, distinguished, eminent, famed, famous, illustrious, notable, noted, prominent, well-known.

rent verb charter, hire, lease, let.

reorganise verb change, rationalise, rearrange, reshuffle, restructure, transform. □ **reorganisation** noun change, rationalisation, rearrangement, reshuffle, restructuring, shake-up, transformation.

repair verb darn, fix, mend, overhaul, patch (up), recondition, restore, service.

reparation noun atonement, compensation, damages, indemnity, redress, restitution.

repay verb **1** pay back, recompense, refund, reimburse, remunerate. **2** pay back, reciprocate, requite, return, reward.

repeal verb abrogate, annul, cancel, nullify, rescind, revoke, withdraw.

repeat verb do again, duplicate, echo, quote, recite, redo, reiterate, reproduce, retell, say again, tell again. □ **repeatedly** adverb again and again, continually, frequently, often, over and over, time and time again.

repeat noun rebroadcast, replay, rerun.

repel verb **1** drive away, fend off, force back, keep at bay, parry, repulse, stave off, ward off. **2** disgust, nauseate, offend, put off, revolt, sicken. □ **repellent** adjective disgusting, distasteful, horrible, loathsome, nauseating, offensive, off putting, repugnant, repulsive, revolting, sickening.

repent verb be sorry, bewail, feel remorse, lament, regret, rue. □ **repentant** adjective apologetic, contrite, penitent, regretful, remorseful, rueful, sorry.

repercussion noun after-effect, backlash, consequence, effect, knock-on effect, result, side effect.

repetitive adjective boring, humdrum, monotonous, repetitious, tedious, unchanging, unvaried.

replace verb **1** put back, restore, return. **2** come after, follow, oust, substitute for, succeed, supersede, supplant, take the place of. **3** change, renew, replenish. □ **replacement** noun deputy, locum, proxy, ring-in (Australian informal), stand-in, substitute, successor, surrogate.

replica noun copy, duplicate, facsimile, imitation, likeness, model, reproduction.

reply noun acknowledgement, answer, comeback (informal), rejoinder, response, retort, riposte.

reply *verb* answer, counter, rejoin, respond, retort.

report *verb* **1** announce, communicate, declare, disclose, divulge, document, notify, publish, record, say, state, tell, write up. **2** denounce, dob in (*Australian informal*), grass (on) (*slang*), inform on, shop (*slang*), tell on. **3** front up (*informal*), introduce yourself, present yourself.

report *noun* **1** account, announcement, article, bulletin, communiqué, description, narrative, news, paper, proceedings, record, statement, story, write-up. **2** bang, blast, boom, detonation, explosion, noise.

reporter *noun* correspondent, journalist, writer.

repose *noun* rest, sleep, slumber.

repose *verb* lie, recline, relax, rest, stretch out; see also *SLEEP*.

reprehensible *adjective* blameworthy, culpable, deplorable, despicable, inexcusable, shameful, unworthy, wicked, wrong.

represent *verb* **1** depict, describe, illustrate, picture, portray, present, show. **2** correspond to, denote, express, indicate, mean, signify, stand for, symbolise. **3** act for, act on behalf of, speak for.

representative *noun* agent, ambassador, delegate, deputy, emissary, envoy, mouthpiece, proxy, spokesperson, stand-in, substitute.

representative *adjective* archetypal, characteristic, illustrative, typical.

repress *verb* bottle up, check, control, crush, curb, hold back, inhibit, keep down, oppress, put down, quash, quell, restrain, stifle, subdue, subjugate, suppress.

reprieve *noun* pardon, postponement, remission, stay of execution.

reprieve *verb* let off, pardon, spare.

reprimand *noun* admonition, castigation, dressing down (*informal*), lecture, rebuke, reproach, reproof, rocket (*slang*), scolding, serve (*Australian informal*), talking-to (*informal*), wigging (*informal*).

reprimand *verb* admonish, berate, castigate, censure, chastise, chide (*old use*), go crook at (*Australian informal*), haul over the coals, lecture, rap over the knuckles, rebuke, reproach, reprove, rouse on (*Australian informal*), scold, take to task, tell off (*informal*), tick off (*informal*), upbraid.

reprisal *noun* retaliation, retribution, revenge, vengeance.

reproach *verb* admonish, blame, castigate, censure, chide (*old use*), criticise, rebuke, reprimand, reprove, scold, upbraid. □ **reproach** *noun* condemnation, discredit, disgrace, disrepute, humiliation, ignominy, rebuke, shame.

reproduce *verb* **1** mimic, recreate, repeat, replicate. **2** copy, duplicate, fax, photocopy, print. **3** breed, multiply, procreate, proliferate, propagate. □ **reproduction** *noun* **1** breeding, procreation, proliferation, propagation. **2** copy, duplicate, facsimile, imitation, print, replica.

repudiate *verb* deny, disclaim, disown, reject.

repugnant *adjective* abhorrent, abominable, detestable, disgusting, distasteful, hateful, hideous, horrible, loathsome, nasty, nauseating, objectionable, obnoxious, odious, offensive, off-putting, repulsive, revolting, vile.

repulse *verb* drive back, fend off, force back, repel, ward off.

repulsive *adjective* abominable, disgusting, distasteful, foul, gross (*informal*), hideous, horrible, loathsome, nasty, nauseating, objectionable, obnoxious, odious, offensive, off-putting, repellent, repugnant, revolting, sickening, ugly, vile, yucky (*informal*).

reputable *adjective* above board, honest, honourable, reliable, respectable, respected, trustworthy.

reputation *noun* fame, name, prestige, renown, repute, standing.

reputed *adjective* alleged, putative, supposed.

request *verb* **1** apply for, ask for, beg for, petition for, plead for, seek, solicit. **2** appeal to, ask, beseech, entreat, implore.

request *noun* appeal, application, entreaty, petition, plea, supplication.

require *verb* **1** call for, demand, depend on, necessitate, need, rely on. **2** command, compel, direct, oblige, order. □ **required** *adjective* compulsory, essential, mandatory, necessary, obligatory, prescribed, requisite, set.

requirement *noun* essential, must, necessity, prerequisite, requisite, specification, stipulation.

rescue *verb* deliver, free, liberate, recover, release, retrieve, salvage, save.

rescue *noun* deliverance, liberation, recovery, release, retrieval, salvage, saving.

research *noun* experimentation, exploration, inquiry, investigation, study.

research *verb* delve into, explore, inquire into, investigate, study.

resemblance *noun* affinity, correspondence, likeness, similarity.

resemble *verb* be like, be similar to, look like, take after.

resent *verb* begrudge, dislike, mind, object to, take exception to, take umbrage at. □ **resentful** *adjective* aggrieved, angry, bitter, discontented, disgruntled, envious, grudging, huffy, indignant, jealous, piqued, rancorous, sullen. □ **resentment** *noun* anger, animosity, bitterness, discontent, envy, grudge, hatred, hostility, ill will, indignation, jealousy, pique, rancour.

reservation *noun* **1** arrangement, booking. **2** condition, doubt, hesitation, limitation, misgiving, objection, proviso, qualification, qualm, scruple.

reserve *verb* **1** hoard, hold back, keep, keep back, preserve, put aside, retain, save, spare, withhold. **2** book,

order, prearrange, secure. **3** defer, delay, postpone, suspend, withhold.

reserve *noun* **1** cache, fund, hoard, kitty, pool, reservoir, stock, stockpile, store, supply. **2** backup, deputy, stand-by, stand-in, substitute, understudy. **3** conservation park, game park, preserve, safari park, sanctuary, wildlife park.

reserved *adjective* aloof, bashful, distant, remote, restrained, reticent, shy, standoffish, taciturn, uncommunicative, undemonstrative, unemotional, withdrawn.

reservoir *noun* dam, lake, pond.

reshuffle *noun* rearrangement, reorganisation, shake-up, spill (*Australian informal*).

reside *verb* (*reside in*) dwell in, hang out in (*informal*), inhabit, live in, lodge in, occupy, stay in.

residence *noun* abode (*old use*), domicile, dwelling, habitation, home, house, place.

resident *noun* **1** citizen, denizen, householder, inhabitant, local, native. **2** guest, inmate, lodger, occupant, visitor.

residue *noun* balance, dregs, lees, leftovers, remainder, remains, remnant, rest.

resign verb abdicate, give up, leave, quit, relinquish, stand down from, step down from, vacate. □ **resign yourself to** accept, reconcile yourself to.

resist verb battle against, confront, defy, fight (against), oppose, stand up to, withstand. □ **resistant** adjective immune, impervious, proof, unaffected.

resolute adjective adamant, determined, dogged, firm, persistent, purposeful, resolved, staunch, steadfast, tenacious, unwavering.

resolution noun **1** determination, doggedness, persistence, purpose, resolve, tenacity, willpower. **2** commitment, decision, intention, pledge, promise, resolve. **3** decision, motion, proposition. **4** resolving, settlement, solution, solving, sorting out, working out.

resolve verb **1** decide, determine. **2** clear up, fix, overcome, remedy, settle, solve, sort out, work out.

resolve noun **1** intention, pledge, promise, resolution. **2** determination, doggedness, purpose, resolution, steadfastness, will-power.

resonant adjective booming, echoing, full, resounding, reverberating, rich, sonorous, stentorian, vibrant.

resort verb (resort to) adopt, fa᎐ back on, have recourse to, tur᎐ to, use, utilise.

resort noun centre, haun᎐ holiday centre, retreat, spot.

resound verb echo, resonate reverberate, ring.

resounding adjective enor mous, great, marked, notable outstanding, remarkable striking, tremendous (i᎐ formal).

resource noun (resources assets, capital, funds materials, means, mone᎐ reserves, riches, wealth.

resourceful adjective cleve᎐ creative, enterprising, inge nious, innovative, inventive shrewd.

respect noun **1** admiration awe, esteem, honour, regard reverence, veneration. consideration, courtesy, defe᎐ ence, politeness, regard. aspect, detail, facet, featur᎐ particular, point, regard, wa᎐ **4** reference, regard, relation

respect verb admire, esteem honour, look up to, revere value, venerate.

respectable adjective **1** decen᎐ honest, honourable, la᎐ abiding, presentable, prope᎐ reputable, upright, worthy. acceptable, adequate, fa᎐

passable, reasonable, satisfactory.

respectful *adjective* civil, considerate, courteous, deferential, polite, well-mannered.

respite *noun* break, breather, intermission, let-up, lull, pause, relief, reprieve, rest, spell (*Australian*).

respond *verb* **1** answer, counter, rejoin, reply, retort. **2** act in response, react.

response *noun* **1** answer, comeback, rejoinder, reply, retort, riposte. **2** acknowledgement, feedback, reaction.

responsibility *noun* **1** blame, culpability, fault, guilt, liability. **2** burden, duty, job, obligation, onus, task.

responsible *adjective* **1** accountable, answerable, in charge (of), liable. **2** conscientious, dependable, dutiful, honest, law-abiding, level-headed, mature, reliable, sensible, trustworthy. **3** executive, important, managerial, senior, supervisory. **4** at fault, culpable, guilty, to blame.

responsive *adjective* alert, alive, awake, impressionable, interested, quick, receptive, sensitive, sympathetic.

rest *noun* **1** ease, idleness, inactivity, leisure, relaxation, repose, respite; (*a rest on the sofa*) doze, forty winks, kip (*slang*), lie-down, nap, repose, siesta, sleep, snooze; (*a rest from work*) break, breather, holiday, interlude, intermission, interval, pause, recess, smoko (*Australian informal*), spell (*Australian*), time off, vacation. **2** base, holder, prop, stand, support, tripod. □ **at rest** inactive, inert, motionless, still.

rest *verb* **1** doze, idle, laze, lie down, pause, relax, sleep, slumber, snooze, take it easy. **2** lean, perch, place, prop, stand, support.

rest *noun* balance, excess, leftovers, others, remainder, remnant, residue, surplus.

restaurant *noun* bistro, brasserie, buffet, café, cafeteria, canteen, diner (*American*), eatery (*informal*).

restitution *noun* compensation, indemnification, recompense, redress, reparation.

restless *adjective* agitated, disturbed, edgy, excitable, fidgety, frisky, impatient, lively, nervous, restive, skittish, sleepless, toey (*Australian informal*), unsettled, wakeful.

restore *verb* **1** do up (*informal*), fix, mend, rebuild, recondition, reconstruct, refurbish, rehabilitate, remodel, renovate, repair, resurrect. **2** bring back, give back, hand back, put back, re-establish, reinstate, reintroduce, replace, return.

restrain verb bind, bridle, chain, check, contain, control, curb, curtail, fetter, harness, hold back, keep a tight rein on, keep in check, limit, moderate, muzzle, pinion, rein in, repress, restrict, shackle, strait-jacket, suppress, tie up. □ **restraint** noun control, moderation, self-control, self-discipline, self-restraint.

restrict verb bound, check, circumscribe, confine, cramp, curb, enclose, hamper, handicap, hem in, hinder, impede, limit. □ **restriction** noun condition, constraint, control, limitation, proviso, qualification, stipulation.

result noun 1 consequence, effect, fruit, outcome, output, repercussion, upshot. 2 grade, mark, score. 3 answer, finding, solution.

result verb 1 arise, come about, ensue, follow, happen, occur, originate, spring, stem. 2 (result in) bring about, cause, culminate in, end in, finish in, give rise to, lead to.

resume verb 1 begin again, carry on, continue, recommence, restart. 2 reoccupy, return to, take again.

résumé noun abstract, outline, précis, summary, synopsis.

resurrect verb bring back, reactivate, reintroduce, restore, resuscitate, revive.

retain verb 1 hang on to, hold on to, keep, reserve, save. 2 learn, memorise, recall, recollect, remember.

retaliate verb counter-attack, get even, get your own back (informal), hit back, pay back, reciprocate, seek retribution, take reprisals, take revenge. □ **retaliation** noun counter-attack, reprisal, retribution, revenge, vengeance, vindictiveness.

retard verb delay, hamper, handicap, hinder, impede, inhibit, obstruct, slow down, stunt.

reticent adjective diffident, discreet, quiet, reserved, secretive, shy, silent, taciturn, tight-lipped, uncommunicative, unforthcoming.

retire verb 1 give up work, leave work, quit work, stop working. 2 retreat, withdraw. 3 go to bed, hit the hay (informal), hit the sack (informal), turn in (informal).

retiring adjective bashful, diffident, meek, modest, reserved, shy, timid, uncommunicative, withdrawn.

retort noun answer, comeback, rejoinder, reply, response, riposte.

retort verb answer, counter, react, rejoin, reply, respond.

retrace verb □ **retrace your steps** backtrack, go back, return.

retract verb **1** draw in, pull in. **2** cancel, disclaim, recant, rescind, revoke, take back, withdraw.

retreat verb back away, bolt, depart, escape, flee, go away, leave, retire, run away, shrink back, take flight, withdraw.

retreat noun **1** departure, escape, exit, flight, getaway, withdrawal. **2** asylum, haven, hideout (*informal*), hiding-place, refuge, resort, sanctuary, shelter.

retrench verb **1** cut back, downsize, economise, rationalise, tighten your belt. **2** dismiss, get rid of, lay off, make redundant, sack (*informal*), shed.

retribution noun just deserts, justice, nemesis, punishment, recompense, revenge, vengeance.

retrieve verb bring back, fetch, find, get back, recapture, recover, regain, rescue, salvage, track down.

return verb **1** backtrack, come back, go back, reappear, recur, resurface, revert. **2** bring back, give back, hand back, pay back, put back, reciprocate, repay, replace, requite, restore, send back, take back.

return noun **1** arrival, homecoming, reappearance. **2** earnings, gain, income, interest, profit, revenue, yield.

reunion noun gathering, get-together.

reuse verb recycle, use again.

reveal verb **1** bare, display, expose, show, uncover, unmask, unveil. **2** admit, air, betray, bring to light, confess, declare, disclose, divulge, expose, leak, let out, let slip, make known, proclaim, publish, tell, voice.

revel verb (*revel in*) bask in, delight in, enjoy, glory in, luxuriate in, rejoice in, relish, savour, wallow in.

revelation noun admission, confession, disclosure, discovery, eye-opener, leak.

revelry noun carousing, celebration, festivities, high jinks, jollification, merry-making, orgy, party, revels, roistering, spree, wassailing (*old use*).

revenge noun reprisal, retaliation, retribution, vengeance.

□ **take revenge** avenge yourself, get even, get your own back, pay back, retaliate, take reprisals.

revenue noun income, proceeds, receipts, return, takings.

reverberate verb boom, echo, resonate, resound, ring, thunder.

revere verb admire, adore, esteem, glorify, hold in awe, honour, idolise, look up to, respect, reverence, venerate, worship.

reverence noun admiration, adoration, awe, devotion, esteem, homage, honour, respect, veneration.

reversal noun about-face, about-turn, backflip, change, turn-about, turn-around, U-turn.

reverse noun **1** back, flip side (informal), other side, underside, verso. **2** antithesis, contrary, converse, opposite.

reverse verb **1** invert, transpose, turn round, turn upside down. **2** back, drive backwards. **3** countermand, do a backflip on (informal), override, overrule, overturn, revoke, undo.

revert verb backslide, go back, lapse, regress, retrogress, return.

review noun **1** analysis, assessment, examination, inspection, reappraisal, reassessment, reconsideration, re-examination, stocktaking, study, survey. **2** criticism, critique, notice, write-up.

review verb **1** analyse, assess, examine, go over, inspect, reappraise, reassess, reconsider, re-examine, scrutinise, study, survey, take stock of, think over. **2** appraise, assess, comment on, criticise, evaluate, judge.

revise verb **1** brush up on, cram, go over, learn, study, swot (informal). **2** alter, amend, change, edit, modify, revamp, rework, rewrite, update.

revive verb **1** bring round, come round, rally, recover, regain consciousness, resuscitate. **2** bring back, re-establish, reintroduce, restore, resurrect. □ **revival** noun reawakening, rebirth, renaissance, renewal, restoration, resurgence, resurrection.

revoke verb abrogate, annul, cancel, nullify, quash, repeal, rescind, retract, take back, withdraw.

revolt verb **1** disobey, mutiny, rebel, rise up. **2** appal, disgust, horrify, nauseate, offend, repel, shock, sicken.

revolt noun insurrection, mutiny, rebellion, revolution, rising, uprising.

revolting adjective abhorrent, abominable, detestable, disgusting, distasteful, foul, gross (informal), gruesome, hateful, hideous, horrible, loathsome, nasty, nauseating, objectionable, obnoxious, obscene, odious, offensive, off-putting, repellent, repugnant, repulsive, vile, yucky (informal).

revolution noun **1** coup, coup d'état, insurrection, mutiny, rebellion, revolt, rising, uprising. **2** change, reformation, shift, transformation, upheaval. **3** circuit, orbit, rotation, spin, turn.

revolve verb circle, go round, orbit.

reward noun award, bounty, compensation, payment, prize, recompense, remuneration.

reward verb compensate, pay, recompense, remunerate, repay. □ **rewarding** adjective fulfilling, gratifying, profitable, satisfying, worthwhile.

rewrite verb adapt, edit, paraphrase, revamp, revise, rework.

rhetoric noun **1** elocution, eloquence, oratory. **2** bombast, grandiloquence.

rhyme noun jingle, poem, verse.

rhythm noun beat, cadence, lilt, metre, pattern, pulse. □ **rhythmic** adjective metrical, regular, rhythmical, steady.

ribbon noun band, braid, strip, tape.

rich adjective **1** affluent, flush (informal), loaded (informal), moneyed, prosperous, wealthy, well-heeled (informal), well off, well-to-do. **2** abounding, abundant, well endowed, well supplied. **3** costly, expensive, grand, lavish, luxurious, magnificent, opulent, precious, splendid, sumptuous, valuable. **4** deep, full, intense, strong, vibrant, vivid.

riches plural noun affluence, assets, fortune, means, money, opulence, property, prosperity, resources, wealth.

rickety adjective decrepit, dilapidated, flimsy, ramshackle, shaky, tumbledown, unstable, unsteady, weak, wobbly.

ricochet verb bounce, rebound.

rid verb cleanse, clear, free, purge, relieve. □ **get rid of** chuck out (informal), discard, dispense with, dispose of, ditch (informal), drive out, dump, eject, eliminate, eradicate, evict, expel, exterminate, remove, scrap, throw away, throw out, weed out.

riddle noun brainteaser, conundrum, enigma, mystery, poser, problem, puzzle, teaser.

ride verb **1** control, handle, manage. **2** go, journey, travel.

ride noun drive, journey, lift, outing, spin (informal), trip.

rider noun (a horse-rider) equestrian, hoop (Australian slang), horseman, horsewoman, jockey; (a bicycle or motorcycle rider) bicyclist, biker, bikie (Australian informal), cyclist, motorcyclist.

ridge noun brow, crest, hilltop, saddle.

ridicule verb caricature, chiack (Australian informal), deride, gibe at, jeer at, lampoon, laugh at, make fun of, mock, parody, pillory, poke borak at (Australian informal), poke fun at, satirise, scoff at, send up (informal), sling off at (Australian informal), sneer at, take off, take the mickey out of (informal), taunt, tease. □ **ridicule** noun banter, derision, mockery, sarcasm, satire, scorn.

ridiculous adjective absurd, comical, crazy, derisory, droll, farcical, foolish, funny, harebrained, hilarious, idiotic, laughable, ludicrous, mad nonsensical, outrageous preposterous, silly, stupid zany.

rife adjective common, prevalent, rampant, widespread.

rift noun **1** break, chink, cleft crack, crevasse, crevice fissure, fracture, opening, slit split. **2** breach, disagreement division, estrangement schism, split.

rig verb □ **rig out** dress, equip fit out, kit out, outfit.

rig noun **1** installation, platform **2** clothes, gear (informal), get up (informal), kit, outfit, rig out (informal).

right adjective **1** accurate correct, exact, perfect, precise proper, true, valid. **2** decent ethical, fair, good, honest honourable, just, lawful, legal moral, proper, upright virtuous. **3** appropriate, apt fitting, proper, suitable.

right noun **1** starboard. **2** authority, entitlement, licence permission, power, prerogative, privilege.

right verb correct, put right rectify, redress, repair, set right, set upright, stand upright, straighten up.

righteous adjective blameless ethical, good, holy, honest honourable, just, law-abiding, moral, upright, virtuous.

rightful adjective lawful, legal, legitimate, proper, true.

rigid adjective **1** firm, hard, inflexible, stiff, unbending. **2** (rigid rules) cut and dried, firm, hard and fast, inflexible, rigorous, strict, stringent; (a rigid master) harsh, intransigent, stern, strict, stubborn, uncompromising, unyielding.

rigorous adjective austere, harsh, rigid, severe, stern, strict, stringent, tough, uncompromising.

rile verb anger, annoy, exasperate, infuriate, irk, irritate, madden, nark (informal), provoke, vex.

rim noun border, brim, brink, circumference, edge, lip, perimeter, verge.

rind noun crust, husk, peel, skin.

ring noun **1** band, circle, disc, halo, hoop, loop. **2** arena, enclosure.

ring verb circle, encircle, enclose, encompass, hem in, surround.

ring verb **1** chime, clang, ding, dong, jingle, peal, tinkle, toll. **2** echo, resonate, resound, reverberate. **3** call, phone, ring up, telephone.

ring noun **1** chime, clang, jingle, knell, peal, tinkle, toll. **2** bell (informal), buzz (informal), call, phone call.

ring-in noun impostor, phoney (informal), replacement, substitute, swap.

rinse verb clean, swill, wash.

riot noun brawl, commotion, disorder, disturbance, fracas, mêlée, mutiny, pandemonium, revolt, rising, tumult, turmoil, uprising, uproar.

riot verb mutiny, rampage, rebel, revolt, run amok, run riot.

riotous adjective anarchic, boisterous, disorderly, lawless, mutinous, rebellious, rowdy, unruly, wild.

rip verb gash, lacerate, rupture, sever, slash, slit, split, tear. ☐ **rip off** cheat, con (informal), defraud, diddle (informal), fleece, rob, rook, swindle, take for a ride (informal). ☐ **rip-off** noun con (informal), swindle, swizz (informal).

rip noun gash, laceration, rupture, slash, slit, split, tear.

ripe adjective **1** in season, mature, mellow, ready. **2** advanced, mature, old.

ripen verb age, develop, mature, mellow.

ripple noun wave, wavelet.

ripple verb agitate, disturb, ruffle, stir.

rise verb 1 ascend, climb, go up, lift, mount, soar. 2 arise (old use), get up, stand up. 3 mutiny, rebel, revolt, take up arms. 4 begin, commence, flow from, originate, spring from, start. 5 appreciate, escalate, go up, grow, increase, jump, rocket, shoot up, skyrocket, soar, swell.

rise noun 1 ascent, climb. 2 gain, increase, increment, raise. 3 elevation, hill, hillock, incline, slope.

risk noun chance, danger, possibility. □ **at risk** in danger, in jeopardy, in peril.

risk verb chance, endanger, gamble, hazard, imperil, jeopardise, stake, venture.

risky adjective chancy, dangerous, dicey (slang), dodgy (informal), hairy (slang), hazardous, perilous, precarious, tricky, uncertain, unsafe.

ritual noun ceremony, practice, procedure, rite, routine, service, tradition.

rival noun adversary, antagonist, challenger, competitor, contender, enemy, foe, opponent.

rival verb compare with, compete with, contend with,

contest, equal, match, measure up to, oppose, vie with.

river noun brook, creek, rill, rivulet, stream, tributary, watercourse, waterway.

road noun 1 alley, avenue, boulevard, bypass, byway, causeway, clearway, close, crescent, cul-de-sac, dead end, drive, expressway, freeway, highway, lane, motorway, orbital, parade, ring road, route, street, thoroughfare, tollway, track, turnpike (historical & American), way. 2 path, route, way. □ **roadside** noun edge, kerb, verge, wayside. □ **roadway** noun carriageway, road. □ **road train** juggernaut (informal), lorry, semi (Australia informal), semitrailer, truck.

roam verb meander, ramble, range, rove, saunter, stroll, tootle around (informal), travel, wander.

roar noun 1 bellow, howl, shout, rumble, thunder, yell. 2 guffaw, hoot (informal), howl, scream, shout, shriek.

roar verb 1 bawl, bellow, howl, rumble, scream, shout, thunder, yell. 2 guffaw, laugh.

roast verb bake.

rob verb burgle, hold up, loot, mug, pilfer from, plunder,

ransack, steal from, stick up (*informal*); see also *SWINDLE*.
□ **robber** noun bandit, brigand, buccaneer, burglar, bushranger, crook (*informal*), highwayman, housebreaker, looter, marauder, mugger, pickpocket, pilferer, pirate, plunderer, shoplifter, thief.
□ **robbery** noun burglary, heist (*informal*), hold-up, larceny, looting, mugging, pillage, plunder, stealing, stick-up (*informal*), theft.

robe noun bathrobe, cassock, dress, dressing gown, gown, habit, kimono, vestment.

robot noun android, automaton, machine.

robust adjective brawny, hardy, healthy, muscular, powerful, strapping, strong, sturdy, tough, vigorous.

rock noun boulder, crag, outcrop, pebble, stone.

rock verb 1 move to and fro, sway, swing. 2 lurch, pitch, reel, roll, shake, toss, totter, wobble.

rocky adjective craggy, gravelly, pebbly, rugged, stony.

rocky adjective precarious, shaky, uncertain, unstable, unsteady.

rod noun bar, baton, cane, cue, dowel, mace, poker, pole, sceptre, staff, stick, wand.

rogue noun 1 blackguard, con man (*informal*), crook (*informal*), good-for-nothing, knave (*old use*), miscreant, rascal, rotter, scoundrel, villain, wretch. 2 devil, imp, monkey, rascal, scallywag, scamp, wag.

role noun 1 character, part. 2 function, job, part, place.

roll verb 1 go round, revolve, rotate, somersault, spin, trundle, tumble, turn, twirl, wheel, whirl. 2 coil, curl, furl, twist, wind, wrap. 3 flatten, level, smooth. 4 lurch, pitch, reel, rock, sway, toss, totter.

roll noun 1 cylinder, reel, spool. 2 bagel, bap, bun. 3 list, register. 4 boom, reverberation, rumble, thunder.

roller coaster big dipper, switchback.

romance noun 1 love story. 2 affair, courtship, liaison, love affair, relationship.
□ **romantic** adjective 1 amorous, emotional, loving, mushy, nostalgic, passionate, sentimental, sloppy, soppy (*informal*), tender. 2 idealistic, impractical, quixotic, starry-eyed, unrealistic, Utopian, visionary.

romp verb caper, dance, frisk, frolic, gambol, jump, play, prance, run, skip.

rook verb cheat, defraud, diddle (informal), have (slang), overcharge, rip off (informal), swindle.

room noun **1** cell, chamber (old use), office. **2** area, elbow room, space.

roomy adjective ample, big, capacious, commodious, huge, large, spacious, vast.

roost verb nest, perch, settle, sleep.

rooster noun cock, cockerel.

root noun **1** radicle, rhizome, rootlet, tuber. **2** basis, bottom, cause, foundation, origin, source. □ **take root** become established, catch on, take hold.

root verb **1** grow roots, take root. **2** anchor, fix, stick. □ **root out** eliminate, eradicate, get rid of, remove, weed out.

rope noun cable, cord, guy, hawser, lanyard, lariat, lasso, line, noose, painter, stay, tether.

rope verb attach, bind, fasten, hitch, secure, tie.

rort noun dodge (informal), lurk (Australian informal), racket, scam (slang), scheme, swindle.

roster noun list, rota.

rostrum noun dais, platform, podium, stage, stand.

rosy adjective **1** blushing, florid, flushed, glowing, pink, red, rose, rubicund, ruddy. **2** auspicious, bright, cheerful, encouraging, hopeful, optimistic, promising.

rot verb decay, decompose, disintegrate, fester, go bad, go off, moulder, perish, putrefy, spoil.

rot noun **1** decay, decomposition, disintegration, mould, putrefaction. **2** see NONSENSE.

rotate verb **1** go round, gyrate, revolve, spin, swivel, turn, twirl, whirl. **2** alternate, swap, take turns at.

rotten adjective **1** bad, crumbling, decayed, decomposed, disintegrating, mouldy, off, perished, putrid, rancid, rank, stinking. **2** (a rotten thing to do) beastly, contemptible, despicable, lousy (informal), low-down, mean, nasty, unkind; (rotten weather) abysmal (informal), appalling (informal), atrocious (informal), bad, dreadful (informal), foul, shocking (informal), terrible (informal); (feeling rotten) ill, miserable, poorly, seedy (informal), sick, unwell, wretched.

rotund adjective chubby, corpulent, fat, obese, overweight, plump, podgy, portly, stout, tubby.

rough adjective **1** (*a rough surface*) broken, bumpy, coarse, craggy, irregular, jagged, knobbly, pitted, ragged, rocky, rugged, stony, uneven; (*rough skin*) bristly, calloused, chapped, hard, leathery, scaly, unshaven. **2** (*a rough voice*) grating, gruff, harsh, hoarse, husky, rasping, raucous, strident; (*rough play*) boisterous, lively, rowdy, unrestrained, wild; (*rough weather*) blustery, inclement, squally, stormy, tempestuous, turbulent, violent, wild. **3** careless, clumsy, crude, hasty, imperfect, makeshift, patchy, rough-and-ready, rudimentary, unfinished. **4** approximate, ballpark (*informal*), general, hazy, imprecise, inexact, sketchy, vague. □ **roughly** adverb about, approximately, around, close to, in the vicinity of, nearly, round about.

round adjective **1** bulbous, circular, curved, globular, rotund, spherical. **2** complete, entire, full, whole.

round noun **1** course, cycle, series, succession. **2** bout, division, game, heat, section, stage.

round verb go round, turn. □ **round off** bring to a close, close, complete, conclude, end, finish, terminate. □ **round up** assemble, collect, gather, herd, muster.

roundabout noun carousel, merry-go-round, whirligig.

roundabout adjective circuitous, circumlocutory, devious, indirect, meandering, oblique, tortuous.

rouse verb **1** arouse, awaken, stir, waken, wake up. **2** excite, incite, move, provoke, stimulate.

rouseabout noun blue tongue (*Australian informal*), handyman, knockabout (*Australian*), loppy (*Australian*), odd-job man.

rousing adjective exciting, inspiring, moving, powerful, provoking, stirring.

rout verb beat, conquer, crush, defeat, overpower, overthrow, put to flight, scatter, thrash, trounce, vanquish.

route noun course, itinerary, path, road, way.

routine noun custom, habit, method, pattern, practice, procedure, ritual, system, way. □ **routine** adjective customary, familiar, habitual, humdrum, mechanical, monotonous, normal, ordinary, predictable, regular, scheduled, standard, usual.

rove *verb* prowl, ramble, roam, stray, wander. □ **rover** *noun* gypsy, itinerant, nomad, traveller, vagabond, wanderer, wayfarer.

row *noun* chain, column, file, line, queue, rank, sequence, series, string, tier.

row *verb* paddle, propel, scull.

row *noun* **1** clamour, commotion, din, disturbance, fuss, hubbub, hullabaloo, noise, racket, ruckus, rumpus, shindy (*informal*), tumult, uproar. **2** altercation, argument, barney (*informal*), blue (*Australian informal*), bust-up (*informal*), disagreement, dispute, fight, fracas, quarrel, run-in, scrap (*informal*), squabble, tiff, wrangle.

rowdy *adjective* boisterous, disorderly, lawless, noisy, obstreperous, riotous, rough, unruly, wild.

royal *adjective* kingly, monarchic, queenly, regal, sovereign.

rub *verb* **1** caress, massage, pat, stroke. **2** apply, smear, spread, wipe, work in. **3** buff, burnish, polish, shine, wipe. **4** abrade, chafe, gall, wear away. □ **rub out** blot out, cancel, delete, efface, erase, expunge, obliterate, remove, wipe out.

rubbish *noun* **1** debris, detritus, dross, garbage, junk, litter, muck (*informal*), mullock (*Australian*), refuse, rubble, scrap, trash, waste. **2** balderdash, boloney (*informal*), bunkum, claptrap, cobblers (*slang*), codswallop (*slang*), drivel, garbage, gibberish, gobbledegook (*informal*), guff (*slang*), hogwash (*informal*), humbug, nonsense, piffle (*informal*), poppycock (*slang*), rot (*slang*), stuff and nonsense, tommyrot (*slang*), tripe (*informal*), twaddle.

rubbish *verb* bag (*Australian informal*), belittle, criticise, disparage, knock (*informal*), pan (*informal*), pick holes in, pooh-pooh, run down, scoff at, slate (*informal*), tear to pieces.

rubble *noun* debris.

rucksack *noun* backpack, haversack, knapsack, pack.

ruddy *adjective* florid, flushed, red, rosy, rubicund.

rude *adjective* **1** abrupt, abusive, bad-mannered, boorish, brazen, brusque, cheeky, churlish, curt, discourteous, disrespectful, foul-mouthed, ill-mannered, impertinent, impolite, impudent, inconsiderate, insolent, insulting, loutish, offensive, offhand, rough, saucy, surly, uncivil, uncouth, vulgar. **2** blue, coarse, crude, dirty, filthy, foul, improper, indecent, lewd, obscene, offensive, pornographic, smutty, tasteless, unprintable, vulgar. **3** crude, makeshift, primitive, rough, simple.

rudimentary *adjective* **1** basic, elementary, fundamental, primary. **2** immature, incomplete, undeveloped, vestigial.

rudiments *plural noun* ABC, basics, elements, essentials, fundamentals.

rue *verb* lament, mourn, regret, repent.

rueful *adjective* apologetic, contrite, penitent, regretful, remorseful, repentant, sorrowful, sorry.

ruffian *noun* bully, gangster, hood (*informal*), hoodlum, hooligan, hoon (*Australian informal*), larrikin (*Australian*), lout, mugger, rogue, rough, scoundrel, thug, tough, villain.

ruffle *verb* **1** disturb, ripple, stir. **2** agitate, disconcert, disturb, faze (*informal*), fluster, perturb, rattle (*informal*), unsettle, upset.

ruffle *noun* flounce, frill, ruff.

ruffled *adjective* dishevelled, messed up, rumpled, tangled, tousled, untidy.

rug *noun* **1** mat. **2** blanket, coverlet.

rugged *adjective* **1** bumpy, craggy, irregular, jagged, rocky, rough, stony, uneven, wild. **2** beefy, brawny, burly, hardy, husky, muscular, nuggety (*Australian*), robust, strong, sturdy, tough, vigorous.

ruin *noun* **1** collapse, decay, destruction, devastation, dilapidation, disrepair, downfall, failure, fall, rack and ruin, ruination, undoing. **2** (*ruins*) debris, remains, rubble, shell, wreck, wreckage.

ruin *verb* damage, demolish, destroy, devastate, mess up, muck up, sabotage, scupper (*informal*), shatter, spoil, undermine, vandalise, wreck.

rule *noun* **1** by-law, code, commandment, convention, decree, formula, guideline, instruction, law, order, ordinance, policy, precept, principle, protocol, regulation, ruling, statute. **2** convention, custom, norm, practice, routine, standard. **3** authority, command, control, dominion, government, jurisdiction, leadership, regime, reign, sovereignty. □ **as a rule** for the most part, generally, normally, ordinarily, usually.

rule *verb* **1** administer, command, control, direct,

govern, lead, manage, reign over, rule. **2** adjudicate, decide, decree, determine, find, judge, pronounce.

ruler noun **1** chief, commander, emir, emperor, empress, governor, head, head of state, king, leader, lord, monarch, overlord, potentate, president, prince, princess, queen, sovereign, sultan. **2** measure, rule, yardstick.

rumble verb & noun boom, roar, thunder.

rummage verb comb, ferret, forage, fossick (*Australian informal*), hunt, ransack, rifle, scour, search.

rumour noun bush telegraph, furphy (*Australian informal*), gossip, hearsay, mulga wire (*Australian informal*), tale, whisper.

rumour verb bandy about, gossip, put about, report, say, spread about, whisper.

rumpus noun commotion, din, disturbance, fuss, hullabaloo, pandemonium, protest, racket, row, ruckus, shindy (*informal*), storm, to-do, uproar.

run verb **1** bound, dart, dash, fly, gallop, hasten, hurry, hurtle, jog, race, rush, scamper, scoot, scurry, scuttle, shoot, speed, sprint, spurt, stampede,

streak, sweep, tear, trot, whiz, zip. **2** cascade, drip, flow, gush, issue, leak, pour, roll, spurt, stream, trickle. **3** behave, function, go, operate, perform, work. **4** administer, carry on, conduct, control, direct, govern, look after, maintain, manage, organise, oversee, supervise. **5** convey, drive, take, transport. □ **run after** chase, follow, pursue. □ **run away** abscond, beat it (*slang*), bolt, clear off (*informal*), decamp, depart, disappear, do a runner (*slang*), escape, flee, go away, hightail it (*informal*), leave, make off, nick off (*Australian slang*), retreat, run off, scarper (*informal*), scoot, scram (*informal*), shoot through (*Australian informal*), skedaddle (*informal*), take flight, take off, take to your heels, withdraw. □ **run down** bag (*Australian informal*), belittle, criticise, disparage, knock (*informal*), malign, pan (*informal*), revile, rubbish, slate (*informal*). □ **run into 1** bump into, career into, collide with, crash into, hit, knock into, ram, smash into, strike. **2** bump into, come across, meet, run across. □ **run over 1** brim over, overflow, spill over. **2** hit, knock down, run down. **3** go over, practise, rehearse, run through.

run noun **1** drive, excursion, jaunt, outing, ride, spin (*informal*), trip. **2** sequence, series, spate, string, succession. **3** compound, coop, enclosure, pen. **4** farm, property, station (*Australian*).

runaway noun absconder, bolter, deserter, escapee, fugitive.

run-down noun outline, recap (*informal*), report, review, round-up, summary, survey.

runny adjective fluid, liquid, sloppy, thin, watery.

runway noun airstrip, landing strip.

rupture verb break, burst, split, tear.

rural adjective bucolic, country, pastoral, rustic.

ruse noun artifice, deception, dodge (*informal*), hoax, manoeuvre, ploy (*informal*), stratagem, subterfuge, trick, wile.

rush verb **1** charge, dash, fly, gallop, hasten, hurry, hustle, race, run, scoot, scramble, scurry, shoot off, speed, sprint, storm, tear, whiz, zip, zoom. **2** attack, capture, charge, seize, storm.

rush noun **1** haste, hurry, hustle, race. **2** charge, dash, run, scramble, stampede.

rust verb corrode, oxidise, rot.

rustic adjective bucolic, country, pastoral, rural.

rustle verb & noun swish, whisper.

rut noun **1** channel, furrow, groove, track. **2** grind, habit, routine.

ruthless adjective brutal, callous, cruel, ferocious, harsh, heartless, merciless, pitiless, relentless, remorseless, savage, vicious.

Ss

sabotage noun damage, destruction, disruption, vandalism. □ **sabotage** verb destroy, disrupt, ruin, spoil, undermine, wreck.

sachet noun bag, pack, packet.

sack noun bag, pack, package.

sack verb discharge, dismiss, fire, give notice to, give someone the boot (*slang*), lay off, make redundant.

sack verb destroy, lay waste, loot, pillage, plunder, raid, ransack, ravage.

sacred adjective blessed, consecrated, divine, hallowed, holy, religious, revered, sacrosanct, sanctified, spiritual, venerated.

sacrifice *noun* oblation, offering.

sacrifice *verb* forfeit, forgo, give up, offer, renounce, surrender.

sacrilege *noun* desecration, disrespect, irreverence, profanation, profanity, violation. □ **sacrilegious** *adjective* disrespectful, impious, irreverent, profane; see also *BLASPHEMOUS* (at *BLASPHEMY*).

sacrosanct *adjective* inviolable, protected, respected, sacred.

sad *adjective* **1** blue, brokenhearted, dejected, depressed, desolate, despondent, disconsolate, discontented, dismal, distressed, doleful, downcast, gloomy, glum, heartbroken, heavy-hearted, lugubrious, melancholy, miserable, mournful, rueful, sorrowful, unhappy, woebegone, wretched. **2** dismal, distressing, gloomy, heartbreaking, pessimistic, touching, tragic, upsetting. □ **sadness** *noun* dejection, depression, desolation, despondency, discontent, distress, gloom, glumness, melancholy, misery, sorrow, unhappiness, woe, wretchedness.

sadden *verb* depress, dishearten, dismay, distress, grieve, upset.

sadistic *adjective* brutal, cruel, inhuman, monstrous, vicious.

safari *noun* expedition, tour, trip.

safe *adjective* **1** harmless, innocuous, non-toxic. **2** defended, impregnable, protected, secure, sheltered. **3** certain, dependable, reliable, sound, sure. **4** all right, OK (*informal*), safe and sound, unharmed, uninjured, unscathed. □ **safety** *noun* protection, security.

safe *noun* strongbox, vault.

safeguard *noun* defence, precaution, protection, security.

safeguard *verb* defend, guard, look after, preserve, protect.

sag *verb* bow, droop, flop, sink, slump, subside.

saga *noun* chronicle, epic, history, legend, romance, story, tale.

sage *adjective* judicious, prudent, sagacious, sensible, shrewd, wise.

sage *noun* authority, expert, guru, philosopher, pundit, scholar, wise man.

sail *noun* **1** cruise. **2** journey, trip, voyage.

sail *verb* **1** cruise, embark, put to sea, set out, set sail, weigh anchor. **2** navigate, pilot, skipper, steer. **3** drift, float, glide, scud, sweep, waft.

sailor *noun* mariner, navigator, seafarer, seaman, yachtsman, yachtswoman.

saintly *adjective* blameless, blessed, God-fearing, godly, holy, innocent, pious, righteous, upright, virtuous.

salary *noun* earnings, emolument, income, pay, remuneration, stipend.

sale *noun* **1** selling, vending. **2** auction, clearance, sell-out.

salesperson *noun* sales assistant, salesman, saleswoman, shop assistant.

salient *adjective* conspicuous, noticeable, outstanding, prominent, striking.

saline *adjective* brackish, briny, salt, salty.

saliva *noun* dribble, spit, spittle, sputum.

sallow *adjective* pale, pallid, sickly, wan, yellowish.

salon *noun* establishment, parlour, shop.

salty *adjective* brackish, briny, saline, salt.

salute *verb* **1** acknowledge, greet, nod to. **2** applaud, commend, congratulate, honour, pay tribute to.

salute *noun* greeting, salutation, welcome.

salvage *verb* preserve, recover, recycle, rescue, retrieve, save.

□ **salvage** *noun* recovery, rescue, retrieval.

salvation *noun* deliverance, redemption, rescue, saving.

salve *noun* balm, lotion, ointment.

salve *verb* appease, ease, relieve, soothe.

salvo *noun* firing, report, salute, volley.

same *adjective* **1** alike, identical, indistinguishable, selfsame. **2** constant, unchanged, unchanging, uniform, unvarying. □ **sameness** *noun* evenness, monotony, similarity, uniformity.

sample *noun* example, foretaste, instance, model, specimen, taste.

sample *verb* taste, test, try.

sanatorium *noun* clinic, convalescent home, hospital, nursing home.

sanctify *verb* bless, consecrate, hallow.

sanctimonious *adjective* holier-than-thou, hypocritical, pharisaical, pious, self-righteous.

sanction *noun* **1** approval, authorisation, blessing, consent, go-ahead, OK (*informal*), permission, support. **2** ban, boycott, embargo, penalty.

sanction *verb* allow, approve, authorise, consent to, legalise, permit, support.

sanctity *noun* holiness, inviolability, sacredness.

sanctuary *noun* **1** asylum, haven, protection, refuge, retreat, safety, shelter. **2** chapel, church, sanctum, shrine, temple. **3** conservation park, preserve, reservation, reserve, wildlife park.

sand *verb* polish, sandpaper, smooth.

sandbank *noun* reef, sandbar, shoal.

sandwich *noun* sambo (*Australian slang*), sanger (*Australian slang*).

sandwich *verb* jam, squash, squeeze, wedge.

sane *adjective* **1** all there (*informal*), lucid, normal, of sound mind, rational. **2** logical, rational, reasonable, sensible, sound.

sanguine *adjective* confident, hopeful, optimistic, positive.

sanitary *adjective* antiseptic, aseptic, clean, disinfected, germ-free, healthy, hygienic, sanitised, sterile, sterilised.

sanity *noun* normality, rationality, reason, saneness, sense, soundness.

sap *noun* juice, lifeblood.

sap *verb* deplete, drain, exhaust, rob, weaken.

sarcastic *adjective* derisive, ironic, mocking, sardonic, satirical, scornful, sneering, taunting.

sardonic *adjective* cynical, derisive, mocking, sarcastic, scornful, sneering, wry.

sash *noun* cummerbund, girdle, obi, tie.

satanic *adjective* demonic, devilish, diabolic, diabolical, evil, fiendish, hellish, infernal, wicked.

satchel *noun* backpack, bag, pack, schoolbag.

satellite *noun* moon, space station, sputnik.

satin *adjective* glossy, shiny, smooth.

satire *noun* **1** irony, mockery, ridicule, sarcasm. **2** burlesque, caricature, lampoon, parody, send-up (*informal*), skit, spoof (*informal*), take-off. □ **satirical** *adjective* derisive, ironic, mocking, sarcastic. □ **satirise** *verb* caricature, deride, lampoon, make fun of, parody, ridicule, send up (*informal*), take off.

satisfaction *noun* contentment, delight, fulfilment, gratification, happiness, pleasure, pride.

satisfactory *adjective* acceptable, adequate, all right, enough, fair, fine, OK (*informal*), passable, sufficient, tolerable, up to scratch.

satisfy *verb* **1** (*satisfy a person*) content, fulfil, gratify, please; (*satisfy thirst*) appease, assuage, quench, sate, satiate, slake; (*satisfy requirements*) answer, comply with, fill, fulfil, meet, supply. **2** assure, convince, persuade, reassure. □ **satisfying** *adjective* enjoyable, fulfilling, gratifying, pleasing, rewarding.

saturate *verb* drench, soak, souse, wet through.

sauce *noun* condiment, dressing, gravy, relish.

saucepan *noun* cauldron, pan, pot.

saucy *adjective* bold, brazen, cheeky, forward, fresh, impertinent, impudent, insolent, pert, presumptuous.

saunter *verb* amble, mosey (*slang*), ramble, roam, stroll, wander.

sausage *noun* banger (*slang*), snag (*Australian slang*).

savage *adjective* **1** barbaric, feral, primitive, uncivilised, untamed, wild. **2** brutal, callous, cruel, ferocious, fierce, harsh, inhuman, merciless, ruthless, vicious, violent.

save *verb* **1** deliver, guard, keep safe, liberate, preserve, protect, ransom, redeem, release, rescue, set free, spare. **2** collect, conserve, hoard, hold on to, invest, keep, lay by, preserve, put aside, put by, reserve, retain, salvage, set aside, stockpile, store. **3** be sparing with, economise on, use sparingly.

savings *plural noun* capital, funds, investments, nest egg, reserves.

saviour *noun* deliverer, liberator, protector, redeemer, rescuer. □ **our Saviour** Christ, Jesus, Messiah.

savour *noun* aroma, flavour, smell, taste.

savour *verb* appreciate, delight in, enjoy, relish.

savoury *adjective* **1** piquant, salty. **2** appetising, delectable, delicious, mouth-watering, scrumptious (*informal*), tasty.

saw *noun* (*kinds of saw*) chainsaw, circular saw, fretsaw, hacksaw, jigsaw.

say *verb* **1** affirm, allege, announce, answer, articulate, assert, bellow, blurt out, call out, comment, cry, declare, exclaim, moan, mumble, murmur, mutter, pronounce, recite, remark, repeat, reply, respond, scream, shout, shriek, snap, snarl, speak, splutter, squawk, squeal, stammer, state, stutter, tell, utter, voice, whisper, yell. **2** communicate, convey, disclose, divulge, express, impart, indicate, mention, refer to, report, reveal, speak of, tell.

say noun input, opinion, voice, vote.

saying noun adage, aphorism, axiom, byword, catchphrase, cliché, dictum, epigram, maxim, motto, proverb, quotation, slogan.

scaffold noun gallows, gibbet.

scaffolding noun frame, framework, gantry, platform.

scale noun **1** hierarchy, ladder, progression, range, sequence, series, spectrum. **2** proportion, ratio. **3** dimensions, extent, level, scope, size.

scale verb ascend, clamber up, climb, mount.

scale noun **1** flake, lamina, plate. **2** coating, crust, deposit, encrustation. □ **scaly** adjective flaky, peeling, rough, scurfy.

scale noun □ **scales** balance, weighing machine.

scallywag noun devil, imp, knave, miscreant, rascal, rogue, scamp, wretch.

scamper verb dash, hurry, race, run, rush, scoot, scurry, scuttle, skip.

scan verb **1** examine, look at, scrutinise, study, survey. **2** flick through, flip through, glance at, leaf through, skim.

scandal noun **1** crime, disgrace, outrage, shame, sin. **2** gossip, rumour, tattle, tittle-tattle. □ **scandalous** adjective disgraceful, improper, outrageous, shameful, shocking, unseemly, wicked.

scandalise verb affront, appal, offend, outrage, shock.

scandalmonger noun gossip, muckraker (informal), mudslinger (informal), rumourmonger, tittle-tat.

scanty adjective inadequate, insufficient, limited, little, meagre, minimal, scant, skimpy, sparse.

scapegoat noun bunny (Australian informal), fall guy (slang), victim, whipping boy.

scar noun cicatrice, mark, scratch, wound.

scar verb damage, disfigure, mark, scratch, wound.

scarce adjective in short supply, insufficient, rare, scanty. □ **scarcity** noun dearth, lack, paucity, shortage.

scarcely adverb barely, hardly, only just.

scare verb alarm, dismay, frighten, intimidate, panic, shock, startle, terrify.

terrorise, unnerve. □ **scared** *adjective* afraid, alarmed, fearful, frightened, intimidated, nervous, panic-stricken, petrified, terrified.

scare *noun* alarm, fright, shock, start. □ **scary** *adjective* alarming, creepy, eerie, frightening, hair-raising, spine-chilling, spooky (*informal*), terrifying.

scarf *noun* bandanna, headscarf, kerchief, muffler, neckerchief.

scarp *noun* bluff, cliff, escarpment, precipice, slope.

scathing *adjective* biting, caustic, harsh, savage, severe, withering.

scatter *verb* broadcast, disperse, disseminate, spread, sprinkle, strew, throw about.

scatterbrained *adjective* absent-minded, disorganised, dreamy, forgetful, harebrained, muddle-headed, scatty (*informal*), silly, vague.

scavenge *verb* forage, fossick (*Australian informal*), look, rummage, scrounge, search.

scenario *noun* outline, plot, script, storyline, summary, synopsis.

scene *noun* **1** locale, locality, location, place, setting, site, spot. **2** landscape, outlook, panorama, prospect, scenery, sight, view, vista. **3** exhibition, fuss, incident, outburst, spectacle.

scenery *noun* **1** landscape, panorama, view, vista. **2** backdrop, set.

scenic *adjective* beautiful, panoramic, picturesque, pretty.

scent *noun* **1** aroma, bouquet, fragrance, odour, perfume, redolence, smell, whiff. **2** spoor, track, trail.

sceptical *adjective* disbelieving, distrustful, doubting, dubious, incredulous, mistrustful, questioning, suspicious. □ **scepticism** *noun* disbelief, distrust, doubt, mistrust, suspicion.

schedule *noun* agenda, diary, itinerary, plan, programme, timetable.

schedule *verb* appoint, arrange, book, list, plan, programme, timetable.

scheme *noun* **1** plan, programme, project, strategy. **2** conspiracy, dodge (*informal*), lurk (*Australian informal*), plot, ploy, racket, rort (*Australian slang*), ruse, scam (*slang*), stratagem. **3** arrangement, design, system.

scheme *verb* collude, conspire, intrigue, plan, plot.

scholar *noun* academic, expert, highbrow, intellectual, pundit.

□ **scholarly** adjective academic, bookish, erudite, highbrow, intellectual, learned, studious.

scholarship noun **1** award, bursary, fellowship, grant. **2** erudition, learning, research.

scholastic adjective academic, educational.

school noun **1** academy, college, educational institution, seminary. **2** circle, group, movement, set. □ **schoolchild** noun collegian, pupil, scholar, schoolboy, schoolgirl, student. □ **schoolteacher** noun chalkie (Australian slang), master, mistress, pedagogue (old use), schoolie (Australian informal), schoolmaster, schoolmistress, teacher.

school verb discipline, educate, instruct, teach, train.

schooling noun education, instruction, learning, training, tuition.

scientific adjective analytical, methodical, precise, rigorous, systematic.

scintillating adjective animated, brilliant, lively, sparkling, stimulating, witty.

scissors plural noun clippers, cutters, secateurs, shears, snips.

scoff verb (scoff at) belittle, chiack (Australian informal), deride, disparage, gibe at, jeer at, knock (informal), make fun of, mock, ridicule, rubbish (Australian informal), scorn, sling off at (Australian informal), sneer at.

scold verb admonish, berate, castigate, censure, chastise, chide (old use), go crook at (Australian informal), haul over the coals, rap over the knuckles, rebuke, reprimand, reproach, reprove, rouse on (Australian informal), tell of (informal), tick off (informal), upbraid. □ **scolding** noun dressing down (informal), lecture, rap over the knuckles, rebuke, reprimand, reproof, talking-to (informal), wigging (informal).

scoop noun ladle, shovel, spoon.

scoop verb dig, excavate, gouge, hollow.

scoot verb dart, dash, go, hurry, run, rush.

scope noun **1** capacity, latitude, opportunity, outlet, room. **2** area, bounds, compass, extent, limits, orbit, range.

scorch verb brown, burn, discolour, sear, singe.

score noun grade, mark, points, result, tally.

score verb **1** achieve, gain, get, make, notch up, win. **2** cut, gash, gouge, groove, incise, notch, scratch. **3** arrange, orchestrate, write.

scorn noun contempt, derision, disdain, ridicule. □ **scornful** adjective contemptuous, derisive, disdainful, jeering, mocking, sarcastic, scathing, scoffing, sneering, snide (*informal*).

scorn verb despise, disdain, rebuff, refuse, reject, shun, snub, spurn, turn your nose up at.

scoundrel noun blackguard, cad, crook (*informal*), knave (*old use*), miscreant, rascal, rogue, villain.

scour verb clean, cleanse, polish, rub, scrub.

scour verb comb, rake through, ransack, search.

scourge noun **1** lash, whip. **2** affliction, bane, curse, plague, suffering.

scourge verb beat, flog, lash, thrash, whip.

scout noun lookout, spy, vanguard.

scout verb ferret, fossick (*Australian informal*), hunt, look, search, snoop (*informal*).

scowl verb frown, glare, glower, lour.

scraggy adjective bony, emaciated, gaunt, lean, scrawny, skinny, thin.

scramble verb clamber, climb, crawl, dash, hurry, race, run, rush, scurry, struggle.

scramble noun race, run, rush, scrimmage, struggle, tussle.

scrap noun **1** bit, fragment, piece, rag, remnant, shred, tatter. **2** junk, refuse, rubbish, salvage, trash, waste; (*scraps*) crumbs, leftovers, scrapings.

scrap verb abandon, discard, ditch (*informal*), do away with, drop, get rid of, give up, jettison.

scrap noun altercation, argument, barney (*informal*), dispute, fight, quarrel, row, squabble, tiff.

scrape verb **1** clean, rub, scrub. **2** abrade, bark, grate, graze, rasp, scratch, scuff, skin.

scrape noun **1** abrasion, cut, graze, injury, laceration, scratch. **2** difficulty, plight, predicament, trouble.

scrappy adjective bitty, disjointed, fragmentary.

scratch verb **1** abrade, cut, gouge, graze, lacerate, mark, score, scrape, scuff, skin. **2** remove, withdraw.

scratch noun abrasion, gouge, graze, laceration, mark, score, scrape, scuff, wound.

scrawl verb scribble; see also WRITE.

scrawny adjective bony, emaciated, gaunt, lanky, lean, puny, scraggy, skinny, thin.

scream noun 1 cry, howl, screech, shriek, squawk, squeal, yell, yowl. 2 hoot (informal), laugh, riot (informal).

scream verb bawl, cry out, howl, screech, shriek, squawk, squeal, wail, yell, yowl.

screen noun 1 barrier, blind, cover, curtain, divider, partition, protection, shelter, shield. 2 monitor, VDU, visual display unit.

screen verb 1 camouflage, conceal, hide, protect, shelter, shield. 2 broadcast, present, show. 3 check, examine, investigate, test, vet. 4 filter, riddle, sieve, sift, strain.

screw verb rotate, turn, twist.

scribble verb doodle, scrawl.

scrimp verb economise, save, skimp, stint, tighten your belt.

script noun 1 handwriting, writing. 2 lines, screenplay, text, words.

scripture noun sacred writings. □ **Scripture** the Bible, the Word of God.

scrounge verb beg, bludg (Australian informal), borrow cadge, scab (Australian slang) sponge.

scrub verb 1 clean, scour, wash 2 abandon, call off, cance drop, forget, scrap.

scrub noun bush, mallee mulga.

scrubby adjective low, smal stunted.

scruffy adjective bedraggled dishevelled, messy, shabb slovenly, tatty (informal) unkempt, untidy.

scrumptious adjective appe tising, delectable, delicious luscious, mouth-watering tasty, yummy (informal).

scrunch verb crumple, crunch crush, screw up, squash.

scruple noun compunction doubt, hesitation, misgiving qualm, twinge of conscience

scrupulous adjective 1 carefu conscientious, fastidiou meticulous, painstaking, pa ticular, punctilious, rigorou thorough. 2 ethical, hones honourable, moral, principled upright.

scrutinise verb examine inspect, look over, perus study, survey. □ **scrutiny** nou examination, inspection, in vestigation, perusal, study.

scud *verb* fly, race, speed, sweep.

scuff *verb* mark, rub, scrape, wear away.

scuffle *noun* brawl, fight, fisticuffs, scrap (*informal*), scrimmage, skirmish, stoush (*Australian slang*), struggle, tussle.

sculpture *noun* bust, carving, cast, figure, figurine, statue, statuette. □ **sculpture** *verb* carve, chisel, form, hew, make, model, sculpt (*informal*), shape.

scum *noun* film, foam, froth.

scupper *verb* 1 scuttle, sink. 2 foil, ruin, spoil, stonker (*Australian slang*), thwart, wreck.

scurrilous *adjective* abusive, defamatory, insulting, low, offensive, vilifying.

scurry *verb* flit, hurry, run, rush, scamper, scoot, scramble, scutter, scuttle.

scuttle *noun* bucket, pail.

scuttle *verb* scupper, sink.

sea *noun* 1 the deep, the main (*old use*), ocean. 2 expanse, mass. □ **at sea** baffled, bewildered, confused, perplexed, puzzled, uncertain.

seafaring *adjective* maritime, nautical, naval, sailing, seagoing. □ **seafarer** *noun* mariner, sailor, seaman.

seal *noun* crest, emblem, imprint, insignia, stamp, symbol.

seal *verb* 1 close, fasten, secure, stick down. 2 bituminise, macadamise, surface, tar, tarmac, tar-seal (*Australian*). □ **seal off** block off, close off, cordon off.

seam *noun* 1 join, stitching. 2 layer, lode, stratum, vein.

seaman *noun* mariner, sailor, seafarer.

seamy *adjective* sordid, squalid, unattractive, unpleasant, unsavoury.

sear *verb* brown, burn, scorch, singe.

search *verb* check, comb, examine, explore, ferret, forage, fossick (*Australian informal*), frisk, hunt, inspect, look, look over, look through, probe, ransack, rummage, scour, seek. □ **search** *noun* examination, exploration, hunt, inspection, look, probe, quest.

seasick *adjective* nauseous, queasy, sick.

seaside *noun* beach, coast.

season *noun* period, time. □ **in season** available, ready, ripe.

season *verb* 1 flavour, pepper, salt, spice. 2 age, condition, dry, harden, mature.

seasoning *noun* condiment, flavour, herb, relish, spice.

seat *noun* **1** armchair, bench, chair, couch, form, lounge, pew, place, settee, settle, sofa, stall, stool, throne. **2** backside (*informal*), behind (*informal*), bottom, bum (*slang*), buttocks, rump.

seat *verb* **1** place, position, put, situate. **2** accommodate, hold, take.

secateurs *plural noun* clippers, cutters, pruning shears.

secede *verb* break away, leave, pull out, quit, separate, split, withdraw.

secluded *adjective* hidden, isolated, lonely, private, remote, sheltered, solitary.

second *adjective* **1** following, next, subsequent. **2** additional, alternative, backup, extra, other, substitute, supplementary.

second *noun* flash, instant, jiffy (*informal*), minute, moment, tick (*informal*).

second *verb* back, endorse, support.

secondary *adjective* **1** derivative, derived. **2** lesser, minor, subordinate, subsidiary.

second-hand *adjective* hand-me-down, pre-loved, pre-owned, recycled, used, worn.

secret *adjective* **1** classified, concealed, confidential, hidden, hushed up, hush-hush (*informal*), private, under wraps, undisclosed. **2** arcane, cryptic, mysterious, occult. **3** clandestine, covert, private, stealthy, surreptitious, undercover. □ **secrecy** *noun* confidentiality, furtiveness, mystery, privacy, stealth.

secret *noun* **1** confidence. **2** enigma, mystery, puzzle, riddle. **3** formula, key, recipe.

secrete *verb* **1** conceal, hide, stash. **2** discharge, emit, excrete, exude, give off, ooze, produce.

secretive *adjective* cagey (*informal*), enigmatic, evasive, furtive, mysterious, reticent, tight-lipped, uncommunicative.

sect *noun* cult, denomination, faction, party.

section *noun* bit, branch, chapter, compartment, department, division, fraction, instalment, part, piece, portion, sector, segment, slice, stage, subdivision.

sector *noun* area, district, division, part, quarter, region, section, zone.

secular *adjective* earthly, lay, temporal, worldly.

secure adjective **1** defended, impregnable, protected, safe, sheltered, unassailable. **2** firm, safe, solid, sound, steady, strong. **3** assured, certain, guaranteed, reliable, safe, sure.

secure verb **1** batten down, bolt, defend, fasten, fortify, guard, lock, make safe, protect, safeguard. **2** acquire, come by, get, obtain, procure.

security noun **1** assurance, certainty, confidence, protection, safety. **2** guarantee, pledge, surety.

sedate adjective calm, collected, composed, decorous, dignified, peaceful, placid, serious, sober, staid, tranquil.

sedative noun narcotic, opiate, sleeping pill, tranquilliser.

sedentary adjective inactive, seated, sitting, stationary.

sediment noun deposit, dregs, grounds, lees, precipitate, residue.

seditious adjective insurrectionist, mutinous, rabble-rousing, subversive, treasonous.

seduce verb beguile, corrupt, entice, lead astray, lure, persuade, tempt. □ **seductive** adjective alluring, attractive, enticing, inviting, provocative, sexy, tempting.

see verb **1** behold (old use), discern, distinguish, espy, glimpse, identify, look at, make out, notice, observe, perceive, recognise, regard, spot, view, watch. **2** bump into, call on, chance upon, confer with, consult, encounter, meet (with), run into, speak to, talk to, visit. **3** appreciate, comprehend, get (informal), grasp, perceive, realise, understand. **4** conceive, envisage, foresee, imagine, picture, visualise. **5** consider, decide, ponder, reflect on, think about. **6** ensure, make sure, mind, take care. **7** ascertain, determine, discover, find out, investigate, learn. **8** accompany, conduct, escort, lead, show, take, usher. □ **see to** attend to, deal with, look after, sort out, take care of.

seed noun germ, grain, ovule, pip, spore, stone.

seedy adjective **1** disreputable, scruffy, shabby, untidy. **2** ill, off colour, poorly, queasy, sick, under the weather, unwell.

seek verb ask for, look for, pursue, request, search for, solicit; see also AIM.

seem verb appear, feel, look, sound.

seemly adjective appropriate, becoming, befitting, decorous, fitting, proper, right, suitable.

seep verb dribble, exude, filter, flow, leak, ooze, percolate, trickle.

seer noun augur, clairvoyant, diviner, prophet, sibyl (*female*), soothsayer, visionary.

seethe verb **1** boil, bubble, churn, foam, surge. **2** be furious, be livid, get steamed up (*informal*), boil, fume.

segment noun division, part, piece, portion, section, slice, wedge.

segregate verb isolate, keep apart, separate. □ **segregation** noun apartheid, isolation, separation.

seize verb **1** clutch, grab, grasp, pluck, snatch, take hold of. **2** apprehend, arrest, capture, catch, collar (*informal*), nab (*informal*), nick (*slang*). **3** commandeer, confiscate, impound, take away, take possession of. **4** grab, jump at, make use of, take advantage of, use, utilise. □ **seize up** become stuck, jam, lock up.

seizure noun apoplexy, attack, convulsion, fit, stroke.

seldom adverb hardly ever, infrequently, once in a blue moon, rarely.

select verb appoint, choose, elect, nominate, pick. □ **selection** noun **1** choice, decision, option, pick. **2** assort-ment, collection, mixture, range, variety.

select adjective **1** choice, chosen, hand-picked. **2** closed, elite, exclusive, restricted.

selective adjective careful, choosy (*informal*), discrimin-ating, fussy, particular, picky (*informal*).

self- prefix □ **self-centred** adjective egocentric, egotistic self-absorbed, selfish, self-seeking, wrapped up in yourself. □ **self-confident** adjective assured, bold, con-fident, poised, self-assured □ **self-conscious** adjective awkward, bashful, diffident embarrassed, insecure, shy uncomfortable. □ **self-control** noun restraint, self-discipline self-restraint, will-power □ **self-denial** noun abste-miousness, asceticism, selflessness, self-sacrifice □ **self-important** adjective arrogant, bumptious, con-ceited, egocentric, egotistic high and mighty, pompous self-centred, self-satisfied snobbish, snooty (*informal*) stuck-up (*informal*), vain □ **self-possessed** adjective calm, collected, composed confident, cool, dignified sedate, self-assured, self confident, self-controlled unflappable (*informal*). □ **self-**

respect noun dignity, pride, self-esteem. ☐ **self-righteous** adjective holier-than-thou, pompous, priggish, sanctimonious, self-satisfied, smug. ☐ **self-satisfied** adjective cocky, complacent, conceited, proud, self-important, smug. ☐ **self-sufficient** adjective independent, self-contained, self-reliant, self-supporting. ☐ **self-willed** adjective determined, headstrong, intractable, obstinate, pigheaded, refractory, stubborn, wilful.

selfish adjective egocentric, greedy, inconsiderate, mean, miserly, self-centred, self-seeking, stingy, thoughtless, wrapped up in yourself.

selfless adjective altruistic, generous, kind, self-denying, self-sacrificing, unselfish.

sell verb auction, barter, deal in, flog (slang), handle, hawk, market, peddle, retail, stock, trade in, traffic in, vend. ☐ **seller** noun dealer, hawker, merchant, peddler, pedlar, pusher, retailer, salesman, salesperson, saleswoman, shopkeeper, stockist, supplier, trader, trafficker, vendor, wholesaler.

semblance noun air, appearance, façade, pretence, show.

seminar noun class, discussion group, tutorial.

semitrailer noun articulated vehicle, lorry, road train (Australian), semi (Australian informal), transport, truck.

send verb (send a message, package, etc.) consign, convey, direct, dispatch, email, fax, forward, pass on, post, relay, remit, ship, transmit, write; (send a rocket) discharge, fire, launch, propel, release, shoot. ☐ **send away** see DISMISS. ☐ **send for** ask for, call, order, summon. ☐ **send up** caricature, lampoon, make fun of, mimic, parody, satirise, take off. ☐ **send-up** noun burlesque, caricature, lampoon, parody, satire, spoof (informal), take-off.

senile adjective decrepit, doddery, feeble-minded, infirm.

senior adjective 1 elder, older. 2 higher-ranking, superior.

sensation noun 1 awareness, consciousness, feeling, perception, sense. 2 commotion, excitement, stir. ☐ **sensational** adjective dramatic, electrifying, exciting, lurid, scandalous, shocking, spectacular, startling, striking, stunning, thrilling.

sense noun 1 faculty, perception, power, sensation. 2 awareness, consciousness, perception, recognition. 3 brains (informal), common sense, gumption, intelligence, judgement, nous (*informal*), reason, sagacity, wisdom, wit. **4** denotation, import, meaning, signification.

sense *verb* be aware, detect, discern, feel, perceive, realise, suspect, twig (*informal*).

senseless *adjective* **1** absurd, foolish, inane, mad, meaningless, nonsensical, pointless, silly, stupid. **2** cold (*informal*), insensible, out, unconscious.

sensibility *noun* sensitiveness, sensitivity; (*sensibilities*) emotions, feelings, susceptibilities.

sensible *adjective* **1** intelligent, judicious, level-headed, logical, prudent, rational, realistic, reasonable, sagacious, sage, shrewd, thoughtful, wise. **2** functional, practical, serviceable.

sensitive *adjective* **1** delicate, hypersensitive, reactive, tender, thin-skinned, touchy. **2** affected by, responsive to, susceptible to. **3** considerate, empathetic, perceptive, sympathetic, understanding.

sensual *adjective* bodily, carnal, fleshly, physical, sexual.

sensuous *adjective* appealing, attractive, beautiful, exquisite.

sentence *noun* decision, judgement, penalty, punishment.

sentence *verb* condemn, penalise, punish.

sentiment *noun* **1** attitude, belief, feeling, opinion, thought, view. **2** emotion, feeling, sentimentality.

sentimental *adjective* corny (*informal*), emotional, maudlin, mawkish, mushy, nostalgic, romantic, schmaltzy, soppy (*informal*), weepy (*informal*).

sentry *noun* guard, lookout, sentinel, watchman.

separable *adjective* discrete, distinct.

separate *adjective* autonomous, detached, discrete, distinct, free-standing, independent, individual, single, unconnected, unrelated.

separate *verb* **1** break, break apart, detach, disconnect, dissociate, divide, part, segregate, sever, sort, split, sunder, take apart. **2** break up, divorce, part, split up. □ **separation** *noun* **1** break, detachment, disconnection, dissociation, division, partition, segregation, split. **2** break-up, divorce, parting, split-up.

sequel *noun* continuation, development, follow-up.

sequence *noun* chain, course, order, progression, series, succession, train.

serene adjective calm, composed, peaceful, placid, quiet, tranquil, unperturbed, unruffled.

series noun chain, cycle, group, line, order, progression, row, sequence, set, string, succession, train.

serious adjective **1** earnest, grave, long-faced, pensive, sedate, sober, solemn, staid, steady, thoughtful. **2** determined, earnest, genuine, keen, resolute, sincere. **3** bad, critical, dangerous, grave, life-threatening, major, severe. **4** crucial, important, momentous, vital, weighty.

sermon noun address, homily, talk.

serpentine adjective corkscrew, curving, sinuous, tortuous, twisting, winding.

servant noun attendant, butler, domestic, factotum, footman, help, housekeeper, lackey, maid, maidservant, manservant, menial, minion (derogatory), page, retainer, slave, valet, vassal.

serve verb **1** help, work for. **2** assist, attend to, look after, wait on. **3** dish up, distribute, dole out, give, hand, present. **4** complete, discharge, go through, undergo. **5** act, be suitable, do, function.

service noun **1** employment, labour, work. **2** aid, assistance, benefit, help, use. **3** facility, provision, set-up, supply, system, utility. **4** (services) air force, armed forces, armed services, army, defence forces, forces, marines, military, navy, troops. **5** ceremony, rite, ritual, sacrament. **6** maintenance, overhaul, repair.

service verb check, fix, maintain, overhaul, repair, tune.

serviceable adjective **1** functioning, operative, usable, working. **2** durable, functional, hard-wearing, practical, strong, tough.

serviette noun napkin, table napkin.

servile adjective abject, fawning, grovelling, humble, lowly, menial, obsequious, slavish, submissive, subservient, sycophantic.

servitude noun bondage, enslavement, slavery, subjection.

session noun **1** meeting, sitting. **2** period, spell, time.

set verb **1** bung (informal), deposit, dump, install, lay, leave, park (informal), place, plonk, position, put, rest, stand. **2** embed, fix, install, lodge, mount, stick. **3** adjust, regulate. **4** arrange, lay, prepare. **5** appoint, choose, decide on, determine, establish, fix, name, settle on, specify. **6** congeal, firm, gel, jell, solidify, stiffen. **7** allot, assign, give, prescribe. □ **set about** begin, commence, start. □ **set back** delay, hamper, hinder, hold back, impede, slow. □ **set off 1** depart, leave, set forth, set out, start. **2** cause, spark, start, stimulate, touch off, trigger. **3** detonate, explode, ignite, let off. □ **set out 1** begin, depart, embark, leave, set forth, set off, start. **2** declare, detail, make known, present, state. □ **set sail** depart, leave, put to sea, sail. □ **set up 1** arrange, organise, prepare. **2** begin, create, develop, establish, found, institute, start.

set noun **1** assortment, batch, bunch, class, collection, group, series. **2** apparatus, receiver. **3** backdrop, scene, scenery, setting.

setback noun blow, complication, hiccup, hitch, obstacle, problem, reverse, snag.

settee noun couch, lounge, sofa.

setting noun background, context, environment, locale, locality, place, scene, site, surroundings.

settle verb **1** (*settle on a time etc.*) agree, arrange, choose,

decide, determine, fix; (*settle a problem etc.*) clear up, deal with, reconcile, resolve, sort out, straighten out, work out. **2** calm, pacify, quieten, relax, soothe. **3** establish yourself, immigrate, move, put down roots; see also *POPULATE*. **4** come to rest, descend, fall, land, sink, subside. **5** clear, discharge, liquidate, pay. □ **settler** noun colonist, immigrant, pioneer.

settlement noun **1** agreement, arrangement, reconciliation, resolution. **2** colony, community, outpost, township.

set-up noun arrangement, format, organisation, structure, system.

several adjective a few, a good many, a number of, some.

severe adjective **1** cold, cruel, dour, Draconian, forbidding, grim, hard, harsh, merciless, pitiless, rigorous, ruthless, stern, strict, stringent, tough, unsmiling, unsympathetic. **2** acute, bad, critical, dangerous, drastic, extreme, fierce, forceful, grave, intense, serious, strong, violent. **3** austere, plain, simple, spartan, unadorned.

sew verb baste, darn, embroider, mend, smock, stitch, tack.

sewage noun effluent, waste.

sex *noun* **1** gender. **2** coitus, copulation, intercourse, love-making, mating, sexual intercourse.

sexism *noun* male chauvinism, sexual discrimination; see also *PREJUDICE*.

sexual *adjective* (*sexual organs*) genital, reproductive, sex; (*sexual attraction*) carnal, erotic, physical, sensual.

sexy *adjective* alluring, attractive, erotic, flirtatious, seductive, sensual.

shabby *adjective* **1** (*shabby clothes*) frayed, ragged, scruffy, tattered, tatty (*informal*), threadbare, worn; (*shabby buildings*) dilapidated, dingy, drab, neglected, ramshackle, run-down, seedy, squalid, tumbledown. **2** contemptible, despicable, dirty, dishonourable, low-down, mean, unfair.

shack *noun* cabin, hovel, hut, shanty, weekender (*Australian*).

hackle *noun* (*shackles*) bonds, chains, fetters, handcuffs, irons, manacles.

hackle *verb* bind, chain, fetter, handcuff, manacle, restrain.

hade *noun* **1** semi-darkness, shadow. **2** blind, cover, screen, shield. **3** colour, degree, hue, intensity, tinge, tint, tone.

4 degree, difference, gradation, nuance, variation.

shade *verb* **1** cast shadow on, screen, shelter. **2** darken, hatch.

shadow *noun* **1** outline, shape, silhouette. **2** darkness, dimness, gloom, semi-darkness, shade.

shadow *verb* follow, pursue, stalk, tail (*informal*), track, trail.

shady *adjective* **1** cool, dark, dim, shaded, shadowy. **2** crooked, dishonest, dubious, fishy (*informal*), questionable, shonky (*Australian informal*), suspect, suspicious.

shaft *noun* **1** handle, pole, rod, shank, stem, stick. **2** beam, bolt (*of lightning*), ray, streak. **3** opening, passage, tunnel, well.

shaggy *adjective* **1** hairy, hirsute, long-haired, unshorn. **2** bushy, messy, rough, thick, tousled, unkempt, untidy, woolly.

shake *verb* **1** brandish, jiggle, rock, sway, swing, vibrate, wag, waggle, wave, wiggle, wobble. **2** agitate, disconcert, distress, disturb, jolt, perturb, rattle (*informal*), ruffle, shock, stun, unnerve, unsettle, upset. **3** quake, quaver, quiver, shiver, shudder, tremble, wobble.

shaky *adjective* doddery, quivery, rocky, unsteady, trembling, tremulous, weak, wobbly.

shallow *adjective* empty, frivolous, glib, skin-deep, superficial, trivial.

sham *noun* act, charade, counterfeit, fake, fraud, hoax, imitation, phoney (*informal*), pretence, put-on (*informal*). □ **sham** *adjective* artificial, counterfeit, fake, false, imitation, phoney (*informal*), pseudo, synthetic.

sham *verb* counterfeit, fake, feign, pretend, simulate.

shambles *noun* disaster area (*informal*), mess, muddle, pigsty, shemozzle (*informal*).

shame *noun* 1 embarrassment, guilt, humiliation, ignominy, mortification, regret, remorse. 2 disappointment, pity. □ **shameful** *adjective* contemptible, deplorable, disgraceful, dishonourable, ignominious, reprehensible, scandalous, shocking, unbecoming.

shame *verb* disgrace, embarrass, humble, humiliate, mortify.

shamefaced *adjective* abashed, ashamed, embarrassed, hangdog, humiliated, mortified, sheepish.

shameless *adjective* bold, brazen, cheeky, immodest, impudent, unashamed, unseemly.

shanghai *noun* catapult, ging (*Australian informal*), sling, slingshot.

shanty *noun* hovel, hut, shack.

shape *noun* 1 build, contour, figure, form, outline, profile, silhouette. 2 condition, fettle, form, health, state, trim.

shape *verb* 1 construct, fashion, form, frame, make, model, mould, sculpt, sculpture. 2 develop, evolve, progress, take shape. 3 adapt, adjust, fit, modify, tailor.

shapeless *adjective* amorphous, formless, nebulous, unstructured, vague.

share *noun* allocation, allotment, allowance, bit, cut (*informal*), division, fraction, helping, part, portion, quota, ration, whack (*slang*).

share *verb* allocate, allot, apportion, deal out, distribute, divide.

sharp *adjective* 1 cutting, keen, pointed. 2 alert, astute, bright, clever, intelligent, knowing, perceptive, quick, shrewd, smart. 3 (*a sharp slope*) abrupt, precipitous, sheer, steep, vertical; (*a sharp bend*) acute, hairpin, sudden. 4 acute, excruciating, intense, severe, shooting, stabbing. **5** clear, distinct, well-defined. **6** high-pitched, penetrating, piercing, shrill, strident. **7** acid, acrid, bitter, piquant, pungent, sour, strong, tangy, tart, vinegary. **8** acrimonious, angry, bitter, caustic, cutting, harsh, stinging, unkind.

sharp adverb exactly, on the dot, on the knocker (*Australian informal*), precisely, promptly, punctually.

sharpen verb grind, hone, strop, whet.

shatter verb **1** break, burst, crack, explode, smash, splinter. **2** dash, destroy. **3** crush, devastate, disturb, upset.

shave verb **1** cut off, snip off, trim. **2** pare, plane, scrape, slice, trim, whittle.

shave noun □ **close shave** close call (*informal*), narrow escape.

shawl noun scarf, stole.

sheaf noun bunch, bundle.

shear verb clip, crop, cut, strip, trim.

shears plural noun clippers, cutters, scissors.

sheath noun case, cover, scabbard, sleeve.

shed noun barn, garage, hut, lean-to, outbuilding, outhouse, shelter, workshop.

shed verb cast, cast off, discard, drop, lose, moult, slough, spill, throw off.

sheen noun brightness, gleam, gloss, lustre, polish, shine.

sheep noun ewe (*female*), jumbuck (*Australian*), lamb, ram (*male*), wether (*male*).

sheepish adjective abashed, ashamed, bashful, coy, embarrassed, hangdog, self-conscious, shamefaced, shy, timid.

sheer adjective **1** absolute, complete, pure, total, utter. **2** abrupt, perpendicular, precipitous, sharp, steep, vertical. **3** diaphanous, fine, flimsy, gauzy, see-through, thin, transparent.

sheer verb slew, swerve, turn, veer.

sheet noun **1** (*of paper*) folio, leaf, page; (*of glass*) pane, panel, plate. **2** area, expanse, stretch. **3** coating, cover, covering, film, layer, overlay, veneer.

shelf noun ledge, mantelpiece, sill.

shell noun **1** carapace, case, cover, covering, exterior, hull, husk, outside, pod. **2** body, chassis, frame, framework, hull.

shell verb bomb, bombard, fire on.

shelter noun **1** bunker, haven, hut, refuge, sanctuary, shed. **2** asylum, cover, protection, refuge, safety, sanctuary.

shelter verb **1** conceal, cover, give refuge to, harbour, hide, protect, screen, shield. **2** take cover, take refuge.

shelve verb defer, postpone, put aside, put on the back burner (*informal*), put on hold, suspend.

shield noun **1** buckler, escutcheon, hielaman (*Australian*). **2** barrier, defence, guard, protection, refuge, safeguard, screen, shelter.

shield verb defend, guard, preserve, protect, safeguard, screen, shelter.

shift verb change, move, rearrange, relocate, switch, transfer.

shift noun alteration, change, move, relocation, switch, transfer, transposition, variation.

shifty adjective deceitful, dodgy (*informal*), evasive, shonky (*Australian informal*), slippery, sly, sneaky, underhand, untrustworthy, wily.

shilly-shally verb hesitate, hum and haw, vacillate, waver.

shimmer verb flicker, gleam, glimmer, glisten, sparkle, twinkle.

shindy noun brawl, din, disturbance, fight, fracas, row, rumpus, uproar.

shine verb **1** beam, blaze, dazzle, flash, flicker, gleam, glimmer, glint, glisten, glitter, glow, radiate, reflect, scintillate, shimmer, sparkle, twinkle. **2** do well, excel, stand out. **3** buff, burnish, clean, polish.

shine noun brightness, gleam, glint, gloss, glow, lustre, polish, radiance, sheen, shimmer, sparkle.

shiny adjective bright, burnished, gleaming, glistening, glossy, lustrous, polished, satin, shimmering.

ship noun vessel; (*various ships*) aircraft carrier, battleship, brig, clipper, container ship, corvette, cruiser, destroyer, flagship, freighter, frigate, galleon, galley, gunboat, icebreaker, liner, man-of-war, merchant ship, minesweeper, sailing ship, steamship, submarine, tanker, warship, windjammer; see also *BOAT*.

ship verb consign, convey, dispatch, export, freight, send, transport.

shipment noun cargo, consignment, load.

shirk verb avoid, dodge, duck, evade, get out of, shun, shy away from. □ **shirker** noun bludger (*Australian informal*), idler, layabout, loafer, malingerer, skiver (*informal*), slacker.

shirty adjective angry, annoyed, mad, rude, stroppy (*informal*).

shiver verb quake, quaver, quiver, shake, shudder, tremble.

shoal noun school.

shock noun **1** blow, bolt from the blue, bombshell, surprise. **2** trauma. **3** impact, jolt, quake, shake, tremor.

shock verb **1** amaze, astonish, astound, dumbfound, stagger, stun, surprise, take aback, traumatise, upset. **2** appal, disgust, horrify, offend, outrage, scandalise. □ **shocking** adjective abominable, appalling, atrocious, disgusting, disturbing, dreadful, foul, hideous, horrible, horrific, horrifying, monstrous, outrageous, scandalous, terrible.

shoddy adjective bad, careless, gimcrack, inferior, poor, second-rate, slipshod, sloppy, substandard.

shoe noun (*kinds of shoe*) boot, brogue, clog, court shoe, Loafer (*trade mark*), moccasin, pump, sandal, sandshoe, slipper, sneaker, thong, trainer. □ **shoemaker** noun bootmaker, cobbler, shoe repairer.

shonky adjective crooked, dishonest, dodgy (*informal*), shady (*informal*), underhand, unreliable, untrustworthy.

shoot verb **1** discharge, fire, launch, project, propel. **2** gun down, hit, kill, snipe at, wound. **3** bolt, charge, dash, fly, race, rush, speed, streak, tear. **4** bud, germinate, grow, sprout. **5** film, photograph. □ **shoot through** see LEAVE.

shoot noun branch, bud, offshoot, sprig, sprout, sucker, tendril.

shop noun boutique, department store, emporium, mart, megastore, retailer, salon, store, supermarket.

shore noun beach, coast, foreshore, seashore, seaside, strand (*poetical*).

shore verb brace, buttress, prop, support.

short adjective **1** brief, fleeting, momentary, passing, quick, short-lived. **2** diminutive, dwarf, little, miniature, petite, pygmy, small, squat, stubby, stumpy, stunted, tiny, undersized, wee. **3** deficient, insufficient, lacking, light on (*Australian informal*), limited, low, scanty, scarce, wanting. **4** brief, concise, laconic, pithy, succinct, terse, to the point. **5** abrupt, blunt, brusque, curt, gruff, impatient, sharp, snappy, terse.

short *adverb* abruptly, suddenly, unexpectedly.

shortage *noun* dearth, deficiency, deficit, famine, insufficiency, lack, paucity, scarcity, shortfall, want.

shortcoming *noun* defect, deficiency, failing, fault, flaw, foible, imperfection, limitation, vice, weakness.

shorten *verb* abbreviate, abridge, compress, condense, curtail, cut down, diminish, prune, reduce, truncate.

shortly *adverb* **1** before long, directly, presently, soon. **2** abruptly, brusquely, curtly, gruffly, impatiently, sharply, tersely.

short-sighted *adjective* myopic, near-sighted.

short-tempered *adjective* cross, grumpy, hot-tempered, impatient, irascible, irritable, quick-tempered, snappy, testy, tetchy.

shot *noun* **1** bang, blast, discharge, explosion, report. **2** bullet, pellet, slug. **3** archer, marksman, sharpshooter, shooter, sniper. **4** photo, photograph, picture, snapshot. **5** attempt, chance, go, try. **6** immunisation, injection, jab (*informal*), vaccination.

shoulder *verb* **1** elbow, jostle, push, shove. **2** assume, bear, carry, take on, take upon yourself.

shout *noun* bellow, cry, outcry, roar, scream, screech, shriek, yell.

shout *verb* **1** bawl, bellow, call, cry out, roar, scream, screech, shriek, thunder, yell. **2** pay for, stand, treat.

shove *verb* elbow, jostle, push, shoulder, thrust.

shovel *verb* dig, excavate, scoop, shift.

show *verb* **1** display, exhibit, present. **2** disclose, express, indicate, manifest, reveal. **3** demonstrate, describe, explain, illustrate, instruct, point out, teach. **4** conduct, direct, escort, guide, lead, usher. **5** be visible, stick out. □ **show off 1** display, flaunt, parade. **2** boast, brag, skite (*Australian informal*), swagger, swank (*informal*). □ **show-off** *noun* boaster, braggart, exhibitionist, lair

(*Australian informal*), skite (*Australian informal*). □ **show up 1** expose, highlight, reveal. **2** appear, arrive, be present, come, front up (*informal*), materialise, turn up.

show *noun* **1** display, exhibition, expo (*informal*), exposition, fair, pageant, presentation. **2** entertainment, gig (*informal*), performance, play, production. **3** business, enterprise, operation, undertaking.

showdown *noun* clash, confrontation, crisis, moment of truth.

shower *noun* drizzle, rain, sprinkle.

shower *verb* deluge, flood, inundate, overwhelm, spatter, spray, sprinkle.

showy *adjective* bright, brilliant, conspicuous, flamboyant, flashy, garish, gaudy, lairy (*Australian informal*), ostentatious, striking.

shred *noun* **1** bit, fragment, piece, scrap, strip; (*shreds*) rags, tatters. **2** bit, iota, jot, particle, scrap, skerrick (*Australian informal*), trace.

shred *verb* cut up, destroy, rip up, tear up.

shrew *noun* battleaxe (*informal*), nag, scold (*old use*), termagant, virago.

shrewd *adjective* astute, canny, clever, crafty, cunning, far-sighted, ingenious, intelligent, knowing, perceptive, sagacious, savvy (*informal*), sharp, sly, smart, wily, wise.

shriek *noun* cry, howl, scream, screech, squeal, yell.

shriek *verb* cry (out), howl, scream, screech, squeal, yell.

shrill *adjective* high-pitched, penetrating, piercing, screeching, sharp.

shrine *noun* altar, cenotaph, chapel, church, memorial, monument, mosque, sanctuary, temple.

shrink *verb* **1** contract, decline, diminish, dwindle, reduce. **2** back away, draw back, flinch, recoil, retire, retreat, shy away, withdraw.

shrivel *verb* dehydrate, dry up, shrink, wilt, wither, wrinkle.

shroud *noun* winding-sheet.

shroud *verb* **1** cover, swathe, wrap. **2** cloak, clothe, conceal, cover, envelop, hide, veil.

shrub *noun* bush, plant.

shrug *verb* □ **shrug off** dismiss, disregard, ignore, laugh off, make light of, play down.

shudder *verb* **1** quake, quaver, quiver, shake, shiver, tremble. **2** judder, rock, shake, vibrate. □ **shudder** *noun* convulsion, quake, quiver, shake, shiver, spasm, tremble, tremor, vibration.

shuffle verb **1** drag your feet, hobble, scrape your feet, scuff your feet, shamble. **2** jumble, mix, rearrange, reorganise, scramble, shift.

shun verb avoid, dodge, evade, keep away from, recoil from, shy away from, steer clear of.

shunt verb divert, sidetrack.

shut verb bolt, close, fasten, latch, lock, secure. □ **shut out** bar, exclude, keep out, leave out, lock out. □ **shut up 1** confine, imprison, incarcerate, intern, jail, lock up, put away (informal). **2** be quiet, be silent, stop talking.

shy adjective bashful, coy, diffident, hesitant, nervous, reserved, reticent, retiring, self-conscious, timid, timorous.

shy verb buck, jump, recoil, start. □ **shy away from** avoid, back away from, flinch from, recoil from, shrink from, shun.

shy verb cast, fling, hurl, pitch, throw, toss.

sick adjective **1** ailing, bedridden, crook (Australian informal), diseased, ill, indisposed, infirm, poorly, sickly, unwell. **2** bilious, nauseous, queasy. **3** angry, annoyed, disgusted, dis-

tressed, mad, sickened, upset □ **be sick** barf (slang), chuck (informal), chunder (Australian slang), heave, puke (informal), retch, sick up (informal), spew, throw up, vomit. □ **sick of** bored with, fed up with (informal), jack of (Australian slang), tired of, weary of.

sicken verb appal, disgust, distress, horrify, nauseate, offend, repel, revolt, shock, upset.

sickly adjective **1** ailing, delicate, frail, ill, sick, unhealthy, unwell, weak (looking sickly) ashen, green, grey, pale, pallid, peaky, wan, yellow. **2** cloying, nauseating, over-sweet, saccharine, sugary, syrupy. **3** faint, feeble, weak.

sickness noun **1** ill health, illness, infirmity. **2** affliction, ailment, bug (informal), complaint, disease, disorder, illness, malady. **3** biliousness, nausea, queasiness, vomiting.

side noun **1** face, facet, flank, slope, surface. **2** boundary, brink, edge, fringe, limit, margin, perimeter, periphery, rim, verge. **3** aspect, facet, perspective, position, slant, standpoint, view, viewpoint. camp, faction, party, squad, team.

side adjective lateral.

side verb (side with) ally with, back, defend, go along with, stand up for, stick up for (informal), support.

sideboard noun buffet, cabinet, cupboard, dresser.

sidestep verb avoid, bypass, circumvent, dodge, duck, evade, skirt round.

sideways adjective indirect, oblique, sidelong.

sidle verb creep, cringe, edge, slink.

siege noun blockade. □ **lay siege to** beleaguer, besiege, blockade, encircle, surround.

siesta noun catnap, forty winks, kip, nap, rest, sleep, snooze.

sieve noun colander, filter, riddle, screen, sifter, strainer.

sieve verb filter, riddle, screen, sift, strain.

sift verb 1 filter, riddle, screen, sieve, strain. 2 analyse, examine, investigate, review, sort through, study.

sight noun 1 eyesight, vision. 2 display, scene, spectacle. □ **in sight 1** in view, visible. 2 approaching, at hand, close, imminent, near.

sight verb behold (old use), catch sight of, espy, glimpse, make out, observe, see, spot, spy.

sightless adjective blind, visually impaired.

sightseer noun holidaymaker, tourist, traveller, visitor.

sign noun 1 clue, evidence, forewarning, hint, indication, manifestation, omen, pointer, portent, proof, symptom, token, trace, warning. 2 mark, symbol; see also *BADGE*. 3 notice, placard, plaque, poster, signboard, signpost. 4 cue, gesture, motion, nod, signal, wave.

sign verb 1 beckon, gesture, indicate, motion, nod, signal, wave. 2 autograph, countersign, endorse, undersign. □ **sign up** enlist, enrol, join up, register, sign on, volunteer.

signal noun cue, gesture, indication, nod, semaphore, sign, tip-off, warning, wave.

signal verb beckon, gesture, indicate, motion, nod, sign, wave.

significant adjective 1 eloquent, expressive, knowing, meaningful, pregnant, telling. 2 considerable, great, important, momentous, noteworthy, outstanding, remarkable. □ **significance** noun 1 implication, import, meaning, point, purport, sense, signification. 2 consequence, importance, moment.

signify *verb* **1** be a sign of, betoken, denote, imply, indicate, mean, represent, stand for, symbolise. **2** communicate, convey, demonstrate, express, indicate, intimate, make known, show.

silence *noun* calm, hush, peace, quietness, stillness, tranquillity.

silence *verb* gag, hush, muzzle, quieten.

silent *adjective* **1** calm, hushed, peaceful, quiet, soundless, still, tranquil. **2** dumb, mum (*informal*), mute, quiet, reserved, reticent, speechless, taciturn, tight-lipped, tongue-tied, uncommunicative, unforthcoming, voiceless.

silhouette *noun* contour, form, outline, profile, shadow, shape.

silky *adjective* fine, satiny, sleek, smooth, soft.

sill *noun* ledge.

silly *adjective* absurd, asinine, barmy (*slang*), childish, crazy, daft (*informal*), dopey (*informal*), dotty (*informal*), fatuous, foolhardy, foolish, goofy (*slang*), hare-brained, idiotic, illogical, immature, inane, insane, ludicrous, mad, mindless, naïve, pointless, potty (*informal*), reckless, ridiculous, scatty (*informal*), senseless, stupid, unwise.

silt *verb* (*silt up*) become obstructed, block up, clog up.

similar *adjective* akin, alike, analogous, comparable, equivalent, kindred, like, parallel □ **similarity** *noun* affinity, closeness, correspondence likeness, resemblance, similitude.

simmer *verb* boil, bubble, stew.

simple *adjective* **1** basic, easy elementary, rudimentary straightforward. **2** austere modest, natural, ordinary plain, unadorned, uncomplicated, unpretentious, unsophisticated. **3** backward childish, dumb (*informal*) feeble-minded, naïve, obtuse simple-minded, slow, stupid.

simpleton *noun* ass (*informal*), blockhead, bonehead, clo (*informal*), cretin, dil (*Australian informal*), dimwit (*informal*), dodo (*informal*), dolt, dope (*informal*), drip (*informal*), drongo (*Australian informal*), dunce, fool, half-wit, idiot, imbecile, moron (*informal*), mug (*informal*), muggins (*informal*), nincompoop, ninny, nitwit (*informal*), nong (*Australian informal*), sap (*informal*), twit (*slang*).

simulate *verb* act, fake, feign, imitate, pretend, sham.

simultaneous adjective coexistent, coincident, concurrent, contemporaneous, parallel.

sin noun 1 corruption, crime, evil, immorality, iniquity, sinfulness, ungodliness, unrighteousness, vice, wickedness, wrongdoing. 2 crime, error, fault, iniquity, misdeed, misdemeanour, offence, peccadillo, transgression, trespass (old use), vice, wrong, wrongdoing.

sin verb do wrong, err, go astray, offend, transgress, trespass (old use). □ **sinner** noun evildoer, malefactor, miscreant, offender, transgressor, trespasser (old use), wrongdoer.

sincere adjective artless, authentic, dinkum (Australian informal), dinky-di (Australian informal), earnest, frank, genuine, guileless, heartfelt, honest, natural, open, real, true.

sinful adjective bad, blasphemous, corrupt, depraved, evil, immoral, impious, iniquitous, sacrilegious, ungodly, unrighteous, wicked, wrong.

sing verb carol, chant, croon, serenade, trill, yodel; (of birds) chirp, chirrup, tweet, twitter, warble. □ **singer** noun chorister, crooner, diva, minstrel, prima donna, songster, troubadour, vocalist.

singe verb burn, scorch, sear.

single adjective 1 isolated, lone, odd, one, sole, solitary, unique. 2 individual, separate. 3 unattached, unmarried.

single verb □ **single out** choose, earmark, pick out, select.

single-handed adjective alone, independent, solo, unaided, unassisted.

single-minded adjective determined, dogged, obsessive, purposeful, resolute, unswerving, unwavering.

singular adjective exceptional, extraordinary, outstanding, rare, remarkable, uncommon, unique, unusual; see also STRANGE.

sinister adjective 1 alarming, disturbing, forbidding, frightening, menacing, ominous, threatening. 2 bad, criminal, diabolical, evil, malevolent, malignant, vile, villainous, wicked.

sink verb 1 founder, go down, scupper, scuttle, submerge. 2 descend, dip, droop, drop, fall, go down, slump, subside. 3 bore, dig, drill, excavate. □ **sink in** be absorbed, go in, penetrate, register.

sink noun basin, washbasin.

sip verb drink, sup, taste. □ **sip** noun drink, drop, mouthful, sup, swallow, swig (informal), taste.

siren noun **1** alarm, signal, tocsin, warning. **2** enchantress, seductress, temptress.

sissy noun coward, cry-baby, sook (Australian informal), wimp (informal), wuss (slang).

sit verb **1** be seated, perch yourself, rest, settle, squat. **2** lie, remain, stand, stay. **3** assemble, be in session, convene, meet.

site noun location, place, position, setting, spot, venue.

site verb locate, place, position, situate.

sitting room drawing room, living room, lounge, parlour (old use).

situation noun **1** locality, location, place, position, setting, site, spot. **2** circumstances, plight, position, predicament, state of affairs. **3** employment, job, position, post.

size noun amount, area, bulk, capacity, dimensions, extent, magnitude, measurements, proportions, scale, scope.

size verb □ **size up** appraise, assess, gauge, judge, weigh up (informal).

sizeable adjective ample, big, considerable, generous, handsome, hefty, large, substantial.

sizzle verb hiss, sputter.

skate verb glide, skid, skim, slide.

skeleton noun **1** bones, frame. **2** framework, shell, structure.

skerrick noun bit, crumb, fragment, jot, particle, scrap, shred, trace.

sketch noun **1** design, diagram, drawing, picture. **2** abstract, draft, outline, plan, précis, summary, synopsis. **3** play, skit.

sketchy adjective cursory, incomplete, patchy, rough, superficial, vague.

skew adjective askew, oblique, slanting.

skid verb aquaplane, glide, slide, slip.

skilful adjective able, accomplished, adept, adroit, brilliant, capable, clever, competent, consummate, deft, dexterous, expert, gifted, ingenious, masterly, professional, proficient, skilled, talented.

skill noun ability, adroitness, aptitude, art, capability, cleverness, competence, dexterity, expertise, ingenuity, knack, know-how, mastery, proficiency, prowess, talent.

skim *verb* **1** remove, scrape. **2** fly, glide, sail, sweep. **3** flick, flip, glance, leaf, scan, thumb.

skimp *verb* economise, save, scrimp, stint.

skimpy *adjective* brief, inadequate, insufficient, meagre, scanty, small, tiny.

skin *noun* **1** dermis, epidermis; (*an animal's skin*) coat, fur, hide, pelt. **2** casing, coating, covering, exterior, husk, jacket (*of a potato*) membrane, peel, rind, shell. **3** film, membrane.

skin *verb* abrade, bark, graze, scrape, scratch.

skinflint *noun* cheapskate (*informal*), miser, niggard, Scrooge.

skinny *adjective* bony, emaciated, gaunt, lanky, lean, scraggy, scrawny, slender, thin.

skip *verb* **1** bob, bound, caper, cavort, dance, frisk, gambol, hop, leap, prance, romp, run, trip. **2** flit, jump, pass. **3** leave out, miss, neglect, omit, overlook, pass over. **4** absent yourself from, cut (*informal*), miss, play truant from, wag (*informal*).

skirmish *noun* altercation, argument, brush, clash, conflict, confrontation, fight, scrap (*informal*), scrimmage, scuffle, struggle, tussle.

skirt *verb* **1** border, bound, circle, edge, encircle, fringe, surround. **2** avoid, bypass, circumvent, dodge, evade, sidestep.

skit *noun* burlesque, parody, satire, send-up (*informal*), sketch, spoof (*informal*), take-off.

skite *verb* blow your own trumpet, boast, brag, congratulate yourself, crow, show off, vaunt.

skite *noun* boaster, braggart, show-off.

skittish *adjective* excitable, fidgety, frisky, jumpy, lively, nervous, playful, restive, restless.

skulk *verb* creep, hide, loiter, lurk, prowl.

sky *noun* air, atmosphere, ether, firmament, heavens, stratosphere.

slab *noun* block, chunk, hunk, piece, slice, wedge.

slack *adjective* **1** floppy, limp, loose, relaxed. **2** inactive, quiet, slow, sluggish. **3** careless, casual, lackadaisical, lax, lazy, negligent, offhand, remiss, slapdash, slipshod, sloppy.

slack *verb* be lazy, ease off, idle, let up, take it easy.

slacken *verb* decrease, drop off, ease (off), lessen, let up, loosen, reduce, relax, release, slack, slow down.

slam verb **1** bang, close, shut. **2** bump, crash, knock, ram, run, smash.

slander noun calumny, defamation, denigration, libel, misrepresentation, vilification. □ **slanderous** adjective defamatory, denigratory, libellous, malicious, scurrilous, untrue.

slander verb defame, denigrate, libel, malign, misrepresent, slur, smear, vilify.

slang noun argot, cant, jargon, lingo (informal).

slant verb **1** incline, lean, list, slope, tilt. **2** angle, bias, distort. □ **slant** noun **1** angle, incline, list, slope, tilt. **2** angle, attitude, bias, perspective, prejudice, view.

slap verb cuff, hit, smack, spank, strike, whack. □ **slap** noun blow, cuff, hit, smack, whack.

slapdash adjective careless, haphazard, hasty, perfunctory, slipshod, sloppy.

slash verb **1** cut, gash, hack, rip, slice, slit, tear. **2** cut, drop, lower, reduce.

slash noun **1** cut, gash, incision, laceration, rip, slit. **2** line, oblique, stroke.

slaughter verb **1** butcher, destroy, kill. **2** annihilate,

butcher, execute, exterminate, kill, massacre, murder, slay. □ **slaughter** noun bloodbath, bloodshed, butchery, carnage, killing, massacre, murder, pogrom, slaying.

slave noun serf, servant, vassal. □ **slavery** noun bondage, captivity, enslavement, serfdom, servitude, thraldom, thrall.

slave verb drudge, grind away, labour, slog, sweat, toil, work hard.

slave-driver noun despot, oppressor, taskmaster, tyrant.

slavish adjective **1** obsequious, servile, submissive, subservient. **2** unimaginative, unoriginal.

slay verb assassinate, execute, kill, massacre, murder, put to death, slaughter.

sledge noun bob-sled, bobsleigh, luge, sled, sleigh, toboggan.

sleek adjective glossy, lustrous, shiny, silky, smooth.

sleep noun catnap, dormancy, doze, forty winks, hibernation, kip (slang), nap, repose, rest, shut-eye (informal), siesta, slumber, snooze. □ **sleepy** adjective dopey (informal), dormant, drowsy, inactive, lethargic, peaceful, quiet.

somnolent, tired, torpid, weary.

sleep verb catnap, doze, drop off, kip (*slang*), nap, nod off, rest, slumber, snooze.

sleepless adjective disturbed, insomniac, restless, wakeful.

sleepwalker noun noctambulist, somnambulist.

sleeve noun case, casing, cover, sheath.

sleight noun □ **sleight of hand** conjuring, dexterity, legerdemain, trickery.

slender adjective 1 lean, slight, slim, svelte, thin. 2 faint, feeble, remote, slight, slim, small, weak.

sleuth noun detective, investigator, private eye (*informal*).

slice noun 1 chunk, piece, portion, segment, sliver, wedge. 2 cut, part, portion, proportion, share.

slice verb 1 carve, cut, divide. 2 pare, peel, shave, trim, whittle.

slick adjective clever, cunning, glib, sly, smarmy (*informal*), smooth.

slide verb coast, glide, glissade, skate, skid, slip, slither.

slide noun chute, ramp, slippery dip (*Australian*), slope.

slight adjective imperceptible, infinitesimal, insignificant, little, minor, minute, negligible, small, subtle, superficial, tiny, trivial.

slight verb affront, ignore, insult, rebuff, scorn, snub.

slim adjective 1 lean, slender, slight, svelte, thin. 2 faint, feeble, remote, slender, slight, small.

slim verb diet, lose weight, reduce.

slime noun goo (*informal*), gunge (*informal*), gunk (*informal*), muck, mud, ooze, sludge. □ **slimy** adjective gooey (*informal*), gungy (*informal*), mucky, muddy, oozy, slippery, sludgy, viscous; (*a slimy person*) crawling, obsequious, oily, slick, smarmy (*informal*), smooth, unctuous.

sling noun 1 bandage, belt, strap, support. 2 catapult, shanghai (*Australian*), slingshot.

sling verb 1 dangle, hang, suspend, swing. 2 cast, chuck (*informal*), fling, hurl, throw, toss. □ **sling off at** deride, disparage, gibe at, make fun of, mock, poke borak at (*Australian informal*), poke fun at, ridicule.

slink verb creep, edge, skulk, slip, sneak, steal.

slip *verb* **1** fall, glide, skid, slide, slither. **2** creep, skulk, slink, sneak, steal. **3** detach, release. ☐ **slip up** blunder, err, goof (*slang*), make a mistake.

slip *noun* **1** fall, glide, skid, slide. **2** blue (*Australian informal*), blunder, booboo (*slang*), error, lapse, mistake, slip-up (*informal*). **3** piece, scrap, sheet, strip. **4** case, cover, pillowcase, pillowslip. ☐ **give someone the slip** avoid, dodge, elude, escape, evade, lose.

slippery *adjective* greasy, oily, slick, slithery, smooth, wet.

slipshod *adjective* careless, lax, messy, shoddy, slapdash, sloppy, slovenly, unmethodical.

slit *noun* crack, cut, fissure, gash, hole, incision, opening, rip, slash, slot, split, tear.

slit *verb* cut, gash, rip, slash, split, tear.

slither *verb* slide, slink, slip.

sliver *noun* flake, fragment, piece, shaving, slice, strip.

slobber *verb* dribble, drool, salivate, slaver.

slog *verb* **1** hit, strike, thump, whack. **2** grind, labour, plod, plough, toil, work. **3** plod, tramp, trek, trudge.

slogan *noun* catchphrase, catch-word, jingle, motto.

slop *verb* slosh (*informal*), spill, splash, splatter. ☐ **slops** *plural noun* dregs, refuse, swill, waste.

slope *verb* ascend, bank, descend, drop, incline, rise, slant, tilt, tip.

slope *noun* angle, ascent, bank, descent, escarpment, grade, gradient, hill, hillside, inclination, incline, pitch, rake, ramp, rise, scarp, slant, tilt.

sloppy *adjective* **1** gooey (*informal*), liquid, runny, watery. **2** careless, lax, messy, shoddy, slapdash, slipshod, slovenly, unmethodical, untidy. **3** mushy, romantic, sentimental, soppy (*informal*).

slot *noun* groove, hole, opening, slit.

slothful *adjective* idle, inactive, indolent, lazy, slack, sluggish.

slouch *verb* droop, hunch, loll, sag, slump, stoop.

slovenly *adjective* careless, dirty, disreputable, messy, scruffy, slatternly, unkempt, untidy; see also *SLOPPY*.

slow *adjective* **1** (*a slow pace*) dawdling, deliberate, leisurely, measured, plodding, sluggish, steady, unhurried; (*a slow process*) drawn-out, endless, gradual, interminable, long, painstaking, prolonged, protracted, time-consuming; (

slow response) delayed, dilatory, late, tardy. **2** dense, dim, dull, dumb (*informal*), obtuse, stupid, thick (*informal*). □ **slowly** *adverb* at a snail's pace, gradually, leisurely, sluggishly, steadily, unhurriedly.

slow *verb* brake, decelerate, delay, hinder, hold back, impede, reduce speed, retard.

slowcoach *noun* dawdler, laggard, sluggard, straggler.

sludge *noun* goo (*informal*), mire, muck, mud, silt, slime, slush.

sluggish *adjective* inactive, indolent, inert, lazy, lethargic, listless, phlegmatic, slack, slothful, slow, torpid.

slumber *noun* repose, rest, sleep. □ **slumber** *verb* doze, nap, rest, sleep, snooze.

slump *verb* collapse, crash, decline, drop, fall, flop, nosedive, plummet, plunge, sink, tumble.

slump *noun* collapse, crash, decline, depression, downturn, drop, fall, recession, setback, tumble.

slur *verb* mumble, mutter.

slur *noun* aspersion, blot, insult, libel, slander, slight, smear, stain, stigma.

sly *adjective* **1** artful, crafty, cunning, devious, foxy, furtive, secretive, shifty, shrewd, sneaky, underhand, wily. **2** arch, knowing, mischievous, playful, roguish.

smack *noun* blow, hit, rap, slap, spanking, whack.

smack *verb* belt (*slang*), hit, rap, slap, spank, strike, wallop (*slang*), whack.

smack *adverb* bang, directly, slap, straight.

smack *verb* savour, suggest.

small *adjective* **1** baby, compact, diminutive, dwarf, infinitesimal, little, meagre, measly (*informal*), microscopic, miniature, minuscule, minute, petite, pocket-sized, poky, puny, scant, scanty, short, slender, slight, stunted, teeny, teeny (*informal*), tiny, undersized, wee, weeny (*informal*). **2** insignificant, minimal, negligible, paltry, petty, trifling, trivial, unimportant.

small-minded *adjective* bigoted, hidebound, intolerant, narrow-minded, petty, prejudiced, selfish, ungenerous.

smart *adjective* **1** chic, dapper, dolled up (*informal*), elegant, fashionable, natty (*informal*), neat, posh (*informal*), snappy (*informal*), snazzy (*informal*), spruce, stylish, swanky (*informal*), swish (*informal*), trim. **2** able, astute, brainy, bright, capable, clever, ingenious, intelligent, prudent, sensible, sharp, shrewd, wise. **3** brisk, cracking (*slang*), energetic, fast, jaunty, quick, swift, vigorous.

smart *verb* hurt, sting, throb.

smash *verb* **1** break, crash, shatter, shiver, splinter. **2** bash, batter, break, hammer, hit, knock, pound, strike. **3** (*smash into*) bang into, bump into, collide with, crash into, hit, knock into, ram into, run into, slam into.

smash *noun* accident, bingle (*Australian informal*), collision, crash, pile-up (*informal*), prang (*slang*). □ **smash hit** hit, success, triumph, winner.

smear *verb* **1** coat, cover, daub, plaster, rub, spread. **2** blacken, defame, denigrate, malign, slander, slur, smirch, sully, vilify. □ **smear** *noun* blotch, mark, smudge, splotch, stain, streak.

smell *verb* **1** nose, scent, sniff. **2** pong (*informal*), reek, stink.

smell *noun* **1** aroma, bouquet, fragrance, odour, perfume, redolence, scent, whiff. **2** pong (*informal*), reek, stench, stink. □ **smelly** *adjective* foul-smelling, high, malodorous, noisome (*literary*), on the nose (*Australian informal*), pongy

(*informal*), putrid, rancid rank, reeking, stinking.

smile *noun* grin, simper smirk.

smile *verb* beam, grin, simper smirk.

smirk *noun & verb* grin, simper smile, sneer.

smite *verb* see STRIKE. □ **b** **smitten with** be besotted with be bowled over by, be captivated by, be enchanted by be enthralled by, be infatuate with.

smithereens *plural noun* bits fragments, pieces.

smoke *noun* exhaust, fumes smog.

smoke *verb* fume, smoulder.

smoko *noun* coffee break, res spell (*Australian*), tea break.

smooth *adjective* **1** (*a smoot surface*) even, flat, flush, leve unbroken; (*smooth hair* glossy, shiny, silky, sleek, sof velvety; (*a smooth batter* creamy, flowing, runny (*smooth seas*) calm, even, fla peaceful, still, unruffled **2** flowing, orderly, steady, wel regulated. **3** dulcet, mellov pleasant, soothing, swee **4** facile, glib, persuasive plausible, slick, smarm (*informal*), suave, unctuous □ **smoothly** *adverb* easil straightforwardly, well, without a hitch.

smooth *verb* even, flatten, iron, level, plane, press, sand, sandpaper.

smother *verb* **1** asphyxiate, choke, stifle, suffocate. **2** extinguish, put out, quench, snuff. **3** cover. **4** conceal, hide, hold back, repress, restrain, stifle, suppress.

smoulder *verb* burn, smoke.

smudge *noun* blot, blotch, mark, smear, splash, splotch, spot, stain, streak.

smudge *verb* blot, smear, stain, streak.

smug *adjective* complacent, conceited, self-righteous, self-satisfied, supercilious, superior.

smuggling *noun* bootlegging, contraband, drug running, gunrunning.

snack *noun* **1** playlunch, recess, refreshments. **2** bludge (*Australian informal*), breeze (*informal*), cinch (*informal*), doddle (*informal*), piece of cake (*informal*), pushover (*informal*).

snag *noun* **1** catch, difficulty, hitch, impediment, obstacle, obstruction, problem, stumbling block. **2** hole, ladder, rip, run, tear.

snake *noun* serpent.

snaky *adjective* angry, annoyed, bad-tempered, crabby, irritable, shirty (*informal*).

snap *verb* **1** break, crack, fracture, give way, split. **2** bite, nip. **3** bark, growl, snarl. **4** (*snap up*) accept, grab, nab (*informal*), seize, snatch, take. **5** photograph, shoot.

snap *noun* **1** click, crack, crackle, fracture, pop. **2** photo, photograph, picture, snapshot.

snap *adjective* hasty, precipitate, quick, sudden.

snappy *adjective* **1** crabby, cross, crotchety, grumpy, irascible, irritable, short-tempered, testy, tetchy. **2** brisk, energetic, fast, lively, vigorous, zippy.

snare *noun* gin, net, noose, trap.

snare *verb* capture, catch, ensnare, entrap, trap.

snarl *verb* bare your teeth, growl.

snarl *verb* entangle, entwine, knot, tangle, twist. □ **snarl** *noun* blockage, hold-up, jam, obstruction, tangle.

snatch *verb* grab, nab (*informal*), pluck, seize, snitch (*slang*), steal, swipe (*informal*), take.

sneak *verb* **1** creep, slink, slip, steal, tiptoe. **2** smuggle, snitch (*informal*), steal. **3** betray, dob

(*Australian informal*), grass (*slang*), inform, rat (*informal*), report, shop (*slang*), split (*slang*), tell, tell tales.

sneak noun dobber (*Australian informal*), grass (*slang*), informer, pimp (*Australian slang*), tale-bearer, tell-tale. □ **sneaky** adjective crafty, cunning, deceitful, devious, furtive, secretive, shifty, slippery, sly, stealthy, treacherous, underhand, wily.

sneer verb (*sneer at*) deride, disdain, gibe at, jeer at, laugh at, mock, ridicule, scoff at, scorn, snigger at.

sniff verb **1** sniffle, snivel, snuffle. **2** nose, smell.

sniffle verb & noun sniff, snivel, snuffle.

snigger verb & noun chuckle, giggle, simper, snicker, titter.

snip verb clip, crop, cut, lop, prune, trim.

snipe verb fire, shoot.

snippet noun bit, extract, fragment, part, snatch.

snivel verb blubber, cry, sob, weep, whimper, whine; see also *SNIFFLE*.

snobbish adjective condescending, disdainful, haughty, patronising, pompous, pretentious, snooty (*informal*), stuck-up (*informal*), super-

cilious, superior, toffee-nosed (*informal*).

snoop verb nose about, poke your nose in, pry, spy, stickybeak (*Australian informal*).

snooze noun catnap, doze, forty winks, kip (*slang*), nap, rest, siesta, sleep. □ **snooze** verb catnap, doze, kip (*slang*), nap, rest, sleep.

snub verb cold-shoulder, give someone the brush-off, humiliate, ignore, insult, rebuff, reject, scorn.

snuffle verb & noun sniff, sniffle, snivel.

snug adjective comfortable, comfy (*informal*), cosy, secure, warm.

snuggle verb cuddle, curl up, huddle, nestle.

soak verb drench, immerse, saturate, souse, steep, submerge, wet. □ **soak through** penetrate, permeate, seep through. □ **soak up** absorb, sop up, take up.

soar verb **1** ascend, fly, rise. **2** climb, escalate, increase, mount, rise, rocket.

sob verb bawl, blubber, cry, snivel, wail, weep.

sober adjective **1** abstemious, abstinent, clear-headed, lucid, on the wagon (*informal*), teetotal, temperate. **2** calm, earnest, grave, level-headed, restrained, sedate, self-controlled, sensible, serious, solemn, staid. **3** drab, dreary, dull, inconspicuous, sombre, subdued.

sociable *adjective* affable, communicative, companionable, convivial, extroverted, friendly, gregarious, outgoing, social.

social *adjective* **1** gregarious, interdependent. **2** community, public. **3** see SOCIABLE.

society *noun* **1** civilisation, community, culture, humanity, mankind, nation, people, the public. **2** association, body, club, group, guild, organisation, union. **3** companionship, company, fellowship, presence.

socket *noun* hole, hollow.

sodden *adjective* drenched, saturated, soaked, soggy, sopping, waterlogged, wet.

sofa *noun* couch, settee.

soft *adjective* **1** flabby, flaccid, flexible, floppy, limp, malleable, pliable, spongy, springy, squashy, supple. **2** fleecy, satiny, silky, sleek, smooth, velvety. **3** faint, gentle, hushed, inaudible, low, mellow, muted, quiet, subdued. **4** delicate, light, pale, pastel, restful, subdued. **5** easygoing,

indulgent, lax, lenient, merciful, permissive, tolerant; see also SOFT-HEARTED. **6** comfortable, cosy, cushy (*informal*), easy, undemanding.

soften *verb* buffer, cushion, dampen, deaden, lessen, lower, moderate, quieten, reduce, subdue, tone down.

soft-hearted *adjective* caring, compassionate, generous, gentle, kind, merciful, mild, soft, sympathetic, tender-hearted, understanding, warm-hearted.

soggy *adjective* drenched, moist, saturated, soaked, sodden, sopping, waterlogged, wet.

soil *noun* **1** dirt, earth, ground, loam. **2** country, ground, land, territory.

soil *verb* blacken, dirty, stain.

solace *noun* comfort, consolation, relief.

soldier *noun* commando, conscript, fighter, GI (*American*), marine, mercenary, NCO, private, regular, serviceman, servicewoman, trooper, warrior.

sole *adjective* exclusive, lone, only, single, solitary.

solemn *adjective* **1** earnest, glum, grave, sad, sedate, serious, sober, sombre, staid, unsmiling. **2** awesome,

ceremonial, ceremonious, dignified, formal, grand, important, impressive, stately.

solicit verb appeal for, ask for, beg for, request, seek.

solicitous adjective anxious, concerned, considerate, thoughtful, troubled, worried.

solid adjective **1** compact, dense, firm, hard, rigid, stable. **2** continuous, unbroken, uninterrupted. **3** durable, firm, robust, sound, stout, strong, sturdy, substantial. **4** unanimous, undivided, united.

solidarity noun agreement, harmony, like-mindedness, unanimity, unity.

solidify verb congeal, gel, harden, jell, set.

soliloquy noun monologue; see also *SPEECH*.

solitary adjective **1** alone, lone, single, sole, solo, unaccompanied. **2** isolated, one and only, single, sole. **3** deserted, desolate, empty, isolated, lonely, remote, secluded, unfrequented.

solo adjective & adverb alone, independent, individual, on your own, single-handed, unaccompanied.

solution noun **1** blend, mixture. **2** answer, explanation, key, remedy, resolution, result.

solve verb answer, crack, decipher, figure out, resolve, work out.

sombre adjective dark, dismal, drab, dreary, dull, funereal, gloomy, grave, melancholy, sad, serious, sober, solemn.

sometime adjective erstwhile, former, one-time.

sometimes adverb every so often, from time to time, now and then, occasionally, on and off.

somnolent adjective dopey (*informal*), drowsy, lethargic, sleepy, tired, torpid, weary.

song noun air, anthem, aria, ballad, canticle, carol, chant, chorus, ditty, hymn, jingle, lay (*old use*), lied, lullaby, madrigal, number, psalm, serenade, shanty.

sonorous adjective deep, loud, powerful, resonant, resounding, reverberant, rich.

sook noun baby, coward, crybaby, sissy, softie (*informal*), wimp (*informal*), wuss (*slang*).

sool verb egg on, goad, incite, urge.

soon adverb anon (*old use*), before long, by and by, presently, shortly.

soot noun dirt, grime. ▫ **sooty** adjective black, blackish, charcoal, dirty, grimy.

soothe *verb* alleviate, appease, assuage, calm, ease, mitigate, mollify, pacify, palliate, placate, reduce, relieve.

sophisticated *adjective* **1** cosmopolitan, cultivated, cultured, experienced, knowledgeable, refined, urbane, worldly, worldly-wise. **2** advanced, complex, complicated, elaborate, intricate.

sopping *adjective* drenched, dripping, saturated, soaked, sodden, wet.

sorcerer *noun* enchanter, magician, warlock, wizard. □ **sorceress** *noun* enchantress, magician, witch. □ **sorcery** *noun* black magic, enchantment, magic, witchcraft, wizardry.

sordid *adjective* **1** dirty, filthy, foul, putrid, seamy, seedy, sleazy, squalid. **2** base, dishonourable, mean, mercenary, shabby, vile.

sore *adjective* **1** aching, bruised, chafed, grazed, hurting, inflamed, injured, painful, sensitive, smarting, stinging, tender, uncomfortable. **2** aggrieved, angry, annoyed, distressed, irritated, peeved (*informal*), touchy, upset, vexed.

sore *noun* abrasion, abscess, blister, boil, burn, graze, inflammation, laceration, scratch, ulcer, wound.

sorrow *noun* affliction, anguish, distress, grief, hardship, heartache, misery, misfortune, regret, sadness, suffering, trial, tribulation, trouble, unhappiness, woe. □ **sorrowful** *adjective* blue, broken-hearted, dejected, depressed, desolate, despondent, disconsolate, discontented, dismal, distressed, doleful, downcast, gloomy, glum, heartbroken, heavy-hearted, lugubrious, melancholy, miserable, mournful, rueful, sad, sorry, unhappy, woebegone, wretched.

sorry *adjective* **1** apologetic, contrite, penitent, regretful, remorseful, repentant, rueful, sad, sorrowful. **2** compassionate, pitying, sympathetic, understanding. **3** bad, deplorable, dreadful, lamentable, miserable, pitiful, terrible, woeful, wretched.

sort *noun* brand, breed, category, class, form, genus, group, kind, make, species, style, type, variety.

sort *verb* arrange, categorise, class, classify, divide, grade, group, organise, separate. □ **sort out 1** disentangle, organise, straighten out, tidy. **2** pick out, segregate, select, separate, sift. **3** attend to, clear up, deal with, handle, resolve, solve.

soul noun **1** psyche, spirit. **2** creature, individual, person.

soulful adjective emotional, expressive, inspiring, moving, passionate, profound, stirring.

sound noun noise.

sound verb **1** enunciate, pronounce, speak, utter, voice. **2** appear, seem.

sound verb fathom, measure, plumb, probe, test. □ **sound out** see QUESTION.

sound adjective **1** intact, solid, strong, sturdy, undamaged, well-built. **2** fit, healthy, robust, well. **3** cogent, coherent, logical, rational, reasonable, solid, well-founded. **4** reliable, safe, secure, solid. **5** continuous, deep, thorough, unbroken, uninterrupted.

soup noun bisque, broth, chowder, consommé.

sour adjective **1** acid, acidic, astringent, mouth-puckering, sharp, tangy, tart, vinegary. **2** bad, curdled, fermented, off, rancid, stale. **3** bad-tempered, bitter, crabby, disagreeable, embittered, grouchy (informal), irritable, nasty, peevish, sullen, surly, testy, tetchy, unpleasant.

source noun **1** beginning, cause, derivation, head, origin, root, spring, start. **2** authority, informant.

souvenir noun keepsake, memento, reminder.

sovereign noun emperor, empress, king, monarch, potentate, queen, ruler, sultan.

sovereign adjective **1** absolute, paramount, supreme, unlimited. **2** autonomous, independent, self-governing, self-ruling.

sow verb broadcast, disseminate, plant, scatter, spread, strew.

space noun **1** the heavens, outer space, the universe. **2** area, capacity, room, volume. **3** blank, break, distance, gap, hiatus, hole, interval, opening. **4** duration, interval, period, span, stretch. □ **space traveller** astronaut, cosmonaut.

space verb arrange, place, position, separate, spread.

spacecraft noun space probe, spaceship, space shuttle.

spacious adjective big, capacious, commodious, enormous, extensive, large, roomy, sizeable, vast.

span noun **1** breadth, distance, extent, length, measure, reach, spread, stretch. **2** duration, interval, length, period, space, spell, stretch, term.

span *verb* bridge, cross, extend across, straddle, stretch across, traverse.

spank *verb* hit, slap, smack.

spar *verb* **1** box, fight. **2** argue, be at loggerheads, bicker, fight, quarrel, squabble, wrangle.

spare *verb* **1** afford, give, grant, part with. **2** protect from, relieve of, save, shield from.

spare *adjective* **1** additional, available, extra, free, in reserve, leftover, surplus, unoccupied. **2** lanky, lean, skinny, slim, thin, weedy, wiry.

sparing *adjective* careful, economical, frugal, miserly, niggardly, parsimonious, penny-pinching, stingy, thrifty.

spark *noun* flash, flicker, glimmer, glint, sparkle.

spark *verb* □ **spark off** provoke, set off, start, stimulate, touch off, trigger off.

sparkle *verb* flash, gleam, glint, glitter, scintillate, shimmer, shine, twinkle.

sparkling *adjective* aerated, bubbly, carbonated, effervescent, fizzy.

sparse *adjective* meagre, scanty, scarce, scattered, sporadic, thin.

spartan *adjective* ascetic, austere, frugal, hard, harsh, severe, simple, strict.

spasm *noun* **1** contraction, convulsion, cramp, fit, jerk, seizure, shudder, tic, twitch. **2** attack, bout, burst, fit, outburst, spell, spurt.

spasmodic *adjective* erratic, fitful, intermittent, irregular, occasional, sporadic.

spate *noun* deluge, flood, inundation, run, rush, torrent.

spatter *verb* shower, splash, splatter, spot, spray, sprinkle, stain.

spawn *verb* beget, bring about, engender, generate, give rise to, produce, yield.

spay *verb* de-sex, doctor, neuter, sterilise.

speak *verb* **1** articulate, communicate, declare, enunciate, express, pronounce, say, state, talk, utter, vocalise, voice. **2** chat, communicate, confer, converse, talk. **3** address, hold forth, lecture, preach, talk. □ **speak of** allude to, discuss, mention, refer to, talk about. □ **speak out** be outspoken, sound off (*informal*), speak up, speak your mind.

speaker *noun* lecturer, orator, preacher, spokesman, spokesperson, spokeswoman, talker.

spear *noun* harpoon, javelin, lance, pike, trident.

spear *verb* harpoon, impale, lance, pierce, stab.

special *adjective* **1** certain, characteristic, distinctive, individual, particular, specific, unique. **2** exceptional, extraordinary, outstanding, rare, remarkable, singular, uncommon, unusual.

specialist *noun* authority, connoisseur, consultant, expert, master, professional.

speciality *noun* forte, line, specialty, strength, strong point, talent, thing (*informal*).

species *noun* **1** breed, class, classification, strain. **2** see SORT.

specific *adjective* **1** definite, exact, explicit, express, precise, unambiguous. **2** individual, particular, special, unique.

specify *verb* detail, identify, itemise, list, mention, name, spell out, state, stipulate.

specimen *noun* example, instance, model, representative, sample.

specious *adjective* deceptive, misleading, plausible.

speck *noun* bit, fleck, grain, particle, skerrick (*Australian informal*), speckle, spot, trace.

speckled *adjective* brindled, dotted, flecked, freckled, mottled, spotted.

spectacle *noun* **1** display, scene, sight. **2** exhibition, exposition, extravaganza, pageant, show, spectacular. □ **spectacles** *plural noun* eyeglasses, glasses, specs (*informal*).

spectacular *adjective* amazing, breathtaking, dramatic, electrifying, exciting, impressive, magnificent, marvellous, sensational, splendid, stunning, thrilling.

spectator *noun* bystander, eyewitness, looker-on, observer, onlooker, viewer, witness, (*spectators*) audience, crowd.

spectre *noun* apparition, ghost, phantom, poltergeist, spirit, spook (*informal*), vision, wraith.

spectrum *noun* compass, gamut, range, span, spread.

speculate *verb* conjecture, guess, hypothesise, surmise, theorise, wonder. □ **speculative** *adjective* **1** conjectural, hypothetical, suppositional, theoretical. **2** dicey (*slang*), dodgy (*informal*), hazardous, risky, uncertain, unreliable.

speech *noun* **1** articulation, communication, diction, elocution, enunciation, language, pronunciation, speaking, talking, utterance. **2** address, discourse, harangue, homily, lecture, monologue, sermon, soliloquy, spiel (*slang*), talk, tirade.

speechless *adjective* dumb, dumbfounded, inarticulate, mute, silent, thunderstruck, tongue-tied.

speed *noun* **1** pace, rate, velocity. **2** alacrity, briskness, dispatch, haste, promptness, quickness, rapidity, swiftness.

speed *verb* **1** bolt, dash, fly, gallop, hasten, hurry, race, run, rush, scoot, scurry, shoot, streak, tear, zip, zoom. **2** (*speed up*) accelerate, expedite, fast-track (*informal*), get a move on (*informal*), hasten, hurry along, hurry up, quicken, step on it (*informal*).

speedy *adjective* expeditious, express, fast, immediate, prompt, quick, rapid, swift.

spell *noun* charm, curse, hex, incantation.

spell *noun* **1** interval, period, time, while. **2** bout, period, session, shift, stint, stretch, term, turn. **3** break, breather, pause, rest, smoko (*Australian informal*).

spell *verb* mean, portend, result in, signal, signify. □ **spell out** detail, explain, set out, specify.

spellbound *adjective* bewitched, captivated, charmed, enchanted, enraptured, enthralled, entranced, fascinated, hypnotised, mesmerised, rapt, riveted.

spend *verb* **1** blow (*slang*), consume, cough up (*slang*), fork out (*slang*), lash out, outlay, pay out, shell out (*informal*), splash out, splurge, squander, use up. **2** devote, fill, occupy, pass, use (up), while away.

spendthrift *noun* prodigal, profligate, squanderer, wastrel.

spew *verb* **1** barf (*slang*), be sick, chuck (*informal*), chunder (*Australian slang*), puke (*informal*), sick up (*informal*), throw up, vomit. **2** discharge, disgorge, eject, expel, spit out, spurt.

sphere *noun* **1** ball, globe, orb. **2** area, circle, domain, field, range, scope. □ **spherical** *adjective* globular, round.

spice *noun* condiment, flavouring, herb, seasoning. □ **spicy** *adjective* aromatic, fragrant, hot, piquant, pungent, sharp, strong.

spick and span clean, neat, orderly, shipshape, smart, tidy.

spike noun barb, point, prong, spine, stake, thorn.

spike verb impale, pierce, skewer, spear, stab.

spill verb 1 knock over, overturn, slop, tip over, upset. 2 brim over, fall out, overflow, pour, run over, slop.

spin verb 1 gyrate, pirouette, revolve, rotate, swirl, turn, twirl, twist, wheel, whirl. 2 concoct, invent, make up, narrate, relate, tell. □ **spin out** drag out, draw out, extend, prolong, protract.

spin noun drive, ride, run, trip.

spindle noun axle, pin, rod, shaft.

spindly adjective lanky, long, skinny, thin.

spine noun 1 backbone, spinal column, vertebral column. 2 barb, bristle, needle, prickle, quill, spike, thorn.

spine-chilling adjective blood-curdling, chilling, frightening, hair-raising, horrifying, scary, terrifying.

spineless adjective chicken (informal), cowardly, fearful, gutless (informal), irresolute, lily-livered, pusillanimous, timid, timorous, weak.

spin-off noun by-product, offshoot, side benefit.

spiral noun coil, corkscrew, helix, twist, whorl.

spirit noun 1 mind, psyche, soul. 2 (spirits) feelings, frame of mind, humour, mood, morale, temper. 3 apparition, bogy, genie, ghost, gremlin (informal), phantom, poltergeist, spectre, spook (informal), sprite. 4 animation, courage, dash, determination, drive, endurance, energy, enthusiasm, fearlessness, grit, gusto, guts (informal), liveliness, mettle, passion, pluck, spunk (informal), verve, vigour, vivacity, will, zeal, zest. 5 atmosphere, attitude, feeling, mood. 6 character, disposition, heart, make-up, nature, temperament.

spirited adjective animated, ardent, bold, brave, courageous, daring, determined, energetic, fearless, feisty (informal), fervent, intrepid, lively, mettlesome, passionate, plucky, vigorous.

spiritual adjective 1 emotional, inner, mental, psychic, psychological. 2 divine, ecclesiastical, religious, sacred.

spit noun saliva, slag (Australian slang), spittle, sputum. □ **dead spit** double, image, likeness, look-alike, ringer (informal), spitting image.

spit *noun* peninsula, point, promontory.

spite *noun* animosity, bitterness, hatred, hostility, ill will, malevolence, malice, rancour, resentment, revenge, spleen, vengeance, vindictiveness. □ **spiteful** *adjective* bitchy (*informal*), bitter, catty, malevolent, malicious, nasty, rancorous, resentful, revengeful, unkind, vengeful, venomous, vindictive. □ **in spite of** despite, notwithstanding, regardless of.

splash *verb* shower, slosh (*informal*), spatter, splatter, spray.

splash *noun* blob, blotch, mark, smear, smudge, splotch, stain, streak.

spleen *noun* anger, animosity, bitterness, gall, hostility, irritability, malice, rancour, spite, wrath.

splendid *adjective* **1** beautiful, brilliant, dazzling, fine, glittering, glorious, gorgeous, grand, imposing, impressive, lavish, magnificent, resplendent, rich, showy, spectacular, sumptuous, superb. **2** brilliant, excellent, exceptional, fabulous (*informal*), fantastic (*informal*), first-rate, great, marvellous, outstanding, remarkable, stupendous, super

(*informal*), superb, terrific (*informal*), wonderful.

splendour *noun* beauty, brilliance, glory, grandeur, greatness, magnificence, majesty, resplendence, richness, show, sumptuousness.

splice *verb* braid, intertwine, interweave, join, plait.

splinter *noun* fragment, shard, shiver, sliver.

splinter *verb* fracture, shatter, split.

split *verb* **1** break, burst, chop, cleave, come apart, crack, fracture, hew, rip, splinter, tear. **2** allocate, apportion, carve up, distribute, divide, dole out, share. □ **split up** break up, divorce, part, separate.

split *noun* **1** breach, division, rift, rupture, schism. **2** breach, break, cleft, crack, fissure, fracture, slit.

splutter *verb* **1** hiss, sizzle, spit, sputter. **2** mumble, stammer, stutter.

spoil *verb* **1** blight, botch, bungle, damage, destroy, harm, mar, mess up, ruin, undo, upset, wreck. **2** cosset, indulge, lavish, mollycoddle, overindulge, pamper. **3** decay, decompose, deteriorate, go bad, go off, perish, putrefy, rot.

spoil noun booty, loot, pillage, plunder, prizes, spoils, swag (*informal*).

spoilsport noun damper, killjoy, nark (*Australian informal*), party-pooper (*informal*), wet blanket (*informal*), wowser (*Australian informal*).

spoken adjective oral, unwritten, verbal.

spokesperson noun delegate, mouthpiece, representative, speaker, spokesman, spokeswoman.

sponge verb 1 clean, mop, wash, wipe. 2 (*sponge off, on*) bludge on (*Australian informal*), cadge from, impose on, live off, scrounge from. □ **sponger** noun bludger (*Australian informal*), cadger, freeloader (*informal*), hanger-on, parasite, scrounger.

spongy adjective absorbent, boggy, marshy, porous, soft, springy, swampy.

sponsor noun backer, benefactor, financier, patron, promoter, supporter.

sponsor verb back, finance, fund, promote, subsidise, support.

spontaneous adjective ad lib, automatic, extempore, impetuous, impromptu, impulsive, instinctive, involuntary, natural, off-the-cuff, reflex, unconscious, unforced, unplanned, unprepared, unrehearsed, voluntary.

spooky adjective creepy, eerie, frightening, ghostly, scary, uncanny, weird.

spool noun bobbin, reel.

sporadic adjective fitful, infrequent, intermittent, irregular, isolated, occasional, random, scattered, spasmodic.

sport noun 1 diversion, game, pastime, physical activity, recreation. 2 sportsman, sportswoman.

sporting adjective considerate, decent, fair, generous, sportsmanlike.

sportsground noun arena, field, ground, oval, pitch, playing field, stadium.

sportsman, sportswoman noun contestant, participant, player, sportsperson.

spot noun 1 blot, blotch, dot, fleck, mark, patch, smudge, speck, speckle, splash, splotch, stain. 2 birthmark, blackhead, blemish, freckle, mole, pimple, whitehead, zit (*informal*) (*spots*) rash. 3 area, district, locality, location, neighbourhood, place, position, region, setting, site, situation. 4 bead, blob, drop. □ **on the spot** at the scene, immediately, right away, straight away, then and there.

spot verb **1** dot, mark, smudge, soil, spatter, speckle, splash, splotch, spray, stain. **2** catch sight of, detect, discover, distinguish, espy, find, identify, locate, notice, pick out, recognise, see.

spotless adjective clean, faultless, flawless, immaculate, impeccable, perfect, unblemished, unstained, untarnished.

spotty adjective blotchy, brindled, dappled, dotted, flecked, freckled, mottled, pimply, speckled, splotchy, spotted.

spouse noun consort, husband, mate (informal), partner, wife.

spout noun jet, nozzle, outlet.

spout verb **1** flow, gush, jet, spray, spurt, squirt, stream. **2** carry on (informal), declaim, go on (informal), hold forth, pontificate, rant, rave, sermonise.

sprain verb twist, wrench.

sprawl verb flop, lie spread-eagled, loll, lounge, recline, slouch, slump, spread yourself out, stretch out.

spray verb shower, spatter, splash, sprinkle, wet.

spray noun **1** drizzle, droplets, mist, shower, vapour. **2** aerosol, atomiser, vaporiser.

spray noun bouquet, bunch, corsage, nosegay, posy, sprig.

spread verb **1** lay out, open out, stretch out, unfold, unfurl, unroll. **2** apply, coat, lay on, paste, plaster, smear. **3** enlarge, expand, extend, grow, increase, multiply, permeate, pervade, proliferate, sprawl, widen. **4** broadcast, circulate, diffuse, disperse, disseminate, distribute, promulgate, publicise, scatter, sprinkle, strew, transmit.

spread noun **1** advance, enlargement, expansion, extension, growth, increase, proliferation. **2** breadth, compass, coverage, expanse, extent, range, reach, scope, span, stretch, sweep, width. **3** banquet, feast, meal.

spree noun bender (slang), binge (slang), field day, fling, orgy, outing, revel, splurge.

sprig noun branch, shoot, spray.

sprightly adjective active, agile, dynamic, energetic, hale, lively, nimble, perky, spry, vivacious.

spring verb **1** bounce, bound, dart, hop, jump, leap, pounce, shoot out, vault. **2** arise, derive, emanate, grow, originate, proceed, stem. **3** appear, burst forth, come up, emerge, grow, shoot up, sprout. □ **spring back** bounce back, fly back, rebound, recoil.

spring noun **1** bound, hop, jump, leap, vault. **2** fountain, geyser, spa, well-spring.

springy adjective bouncy, elastic, resilient, spongy. □ **springiness** noun bounce, elasticity, resilience, spring.

sprinkle verb dust, scatter, shower, spatter, splash, spray, strew.

sprinkling noun few, handful.

sprint verb dash, race, run, rush, speed, tear.

sprite noun elf, fairy, goblin, hobgoblin, imp, leprechaun, pixie, spirit.

sprout verb bud, develop, germinate, grow, shoot.

spruce adjective chic, dapper, neat, smart, tidy, trim, well-groomed.

spruce verb clean up, groom, neaten, smarten, tidy, titivate (informal).

spruiker noun barker, tout.

spry adjective active, agile, dynamic, energetic, hale, lively, nimble, sprightly.

spur verb egg on, encourage, goad, motivate, prompt, stimulate, urge.

spurious adjective bogus, counterfeit, fake, false, phoney (informal).

spurn verb disdain, rebuff, refuse, reject, repudiate, scorn, turn your nose up at.

spurt verb **1** burst, flow, gush, jet, shoot, spout, spray, squirt, stream, surge. **2** dash, race, shoot, speed, sprint, tear.

spurt noun burst, gush, jet, rush, spray, squirt, stream, surge.

sputter verb hiss, sizzle, spit, splutter.

spy noun double agent, informer, intelligence agent, mole, secret agent, undercover agent.

spy verb **1** (spy on) keep under surveillance, keep watch on, observe, peep on, shadow, snoop on (informal), tail (informal), watch. **2** catch sight of, discern, discover, espy, make out, notice, observe, perceive, see, spot. □ **spying** noun espionage, intelligence, surveillance.

squabble verb argue, bicker, fight, quarrel, scrap (informal), wrangle. □ **squabble** noun altercation, argument, barney (informal), dispute, fight, quarrel, row, scrap (informal), tiff, wrangle.

squad noun band, force, gang, group, team, unit.

squalid adjective dilapidated, dirty, filthy, run-down, seedy, shabby, sordid, wretched.

squall noun gust, storm, wind.

squander verb blow (slang), dissipate, fritter away, throw away, waste.

square noun conservative, fuddy-duddy (informal), old fogy, stick-in-the-mud (informal).

square adjective **1** equal, even, level, tied. **2** above board, decent, equitable, fair, honest, just, straight. **3** conservative, conventional, old-fashioned, out of date, out of touch.

square verb agree, be consistent, correspond, fit, match, tally.

squash verb **1** compress, crush, flatten, mangle, mash, press, pulp, smash, squeeze. **2** cram, crowd, crush, jam, pack, squeeze. **3** crush, put down, quash, quell, suppress.

squat verb crouch.

squat adjective dumpy, nuggety (Australian), short, stocky, stubby, thickset.

squatter noun grazier, pastoralist, sheep farmer.

squawk verb & noun cry, scream, screech.

squeak verb & noun cheep, chirp, cry, peep, screech, shriek, squeal, yelp.

squeal verb & noun cry, scream, screech, shriek, wail, yell.

squeamish adjective easily nauseated, queasy.

squeeze verb **1** compact, compress, crush, press, squash, wring. **2** cram, crowd, force, jam, pack, pile, push, squash.

squeeze noun clasp, cuddle, embrace, hug.

squirm verb fidget, twist, wiggle, wriggle, writhe.

squirt verb gush, shoot, shower, spatter, splash, splatter, spray, sprinkle, spurt, syringe.

stab verb jab, knife, lance, pierce, spear, spike, wound.

stab noun **1** jab, pang, prick, tweak, twinge. **2** attempt, bash (informal), crack (informal), go (Australian informal), shot (informal), try.

stable adjective anchored, balanced, constant, enduring, established, firm, fixed, lasting, permanent, reliable, secure, solid, sound, steady, strong, sturdy, unchanged.

stable noun stall.

stack noun **1** bundle, heap, load, mound, mountain, pile. **2** cock, haycock, hayrick, haystack, rick. **3** heap, load, lot (informal), mass, mountain, pile (informal), plenty, ton (informal).

stack verb collect, heap, pile.

stadium noun amphitheatre, arena, ground, sportsground.

staff noun 1 crew, employees, manpower, personnel, team, workers, workforce. 2 baton, cane, crook, crosier, crutch, mace, pole, rod, sceptre, stick, truncheon.

staff verb man, run, service.

stage noun 1 dais, platform, podium, rostrum. 2 juncture, leg, part, period, phase, point, section.

stage verb 1 mount, perform, present, produce, put on. 2 arrange, carry out, hold, organise, plan.

stagger verb 1 falter, lurch, reel, stumble, teeter, totter. 2 astonish, astound, confound, dumbfound, flabbergast, nonplus, overwhelm, shake, shock, startle, stun, surprise, take aback.

stagnant adjective motionless, sluggish, stale, standing, static, still.

stagnate verb become stale, idle, languish, mark time, vegetate.

staid adjective dignified, earnest, grave, restrained, sedate, serious, settled, sober, steady.

stain noun 1 blotch, discoloration, mark, smudge, speck, splotch, spot. 2 blemish, blot, flaw, stigma, taint, tarnish. 3 dye, tint.

stain verb discolour, mark, smear, smudge, soil, spot.

stake noun 1 picket, pole, post, spike, stick. 2 bet, wager. 3 concern, interest, investment, share.

stake verb 1 brace, prop, support. 2 bet, chance, gamble, hazard, risk, wager.

stale adjective (stale bread) dry, hard, mouldy, old; (stale air) close, fusty, musty, stuffy.

stalemate noun deadlock, impasse, stand-off, standstill.

stalk noun shoot, stem.

stalk verb 1 follow, hound, hunt, prowl after, pursue, shadow, tail (informal), track, trail. 2 march, stride, strut.

stall noun 1 booth, counter, kiosk, stand, table. 2 compartment, cubicle, enclosure, pen.

stall verb block, delay, hedge, obstruct, play for time, procrastinate, put off, stave off, temporise.

stalwart adjective dependable, faithful, firm, loyal, reliable, staunch, steadfast, strong.

stamina noun endurance, energy, fortitude, perseverance, staying power, strength, vigour.

stammer verb falter, splutter, stumble, stutter.

stamp noun **1** brand, hallmark, imprint, logo, mark, seal, trade mark. **2** characteristic, hallmark, mark. □ **stamp-collecting** noun philately.

stamp verb **1** crush, flatten, squash, step, stomp, tramp, trample, tread. **2** brand, emboss, engrave, imprint, inscribe, print. □ **stamp out** abolish, eliminate, eradicate, put an end to, stop.

stampede noun charge, dash, race, run, rush. □ **stampede** verb bolt, charge, dash, race, rush.

stance noun **1** bearing, carriage, deportment, position, posture. **2** attitude, line, opinion, position, stand, standpoint, viewpoint.

stand verb **1** get up, rise. **2** deposit, place, position, put, set. **3** continue, remain, stay. **4** abide, bear, cope with, endure, face, handle, put up with, stomach, suffer, take, tolerate, undergo, weather, withstand. **5** pay for, provide, shout (Australian informal), treat to. □ **stand down 1** resign, step down, withdraw. **2** lay off, stand off, suspend. □ **stand for 1** be short for, denote, indicate, mean, represent, signify, symbolise. **2** brook, endure, put up with, suffer, take, tolerate. □ **stand in for** cover for, deputise for, fill in for, relieve, replace, substitute for, take the place of. □ **stand-in** noun deputy, locum, relief, replacement, reserve, stand-by, substitute, surrogate. □ **stand out** be conspicuous, be noticeable, be prominent, stick out. □ **stand up for** defend, speak up for, stand by, stick up for, support. □ **stand up to 1** challenge, confront, defy, face up to, oppose, resist. **2** endure, last through, resist, survive, withstand.

stand noun **1** base, pedestal, rack, shelf, support, tripod. **2** booth, counter, kiosk, stall. **3** place, position.

standard noun **1** grade, level, quality. **2** benchmark, criterion, guideline, requirement, specification, touchstone, yardstick. **3** banner, ensign, flag, pennant.

standard adjective **1** common, conventional, customary, normal, ordinary, orthodox, regular, routine, set, stock, usual. **2** accepted, approved, authoritative, classic, definitive, established, official, prescribed, recognised.

standover adjective bullying, intimidating, threatening.

standpoint noun angle, attitude, opinion, point of

view, position, stance, stand, viewpoint.

standstill *noun* halt, impasse, stop.

staple *adjective* basic, chief, essential, main, primary, principal, standard.

star *noun* **1** celestial body, heavenly body; (*group of stars*) constellation, galaxy. **2** asterisk, pentagram. **3** celebrity, idol, megastar (*informal*), superstar.

star *verb* act, appear, feature, perform, play.

stare *verb* gape, gawk (*informal*), gawp (*informal*), gaze, glare, goggle, look, peer, watch. □ **stare** *noun* gape, gaze, glare, look.

stark *adjective* **1** absolute, complete, downright, pure, sheer, total, utter. **2** austere, bare, bleak, desolate, grim, harsh, plain, severe, simple, spartan.

stark *adverb* absolutely, altogether, completely, quite, totally, utterly, wholly.

start *verb* **1** activate, begin, commence, embark on, enter upon, switch on, take up, turn on. **2** create, establish, found, inaugurate, initiate, institute, launch, originate, pioneer, set up. **3** depart, get going, leave, set off, set out. **4** blench, flinch,

jump, leap, recoil, spring, twitch, wince.

start *noun* **1** beginning, birth, commencement, dawn, genesis, inauguration, inception, kick-off (*informal*), launch, onset, opening, origin, outset. **2** advantage, break (*informal*), chance, edge, head start, lead, opening, opportunity. **3** jolt, jump, shock, surprise.

starting point base, basis, beginning, foundation, premise.

startle *verb* alarm, disturb, frighten, scare, shake, surprise, unsettle, upset. □ **startling** *adjective* alarming, astonishing, disturbing, dramatic, remarkable, shocking, staggering, surprising, unexpected.

starvation *noun* famine, hunger, malnutrition, under-nourishment.

starving *adjective* famished, hungry, ravenous.

state *noun* **1** circumstances, condition, frame of mind, health, mood, shape, situation. **2** country, kingdom, land, nation, principality, republic. **3** government. **4** dither, flap (*informal*), fluster, panic, stew (*informal*), tizzy (*informal*).

state *verb* affirm, announce, assert, declare, express, proclaim, report, say, voice.

stately *adjective* dignified, grand, imposing, impressive, magnificent, majestic.

statement *noun* **1** account, affidavit, affirmation, announcement, assertion, comment, communication, communiqué, confession, declaration, proclamation, remark, report, utterance. **2** account, bill, invoice.

static *adjective* constant, fixed, frozen, pegged, stable, stationary, steady, unchanging, unvarying.

station *noun* **1** location, place, position, post, site. **2** depot, stop, terminal, terminus. **3** broadcaster, channel. **4** estate, property, ranch (*American*), run (*Australian*).

station *verb* assign, base, locate, place, position, post.

stationary *adjective* immobile, motionless, parked, standing, static, still, unmoving.

statue *noun* bust, carving, cast, figurine, sculpture, statuette.

stature *noun* **1** height, size, tallness. **2** calibre, eminence, greatness, importance, prominence, standing.

status *noun* **1** level, position, rank, standing, station. **2** distinction, importance, prestige, recognition.

statute *noun* act, law, regulation, rule.

staunch *adjective* dependable, faithful, firm, loyal, reliable, steadfast, strong, trustworthy.

stave *verb* □ **stave off** avert, defer, fend off, prevent, ward off.

stay *verb* **1** continue, hang around, keep on, linger, remain, stick around (*informal*), tarry, wait. **2** dwell, live, lodge, reside, sleep, sleep over, sojourn, visit.

stay *noun* **1** holiday, sojourn, stop, stopover, time, visit. **2** deferment, postponement, reprieve.

stay *noun* brace, line, prop, rope, support.

steadfast *adjective* constant, determined, firm, persistent, resolute, staunch, steady, sure, unchanging, unshakeable.

steady *adjective* **1** balanced, firm, immovable, secure, stable. **2** consistent, constant, continuous, even, invariable, regular, unchanging, uniform.

steady *verb* balance, control, secure, stabilise, support.

steal *verb* **1** appropriate, duff (*Australian*), embezzle, filch, help yourself to, knock off (*slang*), lift (*informal*), make off with, misappropriate, nick (*slang*), pilfer, pinch (*informal*), poach, pocket, purloin, seize, snaffle (*informal*), snatch, snavel (*Australian informal*), snitch (*slang*), souvenir (*slang*), swipe (*informal*), take, thieve. **2** creep, flit, skulk, slink, slip, sneak, tiptoe. □ **stealing** *noun* see *THEFT*.

stealthy *adjective* covert, furtive, secret, secretive, sly, sneaky, surreptitious, under-cover, unobtrusive.

steam *noun* **1** mist, vapour. **2** energy, momentum, power, puff (*informal*), stamina.

steep *adjective* **1** abrupt, precipitous, sharp, sheer, vertical. **2** dear, excessive, exorbitant, expensive, extortionate, high.

steep *verb* immerse, impregnate, marinade, saturate, soak, souse, submerge.

steer *verb* conduct, direct, guide, lead, navigate, pilot.

stem *noun* cane, stalk, stock, trunk.

stem *verb* arise, derive, issue, originate, result, spring.

stem *verb* check, curb, halt, hold back, stanch, stop.

stench *noun* pong (*informal*), reek, stink.

step *noun* **1** pace, stride. **2** footstep, gait, tread, walk. **3** rung, stair, tread. **4** action,

initiative, measure, move. □ **steps** *plural noun* ladder staircase, stairs, stepladder.

step *verb* trample, tread, walk □ **step in** intercede, interfere intervene. □ **step on it** see *HURRY*. □ **step up** boost, build up, increase, raise.

stereotyped *adjective* clichéd conventional, hackneyed standardised, typecast.

sterile *adjective* **1** arid, bare barren, desert, fruitless infertile, unfruitful, unproductive, waste. **2** antiseptic aseptic, clean, disinfected germ-free, hygienic, sanitary sterilised.

sterilise *verb* **1** clean, disinfect fumigate, pasteurise, purify sanitise. **2** castrate, de-sex doctor, geld, neuter, spay.

sterling *adjective* **1** genuine pure, real. **2** see *EXCELLENT*.

stern *adjective* austere authoritarian, dour, forbidding, grim, hard, harsh inflexible, rigid, severe, strict tyrannical.

stern *noun* back, poop, rear.

stevedore *noun* docker, water sider (*Australian*), waterside worker, wharfie (*Australian informal*), wharf labourer.

stew *verb* braise, casserole.

stew *noun* casserole, fricassee goulash, hotpot, ragout. □ **in a**

stew in a dither, in a flap (*informal*), in a fluster, in a panic, in a state, in a tizzy (*informal*).

steward noun **1** attendant. **2** agent, bailiff, manager.

stick noun **1** baton, bludgeon, cane, club, cudgel, pole, rod, stake, truncheon, twig, waddy (*Australian*), wand. **2** cane, crook, staff, walking-stick. **3** bat, club, cue. □ **the sticks** the backblocks (*Australian*), the back of beyond, the backwoods, the bush, the country, the outback (*Australian*), Woop Woop (*Australian informal*).

stick verb **1** insert, jab, poke, push, thrust. **2** adhere, affix, attach, bind, bond, cement, fasten, fix, fuse, glue, gum, join, paste, seal, tape, weld. **3** become immobilised, become trapped, become wedged, catch, jam, lodge. **4** keep, remain, stay. □ **stick at** continue, keep at, last at, persevere with, persist at. □ **stick out 1** extend, jut out, poke out, project, protrude, stand out. **2** be conspicuous, be noticeable, stand out. □ **stick to** abide by, adhere to, follow, keep to. □ **stick up for** back, back up, defend, side with, stand by, stand up for, support.

sticker noun label, notice, seal, sign.

sticky adjective **1** adhesive, glued, gluey, glutinous, gooey (*informal*), gummed, tacky, viscous. **2** clammy, close, humid, muggy, steamy, sultry. **3** awkward, delicate, difficult, ticklish, tricky.

stickybeak noun busybody, Nosy Parker (*informal*), snooper (*informal*).

stiff adjective **1** firm, hard, inflexible, rigid, taut, tense, tight. **2** dense, firm, heavy, solid, thick. **3** arduous, challenging, difficult, exacting, formidable, hard, rigorous, tough. **4** aloof, austere, cold, cool, formal, prim, reserved, stand-offish, starchy, stilted, strait-laced, unfriendly, wooden. **5** brisk, keen, potent, powerful, strong. **6** Draconian, drastic, hard, harsh, merciless, severe, tough.

stiffen verb coagulate, congeal, firm up, harden, jell (*informal*), set, solidify, thicken.

stifle verb **1** asphyxiate, smother, suffocate. **2** hold back, restrain, smother, suppress.

stigmatise verb brand, condemn, denounce, label.

still adjective **1** calm, immobile, inert, motionless, static, stagnant, stationary, stock-still, undisturbed. **2** calm, noiseless, peaceful, quiet, silent, soundless, tranquil. □ **stillness** noun calm, peace, quietness, silence, tranquillity.

still verb allay, appease, calm, lull, pacify, quieten, settle, soothe, subdue.

stilted adjective artificial, awkward, forced, formal, laboured, pompous, stiff, unnatural.

stilts plural noun blocks, piles, pillars, posts.

stimulate verb activate, arouse, awaken, encourage, excite, inspire, kindle, prompt, provoke, rouse, spur, stir up, whet.

stimulus noun encouragement, goad, incentive, inducement, shot in the arm, spur.

sting noun bite, prick, tingle, wound.

sting verb **1** bite, nip, prick, wound. **2** burn, hurt, smart, tingle. **3** goad, incite, provoke, spur, stimulate, stir.

stingy adjective (a stingy person) close-fisted, mean, mingy (informal), miserly, niggardly, parsimonious, penny-pinching, tight, tight-fisted; (a stingy amount) beggarly, inadequate, insufficient, meagre, measly

(informal), paltry, scanty, skimpy, small.

stink noun pong (informal), reek, stench.

stink verb pong (informal), reek. □ **stinking** adjective see SMELLY (at SMELL).

stint noun period, quota, shift, spell, stretch, term, turn.

stint verb be niggardly, be stingy, economise, pinch, skimp.

stipend noun allowance, emolument, income, pay, salary.

stipulate verb demand, designate, insist on, lay down, specify, state. □ **stipulation** noun condition, demand, proviso, requirement, specification.

stir verb **1** agitate, beat, blend, mix, whip, whisk. **2** flutter, move, quiver, rustle, twitch. **3** arouse, awaken, excite, inspire, kindle, provoke, quicken, rouse, stimulate. □ **stirring** adjective exciting, inspiring, moving, provocative, rousing, stimulating.

stir noun commotion, disturbance, excitement, fuss, kerfuffle (informal), sensation, to-do.

stitch verb baste, darn, embroider, mend, sew, tack.

stock noun **1** accumulation, cache, hoard, quantity, reserve, stockpile, store, supply. **2** animals, beasts, livestock. **3** ancestry, background, blood, descent, extraction, lineage. **4** bouillon, broth.

stock verb carry, handle, have, keep, sell. □ **stock up on** accumulate, amass, buy up, hoard, lay in, stockpile.

stocking noun (stockings) hosiery, pantihose, tights.

stockman noun drover (Australian), herdsman, stockrider (Australian).

stocky adjective burly, dumpy, nuggety (Australian), solid, stout, sturdy, thickset.

stodgy adjective **1** heavy, indigestible, starchy. **2** boring, dreary, dull, tedious, uninteresting.

stoical adjective calm, fatalistic, impassive, patient, philosophical, resigned, self-controlled, uncomplaining.

stole noun scarf, shawl, wrap.

stolid adjective apathetic, dull, impassive, indifferent, phlegmatic, unemotional, unexcitable, uninterested.

stomach noun abdomen, belly, gut, insides (informal), paunch, tummy (informal).

stomach verb abide, bear, endure, put up with, stand, take, tolerate.

stone noun **1** boulder, cobble, gibber (Australian), pebble, rock; (stones) gravel, scree, shingle. **2** gem, jewel. **3** pip, pit, seed.

stoned adjective see INTOXICATED.

stonker verb beat, defeat, euchre, get the better of, outwit, thwart.

stony adjective **1** cobbled, gravelly, pebbly, rocky, rough, rugged, shingly. **2** blank, chilly, cold, fixed, frosty, hard, icy, indifferent, unfeeling, unresponsive, unsympathetic.

stooge noun butt, fall guy (slang), foil, straight man.

stoop verb **1** bend down, crouch, duck, kneel, lean over. **2** demean yourself, descend, fall, lower yourself, resort, sink. □ **stoop** noun droop, hunch, slouch.

stop verb **1** abandon, break off, cease, come to an end, conclude, desist, discontinue, end, expire, finish, give up, halt, interrupt, knock off (informal), leave off, pause, peter out, pull up, put an end to, quit, refrain from, run out, stall, switch off, terminate, turn off. **2** put up, rest, sojourn, stay, stop off, stop over. **3** arrest, bar, block, check, curb, halt, hamper, hinder, immobilise, impede, interrupt, obstruct, preclude, prevent, stanch, stem. **4** block, bung, close, fill, plug, seal. □ **stoppage** *noun* interruption, shut-down, strike, walk-out.

stop *noun* break, cessation, close, conclusion, end, finish, halt, interlude, intermission, pause, recess, rest, standstill, suspension, termination.

stopgap *noun* fill-in, relief, stand-in (*informal*), substitute, temporary.

stopper *noun* bung, cork, plug.

store *noun* **1** accumulation, cache, collection, hoard, pile, reserve, stock, stockpile, supply. **2** depot, storehouse, warehouse. **3** department store, emporium, general store, megastore, retailer, shop, supermarket.

store *verb* accumulate, collect, hoard, keep, lay up, preserve, put aside, put away, reserve, save, stash (*informal*), stockpile, stow.

storey *noun* floor, level.

storm *noun* **1** blizzard, cloudburst, cyclone, deluge, downpour, dust storm, gale, hailstorm, hurricane, rainstorm, sandstorm, snowstorm, squall, tempest, thunderstorm, tornado, typhoon, willy willy (*Australian*). **2** commotion, furore, fuss, outcry,

row, rumpus, stir, to-do, uproar. □ **stormy** *adjective* blustery, foul, gusty, inclement, squally, tempestuous, turbulent, violent, wild, windy.

storm *verb* **1** charge, rush, stamp, stomp, tear. **2** attack, charge, invade, raid, rush, take by storm, take over.

story *noun* **1** account, allegory, anecdote, chronicle, fable, legend, myth, narrative, novel, parable, record, report, statement, tale, version, yarn. **2** plot, scenario, storyline. **3** falsehood, fib, fiction, furphy (*Australian informal*), lie, untruth.

stout *adjective* **1** burly, corpulent, fat, obese, overweight, plump, portly, rotund, stocky, tubby. **2** fat, solid, strong, sturdy, thick. **3** bold, brave, courageous, determined, fearless, resolute, valiant.

stow *verb* load, pack, put, stash (*informal*), store, stuff.

straggle *verb* dawdle, lag, loiter, stray, trail. □ **straggler** *noun* dawdler, laggard, loiterer, slowcoach, stray. □ **straggly** *adjective* lank, loose, unkempt, untidy.

straight *adjective* **1** direct, unbending, unswerving. **2** aligned, level, neat, orderly, shipshape, square, tidy. **3**

candid, direct, frank, honest, straightforward, truthful, upfront (*informal*).

straight *adverb* candidly, directly, frankly, honestly, without beating about the bush. □ **straight away** at once, directly, immediately, instantly, on the spot, right away, without delay.

straightforward *adjective* **1** easy, simple, uncomplicated. **2** candid, direct, frank, honest, open, straight, truthful.

strain *verb* **1** pull, stretch, tauten, tense, tighten. **2** damage, injure, overtax, overwork, pull, rick, sprain, tax, wrench. **3** exert yourself, heave, push, strive, struggle, try. **4** filter, percolate, riddle, screen, sieve, sift.

strain *noun* **1** injury, pull, rick, sprain, wrench. **2** burden, drag, effort, exertion, pressure, stress, struggle, tax, tension, worry. **3** air, melody, song, tune.

strain *noun* breed, kind, type, variety.

strainer *noun* colander, filter, sieve, sifter.

strait *noun* channel, narrows, passage, sound. □ **in dire straits** in a mess, in a predicament, in a spot (*informal*), in difficulties, in distress, in

need, in strife (*Australian informal*), in trouble.

strait-laced *adjective* old-fashioned, prim, proper, prudish, puritanical, stuffy.

strand *noun* fibre, filament, thread.

strand *verb* □ **stranded** *adjective* **1** beached, grounded, shipwrecked. **2** abandoned, deserted, high and dry, in the lurch, marooned.

strange *adjective* **1** abnormal, bizarre, curious, eccentric, extraordinary, funny, odd, outlandish, peculiar, queer, singular, surprising, uncanny, unconventional, unusual, way-out (*informal*), weird, zany. **2** alien, exotic, foreign, new, novel, unfamiliar, unknown.

stranger *noun* alien, foreigner, newcomer, outsider, visitor.

strangle *verb* asphyxiate, choke, garrotte, suffocate, throttle.

strap *noun* band, belt, bowyang (*Australian*), cord, thong, tie.

strap *verb* attach, bind, fasten, lash, secure, tie, truss.

strapping *adjective* healthy, husky, robust, strong, sturdy, tall, vigorous.

stratagem *noun* artifice, dodge, manoeuvre, plan, ploy (*informal*), ruse, scheme, subterfuge, tactic, trick.

strategic *adjective* calculated, planned, politic, tactical.

strategy *noun* approach, method, plan, policy, scheme, tactics.

stratum *noun* **1** layer, lode, seam, vein. **2** class, echelon, level, rank, station.

stray *verb* deviate, digress, diverge, drift, go astray, roam, rove, straggle, wander.

stray *adjective* abandoned, homeless, lost, roaming, wandering.

streak *noun* **1** band, line, strip, stripe. **2** element, side, strain, vein.

streak *verb* **1** mark, smear, stain, stripe. **2** dart, dash, run, rush, speed, tear, whiz, zoom.

stream *noun* **1** brook, creek, rill, river, rivulet, tributary, watercourse. **2** current, flood, flow, gush, jet, rush, surge, tide, torrent.

stream *verb* flood, gush, issue, pour, run, rush, shoot, spill, spout, spurt, surge.

streamer *noun* bunting, flag, pennant, ribbon.

streamlined *adjective* **1** aerodynamic, sleek, smooth. **2** efficient, rationalised, simplified, smooth.

street *noun* alley, avenue, boulevard, close, crescent, cul-de-sac, drive, highway, lane, place, road, terrace, thoroughfare.

strength *noun* **1** brawn, endurance, force, intensity, might, muscle, potency, power, robustness, stamina, toughness, vigour. **2** asset, forte, strong point.

strengthen *verb* bolster, boost, brace, build up, buttress, enhance, fortify, heighten, increase, intensify, prop up, reinforce, shore up, support, toughen.

strenuous *adjective* **1** arduous, demanding, difficult, exhausting, hard, herculean, laborious, taxing, tough, uphill. **2** dynamic, energetic, enthusiastic, hard-working, indefatigable, industrious, persistent, sedulous, tenacious, untiring.

stress *noun* **1** anxiety, pressure, strain, tension, worry. **2** accent, beat, emphasis, force, importance, priority, value, weight. □ **stressful** *adjective* demanding, difficult, draining, exhausting, onerous, pressured, taxing, tense, trying, worrying.

stress *verb* accentuate, dwell on, emphasise, highlight, impress, insist on, labour, underline.

stretch *verb* **1** broaden, distend, draw out, elongate, expand, extend, inflate, lengthen, pull out, widen. **2** continue, cover, extend, reach, spread.

stretch noun **1** elasticity, give, stretchiness. **2** (*a stretch of time*) period, spell, stint, term; (*a stretch of land*) area, distance, expanse, length, section, tract.

stretcher noun camp bed, camp stretcher, folding bed.

stricken adjective affected, afflicted, smitten, struck down.

strict adjective **1** (*a strict teacher*) authoritarian, firm, inflexible, rigid, severe, stern, tough, uncompromising; (*strict rules*) absolute, binding, firm, hard and fast, inflexible, rigid, stringent. **2** close, exact, faithful, literal, meticulous, precise, scrupulous.

stride verb march, pace, stalk, walk.

stride noun pace, step.

strident adjective discordant, grating, harsh, loud, rasping, raucous.

strife noun conflict, disagreement, discord, dissension, friction, trouble, unrest. □ **in strife** in a mess, in difficulties, in hot water (*informal*), in the soup (*slang*), in trouble.

strike verb **1** bash, batter, beat, belt (*slang*), box, clobber (*slang*), clout (*informal*), cuff, dong (*Australian informal*), flog, hit, job (*informal*), knock, lash, punch, quilt (*Australian slang*), rap, slap, smack, smite, sock (*slang*), spank, stoush (*Australian slang*), swipe (*informal*), tap, thrash, thump, thwack, trounce, wallop (*slang*), whack, whip; (*of a vehicle, etc.*) bump into, collide with, crash into, hit, knock into, ram into, run into, smash into. **2** affect, afflict, assail, assault, attack, hit. **3** chime, peal, sound, toll. **4** appear to, come across (*informal*), impress, seem to. **5** come upon, discover, find, reach, stumble on. **6** down tools (*informal*), go on strike, stop work, take industrial action, walk out.

strike noun **1** assault, attack, blitz, bombardment, offensive, onslaught, raid. **2** industrial action, stoppage, walk-out.

striking adjective amazing, astounding, conspicuous, extraordinary, impressive, noticeable, obvious, remarkable.

string noun **1** cord, rope, strand, twine. **2** chain, column, file, line, queue, row, sequence, series, succession.

string verb **1** fasten, hang, sling, stretch, suspend, tie. **2** lace, thread.

stringent adjective firm, inflexible, rigid, rigorous, strict, tough, uncompromising.

strip verb **1** peel off, remove, shave off, take off. **2** disrobe, expose yourself, undress.

strip noun band, bar, belt, ribbon, stripe.

stripe noun band, bar, chevron, line, strip. □ **striped** adjective banded, lined, striated, stripy.

strive verb **1** aim, attempt, endeavour, make an effort, try. **2** battle, contend, fight, struggle.

stroke noun **1** blow, hit, lash, whack. **2** apoplexy, brain attack, cerebrovascular accident, seizure.

stroke verb caress, massage, pat, rub, touch.

stroll verb amble, promenade, ramble, saunter, walk, wander.

stroller noun pushchair, pusher (Australian).

strong adjective **1** (a strong man) brawny, burly, hardy, hefty, mighty, muscular, powerful, robust, sinewy, stalwart, sturdy, tough; (a strong argument) cogent, compelling, convincing, forceful, irrefutable, persuasive, powerful, solid, sound, weighty; (a strong wind) destructive, mighty, powerful, violent; (strong measures) drastic, extreme, firm, harsh, severe, stiff, stringent. **2** (strong furniture) durable, hard-wearing, heavy-duty, indestructible, sound, stout, sturdy, tough, unbreakable; (a strong opponent) formidable, invincible, powerful, unbeatable, unconquerable. **3** (a strong faith) ardent, earnest, fervent, firm, intense, keen, passionate, powerful, steadfast, unshakeable. **4** (a strong flavour) aromatic, hot, piquant, pungent, sharp, spicy; (a strong drink) alcoholic, concentrated, fortified, heady, intoxicating, potent, stiff; (strong colours) bold, bright, dark, deep, intense, loud, solid, vivid; (a strong accent) clear, definite, distinct, marked, noticeable, obvious, pronounced, unmistakable. □ **strong point** asset, forte, speciality, strength.

stronghold noun bastion, castle, citadel, fort, fortification, fortress.

stroppy adjective bad-tempered, difficult, irritable, obstreperous, perverse, snaky

(*Australian informal*), uncooperative.

structure noun **1** building, construction, edifice. **2** arrangement, composition, configuration, constitution, design, form, framework, layout, make-up, organisation, shape. □ **structure** verb arrange, design, construct, organise, put together.

struggle verb **1** endeavour, labour, strain, strive, toil, try, work hard. **2** battle, contend, fight, grapple, scuffle, spar, tussle, vie, wrestle.

struggle noun **1** effort, exertion, grind, hassle (*informal*), strain, trial. **2** battle, conflict, confrontation, contest, fight, scuffle, skirmish, tussle.

strut verb flounce, parade, prance, stride, swagger.

stub noun **1** butt, end, remains, remnant, stump. **2** butt, counterfoil.

stub verb bump, hit, knock, strike. □ **stub out** extinguish, put out, snuff.

stubborn adjective adamant, defiant, dogged, headstrong, inflexible, intractable, intransigent, obstinate, pigheaded, recalcitrant, refractory, strong-minded, uncompromising, unyielding.

stuck-up adjective arrogant, conceited, condescending, haughty, high and mighty, hoity-toity, patronising, pretentious, proud, snobbish, snooty (*informal*), toffee-nosed (*informal*), uppity (*informal*).

student noun apprentice, learner, postgraduate, pupil, scholar, schoolboy, schoolchild, schoolgirl, trainee, undergraduate.

studio noun workroom, workshop.

studious adjective academic, bookish, diligent, intellectual, scholarly.

study verb **1** cram, learn, memorise, revise, swot (*informal*). **2** analyse, examine, inquire into, investigate, look at, research, survey.

study noun **1** education, instruction, learning, research, scholarship, training. **2** analysis, examination, inquiry, investigation, review, survey. **3** den, office, studio, workroom.

stuff noun **1** material, matter, substance. **2** belongings, bits and pieces, effects, gear, goods, junk (*informal*), odds and ends, paraphernalia, possessions, things.

stuff verb **1** cram, jam, pack, ram, squash, squeeze. **2** fill, pack, pad, wad. **3** push, put, shove (*informal*), stash (*informal*), stick (*informal*), stow, thrust. **4** fill, gorge, sate, satiate.

stuffing noun **1** filling, padding, wadding. **2** filling, seasoning.

stuffy adjective **1** airless, close, fusty, humid, muggy, musty, oppressive, stale, stifling, suffocating, sultry, unventilated. **2** blocked up, clogged up, congested, stuffed up. **3** conventional, dreary, dull, narrow-minded, old-fashioned, priggish, prim, staid, strait-laced.

stumble verb **1** fall, falter, flounder, lurch, reel, sprawl, stagger, topple, totter, trip. **2** blunder, falter, flounder. □ **stumble on** chance on, come across, discover, find, happen on, hit on.

stumbling block difficulty, hindrance, hitch, hurdle, impediment, obstacle, snag.

stump noun base, butt, end, remnant, stub.

stump verb baffle, bewilder, confound, mystify, perplex, puzzle, throw (*informal*).

stun verb **1** daze, knock out, stupefy. **2** amaze, astonish, astound, bewilder, bowl over, daze, dumbfound, flabbergast, floor, overwhelm, shock, stagger, stupefy, surprise.

stunt verb check, curb, hamper, hinder, impede, inhibit, restrict, retard.

stunt noun act, exploit, feat, performance, trick.

stupefy verb amaze, astonish, astound, bewilder, confound, daze, flabbergast, numb, overwhelm, shock, stagger, stun, surprise.

stupendous adjective amazing, astonishing, astounding, colossal, enormous, exciting, extraordinary, great, huge, immense, incredible, marvellous, phenomenal, prodigious, sensational (*informal*), spectacular, stunning (*informal*), terrific (*informal*), tremendous (*informal*), unbelievable, unreal (*slang*), wonderful.

stupid adjective (*a stupid person*) asinine, bovine, brainless, clueless (*informal*), dense, dim (*informal*), dim-witted, dopey (*informal*), dull, dumb (*informal*), feeble-minded, foolish, half-witted, idiotic, obtuse, simple-minded, slow, thick, unintelligent; (*a stupid thing to do*) absurd, crazy, foolhardy, foolish, idiotic, imprudent, inane, irrational, ludicrous, mad, mindless nonsensical, reckless, senseless, silly, unwise.

sturdy adjective **1** brawny, burly, hardy, hefty, husky, mighty, muscular, nuggety (*Australian*), robust, stalwart, stout, strapping, strong, tough, vigorous. **2** durable, indestructible, solid, sound, strong, tough, unbreakable.

stutter verb falter, stammer, stumble.

style noun **1** (*a style of painting*) approach, genre, manner, method, mode, technique, way; (*a style of writing*) expression, language, phraseology, wording. **2** design, fashion, kind, pattern, shape, sort, type, version. **3** chic, class, elegance, flair, panache, polish, sophistication.

style verb arrange, cut, design, shape.

stylish adjective chic, classy (*informal*), elegant, fashionable, smart, snazzy (*informal*), trendy (*informal*), up to date, with it (*informal*).

suave adjective bland, charming, debonair, diplomatic, gracious, polite, smooth, sophisticated, urbane.

subconscious adjective instinctive, intuitive, unconscious.

subdue verb **1** control, defeat, overcome, overpower, quell, repress, restrain, suppress. **2** hush, lower, moderate, mute, quieten, soften, tone down.

subject noun **1** issue, matter, substance, theme, topic. **2** course, discipline, field. **3** citizen, national, subordinate, vassal.

subject adjective □ **subject to 1** accountable to, amenable to, answerable to, bound by. **2** liable to, prone to, susceptible to, vulnerable to. **3** conditional upon, contingent on, dependent upon.

subject verb expose, put through, submit, treat.

subjective adjective biased, idiosyncratic, individual, personal, prejudiced.

subjugate verb conquer, overpower, quell, subdue, subject, vanquish.

sublime adjective **1** awe-inspiring, elevated, exalted, glorious, grand, lofty, magnificent, majestic, noble, wonderful. **2** complete, extreme, supreme, total, utter.

submerge verb cover, dip, dive, drown, duck, dunk, engulf, flood, go under, immerse, inundate, plunge, sink, soak, souse, steep, swamp.

submissive *adjective* accommodating, acquiescent, compliant, deferential, docile, humble, meek, obedient, passive, servile, tractable, unassertive, yielding.

submit *verb* **1** bow, capitulate, give in, succumb, surrender, throw in the towel, yield. **2** give in, hand in, offer, present, proffer, propose, put forward, tender. □ **submission** *noun* **1** capitulation, compliance, deference, humility, meekness, obedience, passivity, surrender. **2** entry, presentation, proposal, suggestion, tender.

subordinate *adjective* **1** lesser, secondary, subsidiary. **2** inferior, junior, lower.

subpoena *noun* order, summons, writ.

subscribe *verb* **1** (*subscribe to*) contribute to, donate to, give to, help, support. **2** (*subscribe to*) accept, agree with, approve of, believe in, endorse, go along with, hold with (*informal*), support. □ **subscription** *noun* contribution, dues, fee, membership fee, sub (*informal*).

subsequent *adjective* ensuing, following, later, succeeding.

subservient *adjective* deferential, fawning, obsequious, servile, slavish, submissive, sycophantic, toadying, truckling.

subside *verb* **1** cave in, collapse, drop, settle, sink. **2** abate, decrease, die down, diminish, ebb, lessen, let up, moderate, recede, wane, weaken.

subsidiary *adjective* additional, extra, lesser, minor, secondary, subordinate, supplementary.

subsidise *verb* back, contribute to, finance, fund, sponsor, support, underwrite.

subsidy *noun* assistance, contribution, grant.

subsist *verb* exist, live, survive.

substance *noun* **1** material, matter, stuff. **2** essence, gist, heart, nub, pith, thrust.

substantial *adjective* **1** big, considerable, large, significant, sizeable, tidy (*informal*). **2** solid, strong, well-built.

substantiate *verb* authenticate, back up, confirm, corroborate, prove, support, validate, verify.

substitute *noun* deputy, fill-in, locum, proxy, relief, replacement, reserve, ring-in (*Australian informal*), stand-in, stopgap, sub (*informal*), surrogate, understudy.

substitute *verb* exchange, interchange, replace, swap, switch; (*substitute for*) cover for, deputise for, fill in for, relieve for, replace, stand in for.

subterfuge noun artifice, deception, dodge (*informal*), lurk (*Australian informal*), plan, ploy, pretext, ruse, scheme, stratagem, trick, wile.

subtle adjective **1** fine, imperceptible, minor, slight, tiny. **2** delicate, faint, gentle, mild, understated. **3** clever, cunning, devious, ingenious, sly, sneaky, wily.

subtract verb deduct, remove, take away, take off.

suburb noun area, community, district, neighbourhood.

subvert verb destroy, overthrow, overturn, sabotage, topple, undermine.

subway noun tunnel, underpass.

succeed verb **1** achieve success, bear fruit, be effective, be successful, do well, make good, make it, prosper, work. **2** come after, follow, replace, supplant, take over from.

success noun **1** achievement, attainment, prosperity, triumph, victory. **2** hit, sell-out (*informal*), sensation, smash hit (*informal*), triumph, winner.

successful adjective booming, effective, flourishing, fruitful, productive, profitable, prosperous, thriving, triumphant, victorious, winning.

succession noun chain, cycle, line, round, run, sequence, series, string, train. □ **in succession** consecutively, in a row, one after the other, running, successively.

successive adjective consecutive, straight, uninterrupted.

succinct adjective brief, concise, condensed, laconic, pithy, terse.

succour noun aid, assistance, help, relief. □ **succour** verb aid, assist, help, minister to, relieve.

succulent adjective juicy, luscious, moist, tasty.

succumb verb bow, capitulate, give in, give way, submit, surrender, yield.

suck verb □ **suck up to** crawl to (*informal*), fawn on, flatter, grovel to, kowtow to, play up to, toady to.

sucker noun dupe, mug (*informal*), muggins (*informal*), pushover (*informal*), sap (*informal*).

suckle verb breastfeed, feed, nurse.

sudden adjective abrupt, hasty, impetuous, instant, precipitate, quick, rapid, rash, snap, surprise, swift, unexpected, whirlwind. ☐ **all of a sudden** abruptly, all at once, in an instant, in the twinkling of an eye, out of the blue, quickly, suddenly, unexpectedly, without warning.

suds *plural noun* bubbles, foam, froth, lather.

suffer *verb* **1** be in pain, feel pain, hurt. **2** bear, cope with, endure, experience, feel, go through, put up with, undergo. **3** allow, permit, put up with, stand, take, tolerate. ☐ **suffering** *noun* affliction, agony, anguish, discomfort, distress, grief, hardship, heartache, hurt, misery, pain, sorrow, torment, torture, tribulation, woe.

suffice *verb* answer, be adequate, be ample, be enough, be sufficient, do, satisfy, serve.

sufficient *adjective* adequate, ample, enough.

suffocate *verb* asphyxiate, choke, smother, stifle, strangle, throttle.

sugary *adjective* cloying, saccharine, sickly, sweet.

suggest *verb* **1** advise, advocate, propose, put forward, recommend. **2** hint, imply, indicate, insinuate, intimate. ☐ **suggestion** *noun* advice, proposal, recommendation, tip.

suicidal *adjective* self-destructive.

suit *noun* **1** costume, ensemble, outfit. **2** action, case, lawsuit, proceedings.

suit *verb* **1** be acceptable to, be convenient for, be right for, be suitable for, fit in with, please. **2** become, look good on.

suitable *adjective* acceptable, apposite, appropriate, apt, becoming, befitting, convenient, fitting, meet (*old use*), pertinent, proper, relevant, right, satisfactory, seemly, timely.

suitcase *noun* bag, case, grip, port (*Australian*), portmanteau, trunk, valise.

suitor *noun* admirer, beau, boyfriend, lover, swain (*old use*), sweetheart.

sulky *adjective* bad-tempered, brooding, disgruntled, moody, peevish, petulant, pouting, resentful, scowling, sullen.

sullen *adjective* bad-tempered, brooding, dismal, gloomy, grouchy (*informal*), grumpy, melancholy, moody, morose, resentful, sour, sulky, surly, unsociable.

sully *verb* blemish, disgrace, smirch, soil, spoil, stain, taint, tarnish.

sultry *adjective* close, hot, humid, muggy, oppressive.

sticky, stifling, stuffy, suffocating.

sum noun **1** addition, aggregate, subtotal, total. **2** calculation, problem. **3** amount, quantity.

sum verb □ **sum up 1** précis, recap (informal), recapitulate, review, summarise. **2** assess, judge, size up.

summarise verb précis, recap (informal), recapitulate, review, sum up.

summary noun abstract, digest, outline, précis, recap (informal), recapitulation, résumé, synopsis.

summary adjective **1** brief, concise, condensed, short, succinct. **2** hasty, instant, instantaneous, prompt.

summit noun apex, crest, crown, peak, pinnacle, top, zenith.

summon verb call, command, order, send for, subpoena, summons. □ **summon up** call on, draw on, gather, invoke, muster.

summons noun command, demand, order, subpoena, writ.

sumptuous adjective costly, expensive, extravagant, grand, lavish, luxurious, magnificent, opulent, posh (informal), splendid.

sunbathe verb bask, sunbake, sun yourself.

sundry adjective assorted, diverse, miscellaneous, several, various.

sunny adjective **1** bright, clear, cloudless, fair, fine, sunlit. **2** blithe, bright, buoyant, cheerful, gay, genial, happy, jovial, joyful, light-hearted, smiling.

sunrise noun cock-crow, dawn, daybreak, first light, sun-up.

sunset noun dusk, evening, gloaming, nightfall, sundown, twilight.

sunshade noun awning, canopy, parasol.

superb adjective brilliant (informal), cool (informal), excellent, exceptional, fabulous (informal), fantastic (informal), fine, first-class, first-rate, grand, great, impressive, magnificent, marvellous, outstanding, remarkable, splendid, stupendous, super (informal), superlative, terrific (informal), top-notch (informal), wonderful.

supercilious adjective arrogant, condescending, disdainful, haughty, hoity-toity, lofty, lordly, patronising, proud, scornful, self-important, snobbish, stuck-up (informal), superior.

superficial adjective **1** exterior, external, shallow, skin-deep, slight, surface. **2** cursory, hasty, hurried, perfunctory, quick, sketchy.

superfluous adjective excess, extra, redundant, spare, surplus, unnecessary, unneeded.

superhuman adjective divine, miraculous, prodigious, supernatural.

superintend verb administer, control, direct, manage, organise, oversee, preside over, run, supervise. □ **superintendent** noun administrator, boss, chief, foreman, head, manager, overseer, supervisor, warden.

superior adjective **1** higher, senior. **2** better, excellent, first-class, greater, outstanding, super (informal), top, unequalled. **3** arrogant, condescending, disdainful, haughty, high and mighty, hoity-toity, lofty, patronising, self-important, smug, snobbish, stuck-up (informal), supercilious.

superlative adjective consummate, excellent, first-class, incomparable, magnificent, matchless, outstanding, superb, supreme, unparalleled, unsurpassed.

supernatural adjective extraordinary, metaphysical, miraculous, mysterious, mystic, occult, paranormal, psychic, unearthly.

supersede verb displace, oust, replace, supplant, take the place of.

supervise verb administer, control, direct, head, manage, organise, oversee, preside over, run, stage-manage, superintend, watch over. □ **supervision** noun administration, control, direction, management, observation, organisation, oversight, scrutiny, surveillance, watch. □ **supervisor** noun administrator, boss, chief, director, foreman, head, manager, overseer, superintendent, superior.

supine adjective face upwards, flat on your back; see also HORIZONTAL.

supplant verb displace, oust, replace, supersede, take the place of.

supple adjective flexible, limber, lithe, pliable.

supplement noun **1** addition, additive, add-on, extra, surcharge. **2** addendum, addition, appendix, codicil, insert, postscript, rider. □ **supplementary** adjective additional, extra.

supplement verb add to, augment, boost, increase, top up.

supplication noun appeal, entreaty, petition, plea, prayer, request.

supply verb equip, furnish, give, provide. □ **supplier** noun dealer, distributor, merchant, retailer, seller, shopkeeper, stockist, vendor, wholesaler.

supply noun 1 hoard, reserve, stock, stockpile, store. 2 delivery, provision.

support verb 1 bear, bolster, brace, buttress, carry, hold up, prop up, reinforce, shore up. 2 assist, back, barrack for (Australian), champion, comfort, contribute to, defend, encourage, finance, help, patronise, side with, sponsor, stand by, stand up for, stick by, stick up for, subsidise, succour, sustain. 3 finance, fund, keep, maintain, provide for. 4 back up, confirm, corroborate, endorse, substantiate, uphold, verify. □ **supporter** noun ally, backer, benefactor, champion, fan, follower, helper, patron, well-wisher. □ **supportive** adjective caring, encouraging, helpful, sympathetic, understanding.

support noun 1 aid, assistance, backing, help, patronage, sponsorship. 2 bolster, brace,

bracket, buttress, calliper, column, crutch, foundation, joist, pillar, post, prop, stanchion, stay, stilt, strut.

suppose verb assume, believe, expect, fancy, guess, imagine, presume, surmise, think. □ **supposition** noun assumption, conjecture, guess, hypothesis, opinion, presumption, speculation, surmise, theory. □ **be supposed to** be expected to, be meant to, be obliged to.

suppress verb 1 crush, overcome, overpower, put an end to, quash, quell, squash, stop. 2 bottle up, censor, conceal, contain, control, cover up, hide, keep in check, keep secret, repress, restrain, silence, stifle, withhold.

supreme adjective 1 chief, highest, leading, paramount, principal, sovereign. 2 consummate, extreme, greatest, highest, utmost, uttermost.

sure adjective 1 assured, certain, confident, convinced, persuaded, positive. 2 bound, certain, guaranteed. 3 certain, dependable, fail-safe, infallible, reliable, sure-fire (informal), trustworthy, unfailing. 4 certain, clear, definite, indisputable, true, undeniable. □ **make sure** ascertain, check, confirm, double-check, make certain, verify.

surf noun foam, spume; see also WAVE.

surface noun coating, covering, exterior, façade, finish, outside, shell, skin, top, veneer.

surface verb come up, emerge, rise.

surge verb billow, heave, push, roll, rush, stream, swell. □ **surge** noun flow, gush, rush, stream, upsurge, wave.

surly adjective bad-tempered, churlish, crabby, crotchety, crusty, grouchy (informal), gruff, grumpy, rude, snaky (Australian informal), sullen, testy, unfriendly.

surmise verb assume, conjecture, guess, infer, presume, speculate, suppose, suspect.

surmount verb **1** conquer, get over, overcome, prevail over, triumph over. **2** cap, crown, top.

surname noun family name, last name.

surpass verb beat, do better than, eclipse, exceed, excel, go beyond, outclass, outdo, outshine, outstrip, overshadow, top, transcend.

surplus noun excess, glut, residue, surfeit.

surprise noun **1** bolt from the blue, bombshell, shock. **2** amazement, astonishment, in credulity, shock, wonder.

surprise verb **1** amaze, astonish, astound, confound, dumbfound, flabbergast, non plus, shock, stagger, startle, stun, take aback. **2** catch, catch red-handed, discover, spring (Australian informal), take unawares. □ **surprising** adjective amazing, astonishing, astounding, incredible, mind boggling (informal), stag gering, startling, unexpected, unforeseen.

surrender verb **1** capitulate, give in, give yourself up, submit, throw in the towel, yield. **2** give, hand over, part with, relinquish.

surreptitious adjective clan destine, covert, furtive, secret, secretive, sly, stealthy, sneaky, underhand.

surround verb beset, besiege, encircle, enclose, encompass, envelop, hem in, ring, skirt.

surroundings plural noun en vironment, environs, milieu, setting.

surveillance noun observa tion, scrutiny, supervision, watch.

survey noun examination, inquiry, inspection, investiga

tion, overview, poll, review, study.

survey *verb* **1** consider, contemplate, examine, explore, inspect, investigate, look at, look over, observe, review, scrutinise, study, view. **2** map out, measure, plot.

survive *verb* **1** continue, endure, exist, keep on, last, live (on), persist, subsist. **2** come through, live through, outlast, outlive, weather. □ **survival** *noun* existence, life, subsistence.

susceptible *adjective* (*susceptible to*) inclined to, liable to, open to, predisposed to, prone to, receptive to, responsive to, sensitive to, subject to, vulnerable to.

suspect *verb* **1** distrust, doubt, have misgivings about, mistrust, question. **2** believe, fancy, guess, have a feeling, have a hunch, imagine, suppose, surmise, think.

suspend *verb* **1** dangle, hang, sling. **2** adjourn, defer, delay, discontinue, interrupt, postpone, put off, shelve. **3** lay off, stand down.

suspense *noun* anticipation, expectation, tension, uncertainty, waiting.

suspicion *noun* **1** distrust, doubt, misgiving, mistrust,

scepticism. **2** feeling, hunch, idea, notion.

suspicious *adjective* **1** disbelieving, distrustful, doubting, incredulous, mistrustful, sceptical, wary. **2** dubious, fishy (*informal*), questionable, shady, suspect, untrustworthy.

sustain *verb* **1** bear, carry, hold, support, take. **2** keep alive, keep going, nourish. **3** continue, keep up, maintain, prolong. **4** experience, suffer, undergo.

swag *noun* **1** booty, loot, plunder, spoils, takings. **2** bluey (*Australian*), drum (*Australian*), matilda (*Australian*), shiralee (*Australian*). **3** heap (*informal*), lot, masses, mountain, pile (*informal*).

swagger *verb* parade, prance, strut.

swagman *noun* bagman (*Australian*), sundowner (*Australian*), swaggie (*Australian*), tramp.

swallow *verb* **1** consume, devour, down (*informal*), eat, gobble, gulp, guzzle, imbibe, ingest, quaff, scoff (*informal*), swig (*informal*), swill. **2** accept, believe, buy (*slang*), fall for (*informal*). □ **swallow up** absorb, assimilate, engulf, swamp.

swamp *noun* bog, fen, marsh, morass, quagmire, slough.

swamp *verb* **1** deluge, engulf, fill, flood, inundate, submerge. **2** deluge, flood, inundate, overwhelm, snow under.

swan *noun* cob (*male*), cygnet (*young*), pen (*female*).

swap *verb* barter, exchange, interchange, substitute, switch, trade. □ **swap** *noun* exchange, substitution.

swarm *noun* army, cluster, crowd, drove, flock, herd, host, mass, mob, multitude, myriad, throng.

swarm *verb* **1** cluster, congregate, crowd, flock, herd, mass, mob, pour, stream, surge, throng. **2** (*swarm with*) be alive with, be crowded with, be overflowing with, be overrun by, crawl with, teem with.

swarthy *adjective* dark, tanned.

swathe *verb* bandage, bind up, cover, envelop, swaddle, wrap.

sway *verb* **1** lurch, reel, rock, stagger, swing, totter, wobble. **2** influence, move, persuade, win over.

swear *verb* **1** pledge, promise, vow. **2** blaspheme, curse. □ **swear-word** *noun* blasphemy, expletive, four-letter word (*informal*), obscenity, profanity.

sweat *noun* lather, perspiration.

sweat *verb* perspire.

sweater *noun* jersey, jumper, pullover, skivvy (*Australian*), sweatshirt, top, windcheater.

sweep *verb* **1** brush, clean, clear. **2** belt (*slang*), charge, dash, fly, race, rush, sail, speed, tear, zoom.

sweeping *adjective* broad, comprehensive, extensive, far-reaching, general, huge, massive, radical, wholesale, wide-ranging.

sweet *adjective* **1** cloying, luscious, saccharine, sickly, sugary, syrupy. **2** balmy, fragrant, perfumed, scented. **3** dulcet, euphonious, harmonious, mellifluous, mellow, melodious, pleasant, tuneful. **4** amiable, appealing, charming, considerate, dear, delightful, endearing, generous, gentle, good-natured, kind, likeable, lovable, lovely, nice, pleasant, thoughtful.

sweet *noun* **1** candy (*American*), confection, lolly (*Australian*), toffee. **2** afters (*informal*), dessert, pudding (*British*).

sweetheart *noun* beloved, boyfriend, darling, dear, fiancé, fiancée, girlfriend, love, lover.

swell verb augment, balloon, billow, bloat, blow up, boost, build up, bulge, distend, expand, grow, grow louder, heighten, increase, inflate, intensify, mount, multiply, puff up, rise, surge.

swell noun **1** increase, rise, surge, upsurge. **2** billows, surge, waves.

swelling noun blister, boil, bulge, bump, inflammation, lump, protuberance.

sweltering adjective boiling, hot, scorching, stifling, sultry, torrid.

swerve verb deviate, sheer, turn, veer.

swift adjective brisk, expeditious, fast, fleet, nimble, nippy (*informal*), prompt, quick, rapid, speedy.

swig verb drink, gulp, guzzle, quaff, swallow, swill. □ **swig** noun draught, gulp, mouthful.

swill verb clean, rinse, wash.

swill noun pigswill, slop.

swim verb bathe, bogey (*Australian*), have a dip. □ **swimming costume** bathers (*Australian*), bathing suit, bikini, cossie (*Australian informal*), swimmers (*Australian*), swimsuit, togs (*Australian informal*), trunks. □ **swimming pool** aquatic centre, baths, pool.

swindle verb cheat, con (*informal*), deceive, defraud, diddle (*informal*), dupe, fleece, hoax, hoodwink, rip off (*informal*), rook, trick. □ **swindle** noun con (*informal*), confidence trick, deception, fraud, hoax, racket, rip-off (*informal*), rort (*Australian slang*), scam (*slang*), swizz (*informal*), trick. □ **swindler** noun charlatan, cheat, con man (*informal*), crook (*informal*), fraud, racketeer, rogue, shark, sharper, shicer (*Australian slang*), shyster (*informal*), trickster.

swing verb **1** be suspended, dangle, flap, oscillate, rock, rotate, see-saw, spin, sway, swivel, turn. **2** alter, change, fluctuate, oscillate, shift, switch, vary, waver.

swing noun **1** stroke, sweep, swipe (*informal*). **2** change, movement, shift, turnaround.

swipe verb **1** belt (*slang*), hit, strike, swing at, whack. **2** grab, nab (*informal*), nick (*slang*), pinch (*informal*), seize, snatch, snitch (*slang*), steal. □ **swipe** noun hit, stroke, swing.

swirl verb eddy, revolve, spin, spiral, twirl, twist, whirl.

swish adjective elegant, fashionable, posh (*informal*), smart, snazzy (*informal*), swanky (*informal*).

switch noun **1** about-face, change, changeover, shift, U-turn, variation. **2** lash, rod, stick, whip.

switch verb **1** flick, turn. **2** change, exchange, interchange, substitute, swap.

swivel verb pivot, revolve, rotate, spin, turn, twirl, whirl.

swollen adjective bloated, bulging, distended, inflated, puffed-up, puffy.

swoop verb **1** descend, dive, plunge, pounce, spring. **2** (*swoop on*) attack, descend on, raid, rush, storm.

sword noun blade, broadsword, claymore, cutlass, foil, rapier, sabre, scimitar, steel (*literary*).

sycophant noun crawler (*informal*), fawner, flatterer, lackey, toady, truckler, yes-man.

symbol noun **1** badge, emblem, insignia, logo, sign, token, trade mark. **2** character, figure, ideogram, letter, mark, pictogram, sign. □ **symbolic** adjective allegorical, figurative, metaphorical.

symbolise verb betoken, denote, express, indicate, mean, represent, signify, stand for.

symmetrical adjective balanced, even, regular. □ **symmetry** noun balance, evenness, harmony, regularity.

sympathise verb **1** (*sympathise with*) commiserate with, empathise with, feel compassion for, feel for, feel sorry for, identify with, offer condolences to, pity, relate to, understand. **2** (*sympathise with*) agree with, approve of, go along with, side with, support. □ **sympathiser** noun comrade, fellow-traveller, supporter.

sympathy noun commiseration, compassion, concern, condolences, empathy, feeling, pity, tenderness, understanding. □ **sympathetic** adjective caring, compassionate, concerned, humane, kind, kindly, merciful, supportive, tender-hearted, understanding, warm-hearted.

symptom noun feature, indication, mark, pointer (*informal*), sign, signal.

syndicate noun alliance, association, cartel, consortium, federation, group, league.

synopsis noun abstract, outline, précis, résumé, summary.

synthesis noun amalgamation, blend, combination, fusion, mixture, union.

synthetic *adjective* artificial, fake, imitation, man-made, manufactured.

syringe *noun* hypodermic, needle.

system *noun* **1** arrangement, network, organisation, set-up, structure. **2** approach, method, methodology, order, plan, procedure, routine, scheme, structure, technique, way.

systematic *adjective* business-like, efficient, logical, methodical, ordered, orderly, organised, planned, scientific.

Tt

table *noun* **1** altar, bar, bench, buffet, counter, desk, lectern, stand. **2** chart, list, tabulation.

tableland *noun* highland, plateau.

tablet *noun* **1** capsule, lozenge, pill. **2** panel, plaque, plate, slab.

taboo *adjective* banned, forbidden, prohibited, proscribed, unacceptable, unmentionable.

tacit *adjective* implicit, implied, silent, unspoken, unstated.

taciturn *adjective* quiet, reserved, reticent, silent, uncommunicative, unforthcoming.

tack *noun* **1** drawing pin, nail, pin, staple. **2** approach, course, direction, method, policy, strategy, tactic.

tack *verb* **1** fasten, fix, nail, pin, staple. **2** baste, sew, stitch. □ **tack on** add, annex, append, attach, tag on.

tackle *verb* **1** address, approach, attack, deal with, grapple with, handle, manage, set about. **2** attack, challenge, intercept, take on.

tackle *noun* apparatus, equipment, gear, kit, rig.

tacky *adjective* **1** sticky, wet. **2** cheap, kitsch, shabby, tasteless, tawdry.

tact *noun* courtesy, delicacy, diplomacy, discretion, sensitivity. □ **tactful** *adjective* considerate, courteous, diplomatic, discreet, polite, politic, sensitive, thoughtful. □ **tactless** *adjective* impolite, impolitic, inconsiderate, indiscreet, insensitive, thoughtless, undiplomatic.

tactic *noun* approach, manoeuvre, plan, ploy (*informal*), policy, scheme, strategy, tack.

tag *noun* label, sticker, tab, ticket.

tag verb **1** identify, label, mark, ticket. **2** add, append, attach, tack. **3** (*tag along with*) accompany, come with, follow, go with, trail after.

tail noun **1** brush, dock, scut. **2** back, end, rear.

tail verb dog, follow, pursue, shadow, stalk, track, trail.

tailor noun clothier, couturier, dressmaker, outfitter.

taint verb (*taint the water*) contaminate, infect, poison, pollute, spoil; (*taint a reputation*) blacken, blemish, blot, stain, sully, tarnish.

take verb **1** clasp, clutch, grab, grasp, hold, pluck, seize, snatch. **2** acquire, gain, get, obtain, receive, scoop up, secure, win. **3** abduct, capture, carry off, catch, detain, seize. **4** catch, travel by, use. **5** accompany, bring, carry, conduct, convey, deliver, escort, guide, lead, run, transport. **6** appropriate, help yourself to, lift (*informal*), make off with, nick (*slang*), pilfer, pinch (*informal*), poach, pocket, purloin, remove, snaffle (*informal*), snatch, snavel (*Australian informal*), snitch (*slang*), souvenir (*slang*), steal, swipe (*informal*). **7** (*of a student*) learn, read, study; (*of a teacher*) instruct in, lecture in, teach, tutor in.

8 be affected by, experience, feel, get. **9** accept, bear, endure, put up with, stand, stomach, suffer, tolerate, undergo, withstand. **10** call for, demand, need, require. **11** deduct, subtract. **12** assume, conclude, construe, gather, infer, interpret, suppose, understand. □ **take after** be the (spitting) image of, look like, resemble. □ **take away** **1** appropriate, commandeer, confiscate, deprive someone of, impound, remove, seize. **2** deduct, subtract. □ **take back** recant, retract, revoke, withdraw. □ **take in** **1** absorb, assimilate, comprehend, digest, grasp, realise, understand. **2** cheat, con (*informal*), deceive, dupe, fool, have on (*informal*), hoodwink, mislead, trick. □ **take off** **1** doff, peel off, remove, shed, strip off. **2** caricature, imitate, lampoon, mimic, parody, send up (*informal*). □ **take-off** noun caricature, imitation, lampoon, parody, send-up (*informal*), spoof (*informal*). □ **take on** **1** appoint, employ, engage, hire, recruit. **2** accept, assume, shoulder, undertake. □ **take out** draw out, extract, pull out, remove. □ **take place** befall, come about, come to pass, happen, occur. □ **take up** **1** begin, commence, embark on, start. **2** consume, eat up, fill, make inroads into, occupy, use up.

takings *plural noun* earnings, income, proceeds, receipts, revenue.

tale *noun* account, anecdote, fable, fairy tale, legend, myth, narrative, saga, story, yarn (*informal*).

talent *noun* ability, accomplishment, aptitude, bent, capacity, flair, genius, gift, knack, know-how, prowess, skill.

talk *verb* babble, chat, chatter, communicate, confer, converse, gabble, gossip, jabber, lecture, mag (*Australian informal*), natter (*informal*), prattle, preach, rabbit on (*informal*), speak, unburden yourself, verbalise, vocalise, yabber (*Australian informal*), yak (*informal*). □ **talker** *noun* chatterbox, conversationalist, gasbag (*informal*), orator, speaker, windbag (*informal*). □ **talk down to** condescend to, patronise. □ **talk into** cajole into, coax into, convince to, persuade to. □ **talk out of** deter from, discourage from, dissuade from, stop.

talk *noun* **1** chat, chinwag (*informal*), confabulation, conference, consultation, conversation, dialogue, discussion, gossip, natter (*informal*), tête-à-tête, yabber (*Australian informal*), yak (*informal*). **2** address, discourse, lecture, oration, presentation, sermon, speech. **3** gossip, hearsay, report, rumour.

talkative *adjective* chatty, communicative, garrulous, loquacious, voluble.

tall *adjective* (*a tall person*) gangling, gigantic, lanky, leggy; (*a tall building*) high, lofty, multi-storey, towering.

tally *noun* account, count, reckoning, record, score, total.

tally *verb* accord, agree, coincide, concur, conform, correspond, match, square.

tame *adjective* **1** docile, domestic, domesticated, gentle. **2** bland, boring, dull, flat, unexciting, uninteresting.

tame *verb* break in, domesticate, subdue, train.

tamper *verb* tamper with fiddle with, interfere with, meddle with, muck around with, play with, tinker with.

tan *adjective* bronze, brownish-yellow, khaki, tawny, yellowish-brown.

tan *verb* bronze, brown, suntan.

tang *noun* bite, piquancy, pungency, savour, sharpness, spiciness.

tangible *adjective* concrete, definite, objective, palpable, real, solid, substantial.

tangle *verb* confuse, entangle, entwine, knot, ravel, snarl, twist. □ **tangle** *noun* confusion, jumble, jungle, knot, maze, muddle, snarl, web. □ **tangled** *adjective* dishevelled, knotted, knotty, matted, ruffled, tousled, unkempt.

tank *noun* cistern, reservoir, vat.

tantalise *verb* entice, lead on, tease, tempt, torment.

tantamount *adjective* as good as, equal, equivalent, the same as.

tantrum *noun* fit of temper, hysterics, outburst, paddy (*informal*), rage.

tap *noun* faucet, stopcock, valve.

tap *verb* **1** drain, draw off, extract, siphon off. **2** draw on, exploit, make use of, milk, use.

tap *noun* knock, patter, pit-a-pat, rap.

tap *verb* beat, drum, hit, knock, patter, rap, strike.

tape *noun* **1** binding, ribbon, strip. **2** audiotape, cassette, video, videotape.

tape *verb* **1** bind, fasten, fix, seal, sellotape, stick. **2** record, tape-record, video, videotape.

taper *verb* narrow, thin.

target *noun* **1** aim, goal, object, objective. **2** butt, object, scapegoat, victim.

tariff *noun* charges, fees, prices, rates.

tarnish *verb* **1** blacken, discolour, dull, stain. **2** besmirch, blacken, blemish, mar, smirch, spoil, stain, sully, taint.

tart *noun* flan, pastry, pie, quiche, tartlet.

tart *adjective* **1** acid, acidic, astringent, piquant, pungent, sharp, sour, tangy. **2** acid, biting, caustic, cutting, sharp, trenchant.

task *noun* assignment, charge, chore, commission, duty, errand, function, job, mission, work. □ **take to task** admonish, castigate, censure, chastise, chide (*old use*), criticise, rebuke, reprimand, reproach, reprove, scold, tell off (*informal*), tick off (*informal*), upbraid.

taskmaster *noun* boss, disciplinarian, martinet, slave driver, tyrant.

taste *verb* sample, savour, sip, test, try.

taste *noun* **1** flavour, savour, tang. **2** discernment, discrimination, judgement, refinement, style. **3** appetite fondness, inclination, liking, love, partiality, penchant, predilection. **4** bit, bite, morsel, mouthful, nibble, piece, sample, sip, swallow, titbit.

tasteful *adjective* aesthetic, artistic, attractive, elegant, graceful, handsome, refined, stylish.

tasteless *adjective* **1** bland, flavourless, insipid, weak, wishy-washy. **2** cheap, coarse, crude, garish, gaudy, improper, indelicate, inelegant, kitsch, offensive, rude, showy, tacky (*informal*), tawdry, unattractive, unseemly, vulgar.

tasty *adjective* appetising, delectable, delicious, flavoursome, luscious, mouth-watering, palatable, piquant, savoury, scrumptious (*informal*), yummy (*informal*).

tattered *adjective* frayed, holey, ragged, ripped, tatty (*informal*), threadbare, torn, worn-out.

tatters *plural noun* rags, shreds.

tatty *adjective* frayed, holey, moth-eaten, old, patched, ragged, scruffy, shabby, tattered, untidy, worn.

taunt *verb* chiack (*Australian informal*), deride, gibe, jeer at, make fun of, mock, poke borak at (*Australian informal*), poke fun at, ridicule, scoff at, sling off at (*Australian informal*), sneer at, take the mickey out of (*informal*), tease, torment. ◻ **taunt** *noun* barb, dig, gibe, insult, jeer, sneer.

taut *adjective* stretched, tense, tight.

tawdry *adjective* cheap, flashy, garish, gaudy, kitsch, showy, tacky (*informal*), tasteless, tatty (*informal*).

tax *noun* charge, customs, duty, excise, impost, levy, rates, slug (*Australian informal*), tariff, taxation, tithe (*historical*), toll, tribute (*historical*).

tax *verb* burden, challenge, exhaust, overload, overwork, strain, stretch, tire. ◻ **taxing** *adjective* challenging, demanding, difficult, draining, exacting, exhausting, hard, onerous, strenuous, stressful, tiring, tough.

taxi *noun* cab, taxi-cab.

teach *verb* coach, drill, edify, educate, enlighten, implant, inculcate, indoctrinate, inform, instil, instruct, lecture, school, train, tutor.

teacher *noun* chalkie (*Australian slang*), coach, educator, governess, guide, guru, headmaster, headmistress, instructor, lecturer, master, mentor, mistress, pedagogue (*old use*), preacher, principal, professor, rabbi, schoolie (*Australian slang*), schoolmaster, schoolmistress, schoolteacher, trainer, tutor.

teaching noun **1** education, instruction, training, tuition. **2** doctrine, dogma, precept, principle, tenet.

team noun **1** club, line-up, side, squad. **2** band, corps, crew, force, gang, group, staff, unit. □ **teamwork** noun collaboration, cooperation.

team verb (*team up*) band together, collaborate, combine, cooperate, join forces, unite.

tear verb **1** gash, lacerate, ladder, mangle, mutilate, rend, rip, rupture, shred, slash, slit, snag, split. **2** bolt, dart, dash, fly, gallop, hurry, hurtle, race, rip, run, rush, shoot, speed, sprint, spurt, streak, sweep, whiz, zip. **3** grab, pluck, pull, rip, seize, snatch.

tear noun gash, hole, laceration, rent, rip, rupture, slash, slit, split.

tearful adjective crying, emotional, lachrymose, maudlin, sobbing, teary (*informal*), upset, weepy (*informal*).

tease verb annoy, bait, bother, chaff, chiack (*Australian informal*), gibe, make fun of, molest, needle, pay out, pester,

poke borak at (*Australian informal*), poke fun at, provoke, rag, rib (*informal*), ridicule, sling off a (*Australian informal*), stir (*informal*), take the mickey out of (*informal*), tantalise, taunt, torment.

teat noun dug, nipple.

technical adjective **1** applied, mechanical, practical. **2** scientific, specialised, specialist.

technique noun approach, art, craft, knack, manner, method, procedure, skill, system, trick, way.

tedious adjective boring, dreary, dull, humdrum, laborious, long-winded, monotonous, stodgy, tiresome, tiring, unexciting, uninteresting, wearisome.

teem verb **1** abound, be full (of), be overrun, brim, overflow, seethe, swarm. **2** bucket down, pelt, pour, rain, rain cats and dogs (*informal*).

teenager noun adolescent, juvenile, minor, youth.

teeter verb lurch, reel, stagger, sway, totter, wobble.

teetotal adjective abstinent, non-drinking, temperate. □ **teetotaller** noun abstainer, non-drinker, wowser (*Australian*).

telepathic *adjective* psychic.

telephone *noun* blower (*informal*), phone.

telephone *verb* call, dial, give someone a bell (*informal*), give someone a buzz (*informal*), give someone a call, phone, ring (up).

televise *verb* broadcast, screen, telecast, transmit.

television *noun* television receiver, television set, telly (*informal*), the box (*informal*), TV.

tell *verb* **1** acquaint (with), advise, announce, apprise (*formal*), broadcast, chronicle, communicate, confess, describe, disclose, divulge, explain, impart, inform, make known, mention, narrate, notify, proclaim, recite, recount, relate, report, reveal, state, warn. **2** say, speak, utter. **3** bid, command, direct, instruct, order. **4** blab, give the show away, let the cat out of the bag, spill the beans (*slang*), squeal (*slang*), talk, tittle-tattle; (*tell on*) betray, blow the whistle on (*informal*), dob in (*Australian informal*), grass (on) (*slang*), inform on, rat on (*slang*), report, shop (*slang*), sneak on (*slang*), split on (*slang*). **5** determine, discern, discover, distinguish, identify,

make out, recognise. □ **tell off** admonish, blast (*informal*), castigate, censure, chastise, go crook at (*Australian informal*), lecture, rebuke, reprimand, reproach, rouse on (*Australian informal*), scold, tick off (*informal*).

telling *adjective* effective, forceful, powerful, significant, strong, weighty.

tell-tale *noun* blabbermouth, dobber (*Australian informal*), grass (*slang*), informer, sneak (*informal*), tale-bearer.

tell-tale *adjective* give-away (*informal*), indicative, meaningful, revealing, significant.

temerity *noun* audacity, boldness, cheek, effrontery, gall, hide, impertinence, impudence, nerve, presumption, rashness.

temper *noun* **1** disposition, frame of mind, humour, mood. **2** anger, fury, hotheadedness, irascibility, ire, irritation, paddy (*informal*), peevishness, petulance, pique, rage, tantrum, wrath.

temper *verb* mitigate, moderate, palliate, soften, tone down.

temperament *noun* character, disposition, make-up, nature, personality, spirit, temper.

temperamental *adjective* capricious, changeable, emotional, erratic, excitable, fickle, highly-strung, hotheaded, mercurial, moody, touchy, unpredictable, volatile.

temperate *adjective* gentle, mild, moderate.

tempest *noun* cyclone, gale, hurricane, storm, tornado, typhoon.

tempestuous *adjective* blustery, rough, squally, stormy, turbulent, violent, wild, windy.

temple *noun* church, gurdwara, mosque, pagoda, sanctuary, shrine, stupa, synagogue, tabernacle.

tempo *noun* pace, rate, speed.

temporary *adjective* brief, ephemeral, fleeting, impermanent, interim, makeshift, momentary, passing, provisional, short-lived, short-term, stopgap, transient, transitory.

tempt *verb* allure, attract, bait, coax, entice, inveigle, lure, seduce, tantalise. □ **temptation** *noun* attraction, bait, draw, enticement, incentive, inducement, lure. □ **tempting** *adjective* alluring, appealing, attractive, enticing, inviting, irresistible, seductive.

tenable *adjective* arguable, defensible, plausible, reasonable, supportable.

tenacious *adjective* **1** firm, iron, powerful, strong, tight. **2** determined, dogged, obstinate, persistent, resolute, staunch, stubborn, unyielding.

tenant *noun* inhabitant, lessee, occupant, resident.

tend *verb* be apt, be disposed, be inclined, be liable, be prone.

tend *verb* attend to, care for, cherish, keep an eye on, keep watch over, look after, mind, nurse, take care of, watch.

tendency *noun* disposition, inclination, penchant, predilection, predisposition, proclivity, propensity, readiness.

tender *adjective* **1** edible, soft, succulent. **2** delicate, fragile, frail, sensitive, vulnerable. **3** affectionate, compassionate, fond, gentle, kind, loving.

tender *verb* give, hand in, offer, present, proffer, submit.

tender *noun* bid, offer, proposal, quotation, quote (*informal*).

tender-hearted *adjective* caring, compassionate, humane, kind, kind-hearted, kindly, merciful, soft-hearted, sympathetic, warm-hearted.

tenet *noun* belief, creed, doctrine, dogma, precept, principle, teaching.

tense *adjective* **1** stiff, strained, stretched, taut, tight

2 anxious, apprehensive, edgy, highly-strung, jumpy, keyed up, nervous, nervy, uneasy, uptight (*informal*). **3** explosive, fraught, nerve-racking, strained, stressful, uneasy, volatile.

tension *noun* **1** stiffness, tautness, tightness. **2** anxiety, apprehension, strain, stress, suspense, uneasiness.

tent *noun* big top, marquee, tepee, wigwam.

tentative *adjective* cautious, experimental, hesitant, provisional, trial, unconfirmed.

term *noun* **1** semester, trimester. **2** course, duration, period, session, spell, stint, stretch, time. **3** expression, name, phrase, word. □ **terms** *plural noun* **1** footing, relations, standing. **2** conditions, provisions, specifications, stipulations. **3** charges, fees, prices, rates.

term *verb* call, designate, label, name.

terminal *noun* depot, station, terminus.

terminal *adjective* deadly, fatal, incurable, mortal.

terminate *verb* cease, close, come to an end, conclude, cut off, end, finish, round off, stop, wind up.

terminology *noun* jargon, language, lingo (*informal*), nomenclature, phraseology, terms, vocabulary, words.

terminus *noun* depot, last stop, station, terminal.

terrain *noun* country, ground, land, landscape, region, territory.

terrible *adjective* abominable, abysmal, appalling, atrocious, awful, bad, catastrophic, disastrous, distressing, dreadful, excruciating, frightful, ghastly, gruesome, hideous, horrendous, horrible, horrific, intolerable, lousy (*informal*), miserable, nasty, rotten (*informal*), shocking, terrifying, unbearable, woeful.

terrific *adjective* **1** astronomical, colossal, enormous, excessive, exorbitant, extravagant, extreme, fierce, huge, intense, large, mighty, monumental, severe, staggering, stupendous, tremendous. **2** admirable, brilliant, excellent, extraordinary, fabulous (*informal*), fantastic (*informal*), fine, first-class, great, incredible, magnificent, marvellous, outstanding, phenomenal, remarkable, sensational, spectacular, splendid, super (*informal*), superb, unbelievable, wonderful.

terrify verb alarm, appal, dismay, freak out (informal), frighten, horrify, petrify, scare, terrorise. □ **terrifying** adjective alarming, frightening, hair-raising, horrifying, nightmarish, scary, spine-chilling.

territory noun area, country, district, domain, land, province, region, state, terrain, tract, zone.

terror noun alarm, consternation, dismay, dread, fear, fright, horror, panic, trepidation.

terrorise verb bully, frighten, intimidate, menace, persecute, terrify, torment.

terse adjective abrupt, brief, brusque, compact, concise, crisp, curt, laconic, pithy, short, snappy (informal), succinct.

test noun analysis, appraisal, assessment, audition, check, evaluation, exam (informal), examination, experiment, quiz, trial, try-out.

test verb appraise, assess, audition, check, evaluate, examine, experiment with, question, quiz, sample, screen, trial, try out.

testify verb affirm, attest, bear witness, declare, give evidence, state under oath, swear.

testimony noun 1 affidavit, declaration, deposition, evidence, statement. 2 demonstration, evidence, indication, manifestation, proof.

testy adjective bad-tempered, cranky, cross, crotchety, grouchy (informal), grumpy, irritable, peevish, petulant, prickly, querulous, shirty (informal), short-tempered, snaky (Australian informal), stroppy (informal), surly, tetchy, touchy.

tether verb chain up, secure, tie up.

tether noun chain, halter, lead, leash, rope. □ **at the end of your tether** at the end of your patience, at your wits' end, desperate.

text noun 1 content, matter, script, transcript, wording, words. 2 passage, quotation, sentence, verse.

textbook noun manual, primer, schoolbook, text.

textiles plural noun cloths, fabrics, materials.

texture noun appearance, composition, consistency, feel, grain, structure, weave.

thank verb acknowledge, express appreciation to, express gratitude to.

thankful *adjective* appreciative, grateful, indebted, obliged, pleased.

thankless *adjective* unappreciated, unrewarding, useless, vain.

thanks *plural noun* acknowledgement, appreciation, gratefulness, gratitude, thankfulness.

thaw *verb* defrost, liquefy, melt, soften, unfreeze.

theatre *noun* auditorium, hall, playhouse.

theatrical *adjective* dramatic, stage.

theft *noun* burglary, embezzlement, larceny, misappropriation, pilfering, poaching, robbery, shoplifting, stealing, thieving.

theme *noun* **1** argument, keynote, matter, subject, topic. **2** air, melody, motif, tune.

theology *noun* divinity, religion.

theoretical *adjective* abstract, academic, conjectural, hypothetical, notional, unproven, untested.

theory *noun* **1** argument, assumption, conjecture, explanation, hypothesis, idea, notion, supposition, surmise, thesis, view. **2** laws, principles, rules, science, system.

therapeutic *adjective* curative, healing, medicinal, remedial, restorative.

therapy *noun* cure, healing, remedy, treatment.

therefore *adverb* accordingly, consequently, hence, so, thus.

thick *adjective* **1** broad, bulky, chunky, deep, fat, solid, squat, stout, stubby, stumpy, wide. **2** broad, fat, wide. **3** abundant, bushy, dense, impenetrable, lush, luxuriant, profuse, rank. **4** concentrated, condensed, heavy, solid, stiff, viscous. **5** dense, dim (*informal*), dull, dumb (*informal*), half-witted, obtuse, slow, stupid, unintelligent. □ **thickness** *noun* **1** breadth, depth, diameter, width. **2** layer, ply.

thicken *verb* clot, coagulate, concentrate, condense, congeal, reduce, set, solidify, stiffen.

thicket *noun* bushes, copse, grove, spinney, wood.

thickset *adjective* beefy, brawny, burly, heavy, husky, nuggety (*Australian*), solid, stocky, sturdy.

thief *noun* bandit, brigand, burglar, bushranger, crook (*informal*), highwayman, housebreaker, kleptomaniac, looter, mugger, pickpocket, pilferer, robber, shoplifter.

thin adjective **1** fine, narrow. **2** delicate, diaphanous, fine, flimsy, fragile, light, see-through, sheer, transparent. **3** bony, emaciated, gangling, gaunt, lanky, lean, puny, scraggy, scrawny, skinny, slender, slight, slim, spare, spindly, weedy, wiry. **4** light, meagre, scant, scanty, sparse, wispy. **5** dilute, runny, watery. **6** feeble, flimsy, inadequate, lame.

thin verb dilute, water down, weaken.

thing noun **1** article, commodity, device, item, object, product. **2** (a thing to happen, do, etc.) act, affair, business, deed, doing, event, feat, happening, incident, occurrence, phenomenon; (a thing to discuss) aspect, concern, detail, fact, feature, item, matter, particular. □ **things** plural noun **1** belongings, bits and pieces, chattels, clothes, effects, equipment, gear, goods, paraphernalia, possessions, property, stuff. **2** circumstances, conditions, matters, the situation.

think verb **1** brood, cogitate, consider, contemplate, deliberate, meditate, mull over, muse, ponder, rack your brains, reason, reflect,

ruminate. **2** assume, believe, conjecture, consider, deem, expect, hold, imagine, judge, reckon, regard, suppose, surmise. □ **think up** conceive, concoct, create, devise, dream up, invent, make up.

thirst noun appetite, craving, desire, fancy, hankering, hunger, longing, lust, passion, yearning. □ **thirsty** adjective dehydrated, dry, parched.

thong noun belt, lash, strap, strip.

thorn noun barb, needle, prickle, spike, spine.

thorny adjective **1** barbed, prickly, spiky, spiny. **2** complicated, difficult, hard, intricate, knotty, problematic, ticklish, troublesome.

thorough adjective **1** (a thorough account) blow-by-blow, close, complete, comprehensive, detailed, exhaustive, extensive, full, in-depth, minute; (a thorough worker) careful, conscientious, diligent, methodical, meticulous, painstaking, punctilious, rigorous, scrupulous, systematic. **2** absolute, complete, downright, out-and-out, outright, total, utter.

thoroughbred adjective pedigree, pure-bred.

thought noun **1** belief, concept, idea, notion, opinion, sentiment, view. **2** contemplation, daydreaming, deliberation, introspection, meditation, reasoning, reflection, reverie, rumination, thinking.

thoughtful adjective **1** absorbed, broody, contemplative, introspective, pensive, reflective, serious, wistful. **2** attentive, caring, concerned, considerate, helpful, kind, obliging, solicitous.

thoughtless adjective **1** absentminded, careless, forgetful, heedless, negligent, scatterbrained, unthinking. **2** inconsiderate, indiscreet, insensitive, rude, selfish, tactless, unfeeling.

thrash verb **1** beat, belt (*slang*), cane, flog, hit, lash, lay into (*informal*), quilt (*Australian slang*), scourge, tan (*slang*), wallop (*slang*), whack, whip. **2** beat, clobber (*slang*), defeat, drub, lick (*informal*), overwhelm, paste (*slang*), pulverise, rout, slaughter, trounce.

thread noun fibre, filament, strand, yarn.

threadbare adjective frayed, holey, ragged, shabby, tattered, tatty (*informal*), thin, worn.

threat noun **1** intimidation, menace, warning. **2** danger, hazard, menace, risk.

threaten verb **1** bully, intimidate, menace, terrorise. **2** endanger, imperil, jeopardise, put at risk.

threshold noun **1** doorstep, doorway, entrance. **2** beginning, brink, dawn, outset, start, verge.

thrifty adjective economical, frugal, provident, sparing.

thrill noun buzz (*informal*), enjoyment, excitement, kick (*informal*), pleasure, quiver, shiver, tingle.

thrill verb delight, electrify, excite, rouse, stir, wow (*slang*). □ **thrilling** adjective electrifying, exciting, exhilarating, heady, rousing, sensational, stirring.

thrive verb boom, burgeon, do well, flourish, grow, prosper, succeed.

throat noun gullet, oesophagus, trachea, windpipe.

throaty adjective deep, gruff, guttural, hoarse, husky, rasping.

throb verb beat, palpitate, pound, pulsate, pulse, thump, vibrate.

throng noun crowd, gathering, herd, horde, host, mass, mob, multitude, swarm.

throng verb congregate, crowd, flock, gather, herd, mill, press, swarm.

throttle verb choke, garrotte, strangle, suffocate.

throw verb **1** bowl, cast, chuck (*informal*), fling, heave, hurl, launch, lob, pelt, pitch, project, propel, shy, sling, toss. **2** bung (*informal*), chuck (*informal*), dump, plonk, slam, toss. □ **throw** noun delivery, fling, hurl, launch, lob, pitch, shot, shy, toss. □ **throw away 1** cast off, chuck out (*informal*), discard, dispose of, ditch (*slang*), dump, get rid of, jettison, reject, scrap, throw out. **2** blow (*informal*), squander, waste. □ **throw up** barf (*slang*), be ill, be sick, chuck (*informal*), chunder (*Australian slang*), puke (*informal*), sick up (*informal*), spew, vomit.

thrust verb **1** drive, elbow, force, jostle, propel, push, ram, shoulder, shove. **2** jab, lunge, pierce, plunge, poke, stab, stick.

thud verb & noun bump, clunk, crash, thump.

thug noun bully, delinquent, gangster, hoodlum, hooligan, mugger, rough, ruffian, tough.

thumb verb browse, flick, flip, leaf, skim.

thump verb **1** bash, batter, beat, clobber (*slang*), clout (*informal*), hammer, hit, knock, pound, punch, quilt (*Australian slang*), slog, slug, sock (*slang*), stoush (*Australian slang*), strike, thwack, wallop (*slang*), whack. **2** bang, bump, clunk, crash, thud.

thunder noun boom, roar, roll, rumble.

thus adverb accordingly, consequently, hence, so, therefore.

thwart verb baulk, block, foil, frustrate, hamper, hinder, obstruct, prevent, stonker (*Australian slang*), stymie (*informal*).

tic noun spasm, twitch.

tick noun flash, instant, jiffy, minute, moment, second, trice.

tick verb □ **tick off** admonish, castigate, censure, chastise, chide (*old use*), lecture, rap over the knuckles, rebuke, reprimand, reproach, scold, tell off (*informal*), upbraid.

ticket noun **1** coupon, pass, permit, token, voucher. **2** label, tab, tag.

tickle verb **1** stroke, touch. **2** itch, tingle. **3** amuse, delight, divert, entertain, please, titillate.

ticklish adjective awkward, delicate, difficult, knotty, problematic, thorny, tricky.

tide noun current, ebb and flow.

tidy adjective **1** methodical, neat, orderly, presentable, shipshape, smart, spick and span, spruce, straight, systematic, trim, uncluttered, well-groomed. **2** considerable, goodly, handsome, sizeable, substantial.

tidy verb arrange, clean up, groom, neaten, organise, smarten up, sort out, spruce up, straighten, titivate (*informal*).

tie verb **1** attach, bind, connect, couple, fasten, hitch, join, knot, lace, lash, link, moor, secure, strap, tether, truss, unite, yoke. **2** be equal, be even, be level, be neck and neck, draw.

tie noun **1** bow tie, cravat, necktie. **2** dead heat, draw, stalemate.

tier noun bank, layer, level, line, rank, row.

tiff noun altercation, argument, barney (*informal*), blue (*Australian informal*), disagreement, quarrel, row, squabble.

tight adjective **1** close-fitting, skintight, snug. **2** fast, firm, fixed, secure. **3** stiff, stretched, taut, tense. **4** mean, miserly, niggardly, parsimonious, penny-pinching, stingy, tight-fisted.

tighten verb constrict, contract, narrow, stiffen, stretch, tauten, tense.

till noun cash drawer, cash register, peter (*Australian slang*).

till verb cultivate, farm, plough, work.

tilt verb bank, cant, heel over, incline, keel over, lean, list, slope, sway, tip.

tilt noun cant, incline, rake, slant, slope.

timber noun beams, boards, logs, lumber, planks, wood.

time noun **1** age, days, epoch, era, period. **2** date, day, hour, instant, juncture, moment, point, stage. **3** moment, occasion, opportunity. **4** duration, interval, period, phase, season, session, span, spell, stretch, term, while. □ **on time** on schedule, on the dot, on the knocker (*Australian informal*), punctually.

timeless adjective abiding, ageless, enduring, eternal, everlasting, immutable, indestructible, permanent, unchanging.

timely adjective opportune, seasonable, well-timed.

timetable noun programme, schedule.

timid adjective bashful, chicken (*informal*), cowardly, coy, diffident, faint-hearted, fearful, frightened, mousy, nervous, pusillanimous, sheepish, shy, sooky (*Australian informal*), timorous, underconfident, unheroic, wussy (*slang*).

tin noun can, canister.

tinge verb colour, dye, shade, stain, tint. □ **tinge** noun colour, shade, tincture, tint; (*a tinge of sadness, etc.*) hint, suggestion, touch, trace.

tingle verb prickle, sting, tickle.

tinker verb fiddle, mess about, play, potter, toy.

tinkle verb & noun chime, ding, jingle, peal, ring.

tint noun colour, dye, hue, pigment, shade, stain, tincture, tinge, tone.

tiny adjective baby, compact, diminutive, dwarf, imperceptible, infinitesimal, insignificant, little, microscopic, midget, miniature, minuscule, minute, negligible, piccaninny, pocket-sized, pygmy, skimpy, small, teeny (*informal*), trifling, undersized, wee (*informal*), weeny (*informal*).

tip noun apex, cap, crest, crown, end, extremity, peak, pinnacle, point, summit, top.

tip noun **1** gift, gratuity, present. **2** advice, clue, hint, pointer, suggestion, warning, wrinkle (*informal*).

tip verb cant, heel over, incline, lean, list, tilt. □ **tip over** capsize, keel over, knock over, overturn, spill, topple over, upend, upset, upturn.

tip noun dump, garbage dump, refuse dump, rubbish dump.

tipsy adjective inebriated, intoxicated, jolly, merry (*informal*), slightly drunk, tiddly (*informal*).

tirade noun denunciation, diatribe, harangue, lecture.

tire verb drain, exhaust, fatigue, wear out, weary. □ **tiring** adjective arduous, exacting, exhausting, hard, laborious, onerous, strenuous, taxing, tiresome, wearing, wearisome, wearying.

tired adjective all in (*informal*), beat (*slang*), bushed (*informal*), dog-tired, done in (*informal*), drained, drowsy, exhausted, fagged (*informal*), fatigued, jaded, languid, listless, pooped (*informal*), sapped, sleepy, weary, whacked (*informal*), worn out, zapped (*slang*), zonked (*slang*). □ **tiredness** noun drowsiness, exhaustion, fatigue, languor, lassitude, lethargy, listlessness, sleepiness, weariness. □ **tired of** bored of, browned off with (*slang*), fed up with, jack of (*Australian slang*), sick of.

tireless *adjective* energetic, hard-working, indefatigable, industrious, unflagging, untiring.

tiresome *adjective* annoying, boring, bothersome, dreary, dull, exasperating, irksome, irritating, tedious, troublesome, uninteresting, wearisome.

titbit *noun* bit, delicacy, morsel, nibble, snack.

titillate *verb* arouse, excite, stimulate, tantalise, tickle, turn on (*informal*).

title *noun* **1** caption, heading, inscription, name. **2** appellation, designation, position, rank, status.

titter *verb* & *noun* chuckle, giggle, snicker, snigger.

toady *verb* crawl (*informal*), curry favour (with), fawn (on), grovel, kowtow, play up, suck up (*informal*), truckle. □ **toady** *noun* crawler (*informal*), flatterer, flunkey, hanger-on, lackey, parasite, sycophant, truckler, yes-man.

toast *verb* **1** brown, cook, grill. **2** drink to, raise your glass to, salute.

toboggan *noun* luge, sled, sledge.

toddler *noun* baby, child, infant, preschooler.

to-do *noun* bother, commotion, disturbance, excitement, furore, fuss, hue and cry, hullabaloo, kerfuffle (*informal*), outcry, palaver (*informal*), rumpus, stir, storm, turmoil, uproar.

toey *adjective* agitated, anxious, impatient, nervous, restive, restless, uneasy.

together *adverb* **1** closely, cooperatively, in collaboration, jointly, side by side. **2** as one, in chorus, in unison, simultaneously.

toil *verb* beaver away, drudge, labour, slave, slog, strive, sweat, work.

toil *noun* drudgery, effort, exertion, grind, industry, labour, slog, sweat (*informal*), travail (*old use*), work, yakka (*Australian informal*).

toilet *noun* bathroom, convenience, dunny (*Australian slang*), Gents (*informal*), Ladies, latrine, lavatory, loo (*informal*), men's, powder room, privy, rest room, toot (*Australian informal*), urinal, washroom, water closet, WC, women's.

token *noun* **1** counter, disc. **2** coupon, voucher. **3** evidence, expression, indication, keepsake, mark, memento, sign, symbol.

tolerable adjective **1** bearable, endurable. **2** acceptable, adequate, fair, OK (*informal*), passable, reasonable, satisfactory, so-so (*informal*).

tolerant adjective broadminded, charitable, easygoing, forbearing, forgiving, indulgent, lenient, liberal, long-suffering, open-minded, patient, permissive, understanding.

tolerate verb abide, accept, admit, allow, bear, brook, condone, cope with, endure, permit, put up with, sanction, stand, stomach, suffer, take.

toll noun **1** charge, fee, levy, payment, tax. **2** cost, damage, loss.

toll verb chime, peal, ring, sound, strike.

tomb noun crypt, grave, mausoleum, sepulchre, vault.

tombstone noun gravestone, headstone, monument.

tone noun **1** inflection, intonation, modulation, note, pitch, sound, timbre. **2** colour, hue, shade, tinge, tint. **3** atmosphere, character, expression, feeling, manner, mood, note, quality, spirit, style, vein.

tone verb blend, harmonise, match. □ **tone down** moderate, modulate, play down, soften, subdue, temper.

tongue-tied adjective dumb, inarticulate, mute, silent, speechless.

too adverb **1** also, as well, besides, furthermore, in addition. **2** excessively, extremely, overly, unduly.

tool noun apparatus, appliance, contraption, device, gadget, implement, instrument, machine, utensil; (*tools*) equipment, gear, hardware.

toot noun & verb beep, blast, honk, hoot, sound.

top noun **1** apex, brow, crest, crown, head, peak, pinnacle, summit, tip, vertex, zenith. **2** cap, cover, covering, lid, stopper.

top adjective (*the top level*) highest, maximum, supreme, topmost, uppermost; (*the top designers, etc.*) best, foremost, greatest, leading, outstanding, pre-eminent.

top verb **1** cap, cover, crown, finish, garnish. **2** (*top the list*) head, lead; (*top their score*) beat, better, exceed, improve on, outdo, surpass.

topic noun issue, matter, point, subject, theme.

topical *adjective* contemporary, current, live, up to date, up to the minute.

topple *verb* **1** collapse, crash, fall, stumble, tip over, totter, tumble. **2** bring down, oust, overthrow, overturn, unseat.

topsy-turvy *adjective* chaotic, confused, disorderly, higgledy-piggledy, messy, mixed-up, muddled, upside-down.

torch *noun* flashlight.

toreador *noun* bullfighter, matador, picador.

torment *verb* **1** afflict, bedevil, distress, haunt, plague, rack, torture, trouble, worry. **2** annoy, bait, harass, intimidate, molest, oppress, persecute, pester, plague, provoke, tease, victimise.

torment *noun* agony, anguish, distress, hell, misery, pain, suffering, torture.

torn *adjective* holey, ragged, rent, ripped, slit, split, tattered, tatty (*informal*).

tornado *noun* twister (*American*), whirlwind; see also *STORM*.

torpor *noun* drowsiness, inertia, languor, lassitude, lethargy, listlessness, sleepiness, sluggishness, somnolence.

torrent *noun* **1** cascade, deluge, flood, rush, spate, stream. **2** deluge, downpour.

tortuous *adjective* circuitous, convoluted, crooked, serpentine, sinuous, twisting, winding, zigzag.

torture *verb* abuse, afflict, distress, maltreat, mistreat, persecute, plague, punish, rack, torment, trouble, worry. □ **torture** *noun* agony, anguish, pain, suffering, torment.

toss *verb* **1** bowl, cast, chuck (*informal*), fling, heave, hurl, launch, lob, pitch, propel, shy, sling, throw. **2** bob, bounce, lurch, pitch, reel, rock, roll, squirm, thrash, welter, wriggle, writhe. □ **toss** *noun* delivery, fling, hurl, launch, lob, pitch, throw.

total *adjective* **1** aggregate, combined, complete, cumulative, entire, full, overall, whole. **2** absolute, complete, outright, perfect, pure, sheer, thorough, utter. □ **totally** *adverb* absolutely, completely, entirely, fully, to the hilt, utterly, wholly.

total *noun* aggregate, amount, sum, sum total, whole.

total *verb* **1** add up, calculate, compute, sum, tot up (*informal*), work out. **2** add up to, amount to, come to, make, tot up to (*informal*).

totter *verb* dodder, falter, reel, rock, shake, stagger, stumble, sway, teeter, wobble.

touch *verb* **1** be in contact with, brush, caress, dab, feel, finger, fondle, graze, handle, manipulate, massage, maul, nudge, pat, paw, poke, press, prod, rub, strike, stroke, tap, tickle. **2** fiddle with, interfere with, meddle with, play with, tamper with, tinker with. **3** affect, impress, move, stir. □ **touch-and-go** *adjective* chancy, dicey (*slang*), doubtful, iffy (*informal*), precarious, risky, uncertain. □ **touch down** arrive, land. □ **touch up** enhance, fix up, improve, repair.

touch *noun* **1** dash, hint, pinch, soupçon, suggestion, suspicion, tinge, trace, whiff. **2** ability, dexterity, finesse, flair, knack, skill, technique. **3** contact, communication, correspondence.

touching *adjective* emotional, moving, poignant, rousing, stirring.

touchy *adjective* over-sensitive, prickly, sensitive, thin-skinned.

tough *adjective* **1** durable, hard-wearing, hardy, heavy-duty, indestructible, resistant, serviceable, strong, sturdy, unbreakable. **2** chewy, gristly, leathery. **3** beefy, brawny, burly, fit, hardy, robust, rugged, strapping, strong, sturdy. **4** firm, inflexible, merciless, rigid, strict, stubborn, uncompromising. **5** arduous, challenging, demanding, difficult, exacting, formidable, gruelling, hard, laborious, onerous, stiff, strenuous, taxing, uphill.

toughen *verb* fortify, harden, reinforce, strengthen.

tour *noun* excursion, expedition, jaunt, journey, outing, trip.

tour *verb* explore, go round, holiday in, travel round, visit.

tourist *noun* globe-trotter, holidaymaker, sightseer, traveller, tripper, visitor.

tournament *noun* championship, competition, contest, event, series.

tow *verb* drag, draw, haul, pull, tug.

tower *noun* belfry, keep, minaret, pagoda, skyscraper, steeple, turret.

tower *verb* loom, rise, soar, stand out, stick up.

town *noun* big smoke (*informal*), city, community, metropolis, settlement, township.

toxic *adjective* deadly, lethal, poisonous.

toy *noun* game, plaything.

toy *verb* □ **toy with** fiddle with, flirt with, play with, trifle with, twiddle with.

trace *noun* **1** evidence, indication, mark, sign, track, trail. **2** bit, dash, drop, element, hint, overtone, pinch, shade, shadow, suggestion, suspicion, tinge, touch.

trace *verb* **1** copy, draw over. **2** discover, find, follow, hunt down, locate, pursue, recover, retrieve, track down.

track *noun* **1** footprint, mark, print, scent, spoor, trace, trail. **2** lane, path, road, trail, way. **3** circuit, course, racecourse, racetrack. **4** line, rails, railway line.

track *verb* follow, hunt, pursue, shadow, stalk, tail (*informal*), trail. □ **track down** discover, find, locate, recover, retrieve, trace.

tract *noun* area, expanse, region, stretch, zone.

trade *noun* **1** barter, business, buying and selling, commerce, dealing, exchange, traffic, transactions. **2** business, field, industry. **3** calling, career, craft, employment, job, occupation, vocation, work. □ **trade mark** brand, crest,

emblem, hallmark, logo, name, proprietary name, symbol.

trade *verb* barter, buy and sell, deal, do business, exchange, market, swap, traffic. □ **trader** *noun* dealer, merchant, retailer, seller, shopkeeper, supplier, vendor.

tradesman *noun* artisan, craftsman, workman.

tradition *noun* convention, custom, habit, institution, practice, ritual. □ **traditional** *adjective* classical, conventional, customary, established, habitual, orthodox, set, standard, time-honoured.

traffic *verb* deal, peddle, push (*informal*), sell, trade.

tragedy *noun* calamity, catastrophe, disaster, misfortune.

tragic *adjective* appalling, calamitous, catastrophic, dire, disastrous, distressing, ghastly, heartbreaking, pathetic, pitiful, sad, terrible, unfortunate, wretched.

trail *noun* **1** footmarks, footprints, marks, scent, spoor, traces, track, wake. **2** lane, path, track.

trail *verb* **1** follow, hound, pursue, shadow, stalk, tail (*informal*), track. **2** drag, draw, haul, pull, tow. **3** dally, dawdle, drop behind, fall behind, lag, straggle. **4** dangle, drag, hang, sweep.

trailer noun advertisement, clip, extract, preview.

train noun **1** caravan, cavalcade, column, convoy, cortège, file, line, motorcade, procession. **2** chain, sequence, series, set, string, succession.

train verb **1** coach, condition, discipline, drill, educate, instruct, teach. **2** exercise, practise, prepare, work out. **3** aim, direct, focus, level, point.

trainee noun apprentice, beginner, cadet, learner, novice, student.

trainer noun coach, instructor, teacher, tutor.

traipse verb plod, tramp, trek, trudge, walk.

trait noun attribute, characteristic, feature, idiosyncrasy, peculiarity, quality.

traitor noun betrayer, collaborator, deserter, informer, Judas, quisling, renegade, snake in the grass, turncoat.

tramp noun beggar, down-and-out, hobo, sundowner (Australian), swagman (Australian), vagabond, vagrant.

tramp verb **1** clomp, clump, stamp, stomp, stride. **2** hike, march, plod, ramble, slog,

traipse (informal), trek trudge, walk.

trample verb crush, flatten squash, stamp on, step on tramp on, tread on, walk on.

tranquil adjective calm collected, composed, peaceful placid, quiet, restful, sedate serene, still, undisturbed unflappable (informal), un troubled.

transact verb carry out conduct, execute, handle manage, negotiate, perform ☐ **transaction** noun deal dealing, negotiation, under taking.

transcend verb eclipse, exceed go beyond, outshine, outstrip overshadow, surpass.

transfer verb carry, convey deliver, move, relocate remove, shift, shunt, switch take, transplant, transport.

transfix verb **1** impale, pierce skewer, spike, stab. **2** freeze paralyse, petrify, rivet, root to the spot.

transform verb alter, change convert, metamorphose modify, remodel, turn ☐ **transformation** noun altera tion, change, conversion facelift, makeover, meta morphosis, revolution.

transgress verb **1** breach break, contravene, infringe offend against, violate. **2** do wrong, err, go astray, sin, trespass (*old use*).

transient *adjective* brief, ephemeral, fleeting, impermanent, momentary, passing, short-lived, temporary, transitory.

transit *noun* conveyance, movement, passage, shipment, transfer, transport, transportation.

transition *noun* change, changeover, conversion, development, evolution, metamorphosis, move, progression, shift, switch, transformation.

translate *verb* change, convert, decipher, decode, interpret, paraphrase, render, rephrase, reword.

transmit *verb* **1** carry, communicate, convey, dispatch, forward, pass on, relay, send, spread, transfer. **2** broadcast, relay, send out.

transparent *adjective* clear, crystal-clear, diaphanous, filmy, gauzy, limpid, see-through, sheer.

transpire *verb* become known, be disclosed, be revealed, come to light, emerge, leak out.

transplant *verb* move, relocate, shift, transfer.

transport *verb* **1** bear, bring, carry, cart, convey, deliver, ferry, fetch, forward, freight, haul, move, shift, ship, take, transfer. **2** banish, deport, exile, expatriate. □ **transportable** *adjective* demountable, mobile, portable.

transport *noun* **1** carriage, conveyance, freight, haulage, shipping, transportation. **2** conveyance, transportation, vehicle, wheels (*slang*).

transpose *verb* interchange, reverse, switch.

trap *noun* **1** gin, net, noose, pitfall, snare. **2** ambush, booby trap, pitfall, snare, trick.

trap *verb* **1** capture, catch, corner, ensnare, snare. **2** catch (out), deceive, dupe, set up (*informal*), trick.

trash *noun* garbage, junk, litter, refuse, rubbish, scraps, waste; see also *NONSENSE*.

traumatic *adjective* distressing, disturbing, painful, shocking, upsetting.

travel *verb* commute, cross, go, journey, move, progress, roam, rove, tour, trek, voyage, wander. □ **travels** *plural noun* excursion, expedition, exploration, globe-trotting, journey, peregrination, pilgrimage, tour, trip, voyage, wandering. □ **traveller** *noun* backpacker, commuter, explorer, globetrotter, gypsy, holidaymaker, nomad, passenger, sightseer, tourist, tripper, vagabond, visitor, voyager, wanderer, wayfarer. □ **travelling** *adjective* itinerant, peripatetic, roving, touring, vagabond, wandering.

traverse *verb* bridge, cross, extend across, go across, pass over, span.

travesty *noun* burlesque, misrepresentation, mockery, parody, perversion.

treacherous *adjective* **1** deceitful, disloyal, duplicitous, false, perfidious, sneaky, traitorous, two-faced, untrustworthy. **2** dangerous, hazardous, perilous, precarious, unsafe. □ **treachery** *noun* betrayal, disloyalty, duplicity, perfidy, treason.

tread *verb* stamp, step, tramp, trample, walk.

treason *noun* betrayal, disloyalty, high treason, traitorousness, treachery.

treasure *noun* cache, fortune, hoard, riches, valuables, wealth.

treasure *verb* appreciate, cherish, esteem, love, prize, value.

treat *verb* **1** behave towards, consider, deal with, handle, look upon, manage, regard, view. **2** deal with, discuss, handle, present, tackle. **3** attend to, care for, look after, minister to, nurse, tend. **4** coat, dress, impregnate, process. **5** buy for, pay for, shout (*Australian informal*), stand.

treat *noun* **1** delight, joy, luxury, pleasure, thrill. **2** gift, present, shout (*Australian informal*).

treatise *noun* article, discourse, dissertation, essay, monograph, paper, study, thesis.

treatment *noun* care, cure, medication, remedy, therapy.

treaty *noun* agreement, alliance, armistice, compact, convention, covenant, deal, pact.

trek *noun* excursion, expedition, hike, journey, tramp, walk.

trek *verb* hike, journey, slog, traipse (*informal*), tramp, trudge, walk.

trellis *noun* frame, grid, grille, lattice.

tremble *verb* quake, quaver, quiver, shake, shiver, shudder, vibrate, wobble. □ **tremble** *noun* quaver, quiver, shake, shiver, shudder, tremor, vibration, wobble.

tremendous *adjective* **1** big, colossal, enormous, gigantic, huge, immense, large, mammoth, massive, terrific (*informal*), vast. **2** excellent, exceptional, fabulous (*informal*), fantastic (*informal*), fine, great, impressive, magnificent, marvellous, remarkable, stupendous, superb, terrific (*informal*), wonderful.

tremor *noun* quaver, quiver, shake, shiver, shudder, tremble, vibration, wobble; (*earth tremor*) earthquake, quake (*informal*), shock.

tremulous *adjective* nervous, quavering, quivering, shaky, shivering, timid, trembling.

trench *noun* ditch, furrow, sap.

trend *noun* **1** direction, drift, inclination, movement, shift, tendency. **2** craze, fad, fashion, mode, style, vogue.

trendy *adjective* contemporary, cool (*informal*), fashionable, in, modern, stylish, up to date, with it (*informal*).

trepidation *noun* alarm, anxiety, apprehension, consternation, dismay, dread, fear, nervousness, panic, uneasiness.

trespass *verb* **1** encroach, intrude, invade. **2** err, offend, sin, transgress.

trespass *noun* iniquity, misdeed, offence, sin, transgression, wrong, wrongdoing.

trial *noun* **1** check, evaluation, experiment, test, try-out. **2** case, examination, hearing, inquiry. **3** adversity, affliction, hardship, ordeal, suffering, tribulation, trouble, woe. □ **trial** *adjective* experimental, pilot, probationary, testing.

tribe *noun* clan, community, family, people, race.

tribulation *noun* adversity, affliction, anxiety, distress, hardship, misery, misfortune, ordeal, suffering, trial, trouble, woe, worry.

tribunal *noun* board, committee, court, forum.

tributary *noun* branch, creek, rivulet.

tribute *noun* accolade, commendation, compliment, eulogy, panegyric, testimonial. □ **pay tribute to** commend, compliment, honour, laud (*formal*), pay homage to, praise, salute.

trick *noun* **1** bluff, con (*informal*), confidence trick, deception, dodge (*informal*), fraud, hoax, lurk (*Australian informal*), manoeuvre, ploy, ruse, stratagem, subterfuge, wile. **2** gag, hoax, joke, practical joke, prank. **3** art, knack, method, secret, skill, technique, way. **4** illusion, legerdemain, magic, sleight of hand.

trick verb bluff, cheat, con (*informal*), deceive, defraud, dupe, fool, have on (*informal*), hoax, hoodwink, kid (*informal*), mislead, outwit, pull someone's leg, swindle, take in.

trickery noun artifice, cheating, chicanery, craftiness, cunning, deceit, deceitfulness, deception, fraud, hocus-pocus, pretence, skulduggery, sleight of hand, wiliness.

trickle verb dribble, drip, leak, ooze, percolate, seep.

trickster noun charlatan, cheat, con man (*informal*), crook (*informal*), fraud, racketeer, rogue, shark, sharp (*informal*), shicer (*Australian slang*), swindler.

tricky adjective **1** awkward, complicated, dangerous, delicate, difficult, hard, knotty, problematical, risky, ticklish. **2** artful, crafty, cunning, deceitful, foxy, shifty, slippery, sly, underhand, wily.

trifle noun bagatelle, inessential, little thing, nothing, triviality.

trifle verb dally, flirt, play, toy.

trifling adjective inconsequential, insignificant, little,

minor, negligible, paltry, petty, small, superficial, trivial, unimportant.

trigger verb □ **trigger off** initiate, provoke, set off, spark off, start, touch off.

trim adjective neat, orderly, shipshape, spick and span, spruce, tidy.

trim verb **1** bob, clip, crop, cut, shear, snip. **2** adorn, deck, decorate, ornament.

trim noun **1** condition, fettle, form, health, shape. **2** decoration, ornamentation, trimming.

trinket noun bric-à-brac, jewellery, knick-knack, novelty, ornament, trifle.

trio noun threesome, triad, trilogy, trinity, triplets, triumvirate.

trip verb **1** fall over, slip, sprawl, stumble. **2** caper, dance, frolic, gambol, prance, skip. □ **trip up** blunder, bungle, err, slip up (*informal*), stumble.

trip noun cruise, drive, excursion, expedition, flight, holiday, jaunt, journey, outing, run, tour, trek, visit, voyage.

triple adjective **1** tripartite. **2** threefold, treble.

trite adjective banal, clichéd, commonplace, corny, hackneyed, platitudinous, stereo-typed, stock, unoriginal.

triumph noun accomplishment, achievement, conquest, feat, hit (*informal*), smash hit (*informal*), success, victory, winner. □ **triumphant** *adjective* successful, victorious, winning; see also *EXULTANT* (at *EXULT*).

triumph verb be successful, be victorious, conquer, prevail, succeed, win; (*triumph over*) beat, conquer, defeat, over-come, overpower, vanquish.

trivial adjective inconsequen-tial, insignificant, little, minor, negligible, paltry, petty, small, superficial, trifling, un-important.

troop noun band, company, crew, flock, gang, group, horde, mob, pack. □ **troops** *plural noun* armed forces, army, military, servicemen, service-women, soldiers.

troop verb file, march, parade.

trophy noun award, cup, medal, prize, shield.

trouble noun **1** adversity, anxiety, bother, burden, concern, difficulty, distress, hardship, hassle (*informal*), inconvenience, irritation, mis-fortune, nuisance, problem, sorrow, suffering, trial, tribulation, vexation, woe,

worry. **2** affliction, ailment, breakdown, defect, disease, disorder, fault, illness, malfunction, pain, problem. **3** commotion, conflict, discord, disorder, disturbance, fuss, mischief, row, strife, turmoil, unrest. □ **in trouble** in a fix, in a jam (*informal*), in a mess, in a pickle (*informal*), in a plight, in a predicament, in a scrape, in a spot (*informal*), in difficulties, in dire straits, in hot water (*informal*), in strife (*Australian informal*), in the soup (*informal*), up the creek (*informal*). □ **take trouble** bother, exert yourself, make an effort, take care, take pains.

trouble verb **1** afflict, agitate, ail, annoy, bother, bug (*informal*), concern, distress, disturb, hassle (*informal*), hurt, inconvenience, irritate, oppress, perturb, pester, plague, prey on, put out, upset, vex, weigh down, worry. **2** bother, make the effort, take the time, take the trouble.

troublemaker noun agitator, culprit, delinquent, firebrand, hooligan, mischief-maker, rabble-rouser, ratbag (*Aus-tralian informal*), ringleader, ruffian, stirrer (*Australian*).

troublesome adjective annoy-ing, bothersome, difficult,

distressing, inconvenient, irritating, pesky (*informal*), pestilential, recalcitrant, tiresome, trying, uncooperative, unmanageable, unruly, vexing, worrying.

trough *noun* channel, conduit, culvert, depression, ditch, furrow, gully, gutter, trench.

trounce *verb* **1** beat, belt (*slang*), cane, flog, hit, lash, lay into (*informal*), quilt (*Australian slang*), scourge, tan (*slang*), thrash, wallop (*slang*), whack, whip. **2** beat, clobber (*slang*), defeat, drub, lick (*informal*), overpower, paste (*slang*), rout, slaughter, thrash, vanquish.

troupe *noun* band, company, group.

trousers *plural noun* (*kinds of trousers*) bell-bottoms, breeches, chinos, cords, flares, hipsters, jeans, jodhpurs, knickerbockers, moleskins, pantaloons, pants (*informal*), plus fours, slacks, strides (*informal*).

truant *noun* absentee, malingerer, skiver (*informal*), wag (*informal*). □ **play truant** absent yourself, bludge (*Australian informal*), play hookey (*informal*), skive (*informal*), stay away, wag (*informal*).

truce *noun* armistice, ceasefire, moratorium, peace.

truck *noun* juggernaut, lorry, pick-up, road train (*Australian*), semi (*Australian informal*), semitrailer, van.

trudge *verb* lumber, plod, slog, traipse (*informal*), tramp, trek.

true *adjective* **1** accurate, actual, authentic, correct, exact, factual, faithful, genuine, honest, precise, reliable, right, strict, truthful, veracious. **2** authorised, genuine, legal, legitimate, proper, rightful. **3** accurate, correct, exact, faithful, precise, right, strict. **4** constant, dependable, dinkum (*Australian informal*), dinky-di (*Australian informal*), faithful, loyal, real, reliable, sincere, staunch, true-blue, trustworthy.

trunk *noun* **1** bole, stem, stock. **2** proboscis, snout. **3** box, case, chest, coffer. **4** body, torso. □ **trunks** *plural noun* bathers (*Australian*), costume, shorts, swimmers (*Australian*), togs (*Australian informal*).

truss *verb* bind, secure, tie up.

trust *verb* **1** believe in, depend on, have confidence in, have faith in, rely on. **2** assign, commend, commit, consign, delegate, entrust, hand over. **3** assume, expect, hope presume, take it. □ **trusting** *adjective* credulous, gullible, naïve, trustful, unsuspecting, unsuspicious.

trust *noun* **1** belief, confidence, conviction, credence, faith, reliance. **2** responsibility. □ **trustworthy** *adjective* dependable, faithful, honest, loyal, reliable, responsible, staunch, steadfast, steady, sure, true, trusty (*old use*).

truth *noun* **1** axiom, fact, law, maxim, principle, reality, truism. **2** accuracy, authenticity, genuineness, reliability, truthfulness, veracity.

truthful *adjective* **1** frank, honest, open, sincere, straight, trustworthy, veracious. **2** accurate, correct, factual, faithful, honest, reliable, true.

try *verb* **1** aim, attempt, endeavour, strive, struggle. **2** check out, experiment with, sample, taste, test, try out. **3** adjudicate, examine, hear, judge. **4** strain, tax, test.

try *noun* attempt, bash (*informal*), crack (*informal*), go, shot (*informal*), stab (*informal*), whack (*informal*).

trying *adjective* annoying, demanding, difficult, exasperating, frustrating, irritating, stressful, taxing, tiresome, troublesome, vexing.

tub *noun* barrel, bath, butt, cask, drum, pot.

tubby *adjective* chubby, dumpy, fat, obese, plump, podgy, portly, rotund, stout.

tube *noun* conduit, duct, hose, pipe.

tuberculosis *noun* consumption (*old use*), TB (*informal*).

tuck *verb* insert, push, shove, stick, stuff.

tuck *noun* fold, pin-tuck, pleat.

tuft *noun* bunch, clump, tussock.

tug *verb* **1** jerk, pluck, pull, wrench, yank. **2** drag, draw, haul, pull, tow.

tuition *noun* coaching, education, instruction, lessons, teaching, training.

tumble *verb* collapse, drop, fall, nosedive, plummet, plunge, roll, stumble, topple.

tumbledown *adjective* decrepit, derelict, dilapidated, ramshackle, rickety.

tumour *noun* cancer, carcinoma, growth, lump.

tumult *noun* bedlam, chaos, commotion, confusion, din, disturbance, fracas, hubbub, hullabaloo, kerfuffle (*informal*), mayhem, noise, pandemonium, racket, riot, row, ruckus, rumpus, shindy (*informal*), turmoil, uproar.

tumultuous *adjective* boisterous, excited, noisy, rowdy, uproarious, wild.

tune *noun* air, melody, strain, theme. □ **tuneful** *adjective* catchy, harmonious, melodious, musical, pleasant.

tune *verb* adjust, regulate, set.

tunnel *noun* adit, burrow, hole, mine, passage, shaft, subway, underpass.

tunnel *verb* burrow, dig, excavate.

turbulent *adjective* **1** blustery, gusty, rough, stormy, tempestuous, violent, wild, windy. **2** boisterous, disorderly, obstreperous, restless, riotous, rough, rowdy, unruly, violent, wild.

turf *noun* grass, lawn, sod, sward.

turmoil *noun* agitation, bedlam, chaos, commotion, confusion, disorder, disturbance, mess, pandemonium, tumult, upheaval, uproar.

turn *verb* **1** circle, go round, gyrate, pivot, revolve, rotate, spin, spin round, swing round, swivel, twirl, twist round, veer, wheel round, whirl. **2** flip over, invert, reverse, roll over. **3** become, be transformed, change, metamorphose. **4** adapt, change, convert, make, modify, transform.

5 (*turn off*) cut off, disconnect, switch off; (*turn on*) plug in, put on, start, switch on. □ **turn down** decline, knock back (*informal*), pass up (*informal*), rebuff, refuse, reject, spurn. □ **turn out 1** chuck out (*informal*), eject, evict, expel, kick out (*informal*), remove, throw out, turf out (*informal*). **2** end up, happen, pan out, work out. □ **turn up** appear, arrive, come, front (up) (*informal*), lob in (*Australian informal*), roll up (*informal*), show up.

turn *noun* **1** revolution, rotation, twist, wind. **2** alteration, change, shift. **3** angle, bend, corner, curve, hairpin bend, loop, turning, twist, wind. **4** chance, go, innings, move, opportunity, shot, spell, stint. **5** fright, scare, shock, start, surprise.

turncoat *noun* apostate, defector, deserter, renegade, traitor.

turning point breakthrough, crisis, crossroads, watershed.

tussle *noun* battle, brawl, clash, conflict, fight, fracas, scrap (*informal*), scuffle, set-to, skirmish, squabble, struggle, wrestle.

tussock *noun* clump, tuffet, tuft.

tutor noun coach, educator, instructor, mentor, teacher. □ **tutor** verb coach, instruct, school, teach.

tutorial noun class, discussion group, seminar.

tweak verb jerk, pinch, pull, tug, twist, yank.

tweet verb cheep, chirp, chirrup, peep, twitter.

twiddle verb fiddle with, fidget with, play with, twirl.

twig noun offshoot, shoot, stalk, stem, stick.

twilight noun dusk, evening, gloaming, gloom, nightfall, sundown, sunset.

twin noun clone, double, look-alike, ringer (*informal*), spitting image.

twin verb couple, link, match, pair.

twine noun cord, string, thread.

twine verb coil, entwine, twist, weave, wind.

twinge noun ache, cramp, pain, pang, spasm, stitch, throb.

twinkle verb blink, flash, flicker, glimmer, glitter, shimmer, shine, sparkle.

twirl verb gyrate, loop, pirouette, revolve, rotate, spin, twist, whirl, wind.

twist verb **1** braid, coil, curl, entwine, intertwine, inter-weave, plait, twine, twirl,

weave, wind. **2** (*of a road*) bend, curve, kink, loop, meander, turn, wind, worm, zigzag; (*of a person*) squirm, wriggle, writhe. **3** bend, buckle, contort, crumple, distort, screw up, warp; (*twist an ankle*) rick, sprain, turn, wrench.

twist noun bend, coil, convolution, corkscrew, curve, kink, knot, loop, snarl, tangle, turn, wind, zigzag. □ **twisty** adjective crooked, curved, serpentine, sinuous, tortuous, winding, zigzag.

twit noun see *FOOL*.

twitch verb fidget, flinch, jerk, jump, quiver, start, wince, wriggle. □ **twitch** noun blink, jerk, spasm, tic.

twitter verb cheep, chirp, chirrup, peep, tweet.

two-faced adjective deceitful, dishonest, double-dealing, duplicitous, false, hypocritical, insincere.

tycoon noun baron, magnate, mogul (*informal*).

type noun **1** breed, category, class, form, genus, group, kind, make, model, order, sort, species, strain, style, variety, version. **2** characters, font, print, typeface.

typhoon *noun* hurricane, tropical cyclone; see also *STORM*.

typical *adjective* **1** average, normal, ordinary, regular, representative, standard. **2** characteristic, customary, distinctive, usual.

typify *verb* epitomise, exemplify, represent.

tyrannical *adjective* autocratic, cruel, despotic, dictatorial, domineering, harsh, imperious, oppressive, severe, tyrannous, unjust.

tyrant *noun* autocrat, bully, despot, dictator, martinet, slave-driver.

Uu

ugly *adjective* **1** frightful, ghastly, grotesque, hideous, horrible, monstrous, repulsive, shocking, unattractive, unsightly. **2** belligerent, hostile, menacing, nasty, threatening, unpleasant.

ulterior *adjective* covert, hidden, secret, undisclosed.

ultimate *adjective* **1** concluding, end, final, last. **2** basic, fundamental, primary, root, underlying. □ **ultimately**

adverb eventually, finally, in the end, in the long run.

umbrella *noun* brolly (*informal*), parasol, sunshade.

umpire *noun* adjudicator, arbiter, arbitrator, judge, moderator, ref (*informal*), referee.

umpire *verb* adjudicate, arbitrate, judge, moderate, referee.

unacceptable *adjective* improper, inadmissible, intolerable, objectionable, offensive, taboo, unsatisfactory, unseemly, unsuitable.

unafraid *adjective* bold, brave, courageous, dauntless, fearless, game, intrepid, plucky, undaunted, valiant.

unanimity *noun* accord, agreement, consensus, solidarity, unity.

unassuming *adjective* diffident, modest, quiet, retiring, self-effacing, unassertive, unpretentious.

unattractive *adjective* drab, hideous, inelegant, plain, repulsive, tasteless, ugly, unappealing, unbecoming, unsightly.

unauthorised *adjective* illegal, illicit, pirated, unofficial, unsanctioned.

unavoidable *adjective* **1** certain, destined, fated,

inescapable, inevitable, pre-destined. **2** compulsory, mandatory, necessary, obligatory.

unaware *adjective* ignorant, oblivious, unconscious, uninformed.

unawares *adverb* by surprise, off guard, unexpectedly.

unbalanced *adjective* **1** asymmetrical, lopsided, uneven. **2** biased, one-sided, partisan, prejudiced, unfair. **3** crazy, demented, deranged, insane, mad, unhinged, unsound, unstable.

unbearable *adjective* excruciating, insufferable, intolerable, unendurable.

unbeatable *adjective* invincible, unconquerable, undefeatable, unstoppable.

unbecoming *adjective* **1** unattractive, unflattering, unsuitable. **2** improper, inappropriate, indecorous, ungentlemanly, unladylike, unseemly, unsuitable.

unbelievable *adjective* amazing, astounding, extraordinary, far-fetched, implausible, improbable, incredible, unconvincing.

unbiased *adjective* disinterested, even-handed, fair, impartial, just, neutral, non-partisan, objective, open-minded, unprejudiced.

unblock *verb* clear, free, unclog, unstop.

unbreakable *adjective* indestructible, solid, strong, sturdy, tough.

unbroken *adjective* complete, continuous, entire, intact, uninterrupted, whole.

uncalled-for *adjective* gratuitous, needless, unjustified, unnecessary, unsolicited, unwarranted, unwelcome.

uncanny *adjective* **1** creepy, eerie, frightening, mysterious, scary, spooky (*informal*), strange, unearthly, weird. **2** astonishing, extraordinary, incredible, remarkable, striking, unbelievable.

uncaring *adjective* callous, cold, hard-hearted, heartless, indifferent, insensitive, unfeeling, unsympathetic.

uncertain *adjective* **1** ambivalent, doubtful, dubious, hesitant, indecisive, in two minds, irresolute, undecided, unsure. **2** changeable, erratic, unpredictable, unreliable, variable.

unchangeable *adjective* changeless, consistent, constant, dependable, immutable, invariable, reliable, unvarying.

uncharitable *adjective* mean, unchristian, unfair, ungenerous, unkind.

uncivilised adjective **1** barbarian, barbaric, barbarous, primitive, savage, wild. **2** antisocial, boorish, philistine, rude, uncouth, uncultured, vulgar.

uncomfortable adjective anxious, apprehensive, awkward, disturbed, embarrassed, nervous, painful, troubled, uneasy, worried.

uncommon adjective abnormal, curious, exceptional, extraordinary, infrequent, odd, peculiar, rare, remarkable, singular, special, strange, striking, unfamiliar, unusual.

uncommunicative adjective quiet, reserved, reticent, retiring, secretive, silent, taciturn, tight-lipped, unforthcoming, unsociable.

uncomplimentary adjective critical, derogatory, disparaging, insulting, pejorative, rude, unkind.

uncompromising adjective hard-line, inflexible, intransigent, rigid, strict, stubborn, unbending, unyielding.

unconcerned adjective apathetic, carefree, indifferent, lackadaisical, nonchalant, oblivious, unperturbed, untroubled.

unconditional adjective absolute, complete, unlimited, unqualified, unreserved.

unconnected adjective independent, separate, unrelated.

unconscious adjective **1** blacked out, comatose, insensible, knocked out, senseless. **2** oblivious, unaware. **3** automatic, instinctive, involuntary, mechanical, reflex, unintentional, unthinking, unwitting.

uncontrollable adjective (an uncontrollable person) headstrong, intractable, irrepressible, obstreperous, rebellious, refractory, undisciplined, unmanageable, unruly, wayward, wilful; (an uncontrollable urge) compulsive, irresistible, overwhelming.

unconventional adjective abnormal, eccentric, odd, offbeat, original, peculiar, singular, strange, unorthodox, unusual, way-out, weird.

unconvincing adjective feeble, flimsy, implausible, lame, unbelievable, unsatisfactory, weak.

uncooperative adjective difficult, obstructive, perverse, rebellious, recalcitrant, stroppy (informal), unhelpful.

uncouth adjective bad-mannered, boorish, coarse, loutish, rough, rude, uncivil, unrefined, vulgar.

uncover verb **1** bare, dig up, lay bare, strip, unearth, unwrap. **2** dig up, disclose, discover, expose, reveal, unearth.

uncultivated adjective fallow, unused, virgin, waste, wild.

undecided adjective ambivalent, in two minds, irresolute, open-minded, uncertain, unsure, vacillating.

undeniable adjective certain, incontrovertible, indisputable, indubitable, irrefutable, positive, sure, unquestionable.

under preposition **1** below, beneath, underneath. **2** below, less than, lower than. **3** below, junior to, subordinate to.

undercurrent noun **1** undertow. **2** atmosphere, feeling, hint, undertone, vibes (informal).

underdone adjective rare, undercooked.

underestimate verb misjudge, underrate, undervalue.

undergo verb bear, be subjected to, brave, endure, experience, go through, put up with, submit to, weather.

underground adjective **1** subterranean. **2** clandestine, covert, secret, undercover.

undergrowth noun brush, bushes, ground cover, shrubs.

underhand adjective crafty, crooked (informal), cunning,

deceitful, devious, dishonest, fraudulent, shonky (Australian informal), sly, sneaky, unscrupulous.

underline verb emphasise, highlight, point up, stress.

underling noun flunkey, menial, minion, servant, subordinate.

undermine verb destroy, erode, ruin, sabotage, sap, subvert, weaken.

underneath preposition below, beneath, under.

underpants plural noun boxer shorts, briefs, drawers, jocks (slang), knickers, panties (informal), pants, undies (informal).

underpass noun subway, tunnel.

underprivileged adjective deprived, disadvantaged, needy, poor.

underrate verb sell short, underestimate, undervalue.

underside noun back, bottom, reverse, underneath, wrong side.

undersized adjective diminutive, dwarf, little, midget, puny, pygmy, short, small, stunted, tiny, underdeveloped.

understand verb **1** appreciate, apprehend, comprehend, cotton on to (informal), decipher, decode, fathom, follow, get (*informal*), grasp, interpret, jerry to (*Australian informal*), make head or tail of, make out, know, perceive, realise, recognise, see, take in, tumble to (*informal*), twig (*informal*). **2** accept, appreciate, empathise with, sympathise with, tolerate. **3** believe, gather, have been told, hear.

understanding noun **1** intellect, intelligence, knowledge, mentality, perception, wisdom. **2** appreciation, apprehension, awareness, comprehension, conception, insight, perception, realisation. **3** compassion, consideration, empathy, feeling, sensitivity, sympathy, tolerance. **4** accord, agreement, arrangement, bargain, compromise, deal, entente, pact, settlement.

understanding adjective compassionate, considerate, forbearing, perceptive, sensitive, sympathetic, tolerant.

undertake verb accept, agree to, assume, commit yourself to, consent to, embark on, enter upon, promise to, tackle, take on.

undertaker noun funeral director, mortician (*American*).

undertaking noun **1** endeavour, enterprise, job, project, task, venture, work. **2** assurance, commitment, guarantee, pledge, promise, vow.

undertone noun **1** murmur, whisper. **2** atmosphere, hint, suggestion, trace, undercurrent.

underwater adjective sub-aquatic, submarine, submerged, undersea.

underwear noun lingerie, underclothes, undergarments, undies (*informal*).

underworld noun Hades, hell.

undeserved adjective unearned, unjustified, unmerited, unwarranted.

undesirable adjective objectionable, offensive, repugnant, unacceptable, unsatisfactory.

undeveloped adjective embryonic, immature, primitive, rudimentary.

undisciplined adjective disobedient, disorderly, naughty, obstreperous, recalcitrant, refractory, uncontrolled, unruly, wayward, wild, wilful.

undistinguished adjective mediocre, ordinary, unexceptional, unimpressive, unremarkable.

undivided adjective complete, exclusive, full, total, whole-hearted.

undo verb **1** detach, disconnect, loosen, open, release unbuckle, unbutton, unclasp, unfasten, unhook, unpick, unravel, unscrew, untie, unwrap, unzip. **2** cancel, counteract, destroy, nullify, reverse, ruin, spoil, wreck.

undoubted *adjective* certain, clear, clear-cut, indisputable, sure, undisputed.

undress *verb* disrobe, peel off, strip, uncover yourself. □ **undressed** *adjective* bare, naked, nude, unclothed.

undue *adjective* disproportionate, excessive, inordinate, unjustified, unnecessary, unreasonable.

undying *adjective* abiding, constant, endless, eternal, everlasting, immortal, infinite, never-ending, permanent, perpetual, unending.

unearth *verb* **1** dig up, discover, disinter, excavate, exhume, uncover. **2** dig up, discover, find, uncover.

unearthly *adjective* creepy, eerie, ghostly, spooky (*informal*), supernatural, uncanny, weird.

uneasy *adjective* anxious, apprehensive, edgy, ill at ease, jittery (*informal*), nervous, nervy, tense, uncomfortable, worried.

uneatable *adjective* inedible.

uneconomic *adjective* nonpaying, unprofitable, unviable.

uneducated *adjective* ignorant, illiterate, unschooled, untaught.

unemployed *adjective* jobless, laid off, on the dole (*informal*), out of work, redundant.

unequal *adjective* **1** different, disparate, dissimilar, uneven. **2** biased, inequitable, one-sided, unbalanced, uneven, unfair.

unethical *adjective* dishonest, dishonourable, immoral, shady, shonky (*Australian informal*), underhand, unprincipled, unscrupulous, wrong.

uneven *adjective* **1** bumpy, crooked, irregular, jagged, lumpy, ragged, rough, rugged, undulating, wavy. **2** inequitable, one-sided, unbalanced, unequal, unfair. **3** erratic, inconsistent, patchy, variable.

unexcitable *adjective* calm, cool, impassive, listless, nonchalant, phlegmatic, serene, stolid, unemotional, unflappable (*informal*).

unexciting *adjective* boring, dreary, dull, humdrum, monotonous, mundane, ordinary, run-of-the-mill, tame, tedious, uneventful, uninteresting.

unexpected *adjective* accidental, chance, fortuitous, startling, surprising, undreamed-of, unforeseen, unlooked-for.

unfailing *adjective* constant, dependable, infallible, reliable.

unfair *adjective* biased, inequitable, one-sided, partial, partisan, prejudiced, unjust, unreasonable.

unfaithful *adjective* adulterous, disloyal, false, fickle, inconstant, perfidious, traitorous, treacherous, two-timing (*informal*), untrue. □ **unfaithfulness** *noun* adultery, disloyalty, inconstancy, infidelity, perfidy, treachery, treason.

unfamiliar *adjective* alien, exotic, foreign, new, novel, strange, unheard-of, unknown.

unfashionable *adjective* dated, obsolete, old-fashioned, outdated, outmoded, out-of-date.

unfasten *verb* detach, disconnect, loosen, open, release, unbolt, unbuckle, unbutton, unclasp, undo, unhook, unlatch, unlock, unscrew, untie, unzip.

unfavourable *adjective* adverse, contrary, critical, disadvantageous, discouraging, hostile, inauspicious, negative, unhelpful, unpropitious.

unfeeling *adjective* callous, clinical, cold, cold-hearted, cruel, hard, hard-hearted, harsh, heartless, inhuman, insensitive, merciless, pitiless, ruthless, uncaring, unsympathetic.

unfit *adjective* **1** inadequate, inappropriate, incapable, incompetent, unqualified, unsuitable, unsuited, unusable, useless. **2** out of condition, out of form, out of training, unhealthy.

unflappable *adjective* calm, collected, composed, cool, easygoing, imperturbable, nonchalant, phlegmatic, placid, unexcitable.

unfold *verb* **1** open out, spread out, unfurl. **2** develop, emerge, evolve.

unforgettable *adjective* impressive, memorable, noteworthy, remarkable, striking.

unforgivable *adjective* indefensible, inexcusable, unjustifiable, unpardonable.

unforgiving *adjective* hardhearted, implacable, merciless, pitiless, remorseless, vengeful, vindictive.

unfortunate *adjective* **1** hapless, ill-fated, jinxed (*informal*), luckless, unlucky, wretched. **2** inappropriate, lamentable, regrettable, tactless, unsuitable.

unfounded *adjective* baseless, groundless, needless, unjustified, unwarranted.

unfriendly *adjective* aloof, antagonistic, antisocial, clinical, cool, distant, hostile, icy, inhospitable, stand-offish, surly, uncaring, unfeeling, unkind, unneighbourly, unsociable.

ungainly *adjective* awkward, clumsy, gangling, gawky, inelegant, ungraceful.

ungodly *adjective* evil, godless, immoral, impious, iniquitous, irreligious, sinful, unholy, wicked.

ungrateful *adjective* unappreciative, unthankful. □ **ungratefulness** *noun* ingratitude.

unhappy *adjective* **1** blue, dejected, depressed, despondent, disconsolate, discontented, dismal, dispirited, distressed, doleful, downcast, down-hearted, fed up (*informal*), gloomy, glum, heartbroken, heavy-hearted, melancholy, miserable, mournful, pessimistic, sad, sorrowful, woebegone, wretched. **2** bad, inappropriate, poor, regrettable, unfortunate, unlucky, unsatisfactory, unsuitable.

unharmed *adjective* safe, safe and sound, undamaged, unhurt, uninjured, unscathed.

unhealthy *adjective* **1** ailing, diseased, poorly, sick, sickly, unsound, unwell. **2** deleterious, detrimental, harmful, insalubrious, insanitary, unhygienic, unwholesome.

unhelpful *adjective* obstructive, stroppy (*informal*), uncooperative.

unidentified *adjective* anonymous, incognito, nameless, unknown, unnamed.

uniform *noun* habit, livery, regalia.

uniform *adjective* consistent, constant, even, identical, invariable, regular, same, stable, steady, unchanging.

unify *verb* amalgamate, bind, bring together, combine, consolidate, federate, incorporate, integrate, join, merge, tie, unite.

unimaginative *adjective* colourless, dull, hackneyed, ordinary, pedestrian, prosaic, unexciting, uninspired, unoriginal.

unimportant *adjective* inconsequential, insignificant, irrelevant, minor, obscure, peripheral, petty, trivial.

uninhabited *adjective* deserted, empty, unoccupied, vacant.

uninhibited *adjective* free, reckless, spontaneous, unrepressed, unrestrained, unselfconscious.

unintelligible *adjective* confused, incoherent, incomprehensible, indecipherable, meaningless.

unintentional *adjective* accidental, chance, fortuitous, inadvertent, unforeseen, unintended, unplanned, unpremeditated; see also *INVOLUNTARY.*

uninterested *adjective* apathetic, blasé, bored, detached, indifferent, unconcerned.

uninteresting *adjective* banal, boring, commonplace, dreary, dull, humdrum, monotonous, mundane, ordinary, pedestrian, prosaic, stodgy, tedious, tiresome, uneventful, unexciting, unimaginative, uninspiring, vapid.

uninterrupted *adjective* continuous, non-stop, solid, sound, unbroken, undisturbed.

uninvited *adjective* unasked, unwanted, unwelcome.

uninviting *adjective* inhospitable, unappealing, unattractive, unenticing, unwelcoming.

union *noun* **1** alliance, amalgamation, association, coalition, combination, federation, merger, synthesis, unification. **2** guild, trade union.

unique *adjective* distinctive, inimitable, matchless, one-off, peculiar, singular.

unit *noun* **1** measure, measurement, quantity. **2** component, constituent, element, item, module, part, piece, section; (*a research unit*) group, squad, team; (*a home unit*) apartment, condominium (*American*), flat.

unite *verb* amalgamate, band together, bind, bring together, collaborate, combine, consolidate, cooperate, federate, incorporate, integrate, join, join forces, link, merge, team up, tie, unify.

unity *noun* accord, agreement, cohesion, concord, consensus, harmony, oneness, solidarity, unanimity.

universal *adjective* general, global, international, ubiquitous, widespread, worldwide.

universe *noun* cosmos, Creation, world.

unjust *adjective* biased, inequitable, one-sided, partial, prejudiced, unfair, unjustified, unreasonable, wrong.

unkempt *adjective* bedraggled, dishevelled, messy, scruffy, tousled, untidy.

unkind *adjective* beastly (*informal*), callous, cold-hearted, cruel, hard-hearted, harsh, heartless, hurtful, inconsiderate, inhuman, inhumane, malicious, mean, merciless, nasty, pitiless, ruthless, sadistic, spiteful, stern, thoughtless, uncaring, uncharitable, unfeeling, unfriendly, unneighbourly, unsympathetic, vicious.

unknown *adjective* anonymous, nameless, obscure, undistinguished, unheard-of, unidentified, unnamed.

unlikely *adjective* far-fetched, implausible, improbable, incredible, unbelievable.

unlimited *adjective* absolute, boundless, complete, endless, everlasting, full, inexhaustible, infinite, limitless, never-ending, unconditional, unqualified, unrestricted, vast.

unload *verb* discharge, drop off, dump, empty, offload, remove, unpack.

unlock *verb* open, unbolt, undo, unfasten, unlatch.

unlucky *adjective* accident-prone, hapless, ill-fated, jinxed (*informal*), luckless, unfortunate, wretched.

unmanageable *adjective* (*an unmanageable load*) awkward, cumbersome, unwieldy; (*an unmanageable person*) difficult, intractable, obstreperous, refractory, stroppy (*informal*), uncontrollable, undisciplined, unruly, wayward.

unmarried *adjective* maiden, single, unattached, unwed.

unmentionable *adjective* forbidden, obscene, rude, shocking, taboo, unprintable.

unmistakable *adjective* apparent, blatant, clear, conspicuous, distinct, evident, glaring, manifest, noticeable, obvious, patent, plain, pronounced.

unnatural *adjective* **1** abnormal, bizarre, freakish, odd, peculiar, strange, supernatural, unusual, weird. **2** affected, artificial, contrived, forced, mannered, phoney (*informal*), stilted, studied, theatrical.

unnecessary *adjective* dispensable, excessive, expendable, inessential, needless, nonessential, redundant, superfluous, uncalled-for, unwanted.

unnerve *verb* agitate, disconcert, fluster, frighten, perturb, rattle (*informal*), unsettle, upset.

unoccupied *adjective* deserted, empty, uninhabited, unlived-in, vacant.

unorthodox *adjective* heretical, irregular, non-standard, unconventional.

unpaid *adjective* **1** outstanding, overdue, owing. **2** honorary, unsalaried, unwaged, voluntary.

unparalleled *adjective* incomparable, inimitable, matchless, peerless, supreme, unequalled, unrivalled, unsurpassed.

unplanned *adjective* accidental, chance, fortuitous, unintended, unintentional, unpremeditated, unscheduled.

unpleasant *adjective* abominable, annoying, appalling, atrocious, awful, bad-tempered, beastly (*informal*), diabolical, disagreeable, disgusting, distasteful, dreadful, foul, frightful, ghastly, harsh, hateful, hideous, horrible, horrid, irksome, loathsome, nasty, nauseating, objectionable, obnoxious, offensive, off-putting, repugnant, repulsive, revolting, sickening, sordid, squalid, terrible, troublesome, unattractive, unfriendly, unlikeable, unpalatable, unsightly, upsetting, vile.

unpopular *adjective* disliked, friendless, on the outer (*Australian informal*), shunned, unloved.

unprecedented *adjective* exceptional, extraordinary, unheard-of, unparalleled, unusual.

unpredictable *adjective* capricious, changeable, erratic, fickle, inconstant, mercurial, moody, temperamental, unreliable, volatile.

unprejudiced *adjective* disinterested, fair, impartial, objective, open-minded, unbiased.

unprepared *adjective* ad lib, extempore, impromptu, off the cuff, spontaneous, unrehearsed.

unpretentious *adjective* homely, humble, lowly, modest, plain, simple, unimposing, unostentatious.

unproductive *adjective* barren, fruitless, futile, infertile, sterile, unprofitable, unrewarding, useless, vain.

unprofessional *adjective* **1** amateurish, incompetent, inexpert, shoddy. **2** improper, irresponsible, negligent, unethical, unprincipled.

unprofitable *adjective* fruitless, uncommercial, uneconomic, unproductive, useless, worthless.

unquestionable *adjective* certain, definite, incontrovertible, indisputable, indubitable, irrefutable, sure, undeniable, undisputed.

unravel *verb* disentangle, untangle, untwist.

unreadable *adjective* illegible, indecipherable.

unreal *adjective* artificial, fabulous, false, fantastic, fictitious, hypothetical, illusory, imaginary, make-believe, mythical, non-existent.

unrealistic *adjective* idealistic, impracticable, impractical, unreasonable, unworkable.

unreasonable *adjective* **1** headstrong, illogical, irrational, obstinate, opinionated, perverse, pigheaded, stubborn, wilful. **2** absurd, excessive, exorbitant, extortionate, immoderate, ludicrous, outrageous, preposterous, steep (*informal*), undue, unjust.

unreliable *adjective* chancy, dicey (*slang*), dodgy (*informal*), erratic, fickle, iffy (*informal*), irresponsible, risky, shonky (*Australian informal*), uncertain, undependable, unsound, unsure, untrustworthy.

unrepentant *adjective* hardened, impenitent, remorseless, unashamed.

unreservedly *adverb* absolutely, completely, totally, unconditionally, utterly, wholeheartedly, without reservation.

unrest *noun* agitation, disquiet, dissatisfaction, rebellion, rioting, strife, trouble, turbulence, turmoil, unease, uprising.

unrivalled *adjective* incomparable, matchless, peerless, unequalled, unparalleled, unsurpassed.

unroll *verb* open out, spread out, unfurl.

unruly *adjective* boisterous, disobedient, disorderly, lawless, obstreperous, riotous, rowdy, uncontrollable, undisciplined, unmanageable, wayward, wild.

unsafe *adjective* dangerous, hazardous, perilous, precarious, risky, treacherous.

unsatisfactory *adjective* defective, deficient, disappointing, faulty, inadequate, insufficient, substandard, unacceptable.

unscathed *adjective* safe, safe and sound, undamaged, unharmed, unhurt, uninjured.

unscrupulous *adjective* corrupt, crooked, deceitful, dishonest, dishonourable, immoral, shady, shonky (*Australian informal*), unethical, unprincipled.

unseemly *adjective* improper, inappropriate, indecent, indecorous, offensive, tasteless, unbecoming, unfitting.

unseen *adjective* concealed, hidden, invisible, out of sight, unnoticed.

unselfish *adjective* altruistic, considerate, generous, kind, magnanimous, open-handed, philanthropic, selfless, thoughtful, unstinting.

unsettled *adjective* **1** agitated, disconcerted, disturbed, edgy, flustered, perturbed, rattled (*informal*), restless, ruffled, troubled, uneasy, unnerved, upset. **2** changeable, erratic, patchy, unpredictable, unstable, variable.

unshakeable *adjective* firm, resolute, staunch, steadfast, unwavering.

unsociable *adjective* aloof, antisocial, reclusive, retiring, stand-offish, unfriendly, withdrawn.

unsophisticated *adjective* artless, ingenuous, naïve, natural, simple, unaffected, unpretentious, unrefined, unworldly.

unstable *adjective* changeable, explosive, fluctuating, fluid, unpredictable, volatile.

unsteady *adjective* precarious, rickety, rocky, shaky, unstable, wobbly, wonky (*informal*).

unsuccessful *adjective* abortive, failed, fruitless, futile, ineffective, ineffectual, unavailing, vain.

unsuitable *adjective* inappropriate, out of place, unbecoming, unfitting, unseemly, wrong.

unsure *adjective* see UNCERTAIN.

unsuspecting *adjective* credulous, gullible, ingenuous, naïve, trusting, unsuspicious, unwary.

unsympathetic *adjective* callous, cold, hard-hearted, heartless, indifferent, insensitive, uncaring, uncompassionate, unfeeling.

untamed *adjective* feral, savage, unbroken, undomesticated, warrigal (*Australian*), wild.

untangle *verb* disentangle, unravel, unsnarl, untwist.

unthinkable *adjective* inconceivable, incredible, unbelievable, unimaginable.

unthinking *adjective* careless, heedless, inconsiderate, mindless, negligent, short-sighted, tactless, thoughtless.

untidy *adjective* (*an untidy place*) chaotic, cluttered, disorderly, disorganised, higgledy-piggledy, jumbled, littered, messy, muddled, topsy-turvy; (*an untidy person*) bedraggled, dishevelled, ruffled, rumpled, scruffy, shabby, shaggy, slatternly, sloppy, slovenly, straggly, tatty (*informal*), tousled, unkempt.

untie verb detach, disconnect, loosen, release, undo, unfasten, unknot.

untold adjective countless, immeasurable, incalculable, indescribable, innumerable, myriad, numberless, numerous.

untrue adjective **1** apocryphal, erroneous, false, fictitious, invented, made-up, untruthful, wrong. **2** disloyal, fickle, perfidious, treacherous, unfaithful.

untruth noun fabrication, fairy story, falsehood, fib, fiction, lie, story. □ **untruthful** adjective deceitful, dishonest, false, lying, mendacious.

unused adjective **1** blank, clean, empty, fresh, new, untouched. **2** inexperienced (at), unaccustomed, unfamiliar (with).

unusual adjective abnormal, atypical, bizarre, curious, different, eccentric, exceptional, exotic, extraordinary, freakish, irregular, odd, offbeat, outlandish, peculiar, phenomenal, queer, rare, remarkable, singular, special, strange, surprising, uncommon, unfamiliar, unorthodox, way-out (*informal*), weird.

unwanted adjective excluded, on the outer (*Australian*), rejected, shunned, unpopular, unwelcome; see also *UNNECESSARY*.

unwarranted adjective groundless, indefensible, inexcusable, uncalled-for, unjustified, unnecessary, unreasonable.

unwary adjective imprudent, incautious, unguarded, unsuspecting, unsuspicious.

unwell adjective ailing, bilious, crook (*Australian informal*), funny (*informal*), ill, indisposed, infirm, nauseous, off colour, out of sorts, poorly, queasy, rotten, seedy (*informal*), sick, sickly, under the weather, unhealthy.

unwholesome adjective deleterious, detrimental, harmful, insalubrious, insanitary, unhealthy, unhygienic.

unwieldy adjective awkward, bulky, clumsy, cumbersome, heavy, hefty.

unwilling adjective averse, disinclined, hesitant, loath, reluctant.

unwind verb **1** undo, unravel, unroll. **2** calm down, ease off, relax, take it easy.

unwise adjective crazy, foolish, impolitic, imprudent, inadvisable, injudicious, silly, stupid, unintentional.

unworldly adjective callow, green, inexperienced, innocent, naïve, unsophisticated.

unworthy adjective **1** undeserving. **2** inappropriate, unbecoming, unbefitting, unfitting, unsuitable.

unwritten adjective implicit, oral, spoken, tacit, unstated.

unyielding adjective adamant, firm, inflexible, intransigent, obstinate, relentless, steadfast, stubborn, tenacious, tough, unbending, uncompromising.

up adverb □ **up to date** contemporary, current, fashionable, latest, modern, modernised, new, trendy (*informal*), up to the minute, with it (*informal*).

upbraid verb admonish, berate, castigate, censure, chastise, chide (*old use*), rebuke, reprimand, reproach, reprove, scold, tell off (*informal*), tick off (*informal*).

upbringing noun education, nurture, raising, rearing, training.

update verb modernise, refurbish, remodel, renovate.

upfront adjective direct, forthright, frank, honest, open.

upgrade verb enhance, improve.

upheaval noun change, chaos, disruption, disturbance, havoc, turbulence, turmoil.

uphill adjective arduous, demanding, difficult, exacting, gruelling, hard, laborious, strenuous, tough.

uphold verb confirm, endorse, maintain, stand by, support, sustain.

upkeep noun maintenance, repairs, running.

uplift verb buoy up, encourage, inspire, lift, raise.

upmarket adjective classy (*informal*), de luxe, expensive, luxurious, superior.

upper adjective higher, raised, superior.

uppermost adjective highest, top, topmost.

upright adjective **1** erect, perpendicular, standing, vertical. **2** ethical, good, honest, honourable, just, moral, principled, righteous, trustworthy, upstanding, virtuous.

uprising noun insurrection, mutiny, rebellion, revolt, revolution, rising.

uproar noun bedlam, chaos, clamour, commotion, confusion, disorder, fracas, furore, hullabaloo, kerfuffle (*informal*), mayhem, outcry, pandemonium, protest, riot, row, ruckus, rumpus, stir, storm, to-do, tumult, turmoil.

uproarious *adjective* boisterous, disorderly, noisy, obstreperous, rowdy, tumultuous, unruly.

uproot *verb* dig up, eradicate, get rid of, pull up, remove, root out.

upset *verb* **1** knock over, overturn, spill, tip up, topple, up-end, upturn. **2** agitate, alarm, anger, annoy, bother, distress, disturb, fluster, frighten, grieve, hurt, offend, perturb, provoke, rattle (*informal*), trouble, vex, worry. **3** affect, disrupt, interfere with, mess up.

upset *noun* ailment, bug (*informal*), complaint, disorder, malady.

upshot *noun* consequence, effect, outcome, result.

upside-down *adverb* & *adjective* inverted, topsy-turvy, upturned.

uptight *adjective* anxious, apprehensive, edgy, jittery (*informal*), keyed up, nervous, tense, uneasy, worried.

urban *adjective* city, metropolitan, town.

urge *verb* **1** beseech, coax, encourage, entreat, exhort, implore, plead with, press,

prompt, push, recommend. **2** drive, egg on, force, goad, impel, prod, spur.

urge *noun* compulsion, desire, drive, fancy, impulse, itch, longing, wish, yearning, yen.

urgent *adjective* compelling, desperate, dire, immediate, imperative, important, necessary, pressing, vital.

urinate *verb* excrete, pass water, relieve yourself, void.

usable *adjective* available, functional, operational, working.

usage *noun* **1** handling, treatment, use. **2** convention, custom, habit, practice, use.

use *verb* apply, consume, employ, exercise, exert, expend, exploit, handle, make use of, manipulate, operate, ply, utilise, wield, work. □ **user** *noun* consumer, operator. □ **used to** acclimatised to, accustomed to, familiar with. □ **use up** blow (*slang*), consume, deplete, exhaust, expend, fritter away, go through, spend.

use *noun* **1** handling, usage. **2** application, function. **3** advantage, benefit, good, point, purpose, usefulness, utility, value.

used *adjective* cast-off, hand-me-down, old, recycled, second-hand, worn.

useful *adjective* advantageous, beneficial, constructive, convenient, effective, efficient, functional, handy, helpful, invaluable, positive, practical, productive, profitable, serviceable, usable, utilitarian, valuable, worthwhile.

useless *adjective* (*useless efforts*) fruitless, futile, hopeless, ineffective, ineffectual, pointless, unavailing, unproductive, vain; (*a useless gadget*) bung (*Australian informal*), dud (*informal*), impractical, unusable, worthless.

usher *noun* attendant, escort, guide, sidesman.

usher *verb* conduct, escort, guide, lead, show.

usual *adjective* accustomed, common, conventional, customary, established, everyday, familiar, general, habitual, normal, ordinary, orthodox, regular, routine, set, standard, stock, traditional, typical.

utensil *noun* appliance, device, gadget, implement, instrument, machine, tool.

utilise *verb* see USE.

utilitarian *adjective* functional, practical, serviceable, useful.

utility *noun* convenience, practicality, service, serviceability, use, usefulness.

utmost *adjective* extreme, greatest, highest, maximum, paramount, supreme.

utter *verb* come out with, emit, express, let out, pronounce, say, speak, voice.

utter *adjective* absolute, arrant, complete, downright, out-and-out, perfect, positive, pure, sheer, thorough, total, unmitigated.

U-turn *noun* about-face, about-turn, backflip, reversal.

V v

vacant *adjective* **1** available, clear, deserted, empty, free, spare, unfilled, uninhabited, unoccupied, untenanted, unused, void. **2** absent-minded, blank, deadpan, empty, expressionless, vacuous. □ **vacancy** *noun* job, opening, position, post, situation.

vacate *verb* abandon, depart from, evacuate, leave, quit.

vacation *noun* break, furlough, holiday, leave, time off.

vaccination *noun* booster, immunisation, injection, inoculation, jab (*informal*), shot.

vacillate *verb* dither, fluctuate, hesitate, hum and haw, shilly-shally, swing, waver.

vacuum *noun* emptiness, nothingness, void.

vagabond *noun* beachcomber, gypsy, hobo, itinerant, nomad, rover, swagman (*Australian*), tramp, traveller, vagrant, wanderer, wayfarer.

vagrant *noun* beggar, hobo, homeless person, itinerant, rover, tramp, vagabond.

vague *adjective* ambiguous, amorphous, blurred, dim, equivocal, fuzzy, general, hazy, imprecise, indefinite, indistinct, inexplicit, loose, nebulous, sketchy, uncertain, unclear, woolly.

vain *adjective* **1** arrogant, boastful, cocky, conceited, egotistical, narcissistic, proud, stuck-up (*informal*). **2** abortive, fruitless, futile, hopeless, unavailing, unsuccessful, useless.

valedictory *adjective* farewell, leave-taking, parting.

valiant *adjective* bold, brave, courageous, daring, dauntless, doughty, fearless, gallant, heroic, intrepid, lion-hearted, plucky, spirited, stout-hearted, undaunted, valorous.

valid *adjective* **1** lawful, legal, legitimate, official. **2** accept-able, allowable, cogent, logical, permissible, proper, reasonable, sound.

valley *noun* basin, canyon, dale, dell, glen, gorge, gully (*Australian*), hollow, pass, ravine, vale.

valour *noun* bravery, courage, daring, gallantry, heroism, intrepidity, pluck.

valuable *adjective* (*valuable jewellery*) costly, expensive, precious, priceless, prized, treasured; (*a valuable lesson*) beneficial, constructive, helpful, important, invaluable, profitable, useful, worthwhile.

value *noun* **1** price, worth. **2** advantage, benefit, importance, merit, profit, use, usefulness, worth.

value *verb* **1** appreciate, cherish, esteem, prize, respect, set store by, treasure. **2** appraise, assess, estimate, evaluate, price.

van *noun* **1** lorry, panel van (*Australian*), truck, wagon. **2** campervan, caravan.

vandal *noun* delinquent, hoodlum, hooligan, ruffian, thug.

vanguard *noun* **1** advance guard, front line, spearhead, van. **2** avant-garde, cutting edge, forefront, leaders, pioneers, trailblazers, trend-setters.

vanish verb become invisible, disappear, evaporate, fade away, go away.

vanity noun conceit, egotism, narcissism, pride, self-admiration, self-love.

vanquish verb beat, conquer, defeat, overcome, overpower, overthrow, rout, subdue, subjugate, thrash, triumph over, trounce.

vapour noun fog, fumes, gas, haze, mist, smoke, steam.

variable adjective changeable, erratic, fickle, fitful, fluctuating, inconsistent, mutable, patchy, shifting, temperamental, unpredictable, unreliable.

variant adjective alternative, different.

variation noun alteration, change, deviation, difference, divergence, fluctuation, modification, permutation, shift.

variegated adjective harlequin, marbled, motley, mottled, multicoloured, particoloured.

variety noun 1 array, assortment, collection, combination, miscellany, mixture, range. 2 change, contrast, difference, diversity, variation. 3 breed, class, form, kind, sort, strain, type.

various adjective 1 assorted, different, disparate, diverse, heterogeneous, miscellaneous, varied. 2 many, numerous, several, sundry.

varnish noun coating, glaze, gloss, lacquer.

vary verb 1 adjust, alter, change, fluctuate, modify, modulate. 2 be at odds, conflict, differ, diverge.

vast adjective big, boundless, broad, colossal, enormous, expansive, extensive, gigantic, great, huge, immense, large, massive, sizeable, spacious, stupendous, substantial, tremendous, wide.

vat noun barrel, tank.

vault verb bound over, clear, hurdle, jump over, leap over, spring over.

vault noun 1 bound, jump, leap, spring. 2 basement, cellar, crypt. 3 strongroom.

veer verb bear, diverge, sheer, swerve, swing, turn, wheel.

vegetate verb do nothing, idle, stagnate, veg (informal).

vegetation noun flora, greenery, growth, plants.

vehement adjective ardent, fervent, fierce, fiery, heated, impassioned, intense, passionate, vigorous, violent.

vehicle noun conveyance; (various vehicles) bus, car,

veil noun **1** mantilla, yashmak. **2** cloak, cloud, cover, mantle, mask, screen, shroud.

veil verb conceal, cover, disguise, hide, mask, obscure, screen, shroud.

velocity noun pace, rate, speed.

vendetta noun conflict, dispute, feud, quarrel.

vendor noun see SELLER (at SELL).

veneer noun **1** coating, covering, exterior, finish, overlay, surface. **2** façade, front, mask, pretence, show.

venerable adjective aged, ancient, august, esteemed, honoured, old, respected, revered, venerated.

venerate verb adore, esteem, hallow, honour, look up to, respect, revere, worship.

vengeance noun reprisal, retaliation, retribution, revenge.

venial adjective excusable, forgivable, minor, pardonable, slight.

venom noun poison, toxin. □ **venomous** adjective (venomous snakes) deadly, fatal, lethal, poisonous, toxic; (venomous words) bitter, hostile, malevolent, malicious, malignant, rancorous, spiteful, vicious, virulent.

vent noun aperture, duct, hole, opening, outlet, slit.

vent verb air, express, give vent to, release.

ventilate verb air, freshen.

venture noun endeavour, enterprise, project, undertaking.

venture verb **1** be so bold as, dare, presume, take the liberty; (venture an opinion etc.) advance, offer, proffer, put forward, volunteer. **2** chance, gamble, hazard, risk, stake, wager.

venue noun location, meeting place, place, site.

verbal adjective **1** lexical, linguistic. **2** oral, said, spoken, unwritten.

verbose adjective circumlocutory, lengthy, long-winded, ponderous, tautological, wordy. □ **verbosity** noun long-windedness, loquacity, verbiage, wordiness.

verdict noun adjudication, conclusion, decision, finding, judgement, opinion.

verge noun border, brink, edge, margin, perimeter, rim, side, threshold.

verge verb □ **verge on** approach, border on, come close to.

verify verb authenticate, check, confirm, corroborate, prove, substantiate, support, uphold, validate.

vernacular noun dialect, idiom, jargon, language, lingo (*informal*), parlance, patois, phraseology, speech, tongue.

versatile adjective adaptable, all-round, flexible, handy, multi-skilled.

verse noun 1 poems, poetry; see also *POEM*. 2 stanza.

version noun 1 account, description, narrative, rendition, report, side, story. 2 edition, interpretation, paraphrase, reading, rendering, translation. 3 design, form, model, style, type, variant, variation.

vertex noun acme, apex, pinnacle, summit, top, zenith.

vertical adjective erect, perpendicular, standing, upright; see also *PRECIPITOUS*.

vertigo noun dizziness, giddiness, light-headedness, unsteadiness.

verve noun animation, dash, energy, enthusiasm, gusto, liveliness, spirit, vigour, vim (*informal*), vitality, vivacity, zeal, zing (*informal*), zip.

very adverb awfully, dreadfully (*informal*), especially, exceedingly, exceptionally, extraordinarily, extremely, frightfully, highly, immensely, jolly (*informal*), mightily, most, particularly, really, terribly, thoroughly, tremendously (*informal*), truly.

very adjective actual, exact, precise, selfsame.

vessel noun 1 boat, craft, ship; see *BOAT*, *SHIP*. 2 container, holder, receptacle, utensil; (*various vessels*) crock, ewer, flask, jar, jug, pitcher, pot, urn, vase.

vestibule noun antechamber, ante-room, entrance hall, foyer, hall, porch, lobby.

vestige noun relic, remains, remnant, residue, trace.

vet noun veterinarian, veterinary surgeon.

vet verb check out, examine, investigate, screen.

veteran noun ex-serviceman, ex-servicewoman, returned serviceman, returned servicewoman, vet (*informal*). ◻ **veteran** adjective experienced, long-serving, old, seasoned.

veto noun prohibition, refusal, rejection.

veto verb ban, bar, block, disallow, forbid, give the thumbs down to, prohibit, reject, rule out.

vex *verb* anger, annoy, bother, bug (*informal*), displease, disturb, exasperate, harass, hassle (*informal*), infuriate, irk, irritate, nark (*informal*), needle, peeve (*informal*), perturb, pique, plague, provoke, put out, rile (*informal*), trouble, try, upset, worry.

viable *adjective* feasible, possible, practicable, practical, realistic, workable.

vibrant *adjective* **1** animated, dynamic, energetic, enthusiastic, lively, sparkling, spirited, vivacious. **2** bold, bright, brilliant, intense, radiant, striking, strong, vivid.

vibrate *verb* oscillate, pulsate, quake, quiver, rattle, shake, shudder, throb, tremble, wobble. □ **vibration** *noun* oscillation, quaver, quiver, rattle, shaking, shudder, tremor.

vice *noun* **1** corruption, depravity, evil, immorality, iniquity, sin, wickedness, wrongdoing. **2** defect, failing, fault, flaw, imperfection, shortcoming, weakness.

vice *noun* clamp.

vicinity *noun* area, district, environs, locality, neighbourhood, precincts, proximity, region, zone.

vicious *adjective* atrocious, barbaric, beastly, brutal, callous, cruel, dangerous, depraved, evil, ferocious, fiendish, fierce, heinous, hostile, immoral, inhuman, malevolent, malicious, mean, monstrous, nasty, nefarious, ruthless, sadistic, savage, spiteful, vile, villainous, vindictive, violent, wicked, wild.

victim *noun* **1** casualty, fatality, martyr, prey, quarry, sacrifice, scapegoat, sufferer. **2** bunny (*Australian informal*), dupe, fall guy (*slang*), mug (*informal*), sucker (*informal*).

victimise *verb* bully, cheat, exploit, oppress, persecute, pick on, torment, use.

victor *noun* champion, conqueror, vanquisher, winner.

victory *noun* conquest, success, triumph, walk-over, win. □ **victorious** *adjective* conquering, successful, triumphant, winning.

vie *verb* compete, contend, contest, rival, strive.

view *noun* **1** landscape, outlook, panorama, prospect, scene, scenery, spectacle, vista. **2** sight, vision. **3** attitude, belief, conviction, idea, notion, opinion, sentiment, thought; see also *VIEWPOINT*.

view *verb* **1** behold (*old use*), contemplate, examine, eye, gaze at, inspect, look at, observe, scrutinise, stare at, survey, take in, watch, witness. **2** consider, deem, judge, look upon, regard, see. □ **viewer** *noun* observer, onlooker, spectator, watcher.

viewpoint *noun* angle, attitude, opinion, outlook, perspective, point of view, position, side, slant, stance, stand, standpoint, view.

vigilant *adjective* alert, attentive, awake, careful, observant, on the lookout, on your guard, wary, watchful.

vigorous *adjective* active, dynamic, energetic, fit, forceful, hardy, hearty, intense, keen, lively, robust, spirited, strapping, strenuous, strong, vital, vivacious, zealous.

vigour *noun* animation, dash, drive, dynamism, energy, enthusiasm, gusto, liveliness, pep, power, spirit, stamina, strength, verve, vim (*informal*), vitality, vivacity, zeal, zest, zip.

vile *adjective* **1** disgusting, foul, ghastly, horrible, nasty, nauseating, objectionable, obnoxious, offensive, repugnant, repulsive, revolting, unpleasant. **2** abominable, base, contemptible, depraved, despicable, evil, foul, hateful, heinous, hideous, horrible, ignoble, immoral, loathsome, low, nasty, odious, outrageous, shameful, shocking, sinful, sordid, wicked.

vilify *verb* blacken, defame, denigrate, libel, malign, revile, slander, smear.

village *noun* community, hamlet, settlement, township.

villain *noun* baddy (*informal*), blackguard, criminal, crook (*informal*), knave (*old use*), malefactor, miscreant, rascal, rogue, scoundrel, wrongdoer.

vindicate *verb* **1** absolve, acquit, clear, exculpate, exonerate. **2** defend, justify, support, uphold.

vindictive *adjective* revengeful, spiteful, unforgiving, vengeful.

vintage *noun* **1** grape gathering, grape harvest. **2** date, era, period, year.

violate *verb* **1** break, contravene, defy, disobey, disregard, ignore, infringe, transgress. **2** defile, desecrate, dishonour, profane. □ **violation** *noun* abuse, breach, contravention, disregard, infringement, transgression.

violent *adjective* (*a violent person, assault, etc.*) berserk, bloodthirsty, brutal, cruel, desperate, destructive, ferocious, fierce, frenzied, hotheaded, maniacal, murderous, savage, uncontrollable, vicious, wild; (*a violent argument*) fierce, furious, heated, impassioned, intense, passionate, stormy, tempestuous, vehement; (*a violent storm*) destructive, fierce, intense, mighty, powerful, raging, severe, tempestuous, turbulent, wild.

violin noun fiddle (*informal*).

VIP abbreviation big shot (*informal*), bigwig (*informal*), celebrity, dignitary.

virgin adjective **1** clean, fresh, immaculate, new, pristine, pure, spotless, unblemished. **2** uncultivated, unspoilt, untouched, unused.

virile adjective macho, manly, masculine, red-blooded, robust, strong.

virtually adverb almost, effectively, essentially, more or less, nearly, practically.

virtue noun **1** decency, goodness, honesty, honour, integrity, morality, principle, probity, rectitude, righteousness. **2** advantage, asset, good point, merit, plus, strength, strong point. ◻ **virtuous** adjective blameless, chaste, decent, ethical, good, honest,

honourable, moral, pure, righteous, saintly, upright.

virtuoso noun expert, genius, maestro, master.

virus noun bug (*informal*), germ, microbe, microorganism.

viscous adjective gluey, glutinous, sticky, thick, viscid.

visible adjective apparent, clear, conspicuous, discernible, evident, in sight, in view, manifest, noticeable, observable, obvious, outward, palpable, patent, plain, unmistakable.

vision noun **1** eyesight, sight. **2** conception, dream, idea, mental picture, plan. **3** apparition, ghost, hallucination, illusion, phantom, spectre, spirit, wraith. **4** farsightedness, foresight, imagination, insight.

visit verb **1** call in on, drop in on, go to see, look in on, look up, pop in on, stop by. **2** sojourn, stay. ◻ **visitor** noun blow-in (*Australian informal*), caller, company, guest, holidaymaker, non-resident, sightseer, tourist, traveller.

visit noun call, sojourn, stay, visitation.

vista noun landscape, outlook, panorama, prospect, scene, scenery, view.

visual *adjective* ocular, ophthalmic, optic, optical, sight.

visualise *verb* conceive, envisage, imagine, picture, see.

vital *adjective* basic, critical, crucial, essential, fundamental, important, indispensable, key, necessary, significant.

vitality *noun* animation, dynamism, energy, exuberance, go, gusto, liveliness, pep, strength, verve, vigour, vim (*informal*), vivacity, zeal, zest, zing (*informal*), zip.

vitriolic *adjective* abusive, acrimonious, bitter, caustic, cutting, hostile, savage, scathing, spiteful, stinging, venomous, virulent.

vivacious *adjective* animated, bubbly, exuberant, high-spirited, lively, perky, sparkling, spirited, vital. □ **vivacity** *noun* see VITALITY.

vivid *adjective* (*vivid colours*) bold, bright, brilliant, colourful, deep, garish, gaudy, gay, intense, loud, rich, striking, strong, vibrant; (*a vivid description*) clear, detailed, graphic, lifelike, lively, realistic.

vocabulary *noun* dictionary, glossary, lexicon, word list.

vocal *adjective* oral, spoken, sung.

vocalist *noun* chorister, diva, minstrel, prima donna, singer, songster, troubadour.

vocation *noun* **1** career, job, line of work, occupation, profession, trade. **2** call, calling, mission.

vociferous *adjective* clamorous, insistent, loud, noisy, outspoken, vocal.

vogue *noun* craze, fashion, mode, rage, style, trend. □ **in vogue** fashionable, in, in fashion, popular, trendy (*informal*).

voice *noun* say, vote.

voice *verb* air, articulate, communicate, declare, enunciate, express, speak, state, utter, ventilate.

void *adjective* **1** bare, empty, unoccupied, vacant. **2** invalid, null and void.

void *noun* blank, emptiness, gap, hole, space, vacuum.

volatile *adjective* (*a volatile person*) capricious, changeable, erratic, fickle, inconstant, mercurial, unpredictable, unstable; (*a volatile situation*) charged, explosive, tense, unstable.

volition *noun* □ **of your own volition** by choice, freely, of your own accord, of your own free will, voluntarily, willingly.

volley noun barrage, bombardment, fusillade, hail, salvo, shower.

voluble adjective chatty, fluent, garrulous, glib, loquacious, talkative.

volume noun **1** capacity, dimensions, measure, size. **2** amount, bulk, mass, quantity. **3** loudness, sound. **4** book, part, tome.

voluminous adjective ample, big, billowing, bulky, full, large, roomy, vast.

voluntary adjective **1** non-compulsory, optional, unforced. **2** honorary, unpaid, unsalaried. □ **voluntarily** adverb by choice, freely, of your own accord, of your own free will, of your own volition, willingly.

volunteer verb nominate yourself, offer, step forward; see also *ENLIST*.

vomit verb barf (slang), be sick, bring up, chuck (informal), chunder (Australian slang), puke (informal), sick up (informal), spew, throw up.

voracious adjective **1** greedy, insatiable, ravenous. **2** avid, compulsive, eager, insatiable, keen.

vortex noun eddy, maelstrom, spiral, whirlpool, whirlwind.

vote verb (vote for) choose, elect, opt for, pick, select.

vote noun **1** ballot, election, plebiscite, poll, referendum. **2** franchise, right to vote, suffrage.

vouch verb □ **vouch for** answer for, attest to, confirm, guarantee, swear to.

voucher noun coupon, token.

vow noun oath, pledge, promise.

vow verb declare, give your word, pledge, promise, swear, take an oath.

voyage noun crossing, cruise, journey, passage, sail, trip.

voyage verb cruise, journey, sail, travel.

vulgar adjective bad-mannered, boorish, coarse, common, crude, dirty, ill-mannered, impolite, indecent, lewd, obscene, offensive, risqué, rough, rude, smutty, tasteless, uncouth.

vulnerable adjective defenceless, exposed, insecure, precarious, sensitive, susceptible, unguarded, unprotected, weak.

Ww

wad noun bundle, hunk, lump, mass, pad, plug, roll.

wad verb fill, line, pad, stuff.

waddle verb shuffle, toddle, wobble.

waddy noun bludgeon, club, war club.

wade verb paddle, plod, splash, trek, trudge.

waffle noun hot air (slang), padding, verbiage. □ **waffle** verb prattle, rabbit (informal), ramble, witter (informal).

waft verb drift, float, stream.

wag verb **1** shake, waggle, wave, wiggle. **2** absent yourself from, bludge (Australian informal), play hookey from (informal), play truant from, skive off (informal), stay away from.

wag noun clown, comedian, jester, joker, wit.

wage noun earnings, income, pay, payment, remuneration, wages.

wage verb carry on, conduct, engage in, fight, pursue.

wager noun bet, flutter (informal), gamble, punt, speculation, stake. □ **wager** verb bet, gamble, hazard, punt (informal), risk, stake.

wagon noun cart, dray, wain (old use).

waif noun foundling, homeless person, orphan, stray.

wail verb bawl, caterwaul, cry, groan, howl, moan, shriek, sob, weep, whine, yowl.

waist noun middle, midriff, waistline.

waistcoat noun jerkin, vest.

wait verb **1** bide your time, dally, delay, hang around, hang on, hold on, linger, mark time, pause, remain, rest, sit tight (informal), stand by, stay, stop, tarry. **2** be deferred, be delayed, be postponed, be put off, be shelved. □ **wait on** attend to, serve.

wait noun adjournment, delay, hold-up, interval, pause, postponement, stay.

waive verb abandon, dispense with, forgo, forsake, give up, relinquish, renounce, set aside, surrender, yield.

wake verb **1** awake, get up, stir, surface (informal), wake up. **2** awaken, disturb, rouse, waken, wake up.

wake noun vigil, watch.

wake noun backwash, track, trail, wash. □ **in the wake of** after, behind, following, subsequent to.

wakeful adjective awake, insomniac, restless, sleepless.

walk verb amble, bushwalk (Australian), creep, foot it, go on foot, hike, hobble, limp, march, pace, parade, perambulate, plod, promenade, prowl, ramble, saunter, shamble, shuffle, slink, slog, stagger, stalk, stamp, step, stride, stroll, strut, swagger, tiptoe, toddle, totter, traipse (*informal*), tramp, trample, tread, trek, troop, trudge, waddle, wade. □ **walker** *noun* bushwalker, hiker, pedestrian, rambler. □ **walk out 1** depart, flounce out, leave, storm out. **2** down tools, go on strike, stop work, strike, take industrial action, walk off the job. □ **walk out on** abandon, desert, forsake, leave, leave in the lurch.

walk *noun* **1** amble, bushwalk (*Australian*), constitutional, hike, promenade, ramble, saunter, stroll, tramp, trek, walkabout, wander. **2** gait, pace, step, stride. **3** path, pathway, route, track, trail.

walkover *noun* breeze (*informal*), child's play, cinch (*informal*), doddle (*informal*), piece of cake (*informal*), pushover (*informal*), snack (*Australian informal*), snap (*informal*).

wall *noun* barricade, barrier, battlements, bulkhead, bulwark, dyke, embankment, fence, parapet, partition, rampart, stockade.

wallet *noun* notecase, pocketbook, purse.

wallow *verb* **1** flounder, roll about, splash about. **2** bask, delight, indulge, luxuriate, revel.

wan *adjective* pale, pallid, pasty, peaky, sickly, washed out, waxen.

wand *noun* baton, cane, rod, staff, stick.

wander *verb* **1** meander, mooch (*informal*), mosey (*slang*), prowl, ramble, range, roam, rove, saunter, stroll, tootle (*informal*), traipse (*informal*), travel, walk. **2** deviate, digress, drift, stray.

wanderer *noun* drifter, gypsy, hobo, itinerant, nomad, rambler, rover, swagman (*Australian*), traveller, vagabond, vagrant, wayfarer.

wane *verb* decline, decrease, diminish, dwindle, ebb, fade, lessen, subside, taper off, weaken.

wangle *verb* contrive, engineer, fix (*informal*), get, pull off, swing (*informal*).

want *verb* **1** covet, crave, desire, fancy, hanker after, hunger for, long for, pine for, wish for, yearn for. **2** need, require. **3** be short of, lack, miss.

want *noun* **1** desire, need, requirement, wish. **2** absence, dearth, deficiency, insufficiency, lack, paucity, scarcity, shortage.

wanton *adjective* arbitrary, groundless, irresponsible, malicious, motiveless, reckless, senseless, unprovoked, wilful.

war *noun* **1** battle, combat, conflict, fighting, hostilities, strife, warfare. **2** attack, battle, blitz, campaign, crusade, fight, struggle.

ward *noun* **1** charge, dependant, protégé(e). **2** area, district, division, section.

ward *verb* □ **ward off** avert, beat off, deflect, fend off, keep at bay, parry, repel, repulse, stave off, thwart.

warden *noun* superintendent, supervisor; (*churchwarden*) attendant, sexton, sidesman, steward, verger.

warder *noun* guard, jailer, keeper, prison officer.

wardrobe *noun* closet, cupboard.

ware *noun* □ **wares** commodities, goods, merchandise, products, stock.

warehouse *noun* depot, store, storehouse.

warlike *adjective* **1** aggressive, bellicose, belligerent, combative, hostile, militant, militaristic, pugnacious. **2** martial, military.

warm *adjective* **1** (*warm food*) heated, lukewarm, tepid; (*warm weather*) balmy, mild, sunny. **2** cosy, thermal, thick, woolly. **3** cordial, enthusiastic, friendly, hearty, hospitable, rousing, sincere.

warm *verb* heat, heat up, hot up (*informal*), reheat, scald, warm up.

warm-hearted *adjective* affectionate, amiable, caring, compassionate, friendly, genial, kind, kind-hearted, kindly, loving, sympathetic, tenderhearted, warm.

warn *verb* admonish, advise, alert, apprise (*formal*), caution, counsel, forewarn, inform, make aware, notify, remind, tell, tip off. □ **warning** *noun* admonition, advice, caution, caveat, counsel, forewarning, hint, indication, notice, notification, omen, sign, signal, threat, tip-off.

warp *verb* **1** bend, bow, buckle, contort, curve, distort, twist. **2** corrupt, pervert, twist.

warrant *noun* authorisation, authority, entitlement, licence, permit.

warrant *verb* authorise, call for, excuse, justify, permit, sanction.

warrigal *adjective* feral, unbroken, untamed, wild.

warrior *noun* brave, combatant, fighter, gladiator, soldier.

warship *noun* aircraft carrier, battleship, corvette, cruiser, destroyer, frigate, gunboat, man-of-war, submarine, torpedo boat, trireme (*historical*).

wary *adjective* alert, careful, cautious, chary, circumspect, distrustful, guarded, observant, on the lookout, on your guard, suspicious, vigilant, watchful.

wash *verb* **1** clean, cleanse, douse, drench, flush, launder, mop, rinse, scour, scrub, shampoo, sluice, soak, soap, sponge, swab, swill, wipe; (*wash yourself*) bath, bathe, clean yourself, perform your ablutions, shower. **2** break, flow, splash, sweep. **3** carry, sweep, transport. **4** be accepted, hold water, stand up.

wash *noun* **1** bath, scrub, shower. **2** backwash, wake.

washing *noun* clothes, laundry, wash.

wash-out *noun* damp squib, disaster, failure, fiasco, fizzer (*Australian informal*), flop (*informal*).

waste *verb* **1** blow (*slang*), dissipate, fritter away, misspend, misuse, squander. **2** let slip, miss, throw away. **3** (*waste away*) become emaciated, fade away, grow thin, pine, shrivel, wither.

waste *adjective* **1** discarded, leftover, superfluous, unwanted, useless. **2** arid, barren, desert, uncultivated, unusable, wild.

waste *noun* **1** misuse, squandering. **2** debris, dregs, dross, effluent, garbage, junk, litter, refuse, rubbish, scraps, sewage, trash. **3** desert, wasteland, wilderness.
□ **wasteful** *adjective* extravagant, improvident, prodigal, profligate, uneconomical.

watch *verb* **1** attend to, behold (*old use*), concentrate on, contemplate, eye, gaze at, keep your eyes on, look at, mark, monitor, note, notice, observe, pay attention to, peep at, peer at, regard, scrutinise, stare at, survey, take notice of, view. **2** keep an eye on, keep under observation, keep under surveillance, spy on. **3** be on guard, be on the lookout, be vigilant, be wary, be watchful, keep your eyes open, watch out. **4** guard, keep an eye on, look after, mind, protect, supervise, take care of, tend.

watch *noun* chronometer, pocket watch, stopwatch, timepiece, wristwatch.

watchful *adjective* alert, attentive, careful, eagle-eyed, observant, vigilant, wary.

watchman *noun* guard, night-watchman, patrol, security guard.

watchword *noun* byword, catchphrase, catchword, maxim, motto, slogan.

water *noun* creek, dam, lake, ocean, pond, pool, reservoir, river, sea, stream.

water *verb* **1** dampen, flood, hose, irrigate, moisten, soak, spray, sprinkle, wet. **2** run, stream, weep. □ **water down** adulterate, dilute, thin, weaken.

waterfall *noun* cascade, cataract, falls.

waterhole *noun* **1** pond, pool. **2** claypan (*Australian*), gilgai (*Australian*), gnamma hole (*Australian*), mickery (*Australian*), rockhole, soak, watering hole.

waterlogged *adjective* boggy, marshy, saturated, soaked, sodden, swampy.

waterproof *adjective* impermeable, impervious, showerproof, water-repellent, water-resistant, watertight, weatherproof.

watershed *noun* crossroads, turning point.

watertight *adjective* **1** sealed, waterproof. **2** irrefutable, sound, unassailable.

waterway *noun* canal, channel, river, stream, watercourse.

watery *adjective* **1** aqueous, fluid, liquid. **2** bleary, damp, lachrymose, moist, streaming, tearful, teary, weepy, wet. **3** diluted, runny, thin, watered down, weak, wishy-washy.

wave *noun* **1** billow, boomer, breaker, comber, dumper (*Australian*), ripple, roller, surf, swell, wavelet. **2** gesticulation, gesture, salutation, signal. **3** outbreak, rush, spate, surge, upsurge.

wave *verb* **1** brandish, flap, flourish, flutter, shake, swing, wag, wiggle. **2** gesticulate, gesture, signal. **3** coil, curl, kink, twirl.

waver *verb* **1** falter, flicker, quiver, shake, teeter, totter, tremble, wobble. **2** dither, hesitate, hover, oscillate, shilly-shally, swing, vacillate.

wavy *adjective* crimped, curly, curving, kinky, rippled, squiggly, undulating.

wax *verb* enlarge, grow, increase.

way *noun* **1** course, direction, path, road, route, track, trail. **2** distance, haul, journey. **3** approach, fashion, manner, means, method, mode, procedure, process, style, system, technique; see also *PRACTICE*. **4** aspect, detail, feature, particular, respect, sense. **5** condition, shape, state. □ **give way 1** break, buckle, cave in, collapse, crack, crumble, give, snap. **2** back down, capitulate, concede, give in, submit, succumb, surrender, yield.

wayfarer noun gypsy, rover, traveller, vagabond, walker, wanderer.

waylay verb accost, ambush, assail, bail up (*Australian*), buttonhole, corner, detain, hold up, intercept, lie in wait for, pounce on, set upon.

wayward adjective contrary, disobedient, headstrong, incorrigible, intractable, naughty, obstinate, perverse, rebellious, recalcitrant, refractory, self-willed, stroppy (*informal*), stubborn, unmanageable, unruly, wilful.

weak adjective **1** decrepit, delicate, feeble, flimsy, fragile, rickety, shaky, unsteady. **2** debilitated, delicate, exhausted, feeble, frail, infirm, listless, puny, sickly, weedy. **3** cowardly, feckless, impotent, ineffective, ineffectual, namby-pamby, powerless, pusillanimous, soft, spineless, timo-

rous, unassertive. **4** flimsy, implausible, lame, pathetic, thin, unconvincing, unsatisfactory. **5** dilute, insipid, tasteless, thin, watery, wishy-washy.

weaken verb debilitate, decline, decrease, dilute, diminish, dwindle, ebb, enervate, enfeeble, erode, exhaust, fade, impair, lessen, reduce, sap, undermine, wane, water down.

weakling noun coward, drip (*informal*), milksop, runt, sissy, softie (*informal*), sook (*Australian informal*), weed, wimp (*informal*), wuss (*slang*).

weakness noun **1** debility, decrepitude, feebleness, fragility, frailty. **2** defect, deficiency, failing, fault, flaw, foible, imperfection, shortcoming, weak point. **3** fondness, liking, partiality, passion, penchant, predilection, soft spot.

wealth noun **1** affluence, assets, capital, fortune, means, money, opulence, property, prosperity, riches. **2** abundance, fund, mine, profusion, store.

wealthy adjective affluent, flush (*informal*), loaded (*informal*), moneyed, opulent, prosperous, rich, well-heeled (*informal*), well in (*Australian informal*), well off, well-to-do.

weapon noun (*weapons*) armaments, arms, munitions, weaponry.

wear verb **1** be attired in, clothe yourself in, don, dress in, have on, put on, sport. **2** abrade, corrode, eat away, erode, grind down, rub away, scuff, wear away, wear down. **3** endure, last, stand up, survive. □ **wear off** decrease, diminish, dwindle, fade, lessen, subside. □ **wear out 1** become shabby, become threadbare, fray, wear thin. **2** drain, exhaust, fatigue, tire out, weary.

wear noun **1** apparel (*formal*), attire (*formal*), clobber (*slang*), clothes, clothing, dress, garb, garments, gear (*informal*), raiment (*old use*). **2** damage, deterioration, disrepair, wear and tear.

weary adjective all in (*informal*), beat (*slang*), dog-tired, done in (*informal*), drained, drowsy, exhausted, fagged out (*informal*), fatigued, jaded, knackered (*slang*), pooped (*informal*), sleepy, spent, tired, whacked (*informal*), worn out, zonked (*slang*). □ **weariness** noun exhaustion, fatigue, languor, lassitude, lethargy, listlessness, tiredness.

weary verb drain, exhaust, fatigue, sap, tire, wear out.

weather noun climate, the elements.

weather verb **1** season. **2** brave, come through, endure, ride out, stand up to, survive, withstand.

weave verb **1** braid, entwine, interlace, intertwine, interweave, plait. **2** compose, create, put together, spin. **3** meander, wind, zigzag.

web noun **1** cobweb, gossamer. **2** mesh, net, network.

wed verb get hitched (*informal*), marry, tie the knot (*informal*). □ **wedded** adjective conjugal, marital, married, matrimonial, nuptial.

wedding noun marriage, nuptials.

wedge noun **1** block, chock. **2** chunk, hunk, piece, slab, slice.

wedge verb jam, pack, ram, sandwich, squeeze, stick, stuff.

wedlock noun marriage, matrimony.

weed verb (*weed out*) eliminate, eradicate, get rid of, remove, root out.

weedy adjective **1** overgrown, rank, wild. **2** delicate, frail, puny, scrawny, thin, undersized, weak.

weep verb **1** bawl, blubber, break down, cry, howl, shed tears, snivel, sob, wail. **2** ooze, seep. ◻ **weepy** *adjective* crying, lachrymose, maudlin, tearful, teary.

weigh *verb* **1** measure, tip the scales at. **2** be important, carry weight, count, have an influence, matter. ◻ **weigh down** burden, depress, encumber, load, oppress, overload, saddle, trouble. ◻ **weigh up** assess, balance, compare, consider, evaluate.

weight *noun* **1** heaviness, mass. **2** burden, load, millstone, onus, pressure, strain. **3** authority, clout (*informal*), force, importance, influence, power.

weighty *adjective* **1** burdensome, cumbersome, heavy, hefty, massive, ponderous. **2** grave, important, momentous, pressing, serious.

weir *noun* barrage, dam.

weird *adjective* **1** abnormal, bizarre, curious, eccentric, freakish, funny, kinky (*informal*), odd, offbeat, outlandish, peculiar, queer, strange, unconventional, unusual, wacky (*slang*), wayout (*informal*), zany. **2** creepy, eerie, extraordinary, mysterious, peculiar, queer, spooky (*informal*), strange, supernatural, uncanny, unnatural.

weirdo *noun* crackpot (*informal*), crank, dingbat (*informal*), eccentric, freak, fruitcake (*informal*), nut (*informal*), nutcase (*informal*), oddball (*informal*).

welcome *noun* greeting, reception, salutation.

welcome *adjective* appreciated, gratifying, pleasing.

welcome *verb* accept, admit, greet, hail, let in, meet, receive.

welfare *noun* good, happiness, health, security, well-being.

well *noun* bore, shaft.

well *adverb* **1** ably, commendably, competently, correctly, effectively, fairly, justly, nicely, proficiently, properly, satisfactorily, skilfully, splendidly. **2** carefully, completely, conscientiously, meticulously, scrupulously, thoroughly. ◻ **well off** affluent, comfortable, loaded (*informal*), moneyed, prosperous, rich, wealthy, well-heeled (*informal*), well in (*Australian informal*), well-to-do.

well *adjective* **1** fit, hale and hearty, healthy, robust, sound, strong. **2** all right, fine, OK (*informal*), satisfactory.

well-being *noun* good, happiness, health, welfare.

well-known *adjective* **1** eminent, famous, illustrious, notable, noted, notorious, prominent, renowned. **2** everyday, familiar, household, proverbial.

well-mannered adjective civil, correct, courteous, genteel, polite, refined, respectful, suave, thoughtful, urbane, well-behaved, well-bred.

welt noun ridge, scar, stripe, weal.

wet adjective **1** boggy, clammy, damp, dank, dewy, drenched, dripping, humid, moist, muddy, saturated, soaked, sodden, soggy, sopping, waterlogged. **2** sticky, tacky. **3** drizzly, rainy, showery, stormy. □ **wetness** noun clamminess, condensation, damp, dampness, humidity, liquid, moisture, perspiration, sweat.

wet verb dampen, douse, drench, immerse, moisten, saturate, soak, splash, spray, sprinkle, squirt, water.

wharf noun dock, jetty, landing stage, pier, quay.

wharfie noun docker, longshoreman, stevedore, watersider (Australian), waterside worker (Australian), wharf labourer.

wheel noun castor, circle, disc, ring, roller.

wheel verb **1** push, trundle. **2** circle, gyrate, pivot, revolve, rotate, spin, swing, swivel, turn, veer, whirl.

wheeze verb & noun gasp, pant, puff.

whereabouts plural noun location, position, situation.

whet verb **1** grind, hone, sharpen, strop. **2** arouse, awaken, excite, kindle, stimulate, stir.

whiff noun **1** breath, puff. **2** aroma, fragrance, odour, smell, stink.

while noun period, spell, time.

while verb □ **while away** fill, occupy, pass, spend.

whim noun caprice, desire, fancy, impulse, urge.

whimper verb cry, grizzle (informal), moan, snivel, wail, whine.

whine verb cry, grizzle (informal), moan, wail, whimper, whinge (informal).

whinge verb beef (slang), complain, gripe (informal), grizzle (informal), grumble, moan, whine.

whip noun birch, crop, lash, rawhide, scourge, strap, switch.

whip verb **1** beat, birch, flog, lash, scourge, tan (slang), thrash. **2** beat, mix, whisk. **3** pull, seize, snatch, swipe, whisk.

whirl verb gyrate, reel, revolve, rotate, spin, swirl, swivel, turn, twirl.

whirlpool noun eddy, maelstrom, vortex.

whirlwind noun tornado, twister (*American*), vortex, willy willy (*Australian*).

whirr verb buzz, drone, hum.

whisk verb **1** brush, sweep. **2** beat, mix, whip.

whisker noun (*whiskers*) beard, bristles, facial hair, moustache, sideburns, stubble. □ **whiskery** adjective bristly, hairy, hirsute, stubbly, unshaven, whiskered.

whisper verb breathe, murmur, mutter, say under your breath. □ **whisper** noun hushed tone, murmur, undertone; see also RUMOUR.

whistle noun **1** catcall, hoot. **2** hooter, pipe, siren.

white adjective **1** chalky, cream, hoary, ivory, lily-white, milky, off-white, platinum, silvery, snow-white, snowy. **2** anaemic, ashen, bloodless, colourless, pale, pallid, pasty, wan, waxen.

whiten verb blanch, bleach, fade, lighten, pale.

whiz verb dash, fly, hurry, hurtle, race, shoot, speed, tear, zip, zoom.

whiz-kid noun expert, genius, prodigy, virtuoso, wizard.

whole adjective complete, entire, full, intact, total, unabridged, unbroken, uncut, undamaged, uninjured.

whole noun □ **on the whole** all in all, altogether, by and large, for the most part, generally, in general, in the main.

wholehearted adjective complete, dedicated, devoted, earnest, enthusiastic, full, hearty, sincere, total, unconditional, unreserved.

wholesale adjective comprehensive, extensive, general, large-scale, mass, sweeping, universal, widespread.

wholesome adjective healthy, nourishing, nutritious.

wicked adjective **1** atrocious, bad, base, beastly, contemptible, corrupt, degenerate, depraved, despicable, devilish, diabolical, evil, fiendish, foul, heinous, immoral, incorrigible, infamous, iniquitous, lawless, malicious, monstrous, nefarious, satanic, shameful, sinful, sinister, spiteful, ungodly, unholy, vicious, vile, villainous. **2** arch, devilish, impish, mischievous, naughty, roguish. □ **wickedness** noun depravity, evil, immorality, iniquity, sin, sinfulness, turpitude, ungodliness, un-righteousness, vice, villainy, wrongdoing.

wide adjective **1** big, broad, expansive, extensive, im-mense, large, open, spacious, vast, yawning. **2** big, broad, comprehensive, extensive, far-reaching, global, sweeping, vast, wide-ranging.

widen verb broaden, dilate, enlarge, expand, open out, spread.

widespread adjective common, extensive, general, pervasive, prevalent, rife, ubiquitous, universal, wholesale.

width noun breadth, diameter, girth, span, thickness.

wield verb (wield a weapon) handle, hold, manage, manipulate, ply, swing, use; (wield power) command, exercise, exert, use.

wife noun bride, consort, partner, spouse.

wig noun hairpiece, switch, toupee.

wiggle verb shake, sway, twitch, wag, waggle, wobble, wriggle.

wigwam noun hut, tent, tepee.

wild adjective **1** feral, free, myall (Australian), natural, savage, unbroken, uncultivated, un-domesticated, untamed, war-rigal (Australian). **2** bleak, desolate, rough, rugged, uncultivated, uninhabited, waste. **3** barbarian, barbaric, barbarous, primitive, un-civilised. **4** berserk, bois-terous, crazy, disorderly, excited, frenzied, hysterical, lawless, obstreperous, rebel-lious, reckless, riotous, rowdy, uncontrolled, undisciplined, unrestrained, unruly, violent. **5** blustery, rough, squally, stormy, tempestuous, turbu-lent, violent, windy. **6** absurd, crazy, foolish, hare-brained, impracticable, mad, madcap, rash, ridiculous, silly, unreasonable.

wilderness noun bush, desert, wasteland, wilds.

wilful adjective **1** determined, dogged, headstrong, intrac-table, mulish, obstinate, perverse, pigheaded, recalci-trant, refractory, self-willed, strong-willed, stubborn, way-ward. **2** calculated, deliberate, intentional, premeditated.

will noun **1** will-power. **2** choice, desire, inclination, intention, volition, wish(es). **3** commit-ment, determination, resolu-tion, resolve. **4** testament.

will verb bequeath, hand down, leave, pass on.

willing adjective amenable, consenting, cooperative, dis-posed, eager, enthusiastic, game, happy, inclined, keen, obliging, prepared, ready. □ **willingly** adverb eagerly, happily, like a shot, of your own accord, of your own free will, of your own volition, readily, voluntarily.

will-power noun commitment, determination, resolution, resolve, self-control, self-discipline, will.

wilt verb become limp, deteriorate, droop, flop, languish, shrivel, wither.

wily adjective artful, astute, clever, crafty, cunning, devious, foxy, knowing, scheming, shrewd, sly, tricky, underhand.

wimp noun baby, coward, milksop, sissy, sook (Australian informal), wuss (slang).

win verb 1 be victorious, come first, come top, prevail, succeed, triumph. 2 attain, earn, gain, get, land, obtain, pick up, receive, secure, walk away with (informal). □ **win over** convert, convince, persuade, sway, talk round.

win noun conquest, success, triumph, victory.

wince verb blench, cringe, flinch, grimace, recoil, start.

winch verb hoist, lift, pull.

wind noun 1 air current, blast, breeze, draught, gale, gust, squall, zephyr; (various winds) cyclone, doctor (Australian), hurricane, mistral, monsoon, sirocco, southerly buster (Australian), tornado, typhoon, whirlwind, willy willy (Australian). 2 flatulence, gas. 3 air, breath, puff.

wind verb 1 bend, curl, curve, loop, meander, snake, turn, twist, wander, zigzag. 2 coil, loop, roll, twine, twirl, twist, wrap. □ **wind up 1** close down, dissolve, liquidate. 2 end up, finish up, land.

windfall noun bonanza, godsend.

window noun 1 aperture, opening; (kinds of window) bay window, bow window, casement, dormer window, fanlight, French window, oriel window, porthole, quarter-light, skylight, transom, windscreen. 2 glass, pane.

windy adjective blowy, blustery, breezy, gusty, squally, stormy, tempestuous.

wine noun (informal terms) booze, grog, plonk, vino.

wing noun 1 pinion. 2 branch, faction, section.

wink verb 1 bat an eyelid, blink. 2 blink, flash, flicker, sparkle, twinkle.

winner noun 1 champion, conqueror, victor. 2 hit,

knockout (*informal*), smash hit (*informal*), success.

wipe verb **1** clean, dry, dust, mop, polish, rub, sponge, towel. **2** apply, rub, smear, spread. **3** erase, scrub (*informal*); see also DELETE. □ **wipe out 1** cancel, erase, expunge, get rid of, remove. **2** annihilate, destroy, eliminate, exterminate, kill, obliterate.

wire noun cable, flex, lead.

wiry adjective lean, muscular, sinewy, strong, thin, tough.

wisdom noun astuteness, discernment, insight, intellect, intelligence, judgement, nous (*informal*), prudence, reason, sagacity, sense, shrewdness, understanding.

wise adjective (*a wise person*) astute, discerning, intelligent, knowing, perceptive, prudent, sagacious, sage, savvy (*informal*), sensible, shrewd, smart, understanding; (*a wise decision*) advisable, appropriate, judicious, politic, prudent, sensible, shrewd, smart, sound.

wish verb aspire, crave, desire, fancy, hanker, hope, long, want, yearn.

wish noun ambition, aspiration, craving, desire, fancy, hope,

longing, objective, request, want, whim, yearning, yen.

wistful adjective doleful, forlorn, longing, melancholy, nostalgic, pensive, pining, sad, yearning.

wit noun **1** brains, common sense, intellect, intelligence, judgement, nous (*informal*), sense, understanding, wisdom. **2** banter, humour, jokes, puns, repartee. **3** comedian, comic, humorist, jester, joker, punster, wag.

witch noun enchantress, magician, sorceress. □ **witchcraft** noun black magic, magic, the occult, sorcery, voodoo, witchery, wizardry.

witchdoctor noun medicine man, shaman.

withdraw verb **1** extract, pull out, recall, remove, take away, take back, take out. **2** back off, depart, go, go away, leave, pull out, retire, retreat. **3** cancel, recant, rescind, retract, revoke, take back.

withdrawn adjective antisocial, detached, introverted, reclusive, reserved, retiring, shy, unsociable.

wither verb dehydrate, droop, dry out, dry up, shrivel, wilt.

withhold verb (*withhold permission*) deny, refuse; (*withhold information*) conceal, hide, hold back, keep back, suppress.

withstand verb bear, cope with, endure, oppose, resist, stand up to, survive, tolerate, weather.

witness noun bystander, eyewitness, looker-on, observer, onlooker, spectator, viewer.

witness verb **1** behold (old use), be present at, observe, see, view, watch. **2** countersign, endorse, validate.

witty adjective amusing, clever, droll, funny, humorous, quickwitted, scintillating, sharp-witted.

wizard noun **1** magician, medicine man, sorcerer, warlock (old use), witchdoctor. **2** expert, genius, maestro, master, virtuoso, whiz (informal).

wobble verb quake, quaver, quiver, reel, rock, shake, stagger, sway, teeter, totter, tremble, waver. ▫ **wobbly** adjective loose, rickety, rocky, shaky, unbalanced, unstable, unsteady, wonky (informal).

woe noun **1** anguish, distress, grief, hardship, heartache, misery, misfortune, pain, sorrow, suffering, unhappiness. **2** adversity, affliction, burden, misfortune, problem,

trial, tribulation, trouble.

woman noun bird (informal), chick (slang), dame (old use or American slang), damsel (old use), female, girl, lady, lass, maid (old use), maiden (old use), matron, sheila (Australian slang). ▫ **womanish** adjective effeminate, sissy, unmanly, unmasculine. ▫ **womanly** adjective feminine, ladylike.

wonder noun **1** admiration, amazement, astonishment, awe, bewilderment, fascination, surprise, wonderment. **2** curiosity, marvel, miracle, phenomenon, rarity.

wonder verb **1** ask yourself, be curious, conjecture, muse, ponder, puzzle, question, speculate, think. **2** be amazed, be stunned, be surprised, marvel.

wonderful adjective admirable, amazing, astonishing, astounding, awe-inspiring, awesome, breathtaking, brilliant (informal), excellent, extraordinary, fabulous (informal), fantastic (informal), fine, first-class, impressive, incredible, magnificent, marvellous, miraculous, outstanding, phenomenal, prodigious, remarkable, sensational, spectacular, splendid, staggering, stunning, stupendous, superb, terrific (*informal*), tremendous (*informal*), unbelievable, unreal (*slang*), wondrous (*old use*).

woo verb **1** court, pursue, seek the hand of. **2** attract, seek, seek to win.

wood noun **1** see TIMBER **2** bush, copse, forest, grove, jungle, scrub, spinney, thicket, woodland, woods.

woodcutter noun logger, lumberjack (*American*), sawyer, splitter, tree-feller.

wooded adjective forested, silvan, timbered, tree-covered.

wooden adjective **1** timber, wood. **2** clumsy, leaden, rigid, stiff. **3** blank, deadpan (*informal*), empty, expressionless, glassy, impassive, poker-faced, vacant, vacuous.

woodwork noun cabinet-making, carpentry, joinery.

wool noun **1** fleece, hair. **2** yarn.

woolly adjective **1** fleecy, fluffy, furry, fuzzy, hairy, shaggy. **2** wool, woollen. **3** fuzzy, hazy, imprecise, indefinite, muddled, unclear, vague.

word noun **1** appellation, expression, name, term. **2** assurance, guarantee, pledge, promise, undertaking, vow, word of honour. **3** command, direction, information, order. **4** advice, information, intelligence, message, news, report, tidings. □ **word for word** accurately, exactly, faithfully, literally, precisely, verbatim.

word verb couch, express, formulate, phrase, put.

wording noun expression, language, phraseology, phrasing.

wordy adjective diffuse, garrulous, long-winded, loquacious, rambling, talkative, verbose, voluble.

work noun **1** drudgery, effort, elbow grease, exertion, grind, industry, labour, slog, sweat (*informal*), toil, travail (*old use*), yakka (*Australian informal*). **2** assignment, chore, duty, homework, job, project, task, undertaking. **3** business, career, employment, job, occupation, profession, trade, vocation. **4** (*a literary work*) book, composition, creation, opus, piece, writing.

work verb **1** apply yourself, beaver away, be busy, drudge, exert yourself, graft (*slang*), grind away, labour, peg away, plug away, slave, slog, strive, sweat, toil. **2** be employed, have a job. **3** act, function, go, operate, perform, run. **4** control, handle, manage, manipulate, operate, use, wield. **5** accomplish, achieve, bring about, effect, execute, perform. □ **work out 1** calculate, compute, deduce, fathom, figure out, infer, reason, solve. **2** develop, evolve, go, pan out, turn out. □ **work up** agitate, arouse, excite, get someone het up (*informal*), get someone hot under the collar, incite, stir up, upset.

workable *adjective* feasible, practicable, practical, viable.

worker *noun* artisan, breadwinner, craftsman, craftswoman, employee, hand, labourer, operative, operator, tradesman, tradeswoman, wage-earner, workman; (*workers*) human resources, manpower, personnel, staff, workforce.

workman *noun* handyman, labourer, navvy, tradesman, worker.

workmanship *noun* craftsmanship, handiwork, skill, technique.

workshop *noun* factory, laboratory, mill, plant, workroom, works.

world *noun* **1** earth, globe, planet. **2** cosmos, Creation, universe. **3** area, circle, domain, field, realm, sphere.

worldly *adjective* **1** earthly, material, mundane, secular, temporal. **2** acquisitive, materialistic, mercenary.

worldwide *adjective* global, international, universal.

worm *verb* crawl, slither, squirm, twist, wriggle, writhe.

worn *adjective* **1** dilapidated, frayed, holey, ragged, shabby, tattered, tatty (*informal*), thin, threadbare. **2** careworn, drawn, exhausted, haggard, jaded, tired, weary, worn out.

worried *adjective* afraid, agitated, anxious, apprehensive, concerned, distraught, distressed, fearful, fretful, frightened, nervous, perturbed, troubled, uneasy.

worry *verb* **1** alarm, annoy, bother, distress, disturb, harass, hassle, irritate, perturb, pester, plague, trouble, upset, vex. **2** be agitated, be anxious, be uneasy, brood, fret.

worry *noun* **1** anguish, anxiety, apprehension, bother, concern, disquiet, distress, stress, trouble, uneasiness. **2** bugbear, burden, concern, hassle (*informal*), headache, menace, nightmare (*informal*), problem, trial, trouble, vexation.

worsen *verb* (*make worse*) aggravate, exacerbate; (*become worse*) decline, degenerate, deteriorate, go backwards, go downhill (*informal*), go to the pack (*Australian informal*), retrogress.

worship *verb* admire, adore, deify, dote on, exalt, extol, glorify, hallow, honour, idolise, laud (*informal*), look up to, love, magnify, praise, respect, revere, venerate.

worship *noun* adoration, deification, devotion, exaltation, glorification, homage, honour, praise, respect, reverence, veneration.

worth *adjective* □ **be worth 1** be priced at, be valued at, cost, sell at. **2** be worthy of, deserve, justify, merit.

worth *noun* benefit, good, importance, merit, use, usefulness, value.

worthless *adjective* futile, insignificant, meaningless, pointless, unimportant, unproductive, unprofitable, useless, vain, valueless.

worthwhile *adjective* advantageous, beneficial, important, productive, profitable, rewarding, useful, valuable.

worthy *adjective* admirable, commendable, creditable, deserving, estimable, good, honourable, meritorious, praiseworthy, respectable, worthwhile.

wound *noun* **1** cut, gash, graze, incision, injury, laceration, lesion, scratch, sore. **2** blow, damage, distress, hurt, injury, pain, trauma.

wound *verb* **1** cut, damage, gash, graze, harm, hurt, injure, knife, lacerate, maim, mutilate, shoot, stab. **2** hurt, mortify, offend, pain, sting.

wowser *noun* killjoy, party pooper (*slang*), puritan, spoilsport, teetotaller, wet blanket.

wrangle *verb* argue, bicker, debate, disagree, dispute, fight, haggle, quarrel, quibble, squabble. □ **wrangle** *noun* altercation, argument, barney (*informal*), brawl, clash, controversy, disagreement, dispute, quarrel, row, squabble, tiff.

wrap *verb* bind, cocoon, cover, encase, enclose, enfold, envelop, insulate, lag, muffle, pack, package, parcel up, shroud, surround, swaddle, swathe.

wrap *noun* cape, cloak, coat, mantle, poncho, shawl, stole.

wrapper *noun* case, casing, cover, envelope, jacket, packet, sleeve.

wrath *noun* anger, displeasure, exasperation, fury, indignation, ire, rage, temper.

wreath noun chaplet, festoon, garland, lei.

wreck verb **1** break up, dash, demolish, destroy, devastate, ruin, scupper, scuttle, shatter, shipwreck, smash, trash (*informal*), vandalise. **2** dash, destroy, muck up, ruin, sabotage, shatter, spoil, undermine, undo.

wreckage noun debris, flotsam, remains, remnants, rubble, ruins, wreck.

wrench verb force, jerk, lever, prise, pull, tear, tug, twist, wrest, yank (*informal*).

wrestle verb **1** battle, contend, fight, grapple, scuffle, struggle, tussle. **2** contend, grapple, struggle.

wretch noun **1** beggar, down-and-out, unfortunate. **2** blackguard, miscreant, rascal, ratbag (*informal*), rogue, rotter (*slang*), scoundrel, swine (*informal*), villain.

wretched adjective dejected, depressed, despondent, disconsolate, dismal, forlorn, hapless, hopeless, miserable, pathetic, pitiful, sad, sorrowful, sorry, unfortunate, unhappy, woebegone.

wriggle verb crawl, slither, squirm, twist, wiggle, worm your way, writhe. □ **wriggle out of** avoid, back out of,

escape, evade, extricate yourself from, get out of.

wring verb **1** mangle, press, squeeze, twist. **2** extort, extract, force, obtain, screw, wrest.

wrinkle noun corrugation, crease, crinkle, crow's-foot, crumple, fold, furrow, line, pleat, pucker, ridge.

wrinkle verb crease, crinkle, crumple, pucker, rumple, screw up.

write verb **1** inscribe, pen, pencil, print, scrawl, scribble, sign. **2** compose, create, produce. **3** correspond, drop a line, send a letter. □ **writer** noun author, columnist, correspondent, dramatist, essayist, journalist, novelist, playwright, poet, screenwriter, scribe, scriptwriter. □ **writing** noun **1** calligraphy, copperplate, graffiti, hand, handwriting, hieroglyphics, inscription, longhand, printing, scrawl, scribble, script, shorthand. **2** article, book, composition, diary, document, essay, journal, letter, literature, novel, poem, prose, publication, story, text, work. □ **write down** document, jot down, list, make a note of, note, record, register, take down, transcribe. □ **write off** **1** cancel, erase, forget about, wipe out. **2** destroy, ruin, wreck.

writhe verb squirm, twist, wriggle.

wrong adjective **1** erroneous, fallacious, false, imprecise, inaccurate, incorrect, inexact, mistaken, untrue. **2** bad, corrupt, criminal, crooked, dishonest, evil, illegal, illicit, immoral, improper, iniquitous, naughty, reprehensible, sinful, unethical, unfair, unjust, unlawful, wicked. **3** amiss, awry, defective, faulty, kaput (*informal*), out of order, wonky (*informal*).

wrong noun abuse, crime, evil, immorality, iniquity, injustice, misdeed, misdemeanour, offence, sin, sinfulness, transgression, trespass (*old use*), vice, wickedness, wrongdoing.

wrong verb abuse, harm, illtreat, maltreat, misrepresent, mistreat.

wrongdoer noun baddy (*informal*), criminal, crook (*informal*), culprit, delinquent, evildoer, felon, lawbreaker, malefactor, miscreant, offender, sinner, transgressor, villain.

wry adjective askew, contorted, crooked, distorted, twisted.

Yy

yakka noun effort, exertion, graft (*slang*), grind, labour, slog, sweat, toil, work.

yank verb & noun jerk, pull, tug, wrench.

yap verb & noun bark, yelp.

yard noun backyard, courtyard, garden, quad (*informal*), quadrangle.

yardstick noun benchmark, criterion, gauge, guide, measure, standard, touchstone.

yarn noun **1** fibre, strand, thread. **2** anecdote, narrative, story, tale.

year noun class, form, grade, level. □ **yearly** adjective annual.

yearn verb crave, hanker, have a yen, hunger, long, pine, thirst; see also *DESIRE*.

yell verb bawl, bellow, call, cry, holler (*American*), howl, roar, scream, screech, shout, shriek. □ **yell** noun bellow, cry, howl, roar, scream, screech, shout, shriek.

yellow adjective amber, buttercup, canary, daffodil, gold, golden, jaundiced, lemon, mustard, primrose, saffron.

yelp *verb & noun* bark, cry, howl, squeal.

yen *noun* craving, desire, fancy, hankering, hunger, longing, thirst, yearning.

yield *verb* **1** bow, capitulate, cave in, give in, give way, submit, succumb, surrender. **2** bear, bring forth (*old use*), bring in, earn, generate, net, pay, produce, return.

yield *noun* crop, harvest, output, return.

yob or **yobbo** *noun* hooligan, hoon (*Australian informal*), larrikin (*Australian*), lout, ruffian, thug.

yokel *noun* bushie (*Australian informal*), country bumpkin, countryman, countrywoman, hick (*informal*), hill-billy (*American informal*), rustic.

young *adjective* adolescent, baby, developing, fledgeling, growing, junior, juvenile, new, newborn, undeveloped, youthful.

young *noun* babies, brood, family, litter, offspring, progeny.

youngster *noun* adolescent, boy, child, girl, juvenile, kid (*informal*), lad, lass, teenager, youth.

youth *noun* **1** adolescence, teenage years, teens, young days. **2** adolescent, boy, fellow, juvenile, kid (*informal*), lad, teenager, young man, youngster. **3** kids (*informal*), the young, young people. □ **youthful** *adjective* active, energetic, sprightly, spry, vigorous, young, young-looking.

yucky *adjective* disgusting, gross (*informal*), repulsive, revolting, sickening.

yummy *adjective* appetising, delectable, delicious, mouth-watering, scrumptious (*informal*), tasty.

Zz

zany *adjective* absurd, bizarre, comical, crazy, eccentric, funny, idiotic, mad, odd, offbeat, peculiar, unconventional, unusual, wacky (*slang*), weird.

zeal *noun* ardour, dedication, devotion, diligence, eagerness, earnestness, energy, enthusiasm, fanaticism, fervour, gusto, keenness, passion, verve, vigour, zest. □ **zealous** *adjective* ardent, conscientious, devoted, diligent, eager, earnest, energetic, enthusiastic, fanatical, fervent, keen, passionate.

zealot *noun* bigot, crank, enthusiast, extremist, fanatic.

zenith *noun* acme, apex, climax, height, peak, pinnacle, prime, summit, top.

zero *noun* cipher, duck (*Cricket*), love (*Tennis*), nil, nothing, nought, zilch (*slang*).

zest *noun* eagerness, energy, enjoyment, enthusiasm, excitement, gusto, interest, keenness, liveliness, oomph (*informal*), pleasure, relish, sparkle, spirit, vigour, zeal, zing (*informal*).

zigzag *verb* curve, meander, snake, twist, wind.

zip *noun* energy, go, gusto, life, liveliness, oomph (*informal*), pep, vigour, vim (*informal*), vitality, zest, zing (*informal*).

zip *verb* race, rush, speed, tear, whiz.

zone *noun* area, belt, district, locality, place, region, sector, territory.

zoo *noun* conservation park, menagerie, safari park, sanctuary, wildlife park, zoological gardens.

zoom *verb* dash, fly, hurry, race, rush, speed, tear, whiz, zip.